THE DOCTRINE AND COVENANTS

THE PEARL OF GREAT PRICE

PRESENTED TO

_____

_____

_____

Cover design copyrighted 2004 by Covenant Communications, Inc.

Published by Covenant Communications, Inc.
American Fork, Utah

Copyright © 2004 by Covenant Communications, Inc. All rights reserved. No part of this book may be reproduced in any format or in any medium without the written permission of the publisher, Covenant Communications, Inc., P.O. Box 416, American Fork, UT 84003.

Printed in China
First Printing: October 2004

11 10 09 08 07 06 05 04   10 9 8 7 6 5 4 3 2 1

ISBN 1-59156-560-X

PRIESTHOOD LINE OF AUTHORITY

Name

Date Received Aaronic Priesthood

Ordained by

Date Received Melchizedek Priesthood

Ordained by

Line of Authority

Name

Date Received Aaronic Priesthood

Ordained by

Date Received Melchizedek Priesthood

Ordained by

Line of Authority

Name

Date Received Aaronic Priesthood

Ordained by

Date Received Melchizedek Priesthood

Ordained by

Line of Authority

Name

Date Received Aaronic Priesthood

Ordained by

Date Received Melchizedek Priesthood

Ordained by

Line of Authority

For I have conferred upon you the keys and power of the priesthood, wherein I restore all things, and make known unto you all things in due time. D&C 132:45

Name

Date Received Aaronic Priesthood

Ordained by

Date Received Melchizedek Priesthood

Ordained by

Line of Authority

Name

Date Received Aaronic Priesthood

Ordained by

Date Received Melchizedek Priesthood

Ordained by

Line of Authority

Name

Date Received Aaronic Priesthood

Ordained by

Date Received Melchizedek Priesthood

Ordained by

Line of Authority

Name

Date Received Aaronic Priesthood

Ordained by

Date Received Melchizedek Priesthood

Ordained by

Line of Authority

Name

Date Received Aaronic Priesthood

Ordained by

Date Received Melchizedek Priesthood

Ordained by

Line of Authority

Name

Date Received Aaronic Priesthood

Ordained by

Date Received Melchizedek Priesthood

Ordained by

Line of Authority

PATRIARCHAL BLESSINGS

Name

Age

Date

Patriarch

Stake

Place

Name

Age

Date

Patriarch

Stake

Place

Name

Age

Date

Patriarch

Stake

Place

Name

Age

Date

Patriarch

Stake

Place

And again, verily I say unto you . . . that my servant Hyrum may take the office of . . . Patriarch, which was appointed unto him by his father, by blessing and also by right; That from henceforth he shall hold the keys of patriarchal blessings upon the heads of all my people, That whosoever he blesses shall be blessed . . . D&C 124:91–93

Name

Age

Date

Patriarch

Stake

Place

Name

Age

Date

Patriarch

Stake

Place

Name

Age

Date

Patriarch

Stake

Place

Name

Age

Date

Patriarch

Stake

Place

Name

Age

Date

Patriarch

Stake

Place

Name

Age

Date

Patriarch

Stake

Place

MISSIONARY SERVICE

Name

Type of Mission

Mission

Set Apart

Dates Served

Language Spoken

Mission President(s)

Name

Type of Mission

Mission

Set Apart

Dates Served

Language Spoken

Mission President(s)

Name

Type of Mission

Mission

Set Apart

Dates Served

Language Spoken

Mission President(s)

Name

Type of Mission

Mission

Set Apart

Dates Served

Language Spoken

Mission President(s)

Name

Type of Mission

Mission

Set Apart

Dates Served

Language Spoken

Mission President(s)

Name

Type of Mission

Mission

Set Apart

Dates Served

Language Spoken

Mission President(s)

Name

Type of Mission

Mission

Set Apart

Dates Served

Language Spoken

Mission President(s)

Name

Type of Mission

Mission

Set Apart

Dates Served

Language Spoken

Mission President(s)

Therefore, O ye that embark in the service of God, see that ye serve him with all your heart, might, mind and strength, that ye may stand blameless before God at the last day. D&C 4:2

Name

Type of Mission

Mission

Set Apart

Dates Served

Language Spoken

Mission President(s)

Name

Type of Mission

Mission

Set Apart

Dates Served

Language Spoken

Mission President(s)

Name

Type of Mission

Mission

Set Apart

Dates Served

Language Spoken

Mission President(s)

Name

Type of Mission

Mission

Set Apart

Dates Served

Language Spoken

Mission President(s)

Name

Type of Mission

Mission

Set Apart

Dates Served

Language Spoken

Mission President(s)

Name

Type of Mission

Mission

Set Apart

Dates Served

Language Spoken

Mission President(s)

Name

Type of Mission

Mission

Set Apart

Dates Served

Language Spoken

Mission President(s)

Name

Type of Mission

Mission

Set Apart

Dates Served

Language Spoken

Mission President(s)

Name

Type of Mission

Mission

Set Apart

Dates Served

Language Spoken

Mission President(s)

Name

Type of Mission

Mission

Set Apart

Dates Served

Language Spoken

Mission President(s)

TEMPLES VISITED

Place

Date

Ordinance

Place

Date

Ordinance

Place

Date

Ordinance

Place

Date

Ordinance

Place

Date

Ordinance

Place

Date

Ordinance

Organize yourselves; prepare every needful thing; and establish a house, even a house of prayer, a house of fasting, a house of faith, a house of learning, a house of glory, a house of order, a house of God. D&C 88:119

Place

Date

Ordinance

Place

Date

Ordinance

Place

Date

Ordinance

Place

Date

Ordinance

Place

Date

Ordinance

Place

Date

Ordinance

Place

Date

Ordinance

Place

Date

Ordinance

Place	Place
Date	Date
Ordinance	Ordinance

Place	Place
Date	Date
Ordinance	Ordinance

Place	Place
Date	Date
Ordinance	Ordinance

Place	Place
Date	Date
Ordinance	Ordinance

Place	Place
Date	Date
Ordinance	Ordinance

Place	Place
Date	Date
Ordinance	Ordinance

Place	Place
Date	Date
Ordinance	Ordinance

Place	Place
Date	Date
Ordinance	Ordinance

Place	Place
Date	Date
Ordinance	Ordinance

Place	Place
Date	Date
Ordinance	Ordinance

Place	Place
Date	Date
Ordinance	Ordinance

Place	Place
Date	Date
Ordinance	Ordinance

Place

Date

Ordinance

Place

Date

Ordinance

Place

Date

Ordinance

Place

Date

Ordinance

Place

Date

Ordinance

Place

Date

Ordinance

Place

Date

Ordinance

Place

Date

Ordinance

CHURCH HISTORY SITES VISITED

Place

Date

Place

Date

Place

Date

Place

Date

Place

Date

Place

Date

I retired to the woods . . . It was on the morning of a beautiful, clear day, early in the spring of eighteen hundred and twenty. . . . After I had retired to the place where I had previously designed to go . . . I kneeled down and began to offer up the desires of my heart to God. JS—H 1:14–15

Place

Date

Place

Date

Place

Date

Place

Date

Place

Date

Place

Date

Place

Date

Place

Date

Place	Place
Date	Date

Place	Place
Date	Date

Place	Place
Date	Date

Place	Place
Date	Date

THE
DOCTRINE
AND
COVENANTS

THE PEARL OF GREAT PRICE

Search these commandments, for they are true and faithful, and the prophecies and promises which are in them shall all be fulfilled.

What I the Lord have spoken, I have spoken . . . and my word shall not pass away, but shall all be fulfilled, whether by mine own voice or by the voice of my servants, it is the same.

DOCTRINE & COVENANTS 1:37–38

THE DOCTRINE AND COVENANTS

he Latter-day Saints accept four volumes as the standard works of the Church. These are the Bible, the Book of Mormon, the Doctrine and Covenants, and the Pearl of Great Price. By unanimous vote of a General Conference, these four have been declared to be the established rule, or test, by which the belief, the teachings, and the conduct of men must be judged.

The Doctrine and Covenants is different from the other three volumes. It is in every respect a modern book. It contains revelations given during a period extending from 1823 to 1847. It covers the rise and development of the Church, restored in our day. It enables us to follow the tender watch-care of God over the infant Church, during its days of numerical weakness and the incessant assaults of the adversary, in the form of persecution, temptations, and apostasy, and to watch the retreat of the people of God into the wilderness, where the Church, in the language of the Apocalypse, would be "nourished for a time, and times, and half a time, from the face of the serpent" (Rev. 12:14). It contains "doctrines," "covenants," and "predictions," all of the utmost importance to every nation and every individual on earth. The writings of Moses and the Prophets concerned, in the first place, the Hebrew nation and its neighbors in an age that is past. The writings of the Apostles were intended, in the first place, for the churches and Saints of their age. The Doctrine and Covenants has been given to *us*, for our instruction and salvation. We are interested in it, and should study it diligently and intelligently. Moses directed that the Law, that is, the Books of Moses, be read before all Israel (Deut. 31:11), and that the king should read it every day of his life (Deut. 17:19). In the same spirit Isaiah exhorted the people to search the *Book of the Lord* (Isa. 34:16), which, probably, contained the prophecies then collected, and Paul instructed the churches concerning the reading of his inspired epistles (Col. 4:16). The same instructions may be applied now to the Doctrine and Covenants.

As the name implies, and as already stated, this volume of Scripture contains doctrine and covenants. "Doctrine" means "teaching," "instruction." It denotes more especially what is taught as truth, for us to believe, as distinct from precepts, by which rules, to be obeyed, are given. "Doctrine" refers to belief; precept to conduct.

In the Doctrine and Covenants our Lord teaches us what to believe concerning the Godhead, the Church, the Priesthood, the Millennium, the resurrection, the state of man after death in eternal glory, or the opposite, and many other subjects about which it is necessary to have true information.

The word "Covenant" is a term by which God indicates the settled arrangement between Him and His people. In the great Council in heaven, before the creation of the earth, the Father covenanted with His Son, when He said, "Thou art my Son: this day have I begotten thee. Ask of me, and I shall give thee the heathen for thine inheritance, and the uttermost parts of the earth for thy possession" (Psalms 2:7, 8). It was in pursuance of this decree, that the Son came to redeem the world; wherefore Isaiah (9:6) calls Him "Counsellor," or, as it has been rendered, the "Angel [or Messenger] of the Great Council." This covenant concerning the salvation of the human race, entered into in eternity, was made known to Adam, Noah, Abraham, and others, and, finally, through the Prophet Joseph, to the people of God in our day. It is the "everlasting" covenant, because it is from eternity to eternity. It is the "new" covenant, because it has been revealed anew in greater fulness than at any time before. And so, it is the "new and everlasting" covenant.

In it are revealed the organization of the Church, the authority of the Priesthood, the laws and rules by which, if we obey them, we can obtain citizenship in the kingdom of God, and salvation, both temporal and eternal. The covenant made with Israel has been called the Covenant of Works, and that made with Abraham, the Covenant of Promise. The covenant of the gospel is the covenant of "Truth and Grace." It is the covenant of "Faith," as expressed in obedience to all the laws of God. It is the covenant of a Father with His children, the covenant of adoption and heirship. The nature of this covenant is revealed to us in this precious volume of the word of God. It shows us what obligations we take upon ourselves in baptism, and what blessings we secure; what covenants we renew by partaking of the Sacrament, and what promises accompany that ordinance. In one word, it teaches us how to worship God in Spirit and in truth, and reveals to us the way opened up, back to the presence of God.

Furthermore, the Doctrine and Covenants contains predictions in which every nation in the world is interested. Some of these, as, for instance, that on the Civil War in the United States, have been fulfilled. Others, regarding wars among all nations, are being fulfilled at the present moment. Many are to be fulfilled in the future. These concern the establishment of the kingdom of God, and the events through which this will be accomplished. These predictions are a Voice of Warning to the nations. "Hear, O heavens, and give ear, O earth, for the Lord hath spoken."

Only by such study and application of the Word to our lives will it influence our character and fit us for exaltation hereafter. The mere reading does not avail. The standing before a mirror serves no useful purpose, unless we set ourselves in order, so that we become fit to associate with our fellowmen. It is so with reading the Word of God. If we read so as to govern our lives in accordance with the mind and will of God, our characters will be formed thereby, and we shall be fit to associate with those who are permitted to enter His presence.

It is instructive to note the various places in which the Revelations were given. The first revelation (Sec. 2) was given to the Prophet in his father's house, through an angel, on the 21st of September, 1823. It relates to the restoration of the Priesthood. Some of the Revelations given at Harmony and Fayette concerned the bringing forth of the Book of Mormon, and the establishment of the Church. A number of glorious Revelations were given at Kirtland, including the Word of Wisdom and Section 88, on the future destiny of man. At Hiram, Portage Co., Ohio, many Revelations were given on the correct interpretation of the Scriptures, including I Cor 7:14, and the Revelation by John. There the Prophet Joseph and Sidney Rigdon were favored with the grand vision recorded in Section 76, while they were pondering the meaning of John 5:29. Important Revelations concerning the future of the Church were given at Far West. The Revelation on the eternity of the marriage covenant was first written at Nauvoo. And thus we see a gradual unfoldment of truth, each revelation containing just what the people at each time needed for instruction, encouragement, or correction.

Some of the Revelations, as Sections 2 and 27, were given through heavenly messengers; others, as Sections 76 and 110, through "visions": "The veil was taken from our minds, and the eyes of our understanding were opened" (Sec. 110: 1). Others came through divine inspiration, or quickening of the faculties to keener perception of things spiritual, than enjoyed under ordinary circumstances. By what token the Prophet knew that the Revelations so given were from God, we may judge from what the Lord told Oliver Cowdery concerning translation, "You must study it out in your mind; then you must ask me if it be right, and if it is right, I will cause that your bosom shall burn within you; therefore you shall feel that it is right" (Doc. and Cov. 9: 8). When the Spirit of the Lord burns within, there is no mistaking that sacred fire. The Prophet Joseph says that the visions at times rolled like an overflowing surge before his mind (*History of the Church*, Vol. V., p. 339); and that the "still small voice . . . oftentimes it maketh my bones to quake while it maketh manifest" (Doc. and Cov. 85:6). When God speaks, there is no room for doubt.

Many Revelations were given in the presence of witnesses. Section 29, for instance, contains a Revelation inspired in the presence of six elders. Parley P. Pratt, who was present when the revelation in Section 51 was received, relates how the Prophet caused the Revelations to be committed to writing. He says, "Each sentence was uttered slowly and very distinctly, and with a pause between each, sufficiently long for it to be recorded by an ordinary writer in long hand. This was the manner in which all his written Revelations were dictated and written. There was never any hesitation, reviewing, or reading back, in order to keep the run of the subject; neither did any of these communications undergo revisions, interlinings, or corrections. As he dictated them, so they stood, so far as I have witnessed; and I was present to witness the dictation of several communications of several pages each" (Parley P. Pratt, *Autobiography*, pp. 65-66). This statement Elder Brigham H. Roberts (*History of the Church*, Vol. I., p. 173) supplements by the information that some of the early Revelations published in the Book of Commandments in 1833, were revised by the Prophet himself; errors made by scribes and publishers were corrected, and some additional clauses, which also had been given by revelation, were added. The addition of Verses 65 and 67, in Section 20, is an example.

The Prophet Joseph never entertained any doubt concerning the divine inspiration of the Revelations he received for the guidance of the Church. To some of his associates their authority was not always equally clear. Oliver Cowdery, shortly after the establishment of the Church in 1830, informed the Prophet that he had discovered an error in Section 20, Verse 37. He demanded that it be corrected. He had succeeded in influencing the Whitmers in favor of this view, and the Prophet seemed to face a schism which might become fatal to the Church. Had the Prophet Joseph been conscious of a human origin of the work in which he was engaged, wisdom would have suggested that he yield to his co-laborers; but he knew that the Revelations were not his, to change and alter at will. Consequently, he asked Oliver Cowdery by what authority he commanded him "to alter or erase, to add to, or diminish from, a Revelation or commandment from Almighty God" (*History of the Church*, Vol. I., p. 105). Later, Cowdery and the Whitmers freely acknowledged that they had been in error.

Shortly after the Revelation contained in Section 26 had been received, in July, 1830, the Prophet Joseph began to arrange and copy the Revelations so far given, and in this work John Whitmer assisted him. At a special conference held at Hiram, Portage Co., Ohio, November 1st, 1831, it was decided that ten thousand copies should be printed, and that the title should be, *Book of Commandments*. It was also decided to send Oliver Cowdery to Independence, Mo., to supervise the printing there. The manuscript was to be ready for the press by the 15th of November, that year. It was at this time that Section 1 was given (November 1st), and Section 133, called "The Appendix" (November 3rd). At a conference held at Hiram, on November 12th, 1831, the Saints by vote expressed their appreciation of the Revelations given. Oliver Cowdery and John Whitmer were set apart to publish the book, and the manuscript and the means entrusted to them to carry to Zion were dedicated to the Lord by prayer. At the same time Joseph Smith, Jr., Martin Harris, Oliver Cowdery, John Whitmer, Sidney Rigdon, and William W. Phelps were, by revelation (Doc. and Cov. 70), appointed a committee—"stewards"—to look after the business of the publication and distribution of the book; if they should receive more than needful for their necessities, the surplus was to be consecrated for the benefit of the inhabitants of Zion. On the 26th of April, 1832, a general Council of the Church was held at Independence, Mo., which was in session for several days. On the 1st of May, that year, it was decided that, instead of printing ten thousand copies of the Book of Commandments, the first edition should be limited to three thousand copies. William W. Phelps, Oliver Cowdery, and John Whitmer were appointed to "review and prepare such Revelations for the press as shall be deemed proper for publication, and print them as soon as possible, at Independence, Mo., the announcement to be made that they are published by W. W. Phelps and Co." For the Saints believe all that God "does now reveal," as well as all that He "has revealed," and that the publication of Revelations now given through the inspired servants of the Lord is as necessary as the placing of former-day revelations on record.

After the Revelation in Section 1, called "The Lord's Preface," had been received at Hiram, Portage Co., Ohio, on the 1st of November, 1831, a number of the brethren who were present at the conference arose and testified to the truth of the *Book of Commandments*. But notwithstanding this fact, some of the

JOSEPH SMITH RECEIVES A REVELATION DURING THE ORGANIZATION OF THE CHURCH

brethren criticized the language in which they were recorded, as imperfect. The Prophet Joseph did not take any notice of these critics; if the Lord should select some other instrument through whom to speak to the Church, it would be agreeable to him. But the Lord had no such purpose. He gave the critics a test, in these words, "Now seek ye out of the Book of Commandments, even the least that is among them, and appoint him that is the most wise among you; or, if there be any among you, that shall make one like unto it, then ye are justified in saying. that ye do not know that they are true. But if ye cannot make one like unto it, ye are under condemnation if ye do not bear record that they are true" (Doc. and Cov. 67:6–8). That was the test.

William E. McLellin accepted the challenge and did his best to bring forth a literary production that should compare favorably with the Revelations given through the Prophet. He was regarded as a learned man at that time, and when he utterly failed, the testimony of the elders was strengthened, and they renewed their allegiance to the Lord and their loyalty to the Prophet. Accordingly, the following declaration was drawn up:

"The testimony of the witnesses to the book of the Lord's Commandments, which He gave to His Church through Joseph Smith, Jr., who was appointed by the voice of the Church for this purpose; we therefore feel willing to bear testimony to all the world of mankind, to every creature upon the face of all the earth and upon the islands of the sea, that the Lord has borne record to our souls, through the Holy Ghost, shed forth upon us, that these commandments were given by inspiration of God, and are profitable for all men, and are verily true. We give this testimony unto the world, the Lord being our helper; and it is through the grace of God, the Father, and His Son, Jesus Christ, that we are permitted to have this privilege of bearing this testimony unto the world, that the children of men may be profited thereby."

Among the elders present at the special conference by which this question was decided were: Joseph Smith, Jr., Oliver Cowdery, David Whitmer, John Whitmer, Peter Whitmer, Jr., Sidney Rigdon, William E. McLellin, Orson Hyde, Luke Johnson, and Lyman E. Johnson (*History of the Church*, Vol. I., p. 226). Elder Brigham H. Roberts observes that the reason why this testimony did not appear in the *Book of Commandments* was that the printing press was destroyed by a mob before the printing had been completed.

On the 24th of September, 1834, a general assembly of Saints appointed a committee, consisting of Joseph Smith, Oliver Cowdery, and F. G. Williams to collect and arrange the Revelations so far given. This work was completed, and on August 17th, 1835, it was presented to a general assembly at Kirtland, under the name of The Doctrine and Covenants. It was accepted by unanimous vote, as a "law and a rule of faith and practice to the Church," on motion of Oliver Cowdery, on behalf of the committee. Many testimonies were borne to the truth of the Revelations. W. W. Phelps read the written testimony of the Twelve, which was almost identical with that given previously with reference to the *Book of Commandments*. The Twelve at that time were: Thomas B. Marsh, David W. Patten, Brigham Young, Heber C. Kimball, Orson Hyde, William E. McLellin, Parley P. Pratt, Luke S. Johnson, William Smith, Orson Pratt, John F. Boynton, and Lyman E. Johnson.

After the labors of the committee had been accepted, W. W. Phelps read an article on "Marriage," and Oliver Cowdery read one on "Government and Laws in General." Both were ordered printed, together with the Doctrine and Covenants, though neither was presented as a revelation, but expressive of the belief of the Saints on those subjects, at that time. The article on Government is found in section 134. That on Marriage is not included in recent editions.

On the 5th of May, 1879, Elder Orson Pratt, who was then on a mission in England, received a letter from President John Taylor, informing him that the Twelve had decided that he should obtain electroplates for a new edition of the Doctrine and Covenants. He divided the text into verses, and added the references. He was assisted by Elders John Nicholson, Hugh Findlay, John Rider, and Moroni Snow.

The Christian world should not consider it strange that the Lord, our God, again reveals His will to His children. Ancient prophets, speaking of the last days, declare that the Spirit of God will be poured out upon all flesh, and the result will be visions, dreams, and prophecies (Isaiah 44:3; Ezek. 11:19; 36:27; Joel 2:28; Zech. 12:10; Acts 2:16–20). The pouring out of the Spirit upon all flesh is followed by a general Pentecostal manifestation.

Joseph Smith was a great man, raised up for the work he did. He came at the time when the world was prepared for it. At no other time previously could the Church have been established. He came in the country where the foundations could be laid, because the ground had been prepared by liberal laws and religious influences. In no other country could the foundations of the Church have been laid at that time. He came through a lineage selected for his earthly mission, equipped with the very characteristics, gifts, and graces of a messenger from God and a martyr. God formed him for his mission. Therefore, he was great in his day and generation; towering over his fellowmen, and yet full of love towards all, unconscious of his greatness, willing to serve on all occasions, though mighty in words and deeds.

THE PROPHET JOSEPH CONTEMPLATES HIS SACRED MISSION

Table of Contents
DOCTRINE AND COVENANTS

Section 1	1
Section 2	5
Section 3	7
Section 4	9
Section 5	10
Section 6	13
Section 7	17
Section 8	18
Section 9	20
Section 10	22
Section 11	27
Section 12	29
Section 13	30
Section 14	31
Section 15	34
Section 16	35
Section 17	37
Section 18	39
Section 19	42
Section 20	46
Section 21	51
Section 22	55
Section 23	56
Section 24	57
Section 25	59
Section 26	62
Section 27	63
Section 28	65
Section 29	69
Section 30	73
Section 31	75
Section 32	76
Section 33	77
Section 34	81
Section 35	82
Section 36	84
Section 37	85
Section 38	86
Section 39	89
Section 40	91
Section 41	93
Section 42	94
Section 43	99
Section 44	102

Section 45	103
Section 46	109
Section 47	111
Section 48	112
Section 49	113
Section 50	115
Section 51	118
Section 52	121
Section 53	124
Section 54	125
Section 55	126
Section 56	127
Section 57	129
Section 58	132
Section 59	136
Section 60	138
Section 61	140
Section 62	143
Section 63	144
Section 64	149
Section 65	152
Section 66	153
Section 67	155
Section 68	157
Section 69	160
Section 70	161
Section 71	164
Section 72	165
Section 73	168
Section 74	169
Section 75	170
Section 76	173
Section 77	179
Section 78	182
Section 79	184
Section 80	185
Section 81	186
Section 82	187
Section 83	189
Section 84	191
Section 85	197
Section 86	199
Section 87	200
Section 88	201
Section 89	209
Section 90	212
Section 91	215
Section 92	216
Section 93	217
Section 94	220
Section 95	222
Section 96	226
Section 97	227

Section 98	230
Section 99	233
Section 100	234
Section 101	236
Section 102	243
Section 103	246
Section 104	249
Section 105	255
Section 106	258
Section 107	259
Section 108	266
Section 109	267
Section 110	275
Section 111	277
Section 112	279
Section 113	283
Section 114	284
Section 115	285
Section 116	289
Section 117	290
Section 118	292
Section 119	293
Section 120	294
Section 121	295
Section 122	299
Section 123	303
Section 124	305
Section 125	317
Section 126	319
Section 127	320
Section 128	322
Section 129	327
Section 130	328
Section 131	330
Section 132	331
Section 133	338
Section 134	342
Section 135	345
Section 136	349
Section 137	355
Section 138	357
Official Declaration	361
Excerpts	363
About Official Declaration 2	367
Pearl of Great Price	369
Introductory Note	371
The Book of Moses	373
The Book of Abraham	393
Writings of Joseph Smith	405
Joseph Smith—History	409
The Articles of Faith	423
People in the Doctrine and Covenants	425
Doctrine and Covenants Concordance	435

MY SERVANT JOSEPH

Section 1

This revelation is designated by the Lord as "my preface unto the book of my commandments" (section 1:6), given at the conference assembled in Hiram, Ohio, November 1, 1831 (History of the Church, vol. 1:221–222). The conference was considering publishing many of the revelations given to the Prophet Joseph Smith from the Lord.

1. Hearken, O ye people of my church, saith the voice of him who dwells on high, and whose eyes are upon all men; yea, verily I say, hearken ye people from afar and ye that are upon the islands of the sea, listen together.
2. For verily the voice of the Lord is unto all men, and there is none to escape, and there is no eye that shall not see, neither ear that shall not hear, neither heart that shall not be penetrated.
3. And the rebellious shall be pierced with much sorrow, for their iniquities shall be spoken upon the housetops, and their secret acts shall be revealed.
4. And the voice of warning shall be unto all people, by the mouths of my disciples, whom I have chosen in these last days.
5. And they shall go forth and none shall stay them, for I the Lord have commanded them.
6. Behold, this is mine authority, and the authority of my servants, and my preface unto the book of my commandments, which I have given them to publish unto you, O inhabitants of the earth.
7. Wherefore, fear and tremble, O ye people, for what I the Lord have decreed in them shall be fulfilled.
8. And verily I say unto you, that they who go forth, bearing these tidings unto the inhabitants of the earth, to them is power given to seal both on earth and in heaven, the unbelieving and rebellious;
9. Yea, verily, to seal them up unto the day when the wrath of God shall be poured out upon the wicked without measure,
10. Unto the day when the Lord shall come to recompense unto every man according to his work, and measure to every man according to the measure which he has measured to his fellow man.
11. Wherefore the voice of the Lord is unto the ends of the earth, that all that will hear may hear:
12. Prepare ye, prepare ye for that which is to come, for the Lord is nigh;
13. And the anger of the Lord is kindled, and his sword is bathed in heaven, and it shall fall upon the inhabitants of the earth,

14. And the arm of the Lord shall be revealed; and the day cometh that they who will not hear the voice of the Lord, neither the voice of his servants, neither give heed to the words of the prophets and apostles, shall be cut off from among the people;

15. For they have strayed from mine ordinances, and have broken mine everlasting covenant;

16. They seek not the Lord to establish his righteousness, but every man walketh in his own way, and after the image of his own God, whose image is in the likeness of the world, and whose substance is that of an idol, which waxeth old and shall perish in Babylon, even Babylon the great, which shall fall.

17. Wherefore, I the Lord, knowing the calamity which should come upon the inhabitants of the earth, called upon my servant Joseph Smith, jun., and spake unto him from heaven, and gave him commandments;

18. And also gave commandments to others, that they should proclaim these things unto the world; and all this that it might be fulfilled, which was written by the prophets,

19. The weak things of the world shall come forth and break down the mighty and strong ones, that man should not counsel his fellow man, neither trust in the arm of flesh,

20. But that every man might speak in the name of God the Lord, even the Savior of the world;

21. That faith also might increase in the earth;

22. That mine everlasting covenant might be established;

23. That the fulness of my gospel might be proclaimed by the weak and the simple unto the ends of the world, and before kings and rulers.

24. Behold, I am God and have spoken it: these commandments are of me, and were given unto my servants in their weakness, after the manner of their language, that they might come to understanding.

25. And inasmuch as they erred it might be made known:

26. And inasmuch as they sought wisdom they might be instructed:

27. And inasmuch as they sinned they might be chastened, that they might repent:

28. And inasmuch as they were humble they might be made strong, and blessed from on high, and receive knowledge from time to time:

29. And after having received the record of the Nephites, yea, even my servant Joseph Smith, jun., might have power to translate through the mercy of God, by the power of God, the Book of Mormon.

30. And also those to whom these commandments were given, might have power to lay the foundation of this church, and to bring it forth out of obscurity and out of darkness, the only true and living church upon the face of the whole earth, with which I, the Lord, am well pleased, speaking unto the church collectively and not individually—

31. For I the Lord cannot look upon sin with the least degree of allowance;

32. Nevertheless, he that repents and does the commandments of the Lord shall be forgiven;

33. And he that repents not, from him shall be taken even the light which he has received, for my Spirit shall not always strive with man, saith the Lord of Hosts.

34. And again, verily I say unto you, O inhabitants of the earth, I the Lord am willing to make these things known unto all flesh,

35. For I am no respecter of persons, and will that all men shall know that the day speedily cometh; the hour is not yet, but is nigh at hand, when peace shall be taken from the earth, and the devil shall have power over his own dominion,

36. And also the Lord shall have power over his saints, and shall reign in their midst, and shall come down in judgment upon Idumea, or the world.

37. Search these commandments, for they are true and faithful, and the prophecies and promises which are in them shall all be fulfilled.

38. What I the Lord have spoken, I have spoken, and I excuse not myself: and though the heavens and the earth pass away, my word shall not pass away, but shall all be fulfilled, whether by mine own voice or by the voice of my servants, it is the same;

39. For behold, and lo, the Lord is God, and the Spirit beareth record, and the record is true, and the truth abideth forever and ever. Amen.

THE ANGEL MORONI APPEARS TO JOSEPH SMITH, SEPT. 21, 1823

Section 2

On the evening of September 21, 1823, the Angel Moroni appeared to Joseph Smith in his father's home at Manchester, New York. Section two is part of the message the angel delivered to young Joseph that evening (History of the Church, vol. 1:10–12. See also Joseph Smith History 1:29–39).

1. Behold I will reveal unto you the Priesthood, by the hand of Elijah the prophet, before the coming of the great and dreadful day of the Lord;
2. And he shall plant in the hearts of the children the promises made to the fathers, and the hearts of the children shall turn to their fathers;
3. If it were not so, the whole earth would be utterly wasted at its coming.

THE MARTIN HARRIS FARM IN PALMYRA, NEW YORK

Section 3

This revelation was received by the Prophet Joseph Smith at Harmony, Pennsylvania, July 1828, in consequence of the loss of 116 pages of manuscript translated from the Book of Lehi on Mormon's plates (see "Preface," 1st ed. of the Book of Mormon). Joseph Smith allowed Martin Harris, his scribe, to carry the manuscript home to Palmyra, New York. Martin was under covenant to show the writings to only five persons. He showed them to others "and by stratagem they got them away from him" (History of the Church, vol. 1:20–22).

1. The works, and the designs, and the purposes of God cannot be frustrated, neither can they come to naught,
2. For God doth not walk in crooked paths, neither doth he turn to the right hand nor to the left, neither doth he vary from that which he hath said, therefore his paths are straight, and his course is one eternal round.
3. Remember, remember that it is not the work of God that is frustrated, but the work of men;
4. For although a man may have many revelations, and have power to do many mighty works, yet if he boasts in his own strength, and sets at naught the counsels of God, and follows after the dictates of his own will and carnal desires, he must fall and incur the vengeance of a just God upon him.
5. Behold, you have been entrusted with these things, but how strict were your commandments; and remember, also the promises which were made to you, if you did not transgress them;
6. And behold, how oft you have transgressed the commandments and the laws of God, and have gone on in the persuasion of men;
7. For, behold, you should not have feared man more than God, although men set at naught the counsels of God, and despise his words;
8. Yet you should have been faithful, and he would have extended his arm and supported you against all the fiery darts of the adversary; and he would have been with you in every time of trouble.
9. Behold, thou art Joseph, and thou wast chosen to do the work of the Lord, but because of transgression, if thou art not aware thou wilt fall;
10. But remember God is merciful; therefore, repent of that which thou hast done which is contrary to the commandment which I gave you, and thou art still chosen, and art again called to the work;
11. Except thou do this, thou shalt be delivered up and become as other men, and have no more gift.
12. And when thou deliveredst up that which God had given thee sight and power to translate,

thou deliveredst up that which was sacred into the hands of a wicked man,

13. Who has set at naught the counsels of God, and has broken the most sacred promises which were made before God, and has depended upon his own judgment, and boasted in his own wisdom,

14. And this is the reason that thou hast lost thy privileges for a season,

15. For thou hast suffered the counsel of thy director to be trampled upon from the beginning.

16. Nevertheless my work shall go forth, for inasmuch as the knowledge of a Savior has come unto the world, through the testimony of the Jews, even so shall the knowledge of a Savior come unto my people,

17. And to the Nephites, and the Jacobites, and the Josephites, and the Zoramites, through the testimony of their fathers—

18. And this testimony shall come to the knowledge of the Lamanites, and the Lemuelites and the Ishmaelites, who dwindled in unbelief because of the iniquity of their fathers, whom the Lord has suffered to destroy their brethren the Nephites, because of their iniquities and their abominations;

19. And for this very purpose are these plates preserved, which contain these records—that the promises of the Lord might be fulfilled, which he made to his people;

20. And that the Lamanites might come to the knowledge of their fathers, and that they might know the promises of the Lord, and that they may believe the gospel and rely upon the merits of Jesus Christ, and be glorified through faith in his name, and that through their repentance they might be saved. Amen.

Section 4

In February 1829, Joseph Smith, Sen. traveled from Manchester, New York, to visit his son who was residing in Harmony, Pennsylvania. The prophet Joseph Smith recorded: "In the Month of February 1829, my father came to visit us, at which time I received the following revelation for him" (History of the Church, vol. 1:28).

1. Now behold, a marvelous work is about to come forth among the children of men;
2. Therefore, O ye that embark in the service of God, see that ye serve him with all your heart, might, mind and strength, that ye may stand blameless before God at the last day;
3. Therefore, if ye have desires to serve God ye are called to the work,
4. For behold the field is white already to harvest, and lo, he that thrusteth in his sickle with his might, the same layeth up in store that he perish not, but bringeth salvation to his soul;
5. And faith, hope, charity and love, with an eye single to the glory of God, qualify him for the work.
6. Remember faith, virtue, knowledge, temperance, patience, brotherly kindness, godliness, charity, humility, diligence.
7. Ask and ye shall receive, knock and it shall be opened unto you. Amen.

Section 5

Martin Harris desired to receive a witness from the Lord that Joseph Smith had the plates of the Book of Mormon (Section 5:1). This revelation was given to the Prophet Joseph Smith in March 1829 at Harmony, Pennsylvania. "The following I applied for and obtained at the request of the aforementioned Martin Harris" (History of the Church, vol. 1:28).

1. Behold, I say unto you, that as my servant Martin Harris has desired a witness at my hand, that you, my servant Joseph Smith, jun., have got the plates of which you have testified and borne record that you have received of me;

2. And now, behold, this shall you say unto him, he who spake unto you, said unto you, I, the Lord, am God, and have given these things unto you, my servant Joseph Smith, Jun., and have commanded you that you should stand as a witness of these things,

3. And I have caused you that you should enter into a covenant with me, that you should not show them except to those persons to whom I commanded you; and you have no power over them except I grant it unto you.

4. And you have a gift to translate the plates, and this is the first gift that I bestowed upon you, and I have commanded that you should pretend to no other gift, until my purpose is fulfilled in this; for I will grant unto you no other gift until it is finished.

5. Verily, I say unto you, that woe shall come unto the inhabitants of the earth if they will not hearken unto my words;

6. For hereafter you shall be ordained and go forth and deliver my words unto the children of men.

7. Behold, if they will not believe my words, they would not believe you my servant Joseph, if it were possible that you could show them all these things which I have committed unto you.

8. O! this unbelieving and stiffnecked generation, mine anger is kindled against them.

9. Behold, verily I say unto you, I have reserved those things which I have entrusted unto you, my servant Joseph, for a wise purpose in me, and it shall be made known unto future generations;

10. But this generation shall have my word through you;

11. And in addition to your testimony, the testimony of three of my servants, whom I shall call and ordain, unto whom I will show these things, and they shall go forth with my words that are given through you;

12. Yea, they shall know of a surety that these things are true, for from heaven will I declare it unto them.
13. I will give them power that they may behold and view these things as they are;
14. And to none else will I grant this power, to receive this same testimony among this generation, in this the beginning of the rising up and the coming forth of my church out of the wilderness; clear as the moon, and fair as the sun, and terrible as an army with banners.
15. And the testimony of three witnesses will I send forth of my word;
16. And behold, whosoever believeth on my words them will I visit with the manifestation of my Spirit and they shall be born of me, even of water and of the Spirit.
17. And you must wait yet a little while, for ye are not yet ordained;
18. And their testimony shall also go forth unto the condemnation of this generation if they harden their hearts against them;
19. For a desolating scourge shall go forth among the inhabitants of the earth, and shall continue to be poured out from time to time, if they repent not, until the earth is empty, and the inhabitants thereof are consumed away and utterly destroyed by the brightness of my coming.
20. Behold, I tell you these things, even as I also told the people of the destruction of Jerusalem, and my word shall be verified at this time as it hath hitherto been verified.
21. And now I command you my servant Joseph to repent and walk more uprightly before me, and yield to the persuasions of men no more;
22. And that you be firm in keeping the commandments wherewith I have commanded you, and if you do this, behold I grant unto you eternal life, even if you should be slain.
23. And now, again, I speak unto you, my servant Joseph, concerning the man that desires the witness.
24. Behold, I say unto him, he exalts himself and does not humble himself sufficiently before me; but if he will bow down before me, and humble himself in mighty prayer and faith, in the sincerity of his heart, then will I grant unto him a view of the things which he desires to see.
25. And then he shall say unto the people of this generation, behold, I have seen the things which the Lord hath shown unto Joseph Smith, jun., and I know of a surety that they are true, for I have seen them, for they have been shown unto me by the power of God and not of man.
26. And I, the Lord, command him, my servant Martin Harris, that he shall say no more unto them concerning these things, except he shall say I have seen them, and they have been shown unto me by the power of God, and these are the words which he shall say;
27. But if he deny this, he will break the covenant which he has before covenanted with me, and behold, he is condemned.
28. And now, except he humble himself and acknowledge unto me the things that he has done which are wrong, and covenant with me that he will keep my commandments, and exercise faith in me, behold, I say unto him, he shall have no such views, for I will grant unto him no views of the things of which I have spoken.
29. And if this be the case, I command you, my servant Joseph, that you shall say unto him, that he shall do no more, nor trouble me any more concerning this matter.
30. And if this be the case, behold, I say unto thee Joseph, when thou hast translated a few more pages, thou shalt stop for a season, even until I command thee again; then thou mayest translate again.
31. And except you do this, behold, thou shalt have no more gift, and I will take away the things which I have entrusted with thee.
32. And now, because I foresee the lying in wait to destroy thee, yea, I foresee that if my servant

Martin Harris humbleth not himself, and receive a witness from my hand, that he will fall into transgression;

33. And there are many that lie in wait to destroy thee from off the face of the earth, and for this cause, that thy days may be prolonged, I have given unto thee these commandments.

34. Yea, for this cause I have said, stop and stand still until I command thee, and I will provide means whereby thou mayest accomplish the thing which I have commanded thee;

35. And if thou art faithful in keeping my commandments, thou shalt be lifted up at the last day. Amen.

Section 6

This revelation was received by the Prophet Joseph Smith in April, 1829, at Harmony, Pennsylvania. The circumstances preceding the reception of the revelation are as follows: "On the 5th of April, 1829, Oliver Cowdery came to my house, until which time I had never seen him. He stated to me that having been teaching school in the neighborhood where my father resided, and my father being one of those who sent to the school, he went to board for a season at his house, and while there the family related to him the circumstances of my having received the plates, and accordingly he had come to make inquires of me . . . I inquired of the Lord through the Urim and Thummim, and obtained the following" (History of the Church, vol. 1:32–33).

1. A great and marvelous work is about to come forth unto the children of men.
2. Behold, I am God, give heed unto my word, which is quick and powerful, sharper than a two-edged sword, to the dividing asunder of both joints and marrow; therefore give heed unto my words.
3. Behold the field is white already to harvest, therefore whoso desireth to reap, let him thrust in his sickle with his might, and reap while the day lasts, that he may treasure up for his soul everlasting salvation in the kingdom of God:
4. Yea, whosoever will thrust in his sickle and reap, the same is called of God;
5. Therefore, if you will ask of me you shall receive; if you will knock it shall be opened unto you.
6. Now, as you have asked, behold, I say unto you, keep my commandments, and seek to bring forth and establish the cause of Zion,
7. Seek not for riches but for wisdom, and behold, the mysteries of God shall be unfolded unto you, and then shall you be made rich. Behold, he that hath eternal life is rich.
8. Verily, verily, I say unto you, even as you desire of me, so it shall be unto you; and if you desire, you shall be the means of doing much good in this generation.
9. Say nothing but repentance unto this generation, keep my commandments, and assist to bring forth my work, according to my commandments, and you shall be blessed.
10. Behold thou hast a gift, and blessed art thou because of thy gift. Remember it is sacred and cometh from above:
11. And if thou wilt inquire, thou shalt know mysteries which are great and marvelous: therefore thou shalt exercise thy gift, that thou mayest find out mysteries, that thou mayest bring many to the knowledge of the truth; yea, convince them of the error of their ways.

12. Make not thy gift known unto any, save it be those who are of thy faith. Trifle not with sacred things.

13. If thou wilt do good, yea, and hold out faithful to the end, thou shalt be saved in the kingdom of God, which is the greatest of all the gifts of God; for there is no gift greater than the gift of salvation.

14. Verily, verily, I say unto thee, blessed art thou for what thou hast done, for thou hast inquired of me, and behold as often as thou hast inquired, thou hast received instruction of my Spirit. If it had not been so, thou wouldst not have come to the place where thou art at this time.

15. Behold, thou knowest that thou hast inquired of me, and I did enlighten thy mind; and now I tell thee these things, that thou mayest know that thou hast been enlightened by the Spirit of truth;

16. Yea, I tell thee, that thou mayest know that there is none else save God that knowest thy thoughts and the intents of thy heart:

17. I tell thee these things as a witness unto thee, that the words or the work which thou hast been writing is true.

18. Therefore be diligent, stand by my servant Joseph, faithfully, in whatsoever difficult circumstances he may be for the word's sake.

19. Admonish him in his faults, and also receive admonition of him. Be patient; be sober; be temperate; have patience, faith, hope and charity.

20. Behold, thou art Oliver, and I have spoken unto thee because of thy desires; therefore treasure up these words in thy heart. Be faithful and diligent in keeping the commandments of God, and I will encircle thee in the arms of my love.

21. Behold, I am Jesus Christ, the Son of God. I am the same that came unto my own, and my own received me not. I am the light which shineth in darkness, and the darkness comprehendeth it not.

22. Verily, verily, I say unto you, if you desire a further witness, cast your mind upon the night that you cried unto me in your heart, that you might know concerning the truth of these things.

23. Did I not speak peace to your mind concerning the matter? What greater witness can you have than from God?

24. And now, behold, you have received a witness, for if I have told you things which no man knoweth, have you not received a witness?

25. And, behold, I grant unto you a gift, if you desire of me, to translate even as my servant Joseph.

26. Verily, verily, I say unto you, that there are records which contain much of my gospel, which have been kept back because of the wickedness of the people;

27. And now I command you, that if you have good desires—a desire to lay up treasures for yourself in heaven—then shall you assist in bringing to light, with your gift, those parts of my scriptures which have been hidden because of iniquity.

28. And now, behold, I give unto you, and also unto my servant Joseph, the keys of this gift, which shall bring to light this ministry; and in the mouth of two or three witnesses shall every word be established.

29. Verily, verily, I say unto you, if they reject my words, and this part of my gospel and ministry, blessed are ye, for they can do no more unto you than unto me;

30. And even if they do unto you, even as they have done unto me, blessed are ye, for you shall dwell with me in glory;

31. But if they reject not my words, which shall be established by the testimony which shall be given, blessed are they, and then shall ye have joy in the fruit of your labors.

32. Verily, verily, I say unto you, as I said unto my disciples, where two or three are gathered together in my name, as touching one thing, behold, there will I be in the midst of them, even so am I in the midst of you.

33. Fear not to do good, my sons, for whatsoever ye sow, that shall ye also reap; therefore, if ye sow good, ye shall also reap good for your reward.

34. Therefore, fear not, little flock, do good; let earth and hell combine against you, for if ye are built upon my Rock, they cannot prevail.

35. Behold, I do not condemn you, go your ways and sin no more, perform with soberness the work which I have commanded you;

36. Look unto me in every thought; doubt not, fear not;

37. Behold the wounds which pierced my side, and also the prints of the nails in my hands and feet; be faithful, keep my commandments, and ye shall inherit the kingdom of heaven. Amen.

JOSEPH SMITH AND OLIVER COWDERY TRANSLATING THE BOOK OF MORMON

Section 7

While translating the Book of Mormon, a difference of opinion arose between Oliver Cowdery and Joseph Smith as to whether John the Apostle "died or continued to live." Through the Urim and Thummim they received this revelation in April 1829, at Harmony, Pennsylvania (History of the Church, vol. 1:35–36).

1. And the Lord said unto me, John, my beloved, what desirest thou? For if you shall ask, what you will, it shall be granted unto you.
2. And I said unto him, Lord, give unto me power over death, that I may live and bring souls unto thee.
3. And the Lord said unto me, Verily, verily, I say unto thee, because thou desirest this thou shalt tarry until I come in my glory, and shalt prophesy before nations, kindreds, tongues and people.
4. And for this cause the Lord said unto Peter, If I will that he tarry till I come, what is that to thee? for he desired of me that he might bring souls unto me, but thou desiredst that thou mightest speedily come unto me in my kingdom.
5. I say unto thee, Peter, this was a good desire, but my beloved has desired that he might do more, or a greater work yet among men than what he has before done;
6. Yea, he has undertaken a greater work, therefore I will make him as flaming fire and a ministering angel: he shall minister for those who shall be heirs of salvation who dwell on the earth:
7. And I will make thee to minister for him and for thy brother James; and unto you three I will give this power and the keys of this ministry until I come.
8. Verily, I say unto you, ye shall both have according to your desires, for ye both joy in that which ye have desired.

SECTION 8

One of the gifts granted to Oliver Cowdery by the Lord was the gift of translation (section 6:25). Oliver Cowdery became very anxious to have this gift bestowed upon him. The Prophet Joseph Smith informs us: "... in relation to this desire the following revelations (sections 8 and 9) were obtained," April 1829, at Harmony, Pennsylvania (History of the Church, vol. 1:36–37).

1. Oliver Cowdery, verily, verily, I say unto you, that assuredly as the Lord liveth, who is your God and your Redeemer, even so surely shall you receive a knowledge of whatsoever things you shall ask in faith, with an honest heart, believing that you shall receive a knowledge concerning the engravings of old records, which are ancient, which contain those parts of my scripture of which have been spoken by the manifestation of my Spirit;

2. Yea, behold, I will tell you in your mind and in your heart, by the Holy Ghost, which shall come upon you and which shall dwell in your heart.

3. Now, behold, this is the Spirit of revelation; behold, this is the Spirit by which Moses brought the children of Israel through the Red Sea on dry ground;

4. Therefore this is thy gift; apply unto it, and blessed art thou, for it shall deliver you out of the hands of your enemies, when, if it were not so, they would slay you and bring your soul to destruction.

5. O! remember these words, and keep my commandments. Remember this is your gift.

6. Now this is not all thy gift; for you have another gift, which is the gift of Aaron: behold, it has told you many things;

7. Behold, there is no other power, save the power of God, that can cause this gift of Aaron to be with you;

8. Therefore doubt not, for it is the gift of God, and you shall hold it in your hands, and do marvelous works; and no power shall be able to take it away out of your hands, for it is the work of God.

9. And, therefore, whatsoever you shall ask me to tell you, by that means, that will I grant unto you, and you shall have knowledge concerning it:

10. Remember that without faith you can do nothing, therefore ask in faith. Trifle not with these things; do not ask for that which you ought not:

11. Ask that you may know the mysteries of God, and that you may translate and receive knowledge from all those ancient records which have

been hid up, that are sacred, and according to your faith shall it be done unto you.

12. Behold, it is I that have spoken it; and I am the same that spake unto you from the beginning. Amen.

Section 9

The Prophet Joseph received this revelation April 1829, at Harmony, Pennsylvania (see historical background, section 8).

1. Behold, I say unto you, my son, that because you did not translate according to that which you desired of me, and did commence again to write for my servant, Joseph Smith, jun., even so I would that ye should continue until you have finished this record, which I have entrusted unto him:
2. And then, behold, other records have I, that I will give unto you power that you may assist to translate.
3. Be patient, my son, for it is wisdom in me, and it is not expedient that you should translate at this present time.
4. Behold, the work which you are called to do, is to write for my servant Joseph;
5. And, behold, it is because that you did not continue as you commenced, when you began to translate, that I have taken away this privilege from you.
6. Do not murmur, my son, for it is wisdom in me that I have dealt with you after this manner.
7. Behold, you have not understood; you have supposed that I would give it unto you, when you took no thought, save it was to ask me;
8. But, behold, I say unto you, that you must study it out in your mind; then you must ask me if it be right, and if it is right I will cause that your bosom shall burn within you; therefore, you shall feel that it is right;
9. But if it be not right, you shall have no such feelings, but you shall have a stupor of thought, that shall cause you to forget the thing which is wrong: therefore, you cannot write that which is sacred, save it be given you from me.
10. Now if you had known this, you could have translated; nevertheless, it is not expedient that you should translate now.
11. Behold, it was expedient when you commenced, but you feared and the time is past, and it is not expedient now;
12. For, do you not behold that I have given unto my servant Joseph sufficient strength, whereby it is made up; and neither of you have I condemned.
13. Do this thing which I have commanded you, and you shall prosper. Be faithful, and yield to no temptation.

14. Stand fast in the work wherewith I have called you, and a hair of your head shall not be lost, and you shall be lifted up at the last day. Amen.

ECTION 10

In consequence of the loss of 116 pages of the manuscript of the Book of Mormon (section 3), an angel of the Lord took the plates and the Urim and Thummim from the Prophet Joseph. In a few days they were returned to him, and the Prophet ". . . inquired of the Lord, and the Lord said thus unto me." This revelation was received in the summer of 1828, at Harmony, Pennsylvania (History of the Church, vol. 1:23).

1. Now, behold, I say unto you, that because you delivered up those writings which you had power given unto you to translate, by the means of the Urim and Thummim, into the hands of a wicked man, you have lost them;
2. And you also lost your gift at the same time, and your mind became darkened;
3. Nevertheless, it is now restored unto you again, therefore see that you are faithful and continue on unto the finishing of the remainder of the work of translation as you have begun:
4. Do not run faster, or labor more than you have strength and means provided to enable you to translate; but be diligent unto the end:
5. Pray always, that you may come off conqueror; yea, that you may conquer Satan, and that you may escape the hands of the servants of Satan, that do uphold his work.
6. Behold, they have sought to destroy you; yea, even the man in whom you have trusted, has sought to destroy you.
7. And for this cause I said that he is a wicked man, for he has sought to take away the things wherewith you have been entrusted; and he has also sought to destroy your gift;
8. And because you have delivered the writings into his hands, behold, wicked men have taken them from you:
9. Therefore, you have delivered them up; yea, that which was sacred unto wickedness.
10. And, behold, Satan has put it into their hearts to alter the words which you have caused to be written, or which you have translated, which have gone out of your hands.
11. And, behold, I say unto you, that because they have altered the words, they read contrary from that which you translated and caused to be written;
12. And, on this wise, the devil has sought to lay a cunning plan, that he may destroy this work;
13. For he has put into their hearts to do this, that by lying they may say they have caught you in the words which you have pretended to translate.

14. Verily, I say unto you, that I will not suffer that Satan shall accomplish his evil design in this thing,

15. For, behold, he has put it into their hearts to get thee to tempt the Lord thy God, in asking to translate it over again;

16. And then, behold, they say and think in their hearts, we will see if God has given him power to translate, if so, he will also give him power again;

17. And if God giveth him power again, or if he translates again, or in other words, if he bringeth forth the same words, behold, we have the same with us, and we have altered them:

18. Therefore, they will not agree, and we will say that he has lied in his words, and that he has no gift, and that he has no power:

19. Therefore, we will destroy him, and also the work, and will do this that we may not be ashamed in the end, and that we may get glory of the world.

20. Verily, verily, I say unto you, that Satan has great hold upon their hearts; he stirreth them up to iniquity against that which is good,

21. And their hearts are corrupt, and full of wickedness and abominations, and they love darkness rather than light, because their deeds are evil: therefore they will not ask of me.

22. Satan stirreth them up, that he may lead their souls to destruction.

23. And thus he has laid a cunning plan, thinking to destroy the work of God, but I will require this at their hands, and it shall turn to their shame and condemnation in the day of judgment;

24. Yea, he stirreth up their hearts to anger against this work;

25. Yea, he saith unto them, Deceive and lie in wait to catch, that ye may destroy: behold, this is no harm, and thus he flattereth them, and telleth them that it is no sin to lie, that they may catch a man in a lie, that they may destroy him;

26. And thus he flattereth them, and leadeth them along until he draggeth their souls down to hell; and thus he causeth them to catch themselves in their own snare;

27. And thus he goeth up and down, to and fro in the earth, seeking to destroy the souls of men.

28. Verily, verily, I say unto you, wo be unto him that lieth to deceive, because he supposeth that another lieth to deceive; for such are not exempt from the justice of God.

29. Now, behold, they have altered these words, because Satan saith unto them, He hath deceived you: and thus he flattereth them away to do iniquity, to get thee to tempt the Lord thy God.

30. Behold, I say unto you, that you shall not translate again those words which have gone forth out of your hands;

31. For, behold, they shall not accomplish their evil designs in lying against those words. For, behold, if you should bring forth the same words they will say that you have lied; that you have pretended to translate, but that you have contradicted yourself:

32. And, behold, they will publish this, and Satan will harden the hearts of the people to stir them up to anger against you, that they will not believe my words.

33. Thus Satan thinketh to overpower your testimony in this generation, that the work may not come forth in this generation:

34. But behold, here is wisdom, and because I show unto you wisdom, and give you commandments concerning these things, what you shall do, show it not unto the world until you have accomplished the work of translation.

35. Marvel not that I said unto you, here is wisdom, show it not unto the world, for I said, show it not unto the world, that you may be preserved.

36. Behold, I do not say that you shall not show it unto the righteous;

37. But as you cannot always judge the righteous, or as you cannot always tell the wicked from the righteous, therefore I say unto you, hold your peace until I shall see fit to make all things known unto the world concerning the matter.

38. And now, verily I say unto you, that an account of those things that you have written, which have gone out of your hands, are engraven upon the plates of Nephi;

39. Yea, and you remember it was said in those writings that a more particular account was given of these things upon the plates of Nephi.

40. And now, because the account which is engraven upon the plates of Nephi is more particular concerning the things which, in my wisdom, I would bring to the knowledge of the people in this account;

41. Therefore, you shall translate the engravings which are on the plates of Nephi, down even till you come to the reign of king Benjamin, or until you come to that which you have translated, which you have retained;

42. And behold, you shall publish it as the record of Nephi, and thus I will confound those who have altered my words.

43. I will not suffer that they shall destroy my work; yea, I will show unto them that my wisdom is greater than the cunning of the devil.

44. Behold, they have only got a part, or an abridgment of the account of Nephi.

45. Behold, there are many things engraven on the plates of Nephi which do throw greater views upon my gospel; therefore, it is wisdom in me that you should translate this first part of the engravings of Nephi, and send forth in this work.

46. And, behold, all the remainder of this work does contain all those parts of my gospel which my holy prophets, yea, and also my disciples, desired in their prayers should come forth unto this people.

47. And I said unto them, that it should be granted unto them according to their faith in their prayers;

48. Yea, and this was their faith, that my gospel, which I gave unto them, that they might preach in their days, might come unto their brethren the Lamanites, and also all that had become Lamanites, because of their dissensions.

49. Now, this is not all—their faith in their prayers was, that this gospel should be made known also, if it were possible that other nations should possess this land;

50. And thus they did leave a blessing upon this land in their prayers, that whosoever should believe in this gospel in this land, might have eternal life;

51. Yea, that it might be free unto all of whatsoever nation, kindred, tongue, or people they may be.

52. And now, behold, according to their faith in their prayers will I bring this part of my gospel to the knowledge of my people. Behold, I do not bring it to destroy that which they have received, but to build it up.

53. And for this cause have I said; if this generation harden not their hearts, I will establish my church among them.

54. Now I do not say this to destroy my church, but I say this to build up my church;

55. Therefore, whosoever belongeth to my church need not fear, for such shall inherit the kingdom of heaven;

56. But it is they who do not fear me, neither keep my commandments, but build up churches unto themselves to get gain, yea, and all those that do wickedly and build up the kingdom of the devil; yea, verily, verily, I say unto you, that it is they that I will disturb, and cause to tremble and shake to the center.

57. Behold, I am Jesus Christ, the Son of God. I came unto my own, and my own received me not.

58. I am the light which shineth in darkness, and the darkness comprehendeth it not.

59. I am he who said, other sheep have I which are not of this fold, unto my disciples, and many there were that understood me not.

60. And I will show unto this people that I had other sheep, and that they were a branch of the house of Jacob;

61. And I will bring to light their marvelous works, which they did in my name;

62. Yea, and I will also bring to light my gospel which was ministered unto them, and, behold, they shall not deny that which you have received, but they shall build it up, and shall bring to light the true points of my doctrine, yea, and the only doctrine which is in me;

63. And this I do that I may establish my gospel, that there may not be so much contention; yea, Satan doth stir up the hearts of the people to contention concerning the points of my doctrine; and in these things they do err, for they do wrest the scriptures and do not understand them;

64. Therefore, I will unfold unto them this great mystery;

65. For, behold, I will gather them as a hen gathereth her chickens under her wings, if they will not harden their hearts,

66. Yea, if they will come, they may, and partake of the waters of life freely.

67. Behold, this is my doctrine: whosoever repenteth and cometh unto me, the same is my church.

68. Whosoever declareth more or less than this, the same is not of me, but is against me; therefore he is not of my church.

69. And now, behold, whosoever is of my church, and endureth of my church to the end, him will I establish upon my rock, and the gates of hell shall not prevail against them.

70. And now, remember the words of him who is the life and light of the world, your Redeemer, your Lord and your God. Amen.

HYRUM SMITH, BROTHER OF THE PROPHET JOSEPH SMITH

Section 11

In May 1829, Hyrum Smith, brother to Joseph Smith, traveled from Manchester, New York, to Harmony, Pennsylvania, to inquire of his brother concerning the work in which he was engaged. At his "earnest request" Joseph Smith sought the Lord through the Urim and Thummim and received for Hyrum this revelation (History of the Church, vol. 1:44–45).

1. A great and marvelous work is about to come forth among the children of men.
2. Behold, I am God, and give heed to my word, which is quick and powerful, sharper than a two-edged sword, to the dividing asunder of both joints and marrow; therefore give heed unto my word.
3. Behold, the field is white already to harvest, therefore, whoso desireth to reap, let him thrust in his sickle with his might, and reap while the day lasts, that he may treasure up for his soul everlasting salvation in the kingdom of God;
4. Yea, whosoever will thrust in his sickle and reap, the same is called of God;
5. Therefore, if you will ask of me, you shall receive, if you will knock, it shall be opened unto you.
6. Now, as you have asked, behold, I say unto you, keep my commandments, and seek to bring forth and establish the cause of Zion.
7. Seek not for riches but for wisdom, and, behold, the mysteries of God, shall be unfolded unto you, and then shall you be made rich: behold, he that hath eternal life is rich.
8. Verily, verily, I say unto you, even as you desire of me, so it shall be done unto you: and, if you desire, you shall be the means of doing much good in this generation.
9. Say nothing but repentance unto this generation. Keep my commandments, and assist to bring forth my work, according to my commandments, and you shall be blessed.
10. Behold, thou hast a gift, or thou shalt have a gift if thou wilt desire of me in faith, with an honest heart, believing in the power of Jesus Christ, or in my power which speaketh unto thee;
11. For, behold, it is I that speak; behold, I am the light which shineth in darkness, and by my power I give these words unto thee.
12. And now, verily, verily, I say unto thee, put your trust in that Spirit which leadeth to do good: yea, to do justly, to walk humbly, to judge righteously, and this is my Spirit.
13. Verily, verily, I say unto you, I will impart unto you of my Spirit; which shall enlighten your mind, which shall fill your soul with joy,

14. And then shall ye know, or by this shall you know all things whatsoever you desire of me, which are pertaining unto things of righteousness, in faith believing in me that you shall receive.
15. Behold, I command you, that you need not suppose that you are called to preach until you are called:
16. Wait a little longer, until you shall have my word, my rock, my church, and my gospel, that you may know of a surety my doctrine;
17. And then behold, according to your desires, yea, even according to your faith shall it be done unto you.
18. Keep my commandments, hold your peace, appeal unto my Spirit;
19. Yea, cleave unto me with all your heart, that you may assist in bringing to light those things of which has been spoken; yea, the translation of my work; be patient until you shall accomplish it.
20. Behold, this is your work, to keep my commandments, yea, with all your might, mind, and strength;
21. Seek not to declare my word, but first seek to obtain my word, and then shall your tongue be loosed; then, if you desire, you shall have my Spirit and my word, yea, the power of God unto the convincing of men;
22. But now hold your peace, study my word which hath gone forth among the children of men, and also study my word which shall come forth among the children of men, or that which is now translating, yea, until you have obtained all which I shall grant unto the children of men, in this generation, and then shall all things be added thereunto.
23. Behold thou art Hyrum, my son, seek the kingdom of God, and all things shall be added according to that which is just.
24. Build upon my rock, which is my gospel;
25. Deny not the Spirit of revelation, nor the Spirit of prophecy, for wo unto him that denieth these things;
26. Therefore, treasure up in your heart until the time which is in my wisdom that you shall go forth.
27. Behold, I speak unto all who have good desires, and have thrust in their sickle to reap.
28. Behold, I am Jesus Christ, the Son of God. I am the life and the light of the world.
29. I am the same who came unto my own and my own received me not;
30. But verily, verily, I say unto you, that as many as receive me, to them will I give power to become the sons of God, even to them that believe on my name. Amen.

Section 12

Joseph Knight, Sen., of Colesville, New York, a friend of the Smith family, brought several "quantity of provisions" to Joseph Smith to aid him in the translation. He was desirous to know of the Lord his duty pertaining to the work. This revelation was received in May 1829, at Harmony, Pennsylvania (History of the Church, vol. 1:47–48).

1. A great and marvelous work is about to come forth among the children of men.
2. Behold, I am God, and give heed to my word, which is quick and powerful, sharper than a two-edged sword, to the dividing asunder of both joints and marrow; therefore, give heed unto my word.
3. Behold, the field is white already to harvest, therefore, whoso desireth to reap, let him thrust in his sickle with his might, and reap while the day lasts, that he may treasure up for his soul everlasting salvation in the kingdom of God;
4. Yea, whosoever will thrust in his sickle and reap, the same is called of God;
5. Therefore, if you will ask of me you shall receive, if you will knock it shall be opened unto you.
6. Now, as you have asked, behold, I say unto you, keep my commandments, and seek to bring forth and establish the cause of Zion.
7. Behold, I speak unto you, and also to all those who have desires to bring forth and establish this work,
8. And no one can assist in this work, except he shall be humble and full of love, having faith, hope, and charity, being temperate in all things, whatsoever shall be entrusted to his care.
9. Behold, I am the light and the life of the world, that speak these words, therefore give heed with your might, and then you are called. Amen.

SECTION 13

While translating the Book of Mormon, Joseph Smith and Oliver Cowdery learned that baptism was necessary for the remission of sins. These two brethren sought seclusion in the woods along the banks of the Susquehanna River and through prayer inquired of the Lord concerning this matter. John the Baptist appeared, and by the laying on of hands conferred the Aaronic Priesthood upon them. Section 13 contains the words spoken by John the Baptist when conferring this priesthood. The date of this confirmation was May 15, 1829, near Harmony, Pennsylvania. John the Baptist informed Joseph Smith and Oliver Cowdery that he was acting under the direction of Peter, James, and John, who held the keys of the Melchizedek Priesthood. He also informed them that this priesthood would ". . . in due time be conferred on (them) . . ." (History of the Church, vol. 1:39–41).

1. Upon you my fellow servants, in the name of Messiah, I confer the Priesthood of Aaron, which holds the keys of the ministering of angels, and of the gospel of repentance, and of baptism by immersion for the remission of sins; and this shall never be taken again from the earth, until the sons of Levi do offer again an offering unto the Lord in righteousness.

Section 14

In June 1829, Joseph Smith's family and Oliver Cowdery moved to Fayette, New York, to reside with the Peter Whitmer, Sen. family until the translating of the plates of the Book of Mormon was completed. The sons of Peter Whitmer, Sen., namely, David, John, and Peter, Jun. ". . . being anxious to know their respective duties, and having desired with much earnestness that I should inquire of the Lord concerning them, I did so, through the means of the Urim and Thummim, and obtained for them in succession the following revelations." These three revelations were received in June 1829, at Fayette, New York (History of the Church, vol. 1:48–49). This revelation was given to David Whitmer.

1. A great and marvelous work is about to come forth unto the children of men.
2. Behold, I am God, and give heed to my word, which is quick and powerful, sharper than a two-edged sword, to the dividing asunder of both joints and marrow; therefore give heed unto my word.
3. Behold, the field is white already to harvest, therefore, whoso desireth to reap let him thrust in his sickle with his might, and reap while the day lasts, that he may treasure up for his soul everlasting salvation in the kingdom of God,
4. Yea, whosoever will thrust in his sickle and reap, the same is called of God.
5. Therefore, if you will ask of me you shall receive, if you will knock it shall be opened unto you.
6. Seek to bring forth and establish my Zion. Keep my commandments in all things,
7. And, if you keep my commandments and endure to the end you shall have eternal life, which gift is the greatest of all the gifts of God.
8. And it shall come to pass, that if you shall ask the Father in my name, in faith believing, you shall receive the Holy Ghost, which giveth utterance, that you may stand as a witness of the things of which you shall both hear and see, and also that you may declare repentance unto this generation.
9. Behold, I am Jesus Christ the Son of the living God, who created the heavens and the earth; a light which cannot be hid in darkness;
10. Wherefore, I must bring forth the fulness of my gospel from the Gentiles unto the house of Israel.
11. And behold, thou art David, and thou art called to assist; which thing if ye do, and are faithful, ye shall be blessed both spiritually and temporally, and great shall be your reward. Amen.

THE SUSQUEHANNA RIVER

Upon you, my fellow servants, in the name of Messiah I confer the priesthood of Aaron, which holds the keys of the ministering of angels, and of the gospel of repentance, and of baptism by immersion for the remission of sins . . .

D&C 13:1

 SECTION 15

This revelation was given to John Whitmer, June 1829, at Fayette, New York (see historical background, section 14).

1. Hearken, my servant John, and listen to the words of Jesus Christ, your Lord and your Redeemer,
2. For behold, I speak unto you with sharpness and with power, for mine arm is over all the earth,
3. And I will tell you that which no man knoweth save me and thee alone,
4. For many times you have desired of me to know that which would be of the most worth unto you.
5. Behold, blessed are you for this thing, and for speaking my words which I have given you, according to my commandments.
6. And now, behold, I say unto you, that the thing which will be of the most worth unto you, will be to declare repentance unto this people, that you may bring souls unto me, that you may rest with them in the kingdom of my Father. Amen.

SECTION 16

This revelation was given to Peter Whitmer, Jun., June 1829, at Fayette, New York (see historical background, section 14).

1. Hearken my servant Peter, and listen to the words of Jesus Christ, your Lord and your Redeemer,
2. For behold, I speak unto you with sharpness and with power, for mine arm is over all the earth,
3. And I will tell you that which no man knoweth save me and thee alone,
4. For many times you have desired of me to know that which would be of the most worth unto you.
5. Behold, blessed are you for this thing, and for speaking my words which I have given unto you according to my commandments.
6. And now, behold, I say unto you, that the thing which will be of the most worth unto you, will be to declare repentance unto this people, that you may bring souls unto me, that you may rest with them in the kingdom of my Father. Amen.

THE ANGEL MORONI SHOWS THE GOLD PLATES TO DAVID WHITMER AND OLIVER COWDERY IN THE PRESENCE OF THE PROPHET JOSEPH SMITH.

SECTION 17

While translating the plates of the Book of Mormon, Joseph Smith and Oliver Cowdery learned that the Lord would give to three special witnesses a view of the plates. Oliver Cowdery, David Whitmer, and Martin Harris asked Joseph Smith to inquire of the Lord to ascertain if perchance they might be the three witnesses. Through the Urim and Thummim, Joseph Smith received this revelation in June 1829, at Fayette, New York (History of the Church, vol. 1:52–53).

1. Behold, I say unto you, that you must rely upon my word, which if you do, with full purpose of heart, you shall have a view of the plates, and also of the breast plate, the sword of Laban, the Urim and Thummim, which were given to the brother of Jared upon the mount, when he talked with the Lord face to face, and the miraculous directors which were given to Lehi while in the wilderness, on the borders of the Red Sea;

2. And it is by your faith that you shall obtain a view of them, even by that faith which was had by the prophets of old.

3. And after that you have obtained faith, and have seen them with your eyes, you shall testify of them, by the power of God;

4. And this you shall do that my servant Joseph Smith, jun., may not be destroyed, that I may bring about my righteous purposes unto the children of men in this work.

5. And ye shall testify that you have seen them, even as my servant Joseph Smith, jun., has seen them, for it is by my power that he has seen them, and it is because he had faith;

6. And he has translated the book, even that part which I have commanded him, and as your Lord and your God liveth it is true.

7. Wherefore you have received the same power, and the same faith, and the same gift like unto him;

8. And if you do these last commandments of mine, which I have given you, the gates of hell shall not prevail against you; for my grace is sufficient for you, and you shall be lifted up at the last day.

9. And I, Jesus Christ, your Lord and your God, have spoken it unto you, that I might bring about my righteous purposes unto the children of men. Amen.

JOSEPH SMITH AND OLIVER COWDERY HUMBLY PETITION THE LORD

Section 18

When the Aaronic Priesthood was conferred upon Joseph Smith and Oliver Cowdery, they were informed that there was a "Priesthood of Melchizedek," which Priesthood would be conferred upon them in "due time." Being anxious to receive the Melchizedek Priesthood, Joseph Smith and Oliver Cowdery "made this matter a subject of humble prayer." This revelation was received in June 1829, at Fayette, New York (History of the Church, vol. 1:60–62).

1. Now, behold, because of the thing which you, my servant Oliver Cowdery, have desired to know of me, I give unto you these words:
2. Behold, I have manifested unto you, by my Spirit in many instances, that the things which you have written are true; wherefore you know that they are true;
3. And if you know that they are true, behold, I give unto you a commandment, that you rely upon the things which are written;
4. For in them are all things written concerning the foundation of my church, my gospel, and my rock;
5. Wherefore, if you shall build up my church, upon the foundation of my gospel and my rock, the gates of hell shall not prevail against you.
6. Behold, the world is ripening in iniquity, and it must needs be that the children of men are stirred up unto repentance, both the Gentiles and also the house of Israel:
7. Wherefore, as thou hast been baptized by the hands of my servant Joseph Smith, jun., according to that which I have commanded him, he hath fulfilled the thing which I commanded him.
8. And now marvel not that I have called him unto mine own purpose, which purpose is known in me; wherefore, if he shall be diligent in keeping my commandments, he shall be blessed unto eternal life, and his name is Joseph.
9. And now, Oliver Cowdery, I speak unto you, and also unto David Whitmer, by the way of commandment; for, behold, I command all men everywhere to repent, and I speak unto you, even as unto Paul, mine apostle, for you are called even with that same calling with which he was called.
10. Remember the worth of souls is great in the sight of God;
11. For, behold, the Lord your Redeemer suffered death in the flesh; wherefore he suffered the pain of all men, that all men might repent and come unto him.
12. And he hath risen again from the dead, that he might bring all men unto him, on conditions of repentance;

13. And how great is his joy in the soul that repenteth.

14. Wherefore, you are called to cry repentance unto this people;

15. And if it so be that you should labor all your days in crying repentance unto this people, and bring, save it be one soul unto me, how great shall be your joy with him in the kingdom of my Father?

16. And now, if your joy will be great with one soul that you have brought unto me into the kingdom of my Father, how great will be your joy if you should bring many souls unto me!

17. Behold, you have my gospel before you, and my rock, and my salvation.

18. Ask the Father in my name, in faith believing that you shall receive, and you shall have the Holy Ghost, which manifesteth all things which are expedient unto the children of men.

19. And if you have not faith, hope, and charity, you can do nothing.

20. Contend against no church, save it be the church of the devil.

21. Take upon you the name of Christ, and speak the truth in soberness;

22. And as many as repent, and are baptized in my name, which is Jesus Christ, and endure to the end, the same shall be saved.

23. Behold, Jesus Christ is the name which is given of the Father, and there is none other name given whereby man can be saved;

24. Wherefore, all men must take upon them the name which is given of the Father, for in that name shall they be called at the last day;

25. Wherefore, if they know not the name by which they are called, they cannot have place in the kingdom of my Father.

26. And now, behold, there are others who are called to declare my gospel, both unto Gentile and unto Jew;

27. Yea, even Twelve, and the Twelve shall be my disciples, and they shall take upon them my name; and the Twelve are they who shall desire to take upon them my name with full purpose of heart;

28. And if they desire to take upon them my name with full purpose of heart, they are called to go into all the world to preach my gospel unto every creature;

29. And they are they who are ordained of me to baptize in my name, according to that which is written;

30. And you have that which is written before you; wherefore you must perform it according to the words which are written.

31. And now I speak unto you, the Twelve—Behold, my grace is sufficient for you: you must walk uprightly before me and sin not.

32. And, behold, you are they who are ordained of me to ordain priests and teachers; to declare my gospel, according to the power of the Holy Ghost which is in you, and according to the callings and gifts of God unto men;

33. And I, Jesus Christ, your Lord and your God, have spoken it.

34. These words are not of men, nor of man, but of me; wherefore, you shall testify they are of me, and not of man;

35. For it is my voice which speaketh them unto you, for they are given by my Spirit unto you, and by my power you can read them one to another, and save it were by my power, you could not have them;

36. Wherefore you can testify that you have heard my voice, and know my words.

37. And now, behold, I give unto you Oliver Cowdery, and also unto David Whitmer, that you shall search out the Twelve, who shall have the desires of which I have spoken;

38. And by their desires and their works you shall know them;

39. And when you have found them you shall show these things unto them.

40. And you shall fall down and worship the Father in my name;

41. And you must preach unto the world, saying, you must repent and be baptized, in the name of Jesus Christ;

42. For all men must repent and be baptized, and not only men, but women, and children who have arrived at the years of accountability.

43. And now, after that you have received this, you must keep my commandments in all things;

44. And by your hands I will work a marvelous work among the children of men, unto the convincing of many of their sins, that they may come unto repentance, and that they may come unto the kingdom of my Father;

45. Wherefore, the blessings which I give unto you are above all things.

46. And after that you have received this, if you keep not my commandments you cannot be saved in the kingdom of my Father.

47. Behold, I, Jesus Christ, your Lord and your God, and your Redeemer, by the power of my Spirit have spoken it. Amen.

ection 19

"No words of the Prophet introduce this revelation in his History. Nothing is known of the circumstances which called it forth . . ." (History of the Church, *vol. 1:72*). Speaking of this revelation, the Prophet Joseph Smith said it was *"A Commandment of God and not of man, to Martin Harris, given (Manchester, New York, March, 1830) by Him who is Eternal"* (History of the Church, *vol. 1:72*).

1. I am Alpha and Omega, Christ the Lord; yea, even I am He, the beginning and the end, the Redeemer of the world.

2. I, having accomplished and finished the will of him whose I am, even the Father, concerning me—having done this that I might subdue all things unto myself—

3. Retaining all power, even to the destroying of Satan and his works at the end of the world, and the last great day of judgment, which I shall pass upon the inhabitants thereof, judging every man according to his works and the deeds which he hath done.

4. And surely every man must repent or suffer, for I, God, am endless;

5. Wherefore, I revoke not the judgments which I shall pass, but woes shall go forth, weeping, wailing and gnashing of teeth, yea, to those who are found on my left hand;

6. Nevertheless it is not written that there shall be no end to this torment, but it is written endless torment.

7. Again, it is written eternal damnation; wherefore it is more express than other scriptures, that it might work upon the hearts of the children of men-altogether for my name's glory;

8. Wherefore I will explain unto you this mystery, for it is meet unto you to know even as mine apostles.

9. I speak unto you that are chosen in this thing, even as one, that you may enter into my rest;

10. For, behold, the mystery of Godliness, how great is it? for, behold, I am endless, and the punishment which is given from my hand, is endless punishment, for endless is my name: Wherefore—

11. Eternal punishment is God's punishment.

12. Endless punishment is God's punishment.

13. Wherefore I command you to repent, and keep the commandments which you have received by the hand of my servant Joseph Smith, jun., in my name;

14. And it is by my almighty power that you have received them;

15. Therefore I command you to repent—repent, lest I smite you by the rod of my mouth, and by my wrath, and by my anger, and your sufferings be sore—how sore you know not! how exquisite you know not! yea, how hard to bear you know not!

16. For behold, I, God, have suffered these things for all, that they might not suffer if they would repent,

17. But if they would not repent, they must suffer even as I,

18. Which suffering caused myself, even God, the greatest of all, to tremble because of pain, and to bleed at every pore, and to suffer both body and spirit; and would that I might not drink the bitter cup and shrink—

19. Nevertheless, glory be to the Father, and I partook and finished my preparations unto the children of men;

20. Wherefore, I command you again to repent, lest I humble you with my almighty power, and that you confess your sins, lest you suffer these punishments of which I have spoken, of which in the smallest, yea, even in the least degree you have tasted at the time I withdrew my spirit.

21. And I command you, that you preach naught but repentance, and show not these things unto the world until it is wisdom in me.

22. For they cannot bear meat now, but milk they must receive; wherefore, they must not know these things lest they perish.

23. Learn of me, and listen to my words; walk in the meekness of my Spirit, and you shall have peace in me.

24. I am Jesus Christ; I came by the will of the Father, and I do his will.

25. And again, I command thee that thou shalt not covet thy neighbor's wife; nor seek thy neighbor's life.

26. And again, I command thee that thou shalt not covet thine own property, but impart it freely to the printing of the Book of Mormon, which contains the truth and the word of God,

27. Which is my word to the Gentile, that soon it may go to the Jew, of whom the Lamanites are a remnant, that they may believe the gospel, and look not for a Messiah to come who has already come.

28. And again, I command thee that thou shalt pray vocally as well as in thy heart; yea, before the world as well as in secret, in public as well as in private.

29. And thou shalt declare glad tidings, yea, publish it upon the mountains, and upon every high place, and among every people that thou shalt be permitted to see.

30. And thou shalt do it with all humility, trusting in me, reviling not against revilers.

31. And of tenets thou shalt not talk, but thou shalt declare repentance and faith on the Savior and remission of sins by baptism and by fire, yea, even the Holy Ghost.

32. Behold, this is a great and the last commandment which I shall give unto you concerning this matter; for this shall suffice for thy daily walk, even unto the end of thy life.

33. And misery thou shalt receive if thou wilt slight these counsels; yea, even the destruction of thyself and property.

34. Impart a portion of thy property; yea, even part of thy lands, and all save the support of thy family.

35. Pay the debt thou hast contracted with the printer. Release thyself from bondage.

36. Leave thy house and home, except when thou shalt desire to see thy family:

37. And speak freely to all: yea, preach, exhort, declare the truth, even with a loud voice, with a sound of rejoicing, crying—Hosanna, hosanna! blessed be the name of the Lord God.

38. Pray always, and I will pour out my Spirit upon you, and great shall be your blessing; yea,

THE FIRST PRINTING OF THE BOOK OF MORMON

even more than if you should obtain treasures of earth and corruptibleness to the extent thereof.

39. Behold, canst thou read this without rejoicing and lifting up thy heart for gladness?

40. Or canst thou run about longer as a blind guide?

41. Or canst thou be humble and meek, and conduct thyself wisely before me? yea, come unto me thy Savior. Amen.

Section 20

After receiving the revelation pertaining to the workings of the Melchizedek Priesthood, the Prophet informs us, "In this manner did the Lord continue to give us instructions from time to time, concerning the duties which now devolved upon us; and among many other things of the kind, we obtained of Him the following, by the spirit of prophecy and revelation; which not only gave us much information, but also pointed out to us the precise day upon which, according to His will and commandment, we should proceed to organize His Church once more here upon the earth." This revelation was received April 1830 (History of the Church, vol. 1:64).

1. The rise of the church of Christ in these last days, being one thousand eight hundred and thirty years since the coming of our Lord and Savior Jesus Christ in the flesh, it being regularly organized and established agreeable to the laws of our country, by the will and commandments of God, in the fourth month, and on the sixth day of the month which is called April;

2. Which commandments were given to Joseph Smith, jun., who was called of God, and ordained an apostle of Jesus Christ, to be the first elder of this church;

3. And to Oliver Cowdery, who was also called of God, an apostle of Jesus Christ, to be the second elder of this church, and ordained under his hand;

4. And this according to the grace of our Lord and Savior Jesus Christ, to whom be all glory, both now and for ever. Amen.

5. After it was truly manifested unto this first elder that he had received a remission of his sins, he was entangled again in the vanities of the world;

6. But after repenting, and humbling himself sincerely, through faith God ministered unto him by an holy angel, whose countenance was as lightning, and whose garments were pure and white above all other whiteness;

7. And gave unto him commandments which inspired him;

8. And gave him power from on high, by the means which were before prepared, to translate the Book of Mormon,

9. Which contains a record of a fallen people, and the fulness of the gospel of Jesus Christ to the Gentiles and to the Jews also,

10. Which was given by inspiration, and is confirmed to others by the ministering of angels, and is declared unto the world by them,

11. Proving to the world that the Holy Scriptures are true, and that God does inspire men and call

them to his holy work in this age and generation, as well as in generations of old,

12. Thereby showing that he is the same God yesterday, to-day, and for ever. Amen.

13. Therefore, having so great witnesses, by them shall the world be judged, even as many as shall hereafter come to a knowledge of this work;

14. And those who receive it in faith, and work righteousness, shall receive a crown of eternal life;

15. But those who harden their hearts in unbelief, and reject it, it shall turn to their own condemnation,

16. For the Lord God has spoken it; and we, the elders of the church, have heard and bear witness to the words of the glorious Majesty on high, to whom be glory forever and ever. Amen.

17. By these things we know that there is a God in heaven, who is infinite and eternal, from everlasting to everlasting the same unchangeable God, the framer of heaven and earth, and all things which are in them;

18. And that he created man, male and female, after his own image and in his own likeness, created he them,

19. And gave unto them commandments that they should love and serve him, the only living and true God, and that he should be the only being whom they should worship.

20. But by the transgression of these holy laws, man became sensual and devilish, and became fallen man.

21. Wherefore, the Almighty God gave his Only Begotten Son, as it is written in those scriptures which have been given of him.

22. He suffered temptations but gave no heed unto them;

23. He was crucified, died, and rose again the third day;

24. And ascended into heaven, to sit down on the right hand of the Father, to reign with almighty power according to the will of the Father,

25. That as many as would believe and be baptized in his holy name, and endure in faith to the end, should be saved:

26. Not only those who believed after he came in the meridian of time, in the flesh, but all those from the beginning, even as many as were before he came, who believed in the words of the holy prophets, who spake as they were inspired by the gift of the Holy Ghost, who truly testified of him in all things, should have eternal life,

27. As well as those who should come after, who should believe in the gifts and callings of God by the Holy Ghost, which beareth record of the Father, and of the Son;

28. Which Father, Son, and Holy Ghost are one God, infinite and eternal, without end. Amen.

29. And we know that all men must repent and believe on the name of Jesus Christ, and worship the Father in his name, and endure in faith on his name to the end, or they cannot be saved in the kingdom of God.

30. And we know that justification through the grace of our Lord and Savior Jesus Christ is just and true;

31. And we know also, that sanctification through the grace of our Lord and Savior Jesus Christ, is just and true to all those who love and serve God with all their mights, minds, and strength.

32. But there is a possibility that man may fall from grace and depart from the living God;

33. Therefore let the church take heed and pray always, lest they fall into temptation;

34. Yea, and even let those who are sanctified take heed also.

35. And we know that these things are true and according to the revelations of John, neither adding to, or diminishing from the prophecy of his book, the Holy Scriptures, or the revelations of God which shall come hereafter by the gift and power of the Holy Ghost, the voice of God, or the ministering of angels.

36. And the Lord God has spoken it; and honor, power, and glory, be rendered to his holy name, both now and ever. Amen.

37. *And again, by way of commandment to the church concerning the manner of baptism.*—All those who humble themselves before God, and desire to be baptized and come forth with broken hearts and contrite spirits, and witness before the church that they have truly repented of all their sins, and are willing to take upon them the name of Jesus Christ, having a determination to serve him to the end, and truly manifest by their works that they have received of the Spirit of Christ unto the remission of their sins, shall be received by baptism into his church.

38. *The duty of the elders, priests, teachers, deacons, and members of the church of Christ.*—An apostle is an elder, and it is his calling to baptize.

39. And to ordain other elders, priests, teachers, and deacons,

40. And to administer bread and wine—the emblems of the flesh and blood of Christ—

41. And to confirm those who are baptized into the church, by the laying on of hands for the baptism of fire and the Holy Ghost, according to the scriptures;

42. And to teach, expound, exhort, baptize, and watch over the church;

43. And to confirm the church by the laying on of the hands, and the giving of the Holy Ghost;

44. And to take the lead of all meetings.

45. The elders are to conduct the meetings as they are led by the Holy Ghost, according to the commandments and revelations of God.

46. The priest's duty is to preach, teach, expound, exhort, and baptize, and administer the sacrament,

47. And visit the house of each member, and exhort them to pray vocally and in secret, and attend to all family duties;

48. And he may also ordain other priests, teachers, and deacons.

49. And he is to take the lead of meetings when there is no elder present;

50. But when there is an elder present, he is only to preach, teach, expound, exhort, and baptize,

51. And visit the house of each member, exhorting them to pray vocally and in secret, and attend to all family duties.

52. In all these duties the priest is to assist the elder if occasion requires.

53. The teacher's duty is to watch over the church always, and be with and strengthen them,

54. And see that there is no iniquity in the church—neither hardness with each other—neither lying, backbiting, nor evil speaking;

55. And see that the church meet together often, and also see that all the members do their duty;

56. And he is to take the lead of meetings in the absence of the elder or priest—

57. And is to be assisted always, in all his duties in the church, by the deacons, if occasion requires;

58. But neither teachers nor deacons have authority to baptize, administer the sacrament, or lay on hands:

59. They are, however, to warn, expound, exhort, and teach and invite all to come unto Christ.

60. Every elder, priest, teacher, or deacon, is to be ordained according to the gifts and callings of God unto him; and he is to be ordained by the power of the Holy Ghost, which is in the one who ordains him.

61. The several elders, composing this church of Christ are to meet in conference once in three months, or from time to time as said conferences shall direct or appoint;

62. And said conferences are to do whatever church business is necessary to be done at the time.

63. The elders are to receive their licenses from other elders, by vote of the church to which they belong, or from the conferences.

64. Each priest, teacher, or deacon, who is ordained by a priest may take a certificate from him at the time, which certificate when presented to an elder, shall entitle him to a license, which shall authorize him to perform the duties of his calling, or he may receive it from a conference.

65. No person is to be ordained to any office in this church, where there is a regularly organized branch of the same, without the vote of that church;

66. But the presiding elders, traveling bishops, High Councilors, High Priests, and elders, may have the privilege of ordaining, where there is no branch of the church that a vote may be called.

67. Every President of the High Priesthood (or presiding elder), bishop, High Councilor, and High Priest, is to be ordained by the direction of a High Council or general conference.

68. *The duty of the members after they are received by baptism.*—The elders or priests are to have a sufficient time to expound all things concerning the church of Christ to their understanding, previous to their partaking of the sacrament and being confirmed by the laying on of the hands of the elders, so that all things may be done in order.

69. And the members shall manifest before the church, and also before the elders, by a Godly walk and conversation, that they are worthy of it, that there may be works and faith agreeable to the Holy Scriptures—walking in holiness before the Lord.

70. Every member of the church of Christ having children, is to bring them unto the elders before the church, who are to lay their hands upon them in the name of Jesus Christ, and bless them in his name.

71. No one can be received into the church of Christ unless he has arrived unto the years of accountability before God, and is capable of repentance.

72. Baptism is to be administered in the following manner unto all those who repent:

73. The person who is called of God, and has authority from Jesus Christ to baptize, shall go down into the water with the person who has presented himself or herself for baptism, and shall say, calling him or her by name—Having been commissioned of Jesus Christ, I baptize you in the name of the Father, and of the Son, and of the Holy Ghost. Amen.

74. Then shall he immerse him or her in the water, and come forth again out of the water.

75. It is expedient that the church meet together often to partake of bread and wine in the remembrance of the Lord Jesus;

76. And the elder or priest shall administer it; and after this manner shall he administer it—he shall kneel with the church and call upon the Father in solemn prayer, saying—

77. O God, the eternal Father, we ask thee in the name of thy Son, Jesus Christ, to bless and sanctify this bread to the souls of all those who partake of it, that they may eat in remembrance of the body of thy Son, and witness unto thee, O God, the eternal Father, that they are willing to take upon them the name of thy Son, and always remember him and keep his commandments which he has given them, that they may always have his Spirit to be with them. Amen.

78. *The manner of administering the wine.*—He shall take the cup also, and say—

79. O God, the eternal Father, we ask thee in the name of thy Son, Jesus Christ, to bless and sanctify this wine to the souls of all those who drink of it, that they may do it in remembrance of the blood of thy Son, which was shed for them; that they may witness unto thee, O God, the eternal Father, that they do always remember him, that they may have his Spirit to be with them. Amen.

80. Any member of the church of Christ transgressing, or being overtaken in a fault, shall be dealt with as the scriptures direct.

81. It shall be the duty of the several churches composing the church of Christ, to send one or more of their teachers to attend the several conferences held by the elders of the church,

82. With a list of the names of the several members uniting themselves with the church since the last conference, or send by the hand of some priest, so that a regular list of all the names of the whole church may be kept in a book by one of the elders, whosoever the other elders shall appoint from time to time;

83. And also if any have been expelled from the church, so that their names may be blotted out of the general church record of names.

84. All members removing from the church where they reside, if going to a church where they are not known, may take a letter certifying that they are regular members and in good standing, which certificate may be signed by any elder or priest, if the member receiving the letter is personally acquainted with the elder or priest, or it may be signed by the teachers or deacons of the church.

Section 21

The Prophet Joseph Smith and a number of the brethren met together at the house of Peter Whitmer, Sen., April 6, 1830, Fayette, New York, to organize the Church. To be in accordance with the laws of the state of New York, six men participated in the organization. According to the narrative of the Prophet, the following took place. "Having opened the meeting by solemn prayer to our Heavenly Father, we proceeded, according to previous commandment, to call on our brethren to know whether they accepted us as their teachers in the things of the Kingdom of God, and whether they were satisfied that we should proceed and be organized as a Church according to said commandment which we had received. To these several propositions they consented by a unanimous vote. I then laid my hands upon Oliver Cowdery, and ordained him an Elder of the 'Church of Jesus Christ of Latter-day Saints;' after which, he ordained me also to the office of an Elder of said Church. We then took bread, blessed it, and brake it with them; also wine, blessed it, and drank it with them. We then laid our hands on each individual member of the Church present, that they might receive the gift of the Holy Ghost, and be confirmed members of the Church of Christ. . . . Whilst yet together, I received the following commandment" (History of the Church, vol. 1:77–78).

1. Behold there shall be a record kept among you, and in it thou shalt be called a seer, a translator, a prophet, an apostle of Jesus Christ, an elder of the church through the will of God the Father, and the grace of your Lord Jesus Christ,

2. Being inspired of the Holy Ghost to lay the foundation thereof, and to build it up unto the most holy faith,

3. Which church was organized and established in the year of your Lord eighteen hundred and thirty, in the fourth month, and on the sixth day of the month, which is called April.

4. Wherefore, meaning the church, thou shalt give heed unto all his words and commandments which he shall give unto you as he receiveth them, walking in all holiness before me;

5. For his word ye shall receive, as if from mine own mouth, in all patience and faith;

6. For by doing these things the gates of hell shall not prevail against you; yea, and the Lord God will disperse the powers of darkness from before you, and cause the heavens to shake for your good, and his name's glory.

7. For thus saith the Lord God, him have I inspired to move the cause of Zion in mighty power for good, and his diligence I know, and his prayers I have heard.

8. Yea his weeping for Zion I have seen, and I will cause that he shall mourn for her no longer, for his days of rejoicing are come unto the remission of his sins, and the manifestations of my blessings upon his works.

ORGANIZATION OF THE CHURCH OF JESUS CHRIST OF LATTER-DAY SAINTS, APRIL 6, 1830

9. For, behold, I will bless all those who labor in my vineyard with a mighty blessing, and they shall believe on his words, which are given him through me by the Comforter, which manifesteth that Jesus was crucified by sinful men for the sins of the world, yea, for the remission of sins unto the contrite heart.

10. Wherefore it behooveth me that he should be ordained by you, Oliver Cowdery, mine apostle;

11. This being an ordinance unto you, that you are an elder under his hand, he being the first unto you, that you might be an elder unto this church of Christ, bearing my name,

12. And the first preacher of this church unto the church, and before the world, yea, before the Gentiles; yea, and thus saith the Lord God, lo, lo! to the Jews also. Amen.

THE PROPHET JOSEPH EMBRACES HIS FATHER, JOSEPH SR., AFTER BAPTISM

SECTION 22

After the Church was organized, there were those who were desirous to be baptized and join the Church. A number of these people belonged to churches that baptized by immersion. They wondered why they needed to be baptized again by immersion to receive membership in the newly organized church. Obviously, the principle of divine authority was not fully understood. This revelation was received at Manchester, New York, April 1830 (History of the Church, vol. 1:79).

1. Behold, I say unto you, that all old covenants have I caused to be done away in this thing, and this is a new and an everlasting covenant, even that which was from the beginning.
2. Wherefore, although a man should be baptized an hundred times, it availeth him nothing, for you cannot enter in at the strait gate by the law of Moses, neither by your dead works;
3. For it is because of your dead works, that I have caused this last covenant and this church to be built up unto me, even as in days of old.
4. Wherefore, enter ye in at the gate, as I have commanded, and seek not to counsel your God. Amen.

ection 23

Now that the Church was organized, Oliver Cowdery, Hyrum Smith, Samuel H. Smith, Joseph Smith, Sen., and Joseph Knight, Sen. were ". . . anxious to know of the Lord what might be their respective duties in relation to this work." The Prophet Joseph Smith inquired of the Lord and received this revelation April, 1830, at Manchester, New York (History of the Church, vol. 1:80).

1. Behold, I speak unto you, Oliver, a few words. Behold, thou art blessed, and art under no condemnation. But beware of pride, lest thou shouldst enter into temptation.

2. Make known thy calling unto the church, and also before the world, and thy heart shall be opened to preach the truth from henceforth and forever. Amen.

3. Behold, I speak unto you, Hyrum, a few words: for thou also art under no condemnation, and thy heart is opened, and thy tongue loosed; and thy calling is to exhortation, and to strengthen the church continually. Wherefore thy duty is unto the church for ever, and this because of thy family. Amen.

4. Behold, I speak a few words unto you, Samuel, for thou also art under no condemnation, and thy calling is to exhortation, and to strengthen the church, and thou art not as yet called to preach before the world. Amen.

5. Behold, I speak a few words unto you, Joseph, for thou also art under no condemnation, and thy calling also is to exhortation, and to strengthen the church; and this is thy duty from henceforth and forever. Amen.

6. Behold, I manifest unto you, Joseph Knight, by these words, that you must take up your cross, in the which you must pray vocally before the world as well as in secret, and in your family, and among your friends, and in all places.

7. And, behold, it is your duty to unite with the true church, and give your language to exhortation continually, that you may receive the reward of the laborer. Amen.

Section 24

After the Church was organized, missionary efforts commenced in and around Colesville, New York, and several people were baptized. Persecution raised its ugly head and the Prophet Joseph Smith was arrested ". . . on the charge of being a disorderly person, of setting the country in an uproar by preaching the Book of Mormon, etc." (History of the Church, Vol. 1:88). Inasmuch as there was no substance to the charges, Joseph Smith was acquitted. Joseph Smith and Oliver Cowdery returned to the Prophet's home at Harmony, Pennsylvania, where they received the revelations in sections 24, 25, and 26, July 1830 (History of the Church, vol. 1:101–104).

1. Behold, thou wast called and chosen to write the Book of Mormon, and to my ministry; and I have lifted thee up out of thy afflictions, and have counseled thee, that thou hast been delivered from all thine enemies, and thou hast been delivered from the powers of Satan and from darkness!

2. Nevertheless, thou art not excusable in thy transgressions; nevertheless, go thy way and sin no more.

3. Magnify thine office; and after thou hast sowed thy fields and secured them, go speedily unto the church which is in Colesville, Fayette and Manchester, and they shall support thee; and I will bless them both spiritually and temporally;

4. But if they receive thee not, I will send upon them a cursing instead of a blessing.

5. And thou shalt continue in calling upon God in my name, and writing the things which shall be given thee by the Comforter, and expounding all scriptures unto the church;

6. And it shall be given thee in the very moment what thou shalt speak and write, and they shall hear it, or I will send unto them a cursing instead of a blessing.

7. For thou shalt devote all thy service in Zion; and in this thou shalt have strength.

8. Be patient in afflictions, for thou shalt have many; but endure them, for, lo, I am with thee, even unto the end of thy days.

9. And in temporal labors thou shalt not have strength, for this is not thy calling. Attend to thy calling and thou shalt have wherewith to magnify thine office, and to expound all scriptures, and continue in laying on of the hands and confirming the churches.

10. And thy brother Oliver shall continue in bearing my name before the world, and also to the church. And he shall not suppose that he can say enough in my cause; and lo, I am with him to the end.

11. In me he shall have glory, and not of himself, whether in weakness or in strength, whether in bonds or free,

12. And at all times, and in all places, he shall open his mouth and declare my gospel as with the voice of a trump, both day and night. And I will give unto him strength such as is not known among men.

13. Require not miracles, except I shall command you, except casting out devils, healing the sick, and against poisonous serpents, and against deadly poisons;

14. And these things ye shall not do, except it be required of you by them who desire it, that the scriptures might be fulfilled; for ye shall do according to that which is written.

15. And in whatsoever place ye shall enter, and they receive you not in my name, ye shall leave a cursing instead of a blessing, by casting off the dust of your feet against them as a testimony, and cleansing your feet by the wayside.

16. And it shall come to pass that whosoever shall lay their hands upon you by violence, ye shall command to be smitten in my name; and, behold, I will smite them according to your words, in mine own due time.

17. And whosoever shall go to law with thee shall be cursed by the law.

18. And thou shalt take no purse nor scrip, neither staves, neither two coats, for the church shall give unto thee in the very hour what thou needest for food and for raiment, and for shoes and for money, and for scrip;

19. For thou art called to prune my vineyard with a mighty pruning, yea, even for the last time; yea, and also all those whom thou hast ordained, and they shall do even according to this pattern. Amen.

SECTION 25

This revelation was received at Harmony, Pennsylvania, July 1830. It is one of three revelations received at this time (see historical background, section 24). This revelation was given to Emma Smith, the wife of the Prophet Joseph Smith. It contains specific counsel to her and also counsel and information to all women (section 25:16), (History of the Church, vol. 1:101–104).

1. Hearken unto the voice of the Lord your God, while I speak unto you, Emma Smith, my daughter, for verily I say unto you, all those who receive my gospel are sons and daughters in my kingdom.

2. A revelation I give unto you concerning my will, and if thou art faithful and walk in the paths of virtue before me, I will preserve thy life, and thou shalt receive an inheritance in Zion.

3. Behold, thy sins are forgiven thee, and thou art an elect lady, whom I have called.

4. Murmur not because of the things which thou hast not seen, for they are withheld from thee and from the world, which is wisdom in me in a time to come.

5. And the office of thy calling shall be for a comfort unto my servant, Joseph Smith, jun., thy husband, in his afflictions with consoling words, in the spirit of meekness.

6. And thou shalt go with him at the time of his going, and be unto him for a scribe, while there is no one to be a scribe for him, that I may send my servant, Oliver Cowdery, whithersoever I will.

7. And thou shalt be ordained under his hand to expound scriptures, and to exhort the church, according as it shall be given thee by my Spirit:

8. For he shall lay his hands upon thee, and thou shalt receive the Holy Ghost, and thy time shall be given to writing, and to learning much.

9. And thou needest not fear, for thy husband shall support thee in the church; for unto them is his calling, that all things might be revealed unto them, whatsoever I will, according to their faith.

10. And verily I say unto thee that thou shalt lay aside the things of this world, and seek for the things of a better.

11. And it shall be given thee, also, to make a selection of sacred hymns, as it shall be given thee, which is pleasing unto me, to be had in my church;

12. For my soul delighteth in the song of the heart, yea, the song of the righteous is a prayer unto me, and it shall be answered with a blessing upon their heads.

13. Wherefore, lift up thy heart and rejoice, and cleave unto the covenants which thou hast made.

EMMA RECEIVES COUNSEL FROM THE LORD AND IS INSTRUCTED TO MAKE A SELECTION OF SACRED HYMNS.

14. Continue in the spirit of meekness, and beware of pride. Let thy soul delight in thy husband, and the glory which shall come upon him.
15. Keep my commandments continually, and a crown of righteousness thou shalt receive. And except thou do this, where I am you cannot come.
16. And verily, verily I say unto you, that this is my voice unto all. Amen.

SECTION 26

This revelation was received at Harmony, Pennsylvania, July 1830. It is one of three revelations received at this time (see historical background, section 24). This revelation contains specific counsel to Joseph Smith, John Whitmer, and Oliver Cowdery (History of the Church, *vol. 1:101–104).*

1. Behold, I say unto you, that you shall let your time be devoted to the studying of the scriptures, and to preaching, and to confirming the church at Colesville, and to performing your labors on the land, such as is required, until after you shall go to the west to hold the next conference; and then it shall be made known what you shall do.
2. And all things shall be done by common consent in the church, by much prayer and faith, for all things you shall receive by faith. Amen.

ECTION 27

Newel Knight and his wife paid a visit to the Joseph Smith family in Harmony, Pennsylvania. Neither Joseph Smith's wife nor Newel Knight's wife had been confirmed members of the Church after their baptism. The Prophet Joseph Smith states that ". . . it was proposed that we should confirm them, and partake together of the Sacrament, before he and his wife should leave us. In order to prepare for this I set out to procure some wine for the occasion, but had gone only a short distance when I was met by a heavenly messenger, and received the following revelation, the first four paragraphs of which were written at this time, and the remainder in the September following." This revelation was received August 1830, at Harmony, Pennsylvania (History of the Church, vol. 1:106).

1. Listen to the voice of Jesus Christ, your Lord, your God, and your Redeemer, whose word is quick and powerful.

2. For, behold, I say unto you, that it mattereth not what ye shall eat, or what ye shall drink, when ye partake of the sacrament, if it so be that ye do it with an eye single to my glory; remembering unto the Father my body which was laid down for you, and my blood which was shed for the remission of your sins:

3. Wherefore, a commandment I give unto you, that you shall not purchase wine, neither strong drink of your enemies:

4. Wherefore, you shall partake of none, except it is made new among you; yea, in this my Father's kingdom which shall be built up on the earth.

5. Behold, this is wisdom in me: wherefore, marvel not, for the hour cometh that I will drink of the fruit of the vine with you on the earth, and with Moroni, whom I have sent unto you to reveal the Book of Mormon, containing the fulness of my everlasting gospel, to whom I have committed the keys of the record of the stick of Ephraim;

6. And also with Elias, to whom I have committed the keys of bringing to pass the restoration of all things, spoken by the mouth of all the holy prophets since the world began, concerning the last days:

7. And also John the son of Zacharias, which Zacharias he (Elias) visited and gave promise that he should have a son, and his name should be John, and he should be filled with the spirit of Elias;

8. Which John I have sent unto you, my servants, Joseph Smith, jun., and Oliver Cowdery, to ordain you unto this first priesthood which you have received, that you might be called and ordained even as Aaron:

9. And also Elijah, unto whom I have committed the keys of the power of turning the hearts of the fathers to the children, and the hearts of the children to the fathers, that the whole earth may not be smitten with a curse:

10. And also with Joseph and Jacob, and Isaac, and Abraham, your fathers, by whom the promises remain;

11. And also with Michael, or Adam, the father of all, the prince of all, the ancient of days.

12. And also with Peter, and James, and John, whom I have sent unto you, by whom I have ordained you and confirmed you to be apostles, and especial witnesses of my name, and bear the keys of your ministry, and of the same things which I revealed unto them:

13. Unto whom I have committed the keys of my kingdom, and a dispensation of the gospel for the last times; and for the fulness of times, in the which I will gather together in one all things, both which are in heaven, and which are on earth:

14. And also with all those whom my Father hath given me out of the world:

15. Wherefore, lift up your hearts and rejoice, and gird up your loins, and take upon you my whole armor, that ye may be able to withstand the evil day, having done all ye may be able to stand.

16. Stand, therefore, having your loins girt about with truth, having on the breastplate of righteousness, and your feet shod with the preparation of the gospel of peace, which I have sent mine angels to commit unto you,

17. Taking the shield of faith wherewith ye shall be able to quench all the fiery darts of the wicked;

18. And take the helmet of salvation, and the sword of my Spirit, which I will pour out upon you, and my word which I reveal unto you, and be agreed as touching all things whatsoever ye ask of me, and be faithful until I come, and ye shall be caught up, that where I am ye shall be also. Amen.

Section 28

Because of persecution against the Prophet Joseph at Harmony, Pennsylvania, Peter Whitmer, Sen. invited the Prophet Joseph's family to move to Fayette, New York, to live with them. Soon after the Prophet's arrival at Fayette, he discovered "that Satan had been lying in wait to deceive, and seeking whom he might devour. Brother Hiram Page had in his possession a certain stone, by which he had obtained certain 'revelations' concerning the building up of Zion, the order of the Church, etc., all of which were entirely at variance with the order of God's House." Because several members of the Church were believing in these false revelations, the Prophet Joseph Smith inquired of the Lord and received this revelation, September 1830, at Fayette, New York (History of the Church, vol. 1:109–110).

1. Behold, I say unto thee, Oliver, that it shall be given unto thee, that thou shalt be heard by the church in all things whatsoever thou shalt teach them by the Comforter, concerning the revelations and commandments which I have given.

2. But, behold, verily, verily, I say unto thee, no one shall be appointed to receive commandments and revelations in this church, excepting my servant Joseph Smith, jun., for he receiveth them even as Moses;

3. And thou shalt be obedient unto the things which I shall give unto him, even as Aaron, to declare faithfully the commandments and the revelations, with power and authority unto the church.

4. And if thou art led at any time by the Comforter, to speak or teach, or at all times by the way of commandment unto the church, thou mayest do it.

5. But thou shalt not write by way of commandment, but by wisdom:

6. And thou shalt not command him who is at thy head, and at the head of the church,

7. For I have given him the keys of the mysteries, and the revelations which are sealed, until I shall appoint unto them another in his stead.

8. And now, behold, I say unto you, that you shall go unto the Lamanites and preach my gospel unto them; and inasmuch as they receive thy teachings, thou shalt cause my church to be established among them, and thou shalt have revelations, but write them not by way of commandment.

9. And now, behold, I say unto you, that it is not revealed, and no man knoweth where the city shall be built, but it shall be given hereafter. Behold, I say unto you that it shall be on the borders by the Lamanites.

THE HOME OF PETER WHITMER, SR., IN FAYETTE, NEW YORK

10. Thou shalt not leave this place until after the conference, and my servant Joseph shall be appointed to preside over the conference by the voice of it, and what he saith to thee thou shalt tell.

11. And again, thou shalt take thy brother, Hiram Page, between him and thee alone, and tell him that those things which he hath written from that stone, are not of me, and that Satan deceiveth him;

12. For, behold, these things have not been appointed unto him, neither shall anything be appointed unto any of this church contrary to the church covenants.

13. For all things must be done in order, and by common consent in the church, by the prayer of faith.

14. And thou shalt assist to settle all these things according to the covenants of the church before thou shalt take thy journey among the Lamanites.

15. And it shall be given thee from the time thou shalt go, until the time thou shalt return, what thou shalt do.

16. And thou must open thy mouth at all times declaring my gospel with the sound of rejoicing. Amen.

ECTION 29

The only indication as to why this revelation was received appears in the superscription of the 1833 edition of The Book of Commandments *as follows: "A Revelation to the church of Christ, given in the presence of six elders, in Fayette, New York, September, 1830" (The Book of Commandments, 1833 ed., p. 61), (History of the Church, vol. 1:111). This revelation was received a few days before the convening of the Conference of the Church on September 26, 1830. Many wonderful truths were revealed to the Church in this revelation, such as: the gathering of the Lord's elect, the Lord's Second Coming, events following the Millennium, the fall and the Atonement, etc.*

1. Listen to the voice of Jesus Christ, your Redeemer, the Great I AM, whose arm of mercy hath atoned for your sins;
2. Who will gather his people even as a hen gathereth her chickens under her wings, even as many as will hearken to my voice and humble themselves before me, and call upon me in mighty prayer.
3. Behold, verily, verily, I say unto you, that at this time your sins are forgiven you, therefore ye receive these things; but remember to sin no more, lest perils shall come upon you.
4. Verily, I say unto you, that ye are chosen out of the world to declare my gospel with the sound of rejoicing, as with the voice of a trump:
5. Lift up your hearts and be glad, for I am in your midst, and am your advocate with the Father; and it is his good will to give you the kingdom;
6. And as it is written, Whatsoever ye shall ask in faith, being united in prayer according to my command, ye shall receive;
7. And ye are called to bring to pass the gathering of mine elect, for mine elect hear my voice and harden not their hearts;
8. Wherefore the decree hath gone forth from the Father, that they shall be gathered in unto one place upon the face of this land, to prepare their hearts and be prepared in all things against the day when tribulation and desolation are sent forth upon the wicked;
9. For the hour is nigh and the day soon at hand when the earth is ripe: and all the proud, and they that do wickedly, shall be as stubble, and I will burn them up, saith the Lord of Hosts, that wickedness shall not be upon the earth;
10. For the hour is nigh, and that which was spoken by mine apostles must be fulfilled; for as they spoke so shall it come to pass;

11. For I will reveal myself from heaven with power and great glory, with all the hosts thereof, and dwell in righteousness with men on earth a thousand years, and the wicked shall not stand.

12. And again, verily, verily, I say unto you, and it hath gone forth in a firm decree, by the will of the Father, that mine apostles, the Twelve which were with me in my ministry at Jerusalem, shall stand at my right hand at the day of my coming in a pillar of fire, being clothed with robes of righteousness, with crowns upon their heads, in glory even as I am, to judge the whole house of Israel, even as many as have loved me and kept my commandments, and none else;

13. For a trump shall sound both long and loud, even as upon Mount Sinai, and all the earth shall quake, and they shall come forth: yea, even the dead which died in me, to receive a crown of righteousness, and to be clothed upon, even as I am, to be with me, that we may be one.

14. But, behold, I say unto you, that before this great day shall come, the sun shall be darkened, and the moon shall be turned into blood, and the stars shall fall from heaven, and there shall be greater signs in heaven above, and in the earth beneath;

15. And there shall be weeping and wailing among the hosts of men;

16. And there shall be a great hailstorm sent forth to destroy the crops of the earth;

17. And it shall come to pass, because of the wickedness of the world, that I will take vengeance upon the wicked, for they will not repent; for the cup of mine indignation is full; for behold my blood shall not cleanse them if they hear me not.

18. Wherefore, I the Lord God will send forth flies upon the face of the earth, which shall take hold of the inhabitants thereof, and shall eat their flesh, and shall cause maggots to come in upon them;

19. And their tongues shall be stayed that they shall not utter against me; and their flesh shall fall from off their bones, and their eyes from their sockets:

20. And it shall come to pass that the beasts of the forest, and the fowls of the air shall devour them up;

21. And the great and abominable church, which is the whore of all the earth, shall be cast down by devouring fire, according as it is spoken by the mouth of Ezekiel the prophet, who spoke of these things, which have not come to pass, but surely must, as I live, for abominations shall not reign.

22. And again, verily, verily, I say unto you, that when the thousand years are ended, and men again begin to deny their God, then will I spare the earth but for a little season;

23. And the end shall come, and the heaven and the earth shall be consumed and pass away, and there shall be a new heaven and a new earth,

24. For all old things shall pass away, and all things shall become new, even the heaven and the earth, and all the fulness thereof, both men and beasts, the fowls of the air, and the fishes of the sea;

25. And not one hair, neither mote, shall be lost, for it is the workmanship of mine hand.

26. But, behold, verily I say unto you, before the earth shall pass away, Michael, mine archangel, shall sound his trump, and then shall all the dead awake, for their graves shall be opened, and they shall come forth; yea, even all.

27. And the righteous shall be gathered on my right hand unto eternal life; and the wicked on my left hand will I be ashamed to own before the Father;

28. Wherefore I will say unto them—Depart from me, ye cursed, into everlasting fire, prepared for the devil and his angels.

29. And now, behold, I say unto you, never at any time, have I declared from mine own mouth that

they should return, for where I am they cannot come, for they have no power;

30. But remember that all my judgments are not given unto men; and as the words have gone forth out of my mouth even so shall they be fulfilled, that the first shall be last, and that the last shall be first in all things whatsoever I have created by the word of my power, which is the power of my Spirit;

31. For by the power of my Spirit created I them; yea, all things both spiritual and temporal:

32. Firstly, spiritual—secondly, temporal, which is the beginning of my work; and again, firstly, temporal—and secondly, spiritual, which is the last of my work:

33. Speaking unto you that you may naturally understand, but unto myself my works have no end, neither beginning; but it is given unto you that ye may understand, because ye have asked it of me and are agreed.

34. Wherefore, verily I say unto you, that all things unto me are spiritual, and not at any time have I given unto you a law which was temporal; neither any man, nor the children of men; neither Adam, your father, whom I created.

35. Behold, I gave unto him that he should be an agent unto himself; and I gave unto him commandment, but no temporal commandment gave I unto him, for my commandments are spiritual; they are not natural nor temporal, neither carnal nor sensual.

36. And it came to pass, that Adam, being tempted of the devil (for, behold, the devil was before Adam, for he rebelled against me, saying, Give me thine honor, which is my power: and also a third part of the hosts of heaven turned he away from me because of their agency;

37. And they were thrust down, and thus came the devil and his angels.

38. And, behold, there is a place prepared for them from the beginning, which place is hell:

39. And it must needs be that the devil should tempt the children of men, or they could not be agents unto themselves, for if they never should have bitter, they could not know the sweet)

40. Wherefore, it came to pass that the devil tempted Adam, and he partook of the forbidden fruit and transgressed the commandment, wherein he became subject to the will of the devil, because he yielded unto temptation.

41. Wherefore I the Lord God, caused that he should be cast out from the Garden of Eden, from my presence, because of his transgression, wherein he became spiritually dead, which is the first death, even that same death, which is the last death, which is spiritual, which shall be pronounced upon the wicked when I shall say—Depart, ye cursed.

42. But, behold, I say unto you, that I, the Lord God, gave unto Adam and unto his seed, that they should not die as to the temporal death, until I the Lord God should send forth angels to declare unto them repentance and redemption, through faith on the name of mine Only Begotten Son.

43. And thus did I, the Lord God, appoint unto man the days of his probation; that by his natural death he might be raised in immortality unto eternal life, even as many as would believe;

44. And they that believe not unto eternal damnation, for they cannot be redeemed from their spiritual fall, because they repent not;

45. For they will love darkness rather than light, and their deeds are evil, and they receive their wages of whom they list to obey.

46. But behold, I say unto you, that little children are redeemed from the foundation of the world through mine Only Begotten:

47. Wherefore, they cannot sin, for power is not given unto Satan to tempt little children, until they begin to become accountable before me;

48. For it is given unto them even as I will, according to mine own pleasure, that great things may be required at the hand of their fathers.

49. And, again, I say unto you, that whoso having knowledge, have I not commanded to repent?
50. And he that hath no understanding, it remaineth in me to do according as it is written. And now I declare no more unto you at this time. Amen.

Section 30

The Church convened a conference on September 26, 1830, at Fayette, New York. The false revelations of Hiram Page were denounced and the affairs of the Church were put in order. At the conclusion of this conference, the Prophet Joseph Smith received two revelations. The first was given to David Whitmer, Peter Whitmer, Jun., and John Whitmer. The second was given to Thomas B. Marsh (History of the Church, vol. 1:115–117).

1. Behold, I say unto you, David, that you have feared man and have not relied on me for strength as you ought:

2. But your mind has been on the things of the earth more than on the things of me, your Maker, and the ministry whereunto you have been called; and you have not given heed unto my Spirit, and to those who were set over you, but have been persuaded by those whom I have not commanded:

3. Wherefore, you are left to inquire for yourself, at my hand, and ponder upon the things which you have received.

4. And your home shall be at your father's house, until I give unto you further commandments. And you shall attend to the ministry in the church, and before the world, and in the regions round about. Amen.

5. Behold, I say unto you, Peter, that you shall take your journey with your brother Oliver, for the time has come that it is expedient in me that you shall open your mouth to declare my gospel; therefore, fear not, but give heed unto the words and advice of your brother, which he shall give you.

6. And be you afflicted in all his afflictions, ever lifting up your heart unto me in prayer, and faith, for his and your deliverance: for I have given unto him power to build up my church among the Lamanites:

7. And none have I appointed to be his counselor over him in the church, concerning church matters, except it is his brother, Joseph Smith, jun.

8. Wherefore, give heed unto these things and be diligent in keeping my commandments, and you shall be blessed unto eternal life. Amen.

9. Behold, I say unto you, my servant John, that thou shalt commence from this time forth to proclaim my gospel, as with the voice of a trump.

10. And your labor shall be at your brother Philip Burrough's, and in that region round about; yea, wherever you can be heard, until I command you to go from hence.

11. And your whole labor shall be in Zion, with all your soul, from henceforth; yea, you shall ever open your mouth in my cause, not fearing what man can do, for I am with you. Amen.

Section 31

This revelation was given to the Prophet Joseph Smith at the conclusion of the conference September 26, 1830, at Fayette, New York (see historical background, section 30). It is addressed to Thomas B. Marsh, approximately five years before his call to be the President of the First Quorum of the Twelve Apostles of the newly organized Church (History of the Church, vol. 1:115–117).

1. Thomas, my son, blessed are you because of your faith in my work.

2. Behold, you have had many afflictions because of your family: nevertheless, I will bless you and your family; yea, your little ones, and the day cometh that they will believe and know the truth and be one with you in my church.

3. Lift up your heart and rejoice, for the hour of your mission is come: and your tongue shall be loosed; and you shall declare glad tidings of great joy unto this generation.

4. You shall declare the things which have been revealed to my servant, Joseph Smith, jun. You shall begin to preach from this time forth; yea, to reap in the field which is white already to be burned:

5. Therefore, thrust in your sickle with all your soul, and your sins are forgiven you, and you shall be laden with sheaves upon your back, for the laborer is worthy of his hire. Wherefore, your family shall live.

6. Behold, verily I say unto you, go from them only for a little time, and declare my word, and I will prepare a place for them;

7. Yea, I will open the hearts of the people, and they will receive you. And I will establish a church by your hand;

8. And you shall strengthen them and prepare them against the time when they shall be gathered.

9. Be patient in afflictions, revile not against those that revile. Govern your house in meekness, and be steadfast.

10. Behold, I say unto you, that you shall be a physician unto the church, but not unto the world, for they will not receive you.

11. Go your way whithersoever I will, and it shall be given you by the Comforter what you shall do, and whither you shall go.

12. Pray always, lest you enter into temptation, and lose your reward.

13. Be faithful unto the end, and lo, I am with you. These words are not of man nor of men, but of me, even Jesus Christ, your Redeemer, by the will of the Father. Amen.

SECTION 32

After the conclusion of the conference September 26, 1830, ". . . a great desire was manifested by several of the Elders respecting the remnants of the house of Joseph, the Lamanites, residing in the west." They were so eager to engage in missionary work among the Lamanites that the Prophet Joseph Smith inquired of the Lord if several Elders might labor among them. This revelation was given through the Prophet Joseph Smith, October 1830, to Parley P. Pratt and Ziba Peterson, calling them to do missionary work among the Lamanites (History of the Church, vol. 1:118).

1. And now concerning my servant Parley P. Pratt, behold, I say unto him, that as I live I will that he shall declare my gospel and learn of me, and be meek and lowly of heart;
2. And that which I have appointed unto him is that he shall go with my servants Oliver Cowdery and Peter Whitmer, jun., into the wilderness among the Lamanites.
3. And Ziba Peterson, also, shall go with them, and I myself will go with them and be in their midst; and I am their advocate with the Father, and nothing shall prevail against them.
4. And they shall give heed to that which is written and pretend to no other revelation and they shall pray always that I may unfold the same to their understanding.
5. And they shall give heed unto these words and trifle not, and I will bless them. Amen.

Section 33

Ezra Thayer and Northrop Sweet accepted the gospel as it was presented to them by the missionaries set apart to preach to the Lamanites. The Prophet Joseph Smith recorded the following: "The Lord, who is ever ready to instruct such as diligently seek in faith, gave the following revelation at Fayette, New York: Revelation to Ezra Thayer and Northrop Sweet, given October 1830" (History of the Church, vol. 1:126).

1. Behold, I say unto you, my servants Ezra and Northrop, open ye your ears and hearken to the voice of the Lord your God, whose word is quick and powerful, sharper than a two-edged sword, to the dividing asunder of the joints and marrow, soul and spirit; and is a discerner of the thoughts and intents of the heart.

2. For verily, verily, I say unto you, that ye are called to lift up your voices as with the sound of a trump, to declare my gospel unto a crooked and perverse generation:

3. For behold, the field is white already to harvest: and it is the eleventh hour, and for the last time that I shall call laborers into my vineyard.

4. And my vineyard has become corrupted every whit; and there is none which doeth good save it be a few; and they err in many instances, because of priestcrafts, all having corrupt minds.

5. And verily, verily, I say unto you, that this church have I established and called forth out of the wilderness:

6. And even so will I gather mine elect from the four quarters of the earth, even as many as will believe in me, and hearken unto my voice:

7. Yea, verily, verily, I say unto you, that the field is white already to harvest; wherefore, thrust in your sickles, and reap with all your might, mind, and strength.

8. Open your mouths and they shall be filled, and you shall become even as Nephi of old, who journeyed from Jerusalem in the wilderness:

9. Yea, open your mouths and spare not, and you shall be laden with sheaves upon your backs, for lo, I am with you:

10. Yea, open your mouths and they shall be filled, saying—Repent, repent, and prepare ye the way of the Lord, and make his paths straight; for the kingdom of heaven is at hand;

11. Yea, repent and be baptized, every one of you, for a remission of your sins; yea, be baptized even by water, and then cometh the baptism of fire and of the Holy Ghost.

SEVERAL ELDERS OF THE CHURCH SET FORTH TO DO MISSIONARY WORK AMONG THE LAMANITES

12. Behold, verily, verily, I say unto you, this is my gospel, and remember that they shall have faith in me, or they can in nowise be saved;

13. And upon this rock I will build my church; yea, upon this rock ye are built, and if ye continue, the gates of hell shall not prevail against you;

14. And ye shall remember the church articles and covenants to keep them;

15. And whoso having faith you shall confirm in my church, by the laying on of the hands, and I will bestow the gift of the Holy Ghost upon them.

16. And the Book of Mormon and the Holy Scriptures, are given of me for your instruction; and the power of my Spirit quickeneth all things:

17. Wherefore, be faithful, praying always, having your lamps trimmed and burning, and oil with you, that you may be ready at the coming of the bridegroom:

18. For behold, verily, verily, I say unto you, that I come quickly. Even so. Amen.

ection 34

Orson Pratt, a young man nineteen years of age, was converted to the Church by the preaching of his brother Parley P. Pratt. Young Orson asked the Prophet Joseph Smith to inquire of the Lord to ascertain what his duty was. This revelation was given through the Prophet Joseph Smith to Orson Pratt, November 1830, at Fayette, New York (History of the Church, vol. 1:127–128).

1. My son Orson, hearken and hear and behold what I, the Lord God, shall say unto you, even Jesus Christ your Redeemer;

2. The light and the life of the world; a light which shineth in darkness and the darkness comprehendeth it not;

3. Who so loved the world that he gave his own life, that as many as would believe might become the sons of God; wherefore you are my son,

4. And blessed are you because you have believed;

5. And more blessed are you because you are called of me to preach my gospel,

6. To lift up your voice as with the sound of a trump, both long and loud, and cry repentance unto a crooked and perverse generation, preparing the way of the Lord for his second coming;

7. For behold, verily, verily, I say unto you, the time is soon at hand that I shall come in a cloud with power and great glory,

8. And it shall be a great day at the time of my coming, for all nations shall tremble.

9. But before that great day shall come, the sun shall be darkened, and the moon be turned into blood, and the stars shall refuse their shining, and some shall fall, and great destructions await the wicked:

10. Wherefore lift up your voice and spare not, for the Lord God hath spoken; therefore prophesy, and it shall be given by the power of the Holy Ghost;

11. And if you are faithful, behold, I am with you until I come:

12. And verily, verily, I say unto you, I come quickly. I am your Lord and your Redeemer. Even so. Amen.

Section 35

Several missionaries traveled through Ohio on their way to Missouri to preach to the Lamanites. At Mentor, Ohio, many people became interested in their message, and several were baptized, including Sidney Rigdon. In December 1830, Sidney Rigdon and Edward Partridge traveled from Ohio to Fayette, New York, to meet the Prophet. This revelation was given through the Prophet Joseph Smith to Sidney Rigdon, December 1830, at Fayette, New York (History of the Church, vol. 1:128–129).

1. Listen to the voice of the Lord your God, even Alpha and Omega, the beginning and the end, whose course is one eternal round, the same today as yesterday, and for ever.

2. I am Jesus Christ, the Son of God, who was crucified for the sins of the world, even as many as will believe on my name, that they may become the sons of God, even one in me as I am one in the Father, as the Father is one in me, that we may be one.

3. Behold, verily, verily, I say unto my servant Sidney, I have looked upon thee and thy works. I have heard thy prayers, and prepared thee for a greater work.

4. Thou art blessed, for thou shalt do great things. Behold thou wast sent forth, even as John, to prepare the way before me, and before Elijah which should come, and thou knewest it not.

5. Thou didst baptize by water unto repentance, but they received not the Holy Ghost;

6. But now I give unto thee a commandment, that thou shalt baptize by water, and they shall receive the Holy Ghost by the laying on of the hands, even as the apostles of old.

7. And it shall come to pass that there shall be a great work in the land, among the Gentiles, for their folly and their abominations shall be made manifest in the eyes of all people;

8. For I am God, and mine arm is not shortened; and I will show miracles, signs, and wonders, unto all those who believe on my name.

9. And whoso shall ask it in my name in faith, they shall cast out devils; they shall heal the sick; they shall cause the blind to receive their sight, and the deaf to hear, and the dumb to speak, and the lame to walk;

10. And the time speedily cometh that great things are to be shown forth unto the children of men;

11. But without faith shall not anything be shown forth except desolations upon Babylon, the same which has made all nations drink of the wine of the wrath of her fornication.

12. And there are none that doeth good, except those who are ready to receive the fulness of

my gospel which I have sent forth unto this generation.

13. Wherefore I have called upon the weak things of the world, those who are unlearned and despised, to thresh the nations, by the power of my Spirit:

14. And their arm shall be my arm, and I will be their shield and their buckler; and I will gird up their loins, and they shall fight manfully for me; and their enemies shall be under their feet; and I will let fall the sword in their behalf, and by the fire of mine indignation will I preserve them.

15. And the poor and the meek shall have the gospel preached unto them, and they shall be looking forth for the time of my coming, for it is nigh at hand:

16. And they shall learn the parable of the fig-tree, for even now already summer is nigh,

17. And I have sent forth the fulness of my gospel by the hand of my servant Joseph; and in weakness have I blessed him,

18. And I have given unto him the keys of the mystery of those things which have been sealed, even things which were from the foundation of the world, and the things which shall come from this time until the time of my coming, if he abide in me, and if not, another will I plant in his stead.

19. Wherefore, watch over him that his faith fail not, and it shall be given by the Comforter, the Holy Ghost, that knoweth all things:

20. And a commandment I give unto thee, that thou shalt write for him; and the scriptures shall be given, even as they are in mine own bosom, to the salvation of mine own elect;

21. For they will hear my voice, and shall see me, and shall not be asleep, and shall abide the day of my coming, for they shall be purified, even as I am pure.

22. And now I say unto you, tarry with him, and he shall journey with you; forsake him not, and surely these things shall be fulfilled.

23. And inasmuch as ye do not write, behold, it shall be given unto him to prophesy: and thou shalt preach my gospel and call on the holy prophets to prove his words, as they shall be given him.

24. Keep all the commandments and covenants by which ye are bound; and I will cause the heavens to shake for your good, and Satan shall tremble and Zion shall rejoice upon the hills and flourish,

25. And Israel shall be saved in mine own due time; and by the keys which I have given shall they be led, and no more be confounded at all.

26. Lift up your hearts and be glad, your redemption draweth nigh.

27. Fear not, little flock, the kingdom is yours until I come. Behold I come quickly. Even so. Amen.

ection 36

This revelation, "the voice of the Lord to Edward Partridge," was given through the Prophet Joseph Smith, December 1830, at Fayette, New York (see historical background, section 35), (History of the Church, vol. 1:131).

1. Thus saith the Lord God, the Mighty One of Israel, Behold, I say unto you, my servant Edward, that you are blessed, and your sins are forgiven you, and you are called to preach my gospel as with the voice of a trump;
2. And I will lay my hand upon you by the hand of my servant Sidney Rigdon, and you shall receive my Spirit, the Holy Ghost, even the Comforter, which shall teach you the peaceable things of the kingdom;
3. And you shall declare it with a loud voice, saying, Hosanna, blessed be the name of the most high God.
4. And now this calling and commandment give I unto you concerning all men,
5. That as many as shall come before my servants Sidney Rigdon and Joseph Smith, jun., embracing this calling and commandment, shall be ordained and sent forth to preach the everlasting gospel among the nations,
6. Crying repentance, saying, Save yourselves from this untoward generation, and come forth out of the fire, hating even the garments spotted with the flesh.
7. And this commandment shall be given unto the elders of my church, that every man which will embrace it with singleness of heart, may be ordained and sent forth, even as I have spoken.
8. I am Jesus Christ the Son of God: wherefore, gird up your loins and I will suddenly come to my temple. Even so. Amen.

Section 37

This revelation was given to the Prophet Joseph Smith and Sidney Rigdon, December 1830, at Fayette, New York. They were commanded to cease the work of translating the Bible until they moved to Ohio (History of the Church, vol. 1:139).

1. Behold, I say unto you, that it is not expedient in me that ye should translate any more until ye shall go to the Ohio, and this because of the enemy and for your sakes.
2. And again, I say unto you, that ye shall not go, until ye have preached my gospel in those parts, and have strengthened up the church whithersoever it is found, and more especially in Colesville; for, behold, they pray unto me in much faith.
3. And again, a commandment I give unto the church, that it is expedient in me that they should assemble together at the Ohio, against the time that my servant Oliver Cowdery shall return unto them.
4. Behold, here is wisdom, and let every man choose for himself until I come. Even so. Amen.

Section 38

Prior to the Prophet Joseph Smith moving to Ohio, a conference of the Church convened January 2, 1831, at Fayette, New York. Joseph Smith informs us: ". . . the ordinary business of the Church was transacted; and in addition, the following revelation was received" (History of the Church, vol. 1:140).

1. Thus saith the Lord your God, even Jesus Christ, the Great I AM, Alpha and Omega, the beginning and the end, the same which looked upon the wide expanse of eternity, and all the seraphic hosts of heaven, before the world was made:

2. The same which knoweth all things, for all things are present before mine eyes;

3. I am the same which spake, and the world was made, and all things came by me:

4. I am the same which have taken the Zion of Enoch into mine own bosom; and verily, I say, even as many as have believed in my name, for I am Christ, and in mine own name, by the virtue of the blood which I have spilt, have I pleaded before the Father for them;

5. But behold, the residue of the wicked have I kept in chains of darkness until the judgment of the great day, which shall come at the end of the earth;

6. And even so will I cause the wicked to be kept, that will not hear my voice but harden their hearts, and wo, wo, wo, is their doom.

7. But behold, verily, verily, I say unto you that mine eyes are upon you. I am in your midst and ye cannot see me;

8. But the day soon cometh that ye shall see me, and know that I am; for the veil of darkness shall soon be rent, and he that is not purified shall not abide the day:

9. Wherefore, gird up your loins and be prepared. Behold, the kingdom is yours, and the enemy shall not overcome.

10. Verily, I say unto you, ye are clean, but not all; and there is none else with whom I am well pleased,

11. For all flesh is corrupted before me; and the powers of darkness prevail upon the earth, among the children of men, in the presence of all the hosts of heaven,

12. Which causeth silence to reign, and all eternity is pained, and the angels are waiting the great command to reap down the earth, to gather the tares that they may be burned; and, behold, the enemy is combined.

13. And now I show unto you a mystery, a thing which is had in secret chambers, to bring to pass even your destruction in process of time, and ye knew it not;

14. But now I tell it unto you, and ye are blessed, not because of your iniquity, neither your hearts of unbelief; for verily some of you are guilty before me, but I will be merciful unto your weakness.

15. Therefore, be ye strong from henceforth; fear not, for the kingdom is yours:

16. And for your salvation I give unto you a commandment, for I have heard your prayers, and the poor have complained before me, and the rich have I made, and all flesh is mine, and I am no respecter of persons.

17. And I have made the earth rich, and behold it is my footstool, wherefore, again I will stand upon it;

18. And I hold forth and design to give unto you greater riches, even a land of promise, a land flowing with milk and honey, upon which there shall be no curse when the Lord cometh:

19. And I will give it unto you for the land of your inheritance, if you seek it with all your hearts:

20. And this shall be my covenant with you, ye shall have it for the land of your inheritance, and for the inheritance of your children forever, while the earth shall stand, and ye shall possess it again in eternity, no more to pass away.

21. But, verily, I say unto you, that in time ye shall have no king nor ruler, for I will be your king and watch over you.

22. Wherefore, hear my voice and follow me, and you shall be a free people, and ye shall have no laws but my laws when I come, for I am your Lawgiver, and what can stay my hand?

23. But, verily, I say unto you, teach one another according to the office wherewith I have appointed you,

24. And let every man esteem his brother as himself, and practice virtue and holiness before me.

25. And again I say unto you, let every men esteem his brother as himself;

26. For what man among you having twelve sons, and is no respecter of them, and they serve him obediently, and he saith unto the one, be thou clothed in robes and sit thou here; and to the other, be thou clothed in rags and sit thou there, and looketh upon his sons and saith I am just.

27. Behold, this I have given unto you a parable, and it is even as I am: I say unto you, be one; and if ye are not one, ye are not mine.

28. And again I say unto you, that the enemy in the secret chambers seeketh your lives.

29. Ye hear of wars in far countries, and you say that there will soon be great wars in far countries, but ye know not the hearts of men in your own land.

30. I tell you these things because of your prayers; wherefore treasure up wisdom in your bosoms, lest the wickedness of men reveal these things unto you by their wickedness, in a manner which shall speak in your ears with a voice louder than that which shall shake the earth; but if ye are prepared, ye shall not fear.

31. And that ye might escape the power of the enemy, and be gathered unto me a righteous people, without spot and blameless:

32. Wherefore, for this cause I gave unto you the commandment that ye should go to the Ohio; and there I will give unto you my law; and there you shall be endowed with power from on high;

33. And from thence, whosoever I will, shall go forth among all nations, and it shall be told them what they shall do; for I have a great work laid up in store, for Israel shall be saved, and I will lead them whithersoever I will, and no power shall stay my hand.

34. And now I give unto the church in these parts a commandment, that certain men among them shall be appointed, and they shall be appointed by the voice of the church;

35. And they shall look to the poor and the needy, and administer to their relief, that they shall not suffer; and send them forth to the place which I have commanded them;

36. And this shall be their work, to govern the affairs of the property of this church.

37. And they that have farms that cannot be sold, let them be left or rented as seemeth them good.

38. See that all things are preserved; and when men are endowed with power from on high and sent forth, all these things shall be gathered unto the bosom of the church.

39. And if ye seek the riches which it is the will of the Father to give unto you, ye shall be the richest of all people, for ye shall have the riches of eternity; and it must needs be that the riches of the earth are mine to give; but beware of pride, lest ye become as the Nephites of old.

40. And again, I say unto you, I give unto you a commandment, that every man, both elder, priest, teacher, and also member, go to with his might, with the labor of his hands, to prepare and accomplish the things which I have commanded.

41. And let your preaching be the warning voice, every man to his neighbor, in mildness and in meekness.

42. And go ye out from among the wicked. Save yourselves. Be ye clean that bear the vessels of the Lord. Even so. Amen.

Section 39

Shortly after the conference of January 2, 1831 closed, James Covill, who had been a Baptist minister for about forty years, sought the Prophet Joseph Smith and declared ". . . that he would obey any command that the Lord would give to him through [Joseph], as His servant." This revelation was given through the Prophet Joseph Smith to James Covill at Fayette, New York, January 5, 1831 (History of the Church, vol. 1:143).

1. Hearken and listen to the voice of him who is from all eternity to all eternity, the Great I AM, even Jesus Christ,
2. The light and the life of the world; a light which shineth in darkness and the darkness comprehendeth it not:
3. The same which came in the meridian of time unto my own, and my own received me not;
4. But to as many as received me, gave I power to become my sons, and even so will I give unto as many as will receive me, power to become my sons.
5. And verily, verily, I say unto you, he that receiveth my gospel, receiveth me; and he that receiveth not my gospel receiveth not me.
6. And this is my gospel: repentance and baptism by water, and then cometh the baptism of fire and the Holy Ghost, even the Comforter, which showeth all things, and teacheth the peaceable things of the kingdom.
7. And now, behold, I say unto you, my servant James, I have looked upon thy works and I know thee:
8. And verily I say unto thee, thine heart is now right before me at this time, and, behold, I have bestowed great blessings upon thy head:
9. Nevertheless thou hast seen great sorrow, for thou hast rejected me many times because of pride and the cares of the world;
10. But, behold, the days of thy deliverance are come, if thou wilt hearken to my voice, which saith unto thee, arise and be baptized, and wash away your sins, calling on my name, and you shall receive my Spirit, and a blessing so great as you never have known.
11. And if thou do this, I have prepared thee for a greater work. Thou shalt preach the fulness of my gospel which I have sent forth in these last days; the covenant which I have sent forth to recover my people, which are of the house of Israel.
12. And it shall come to pass that power shall rest upon thee; thou shalt have great faith, and I will be with thee and go before thy face.
13. Thou art called to labor in my vineyard, and to build up my church, and to bring forth

Zion, that it may rejoice upon the hills and flourish.

14. Behold, verily, verily, I say unto thee, thou art not called to go into the eastern countries, but thou art called to go to the Ohio.

15. And inasmuch as my people shall assemble themselves to the Ohio, I have kept in store a blessing such as is not known among the children of men, and it shall be poured forth upon their heads. And from thence men shall go forth into all nations.

16. Behold, verily, verily, I say unto you, that the people in Ohio call upon me in much faith, thinking I will stay my hand in judgment upon the nations, but I cannot deny my word:

17. Wherefore lay to with your might and call faithful laborers into my vineyard, that it may be pruned for the last time.

18. And inasmuch as they do repent and receive the fulness of my gospel, and become sanctified, I will stay mine hand in judgment:

19. Wherefore, go forth, crying with a loud voice, saying, the kingdom of heaven is at hand; crying Hosanna! blessed be the name of the most high God.

20. Go forth baptizing with water, preparing the way before my face, for the time of my coming;

21. For the time is at hand; the day nor the hour no man knoweth; but it surely shall come,

22. And he that receiveth these things receiveth me; and they shall be gathered unto me in time and in eternity.

23. And again, it shall come to pass, that on as many as ye shall baptize with water, ye shall lay your hands, and they shall receive the gift of the Holy Ghost, and shall be looking forth for the signs of my coming, and shall know me.

24. Behold, I come quickly. Even so. Amen.

SECTION 40

James Covill rejected the revelation given to him of the Lord (see historical background, section 39). In this revelation (section 40) given to the Prophet Joseph Smith in January 1831, at Fayette, New York, the Lord explains why James Covill rejected His word (History of the Church, vol. 1:145).

1. Behold, verily I say unto you, that the heart of my servant James Covill was right before me, for he covenanted with me that he would obey my word.

2. And he received the word with gladness, but straightway Satan tempted him; and the fear of persecution, and the cares of the world, caused him to reject the word;

3. Wherefore he broke my covenant, and it remaineth with me to do with him as seemeth me good. Amen.

HYRUM SMITH BEGINS TO CLEAR LAND FOR THE BUILDING OF THE KIRTLAND TEMPLE

Section 41

Obedient to the command of the Lord to move to Ohio (section 37:1), the Prophet Joseph Smith arrived in Kirtland, Ohio, in the latter part of January 1831. Joseph and his family lived with the Newell K. Whitney family for several weeks. The membership of the Church in the Kirtland area had reached nearly one hundred souls. Correcting some problems pertaining to Church procedure, the Prophet received this revelation in Kirtland, Ohio, February 4, 1831. This is the first recorded revelation received in Ohio (History of the Church, vol. 1:145–147).

1. Hearken and hear, O ye my people, saith the Lord and your God, ye whom I delight to bless with the greatest blessings, ye that hear me; and ye that hear me not will I curse, that have professed my name, with the heaviest of all cursings.

2. Hearken, O ye elders of my church whom I have called: behold I give unto you a commandment, that ye shall assemble yourselves together to agree upon my word,

3. And by the prayer of your faith ye shall receive my law, that ye may know how to govern my church, and have all things right before me.

4. And I will be your Ruler when I come; and behold, I come quickly, and ye shall see that my law is kept.

5. He that receiveth my law and doeth it, the same is my disciple; and he that saith he receiveth it and doeth it not, the same is not my disciple, and shall be cast out from among you:

6. For it is not meet that the things which belong to the children of the kingdom, should be given to them that are not worthy, or to dogs, or the pearls to be cast before swine.

7. And again, it is meet that my servant Joseph Smith, jun., should have a house built, in which to live and translate.

8. And again, it is meet that my servant Sidney Rigdon should live as seemeth him good, inasmuch as he keepeth my commandments.

9. And again, I have called my servant Edward Partridge, and give a commandment, that he should be appointed by the voice of the church, and ordained a bishop unto the church, to leave his merchandise and to spend all his time in the labors of the church:

10. To see to all things as it shall be appointed unto him, in my laws in the day that I shall give them.

11. And this because his heart is pure before me, for he is like unto Nathanael of old, in whom there is no guile.

12. These words are given unto you, and they are pure before me; wherefore beware how you hold them, for they are to be answered upon your souls in the day of judgment. Even so. Amen.

Section 42

The Lord promised the Saints that if they were obedient and moved to Ohio, He would give His law unto the Church (section 38:31–32). On February 7, 1831, at Kirtland, Ohio, in the presence of twelve Elders, Joseph Smith received this revelation (History of the Church, vol. 1:148).

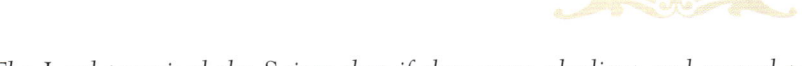

1. Hearken, O ye elders of my church, who have assembled yourselves together in my name, even Jesus Christ the Son of the living God, the Savior of the world: inasmuch as ye believe on my name and keep my commandments,

2. Again, I say unto you, hearken and hear and obey the law which I shall give unto you;

3. For verily I say, as ye have assembled yourselves together according to the commandment wherewith I commanded you, and are agreed as touching this one thing, and have asked the Father in my name, even so ye shall receive.

4. Behold, verily I say unto you, I give unto you this first commandment, that ye shall go forth in my name, every one of you, excepting my servants Joseph Smith, jun., and Sidney Rigdon.

5. And I give unto them a commandment that they shall go forth for a little season, and it shall be given by the power of my Spirit when they shall return;

6. And ye shall go forth in the power of my Spirit, preaching my gospel, two by two, in my name, lifting up your voices as with the voice of a trump, declaring my word like unto angels of God;

7. And ye shall go forth baptizing with water, saying—Repent ye, repent ye, for the kingdom of heaven is at hand.

8. And from this place ye shall go forth into the regions westward; and inasmuch as ye shall find them that will receive you, ye shall build up my church in every region,

9. Until the time shall come when it shall be revealed unto you from on high, when the city of the New Jerusalem shall be prepared, that ye may be gathered in one, that ye may be my people and I will be your God.

10. And again, I say unto you, that my servant Edward Partridge shall stand in the office wherewith I have appointed him. And it shall come to pass, that if he transgress, another shall be appointed in his stead. Even so. Amen.

11. Again, I say unto you, that it shall not be given to any one to go forth to preach my gospel, or to build up my church, except he be ordained

by some one who has authority, and it is known to the church that he has authority, and has been regularly ordained by the heads of the church.

12. And again, the elders, priests, and teachers of this church shall teach the principles of my gospel, which are in the Bible and the Book of Mormon, in the which is the fulness of the gospel;

13. And they shall observe the covenants and church articles to do them, and these shall be their teachings, as they shall be directed by the Spirit;

14. And the Spirit shall be given unto you by the prayer of faith, and if ye receive not the Spirit, ye shall not teach.

15. And all this ye shall observe to do as I have commanded concerning your teaching, until the fulness of my scriptures is given.

16. And as ye shall lift up your voices by the Comforter, ye shall speak and prophesy as seemeth me good;

17. For, behold, the Comforter knoweth all things, and beareth record of the Father and of the Son.

18. And now, behold, I speak unto the church. Thou shalt not kill; and he that kills shall not have forgiveness in this world, nor in the world to come.

19. And again, I say, thou shalt not kill; but he that killeth shall die.

20. Thou shalt not steal; and he that stealeth and will not repent, shall be cast out.

21. Thou shalt not lie; he that lieth and will not repent, shall be cast out.

22. Thou shalt love thy wife with all thy heart, and shalt cleave unto her and none else;

23. And he that looketh upon a woman to lust after her, shall deny the faith, and shall not have the Spirit, and if he repents not he shall be cast out.

24. Thou shalt not commit adultery; and he that committeth adultery, and repenteth not, shall be cast out,

25. But he that has committed adultery and repents with all his heart, and forsaketh it, and doeth it no more, thou shalt forgive;

26. But if he doeth it again, he shall not be forgiven, but shall be cast out.

27. Thou shalt not speak evil of thy neighbor, nor do him any harm.

28. Thou knowest my laws concerning these things are given in my scriptures; he that sinneth and repenteth not, shall be cast out.

29. If thou lovest me thou shalt serve me and keep all my commandments.

30. And behold, thou wilt remember the poor, and consecrate of thy properties for their support that which thou hast to impart unto them with a covenant and a deed which cannot be broken;

31. And inasmuch as ye impart of your substance unto the poor, ye will do it unto me, and they shall be laid before the bishop of my church and his counselors, two of the elders, or High Priests, such as he shall or has appointed and set apart for that purpose.

32. And it shall come to pass, that after they are laid before the bishop of my church, and after that he has received these testimonies concerning the consecration of the properties of my church, that they cannot be taken from the church agreeable to my commandments; every man shall be made accountable unto me, a steward over his own property, or that which he has received by consecration, as much as is sufficient for himself and family.

33. And again, if there shall be properties in the hands of the church, or any individuals of it, more than is necessary for their support, after this first consecration, which is a residue to be consecrated unto the bishop, it shall be kept to administer to those who have not, from time to time, that every man who has need may be amply supplied, and receive according to his wants.

34. Therefore, the residue shall be kept in my storehouse, to administer to the poor and the needy, as shall be appointed by the High Council of the church, and the bishop and his council,

35. And for the purpose of purchasing lands for the public benefit of the church, and building houses of worship, and building up of the New Jerusalem which is hereafter to be revealed,

36. That my covenant people may be gathered in one in that day when I shall come to my temple. And this I do for the salvation of my people.

37. And it shall come to pass, that he that sinneth and repenteth not shall be cast out of the church, and shall not receive again that which he has consecrated unto the poor and the needy of my church; or in other words, unto me;

38. For inasmuch as ye do it unto the least of these, ye do it unto me;

39. For it shall come to pass, that which I spake by the mouths of my prophets, shall be fulfilled; for I will consecrate of the riches of those who embrace my gospel among the Gentiles, unto the poor of my people who are of the house of Israel.

40. And again, thou shalt not be proud in thy heart; let all thy garments be plain, and their beauty the beauty of the work of thine own hands;

41. And let all things be done in cleanliness before me.

42. Thou shalt not be idle; for he that is idle shall not eat the bread nor wear the garments of the laborer.

43. And whosoever among you are sick, and have not faith to be healed, but believe, shall be nourished with all tenderness, with herbs and mild food, and that not by the hand of an enemy.

44. And the elders of the church, two or more, shall be called, and shall pray for and lay their hands upon them in my name; and if they die they shall die unto me, and if they live they shall live unto me.

45. Thou shalt live together in love, insomuch that thou shalt weep for the loss of them that die, and more especially for those that have not hope of a glorious resurrection.

46. And it shall come to pass that those that die in me, shall not taste of death, for it shall be sweet unto them;

47. And they that die not in me, wo unto them, for their death is bitter.

48. And again, it shall come to pass that he that hath faith in me to be healed, and is not appointed unto death, shall be healed;

49. He who hath faith to see shall see;

50. He who hath faith to hear shall hear;

51. The lame who hath faith to leap shall leap;

52. And they who have not faith to do these things, but believe in me, have power to become my sons, and inasmuch as they break not my laws, thou shalt bear their infirmities.

53. Thou shalt stand in the place of thy stewardship;

54. Thou shalt not take thy brother's garment; thou shalt pay for that which thou shalt receive of thy brother;

55. And if thou obtainest more than that which would be for thy support, thou shalt give it into my store-house, that all things may be done according to that which I have said.

56. Thou shalt ask, and my Scriptures shall be given as I have appointed, and they shall be preserved in safety;

57. And it is expedient that thou shouldst hold thy peace concerning them, and not teach them until ye have received them in full.

58. And I give unto you a commandment that then ye shall teach them unto all men; for they shall be taught unto all nations, kindreds, tongues and people.

59. Thou shalt take the things which thou hast received, which have been given unto thee in my Scriptures for a law, to be my law to govern my church;

Section 43

A woman by the name of Hubble claimed to be a prophetess of the Lord and the recipient of many revelations. She deceived some and was the cause of some consternation to the Church. Because of this problem, the Prophet Joseph Smith inquired of the Lord and received this revelation, February 1831, at Kirtland, Ohio (History of the Church, vol. 1:154).

1. O hearken, ye elders of my church, and give an ear to the words which I shall speak unto you;
2. For behold, verily, verily, I say unto you, that ye have received a commandment for a law unto my church, through him whom I have appointed unto you, to receive commandments and revelations from my hand.
3. And this ye shall know assuredly that there is none other appointed unto you to receive commandments and revelations until he be taken, if he abide in me.
4. But verily, verily, I say unto you, that none else shall be appointed unto this gift except it be through him, for if it be taken from him, he shall not have power except to appoint another in his stead;
5. And this shall be a law unto you, that ye receive not the teachings of any that shall come before you as revelations or commandments;
6. And this I give unto you that you may not be deceived, that you may know they are not of me.
7. For verily I say unto you, that he that is ordained of me shall come in at the gate and be ordained as I have told you before, to teach those revelations which you have received, and shall receive through him whom I have appointed.
8. And now, behold, I give unto you a commandment, that when ye are assembled together, ye shall instruct and edify each other, that ye may know how to act and direct my church, how to act upon the points of my law and commandments, which I have given;
9. And thus ye shall become instructed in the law of my church, and be sanctified by that which ye have received, and ye shall bind yourselves to act in all holiness before me,
10. That inasmuch as ye do this, glory shall be added to the kingdom which ye have received. Inasmuch as ye do it not, it shall be taken, even that which ye have received.
11. Purge ye out the iniquity which is among you; sanctify yourselves before me,
12. And if ye desire the glories of the kingdom, appoint ye my servant Joseph Smith, jun., and uphold him before me by the prayer of faith.

13. And again, I say unto you, that if ye desire the mysteries of the kingdom, provide for him food and raiment, and whatsoever thing he needeth to accomplish the work, wherewith I have commanded him;

14. And if ye do it not, he shall remain unto them that have received him, that I may reserve unto myself a pure people before me.

15. Again I say, hearken ye elders of my church, whom I have appointed; ye are not sent forth to be taught, but to teach the children of men the things which I have put into your hands by the power of my Spirit;

16. And ye are to be taught from on high. Sanctify yourselves and ye shall be endowed with power, that ye may give even as I have spoken.

17. Hearken ye, for, behold, the great day of the Lord is nigh at hand.

18. For the day cometh that the Lord shall utter his voice out of heaven; the heavens shall shake and the earth shall tremble, and the trump of God shall sound both long and loud, and shall say to the sleeping nations, Ye saints arise and live; ye sinners stay and sleep until I shall call again;

19. Wherefore gird up your loins lest ye be found among the wicked.

20. Lift up your voices and spare not. Call upon the nations to repent, both old and young, both bond and free, saying; prepare yourselves for the great day of the Lord;

21. For if I, who am a man, do lift up my voice and call upon you to repent, and ye hate me, what will ye say when the day cometh when the thunders shall utter their voices from the ends of the earth, speaking to the ears of all that live, saying, Repent, and prepare for the great day of the Lord;

22. Yea, and again, when the lightnings shall streak forth from the east unto the west, and shall utter forth their voices unto all that live, and make the ears of all tingle that hear, saying these words, Repent ye, for the great day of the Lord is come.

23. And again, the Lord shall utter his voice out of heaven, saying, Hearken, O ye nations of the earth, and hear the words of that God who made you.

24. O, ye nations of the earth, how often would I have gathered you together as a hen gathereth her chickens under her wings, but ye would not?

25. How oft have I called upon you by the mouth of my servants, and by the ministering of angels, and by mine own voice, and by the voice of thunderings, and by the voice of lightnings, and by the voice of tempests, and by the voice of earthquakes, and great hailstorms, and by the voice of famines and pestilences of every kind, and by the great sound of a trump, and by the voice of judgment, and by the voice of mercy all the day long, and by the voice of glory, and honor, and the riches of eternal life, and would have saved you with an everlasting salvation, but ye would not?

26. Behold the day has come, when the cup of the wrath of mine indignation is full.

27. Behold, verily I say unto you, that these are the words of the Lord your God;

28. Wherefore labor ye, labor ye in my vineyard for the last time—for the last time call upon the inhabitants of the earth,

29. For in mine own due time will I come upon the earth in judgment, and my people shall be redeemed and shall reign with me on earth;

30. For the great Millennium, of which I have spoken by the mouth of my servants, shall come.

31. For Satan shall be bound, and when he is loosed again he shall only reign for a little season, and then cometh the end of the earth;

32. And he that liveth in righteousness shall be changed in the twinkling of an eye, and the earth shall pass away so as by fire;

33. And the wicked shall go away into

unquenchable fire, and their end no man knoweth on earth, nor ever shall know, until they come before me in judgment.

34. Hearken ye to these words; Behold, I am Jesus Christ, the Savior of the world. Treasure these things up in your hearts, and let the solemnities of eternity rest upon your minds.

35. Be sober. Keep all my commandments. Even so. Amen.

# Section 44

The Prophet Joseph Smith recorded that in "The latter part of February I received the following revelation, which caused the Church to appoint a conference to be held early in the month of June ensuing." The Lord directs the missionaries who are laboring in the various parts of the country to assemble at Kirtland, Ohio, to meet in conference. He promised them that if they were faithful, His spirit would be poured out upon them. This revelation was received in the latter part of February 1831, at Kirtland, Ohio (History of the Church, vol. 1:157).

1. Behold, thus saith the Lord unto you my servants, it is expedient in me that the elders of my church should be called together, from the east and from the west, and from the north and from the south, by letter or some other way.

2. And it shall come to pass, that inasmuch as they are faithful, and exercise faith in me, I will pour out my Spirit upon them in the day that they assemble themselves together.

3. And it shall come to pass that they shall go forth into the regions round about, and preach repentance unto the people,

4. And many shall be converted, insomuch that ye shall obtain power to organize yourselves, according to the laws of man;

5. That your enemies may not have power over you, that you may be preserved in all things; that you may be enabled to keep my laws, that every bond may be broken wherewith the enemy seeketh to destroy my people.

6. Behold I say unto you, that ye must visit the poor and the needy, and administer to their relief, that they may be kept until all things may be done according to my law which ye have received. Amen.

Section 45

The Prophet Joseph Smith explains the circumstances that preceded the reception of this revelation as follows: "At this age of the Church (i.e., early in the spring of 1831), many false reports, lies, and foolish stories were published in the newspapers, and circulated in every direction, to prevent people from investigating the work, or embracing the faith. . . . But to the joy of the Saints who had to struggle against everything that prejudice and wickedness could invent, I received the following." This revelation was received March 7, 1831, at Kirtland, Ohio (History of the Church, vol. 1:158).

1. Hearken, O ye people of my church, to whom the kingdom has been given—hearken ye and give ear to him who laid the foundation of the earth, who made the heavens and all the hosts thereof, and by whom all things were made which live, and move, and have a being.
2. And again I say, hearken unto my voice, lest death shall overtake you; in an hour when ye think not the summer shall be past, and the harvest ended, and your souls not saved.
3. Listen to him who is the advocate with the Father, who is pleading your cause before him,
4. Saying, Father, behold the sufferings and death of him who did no sin, in whom thou wast well pleased; behold the blood of thy Son which was shed—the blood of him whom thou gavest that thyself might be glorified;
5. Wherefore, Father, spare these my brethren that believe on my name, that they may come unto me and have everlasting life.
6. Hearken, O ye people of my church, and ye elders listen together, and hear my voice while it is called to-day, and harden not your hearts,
7. For verily I say unto you that I am Alpha and Omega, the beginning and the end, the light and the life of the world—a light that shineth in darkness and the darkness comprehendeth it not.
8. I came unto mine own, and mine own received me not; but unto as many as received me, gave I power to do many miracles, and to become the sons of God, and even unto them that believed on my name gave I power to obtain eternal life.
9. And even so I have sent mine everlasting covenant into the world, to be a light to the world, and to be a standard for my people and for the Gentiles to seek to it, and to be a messenger before my face to prepare the way before me;
10. Wherefore, come ye unto it, and with him that cometh I will reason as with men in days of old, and I will show unto you my strong reasoning.
11. Wherefore hearken ye together and let me show unto you, even my wisdom—the wisdom of him whom ye say is the God of Enoch, and his brethren,

KIRTLAND VILLAGE SCENE. PICTURED ON THE RIGHT IS THE WHITNEY STORE THAT HOUSED THE SCHOOL OF THE PROPHETS. IT WAS LOCATED NEXT DOOR TO THE TANNERY.

12. Who were separated from the earth, and were received unto myself—a city reserved until a day of righteousness shall come—a day which was sought for by all holy men, and they found it not because of wickedness and abominations;

13. And confessed they were strangers and pilgrims on the earth;

14. But obtained a promise that they should find it and see it in their flesh.

15. Wherefore, hearken and I will reason with you, and I will speak unto you and prophesy, as unto men in days of old;

16. And I will show it plainly as I showed it unto my disciples as I stood before them in the flesh, and spake unto them, saying; as ye have asked of me concerning the signs of my coming, in the day when I shall come in my glory in the clouds of heaven, to fulfil the promises that I have made unto your fathers,

17. For as ye have looked upon the long absence of your spirits from your bodies to be a bondage, I will show unto you how the day of redemption shall come, and also the restoration of the scattered Israel.

18. And now ye behold this temple which is in Jerusalem, which ye call the house of God, and your enemies say that this house shall never fall.

19. But, verily, I say unto you, that desolation shall come upon this generation as a thief in the night, and this people shall be destroyed and scattered among all nations.

20. And this temple which ye now see shall be thrown down that there shall not be left one stone upon another.

21. And it shall come to pass, that this generation of Jews shall not pass away, until every desolation which I have told you concerning them shall come to pass.

22. Ye say that ye know that the end of the world cometh; ye say also that ye know that the heavens and the earth shall pass away;

23. And in this ye say truly, for so it is; but these things which I have told you shall not pass away until all shall be fulfilled,

24. And this I have told you concerning Jerusalem, and when that day shall come, shall a remnant be scattered among all nations;

25. But they shall be gathered again, but they shall remain until the times of the Gentiles be fulfilled.

26. And in that day shall be heard of wars and rumors of wars, and the whole earth shall be in commotion, and men's hearts shall fail them, and they shall say that Christ delayeth his coming until the end of the earth.

27. And the love of men shall wax cold, and iniquity shall abound;

28. And when the times of the Gentiles is come in, a light shall break forth among them that sit in darkness, and it shall be the fulness of my gospel;

29. But they receive it not, for they perceive not the light, and they turn their hearts from me because of the precepts of men;

30. And in that generation shall the times of the Gentiles be fulfilled;

31. And there shall be men standing in that generation, that shall not pass, until they shall see an overflowing scourge; for a desolating sickness shall cover the land;

32. But my disciples shall stand in holy places, and shall not be moved; but among the wicked, men shall lift up their voices, and curse God and die.

33. And there shall be earthquakes also in divers places, and many desolations; yet men will harden their hearts against me, and they will take up the sword, one against another, and they will kill one another.

34. And, now, when I the Lord had spoken these words unto my disciples, they were troubled:

35. And I said unto them, be not troubled, for when all these things shall come to pass, ye may

know that the promises which have been made unto you shall be fulfilled;

36. And when the light shall begin to break forth, it shall be with them like unto a parable which I will show you:

37. Ye look and behold the fig-trees, and ye see them with your eyes, and ye say when they begin to shoot forth, and their leaves are yet tender, that summer is now nigh at hand;

38. Even so it shall be in that day when they shall see all these things, then shall they know that the hour is nigh.

39. And it shall come to pass that he that feareth me shall be looking forth for the great day of the Lord to come, even for the signs of the coming of the Son of man:

40. And they shall see signs and wonders, for they shall be shown forth in the heavens above, and in the earth beneath;

41. And they shall behold blood, and fire, and vapors of smoke;

42. And before the day of the Lord shall come, the sun shall be darkened, and the moon be turned into blood, and stars fall from heaven;

43. And the remnant shall be gathered unto this place,

44. And then they shall look for me, and, behold, I will come; and they shall see me in the clouds of heaven, clothed with power and great glory, with all the holy angels; and he that watches not for me shall be cut off.

45. But before the arm of the Lord shall fall, an angel shall sound his trump, and the saints that have slept shall come forth to meet me in the cloud;

46. Wherefore, if ye have slept in peace blessed are you, for as you now behold me and know that I am, even so shall ye come unto me and your souls shall live, and your redemption shall be perfected, and the saints shall come forth from the four quarters of the earth.

47. Then shall the arm of the Lord fall upon the nations,

48. And then shall the Lord set his foot upon this mount, and it shall cleave in twain, and the earth shall tremble, and reel to and fro, and the heavens also shall shake,

49. And the Lord shall utter his voice, and all the ends of the earth shall hear it, and the nations of the earth shall mourn, and they that have laughed shall see their folly,

50. And calamity shall cover the mocker, and the scorner shall be consumed, and they that have watched for iniquity shall be hewn down and cast into the fire.

51. And then shall the Jews look upon me and say, What are these wounds in thine hands and in thy feet?

52. Then shall they know that I am the Lord; for I will say unto them, These wounds are the wounds with which I was wounded in the house of my friends. I am he who was lifted up. I am Jesus that was crucified. I am the Son of God.

53. And then shall they weep because of their iniquities; then shall they lament because they persecuted their King.

54. And then shall the heathen nations be redeemed, and they that knew no law shall have part in the first resurrection; and it shall be tolerable for them;

55. And Satan shall be bound that he shall have no place in the hearts of the children of men.

56. And at that day, when I shall come in my glory, shall the parable be fulfilled which I spake concerning the ten virgins;

57. For they that are wise and have received the truth, and have taken the Holy Spirit for their guide, and have not been deceived; verily I say unto you, they shall not be hewn down and cast into the fire, but shall abide the day.

58. And the earth shall be given unto them for an inheritance; and they shall multiply and wax

strong, and their children shall grow up without sin unto salvation,

59. For the Lord shall be in their midst, and his glory shall be upon them, and he will be their King and their Lawgiver.

60. And now, behold I say unto you, it shall not be given unto you to know any further concerning this chapter, until the New Testament be translated, and in it all these things shall be made known;

61. Wherefore I give unto you that ye may now translate it, that ye may be prepared for the things to come;

62. For verily I say unto you, that great things await you;

63. Ye hear of wars in foreign lands, but, behold, I say unto you, they are nigh, even at your doors, and not many years hence ye shall hear of wars in your own lands.

64. Wherefore I, the Lord, have said, gather ye out from the eastern lands, assemble ye yourselves together ye elders of my church; go ye forth into the western countries, call upon the inhabitants to repent, and inasmuch as they do repent, build up churches unto me;

65. And with one heart and with one mind, gather up your riches that ye may purchase an inheritance which shall hereafter be appointed unto you,

66. And it shall be called the New Jerusalem, a land of peace, a city of refuge, a place of safety for the saints of the most High God;

67. And the glory of the Lord shall be there, and the terror of the Lord also shall be there, insomuch that the wicked will not come unto it, and it shall be called Zion.

68. And it shall come to pass, among the wicked, that every man that will not take his sword against his neighbor, must needs flee unto Zion for safety.

69. And there shall be gathered unto it out of every nation under heaven; and it shall be the only people that shall not be at war one with another.

70. And it shall be said among the wicked, Let us not go up to battle against Zion, for the inhabitants of Zion are terrible; wherefore we cannot stand.

71. And it shall come to pass that the righteous shall be gathered out from among all nations, and shall come to Zion singing with songs of everlasting joy.

72. And now I say unto you, keep these things from going abroad unto the world, until it is expedient in me that ye may accomplish this work in the eyes of the people, and in the eyes of your enemies, that they may not know your works until ye have accomplished the thing which I have commanded you;

73. That when they shall know it, that they may consider these things;

74. For when the Lord shall appear he shall be terrible unto them, that fear may seize upon them, and they shall stand afar off and tremble;

75. And all nations shall be afraid because of the terror of the Lord, and the power of his might. Even so. Amen.

SECTION 46

John Whitmer, Church historian, recorded: "In the beginning of the Church, while yet in her infancy, the disciples used to exclude unbelievers, which caused some to marvel. . . . Therefore the Lord designed to speak on this subject, that His people might come to understanding" (History of the Church, vol. 1:163–164). This revelation was received one day following the reception of section 45, March 8, 1831, at Kirtland, Ohio (History of the Church, vol. 1:163).

1. Hearken, O ye people of my church, for verily I say unto you, that these things were spoken unto you for your profit and learning;

2. But notwithstanding those things which are written, it always has been given to the elders of my church from the beginning and ever shall be to conduct all meetings as they are directed and guided by the Holy Spirit;

3. Nevertheless ye are commanded never to cast any one out from your public meetings, which are held before the world;

4. Ye are also commanded not to cast any one, who belongeth to the church out of your sacrament meetings; nevertheless, if any have trespassed, let him not partake until he makes reconciliation.

5. And again I say unto you, ye shall not cast any out of your sacrament meetings, who are earnestly seeking the kingdom: I speak this concerning those who are not of the church.

6. And again I say unto you, concerning your confirmation meetings, that if there be any that are not of the church, that are earnestly seeking after the kingdom, ye shall not cast them out;

7. But ye are commanded in all things to ask of God, who giveth liberally; and that which the Spirit testifies unto you, even so I would that ye should do in all holiness of heart, walking uprightly before me, considering the end of your salvation, doing all things with prayer and thanksgiving, that ye may not be seduced by evil spirits, or doctrines of devils, or the commandments of men, for some are of men, and others of devils.

8. Wherefore, beware lest ye are deceived; and that ye may not be deceived, seek ye earnestly the best gifts, always remembering for what they are given;

9. For verily I say unto you, they are given for the benefit of those who love me and keep all my commandments, and him that seeketh so to do, that all may be benefited that seeketh or that asketh of me, that asketh and not for a sign that he may consume it upon his lusts.

10. And again, verily I say unto you, I would that ye should always remember, and always retain in your minds what those gifts are, that are given unto the church,

11. For all have not every gift given unto them; for there are many gifts, and to every man is given a gift by the Spirit of God:

12. To some is given one, and to some is given another, that all may be profited thereby;

13. To some it is given by the Holy Ghost to know that Jesus Christ is the Son of God, and that he was crucified for the sins of the world;

14. To others it is given to believe on their words, that they also might have eternal life if they continue faithful.

15. And again, to some it is given by the Holy Ghost to know the difference of administration, as it will be pleasing unto the same Lord, according as the Lord will, suiting his mercies according to the conditions of the children of men.

16. And again, it is given by the Holy Ghost to some to know the diversities of operations, whether it be of God, that the manifestations of the Spirit may be given to every man to profit withal.

17. And again, verily I say unto you, to some it is given, by the Spirit of God, the word of wisdom;

18. To another is given the word of knowledge, that all may be taught to be wise and to have knowledge.

19. And again, to some it is given to have faith to be healed,

20. And to others it is given to have faith to heal.

21. And again, to some it is given the working of miracles;

22. And to others it is given to prophesy,

23. And to others the discerning of spirits.

24. And again, it is given to some to speak with tongues,

25. And to another is given the interpretation of tongues:

26. And all these gifts come from God, for the benefit of the children of God.

27. And unto the bishop of the church, and unto such as God shall appoint and ordain to watch over the church, and to be elders unto the church, are to have it given unto them to discern all those gifts, lest there shall be any among you professing and yet be not of God.

28. And it shall come to pass that he that asketh in Spirit shall receive in Spirit;

29. That unto some it may be given to have all those gifts, that there may be a head, in order that every member may be profited thereby:

30. He that asketh in the Spirit, asketh according to the will of God, wherefore it is done even as he asketh.

31. And again, I say unto you, all things must be done in the name of Christ, whatsoever you do in the Spirit;

32. And ye must give thanks unto God in the Spirit for whatsoever blessings ye are blessed with;

33. And ye must practice virtue and holiness before me continually. Even so. Amen.

SECTION 47

Oliver Cowdery was called to be the first historian and recorder for the Church. The Lord now calls John Whitmer as historian, ". . . inasmuch as he is faithful." This revelation was received March 8, 1831, at Kirtland, Ohio (History of the Church, vol. 1:166).

1. Behold, it is expedient in me that my servant John should write and keep a regular history, and assist you, my servant Joseph, in transcribing all things which shall be given you, until he is called to further duties.
2. Again, verily I say unto you, that he can also lift up his voice in meetings, whenever it shall be expedient.
3. And again, I say unto you that it shall be appointed unto him to keep the church record and history continually, for Oliver Cowdery I have appointed to another office.
4. Wherefore it shall be given him, inasmuch as he is faithful, by the Comforter, to write these things. Even so. Amen.

ection 48

The Lord commanded the Saints in New York to gather in Ohio (sections 37:1, 3; 38:31–32; 39:15). The Saints in Ohio made inquiries of the Prophet Joseph Smith regarding purchasing lands for the New York Saints to settle on. This revelation was received March 1831, at Kirtland, Ohio (History of the Church, vol. 1:166).

1. It is necessary that ye should remain for the present time in your places of abode, as it shall be suitable to your circumstances;

2. And inasmuch as ye have lands, ye shall impart to the eastern brethren;

3. And inasmuch as ye have not lands, let them buy for the present time in those regions round about as seemeth them good, for it must needs be necessary that they have places to live for the present time.

4. It must needs be necessary, that ye save all the money that ye can, and that ye obtain all that ye can in righteousness, that in time ye may be enabled to purchase land for an inheritance, even the city.

5. The place is not yet to be revealed, but after your brethren come from the east, there are to be certain men appointed, and to them it shall be given to know the place, or to them it shall be revealed.

6. And they shall be appointed to purchase the lands, and to make a commencement to lay the foundation of the city; and then shall ye begin to be gathered with your families, every man according to his family, according to his circumstances, and as is appointed to him by the Presidency and the bishop of the church according to the laws and commandments which ye have received, and which ye shall hereafter receive. Even so. Amen.

Section 49

Leman Copley, a member of the Shaking Quakers, accepted the restored gospel and joined the Church. However, he still embraced some of the teachings of the Shaking Quakers that were not in harmony with the restored truths of the gospel. The Prophet Joseph Smith said, "In order to have more perfect understanding on the subject, I inquired of the Lord, and received the following." This revelation was given to the Prophet Joseph Smith for Sidney Rigdon, Parley P. Pratt, and Leman Copley, March 1831, at Kirtland, Ohio (History of the Church, vol. 1:167).

1. Hearken unto my word, my servants Sidney, and Parley, and Leman, for behold, verily I say unto you, that I give unto you a commandment that you shall go and preach my gospel which ye have received, even as ye have received it, unto the Shakers.

2. Behold, I say unto you, that they desire to know the truth in part, but not all, for they are not right before me and must needs repent;

3. Wherefore, I send you, my servants Sidney and Parley, to preach the gospel unto them;

4. And my servant Leman shall be ordained unto this work, that he may reason with them, not according to that which he has received of them, but according to that which shall be taught him by you my servants, and by so doing I will bless him, otherwise he shall not prosper.

5. Thus saith the Lord, for I am God, and have sent mine Only Begotten Son into the world for the redemption of the world, and have decreed that he that receiveth him shall be saved, and he that receiveth him not shall be damned.

6. And they have done unto the Son of man even as they listed; and he has taken his power on the right hand of his glory, and now reigneth in the heavens, and will reign till he descends on the earth to put all enemies under his feet, which time is nigh at hand:

7. I, the Lord God, have spoken it, but the hour and the day no man knoweth, neither the angels in heaven, nor shall they know until he comes;

8. Wherefore, I will that all men shall repent, for all are under sin, except them which I have reserved unto myself, holy men that ye know not of;

9. Wherefore I say unto you, that I have sent unto you mine everlasting covenant, even that which was from the beginning,

10. And that which I have promised I have so fulfilled, and the nations of the earth shall bow to it; and, if not of themselves, they shall come down, for that which is now exalted of itself shall be laid low of power;

11. Wherefore I give unto you a commandment that ye go among this people and say unto them,

like unto mine apostle of old, whose name was Peter;

12. Believe on the name of the Lord Jesus, who was on the earth, and is to come, the beginning and the end,

13. Repent and be baptized in the name of Jesus Christ, according to the holy commandment, for the remission of sins;

14. And whoso doeth this shall receive the gift of the Holy Ghost, by the laying on of the hands of the elders of this church.

15. And again, I say unto you, that whoso forbiddeth to marry is not ordained of God, for marriage is ordained of God unto man;

16. Wherefore it is lawful that he should have one wife, and they twain shall be one flesh, and all this that the earth might answer the end of its creation,

17. And that it might be filled with the measure of man, according to his creation before the world was made.

18. And whoso forbiddeth to abstain from meats, that man should not eat the same, is not ordained of God;

19. For, behold, the beasts of the field and the fowls of the air, and that which cometh of the earth, is ordained for the use of man for food and for raiment, and that he might have in abundance:

20. But it is not given that one man should possess that which is above another, wherefore the world lieth in sin;

21. And wo be unto man that sheddeth blood or that wasteth flesh and hath no need.

22. And again, verily I say unto you, that the Son of man cometh not in the form of a woman, neither of a man traveling on the earth;

23. Wherefore be not deceived, but continue in steadfastness, looking forth for the heavens to be shaken, and the earth to tremble and to reel to and fro as a drunken man, and for the valleys to be exalted, and for the mountains to be made low, and for the rough places to become smooth; and all this when the angel shall sound his trumpet.

24. But before the great day of the Lord shall come, Jacob shall flourish in the wilderness, and the Lamanites shall blossom as the rose.

25. Zion shall flourish upon the hills and rejoice upon the mountains, and shall be assembled together unto the place which I have appointed.

26. Behold, I say unto you, go forth as I have commanded you—repent of all your sins, ask and ye shall receive, knock and it shall be opened unto you:

27. Behold, I will go before you and be your rearward; and I will be in your midst, and you shall not be confounded;

28. Behold, I am Jesus Christ, and I come quickly. Even so. Amen.

Section 50

This revelation was received in May 1831, at Kirtland, Ohio. Referring to this event, the Prophet Joseph Smith records: "Soon after the Gospel was established in Kirtland, and during the absence of the authorities of the Church, many false spirits were introduced, many strange visions were seen, and wild, enthusiastic notions were entertained" (History of the Church, vol. 4:580). "In May, a number of the Elders being present, and not understanding the different spirits abroad in the earth, I inquired and received from the Lord the following" (History of the Church, vol. 1:170).

1. Hearken, O ye elders of my church, and give ear to the voice of the living God, and attend to the words of wisdom which shall be given unto you, according as ye have asked and are agreed as touching the church, and the spirits which have gone abroad in the earth.
2. Behold, verily I say unto you, that there are many spirits which are false spirits, which have gone forth in the earth, deceiving the world;
3. And also Satan hath sought to deceive you, that he might overthrow you.
4. Behold, I the Lord, have looked upon you, and have seen abominations in the church that profess my name;
5. But blessed are they who are faithful and endure, whether in life or in death, for they shall inherit eternal life.
6. But wo unto them that are deceivers and hypocrites, for, thus saith the Lord, I will bring them to judgment.
7. Behold, verily I say unto you, there are hypocrites among you, who have deceived some, which has given the adversary power, but behold such shall be reclaimed;
8. But the hypocrites shall be detected and shall be cut off, either in life or in death, even as I will; and wo unto them who are cut off from my church, for the same are overcome of the world;
9. Wherefore, let every man beware lest he do that which is not in truth and righteousness before me.
10. And now come, saith the Lord, by the Spirit, unto the elders of his church, and let us reason together, that ye may understand:
11. Let us reason even as a man reasoneth one with another face to face;
12. Now when a man reasoneth he is understood of man because he reasoneth as a man, even so will I, the Lord, reason with you that you may understand;
13. Wherefore, I the Lord, asketh you this question, unto what were ye ordained?
14. To preach my gospel by the Spirit, even the Comforter which was sent forth to teach the truth;

15. And then received ye spirits which ye could not understand, and received them to be of God; and in this are ye justified?

16. Behold ye shall answer this question yourselves; nevertheless I will be merciful unto you—he that is weak among you hereafter shall be made strong.

17. Verily, I say unto you, he that is ordained of me and sent forth to preach the word of truth by the Comforter, in the Spirit of truth, doth he preach it by the Spirit of truth or some other way?

18. And if it be by some other way, it be not of God.

19. And again, he that receiveth the word of truth, doth he receive it by the Spirit of truth or some other way?

20. If it be some other way it be not of God:

21. Therefore, why is it that ye cannot understand and know that he that receiveth the word by the Spirit of truth, receiveth it as it is preached by the Spirit of truth?

22. Wherefore, he that preacheth and he that receiveth, understandeth one another, and both are edified and rejoice together;

23. And that which doth not edify is not of God, and is darkness;

24. That which is of God is light; and he that receiveth light and continueth in God, receiveth more light, and that light groweth brighter and brighter until the perfect day.

25. And again, verily I say unto you, and I say it that you may know the truth, that you may chase darkness from among you;

26. For he that is ordained of God and sent forth the same is appointed to be the greatest, notwithstanding he is the least and the servant of all:

27. Wherefore he is possessor of all things; for all things are subject unto him, both in heaven and on the earth, the life and the light, the Spirit and the power, sent forth by the will of the Father, through Jesus Christ, his Son;

28. But no man is possessor of all things; except he be purified and cleansed from all sin;

29. And if ye are purified and cleansed from all sin, ye shall ask whatsoever you will in the name of Jesus and it shall be done:

30. But know this, it shall be given you what you shall ask, and as ye are appointed to the head, the spirits shall be subject unto you.

31. Wherefore it shall come to pass, that if you behold a spirit manifested that you cannot understand, and you receive not that spirit, ye shall ask of the Father in the name of Jesus, and if he give not unto you that spirit, then you may know that it is not of God:

32. And it shall be given unto you power over that spirit, and you shall proclaim against that spirit with a loud voice that it is not of God:

33. Not with railing accusation, that ye be not overcome, neither with boasting, nor rejoicing, lest you be seized therewith.

34. He that receiveth of God, let him account it of God, and let him rejoice that he is accounted of God worthy to receive,

35. And by giving heed and doing these things which ye have received and which ye shall hereafter receive: and the kingdom is given you of the Father, and power to overcome all things which are not ordained of him.

36. And behold, verily I say unto you, blessed are you who are now hearing these words of mine from the mouth of my servant, for your sins are forgiven you.

37. Let my servant Joseph Wakefield, in whom I am well pleased, and my servant Parley P. Pratt, go forth among the churches and strengthen them by the word of exhortation;

38. And also my servant John Corrill, or as many of my servants as are ordained unto this office, and let them labor in the vineyard; and let no man hinder them of doing that which I have appointed unto them:

39. Wherefore in this thing my servant Edward Partridge is not justified, nevertheless let him repent and he shall be forgiven.

40. Behold, ye are little children and ye cannot bear all things now, ye must grow in grace and in the knowledge of the truth.

41. Fear not, little children, for you are mine, and I have overcome the world, and you are of them that my Father hath given me;

42. And none of them that my Father hath given me shall be lost:

43. And the Father and I are one: I am in the Father and the Father in me: and inasmuch as ye have received me, ye are in me and I in you;

44. Wherefore I am in your midst, and I am the good Shepherd, and the Stone of Israel. He that buildeth upon this rock shall never fall,

45. And the day cometh that you shall hear my voice and see me, and know that I am.

46. Watch, therefore, that ye may be ready. Even so. Amen.

Section 51

In May 1831 the Saints from the state of New York began to arrive at Ohio, obedient to the command of the Lord (sections 37:3; 38:31–32). The Saints in Ohio were counseled by the Lord to divide their lands with the eastern brethren (section 48:2). Bishop Partridge, whose responsibility was "to see to all things as it shall be appointed unto him" (section 41:10) sought counsel from the Prophet Joseph Smith pertaining to the settling of the New York Saints. This revelation was received in May 1831, at Thompson, Ohio (History of the Church, vol. 1:173).

1. Hearken unto me, saith the Lord your God, and I will speak unto my servant Edward Partridge, and give unto him directions, for it must needs be that he receive directions how to organize this people;

2. For it must needs be that they be organized according to my laws—if otherwise, they will be cut off;

3. Wherefore let my servant Edward Partridge, and those whom he has chosen, in whom I am well pleased, appoint unto this people their portions, every man equal according to their families, according to his circumstances, and their wants and needs.

4. And let my servant Edward Partridge, when he shall appoint a man his portion, give unto him a writing that shall secure unto him his portion, that he shall hold it, even this right and this inheritance in the church, until he transgresses and is not accounted worthy by the voice of the church, according to the laws and covenants of the church, to belong to the church;

5. And if he shall transgress and is not accounted worthy to belong to the church, he shall not have power to claim that portion which he has consecrated unto the bishop for the poor and needy of my church; therefore he shall not retain the gift, but shall only have claim on that portion that is deeded unto him.

6. And thus all things shall be made sure, according to the laws of the land.

7. And let that which belongs to this people be appointed unto this people;

8. And the money which is left unto this people, let there be an agent appointed unto this people, to take the money to provide food and raiment, according to the wants of this people.

9. And let every man deal honestly, and be alike among this people, and receive alike, that ye may be one, even as I have commanded you.

10. And let that which belongeth to this people not be taken and given unto that of another church;

11. Wherefore, if another church would receive money of this church, let them pay unto this church again according as they shall agree;

12. And this shall be done through the bishop or the agent, which shall be appointed by the voice of the church.

13. And again, let the bishop appoint a storehouse unto this church, and let all things both in money and in meat, which are more than is needful for the want of this people, be kept in the hands of the bishop.

14. And let him also reserve unto himself for his own wants, and for the wants of his family, as he shall be employed in doing this business.

15. And thus I grant unto this people a privilege of organizing themselves according to my laws;

16. And I consecrate unto them this land for a little season, until I, the Lord, shall provide for them otherwise, and command them to go hence;

17. And the hour and the day is not given unto them, wherefore let them act upon this land as for years, and this shall turn unto them for their good.

18. Behold, this shall be an example unto my servant Edward Partridge, in other places, in all churches.

19. And whoso is found a faithful, a just, and a wise steward, shall enter into the joy of his Lord, and shall inherit eternal life.

20. Verily, I say unto you, I am Jesus Christ, who cometh quickly, in an hour you think not. Even so. Amen.

BRETHREN OF THE SEVENTY

Section 52

In February 1831, the Lord instructed the Prophet Joseph Smith to call the Elders, laboring in the different areas of the country, to a conference (section 44:1). The Prophet Joseph Smith appointed the conference to convene in June 1831 (see historical background section 44). At this conference the Prophet Joseph Smith said: ". . . the Lord displayed His power to the most perfect satisfaction of the saints." The next day after the conference, June 7, 1831, at Kirtland, Ohio, this revelation was received (History of the Church, vol. 1:175–177).

1. Behold, thus saith the Lord unto the elders whom he hath called and chosen in these last days, by the voice of his Spirit,

2. Saying, I, the Lord, will make known unto you what I will that ye shall do from this time until the next conference, which shall be held in Missouri, upon the land which I will consecrate unto my people, which are a remnant of Jacob, and them who are heirs according to the covenant.

3. Wherefore, verily I say unto you, let my servants Joseph Smith, jun., and Sidney Rigdon take their journey as soon as preparations can be made to leave their homes, and journey to the land of Missouri.

4. And inasmuch as they are faithful unto me, it shall be made known unto them what they shall do;

5. And it shall also, inasmuch as they are faithful, be made known unto them the land of your inheritance.

6. And inasmuch as they are not faithful, they shall be cut off, even as I will, as seemeth me good.

7. And again, verily I say unto you, let my servant Lyman Wight, and my servant John Corrill take their journey speedily:

8. And also my servant John Murdock, and my servant Hyrum Smith, take their journey unto the same place by the way of Detroit.

9. And let them journey from thence preaching the word by the way, saying none other things than that which the prophets and apostles have written, and that which is taught them by the Comforter through the prayer of faith.

10. Let them go two by two, and thus let them preach by the way in every congregation, baptizing by water, and the laying on of the hands by the water's side;

11. For thus saith the Lord, I will cut my work short in righteousness, for the days cometh that I will send forth judgment unto victory.

12. And let my servant Lyman Wight beware, for Satan desireth to sift him as chaff.

13. And behold, he that is faithful shall be made ruler over many things.

14. And again, I will give unto you a pattern in all things, that ye may not be deceived, for Satan is abroad in the land, and he goeth forth deceiving the nations;

15. Wherefore he that prayeth whose spirit is contrite, the same is accepted of me if he obey mine ordinances.

16. He that speaketh, whose spirit is contrite, whose language is meek and edifieth, the same is of God if he obey mine ordinances.

17. And again, he that trembleth under my power shall be made strong, and shall bring forth fruits of praise and wisdom, according to the revelations and truths which I have given you.

18. And again, he that is overcome and bringeth not forth fruits, even according to this pattern, is not of me;

19. Wherefore by this pattern ye shall know the spirits in all cases under the whole heavens.

20. And the days have come, according to men's faith it shall be done unto them.

21. Behold, this commandment is given unto all the elders whom I have chosen.

22. And again, verily I say unto you, let my servant Thomas B. Marsh, and my servant Ezra Thayre, take their journey also, preaching the word by the way unto this same land.

23. And again, let my servant Isaac Morley, and my servant Ezra Booth take their journey, also preaching the word by the way unto this same land.

24. And again, let my servants Edward Partridge and Martin Harris take their journey with my servants Sidney Rigdon and Joseph Smith, jun.

25. Let my servants David Whitmer and Harvey Whitlock also take their journey and preach by the way unto this same land.

26. And let my servants Parley P. Pratt and Orson Pratt take their journey and preach by the way, even unto this same land.

27. And let my servants Solomon Hancock and Simeon Carter also take their journey unto this same land, and preach by the way.

28. Let my servants Edson Fuller and Jacob Scott also take their journey.

29. Let my servants Levi W. Hancock and Zebedee Coltrin also take their journey.

30. Let my servants Reynolds Cahoon and Samuel H. Smith also take their journey.

31. Let my servants Wheeler Baldwin and William Carter also take their journey.

32. And let my servants Newel Knight and Selah J. Griffin, both be ordained, and also take their journey;

33. Yea, verily I say, let all these take their journey unto one place, in their several courses, and one man shall not build upon another's foundation, neither journey in another's track.

34. He that is faithful, the same shall be kept and blessed with much fruit.

35. And again, I say unto you, let my servants Joseph Wakefield and Solomon Humphrey take their journey into the eastern lands:

36. Let them labor with their families, declaring none other things than the prophets and apostles, that which they have seen and heard, and most assuredly believe, that the prophecies may be fulfilled.

37. In consequence of transgression, let that which was bestowed upon Heman Basset be taken from him, and placed upon the head of Simonds Ryder.

38. And again, verily I say unto you, let Jared Carter be ordained a priest, and also George James be ordained a priest.

39. Let the residue of the elders watch over the churches, and declare the word in the regions among them: and let them labor with their own hands that there be no idolatry nor wickedness practised.

40. And remember in all things the poor and the needy, the sick and the afflicted, for he that doeth not these things, the same is not my disciple.

41. And again, let my servants Joseph Smith, jun., and Sidney Rigdon, and Edward Partridge, take with them a recommend from the church. And let there be one obtained for my servant Oliver Cowdery also;

42. And thus, even as I have said, if ye are faithful, ye shall assemble yourselves together to rejoice upon the land of Missouri, which is the land of your inheritance, which is now the land of your enemies.

43. But, behold, I the Lord, will hasten the city in its time, and will crown the faithful with joy and with rejoicing.

44. Behold, I am Jesus Christ, the Son of God, and I will lift them up at the last day. Even so. Amen.

ECTION 53

At the request of Algernon Sidney Gilbert, the Prophet Joseph Smith inquired of the Lord and received this revelation, June 1831, at Kirtland, Ohio (History of the Church, vol. 1:179).

1. Behold, I say unto you, my servant Sidney Gilbert, that I have heard your prayers, and you have called upon me that it should be made known unto you, of the Lord your God, concerning your calling and election in this church, which I, the Lord, have raised up in these last days.

2. Behold, I, the Lord, who was crucified for the sins of the world, give unto you a commandment that you shall forsake the world.

3. Take upon you mine ordinaces, even that of an elder, to preach faith and repentance, and remission of sins, according to my word, and the reception of the Holy Spirit by the laying on of hands.

4. And also to be an agent unto this church in the place which shall be appointed by the bishop, according to commandments which shall be given hereafter.

5. And again, verily I say unto you, you shall take your journey with my servants Joseph Smith, jun., and Sidney Rigdon.

6. Behold, these are the first ordinances which you shall receive, and the residue shall be made known in a time to come, according to your labor in my vineyard.

7. And again, I would that ye should learn that it is he only who is saved that endureth unto the end. Even so. Amen.

ection 54

The Colesville, New York, Saints moved to Ohio and settled at Thompson. They organized themselves under the law of consecration and stewardship. It appears that Leman Copley contracted with the Colesville Saints to occupy some of his land in Thompson, Ohio. The Colesville branch began working the land in good faith, but shortly thereafter, Leman Copley broke his contract. The Saints at Thompson, Ohio, asked Joseph Smith to inquire of the Lord pertaining to this matter. This revelation was received in June 1831, at Kirtland, Ohio (History of the Church, vol. 1:180).

1. Behold, thus saith the Lord, even Alpha and Omega, the beginning and the end, even he who was crucified for the sins of the world.

2. Behold, verily, verily I say unto you, my servant Newel Knight, you shall stand fast in the office wherewith I have appointed you;

3. And if your brethren desire to escape their enemies, let them repent of all their sins, and become truly humble before me and contrite;

4. And as the covenant which they made unto me has been broken, even so it has become void and of none effect;

5. And wo to him by whom this offence cometh, for it had been better for him that he had been drowned in the depth of the sea;

6. But blessed are they who have kept the covenant and observed the commandment, for they shall obtain mercy.

7. Wherefore, go to now and flee the land, lest your enemies come upon you; and take your journey, and appoint whom you will to be your leader, and to pay moneys for you.

8. And thus you shall take your journey into the regions westward, unto the land of Missouri, unto the borders of the Lamanites.

9. And after you have done journeying, behold, I say unto you, seek ye a living like unto men, until I prepare a place for you.

10. And again, be patient in tribulation until I come; and, behold, I come quickly, and my reward is with me, and they who have sought me early shall find rest to their souls. Even so. Amen.

SECTION 55

William W. Phelps arrived in Kirtland, Ohio, in June 1831 "to do the will of the Lord." The Prophet Joseph Smith inquired of the Lord concerning William W. Phelps and received this revelation in June 1831, at Kirtland, Ohio (History of the Church, vol. 1:184–185).

1. Behold, thus saith the Lord unto you, my servant William, yea, even the Lord of the whole earth, thou art called and chosen, and after thou hast been baptized by water, which, if you do with an eye single to my glory, you shall have a remission of your sins, and a reception of the Holy Spirit by the laying on of hands;

2. And then thou shalt be ordained by the hand of my servant Joseph Smith, jun., to be an elder unto this church, to preach repentance and remission of sins by way of baptism in the name of Jesus Christ, the Son of the living God;

3. And on whomsoever you shall lay your hands, if they are contrite before me, you shall have power to give the Holy Spirit.

4. And again, you shall be ordained to assist my servant Oliver Cowdery to do the work of printing, and of selecting and writing books for schools in this church, that little children also may receive instruction before me as is pleasing unto me.

5. And again, verily I say unto you, for this cause you shall take your journey with my servants Joseph Smith, jun., and Sidney Rigdon, that you may be planted in the land of your inheritance to do this work.

6. And again, let my servant Joseph Coe also take his journey with them. The residue shall be made known hereafter, even as I will. Amen

Section 56

The Lord called Thomas B. Marsh and Ezra Thayre to serve as missionary companions (section 52:22). Because of worldly concerns, Ezra Thayre would not leave for his mission at the appointed time (section 56:8–10). Thomas B. Marsh sought counsel of the Prophet Joseph Smith, and this revelation was received in June 1831, at Kirtland, Ohio (History of the Church, vol. 1:186).

1. Hearken, O ye people who profess my name, saith the Lord your God, for behold, mine anger is kindled against the rebellious, and they shall know mine arm and mine indignation, in the day of visitation and of wrath upon the nations.
2. And he that will not take up his cross and follow me, and keep my commandments, the same shall not be saved.
3. Behold, I, the Lord, command, and he that will not obey, shall be cut off in mine own due time, after I have commanded, and the commandment is broken;
4. Wherefore I, the Lord, command and revoke, as it seemeth me good; and all this to be answered upon the heads of the rebellious, saith the Lord;
5. Wherefore, I revoke the commandment which was given unto my servants Thomas B. Marsh and Ezra Thayre, and give a new commandment unto my servant Thomas that he shall take up his journey speedily, to the land of Missouri, and my servant Selah J. Griffin shall also go with him;
6. For behold, I revoke the commandment which was given unto my servants Selah J. Griffin and Newel Knight, in consequence of the stiffneckedness of my people which are in Thompson, and their rebellions;
7. Wherefore, let my servant Newel Knight remain with them, and as many as will go may go, that are contrite before me, and be led by him to the land which I have appointed.
8. And again, verily I say unto you, that my servant Ezra Thayre must repent of his pride, and of his selfishness, and obey the former commandment which I have given him concerning the place upon which he lives;
9. And if he will do this, as there shall be no divisions made upon the land, he shall be appointed still to go to the land of Missouri;
10. Otherwise he shall receive the money which he has paid, and shall leave the place, and shall be cut off out of my church, saith the Lord God of hosts;
11. And though the heaven and the earth pass away, these words shall not pass away, but shall be fulfilled.

12. And if my servant Joseph Smith, jun., must needs pay the money; behold, I, the Lord, will pay it unto him again in the land of Missouri, that those of whom he shall receive may be rewarded again, according to that which they do;
13. For according to that which they do, they shall receive, even in lands for their inheritance.
14. Behold, thus saith the Lord unto my people, you have many things to do and to repent of; for behold, your sins have come up unto me, and are not pardoned, because you seek to counsel in your own ways.
15. And your hearts are not satisfied. And ye obey not the truth, but have pleasure in unrighteousness.
16. Wo unto you rich men, that will not give your substance to the poor, for your riches will canker your souls; and this shall be your lamentation in the day of visitation, and of judgment, and of indignation—The harvest is past, the summer is ended, and my soul is not saved!
17. Wo unto you poor men, whose hearts are not broken, whose spirits are not contrite, and whose bellies are not satisfied, and whose hands are not stayed from laying hold upon other men's goods, whose eyes are full of greediness, and who will not labor with your own hands!
18. But blessed are the poor who are pure in heart, whose hearts are broken, and whose spirits are contrite, for they shall see the kingdom of God coming in power and great glory unto their deliverance; for the fatness of the earth shall be theirs.
19. For behold, the Lord shall come, and his recompense shall be with him, and he shall reward every man, and the poor shall rejoice;
20. And their generations shall inherit the earth from generation to generation, forever and ever. And now I make an end of speaking unto you. Even so. Amen.

Section 57

Obedient to the revelation received from the Lord (section 52:3–5), Joseph Smith left Kirtland, Ohio, for Missouri, June 19, 1831. The Prophet Joseph Smith shares the yearning of his heart and the reception of this revelation as follows: "When will the wilderness blossom as the rose? When will Zion be built up in her glory, and where will Thy temple stand, unto which all nations shall come in the last days? Our anxiety was soon relieved by receiving the following." This revelation was received July 1831, at Jackson County, Missouri (History of the Church, vol. 1:188–189).

1. Hearken, O ye elders of my church, saith the Lord your God, who have assembled yourselves together, according to my commandments, in this land, which is the land of Missouri, which is the land which I have appointed and consecrated for the gathering of the saints:

2. Wherefore this is the land of promise, and the place for the city of Zion.

3. And thus saith the Lord your God, if you will receive wisdom, here is wisdom. Behold, the place which is now called Independence, is the center place, and a spot for the temple is lying westward, upon a lot which is not far from the courthouse.

4. Wherefore it is wisdom that the land should be purchased by the saints; and also every tract lying westward, even unto the line running directly between Jew and Gentile.

5. And also every tract bordering by the prairies, inasmuch as my disciples are enabled to buy lands. Behold, this is wisdom, that they may obtain it for an everlasting inheritance.

6. And let my servant Sidney Gilbert stand in the office which I have appointed him, to receive moneys, to be an agent unto the church, to buy land in all the regions round about, inasmuch as can be in righteousness, and as wisdom shall direct.

7. And let my servant Edward Partridge, stand in the office which I have appointed him, to divide the saints their inheritance, even as I have commanded; and also those whom he has appointed to assist him.

8. And again, verily I say unto you, let my servant Sidney Gilbert plant himself in this place, and establish a store, that he may sell goods without fraud, that he may obtain money to buy lands for the good of the saints, and that he may obtain whatsoever things the disciples may need to plant them in their inheritance.

9. And also let my servant Sidney Gilbert obtain a license—(behold here is wisdom, and whoso readeth let him understand)—that he may send goods also unto the people, even by whom he will, as clerks employed in his service,

PAINTING DEPICTING INDEPENDENCE, MISSOURI

10. And thus provide for my saints, that my gospel may be preached unto those who sit in darkness, and in the region and shadow of death.

11. And again, verily I say unto you, let my servant William W. Phelps be planted in this place, and be established as a printer unto the church;

12. And lo, if the world receiveth his writings—(behold here is wisdom)—let him obtain whatsoever he can obtain in righteousness for the good of the saints.

13. And let my servant Oliver Cowdery, assist him, even as I have commanded, in whatsoever place I shall appoint unto him, to copy, and to correct, and select, that all things may be right before me, as it shall be proved by the Spirit through him.

14. And thus let those of whom I have spoken be planted in the land of Zion, as speedily as can be, with their families, to do those things even as I have spoken.

15. And now concerning the gathering. Let the bishop and the agent make preparations for those families which have been commanded to come to this land as soon as possible, and plant them in their inheritance.

16. And unto the residue of both elders and members, further directions shall be given hereafter. Even so. Amen.

SECTION 58

Because Leman Copley and others broke their contract (covenants) with the Colesville Saints (see historical background, section 54), the Lord commanded the Colesville Saints to move to Missouri. A few days after Joseph Smith and company arrived in Missouri, the Colesville Saints arrived. After their arrival, this revelation was received August 1831, at Jackson County, Missouri (History of the Church, *vol. 1:190–191*).

1. Hearken, O ye elders of my church, and give ear to my word, and learn of me what I will concerning you, and also concerning this land unto which I have sent you:
2. For verily I say unto you, blessed is he that keepeth my commandments, whether in life or in death; and he that is faithful in tribulation, the reward of the same is greater in the kingdom of heaven.
3. Ye cannot behold with your natural eyes, for the present time, the design of your God concerning those things which shall come hereafter, and the glory which shall follow after much tribulation.
4. For after much tribulation cometh the blessings. Wherefore the day cometh that ye shall be crowned with much glory; the hour is not yet, but is nigh at hand.
5. Remember this, which I tell you before, that you may lay it to heart, and receive that which shall to follow.
6. Behold, verily I say unto you, for this cause I have sent you that you might be obedient, and that your hearts might be prepared to bear testimony of the things which are to come;
7. And also that you might be honored of laying the foundation, and of bearing record of the land upon which the Zion of God shall stand;
8. And also that a feast of fat things might be prepared for the poor; yea, a feast of fat things, of wine on the lees well refined, that the earth may know that the mouths of the prophets shall not fail;
9. Yea a supper of the house of the Lord, well prepared, unto which all nations shall be invited.
10. Firstly, the rich and the learned, the wise and the noble;
11. And after that cometh the day of my power: then shall the poor, the lame, and the blind, and the deaf, come in unto the marriage of the Lamb, and partake of the supper of the Lord, prepared for the great day to come.
12. Behold, I, the Lord, have spoken it.
13. And that the testimony might go forth from Zion, yea, from the mouth of the city of the heritage of God:

14. Yea, for this cause I have sent you hither, and have selected my servant Edward Partridge, and have appointed unto him his mission in this land;
15. But if he repent not of his sins, which are unbelief and blindness of heart, let him take heed lest he fall.
16. Behold his mission is given unto him, and it shall not be given again.
17. And whoso standeth in his mission is appointed to be a judge in Israel, like as it was in ancient days, to divide the lands of the heritage of God unto his children.
18. And to judge his people by the testimony of the just, and by the assistance of his counselors, according to the laws of the kingdom which are given by the prophets of God;
19. For verily I say unto you, my law shall be kept on this land.
20. Let no man think he is ruler, but let God rule him that judgeth, according to the counsel of his own will; or, in other words, him that counseleth or sitteth upon the judgment seat.
21. Let no man break the laws of the land, for he that keepeth the laws of God hath no need to break the laws of the land:
22. Wherefore, be subject to the powers that be, until He reigns whose right it is to reign, and subdues all enemies under his feet.
23. Behold, the laws which ye have received from my hand are the laws of the church, and in this light ye shall hold them forth. Behold, here is wisdom.
24. And now as I spake concerning my servant Edward Partridge, this land is the land of his residence, and those whom he has appointed for his counselors. And also the land of the residence of him whom I have appointed to keep my store-house;
25. Wherefore let them bring their families to this land, as they shall counsel between themselves and me:
26. For behold, it is not meet that I should command in all things, for he that is compelled in all things, the same is a slothful and not a wise servant; wherefore he receiveth no reward.
27. Verily I say, men should be anxiously engaged in a good cause, and do many things of their own free will, and bring to pass much righteousness;
28. For the power is in them, wherein they are agents unto themselves. And inasmuch as men do good they shall in nowise lose their reward.
29. But he that doeth not anything until he is commanded, and receiveth a commandment with doubtful heart, and keepeth it with slothfulness, the same is damned.
30. Who am I that made man, saith the Lord, that will hold him guiltless that obeys not my commandments?
31. Who am I, saith the Lord, that have promised and have not fulfilled?
32. I command and a man obey not; I revoke and they receive not the blessing;
33. Then they say in their hearts, this is not the work of the Lord, for his promises are not fulfilled. But wo unto such, for their reward lurketh beneath, and not from above.
34. And now I give unto you further directions concerning this land.
35. It is wisdom in me that my servant Martin Harris should be an example unto the church, in laying his moneys before the bishop of the church.
36. And also, this is a law unto every man that cometh unto this land, to receive an inheritance; and he shall do with his moneys according as the law directs.
37. And it is wisdom also, that there should be lands purchased in Independence, for the place of the store-house, and also for the house of the printing.
38. And other directions concerning my servant Martin Harris shall be given him of the Spirit,

that he may receive his inheritance as seemeth him good.

39. And let him repent of his sins, for he seeketh the praise of the world.

40. And also let my servant William W. Phelps stand in the office which I have appointed him, and receive his inheritance in the land;

41. And also he hath need to repent, for I, the Lord, am not well pleased with him, for he seeketh to excel, and he is not sufficiently meek before me.

42. Behold, he who has repented of his sins, the same is forgiven, and I, the Lord, remember them no more.

43. By this ye may know if a man repenteth of his sins. Behold, he will confess them and forsake them.

44. And now, verily, I say, concerning the residue of the elders of my church, the time has not yet come, for many years, for them to receive their inheritance in this land, except they desire it through the prayer of faith, only as it shall be appointed unto them of the Lord.

45. For, behold, they shall push the people together from the ends of the earth;

46. Wherefore, assemble yourselves together, and they who are not appointed to stay in this land, let them preach the gospel in the regions round about, and after that let them return to their homes.

47. Let them preach by the way, and bear testimony of the truth in all places, and call upon the rich, the high and the low, and the poor to repent;

48. And let them build up churches inasmuch as the inhabitants of the earth will repent.

49. And let there be an agent appointed by the voice of the church, unto the church in Ohio, to receive moneys to purchase lands in Zion.

50. And I give unto my servant, Sidney Rigdon, a commandment that he shall write a description of the land of Zion, and a statement of the will of God, as it shall be made known by the Spirit unto him;

51. And an epistle and subscription, to be presented unto all the churches to obtain moneys, to be put into the hands of the bishop to purchase lands for an inheritance for the children of God, of himself or the agent, as seemeth him good or as he shall direct.

52. For, behold, verily I say unto you, the Lord willeth that the disciples and the children of men should open their hearts, even to purchase this whole region of country, as soon as time will permit.

53. Behold, here is wisdom. Let them do this lest they receive none inheritance, save it be by the shedding of blood.

54. And again, inasmuch as there is land obtained, let there be workmen sent forth of all kinds unto this land, to labor for the saints of God.

55. Let all these things be done in order; and let the privileges of the lands be made known from time to time, by the bishop or the agent of the church;

56. And let the work of the gathering be not in haste, nor by flight, but let it be done as it shall be counseled by the elders of the church at the conferences, according to the knowledge which they receive from time to time.

57. And let my servant Sidney Rigdon consecrate and dedicate this land, and the spot of the temple, unto the Lord.

58. And let a conference meeting be called, and after that let my servants Sidney Rigdon and Joseph Smith, jun., return, and also Oliver Cowdery with them, to accomplish the residue of the work which I have appointed unto them in their own land, and the residue as shall be ruled by the conferences.

59. And let no man return from this land, except he bear record by the way of that which he knows and most assuredly believes.

60. Let that which has been bestowed upon Ziba Peterson be taken from him; and let him stand as a member in the church, and labor with his own hands, with the brethren, until he is sufficiently chastened for all his sins, for he confesseth them not, and he thinketh to hide them.

61. Let the residue of the elders of this church, who are coming to this land, some of whom are exceedingly blessed even above measure, also hold a conference upon this land.

62. And let my servant Edward Partridge direct the conference which shall be held by them.

63. And let them also return, preaching the gospel by the way, bearing record of the things which are revealed unto them;

64. For, verily, the sound must go forth from this place into all the world, and unto the uttermost parts of the earth—the gospel must be preached unto every creature, with signs following them that believe.

65. And behold the Son of man cometh. Amen.

Section 59

Joseph Knight, Sen., and his wife Polly were members of the Colesville Branch. During their journey from Ohio to Missouri, sister Knight became very ill. Her only desire was to live long enough to stand upon the land of Zion (Jackson County, Missouri). Soon after her arrival in Missouri she passed away. This was the first death in the Church in that land. After attending her funeral, the Prophet Joseph Smith received this revelation August 7, 1831, at Jackson County, Missouri (History of the Church, vol. 1:199).

1. Behold, blessed, saith the Lord, are they who have come up unto this land with an eye single to my glory, according to my commandments;
2. For them that live shall inherit the earth, and them that die shall rest from all their labors, and their works shall follow them, and they shall receive a crown in the mansions of my Father, which I have prepared for them;
3. Yea, blessed are they whose feet stand upon the land of Zion, who have obeyed my gospel, for they shall receive for their reward the good things of the earth; and it shall bring forth in its strength;
4. And they shall also be crowned with blessings from above, yea, and with commandments not a few; and with revelations in their time: they that are faithful and diligent before me.
5. Wherefore I give unto them a commandment, saying thus: Thou shalt love the Lord thy God with all thy heart, with all thy might, mind, and strength; and in the name of Jesus Christ thou shalt serve him.
6. Thou shalt love thy neighbor as thyself. Thou shalt not steal; neither commit adultery, nor kill, nor do anything like unto it.
7. Thou shalt thank the Lord thy God in all things.
8. Thou shalt offer a sacrifice unto the Lord thy God in righteousness, even that of a broken heart and a contrite spirit.
9. And that thou mayest more fully keep thyself unspotted from the world, thou shalt go to the house of prayer and offer up thy sacraments upon my holy day;
10. For verily this is a day appointed unto you to rest from your labors, and to pay thy devotions unto the Most High;
11. Nevertheless thy vows shall be offered up in righteousness on all days and at all times;
12. But remember that on this the Lord's day, thou shalt offer thine oblations and thy sacraments unto the Most High, confessing thy sins unto thy brethren, and before the Lord.
13. And on this day thou shalt do none other thing, only let thy food be prepared with

singleness of heart that thy fasting may be perfect, or, in other words, that thy joy may be full.

14. Verily, this is fasting and prayer; or in other words, rejoicing and prayer.

15. And inasmuch as ye do these things with thanksgiving, with cheerful hearts and countenances; not with much laughter, for this is sin, but with a glad heart and a cheerful countenance;

16. Verily I say, that inasmuch as ye do this, the fulness of the earth is yours: the beasts of the field and the fowls of the air, and that which climbeth upon the trees and walketh upon the earth;

17. Yea, and the herb, and the good things which cometh of the earth, whether for food or for raiment, or for houses, or for barns, or for orchards, or for gardens, or for vineyards;

18. Yea, all things which come of the earth, in the season thereof, are made for the benefit and the use of man, both to please the eye and to gladden the heart;

19. Yea, for food and for raiment, for taste and for smell, to strengthen the body and to enliven the soul.

20. And it pleaseth God that he hath given all these things unto man; for unto this end were they made to be used with judgment, not to excess, neither by extortion:

21. And in nothing doth man offend God, or against none is his wrath kindled, save those who confess not his hand in all things, and obey not his commandments.

22. Behold, this is according to the law and the prophets: wherefore, trouble me no more concerning this matter,

23. But learn that he who doeth the works of righteousness shall receive his reward, even peace in this world, and eternal life in the world to come.

24. I, the Lord, have spoken it, and the Spirit beareth record. Amen.

ection 60

Having accomplished what the Lord had commanded them to do in Missouri, some of the brethren desired to know of the Prophet Joseph Smith regarding their return journey to Ohio. The Prophet Joseph Smith received this revelation August 8, 1831, at Jackson County, Missouri (History of the Church, vol. 1:201).

1. Behold, thus saith the Lord unto the elders of his church, who are to return speedily to the land from whence they came. Behold, it pleaseth me, that you have come up hither;

2. But with some I am not well pleased, for they will not open their mouths, but hide the talent which I have given unto them, because of the fear of man. Wo unto such, for mine anger is kindled against them.

3. And it shall come to pass, if they are not more faithful unto me, it shall be taken away, even that which they have;

4. For I, the Lord, rule in the heavens above, and among the armies of the earth; and in the day when I shall make up my jewels, all men shall know what it is that bespeaketh the power of God.

5. But verily, I will speak unto you concerning your journey unto the land from whence you came. Let there be a craft made, or bought, as seemeth you good, it mattereth not unto me, and take your journey speedily for the place which is called St. Louis.

6. And from thence let my servant Sidney Rigdon, and Joseph Smith, jr., and Oliver Cowdery, take their journey for Cincinnati;

7. And in this place let them lift up their voice and declare my word with loud voices, without wrath or doubting, lifting up holy hands upon them. For I am able to make you holy, and your sins are forgiven you.

8. And let the residue take their journey from St. Louis, two by two, and preach the word, not in haste, among the congregations of the wicked, until they return to the churches from whence they came.

9. And all this for the good of the churches; for this intent have I sent them.

10. And let my servant Edward Partridge impart of the money which I have given him, a portion unto mine elders who are commanded to return;

11. And he that is able, let him return it by the way of the agent, and he that is not, of him it is not required.

12. And now I speak of the residue who are to come unto this land.

13. Behold, they have been sent to preach my gospel among the congregations of the wicked; wherefore, I give unto them a commandment thus: Thou shalt not idle away thy time, neither shalt thou bury thy talent that it may not be known.

14. And after thou hast come up unto the land of Zion, and hast proclaimed my word, thou shalt speedily return, proclaiming my word among the congregations of the wicked, not in haste, neither in wrath nor with strife;

15. And shake off the dust of thy feet against those who receive thee not; not in their presence, lest thou provoke them, but in secret, and wash thy feet, as a testimony against them in the day of judgment.

16. Behold, this is sufficient for you, and the will of him who hath sent you.

17. And by the mouth of my servant Joseph Smith, jun., it shall be made known concerning Sidney Rigdon and Oliver Cowdery. The residue hereafter. Even so. Amen.

SECTION 61

Leaving Missouri for Ohio, the Prophet Joseph Smith and several of the brethren started down the Missouri River in canoes. Experiencing many dangers upon these waters, and while encamped at McIlwaine's Bend, they encountered the influence of the evil one. The Prophet Joseph Smith received this revelation August 12, 1831 (History of the Church, vol. 1:202–203).

1. Behold, and hearken unto the voice of him who has all power, who is from everlasting to everlasting, even Alpha and Omega, the beginning and the end.
2. Behold, verily thus saith the Lord unto you, O ye elders of my church, who are assembled upon this spot, whose sins are now forgiven you, for I, the Lord, forgive sins, and am merciful unto those who confess their sins with humble hearts;
3. But verily I say unto you, that it is not needful for this whole company of mine elders to be moving swiftly upon the waters, whilst the inhabitants on either side are perishing in unbelief;
4. Nevertheless, I suffered it that ye might bear record; behold, there are many dangers upon the waters, and more especially hereafter;
5. For I, the Lord, have decreed in mine anger, many destructions upon the waters; yea, and especially upon these waters.
6. Nevertheless, all flesh is in mine hand, and he that is faithful among you shall not perish by the waters.
7. Wherefore it is expedient that my servant Sidney Gilbert and my servant William W. Phelps be in haste upon their errand and mission;
8. Nevertheless, I would not suffer that ye should part until you were chastened for all your sins, that you might be one, and you might not perish in wickedness;
9. But now, verily I say, it behooveth me that ye should part, wherefore let my servants Sidney Gilbert and William W. Phelps take their former company, and let them take their journey in haste that they may fill their mission, and through faith they shall overcome;
10. And inasmuch as they are faithful they shall be preserved, and I, the Lord, will be with them.
11. And let the residue take that which is needful for clothing.
12. Let my servant Sidney Gilbert take that which is not needful with him, as you shall agree.
13. And now, behold, for your good I gave unto you a commandment concerning these things;

and I, the Lord, will reason with you as with men in days of old.

14. Behold, I, the Lord, in the beginning blessed the waters, but in the last days, by the mouth of my servant John, I cursed the waters;

15. Wherefore, the days will come that no flesh shall be safe upon the waters,

16. And it shall be said in days to come that none is able to go up to the land of Zion upon the waters, but he that is upright in heart.

17. And, as I, the Lord, in the beginning cursed the land, even so in the last days have I blessed it, in its time, for the use of my saints, that they may partake the fatness thereof.

18. And now I give unto you a commandment that what I say unto one I say unto all, that you shall forewarn your brethren concerning these waters, that they come not in journeying upon them, lest their faith fail and they are caught her snares;

19. I, the Lord, have decreed, and the destroyer rideth upon the face thereof, and I revoke not the decree;

20. I, the Lord, was angry with you yesterday, but to-day mine anger is turned away.

21. Wherefore, let those concerning whom I have spoken, that should take their journey in haste,

22. And it mattereth not unto me, after a little, if it so be that they fill their mission, whether they go by water or by land; let this be as it is made known unto them according to their judgments hereafter.

23. And now, concerning my servants Sidney Rigdon, and Joseph Smith, jun., and Oliver Cowdery, let them come not again upon the waters, save it be upon the canal, while journeying unto their homes, or in other words, they shall not come upon the waters to journey, save upon the canal.

24. Behold, I, the Lord, have appointed a way for the journeying of my saints, and behold, this is the way—that after they leave the canal, they shall journey by land, inasmuch as they are commanded to journey and go up into the land of Zion;

25. And they shall do like unto the children of Israel, pitching their tents by the way.

26. And, behold, this commandment you shall give unto all your brethren;

27. Nevertheless unto whom is given power to command the waters, unto him it is given by the Spirit to know all his ways;

28. Wherefore let him do as the Spirit of the living God commandeth him, whether upon the land or upon the waters, as it remaineth with me to do hereafter;

29. And unto you is given the course for the saints, or the way for the saints of the camp of the Lord, to journey.

30. And again, verily I say unto you, my servants Sidney Rigdon, and Joseph Smith, jun., and Oliver Cowdery, shall not open their mouths in the congregations of the wicked, until they arrive at Cincinnati;

31. And in that place they shall lift up their voices unto God against that people; yea unto him whose anger is kindled against their wickedness; a people who are well-nigh ripened for destruction;

32. And from thence let them journey for the congregations of their brethren, for their labors even now are wanted more abundantly among them, than among the congregations of the wicked.

33. And now concerning the residue, let them journey and declare the word among the congregations of the wicked, inasmuch as it is given;

34. And inasmuch as they do this, they shall rid their garments, and they shall be spotless before me;

35. And let them journey together, or two by two, as seemeth them good, only let my servant Reynolds Cahoon, and my servant Samuel H. Smith, with whom I am well pleased, be not separated until they return to their homes, and this for a wise purpose in me.

36. And now, verily I say unto you, and what I say unto one I say unto all, be of good cheer little children, for I am in your midst, and I have not forsaken you;

37. And inasmuch as you have humbled yourselves before me, the blessings of the kingdom are yours.

38. Gird up your loins and be watchful and be sober, looking forth for the coming of the Son of Man, for he cometh in an hour you think not.

39. Pray always that you enter not into temptation, that you may abide the day of his coming, whether in life or in death. Even so. Amen.

ection 62

As the Prophet Joseph Smith and the brethren continued their journey from Missouri to Ohio, they met several Elders on their way to Zion (Jackson County, Missouri). Before they parted, the Prophet Joseph Smith received this revelation on the banks of the Missouri River, August 13, 1831 (History of the Church, vol. 1:205).

1. Behold, and hearken O ye elders of my church, saith the Lord your God, even Jesus Christ, your advocate, who knoweth the weakness of man and how to succor them who are tempted;
2. And verily mine eyes are upon those who have not as yet gone up unto the land of Zion; wherefore your mission is not yet full;
3. Nevertheless ye are blessed, for the testimony which ye have borne, is recorded in heaven for the angels to look upon, and they rejoice over you, and your sins are forgiven you.
4. And now continue your journey. Assemble yourselves upon the land of Zion, and hold a meeting and rejoice together, and offer a sacrament unto the Most High;
5. And then you may return to bear record, yea, even altogether, or two by two, as seemeth you good, it mattereth not unto me, only be faithful, and declare glad tidings unto the inhabitants of the earth, or among the congregations of the wicked.
6. Behold, I, the Lord, have brought you together that the promise might be fulfilled, that the faithful among you should be preserved and rejoice together in the land of Missouri. I, the Lord, promise the faithful and cannot lie.
7. I, the Lord, am willing, if any among you desireth to ride upon horses, or upon mules, or in chariots, he shall receive this blessing, if he receive it from the hand of the Lord, with a thankful heart in all things.
8. These things remain with you to do according to judgment and the directions of the Spirit.
9. Behold, the kingdom is yours. And behold, and lo, I am with the faithful always. Even so. Amen.

ECTION 63

After a long and tedious journey from Missouri, the Prophet Joseph Smith arrived in Kirtland, Ohio, August 27, 1831. The Saints in Kirtland were anxious to learn more of the Lord about gathering to the land of Zion (Jackson County, Missouri). The Prophet Joseph Smith inquired of the Lord and received this revelation, August 1831 (History of the Church, vol. 1:206–207).

1. Hearken, O ye people, and open your hearts and give ear from afar; and listen, you that call yourselves the people of the Lord, and hear the word of the Lord and his will concerning you:

2. Yea, verily, I say, hear the word of him whose anger is kindled against the wicked and rebellious;

3. Who willeth to take even them whom he will take, and preserveth in life them whom he will preserve;

4. Who buildeth up at his own will and pleasure; and destroyeth when he pleases, and is able to cast the soul down to hell.

5. Behold, I, the Lord, utter my voice, and it shall be obeyed.

6. Wherefore, verily I say, let the wicked take heed, and let the rebellious fear and tremble; and let the unbelieving hold their lips, for the day of wrath shall come upon them as a whirlwind, and all flesh shall know that I am God.

7. And he that seeketh signs shall see signs, but not unto salvation.

8. Verily, I say unto you, there are those among you who seek signs, and there have been such even from the beginning;

9. But, behold, faith cometh not by signs, but signs follow those that believe.

10. Yea, signs come by faith, not by the will of men, nor as they please, but by the will of God.

11. Yea, signs come by faith, unto mighty works, for without faith no man pleaseth God: and with whom God is angry he is not well pleased; wherefore, unto such he showeth no signs, only in wrath unto their condemnation.

12. Wherefore, I, the Lord, am not pleased with those among you who have sought after signs and wonders for faith, and not for the good of men unto my glory;

13. Nevertheless, I give commandments, and many have turned away from my commandments and have not kept them.

14. There were among you adulterers and adulteresses; some of whom have turned away from

you, and others remain with you, that hereafter shall be revealed.

15. Let such beware and repent speedily, lest judgment shall come upon them as a snare, and their folly shall be made manifest, and their works shall follow them in the eyes of the people.
16. And, verily, I say unto you, as I have said before, he that looketh on a woman to lust after her, or if any shall commit adultery in their hearts, they shall not have the Spirit, but shall deny the faith and shall fear:
17. Wherefore, I, the Lord, have said that the fearful, and the unbelieving, and all liars, and whosoever loveth and maketh a lie, and the whoremonger, and the sorcerer, shall have their part in that lake which burneth with fire and brimstone which is the second death.
18. Verily I say, that they shall not have part in the first resurrection.
19. And now, behold, I, the Lord, say unto you, that ye are not justified because these things are among you;
20. Nevertheless, he that endureth in faith and doeth my will, the same shall overcome, and shall receive an inheritance upon the earth when the day of transfiguration shall come;
21. When the earth shall be transfigured, even according to the pattern which was shown unto mine apostles upon the mount; of which account the fulness ye have not received.
22. And now, verily I say unto you, that as I said that I would make known my will unto you, behold I will make it known unto you, not by the way of commandment, for there are many who observe not to keep my commandments;
23. But unto him that keepeth my commandments, I will give the mysteries of my kingdom, and the same shall be in him a well of living water, springing up unto everlasting life.
24. And now, behold, this is the will of the Lord your God concerning his saints, that they should assemble themselves together unto the land of Zion, not in haste, lest there should be confusion, which bringeth pestilence.
25. Behold, the land of Zion, I, the Lord, hold it in mine own hands;
26. Nevertheless, I, the Lord, render unto Caesar the things which are Caesar's:
27. Wherefore I the Lord, will that you should purchase the lands that you may have advantage of the world, that you may have claim on the world, that they may not be stirred up unto anger.
28. For Satan putteth it into their hearts to anger; against you, and to the shedding of blood;
29. Wherefore the land of Zion shall not be obtained but by purchase or by blood, otherwise there is none inheritance for you.
30. And if by purchase, behold you are blessed;
31. And if by blood, as you are forbidden to shed blood, lo, your enemies are upon you, and ye shall be scourged from city to city, and from synagogue to synagogue, and but few shall stand to receive an inheritance.
32. I, the Lord, am angry with the wicked; I am holding my Spirit from the inhabitants of the earth.
33. I have sworn in my wrath, and decreed wars upon the face of the earth, and the wicked shall slay the wicked, and fear shall come upon every man,
34. And the saints also shall hardly escape; nevertheless, I, the Lord, am with them, and will come down in heaven from the presence of my Father and consume the wicked with unquenchable fire,
35. And behold, this is not yet, but by and by;
36. Wherefore, seeing that I, the Lord, have decreed all these things upon the face of the earth, I will that my saints should be assembled upon the land of Zion;
37. And that every man should take righteousness in his hands and faithfulness upon his loins, and lift a warning voice unto the inhabitants of the earth; and declare both by word and by flight that desolation shall come upon the wicked.

38. Wherefore let my disciples in Kirtland arrange their temporal concerns, who dwell upon this farm.

39. Let my servant Titus Billings, who has the care thereof, dispose of the land, that he may be prepared in the coming spring to take his journey up unto the land of Zion, with those that dwell upon the face thereof, excepting those whom I shall reserve unto myself, that shall not go until I shall command them.

40. And let all the monies which can be spared, it mattereth not unto me whether it be little or much, be sent up unto the land of Zion, unto them whom I have appointed to receive.

41. Behold, I, the Lord, will give unto my servant Joseph Smith, jun., power that he shall be enabled to discern by the Spirit those who shall go up unto the land of Zion, and those of my disciples who shall tarry.

42. Let my servant Newel K. Whitney retain his store, or in other words, the store, yet for a little season.

43. Nevertheless, let him impart all the money which he can impart, to be sent up unto the land of Zion.

44. Behold, these things are in his own hands, let him do according to wisdom.

45. Verily I say, let him be ordained as an agent unto the disciples that shall tarry, and let him be ordained unto this power;

46. And now speedily visit the churches, expounding these things unto them, with my servant Oliver Cowdery. Behold, this is my will, obtaining monies even as I have directed.

47. He that is faithful and endureth shall overcome the world.

48. He that sendeth up treasures unto the land of Zion, shall receive an inheritance in this world, and his works shall follow him, and also a reward in the world to come:

49. Yea, and blessed are the dead that die in the Lord from henceforth, when the Lord shall come, and old things shall pass away, and all things become new, they shall rise from the dead and shall not die after, and shall receive an inheritance before the Lord, in the holy city.

50. And he that liveth when the Lord shall come, and has kept the faith, blessed is he; nevertheless it is appointed to him to die at the age of man.

51. Wherefore, children shall grow up until they become old, old men shall die; but they shall not sleep in the dust, but they shall be changed in the twinkling of an eye;

52. Wherefore, for this cause preached the apostles unto the world the resurrection of the dead;

53. These things are the things that ye must look for, and speaking after the manner of the Lord, they are now nigh at hand; and in time to come, even in the day of the coming of the Son of Man.

54. And until that hour there will be foolish virgins among the wise, and at that hour cometh an entire separation of the righteous and the wicked, and in that day will I send mine angels to pluck out the wicked and cast them into unquenchable fire.

55. And now, behold, verily I say unto you, I the Lord, am not pleased with my servant Sidney Rigdon, he exalted himself in his heart, and received not counsel but grieved the Spirit;

56. Wherefore his writing is not acceptable unto the Lord and he shall make another, and if the Lord receive it not, behold he standeth no longer in the office which I have appointed him.

57. And again, verily I say unto you, those who desire in their hearts, in meekness, to warn sinners to repentance, let them be ordained unto this power;

58. For this is a day of warning, and not a day of many words. For I, the Lord, am not to be mocked in the last days.

59. Behold, I am from above, and my power lieth beneath. I am over all, and in all, and through all,

and search all things, and the day cometh that all things shall be subject unto me.

60. Behold, I am Alpha and Omega, even Jesus Christ.

61. Wherefore let all men beware how they take my name in their lips;

62. For, behold, verily I say, that many there be who are under this condemnation, who use the name of the Lord, and use it in vain, having not authority.

63. Wherefore, let the church repent of their sins, and I, the Lord, will own them, otherwise they shall be cut off.

64. Remember that that which cometh from above is sacred, and must be spoken with care, and by constraint of the Spirit, and in this there is no condemnation, and ye receive the Spirit through prayer; wherefore, without this there remaineth condemnation.

65. Let my servants Joseph Smith, jun., and Sidney Rigdon, seek them a home, as they are taught through prayer by the Spirit.

66. These things remain to overcome through patience, that such may receive a more exceeding and eternal weight of glory, otherwise, a greater condemnation. Amen.

THE PROPHET JOSEPH SMITH TRANSLATING THE BIBLE

Section 64

In September 1831, the Prophet Joseph Smith was making preparations to move to Hiram, Ohio, to resume the work of translating the Bible. At the same time, a group of brethren who had been commanded to go to Zion (Jackson County, Missouri) were making preparations to leave. Prior to their departure, the Prophet Joseph Smith received this revelation September 11, 1831, at Kirtland, Ohio (History of the Church, vol. 1:211).

1. Behold, thus saith the Lord your God unto you, O ye elders of my church, hearken ye and hear, and receive my will concerning you;

2. For verily I say unto you, I will that ye should overcome the world; wherefore I will have compassion upon you.

3. There are those among you who have sinned; but verily I say, for this once, for mine own glory, and for the salvation of souls, I have forgiven you your sins.

4. I will be merciful unto you, for I have given unto you the kingdom:

5. And the keys of the mysteries of the kingdom shall not be taken from my servant Joseph Smith, jun., through the means I have appointed, while he liveth, inasmuch as he obeyeth mine ordinances.

6. There are those who have sought occasion against him without cause;

7. Nevertheless he has sinned, but verily I say unto you, I, the Lord, forgive sins unto those who confess their sins before me and ask forgiveness, who have not sinned unto death.

8. My disciples, in days of old, sought occasion against one another and forgave not one another in their hearts, and for this evil they were afflicted and sorely chastened:

9. Wherefore I say unto you, that ye ought to forgive one another, for he that forgiveth not his brother his trespasses, standeth condemned before the Lord, for there remaineth in him the greater sin.

10. I, the Lord, will forgive whom I will forgive, but of you it is required to forgive all men;

11. And ye ought to say in your hearts, let God judge between me and thee, and reward thee according to thy deeds.

12. And he that repenteth not of his sins, and confesseth them not, then ye shall bring him before the church, and do with him as the Scripture saith unto you, either by commandment or by revelation.

13. And this ye shall do that God may be glorified, not because ye forgive not, having not compassion, but that ye may be justified in the eyes of the law, that ye may not offend him who is your Lawgiver.

14. Verily I say, for this cause ye shall do these things.

15. Behold, I, the Lord, was angry with him who was my servant Ezra Booth, and also my servant Isaac Morley, for they kept not the law, neither the commandment;

16. They sought evil in their hearts, and I, the Lord, withheld my Spirit. They condemned for evil that thing in which there was no evil; nevertheless I have forgiven my servant Isaac Morley.

17. And also my servant Edward Partridge, behold, he hath sinned, and Satan seeketh to destroy his soul; but when these things are made known unto them, and they repent of the evil, they shall be forgiven.

18. And now, verily I say, that it is expedient in me that my servant Sidney Gilbert, after a few weeks, should return upon his business, and to his agency in the land of Zion;

19. And that which he hath seen and heard may be made known unto my disciples, that they perish not. And for this cause have I spoken these things.

20. And again, I say unto you, that my servant Isaac Morley may not be tempted above that which he is able to bear, and counsel wrongfully to your hurt, I gave commandment that his farm should be sold.

21. I will not that my servant Frederick G. Williams should sell his farm, for I, the Lord, will to retain a strong hold in the land of Kirtland, for the space of five years, in the which I will not overthrow the wicked, that thereby I may save some;

22. And after that day, I, the Lord, will not hold any guilty that shall go with an open heart up to the land of Zion; for I the Lord, require the hearts of the children of men.

23. Behold, now it is called to-day (until the coming of the Son of man), and verily it is a day of sacrifice, and a day for the tithing of my people; for he that is tithed shall not be burned (at his coming);

24. For after to-day cometh the burning: this is speaking after the manner of the Lord; for verily I say, to-morrow all the proud and they that do wickedly shall be as stubble; and I will burn them up, for I am the Lord of hosts: and I will not spare any that remain in Babylon.

25. Wherefore, if ye believe me, ye will labor while it is called to-day.

26. And it is not meet that my servants, Newel K. Whitney and Sidney Gilbert, should sell their store and their possessions here, for this is not wisdom, until the residue of the church, which remaineth in this place, shall go up unto the land of Zion.

27. Behold, it is said in my laws, or forbidden, to get in debt to thine enemies;

28. But behold, it is not said at any time that the Lord should not take when he please, and pay as seemeth him good:

29. Wherefore as ye are agents, and ye are on the Lord's errand; and whatever ye do according to the will of the Lord is the Lord's business,

30. And he hath set you to provide for his saints in these last days, that they may obtain an inheritance in the land of Zion:

31. And behold, I, the Lord, declare unto you, and my words are sure and shall not fail, that they shall obtain it;

32. But all things must come to pass in their time;

33. Wherefore, be not weary in well-doing, for ye are laying the foundation of a great work. And out of small things proceedeth that which is great.

34. Behold, the Lord requireth the heart and a willing mind; and the willing and obedient shall eat the good of the land of Zion in these last days;

35. And the rebellious shall be cut off out of the land of Zion, and shall be sent away, and shall not inherit the land:

36. For, verily I say that the rebellious are not of the blood of Ephraim, wherefore they shall be plucked out.

37. Behold, I, the Lord, have made my church in these last days like unto a judge sitting on a hill, or in a high place, to judge the nations;

38. For it shall come to pass that the inhabitants of Zion shall judge all things pertaining to Zion;

39. And liars and hypocrites shall be proved by them, and they who are not apostles and prophets shall be known.

40. And even the bishop, who is a judge, and his counselors, if they are not faithful in their stewardships, shall be condemned, and others shall be planted in their stead;

41. For, behold, I say unto you that Zion shall flourish, and the glory of the Lord shall be upon her,

42. And she shall be an ensign unto the people, and there shall come unto her out of every nation under heaven.

43. And the day shall come when the nations of the earth shall tremble because of her, and shall fear because of her terrible ones. The Lord hath spoken it. Amen.

SECTION 65

This revelation is a revealed prayer which the Prophet Joseph Smith received in October 1831, at Hiram, Ohio. In this revelation, the purpose and destiny of the Kingdom of God is revealed (History of the Church, vol. 1:218).

1. Hearken, and lo, a voice as of one from on high, who is mighty and powerful, whose going forth is unto the ends of the earth, yea, whose voice is unto men—Prepare ye the way of the Lord, make his paths straight.

2. The keys of the kingdom of God are committed unto man on the earth, and from thence shall the gospel roll forth unto the ends of the earth, as the stone which is cut out of the mountain without hands shall roll forth, until it has filled the whole earth;

3. Yea, a voice crying—Prepare ye the way of the Lord, prepare ye the supper of the Lamb, make ready for the Bridegroom;

4. Pray unto the Lord, call upon his holy name, make known his wonderful works among the people;

5. Call upon the Lord, that his kingdom may go forth upon the earth, that the inhabitants thereof may receive it, and be prepared for the days to come, in the which the Son of man shall come down in heaven, clothed in the brightness of his glory, to meet the kingdom of God which is set up on the earth;

6. Wherefore may the kingdom of God go forth, that the kingdom of heaven may come, that thou, O God, mayest be glorified in heaven so on earth, that thy enemies may be subdued; for thine is the honor, power and glory, for ever and ever. Amen.

Section 66

William E. M'Lellin was desirous to know the will of the Lord concerning himself. At his request, the Prophet Joseph Smith inquired of the Lord and this revelation was received October 1831, at Orange, Ohio (History of the Church, vol. 1:219–220).

1. Behold, thus saith the Lord unto my servant William E. M'Lellin, Blessed are you, inasmuch as you have turned away from your iniquities, and have received my truths, saith the Lord your Redeemer, the Savior of the world, even of as many as believe on my name.

2. Verily I say unto you, blessed are you for receiving mine everlasting covenant, even the fulness of my gospel, sent forth unto the children of men, that they might have life and be made partakers of the glories which are to be revealed in the last days, as it was written by the prophets and apostles in days of old.

3. Verily I say unto you, my servant William, that you are clean, but not all; repent, therefore of those things which are not pleasing in my sight, saith the Lord, for the Lord will show them unto you.

4. And now, verily, I, the Lord, will show unto you what I will concerning you, or what is my will concerning you;

5. Behold, verily I say unto you, that it is my will that you should proclaim my gospel from land to land, and from city to city; yea, in those regions round about where it has not been proclaimed.

6. Tarry not many days in this place; go not up unto the land of Zion as yet; but inasmuch as you can send, send; otherwise, think not of thy property.

7. Go unto the eastern lands, bear testimony in every place, unto every people, and in their synagogues, reasoning with the people.

8. Let my servant Samuel H. Smith go with you, and forsake him not, and give him thine instructions; and he that is faithful shall be made strong in every place, and I, the Lord, will go with you.

9. Lay your hands upon the sick, and they shall recover. Return not till I the Lord shall send you. Be patient in affliction. Ask and ye shall receive. Knock and it shall be opened unto you.

10. Seek not to be cumbered. Forsake all unrighteousness. Commit not adultery, a temptation with which thou hast been troubled.

11. Keep these sayings, for they are true and faithful, and thou shalt magnify thine office, and

push many people to Zion with songs of everlasting joy upon their heads.

12. Continue in these things even unto the end, and you shall have a crown of eternal life at the right hand of my Father, who is full of grace and truth.

13. Verily, thus saith the Lord your God, your Redeemer, even Jesus Christ. Amen.

SECTION 67

On November 1, 1831, a conference convened to consider important matters of the Church. Foremost was the printing of the Book of Commandments. *On the first day of the conference, the Lord revealed His preface to this Book (section 1). Most of the brethren were willing to testify of the truths of the revelations to be published. However, a few of the brethren suggested that there should be some improvement of the language. Because of this attitude, the Lord gave this revelation, November 1831, at Hiram, Ohio* (History of the Church, *vol. 1:224–226).*

1. Behold and hearken, O ye elders of my church, who have assembled yourselves together, whose prayers I have heard, and whose hearts I know, and whose desires have come up before me.
2. Behold and lo, mine eyes are upon you, and the heavens and the earth are in mine hands, and the riches of eternity are mine to give.
3. Ye endeavored to believe that ye should receive the blessing which was offered unto you; but behold, verily, I say unto you, there were fears in your hearts, and verily this is the reason that ye did not receive.
4. And now I, the Lord, give unto you a testimony of the truth of these commandments which are lying before you;
5. Your eyes have been upon my servant Joseph Smith, jun., and his language you have known, and his imperfections you have known; and you have sought in your hearts knowledge that you might express beyond his language, this you also know.
6. Now seek ye out of the book of Commandments, even the least that is among them, and appoint him that is the most wise among you;
7. Or, if there be any among you, that shall make one like unto it, then ye are justified in saying that ye do not know that they are true;
8. But if ye cannot make one like unto it, ye are under condemnation if ye do not bear record that they are true;
9. For ye know that there is no unrighteousness in them, and that which is righteous cometh down from above, from the Father of lights.
10. And again, verily I say unto you, that it is your privilege, and a promise I give unto you that have been ordained unto this ministry, that inasmuch as you strip yourselves from jealousies and fears, and humble yourselves before me, for ye are not sufficiently humble, the vail shall be rent and you shall see me and know that I AM; not with the carnal, neither natural mind, but with the spiritual;

11. For no man has seen God at any time in the flesh, except quickened by the Spirit of God;

12. Neither can any natural man abide in the presence of God; neither after the carnal mind;

13. Ye are not able to abide the presence of God now, neither the ministering of angels; wherefore continue in patience until ye are perfected.

14. Let not your minds turn back, and when ye are worthy, in mine own due time, ye shall see and know that which was conferred upon you by the hands of my servant Joseph Smith, jun. Amen.

Section 68

Orson Hyde, Luke Johnson, Lyman E. Johnson, and William E. M'Lellin sought the Prophet Joseph Smith, "to know the mind of the Lord concerning themselves." Inquiring of the Lord, the Prophet Joseph Smith received this revelation, November 1831, at Hiram, Ohio (History of the Church, vol. 1:227).

1. My servant, Orson Hyde, was called by his ordination to proclaim the everlasting gospel, by the Spirit of the living God, from people to people, and from land to land, in the congregations of the wicked, in their synagogues, reasoning with and expounding all Scriptures unto them.

2. And behold, and lo, this is an ensample unto all those who were ordained unto this Priesthood, whose mission is appointed unto them to go forth;

3. And this is the ensample unto them, that they shall speak as they are moved upon by the Holy Ghost,

4. And whatsoever they shall speak when moved upon by the Holy Ghost, shall be scripture, shall be the will of the Lord, shall be the mind of the Lord, shall be the word of the Lord, shall be the voice of the Lord, and the power of God unto salvation:

5. Behold this is the promise of the Lord unto you, O ye my servants;

6. Wherefore be of good cheer, and do not fear, for I the Lord am with you, and will stand by you; and ye shall bear record of me, even Jesus Christ, that I am the Son of the living God, that I was, that I am, and that I am to come.

7. This is the word of the Lord unto you my servant, Orson Hyde, and also unto my servant Luke Johnson, and unto my servant Lyman Johnson, and unto my servant William E. M'Lellin, and unto all the faithful elders of my church.

8. Go ye into all the world, preach the gospel to every creature, acting in the authority which I have given you, baptizing in the name of the Father, and of the Son, and of the Holy Ghost;

9. And he that believeth and is baptized shall be saved, and he that believeth not shall be damned;

10. And he that believeth shall be blest with signs following, even as it is written;

11. And unto you it shall be given to know the signs of the times, and the signs of the coming of the Son of man;

12. And of as many as the Father shall bear record, to you shall be given power to seal them up unto eternal life. Amen.

13. And now concerning the items in addition to the covenants and commandments, they are these:—

14. There remaineth hereafter, in the due time of the Lord, other bishops to be set apart unto the church, to minister even according to the first;

15. Wherefore they shall be High Priests who are worthy, and they shall be appointed by the First Presidency of the Melchisedek priesthood, except they be literal descendants of Aaron,

16. And if they be literal descendants of Aaron, they have a legal right to the bishopric, if they are the firstborn among the sons of Aaron;

17. For the firstborn holds the right of the presidency over this priesthood, and the keys of authority of the same.

18. No man has a legal right to this office to hold the keys of this priesthood, except he be a literal descendant and the first born of Aaron.

19. But as a High Priest of the Melchisedek Priesthood has authority to officiate in all the lesser offices, he may officiate in the office of bishop when no literal descendant of Aaron can be found, provided he is called, and set apart and ordained unto this power under the hands of the First Presidency of the Melchisedek Priesthood.

20. And a literal descendant of Aaron, also, must be designated by this Presidency, and found worthy, and anointed, and ordained under the hands of this Presidency, otherwise they are not legally authorized to officiate in their priesthood;

21. But by virtue of the decree concerning their right of the priesthood descending from father to son, they may claim their anointing, if at any time they can prove their lineage, or do ascertain it by revelation from the Lord under the hands of the above named Presidency.

22. And again, no bishop or High Priest who shall be set apart for this ministry, shall be tried or condemned for any crime, save it be before the First Presidency of the church;

23. And inasmuch as he is found guilty before this Presidency, by testimony that cannot be impeached, he shall be condemned;

24. And if he repents he shall be forgiven, according to the covenants and commandments of the church.

25. And again, inasmuch as parents have children in Zion, or in any of her Stakes which are organized, that teach them not to understand the doctrine of repentance, faith in Christ the son of the living God, and of baptism and the gift of the Holy Ghost by the laying on of the hands when eight years old, the sin be upon the heads of the parents;

26. For this shall be a law unto the inhabitants of Zion, or in any of her Stakes which are organized;

27. And their children shall be baptized for the remission of their sins when eight years old, and receive the laying on of the hands;

28. And they shall also teach their children to pray and to walk uprightly before the Lord.

29. And the inhabitants of Zion shall, also, observe the Sabbath day to keep it holy.

30. And the inhabitants of Zion, also, shall remember their labors, inasmuch as they are appointed to labor, in all faithfulness; for the idler shall be had in remembrance before the Lord.

31. Now, I the Lord, am not well pleased with the inhabitants of Zion, for there are idlers among them; and their children are also growing up in wickedness; they also seek not earnestly the riches of eternity, but their eyes are full of greediness.

32. These things ought not to be, and must be done away from among them: wherefore let my servant Oliver Cowdery carry these sayings unto the land of Zion.

33. And a commandment I give unto them, that he that observeth not his prayers before the Lord in the season thereof, let him be had in remembrance before the judge of my people.

34. These sayings are true and faithful; wherefore transgress them not neither take therefrom.
35. Behold, I am Alpha and Omega, and I come quickly. Amen.

Section 69

The revelations to be printed were dedicated through prayer to the Lord. Concerning this printing, the Prophet Joseph Smith sought the Lord and received this revelation, November 1831, at Hiram, Ohio (History of the Church, vol. 1:234).

1. Hearken unto me, saith the Lord your God, for my servant Oliver Cowdery's sake. It is not wisdom in me that he should be entrusted with the commandments and the monies which he shall carry unto the land of Zion, except one go with him who will be true and faithful;

2. Wherefore, I the Lord will that my servant, John Whitmer, should go with my servant Oliver Cowdery;

3. And also that he shall continue in writing and making a history of all the important things which he shall observe and know concerning my church:

4. And also that he receive counsel and assistance from my servant Oliver Cowdery and others.

5. And also my servants who are abroad in the earth, should send forth the accounts of their stewardships to the land of Zion;

6. For the land of Zion shall be a seat and a place to receive and do all these things;

7. Nevertheless, let my servant, John Whitmer, travel many times from place to place, and from church to church, that he may the more easily obtain knowledge;

8. Preaching and expounding, writing, copying, selecting, and obtaining all things which shall be for the good of the church, and for the rising generations, that shall grow up on the land of Zion, to possess it from generation to generation, for ever and ever. Amen.

ECTION 70

The November 1831 conference of the Church voted to prize the revelations, now to be printed, more than the riches of the world. Referring to these revelations, the Prophet Joseph Smith said they were, "the foundation of the Church in these last days." Inquiring of the Lord, pertaining to the stewardship and management of these revelations (The Book of Commandments) the Prophet Joseph Smith received this revelation, November 1831, at Kirtland, Ohio (History of the Church, vol. 1:235–236).

1. Behold, and hearken, O ye inhabitants of Zion, and all ye people of my church, who are far off, and hear the word of the Lord which I give unto my servant Joseph Smith, jun., and also unto my servant Martin Harris, and also unto my servant Oliver Cowdery, and also unto my servant John Whitmer, and also unto my servant Sidney Rigdon, and also unto my servant William W. Phelps, by the way of commandment unto them;
2. For I give unto them a commandment; wherefore hearken and hear, for thus saith the Lord unto them—
3. I, the Lord, have appointed them, and ordained them to be stewards over the revelations and commandments which I have given unto them, and which I shall hereafter give unto them;
4. And an account of this stewardship will I require of them in the day of judgment:
5. Wherefore I have appointed unto them, and this is their business in the church of God, to manage them and the concerns thereof; yea, the benefits thereof.
6. Wherefore a commandment I give unto them, that they shall not give these things unto the church, neither unto the world:
7. Nevertheless, inasmuch as they receive more than is needful for their necessities and their wants, it shall be given into my storehouse,
8. And the benefits shall be consecrated unto the inhabitants of Zion, and unto their generations, inasmuch as they become heirs according to the laws of the kingdom.
9. Behold, this is what the Lord requires of every man in his stewardship, even as I, the Lord, have appointed, or shall hereafter appoint unto any man.
10. And, behold none are exempt from this law who belong to the church of the living God;
11. Yea, neither the bishop, neither the agent who keepeth the Lord's storehouse, neither he who is appointed in a stewardship over temporal things;

PAINTING DEPICTS PORTIONS OF *THE BOOK OF COMMANDMENTS* BEING SAVED FROM A DESTRUCTIVE MOB

12. He who is appointed to administer spiritual things, the same is worthy of his hire, even as those who are appointed to a stewardship, to administer in temporal things;

13. Yea, even more abundantly, which abundance is multiplied unto them through the manifestations of the Spirit;

14. Nevertheless, in your temporal things you shall be equal, and this not grudgingly, otherwise the abundance of the manifestations of the Spirit shall be withheld.

15. Now this commandment I give unto my servants for their benefit while they remain, for a manifestation of my blessings upon their heads, and for a reward of their diligence and for their security;

16. For food and for raiment; for an inheritance; for houses and for lands, in whatsoever circumstances I, the Lord, shall place them, and whithersoever I, the Lord, shall send them;

17. For they have been faithful over many things, and have done well inasmuch as they have not sinned.

18. Behold, I, the Lord, am merciful and will bless them, and they shall enter into the joy of these things. Even so. Amen.

# Section 71

Ezra Booth, who had apostatized, wrote several articles against the Church in the Ravenna Ohio Star *paper. The Lord commanded the Prophet Joseph Smith and Sidney Rigdon to cease translating the Bible for a season. They were to preach the gospel in public and private to confound their enemies. This revelation was received December 1, 1831, at Hiram, Ohio (History of the Church, vol. 1:238).*

1. Behold, thus saith the Lord unto you my servants Joseph Smith, jun., and Sidney Rigdon, that the time has verily come, that it is necessary and expedient in me that you should open your mouths in proclaiming my gospel, the things of the kingdom, expounding the mysteries thereof out of the scriptures, according to that portion of Spirit and power which shall be given unto you, even as I will.

2. Verily, I say unto you, proclaim unto the world in the regions round about, and in the church also, for the space of a season, even until it shall be made known unto you.

3. Verily this is a mission for a season, which I give unto you.

4. Wherefore, labor ye in my vineyard. Call upon the inhabitants of the earth, and bear record, and prepare the way for the commandments and revelations which are to come.

5. Now, behold this is wisdom; whoso readeth, let him understand and receive also;

6. For unto him that receiveth it shall be given more abundantly, even power;

7. Wherefore, confound your enemies; call upon them to meet you both in public and in private; and inasmuch as ye are faithful, their shame shall be made manifest.

8. Wherefore, let them bring forth their strong reasons against the Lord.

9. Verily, thus saith the Lord unto you, there is no weapon that is formed against you shall prosper;

10. And if any man lift his voice against you, he shall be confounded in mine own due time;

11. Wherefore, keep my commandments, they are true and faithful. Even so. Amen.

SECTION 72

Obedient to the command of the Lord to preach the gospel in public and in private to confound their enemies (see historical background, section 71), the Prophet Joseph Smith and Sidney Rigdon traveled from Hiram, Ohio, to Kirtland, Ohio. While in Kirtland a number of members assembled together to learn their duties and to be edified. While thus convened, the Prophet Joseph Smith received this revelation December 4, 1831, at Kirtland, Ohio (History of the Church, vol. 1:239).

1. Hearken and listen to the voice of the Lord, O ye who have assembled yourselves together, who are the High Priests of my church, to whom the kingdom and power have been given.

2. For verily thus saith the Lord, it is expedient in me for a bishop to be appointed unto you, or of you, unto the church in this part of the Lord's vineyard;

3. And verily in this thing ye have done wisely, for it is required of the Lord, at the hand of every steward, to render an account of his stewardship, both in time and in eternity.

4. For he who is faithful and wise in time, is accounted worthy to inherit the mansions prepared for him of my Father.

5. Verily I say unto you, the elders of the church in this part of my vineyard, shall render an account of their stewardship unto the bishop which shall be appointed of me, in this part of my vineyard.

6. These things shall be had on record, to be handed over unto the bishop in Zion;

7. And the duty of the bishop shall be made known by the commandments which have been given, and the voice of the conference.

8. And now, verily I say unto you, my servant Newel K. Whitney is the man who shall be appointed and ordained unto this power. This is the will of the Lord your God, your Redeemer. Even so. Amen.

9. The word of the Lord, in addition to the law which has been given, making known the duty of the bishop which has been ordained unto the church in this part of the vineyard, which is verily this—

10. To keep the Lord's storehouse; to receive the funds of the church in this part of the vineyard;

11. To take an account of the elders as before has been commanded; and to administer to their wants, who shall pay for that which they receive, inasmuch as they have wherewith to pay;

12. That this also may be consecrated to the good of the church, to the poor and needy.

13. And he who hath not wherewith to pay, an account shall be taken and handed over to the

JOSEPH SMITH PREACHES TO A GROUP OF ASSEMBLED SAINTS

bishop of Zion, who shall pay the debt out of that which the Lord shall put into his hands;

14. And the labors of the faithful who labor in spiritual things, in administering the gospel and the things of the kingdom unto the church, and unto the world, shall answer the debt unto the bishop in Zion;

15. Thus it cometh out of the church, for according to the law every man that cometh up to Zion, must lay all things before the bishop in Zion.

16. And now, verily I say unto you, that as every elder in this part of the vineyard must give an account of his stewardship unto the bishop in this part of the vineyard,

17. A certificate from the judge or bishop in this part of the vineyard, unto the bishop in Zion, rendereth every man acceptable, and answereth all things, for an inheritance, and to be received as a wise steward, and as a faithful laborer;

18. Otherwise he shall not be accepted of the bishop of Zion.

19. And now, verily I say unto you, let every elder who shall give an account unto the bishop of the church, in this part of the vineyard be recommended by the church or churches, in which he labors, that he may render himself and his accounts approved in all things.

20. And again, let my servants who are appointed as stewards over the literary concerns of my church have claim for assistance upon the bishop or bishops, in all things,

21. That the revelations may be published, and go forth unto the ends of the earth, that they also may obtain funds which shall benefit the church in all things,

22. That they also may render themselves approved in all things, and be accounted as wise stewards.

23. And now, behold, this shall be an ensample for all the extensive branches of my church, in whatsoever land they shall be established. And now I make an end of my sayings. Amen.

24. A few words in addition to the laws of the kingdom, respecting the members of the church; they that are appointed by the Holy Spirit to go up unto Zion, and they who are privileged to go up unto Zion;

25. Let them carry up unto the bishop a certificate from three elders of the church, or a certificate from the bishop,

26. Otherwise he who shall go up unto the land of Zion, shall not be accounted as a wise steward. This is also an ensample. Amen.

SECTION 73

A conference of the Church was to convene January 25, 1832 at Amherst, Ohio. Several Elders arrived early and, while waiting for the conference gathering, desired to know what the Lord would have them do. This revelation was received January 10, 1832, at Hiram, Ohio (History of the Church, vol. 1:241).

1. For verily thus saith the Lord, it is expedient in me, that they should continue preaching the gospel, and in exhortation to the churches in the regions round about, until conference;

2. And then, behold, it shall be made known unto them, by the voice of the conference, their several missions.

3. Now, verily, I say unto you my servants, Joseph Smith, jun., and Sidney Rigdon, saith the Lord, it is expedient to translate again,

4. And, inasmuch as it is practicable, to preach in the regions round about until conference; and after that it is expedient to continue the work of translation until it be finished.

5. And let this be a pattern unto the elders until further knowledge, even as it is written.

6. Now I give no more unto you at this time. Gird up your loins and be sober. Even so. Amen.

Section 74

The Prophet Joseph Smith received this revelation in January 1832, at Hiram, Ohio, "as an explanation of the First Epistle to the Corinthians, 7th chapter, 14th verse" (History of the Church, vol. 1:242).

1. For the unbelieving husband is sanctified by the wife, and the unbelieving wife is sanctified by the husband, else were your children unclean, but now are they holy.

2. Now in the days of the apostles the law of circumcision was had among all the Jews who believed not the gospel of Jesus Christ.

3. And it came to pass that there arose a great contention among the people concerning the law of circumcision, for the unbelieving husband was desirous that his children should be circumcised and become subject to the law of Moses, which law was fulfilled.

4. And it came to pass that the children, being brought up in subjection to the law of Moses, gave heed to the traditions of their fathers and believed not the gospel of Christ, wherein they became unholy;

5. Wherefore, for this cause the apostle wrote unto the church, giving unto them a commandment, not of the Lord, but of himself, that a believer should not be united to an unbeliever, except the law of Moses should be done away among them,

6. That their children might remain without circumcision; and that the tradition might be done away, which saith that little children are unholy; for it was had among the Jews,

7. But little children are holy, being sanctified through the atonement of Jesus Christ; and this is what the scriptures mean.

Section 75

The Elders attending the Amherst, Ohio, conference were anxious for the Prophet Joseph Smith to inquire of the Lord that they might know, "what would be most pleasing to Him for them to do, in order to bring men to a sense of their condition." This revelation was given to the Prophet Joseph Smith, January 25, 1832, at Amherst, Ohio (History of the Church, vol. 1:242–243).

1. Verily, verily, I say unto you, I who speak even by the voice of my Spirit; even Alpha and Omega, your Lord and your God;
2. Hearken, O ye who have given your names to go forth to proclaim my gospel, and to prune my vineyard.
3. Behold, I say unto you, that it is my will that you should go forth and not tarry, neither be idle, but labor with your mights,
4. Lifting up your voices as with the sound of a trump, proclaiming the truth according to the revelations and commandments which I have given you.
5. And thus if ye are faithful ye shall be laden with many sheaves, and crowned with honor, and glory, and immortality, and eternal life.
6. Therefore, verily I say unto my servant William E. M'Lellin, I revoke the commission which I gave unto him to go unto the eastern countries,
7. And I gave him a new commission and a new commandment, in the which I, the Lord, chasten him for the murmurings of his heart;
8. And he sinned, nevertheless I forgive him, and say unto him again, go ye into the south countries,
9. And let my servant Luke Johnson go with him, and proclaim the things which I have commanded them,
10. Calling on the name of the Lord for the Comforter, which shall teach them all things that are expedient for them,
11. Praying always that they faint not, and inasmuch as they do this, I will be with them even unto the end.
12. Behold, this is the will of the Lord your God concerning you. Even so. Amen.
13. And again, verily thus saith the Lord, let my servant Orson Hyde, and my servant Samuel H. Smith, take their journey into the eastern countries, and proclaim the things which I have commanded them; and inasmuch as they are faithful, lo, I will be with them even unto the end.
14. And again, verily I say unto my servant Lyman Johnson, and unto my servant Orson

Pratt, they shall also take their journey into the eastern countries; and behold, and lo, I am with them also even unto the end.

15. And again, I say unto my servant Asa Dodds, and unto my servant Calves Wilson, that they also shall take their journey unto the western countries, and proclaim my gospel, even as I have commanded them.

16. And he who is faithful shall overcome all things, and shall be lifted up at the last day.

17. And again, I say unto my servant Major N. Ashley, and my servant Burr Riggs, let them take their journey also into the south country;

18. Yea, let all those take their journey as I have commanded them, going from house to house, and from village to village, and from city to city;

19. And in whatsoever house ye enter, and they receive you, leave your blessing upon that house;

20. And in whatsoever house ye enter, and they receive you not, ye shall depart speedily from that house, and shake off the dust of your feet as a testimony against them;

21. And you shall be filled with joy and gladness; and know this, that in the day of judgment you shall be judges of that house, and condemn them;

22. And it shall be more tolerable for the heathen in the day of judgment, than for that house; therefore gird up your loins and be faithful, and ye shall overcome all things, and be lifted up at the last day. Even so. Amen.

23. And again, thus saith the Lord unto you, O ye elders of my church, who have given your names that you might know his will concerning you;

24. Behold, I say unto you, that it is the duty of the church to assist in supporting the families of those, and also to support the families of those who are called and must needs be sent unto the world to proclaim the gospel unto the world;

25. Wherefore, I, the Lord, give unto you this commandment, that ye obtain places for your families, inasmuch as your brethren are willing to open their hearts;

26. And let all such as can obtain places for their families, and support of the church for them, not fail to go into the world, whether to the east or to the west, or to the north, or to the south;

27. Let them ask and they shall receive, knock and it shall be opened unto them, and made known from on high, even by the Comforter, whither they shall go.

28. And again, verily I say unto you, that every man who is obliged to provide for his own family, let him provide, and he shall in no wise lose his crown; and let him labor in the church.

29. Let every man be diligent in all things. And the idler shall not have place in the church, except he repents and mends his ways.

30. Wherefore, let my servant Simeon Carter, and my servant Emer Harris, be united in the ministry;

31. And also my servant Ezra Thayre, and my servant Thomas B. Marsh;

32. Also my servant Hyrum Smith, and my servant Reynolds Cahoon;

33. And also my servant Daniel Stanton, and my servant Seymour Brunson;

34. And also my servant Sylvester Smith, and my servant Gideon Carter;

35. And also my servant Ruggles Eames, and my servant Stephen Burnett;

36. And also my servant Micah B. Welton, and also my servant Eden Smith. Even so. Amen.

THE JOHN JOHNSON FARM WHERE THIS REVELATION WAS RECEIVED

Section 76

While translating the Bible, the Prophet Joseph Smith became aware that many truths had been taken from these writings, or had been lost. Pertaining to the concept of heaven, and the judgment of man, many eternal truths were missing. On February 16, 1832, at Hiram, Ohio, the Prophet Joseph Smith and Sidney Rigdon saw the following vision (History of the Church, vol. 1:245).

1. Hear O ye heavens, and give ear O earth, and rejoice ye inhabitants thereof, for the Lord is God, and beside him there is no Savior:

2. Great is his wisdom, marvelous are his ways, and the extent of his doings none can find out;

3. His purposes fail not, neither are there any who can stay his hand;

4. From eternity to eternity he is the same, and his years never fail.

5. For thus saith the Lord, I, the Lord, am merciful and gracious unto those who fear me, and delight to honor those who serve me in righteousness and in truth unto the end;

6. Great shall be their reward and eternal shall be their glory;

7. And to them will I reveal all mysteries, yea, all the hidden mysteries of my kingdom from days of old, and for ages to come will I make known unto them the good pleasure of my will concerning all things pertaining to my kingdom;

8. Yea, even the wonders of eternity shall they know, and things to come will I show them, even the things of many generations;

9. And their wisdom shall be great, and their understanding reach to heaven: and before them the wisdom of the wise shall perish, and the understanding of the prudent shall come to naught;

10. For by my Spirit will I enlighten them, and by my power will I make known unto them the secrets of my will; yea, even those things which eye has not seen, nor ear heard, nor yet entered into the heart of man.

11. We, Joseph Smith, jun., and Sidney Rigdon, being in the Spirit on the sixteenth of February, in the year of our Lord, one thousand eight hundred and thirty-two,

12. By the power of the Spirit our eyes were opened and our understandings were enlightened, so as to see and understand the things of God—

13. Even those things which were from the beginning before the world was, which were ordained of the Father, through his Only Begotten Son, who was in the bosom of the Father, even from the beginning,

14. Of whom we bear record, and the record which we bear is the fulness of the gospel of Jesus Christ, who is the Son, whom we saw and with whom we conversed in the heavenly vision;

15. For while we were doing the work of translation, which the Lord had appointed unto us, we came to the twenty-ninth verse of the fifth chapter of John, which was given unto us as follows.

16. Speaking of the resurrection of the dead, concerning those who shall hear the voice of the Son of Man,

17. And shall come forth; they who have done good in the resurrection of the just, and they who have done evil in the resurrection of the unjust.

18. Now this caused us to marvel, for it was given unto us of the Spirit.

19. And while we meditated upon these things, the Lord touched the eyes of our understandings and they were opened, and the glory of the Lord shone round about;

20. And we beheld the glory of the Son, on the right hand of the Father, and received of his fulness;

21. And saw the holy angels, and they who are sanctified before his throne, worshiping God, and the Lamb, who worship him forever and ever.

22. And now, after the many testimonies which have been given of him, this is the testimony last of all, which we give of him, that he lives;

23. For we saw him, even on the right hand of God, and we heard the voice bearing record that he is the Only Begotten of the Father—

24. That by him and through him, and of him the worlds are and were created, and the inhabitants thereof are begotten sons and daughters unto God.

25. And this we saw also, and bear record, that an angel of God who was in authority in the presence of God, who rebelled against the Only Begotten Son, whom the Father loved, and who was in the bosom of the Father—was thrust down from the presence of God and the Son,

26. And was called Perdition, for the heavens wept over him—he was Lucifer, a son of the morning.

27. And we beheld, and lo, he is fallen! is fallen! even a son of the morning.

28. And while we were yet in the Spirit, the Lord commanded us that we should write the vision, for we beheld Satan, that old serpent—even the devil—who rebelled against God, and sought to take the kingdom of our God, and his Christ,

29. Wherefore he maketh war with the saints of God, and encompasses them round about.

30. And we saw a vision of the sufferings of those with whom he made war and overcame, for thus came the voice of the Lord unto us.

31. Thus saith the Lord, concerning all those who know my power, and have been made partakers thereof, and suffered themselves, through the power of the devil, to be overcome, and to deny the truth and defy my power—

32. They are they who are the sons of perdition, of whom I say that it had been better for them never to have been born,

33. For they are vessels of wrath, doomed to suffer the wrath of God, with the devil and his angels in eternity;

34. Concerning whom I have said there is no forgiveness in this world nor in the world to come,

35. Having denied the Holy Spirit after having received it, and having denied the Only Begotten Son of the Father—having crucified him unto themselves and put him to an open shame.

36. These are they who shall go away into the lake of fire and brimstone, with the devil and his angels,

37. And the only ones on whom the second death shall have any power;

38. Yea, verily, the only ones who shall not be redeemed in the due time of the Lord, after the sufferings of his wrath;

39. For all the rest shall be brought forth by the resurrection of the dead, through the triumph and the glory of the Lamb, who was slain, who was in the bosom of the Father before the worlds were made.

40. And this is the gospel, the glad tidings which the voice out of the heavens bore record unto us,

41. That he came into the world, even Jesus, to be crucified for the world, and to bear the sins of the world, and to sanctify the world, and to cleanse it from all unrighteousness;

42. That through him all might be saved whom the Father had put into his power and made by him,

43. Who glorifies the Father, and saves all the works of his hands, except those sons of perdition, who deny the Son after the Father has revealed him;

44. Wherefore, he saves all except them: they shall go away into everlasting punishment, which is endless punishment, which is eternal punishment, to reign with the devil and his angels in eternity, where their worm dieth not, and the fire is not quenched, which is their torment;

45. And the end thereof, neither the place thereof, nor their torment, no man knows,

46. Neither was it revealed, neither is, neither will be revealed unto man, except to them who are made partakers thereof:

47. Nevertheless, I, the Lord, show it by vision unto many, but straightway shut it up again;

48. Wherefore the end, the width, the height, the depth, and the misery thereof, they understand not, neither any man except them who are ordained unto this condemnation.

49. And we heard the voice, saying, Write the vision, for lo! this is the end of the vision of the sufferings of the ungodly!

50. And again, we bear record, for we saw and heard, and this is the testimony of the gospel of Christ concerning them who shall come forth in the resurrection of the just;

51. They are they who received the testimony of Jesus, and believed on his name and were baptized after the manner of his burial, being buried in the water in his name, and this according to the commandment which he has given,

52. That by keeping the commandments they might be washed and cleansed from all their sins, and receive the Holy Spirit by the laying on of the hands of him who is ordained and sealed unto this power,

53. And who overcome by faith, and are sealed by the Holy Spirit of promise, which the Father sheds forth upon all those who are just and true.

54. They are they who are the church of the first born.

55. They are they into whose hands the Father has given all things—

56. They are they who are Priests and Kings, who have received of his fulness, and of his glory,

57. And are Priests of the Most High, after the order of Melchisedek, which was after the order of Enoch, which was after the order of the Only Begotten Son;

58. Wherefore, as it is written, they are Gods, even the sons of God—

59. Wherefore all things are theirs, whether life or death, or things present, or things to come, all are theirs and they are Christ's and Christ is God's;

60. And they shall overcome all things;

61. Wherefore let no man glory in man, but rather let him glory in God, who shall subdue all enemies under his feet—

62. These shall dwell in the presence of God and his Christ for ever and ever.

63. These are they whom he shall bring with him, when he shall come in the clouds of heaven, to reign on the earth over his people.

64. These are they who shall have part in the first resurrection.

65. These are they who shall come forth in the resurrection of the just.

66. These are they who are come unto Mount Zion, and unto the city of the living God, the heavenly place, the holiest of all.

67. These are they who have come to an innumerable company of angels, to the general assembly and church of Enoch, and of the first born.

68. These are they whose names are written in heaven, where God and Christ are the judge of all.

69. These are they who are just men made perfect through Jesus the mediator of the new covenant, who wrought out this perfect atonement through the shedding of his own blood.

70. These are they whose bodies are celestial, whose glory is that of the sun, even the glory of God, the highest of all, whose glory the sun of the firmament is written of as being typical.

71. And again, we saw the terrestrial world, and behold and lo, these are they who are of the terrestrial, whose glory differs from that of the church of the first born who have received the fulness of the Father, even as that of the moon differs from the sun in the firmament.

72. Behold, these are they who died without law,

73. And also they who are the spirits of men kept in prison, whom the Son visited, and preached the gospel unto them, that they might be judged according to men in the flesh,

74. Who received not the testimony of Jesus in the flesh, but afterwards received it.

75. These are they who are honorable men of the earth, who were blinded by the craftiness of men.

76. These are they who receive of his glory, but not of his fulness.

77. These are they who receive of the presence of the Son, but not of the fulness of the Father;

78. Wherefore they are bodies terrestrial, and not bodies celestial, and differ in glory as the moon differs from the sun.

79. These are they who are not valiant in the testimony of Jesus; wherefore they obtain not the crown over the kingdom of our God.

80. And now this is the end of the vision which we saw of the terrestrial, that the Lord commanded us to write while we were yet in the Spirit.

81. And again, we saw the glory of the telestial, which glory is that of the lesser, even as the glory of the stars differs from that of the glory of the moon in the firmament.

82. These are they who received not the gospel of Christ, neither the testimony of Jesus.

83. These are they who deny not the Holy Spirit.

84. These are they who are thrust down to hell.

85. These are they who shall not be redeemed from the devil, until the last resurrection, until the Lord, even Christ the Lamb shall have finished his work.

86. These are they who receive not of his fulness in the eternal world, but of the Holy Spirit through the ministration of the terrestrial;

87. And the terrestrial through the ministration of the celestial.

88. And also the telestial receive it of the administering of angels who are appointed to minister for them, or who are appointed to be ministering spirits for them, for they shall be heirs of salvation.

89. And thus we saw, in the heavenly vision, the glory of the telestial, which surpasses all understanding,

90. And no man knows it except him to whom God has revealed it.

91. And thus we saw the glory of the terrestrial, which excels in all things the glory of the telestial, even in glory, and in power, and in might, and in dominion.

92. And thus we saw the glory of the celestial, which excels in all things—where God, even the Father, reigns upon his throne for ever and ever;

93. Before whose throne all things bow in humble reverence and give him glory for ever and ever.

94. They who dwell in his presence are the church of the first born; and they see as they are seen, and know as they are known, having received of his fulness and of his grace;

95. And he makes them equal in power, and in might, and in dominion.

96. And the glory of the celestial is one, even as the glory of the sun is one.

97. And the glory of the terrestrial is one, even as the glory of the moon is one.

98. And the glory of the telestial is one, even as the glory of the stars is one, for as one star differs from another star in glory, even so differs one from another in glory in the telestial world;

99. For these are they who are of Paul, and of Apollos, and of Cephas.

100. These are they who say they are some of one and some of another—some of Christ and some of John, and some of Moses, and some of Elias, and some of Esaias, and some of Isaiah, and some of Enoch;

101. But received not the gospel, neither the testimony of Jesus, neither the prophets, neither the everlasting covenant.

102. Last of all, these all are they who will not be gathered with the saints, to be caught up unto the church of the first born, and received into the cloud.

103. These are they who are liars, and sorcerers, and adulterers, and whoremongers, and whosoever loves and makes a lie.

104. These are they who suffer the wrath of God on the earth.

105. These are they who suffer the vengeance of eternal fire.

106. These are they who are cast down to hell and suffer the wrath of Almighty God, until the fulness of times when Christ shall have subdued all enemies under his feet, and shall have perfected his work,

107. When he shall deliver up the kingdom, and present it unto the Father spotless, saying—I have overcome and have trodden the wine-press alone, even the wine-press of the fierceness of the wrath of Almighty God.

108. Then shall he be crowned with the crown of his glory, to sit on the throne of his power to reign for ever and ever.

109. But behold, and lo, we saw the glory and the inhabitants of the telestial world, that they were as innumerable as the stars in the firmament of heaven, or as the sand upon the sea shore,

110. And heard the voice of the Lord, saying—these all shall bow the knee, and every tongue shall confess to him who sits upon the throne for ever and ever;

111. For they shall be judged according to their works, and every man shall receive according to his own works, his own dominion, in the mansions which are prepared,

112. And they shall be servants of the Most High, but where God and Christ dwell they cannot come, worlds without end.

113. This is the end of the vision which we saw, which we were commanded to write while we were yet in the Spirit.

114. But great and marvelous are the works of the Lord, and the mysteries of his kingdom which he showed unto us, which surpasses all understanding in glory, and in might, and in dominion,

115. Which he commanded us we should not write while we were yet in the Spirit, and are not lawful for man to utter;

116. Neither is man capable to make them known, for they are only to be seen and understood by the power of the Holy Spirit, which God bestows on those who love him, and purify themselves before him;

117. To whom he grants this privilege of seeing and knowing for themselves;

118. That through the power and manifestation of the Spirit, while in the flesh, they may be able to bear his presence in the world of glory.

119. And to God and the Lamb be glory, and honor, and dominion for ever and ever. Amen.

SECTION 77

While translating the Bible, the Prophet Joseph Smith received an "explanation of the Revelation of St. John." This revelation was received in March 1832, at Hiram, Ohio (History of the Church, vol. 1:253).

1. Q.—What is the sea of glass spoken of by John, 4th chapter, and 6th verse of the Revelations?

A.—It is the earth, in its sanctified, immortal, and eternal state.

2. Q.—What are we to understand by the four beasts, spoken of in the same verse?

A.—They are figurative expressions, used by the Revelator John, in describing heaven, the Paradise of God, the happiness of man, and of beasts, and of creeping things, and of the fowls of the air; that, which is spiritual being in the likeness of that which is temporal; and that which is temporal, is in the likeness of that which is spiritual; the spirit of man in the likeness of his person, as also the spirit of the beast, and every other creature which God has created.

3. Q.—Are the four beasts limited to individual beasts, or do they represent classes or orders?

A.—They are limited to four individual beasts, which were shown to John, to represent the glory of the classes of beings, in their destined order or sphere of creation, in the enjoyment of their eternal felicity.

4. Q.—What are we to understand by the eyes, and wings, which the beasts had?

A.—Their eyes are a representation of light and knowledge; that is, they are full of knowledge; and their wings are a representation of power, to move, to act, &c.

5. Q.—What are we to understand by the four and twenty elders, spoken of by John?

A.—We are to understand that these elders whom John saw, were elders who had been faithful in the work of the ministry, and were dead; who belonged to the seven churches,—and were then in the Paradise of God.

6. Q.—What are we to understand by the book which John saw, which was sealed on the back with seven seals?

A.—We are to understand that it contains the revealed will, mysteries, and the works of

God; the hidden things of his economy concerning this earth during the seven thousand years of its continuance, or its temporal existence.

7. Q.—What are we to understand by the seven seals with which it was sealed?

A.—We are to understand that the first seal contains the things of the first thousand years, and the second also of the second thousand years, and so on until the seventh.

8. Q.—What are we to understand by the four angels, spoken of in the 7th chap. and 1st verse of Revelations?

A.—We are to understand that they are four angels sent forth from God, to whom is given power over the four parts of the earth, to save life and to destroy; these are they who have the everlasting gospel to commit to every nation, kindred, tongue, and people; having power to shut up the heavens, to seal up unto life, or to cast down to the regions of darkness.

9. Q.—What are we to understand by the angel ascending from the east, Revelations 7th chap. and 2nd verse?

A.—We are to understand that the angel ascending from the east, is he to whom is given the seal of the living God, over the twelve tribes of Israel; wherefore he crieth unto the four angels having the everlasting gospel, saying, hurt not the earth, neither the sea, nor the trees, till we have sealed the servants of our God in their foreheads; and if you will receive it, this is Elias which was to come to gather together the tribes of Israel and restore all things.

10. Q.—What time are the things spoken of in this chapter to be accomplished?

A.—They are to be accomplished in the sixth thousandth year, or the opening of the sixth seal.

11. Q.—What are we to understand by sealing the one hundred and forty-four thousand, out of all the tribes of Israel; twelve thousand out of every tribe?

A.—We are to understand that those who are sealed are High Priests, ordained unto the holy order of God, to administer the everlasting gospel; for they are they who are ordained out of every nation, kindred, tongue, and people, by the angels to whom is given power over the nations of the earth, to bring as many as will come to the church of the first born.

12. Q.—What are we to understand by the sounding of the trumpets, mentioned in the 8th chapter of Revelations?

A.—We are to understand that as God made the world in six days and on the seventh day he finished his work, and sanctified it, and also formed man out of the dust of the earth even so, in the beginning of the seventh thousand years will the Lord God sanctify the earth, and complete the salvation of man, and judge all things, and shall redeem all things, except that which he hath not put into his power, when he shall have sealed all things, unto the end of all things; and the sounding of the trumpets of the seven angels, are the preparing and finishing of his work, in the beginning of the seventh thousand years; the preparing of the way before the time of his coming.

13. Q.—When are the things to be accomplished, which are written in the 9th chapter of Revelations?

A.—They are to be accomplished after the opening of the seventh seal, before the coming of Christ.

14. Q.—What are we to understand by the little book which was eaten by John, as mentioned in the 10th chapter of Revelations?

A.—We are to understand that it was a mission, and an ordinance, for him to gather the tribes of Israel; behold, this is Elias; who, as it is written, must come and restore all things.

15. Q.—What is to be understood by the two witnesses, in the eleventh chapter of Revelations?

A.—They are two prophets that are to be raised up to the Jewish nation in the last days, at the time of the restoration, and to prophesy to the Jews, after they are gathered, and build the city of Jerusalem, in the land of their fathers.

ECTION 78

The Prophet Joseph Smith recorded the following: "Besides the work of translating, previous to the 20th of March, I received the four following revelations" (sections 78, 79, 80, 81). The 1835 ed. superscription of this revelation reads: "Revelation given March 1832. The Order given of the Lord to Enoch (Joseph Smith, Jun.), for the purpose of establishing the poor." This revelation was received in March 1832, at Hiram, Ohio (History of the Church, vol. 1:255).

1. The Lord spake unto Enoch, (Joseph Smith, jr.,) saying, Hearken unto me, saith the Lord your God, who are ordained unto the high priesthood of my church, who have assembled yourselves together;

2. And listen to the counsel of him who has ordained you from on high, who shall speak in your ears the words of wisdom, that salvation may be unto you in that thing which you have presented before me, saith the Lord God;

3. For verily I say unto you, the time has come, and is now at hand; and behold, and lo, it must needs be that there be an organization of my people, in regulating and establishing the affairs of the storehouse for the poor of my people, both in this place and in the land of Zion,

4. Or in other words, the city of Enoch, (Joseph) for a permanent and everlasting establishment and order unto my church, to advance the cause, which ye have espoused, to the salvation of man, and to the glory of your Father who is in heaven;

5. That you may be equal in the bands of heavenly things; yea, and earthly things also, for the obtaining of heavenly things;

6. For if ye are not equal in earthly things, ye cannot be equal in obtaining heavenly things;

7. For if you will that I give unto you a place in the celestial world, you must prepare yourselves by doing the things which I have commanded you and required of you.

8. And now, verily thus saith the Lord, it is expedient that all things be done unto my glory, by you who are joined together in this order;

9. Or in other words, let my servant Ahashdah (Newel K. Whitney) and my servant Gazelam, or Enoch (Joseph Smith, jr.) and my servant Peloagoram (Sidney Rigdon,) sit in council with the saints which are in Zion;

10. Otherwise Satan seeketh to turn their hearts away from the truth, that they become blinded and understand not the things which are prepared for them.

11. Wherefore, a commandment I give unto you, to prepare and organize yourselves by a bond or everlasting covenant that cannot be broken.

12. And he who breaketh it shall lose his office and standing in the church, and shall be delivered over to the buffetings of Satan until the day of redemption.

13. Behold, this is the preparation wherewith I prepare you, and the foundation, and the ensample which I give unto you, whereby you may accomplish the commandments which are given you,

14. That through my providence, notwithstanding the tribulation which shall descend upon you, that the church may stand independent above all other creatures beneath the celestial world,

15. That you may come up unto the crown prepared for you, and be made rulers over many kingdoms, saith the Lord God, the Holy One of Zion, who hath established the foundations of Adam-ondi-Ahman;

16. Who hath appointed Michael your prince, and established his feet, and set him upon high, and given unto him the keys of salvation under the counsel and direction of the Holy One, who is without beginning of days or end of life.

17. Verily, verily I say unto you, ye are little children, and ye have not as yet understood how great blessings the Father hath in his own hands and prepared for you;

18. And ye cannot bear all things now, nevertheless, be of good cheer, for I will lead you along: The kingdom is yours and the blessings thereof are yours; and the riches of eternity are yours;

19. And he who receiveth all things with thankfulness shall be made glorious; and the things of this earth shall be added unto him, even an hundred fold, yea, more;

20. Wherefore, do the things which I have commanded you, saith your Redeemer, even the Son Ahman, who prepareth all things before he taketh you;

21. For ye are the church of the first born, and he will take you up in a cloud, and appoint every man his portion.

22. And he that is a faithful and wise steward shall inherit all things. Amen.

SECTION 79

(See historical background, section 78.) In this revelation the Lord calls Jared Carter to preach the gospel. This revelation was received in March 1832, at Hiram, Ohio (History of the Church, vol. 1:255, 257).

1. Verily I say unto you, that it is my will that my servant Jared Carter should go again into the eastern countries, from place to place, and from city to city, in the power of the ordination wherewith he has been ordained, proclaiming glad tidings of great joy, even the everlasting gospel;

2. And I will send upon him the Comforter, which shall teach him the truth and the way whither he shall go;

3. And inasmuch as he is faithful, I will crown him again with sheaves;

4. Wherefore, let your heart be glad, my servant Jared Carter, and fear not, saith your Lord, even Jesus Christ. Amen.

SECTION 80

(See historical background, section 78.) This revelation calls Stephen Burnett and Eden Smith to preach the gospel. They were to testify of the truths they had received. This revelation was received by the Prophet Joseph Smith in March 1832, at Hiram, Ohio (History of the Church, vol. 1:255, 257).

1. Verily, thus saith the Lord, unto you my servant Stephen Burnett, go ye, go ye into the world and preach the gospel to every creature that cometh under the sound of your voice;
2. And inasmuch as you desire a companion, I will give unto you my servant Eden Smith;
3. Wherefore go ye and preach my gospel, whether to the north or to the south, to the east or to the west, it mattereth not, for ye cannot go amiss;
4. Therefore, declare the things which ye have heard and verily believe, and know to be true.
5. Behold, this is the will of him who hath called you, your Redeemer, even Jesus Christ. Amen.

Section 81

(See historical background, section 78.) In March 1832, the Lord revealed to the Prophet Joseph Smith that the First Presidency was to be organized. Jesse Gause was called to serve as a counselor in this presidency. When he failed to fulfill his duties and attend to the responsibilities of this office, he was released and Frederick G. Williams was appointed to take his place. This revelation explaining the duties of a counselor serving in the First Presidency was received in March 1832, at Hiram, Ohio (History of the Church, vol. 1:255, 257–258).

1. Verily, verily I say unto you my servant Frederick G. Williams, listen to the voice of him who speaketh, to the word of the Lord your God, and hearken to the calling wherewith you are called, even to be a High Priest in my church, and a counselor unto my servant Joseph Smith, jun.

2. Unto whom I have given the keys of the kingdom, which belongeth always unto the Presidency of the High Priesthood:

3. Therefore, verily I acknowledge him and will bless him, and also thee, inasmuch as thou art faithful in counsel, in the office which I have appointed unto you, in prayer always vocally and in thy heart, in public and in private, also in thy ministry in proclaiming the gospel in the land of the living, and among thy brethren:

4. And in doing these things thou wilt do the greatest good unto thy fellow beings, and wilt promote the glory of him who is your Lord;

5. Wherefore, be faithful, stand in the office which I have appointed unto you, succor the weak, lift up the hands which hang down, and strengthen the feeble knees;

6. And if thou art faithful unto the end, thou shalt have a crown of immortality and eternal life in the mansions which I have prepared in the house of my Father.

7. Behold, and lo, these are the words of Alpha and Omega, even Jesus Christ. Amen.

Section 82

The Prophet Joseph Smith called a general council of the Church in Jackson County, Missouri, April 26, 1832. He was sustained as the President of the High Priesthood, to which he had previously been sustained at the conference held at Amherst, Ohio, January 25, 1832. After helping Bishop Edward Partridge and Sidney Rigdon solve a problem that had existed between them, the Prophet Joseph Smith received this revelation in the afternoon of the conference April 26, 1832, at Jackson County, Missouri (History of the Church, vol. 1:267).

1. Verily, verily I say unto you, my servants, that inasmuch as you have forgiven one another your trespasses, even so I, the Lord, forgive you;

2. Nevertheless there are those among you who have sinned exceedingly; yea, even all of you have sinned, but verily I say unto you, beware from henceforth, and refrain from sin, lest sore judgments fall upon your heads;

3. For unto whom much is given much is required; and he who sins against the greater light shall receive the greater condemnation.

4. Ye call upon my name for revelations, and I give them unto you; and inasmuch as ye keep not my sayings, which I give unto you, ye become transgressors, and justice and judgment are the penalty which is affixed unto my law;

5. Therefore, what I say unto one I say unto all, Watch, for the adversary spreadeth his dominions and darkness reigneth;

6. And the anger of God kindleth against the inhabitants of the earth; and none doeth good, for all have gone out of the way.

7. And now, verily I say unto you, I, the Lord, will not lay any sin to your charge; go your ways and sin no more; but unto that soul who sinneth shall the former sins return, saith the Lord your God.

8. And again, I say unto you, I give unto you a new commandment, that you may understand my will concerning you.

9. Or, in other words, I give unto you directions how you may act before me, that it may turn to you for your salvation.

10. I, the Lord, am bound when ye do what I say, but when ye do not what I say, ye have no promise.

11. Therefore, verily I say unto you, that it is expedient for my servant Alam, and Ahashdah, (Newel K. Whitney,) Mahalaleel, and Pelagoram, (Sidney Rigdon,) and my servant Gazelam, (Joseph Smith,) and Horah, and Olihah, (Oliver Cowdery,) and Shalemanasseh, and Mahemson, (Martin Harris,) to be bound together by a bond and covenant that cannot be broken by transgression, (except judgment shall immediately follow,) in your several stewardships,

12. To manage the affairs of the poor, and all things pertaining to the bishopric both in the land of Zion and in the land of Shinehah, (Kirtland,)

13. For I have consecrated the land of Shinehah, (Kirtland,) in mine own due time for the benefit of the saints of the Most High, and for a Stake to Zion.

14. For Zion must increase in beauty, and in holiness; her borders must be enlarged; her Stakes must be strengthened; yea, verily I say unto you: Zion must arise and put on her beautiful garments.

15. Therefore, I give unto you this commandment, that ye bind yourselves by this covenant, and it shall be done according to the laws of the Lord.

16. Behold, here is wisdom also in me for your good.

17. And you are to be equal, or in other words, you are to have equal claims on the properties, for the benefit of managing the concerns of your stewardships, every man according to his wants and his needs, inasmuch as his wants are just;

18. And all this for the benefit of the church of the living God, that every man may improve upon his talent, that every man may gain other talents, yea, even an hundred fold, to be cast into the Lord's storehouse, to become the common property of the whole church.

19. Every man seeking the interest of his neighbor, and doing all things with an eye single to the glory of God.

20. This order I have appointed to be an everlasting order unto you, and unto your successors, inasmuch as you sin not;

21. And the soul that sins against this covenant, and hardeneth his heart against it, shall be dealt with according to the laws of my church, and shall be delivered over to the buffetings of Satan until the day of redemption.

22. And now, verily I say unto you, and this is wisdom, make unto yourselves friends with the mammon of unrighteousness, and they will not destroy you.

23. Leave judgment alone with me, for it is mine and I will repay. Peace be with you; my blessings continue with you,

24. For even yet the kingdom is yours, and shall be for ever, if you fall not from your steadfastness. Even so. Amen.

Section 83

After the conference which was held in Jackson County, Missouri, April 26, 1832 (see historical background, section 82), the Prophet Joseph Smith visited members of the Church in the surrounding areas west of Independence, Missouri. On April 30, he returned to Independence and received this revelation (History of the Church, vol. 1:269).

1. Verily, thus saith the Lord, in addition to the laws of the church concerning women and children, those who belong to the church, who have lost their husbands or fathers.
2. Women have claim on their husbands for their maintenance, until their husbands are taken, and if they are not found transgressors they shall have fellowship in the church;
3. And if they are not faithful, they shall not have fellowship in the church; yet they may remain upon their inheritances according to the laws of the land.
4. All children have claim upon their parents for their maintenance until they are of age.
5. And after that they have claim upon the church, or in other words upon the Lord's storehouse, if their parents have not wherewith to give them inheritances.
6. And the storehouse shall be kept by the consecrations of the church, and widows and orphans shall be provided for, as also the poor. Amen.

THE PROPHET JOSEPH SMITH AND ORSON PRATT AS MISSIONARIES

Section 84

In September 1832, the Elders who had been serving missions in the eastern states, began to return to Kirtland, Ohio, and report their stewardship. During these sessions of rejoicing together, the Prophet Joseph Smith received this revelation on the priesthood, September 22 and 23, 1832, at Kirtland, Ohio (History of the Church, vol. 1:286–287).

1. A revelation of Jesus Christ unto his servant Joseph Smith, jun., and six elders, as they united their hearts and lifted their voices on high.
2. Yea, the word of the Lord concerning his church, established in the last days for the restoration of his people, as he has spoken by the mouth of his prophets, and for the gathering of his saints to stand upon Mount Zion, which shall be the city of New Jerusalem,
3. Which city shall be built, beginning at the temple lot, which is appointed by the finger of the Lord, in the western boundaries of the state of Missouri, and dedicated by the hand of Joseph Smith, jun., and others with whom the Lord was well pleased.
4. Verily this is the word of the Lord, that the city New Jerusalem shall be built by the gathering of the saints beginning at this place, even the place of the temple, which temple shall be reared in this generation;
5. For verily, this generation shall not all pass away until an house shall be built unto the Lord, and a cloud shall rest upon it, which cloud shall be even the glory of the Lord, which shall fill the house.
6. And the sons of Moses, according to the Holy Priesthood which he received under the hand of his father-in-law, Jethro;
7. And Jethro received it under the hand of Caleb;
8. And Caleb received it under the hand of Elihu;
9. And Elihu under the hand of Jeremy;
10. And Jeremy under the hand of Gad;
11. And Gad under the hand of Esaias;
12. And Esaias received it under the hand of God.
13. Esaias also lived in the days of Abraham, and was blessed of him—
14. Which Abraham received the Priesthood from Melchisedek, who received it through the lineage of his fathers, even till Noah;
15. And from Noah till Enoch, through the lineage of their fathers;

16. And from Enoch to Abel, who was slain by the conspiracy of his brother, who received the Priesthood by the commandments of God, by the hand of his father Adam, who was the first man—
17. Which Priesthood continueth in the church of God in all generations, and is without beginning of days or end of years.
18. And the Lord confirmed a priesthood also upon Aaron and his seed, throughout all their generations—which priesthood also continueth and abideth forever with the Priesthood which is after the holiest order of God.
19. And this greater Priesthood administereth the gospel and holdeth the key of the mysteries of the kingdom even the key of the knowledge of God;
20. Therefore, in the ordinances thereof, the power of godliness is manifest;
21. And without the ordinances thereof, and the authority of the priesthood, the power of godliness is not manifest unto men in the flesh;
22. For without this no man can see the face of God, even the Father, and live.
23. Now this Moses plainly taught to the children of Israel in the wilderness, and sought diligently to sanctify his people that they might behold the face of God;
24. But they hardened their hearts and could not endure his presence; therefore the Lord in his wrath (for his anger was kindled against them) swore that they should not enter into his rest while in the wilderness, which rest is the fulness of his glory.
25. Therefore he took Moses out of their midst, and the Holy Priesthood also;
26. And the lesser priesthood continued, which priesthood holdeth the key of the ministering of angels and the preparatory gospel;
27. Which gospel is the gospel of repentance and of baptism, and the remission of sins, and the law of carnal commandments, which the Lord in his wrath, caused to continue with the house of Aaron among the children of Israel until John, whom God raised up, being filled with the Holy Ghost from his mother's womb;
28. For he was baptized while he was yet in his childhood, and was ordained by the angel of God at the time he was eight days old unto this power, to overthrow the kingdom of the Jews, and to make straight the way of the Lord before the face of his people, to prepare them for the coming of the Lord, in whose hand is given all power.
29. And again, the offices of elder and bishop are necessary appendages belonging unto the High Priesthood.
30. And again, the offices of teacher and deacon are necessary appendages belonging to the lesser priesthood, which priesthood was confirmed upon Aaron and his sons.
31. Therefore, as I said concerning the sons of Moses—for the sons of Moses, and also the sons of Aaron shall offer an acceptable offering and sacrifice in the house of the Lord, which house shall be built unto the Lord in this generation, upon the consecrated spot as I have appointed,
32. And the sons of Moses and of Aaron shall be filled with the glory of the Lord, upon Mount Zion in the Lord's house, whose sons are ye; and also many whom I have called and sent forth to build up my church;
33. For whoso is faithful unto the obtaining these two priesthoods of which I have spoken, and the magnifying their calling, are sanctified by the Spirit unto the renewing of their bodies;
34. They become the sons of Moses and of Aaron and the seed of Abraham, and the church and kingdom, and the elect of God;
35. And also all they who receive this priesthood receive me, saith the Lord;
36. For he that receiveth my servants receiveth me;
37. And he that receiveth me receiveth my Father;
38. And he that receiveth my Father receiveth my Father's kingdom; therefore all that my Father hath shall be given unto him;

39. And this is according to the oath and covenant which belongeth to the Priesthood.

40. Therefore, all those who receive the Priesthood, receive this oath and covenant of my Father, which he cannot break, neither can it be moved;

41. But whoso breaketh this covenant after he hath received it, and altogether turneth therefrom, shall not have forgiveness of sins in this world nor in the world to come.

42. And all those who come not unto this Priesthood which ye have received, which I now confirm upon you who are present this day, by mine own voice out of the heavens, and even I have given the heavenly hosts and mine angels charge concerning you.

43. And I now give unto you a commandment to beware concerning yourselves, to give diligent heed to the words of eternal life:

44. For you shall live by every word that proceedeth forth from the mouth of God.

45. For the word of the Lord is truth, and whatsoever is truth is light, and whatsoever is light is Spirit, even the Spirit of Jesus Christ;

46. And the Spirit giveth light to every man that cometh into the world; and the Spirit enlighteneth every man through the world, that hearkeneth to the voice of the Spirit;

47. And every one that hearkeneth to the voice of the Spirit cometh unto God, even the Father;

48. And the Father teacheth him of the covenant which he has renewed and confirmed upon you, which is confirmed upon you for your sakes, and not for your sakes only, but for the sake of the whole world;

49. And the whole world lieth in sin, and groaneth under darkness and under the bondage of sin;

50. And by this you may know they are under the bondage of sin, because they come not unto me.

51. For whoso cometh not unto me is under the bondage of sin;

52. And whoso receiveth not my voice is not acquainted with my voice, and is not of me;

53. And by this you may know the righteous from the wicked, and that the whole world groaneth under sin and darkness even now.

54. And your minds in times past have been darkened because of unbelief, and because you have treated lightly the things you have received,

55. Which vanity and unbelief have brought the whole church under condemnation.

56. And this condemnation resteth upon the children of Zion, even all:

57. And they shall remain under this condemnation until they repent and remember the new covenant, even the Book of Mormon and the former commandments which I have given them, not only to say, but to do according to that which I have written,

58. That they may bring forth fruit meet for their Father's kingdom, otherwise there remaineth a scourge and judgment to be poured out upon the children of Zion:

59. For shall the children of the kingdom pollute my holy land? Verily, I say unto you, Nay.

60. Verily, verily, I say unto you who now hear my words, which are my voice, blessed are ye inasmuch as you receive these things;

61. For I will forgive you of your sins with this commandment, that you remain steadfast in your minds in solemnity and the spirit of prayer, in bearing testimony to all the world of those things which are communicated unto you.

62. Therefore go ye into all the world, and unto whatsoever place ye cannot go ye shall send, that the testimony may go from you into all the world unto every creature.

63. And as I said unto mine apostles, even so I say unto you, for you are mine apostles, even God's High Priests; ye are they whom my Father hath given me—ye are my friends;

64. Therefore, as I said unto mine apostles I say unto you again, that every soul who believeth on your words, and is baptized by water for the remission of sins, shall receive the Holy Ghost;

65. And these signs shall follow them that believe.

66. In my name they shall do many wonderful works;

67. In my name they shall cast out devils;

68. In my name they shall heal the sick;

69. In my name they shall open the eyes of the blind, and unstop the ears of the deaf;

70. And the tongue of the dumb shall speak;

71. And if any man shall administer poison unto them it shall not hurt them;

72. And the poison of a serpent shall not have power to harm them.

73. But a commandment I give unto them, that they shall not boast themselves of these things, neither speak them before the world, for these things are given unto you for your profit and for salvation.

74. Verily, verily, I say unto you they who believe not on your words, and are not baptized in water, in my name, for the remission of their sins, that they may receive the Holy Ghost, shall be damned, and shall not come into my Father's kingdom, where my Father and I am.

75. And this revelation unto you, and commandment, is in force from this very hour upon all the world, and the gospel is unto all who have not received it.

76. But, verily, I say unto all those to whom the kingdom has been given, from you it must be preached unto them, that they shall repent of their former evil works, for they are to be upbraided for their evil hearts of unbelief; and your brethren in Zion for their rebellion against you at the time I sent you.

77. And again I say unto you, my friends, (for from henceforth I shall call you friends,) it is expedient that I give unto you this commandment, that ye become even as my friends in days when I was with them traveling to preach the gospel in my power,

78. For I suffered them not to have purse or scrip, neither two coats;

79. Behold I send you out to prove the world, and the laborer is worthy of his hire.

80. And any man that shall go and preach this gospel of the kingdom, and fail not to continue faithful in all things shall not be weary in mind, neither darkened, neither in body, limb, nor joint: and an hair of his head shall not fall to the ground unnoticed. And they shall not go hungry, neither athirst.

81. Therefore, take no thought for the morrow, for what ye shall eat, or what ye shall drink, or wherewithal ye shall be clothed;

82. For consider the lilies of the field, how they grow, they toil not, neither do they spin; and the kingdoms of the world, in all their glory, are not arrayed like one of these;

83. For your Father who art in heaven, knoweth that you have need of all these things.

84. Therefore, let the morrow take thought for the things of itself.

85. Neither take ye thought beforehand what ye shall say, but treasure up in your minds continually the words of life, and it shall be given you in the very hour that portion that shall be meted unto every man.

86. Therefore let no man among you, (for this commandment is unto all the faithful who are called of God in the church unto the ministry,) from this hour take purse or scrip, that goeth forth to proclaim this gospel of the kingdom.

87. Behold, I send you out to reprove the world of all their unrighteous deeds, and to teach them of a judgment which is to come.

88. And whoso receiveth you, there I will be also, for I will go before your face: I will be on your

right hand and on your left, and my Spirit shall be in your hearts, and mine angels round about you, to bear you up.

89. Whoso receiveth you receiveth me; and the same will feed you, and clothe you, and give you money.

90. And he who feeds you, or clothes you, or gives you money, shall in nowise lose his reward:

91. And he that doeth not these things is not my disciple; by this you may know my disciples.

92. He that receiveth you not, go away from him alone by yourselves, and cleanse your feet even with water, pure water, whether in heat or in cold, and bear testimony of it unto your Father which is in heaven, and return not again unto that man.

93. And in whatsoever village or city ye enter, do likewise.

94. Nevertheless, search diligently and spare not; and wo unto that house, or that village or city that rejecteth you, or your words, or your testimony concerning me.

95. Wo, I say again, unto that house, or that village or city that rejecteth you, or your words, or your testimony of me;

96. For I, the Almighty, have laid my hands upon the nations, to scourge them for their wickedness:

97. And plagues shall go forth, and they shall not be taken from the earth until I have completed my work which shall be cut short in righteousness,

98. Until all shall know me, who remain, even from the least unto the greatest, and shall be filled with the knowledge of the Lord, and shall see eye to eye, and shall lift up their voice, and with the voice together sing this new song, saying—

99. The Lord hath brought again Zion
     The Lord hath redeemed his people, Israel,
     According to the election of grace,
     Which was brought to pass by the faith
     And covenant of their fathers.

100. The Lord hath redeemed his people,
     And Satan is bound and time is no longer:
     The Lord hath gathered all things in one:
     The Lord hath brought down Zion from above.
     The Lord hath brought up Zion from beneath.

101. The earth hath travailed and brought forth her strength:
     And truth is established in her bowels:
     And the heavens have smiled upon her:
     And she is clothed with the glory of her God:
     For he stands in the midst of his people:

102. Glory, and honor, and power, and might,
     Be ascribed to our God; for he is full of mercy,
     Justice, grace and truth, and peace,
     Forever and ever, Amen.

103. And again, verily, verily, I say unto you, it is expedient that every man who goes forth to proclaim mine everlasting gospel, that inasmuch as they have families and receive money by gift, that they should send it unto them or make use of it for their benefit, as the Lord shall direct them, for thus it seemeth me good.

104. And let all those who have not families, who receive monies, send it up unto the Bishop in Zion, or unto the Bishop in Ohio, that it may be consecrated for the bringing forth of the revelations and the printing thereof, and for establishing Zion.

105. And if any man shall give unto any of you a coat, or a suit, take the old and cast it unto the poor, and go your way rejoicing.

106. And if any man among you be strong in the Spirit, let him take with him him that is weak, that he may be edified in all meekness, that he may become strong also.

107. Therefore, take with you those who are ordained unto the lesser priesthood, and send them before you to make appointments, and to prepare the way, and to fill appointments that you yourselves are not able to fill.

108. Behold, this is the way that mine apostles, in ancient days, built up my church unto me.

109. Therefore, let every man stand in his own office, and labor in his own calling; and let not the head say unto the feet, it hath no need of the feet, for without the feet how shall the body be able to stand?

110. Also the body hath need of every member, that all may be edified together, that the system may be kept perfect.

111. And behold the High Priests should travel, and also the elders, and also the lesser priests; but the deacons and teachers should be appointed to watch over the church, to be standing ministers unto the church.

112. And the bishop, Newel K. Whitney, also should travel round about and among all the churches, searching after the poor to administer to their wants by humbling the rich and the proud;

113. He should also employ an agent to take charge and to do his secular business as he shall direct;

114. Nevertheless, let the bishop go unto the city of New York, also to the city of Albany, and also to the city of Boston, and warn the people of those cities with the sound of the gospel, with a loud voice, of the desolation and utter abolishment which await them if they do reject these things;

115. For if they do reject these things the hour of their judgment is nigh, and their house shall be left unto them desolate.

116. Let him trust in me and he shall not be confounded; and an hair of his head shall not fall to the ground unnoticed.

117. And verily I say unto you, the rest of my servants, go ye forth as your circumstances shall permit, in your several callings unto the great and notable cities and villages, reproving the world in righteousness of all their unrighteous and ungodly deeds, setting forth clearly and understandingly the desolation of abomination in the last days;

118. For, with you saith the Lord Almighty, I will rend their kingdoms: I will not only shake the earth, but the starry heavens shall tremble;

119. For I, the Lord, have put forth my hand to exert the powers of heaven; ye cannot see it now, yet a little while and ye shall see it, and know that I am, and that I will come and reign with my people.

120. I am Alpha and Omega, the beginning and the end. Amen.

Section 85

William W. Phelps, who was living in Independence, Missouri, addressed a letter to the Prophet Joseph Smith expressing concerns that the members of the Church who had gathered to Zion (Jackson County, Missouri) were not receiving their inheritance according to previous directions given to Bishop Edward Partridge. This section is part of a letter in which the Prophet Joseph Smith responded to the concerns of Brother Phelps, written November 27, 1832, at Kirtland, Ohio (History of the Church, vol. 1:297–299).

1. It is the duty of the Lord's clerk, whom he has appointed, to keep a history, and a General Church Record of all things that transpire in Zion, and of all those who consecrate properties, and receive inheritances legally from the bishop;
2. And also their manner of life, their faith, and works; and also of the apostates who apostatize after receiving their inheritances.
3. It is contrary to the will and commandment of God, that those who receive not their inheritance by consecration, agreeable to his law, which he has given, that he may tithe his people, to prepare them against the day of vengeance and burning, should have their names enrolled with the people of God;
4. Neither is their genealogy to be kept, or to be had where it may be found on any of the records or history of the church;
5. Their names shall not be found, neither the names of the fathers, nor the names of the children written in the book of the law of God, saith the Lord of Hosts.
6. Yea, thus saith the still small voice, which whispereth through and pierceth all things, and often times it maketh my bones to quake while it maketh manifest, saying:
7. And it shall come to pass that I, the Lord God, will send one mighty and strong, holding the scepter of power in his hand, clothed with light for a covering, whose mouth shall utter words, eternal words; while his bowels shall be a fountain of truth, to set in order the house of God, and to arrange by lot the inheritances of the saints, whose names are found, and the names of their fathers, and of their children, enrolled in the book of the law of God:
8. While that man, who was called of God and appointed, that putteth forth his hand to steady the ark of God, shall fall by the shaft of death, like as a tree that is smitten by the vivid shaft of lightning;
9. And all they who are not found written in the book of remembrance shall find none inheritance

in that day, but they shall be cut asunder, and their portion shall be appointed them among unbelievers, where are wailing and gnashing of teeth.

10. These things I say not of myself; therefore, as the Lord speaketh, he will also fulfil.

11. And they who are of the High Priesthood, whose names are not found written in the book of the law, or that are found to have apostatized, or to have been cut off from the church; as well as the lesser priesthood, or the members, in that day, shall not find an inheritance among the saints of the Most High;

12. Therefore it shall be done unto them as unto the children of the priest, as will be found recorded in the second chapter and sixty-first and second verses of Ezra.

Section 86

This revelation was received by the Prophet Joseph Smith, December 6, 1832, at Kirtland, Ohio, explaining the parable of the wheat and tares (see Mathew:13:24–30, 36–43), (History of the Church, vol. 1:300).

1. Verily, thus saith the Lord unto you my servants, concerning the parable of the wheat and of the tares.

2. Behold, verily I say, the field was the world, and the apostles were the sowers of the seed;

3. And after they have fallen asleep the great persecutor of the church, the apostate, the whore, even Babylon, that maketh all nations to drink of her cup, in whose hearts the enemy, even Satan, sitteth to reign, behold he soweth the tares, wherefore the tares choke the wheat and drive the church into the wilderness.

4. But behold, in the last days, even now while the Lord is beginning to bring forth the word, and the blade is springing up and is yet tender.

5. Behold, verily I say unto you, the angels are crying unto the Lord day and night, who are ready and waiting to be sent forth to reap down the fields;

6. But the Lord saith unto them, pluck not up the tares while the blade is yet tender, (for verily your faith is weak,) lest you destroy the wheat also.

7. Therefore, let the wheat and the tares grow together until the harvest is fully ripe, then ye shall first gather out the wheat from among the tares, and after the gathering of the wheat, behold and lo! the tares are bound in bundles, and the field remaineth to be burned.

8. Therefore, thus saith the Lord unto you, with whom the Priesthood hath continued through the lineage of your fathers,

9. For ye are lawful heirs, according to the flesh, and have been hid from the world with Christ in God;

10. Therefore your life and the priesthood haveth remained, and must needs remain through you and your lineage, until the restoration of all things spoken by the mouths of all the holy prophets since the world began.

11. Therefore, blessed are ye if ye continue in my goodness, a light unto the Gentiles, and through this Priesthood, a savior unto my people Israel. The Lord hath said it. Amen.

SECTION 87

Reflecting upon the unrest of many nations of the world and the turmoil among various states in the United States of America, the Prophet Joseph Smith received this revelation and prophecy on war, December 25, 1832 (History of the Church, vol. 1:301).

1. Verily, thus saith the Lord, concerning the wars that will shortly come to pass, beginning at the rebellion of South Carolina, which will eventually terminate in the death and misery of many souls.
2. The days will come that war will be poured out upon all nations, beginning at that place.
3. For behold, the Southern States shall be divided against the Northern States, and the Southern States will call on other nations, even the nation of Great Britain, as it is called, and they shall also call upon other nations, in order to defend themselves against other nations; and then war shall be poured out upon all nations.
4. And it shall come to pass, after many days, slaves shall rise up against their masters, who shall be marshalled and disciplined for war:
5. And it shall come to pass also, that the remnants who are left of the land will marshall themselves, and shall become exceedingly angry, and shall vex the Gentiles with a sore vexation;
6. And thus, with the sword, and by bloodshed, the inhabitants of the earth shall mourn; and with famine, and plague, and earthquake, and the thunder of heaven, and the fierce and vivid lightning also, shall the inhabitants of the earth be made to feel the wrath, and indignation and chastening hand of an Almighty God, until the consumption decreed, hath made a full end of all nations;
7. That the cry of the saints, and of the blood of the saints, shall cease to come up into the ears of the Lord of Sabaoth, from the earth, to be avenged of their enemies.
8. Wherefore, stand ye in holy places, and be not moved, until the day of the Lord come; for behold it cometh quickly, saith the Lord. Amen.

Section 88

This revelation was received two days after the reception of the revelation and prophecy on war (section 87). The Prophet Joseph Smith sent a copy of this revelation to William W. Phelps, editor of the Evening and Morning Star *in Jackson County, Missouri, in which he said, "I send you the 'Olive Leaf' which we have plucked from the Tree of Paradise, the Lord's message of peace to us" (History of the Church,* vol. *1:316). This revelation was received December 27, 1832, at Kirtland, Ohio (History of the Church,* vol. *1:302).*

1. Verily, thus saith the Lord unto you who have assembled yourselves together to receive his will concerning you.

2. Behold, this is pleasing unto your Lord, and the angels rejoice over you; the alms of your prayers have come up into the ears of the Lord of Sabaoth, and are recorded in the book of the names of the sanctified: even them of the celestial world.

3. Wherefore, I now send upon you another Comforter, even upon you my friends, that it may abide in your hearts, even the Holy Spirit of promise; which other Comforter is the same that I promised unto my disciples, as is recorded in the testimony of John.

4. This Comforter is the promise which I give unto you of eternal life; even the glory of the celestial kingdom:

5. Which glory is that of the church of the first born, even of God, the holiest of all, through Jesus Christ his Son.

6. He that ascended up on high, as also he descended below all things; in that he comprehended all things, that he might be in all and through all things, the light of truth;

7. Which truth shineth. This is the light of Christ. As also he is in the sun, and the light of the sun, and the power thereof by which it was made.

8. As also he is in the moon and is the light of the moon, and the power thereof by which it was made.

9. As also the light of the stars, and the power thereof by which they were made.

10. And the earth also, and the power thereof; even the earth upon which you stand.

11. And the light which now shineth, which giveth you light, is through him who enlighteneth your eyes, which is the same light that quickeneth your understandings;

12. Which light proceedeth forth from the presence of God to fill the immensity of space.

13. The light which is in all things; which giveth life to all things: which is the law by which all

things are governed: even the power of God who sitteth upon his throne, who is in the bosom of eternity, who is in the midst of all things.

14. Now, verily I say unto you, that through the redemption which is made for you is brought to pass the resurrection from the dead.

15. And the spirit and the body is the soul of man.

16. And the resurrection from the dead is the redemption of the soul;

17. And the redemption of the soul is through him that quickeneth all things, in whose bosom it is decreed that the poor and the meek of the earth shall inherit it.

18. Therefore it must needs be sanctified from all unrighteousness, that it may be prepared for the celestial glory;

19. For after it hath filled the measure of its creation, it shall be crowned with glory, even with the presence of God the Father;

20. That bodies who are of the celestial kingdom may possess it for ever and ever; for, for this intent was it made and created, and for this intent are they sanctified.

21. And they who are not sanctified through the law which I have given unto you, even the law of Christ, must inherit another kingdom, even that of a terrestrial kingdom, or that of a telestial kingdom.

22. For he who is not able to abide the law of a celestial kingdom, cannot abide a celestial glory.

23. And he who cannot abide the law of a terrestrial kingdom, cannot abide a terrestrial glory:

24. And he who cannot abide the law of a telestial kingdom, cannot abide a telestial glory; therefore he is not meet for a kingdom of glory. Therefore he must abide a kingdom which is not a kingdom of glory.

25. And again, verily I say unto you, the earth abideth the law of a celestial kingdom, for it filleth the measure of its creation, and transgresseth not the law.

26. Wherefore it shall be sanctified; yea, notwithstanding it shall die, it shall be quickened again, and shall abide the power by which it is quickened, and the righteous shall inherit it:

27. For notwithstanding they die, they also shall rise again a spiritual body:

28. They who are of a celestial spirit shall receive the same body which was a natural body; even ye shall receive your bodies, and your glory shall be that glory by which your bodies are quickened.

29. Ye who are quickened by a portion of the celestial glory shall then receive of the same, even a fulness;

30. And they who are quickened by a portion of the terrestrial glory, shall then receive of the same, even a fulness:

31. And also they who are quickened by a portion of the telestial glory shall then receive of the same, even a fulness;

32. And they who remain shall also be quickened; nevertheless they shall return again to their own place, to enjoy that which they are willing to receive, because they were not willing to enjoy that which they might have received.

33. For what doth it profit a man if a gift is bestowed upon him, and he receiveth not the gift? Behold, he rejoices not in that which is given unto him, neither rejoices in him who is the giver of the gift.

34. And again, verily I say unto you, that which is governed by law is also preserved by law, and perfected and sanctified by the same.

35. That which breaketh a law, and abideth not by law, but seeketh to become a law unto itself, and willeth to abide in sin, and altogether abideth in sin, cannot be sanctified by law, neither by mercy, justice, nor judgment. Therefore they must remain filthy still.

36. All kingdoms have a law given:

37. And there are many kingdoms; for there is no space in the which there is no kingdom; and

there is no kingdom in which there is no space, either a greater or a lesser kingdom.

38. And unto every kingdom is given a law; and unto every law there are certain bounds also and conditions.

39. All beings who abide not in those conditions are not justified;

40. For intelligence cleaveth unto intelligence; wisdom receiveth wisdom; truth embraceth truth; virtue loveth virtue; light cleaveth unto light; mercy hath compassion on mercy, and claimeth her own; justice continueth its course, and claimeth its own; judgment goeth before the face of him who sitteth upon the throne, and governeth and executeth all things;

41. He comprehendeth all things, and all things are before him, and all things are round about him: and he is above all things, and in all things, and is through all things, and is round about all things; and all things are by him, and of him, even God, for ever and ever.

42. And again, verily I say unto you, he hath given a law unto all things by which they move in their times and their seasons;

43. And their courses are fixed, even the courses of the heavens and the earth, which comprehend the earth and all the planets;

44. And they give light to each other in their times and in their seasons, in their minutes, in their hours, in their days, in their weeks, in their months, in their years: all these are one year with God, but not with man.

45. The earth rolls upon her wings, and the sun giveth his light by day, and the moon giveth her light by night, and the stars also giveth their light, as they roll upon their wings in their glory, in the midst of the power of God.

46. Unto what shall I liken these kingdoms, that ye may understand?

47. Behold, all these are kingdoms, and any man who hath seen any or the least of these, hath seen God moving in his majesty and power.

48. I say unto you, he hath seen him; nevertheless, he who came unto his own was not comprehended.

49. The light shineth in darkness, and the darkness comprehendeth it not; nevertheless, the day shall come when you shall comprehend even God; being quickened in him and by him.

50. Then shall ye know that ye have seen me, that I am, and that I am the true light that is in you, and that you are in me, otherwise ye could not abound.

51. Behold, I will liken these kingdoms unto a man having a field, and he sent forth his servants into the field to dig in the field;

52. And he said unto the first, go ye and labor in the field, and in the first hour I will come unto you, and ye shall behold the joy of my countenance;

53. And he said unto the second, go ye also into the field, and in the second hour I will visit you with the joy of my countenance;

54. And also unto the third saying, I will visit you;

55. And unto the fourth, and so on unto the twelfth.

56. And the lord of the field went unto the first in the first hour, and tarried with him all that hour, and he was made glad with the light of the countenance of his lord;

57. And then he withdrew from the first that he might visit the second also, and the third, and the fourth, and so on unto the twelfth;

58. And thus they all received the light of the countenance of their lord; every man in his hour, and in his time, and in his season;

59. Beginning at the first, and so on unto the last, and from the last unto the first, and from the first unto the last;

60. Every man in his own order, until his hour was finished, even according as his lord had commanded him, that his lord might be glorified in him, and he in him, that they all might be glorified.

61. Therefore, unto this parable I will liken all these kingdoms, and the inhabitants thereof; every kingdom in its hour, and in its time, and in its season; even according to the decree which God hath made.

62. And again, verily I say unto you, my friends, I leave these sayings with you, to ponder in your hearts, with this commandment which I give unto you, that ye shall call upon me while I am near;

63. Draw near unto me and I will draw near unto you: seek me diligently and ye shall find me; ask and ye shall receive; knock and it shall be opened unto you;

64. Whatsoever ye ask the Father in my name it shall be given unto you, that is expedient for you;

65. And if ye ask anything that is not expedient for you, it shall turn unto your condemnation.

66. Behold, that which you hear is as the voice of one crying in the wilderness—in the wilderness, because you cannot see him—my voice, because my voice is Spirit; my Spirit is truth; truth abideth and hath no end; and if it be in you it shall abound.

67. And if your eye be single to my glory, your whole bodies shall be filled with light, and there shall be no darkness in you, and that body which is filled with light comprehendeth all things.

68. Therefore sanctify yourselves that your minds become single to God, and the days will come that you shall see him; for he will unvail his face unto you, and it shall be in his own time, and in his own way, and according to his own will.

69. Remember the great and last promise which I have made unto you; cast away your idle thoughts and your excess of laughter far from you;

70. Tarry ye, tarry ye in this place, and call a solemn assembly even of those who are the first laborers in this last kingdom;

71. And let those whom they have warned in their traveling, call on the Lord, and ponder the warning in their hearts which they have received for a little season.

72. Behold, and lo! I will take care of your flocks, and will raise up elders and send unto them.

73. Behold, I will hasten my work in its time;

74. And I give unto you, who are the first laborers in this last kingdom, a commandment that you assemble yourselves together, and organize yourselves, and prepare yourselves, and sanctify yourselves; yea, purify your hearts, and cleanse your hands and your feet before me, that I may make you clean;

75. That I may testify unto your Father, and your God, and my God, that you are clean from the blood of this wicked generation: that I may fulfil this promise, this great and last promise, which I have made unto you, when I will.

76. Also, I give unto you a commandment, that ye shall continue in prayer and fasting from this time forth.

77. And I give unto you a commandment, that you shall teach one another the doctrine of the kingdom;

78. Teach ye diligently and my grace shall attend you, that you may be instructed more perfectly in theory, in principle, in doctrine, in the law of the gospel, in all things that pertain unto the kingdom of God, that are expedient for you to understand;

79. Of things both in heaven and in the earth, and under the earth; things which have been, things which are, things which must shortly come to pass; things which are at home, things which are abroad; the wars and the perplexities of the nations, and the judgments which are on the land, and a knowledge also of countries and of kingdoms,

80. That ye may be prepared in all things when I shall send you again to magnify the calling whereunto I have called you, and the mission with which I have commissioned you.

81. Behold, I sent you out to testify and warn the people, and it becometh every man who hath been warned, to warn his neighbor.

82. Therefore, they are left without excuse, and their sins are upon their own heads.

83. He that seeketh me early shall find me, and shall not be forsaken.

84. Therefore, tarry ye, and labor diligently, that you may be perfected in your ministry to go forth among the Gentiles for the last time, as many as the mouth of the Lord shall name, to bind up the law and seal up the testimony, and to prepare the saints for the hour of judgment which is to come;

85. That their souls may escape the wrath of God, the desolation of abomination which awaits the wicked, both in this world and in the world to come. Verily, I say unto you, let those who are not the first elders continue in the vineyard until the mouth of the Lord shall call them, for their time is not yet come; their garments are not clean from the blood of this generation.

86. Abide ye in the liberty wherewith ye are made free; entangle not yourselves in sin, but let your hands be clean, until the Lord comes;

87. For not many days hence and the earth shall tremble and reel to and fro as a drunken man, and the sun shall hide his face, and shall refuse to give light, and the moon shall be bathed in blood, and the stars shall become exceeding angry, and shall cast themselves down as a fig that falleth from off a fig tree.

88. And after your testimony cometh wrath and indignation upon the people;

89. For after your testimony cometh the testimony of earthquakes, that shall cause groanings in the midst of her, and men shall fall upon the ground, and shall not be able to stand.

90. And also cometh the testimony of the voice of thunderings, and the voice of lightnings, and the voice of tempests, and the voice of the waves of the sea, heaving themselves beyond their bounds.

91. And all things shall be in commotion; and surely, men's hearts shall fail them; for fear shall come upon all people;

92. And angels shall fly through the midst of heaven, crying with a loud voice, sounding the trump of God, saying, Prepare ye, prepare ye, O inhabitants of the earth; for the judgment of our God is come: behold, and lo! the Bridegroom cometh, go ye out to meet him.

93. And immediately there shall appear a great sign in heaven, and all people shall see it together.

94. And another angel shall sound his trump, saying, That great church, the mother of abominations, that made all nations drink of the wine of the wrath of her fornication, that persecuteth the saints of God, that shed their blood; she who sitteth upon many waters, and upon the islands of the sea; behold, she is the tares of the earth, she is bound in bundles, her bands are made strong, no man can loose them; therefore, she is ready to be burned. And he shall sound his trump both long and loud, and all nations shall hear it.

95. And there shall be silence in heaven for the space of half an hour, and immediately after shall the curtain of heaven be unfolded, as a scroll is unfolded after it is rolled up, and the face of the Lord shall be unvailed;

96. And the saints that are upon the earth, who are alive, shall be quickened, and be caught up to meet him.

97. And they who have slept in their graves shall come forth; for their graves shall be opened, and they also shall be caught up to meet him in the midst of the pillar of heaven:

98. They are Christ's, the first fruits, they who shall descend with him first, and they who are on the earth and in their graves, who are first caught up to meet him: and all this by the voice of the sounding of the trump of the angel of God.

99. And after this another angel shall sound, which is the second trump; and then cometh the redemption of those who are Christ's at his coming; who have received their part in that prison which is prepared for them, that they might

receive the gospel, and be judged according to men in the flesh.

100. And again, another trump shall sound, which is the third trump; and then come the spirits of men who are to be judged, and are found under condemnation:

101. And these are the rest of the dead, and they live not again until the thousand years are ended, neither again, until the end of the earth.

102. And another trump shall sound, which is the fourth trump, saying, There are found among those who are to remain until that great and last day, even the end, who shall remain filthy still.

103. And another trump shall sound, which is the fifth trump, which is the fifth angel who committeth the everlasting gospel, flying through the midst of heaven, unto all nations, kindreds, tongues, and people;

104. And this shall be the sound of his trump, saying, to all people, both in heaven and in earth, and that are under the earth; for every ear shall hear it, and every knee shall bow, and every tongue shall confess, while they hear the sound of the trump, saying, Fear God, and give glory to him who sitteth upon the throne, for ever and ever: for the hour of his judgment is come.

105. And again, another angel shall sound his trump, which is the sixth angel, saying, She is fallen who made all nations drink of the wine of the wrath of her fornication: she is fallen! is fallen!

106. And again, another angel shall sound his trump, which is the seventh angel, saying, It is finished! It is finished! The Lamb of God hath overcome and trodden the wine-press alone, even the wine-press of the fierceness of the wrath of Almighty God;

107. And then shall the angels be crowned with the glory of his might, and the saints shall be filled with his glory, and receive their inheritance and be made equal with him.

108. And then shall the first angel again sound his trump in the ears of all living, and reveal the secret acts of men, and the mighty works of God in the first thousandth year.

109. And then shall the second angel sound his trump, and reveal the secret acts of men, and the thoughts and intents of their hearts, and the mighty works of God in the second thousandth year:

110. And so on, until the seventh angel shall sound his trump: and he shall stand forth upon the land and upon the sea, and swear in the name of him who sitteth upon the throne, that there shall be time no longer; and Satan shall be bound, that old serpent, who is called the devil, and shall not be loosed for the space of a thousand years.

111. And then he shall be loosed for a little season, that he may gather together his armies;

112. And Michael, the seventh angel, even the archangel, shall gather together his armies, even the hosts of heaven.

113. And the devil shall gather together his armies; even the hosts of hell, and shall come up to battle against Michael and his armies:

114. And then cometh the battle of the great God; and the devil and his armies shall be cast away into their own place, that they shall not have power over the saints any more at all;

115. For Michael shall fight their battles, and shall overcome him who seeketh the throne of him who sitteth upon the throne, even the Lamb.

116. This is the glory of God, and the sanctified; and they shall not any more see death.

117. Therefore, verily I say unto you, my friends, call your solemn assembly, as I have commanded you;

118. And as all have not faith, seek ye diligently and teach one another words of wisdom; yea, seek ye out of the best books words of wisdom: seek learning, even by study and also by faith.

119. Organize yourselves, prepare every needful thing, and establish a house, even a house of prayer, a house of fasting, a house of faith, a house of learning, a house of glory, a house of order, a house of God;

120. That your incomings may be in the name of the Lord; that your outgoings may be in the name of the Lord; that all your salutations may be in the name of the Lord, with uplifted hands unto the Most High.

121. Therefore, cease from all your light speeches; from all laughter; from all your lustful desires; from all your pride and light-mindedness, and from all your wicked doings.

122. Appoint among yourselves a teacher, and let not all be spokesmen at once; but let one speak at a time, and let all listen unto his sayings, that when all have spoken, that all may be edified of all, and that every man may have an equal privilege.

123. See that ye love one another; cease to be covetous, learn to impart one to another as the gospel requires;

124. Cease to be idle; cease to be unclean; cease to find fault one with another; cease to sleep longer than is needful; retire to thy bed early, that ye may not be weary; arise early, that your bodies and your minds may be invigorated;

125. And above all things, clothe yourselves with the bond of charity, as with a mantle, which is the bond of perfectness and peace;

126. Pray always, that ye may not faint until I come, behold, and lo, I will come quickly, and receive you unto myself. Amen.

127. And again, the order of the house prepared for the presidency of the school of the prophets, established for their instruction in all things that are expedient for them, even for all the officers of the church, or in other words, those who are called to the ministry in the church, beginning at the High Priests, even down to the deacons:

128. And this shall be the order of the house of the presidency of the school: He that is appointed to be president, or teacher, shall be found standing in his place, in the house which shall be prepared for him.

129. Therefore he shall be first in the house of God, in a place that the congregation in the house may hear his words carefully and distinctly, not with loud speech.

130. And when he cometh into the house of God, (for he should be first in the house, behold, this is beautiful, that he may be an example).

131. Let him offer himself in prayer upon his knees before God, in token or remembrance of the everlasting covenant.

132. And when any shall come in after him, let the teacher arise, and, with uplifted hands to heaven; yea, even directly, salute his brother or brethren with these words:

133. Art thou a brother or brethren? I salute you in the name of the Lord Jesus Christ, in token or remembrance of the everlasting covenant, in which covenant I receive you to fellowship, in a determination that is fixed, immovable, and unchangeable, to be your friend and brother through the grace of God in the bonds of love, to walk in all the commandments of God blameless, in thanksgiving, for ever and ever. Amen.

134. And he that is found unworthy of this salutation shall not have place among you: for ye shall not suffer that mine house shall be polluted by him.

135. And he that cometh in and is faithful before me, and is a brother, or if they be brethren, they shall salute the president or teacher with uplifted hands to heaven, with this same prayer and covenant, or by saying Amen, in token of the same.

136. Behold, verily, I say unto you, this is a sample unto you for a salutation to one another in the house of God, in the school of the prophets.

137. And ye are called to do this by prayer and thanksgiving, as the Spirit shall give utterance in all your doings in the house of the Lord, in the school of the prophets, that it may become a sanctuary, a tabernacle of the Holy Spirit to your edification.

138. And ye shall not receive any among you into this school save he is clean from the blood of this generation:

139. And he shall be received by the ordinance of the washing of feet, for unto this end was the ordinance of the washing of feet instituted.

140. And again, the ordinance of washing feet is to be administered by the President, or Presiding elder of the church.

141. It is to be commenced with prayer, and after partaking of bread and wine, he is to gird himself according to the pattern given in the thirteenth chapter of John's testimony concerning me. Amen.

Section 89

Brigham Young observed that when the brethren gathered together to receive counsel from the Prophet Joseph Smith, some of the men filled the room with tobacco smoke while others would spit tobacco on the floor, which was difficult to clean. The Prophet Joseph Smith inquired of the Lord relating to the conduct of the Elders using tobacco (Journal of Discourses, vol. 12:158). This revelation was received February 27, 1833, at Kirtland, Ohio (History of the Church, vol. 1:327).

1. A Word of Wisdom, for the benefit of the Council of High Priests, assembled in Kirtland, and the church; and also the saints in Zion.
2. To be sent greeting—not by commandment or constraint, but by revelation and the word of wisdom, showing forth the order and will of God in the temporal salvation of all saints in the last days.
3. Given for a principle with promise, adapted to the capacity of the weak and the weakest of all saints, who are or can be called saints.
4. Behold, verily, thus saith the Lord unto you, in consequence of evils and designs which do and will exist in the hearts of conspiring men in the last days, I have warned you, and forewarn you, by giving unto you this word of wisdom by revelation,
5. That inasmuch as any man drinketh wine or strong drink among you, behold it is not good, neither meet in the sight of your Father, only in assembling yourselves together to offer up your sacraments before him.
6. And, behold, this should be wine, yea, pure wine of the grape of the vine, of your own make.
7. And, again, strong drinks are not for the belly, but for the washing of your bodies.
8. And again, tobacco is not for the body, neither for the belly, and is not good for man, but is an herb for bruises and all sick cattle, to be used with judgment and skill.
9. And again, hot drinks are not for the body or belly.
10. And again, verily I say unto you, all wholesome herbs God hath ordained for the constitution, nature, and use of man.
11. Every herb in the season thereof, and every fruit in the season thereof; all these to be used with prudence and thanksgiving.
12. Yea, flesh also of beasts and of the fowls of the air, I, the Lord, have ordained for the use of man with thanksgiving; nevertheless they are to be used sparingly;
13. And it is pleasing unto me that they should not be used only in times of winter, or of cold, or famine.
14. All grain is ordained for the use of man and of beasts, to be the staff of life, not only for man

BRIGHAM YOUNG LISTENS AS JOSEPH SMITH TEACHES AS DIRECTED BY THE LORD

but for the beasts of the field, and the fowls of heaven, and all wild animals that run or creep on the earth;

15. And these hath God made for the use of man only in times of famine and excess of hunger.

16. All grain is good for the food of man, as also the fruit of the vine, that which yieldeth fruit, whether in the ground or above the ground.

17. Nevertheless, wheat for man, and corn for the ox, and oats for the horse, and rye for the fowls and for swine, and for all beasts of the field, and barley for all useful animals, and for mild drinks, as also other grain.

18. And all saints who remember to keep and do these sayings, walking in obedience to the commandments, shall receive health in their navel, and marrow to their bones,

19. And shall find wisdom and great treasures of knowledge, even hidden treasures;

20. And shall run and not be weary, and shall walk and not faint;

21. And I, the Lord, give unto them a promise, that the destroying angel shall pass by them, as the children of Israel, and not slay them. Amen.

SECTION 90

This revelation contains more information about the organization of the First Presidency (see historical background, section 81). The Prophet Joseph Smith received this revelation March 8, 1833, at Kirtland, Ohio (History of the Church, vol. 1:329).

1. Thus saith the Lord, verily, verily I say unto you my son, thy sins are forgiven thee, according to thy petition, for thy prayers and the prayers of thy brethren, have come up into my ears;
2. Therefore thou art blessed from henceforth that bear the keys of the kingdom given unto you; which kingdom is coming forth for the last time.
3. Verily, I say unto you the keys of this kingdom shall never be taken from you, while thou art in the world, neither in the world to come;
4. Nevertheless, through you shall the oracles be given to another; yea, even unto the church.
5. And all they who receive the oracles of God, let them beware how they hold them, lest they are accounted as a light thing, and are brought under condemnation thereby; and stumble and fall when the storms descend, and the winds blow, and the rains descend, and beat upon their house.
6. And again, verily I say unto thy brethren, Sidney Rigdon and Frederick G. Williams, their sins are forgiven them also, and they are accounted as equal with thee in holding the keys of this last kingdom;
7. As also through your administration the keys of the school of the prophets, which I have commanded to be organized,
8. That thereby they may be perfected in their ministry for the salvation of Zion, and of the nations of Israel, and of the Gentiles, as many as will believe,
9. That through your administration they may receive the word, and through their administration the word may go forth unto the ends of the earth, unto the Gentiles first, and then, behold, and lo, they shall turn unto the Jews;
10. And then cometh the day when the arm of the Lord shall be revealed in power in convincing the nations, the heathen nations, the house of Joseph, of the gospel of their salvation.
11. For it shall come to pass in that day, that every man shall hear the fulness of the gospel in his own tongue, and in his own language, through those

who are ordained unto this power, by the administration of the Comforter, shed forth upon them, for the revelation of Jesus Christ.

12. And now, verily I say unto you, I give unto you a commandment, that you continue in the ministry and Presidency,

13. And when you have finished the translation of the prophets, you shall from thenceforth preside over the affairs of the church and the school;

14. And from time to time as shall be manifested by the Comforter, receive revelations to unfold the mysteries of the kingdom,

15. And set in order the churches, and study and learn, and become acquainted with all good books, and with languages, tongues, and people.

16. And this shall be your business and mission in all your lives, to preside in council, and set in order all the affairs of this church and kingdom.

17. Be not ashamed, neither confounded; but be admonished in all your high-mindedness and pride, for it bringeth a snare upon your souls.

18. Set in order your houses; keep slothfulness and uncleanness far from you.

19. Now, verily I say unto you, let there be a place provided as soon as it is possible, for the family of thy counselor and scribe, even Frederick G. Williams:

20. And let mine aged servant, Joseph Smith, sen., continue with his family upon the place where he now lives, and let it not be sold until the mouth of the Lord shall name.

21. And let my counselor, even Sidney Rigdon, remain where he now resides, until the mouth of the Lord shall name.

22. And let the bishop search diligently to obtain an agent, and let it be a man who has got riches in store—a man of God, and of strong faith;

23. That thereby he may be enabled to discharge every debt; that the storehouse of the Lord may not be brought into disrepute before the eyes of the people.

24. Search diligently, pray always, and be believing, and all things shall work together for your good, if ye walk uprightly and remember the covenant wherewith ye have covenanted one with another.

25. Let your families be small, especially mine aged servant Joseph Smith, sen., as pertaining to those who do not belong to your families;

26. That those things that are provided for you, to bring to pass my work, are not taken from you and given to those that are not worthy,

27. And thereby you be hindered in accomplishing those things which I have commanded you.

28. And again, verily I say unto you, it is my will that my handmaid, Vienna Jaques should receive money to bear her expenses, and go up unto the land of Zion;

29. And the residue of the money may be consecrated unto me, and she be rewarded in mine own due time.

30. Verily I say unto you, that it is meet in mine eyes that she should go up unto the land of Zion, and receive an inheritance from the hand of the bishop,

31. That she may settle down in peace inasmuch as she is faithful, and not be idle in her days from thenceforth.

32. And behold, verily I say unto you, that ye shall write this commandment, and say unto your brethren in Zion, in love greeting, that I have called you also to preside over Zion in mine own due time:

33. Therefore, let them cease wearying me concerning this matter.

34. Behold, I say unto you that your brethren in Zion begin to repent, and the angels rejoice over them;

35. Nevertheless, I am not well pleased with many things, and I am not well pleased with my servant William E. M'Lellin, neither with my servant Sidney Gilbert; and the bishop also, and others have many things to repent of;

36. But verily I say unto you, that I, the Lord, will contend with Zion, and plead with her strong ones, and chasten her until she overcomes and is clean before me:

37. For she shall not be removed out of her place. I the Lord, have spoken it. Amen.

Section 91

While translating the Old Testament, the Prophet Joseph Smith inquired of the Lord regarding the Apocrypha. This revelation was received March 9, 1833, at Kirtland, Ohio (History of the Church, vol. 1:331).

1. Verily, thus saith the Lord unto you concerning the Apocrypha, there are many things contained therein that are true, and it is mostly translated correctly;
2. There are many things contained therein that are not true, which are interpolations by the hands of men.
3. Verily, I say unto you, that it is not needful that the Apocrypha should be translated.
4. Therefore, whoso readeth it, let him understand, for the Spirit manifesteth truth;
5. And whoso is enlightened by the Spirit shall obtain benefit therefrom;
6. And whoso receiveth not by the Spirit, cannot be benefited, therefore it is not needful that it should be translated. Amen.

ECTION 92

In a letter addressed to the brethren in Zion (Jackson County, Missouri), the Prophet Joseph Smith said, "For your satisfaction, I here insert a revelation given to Frederick G. Williams the 15th of March, 1833, constituting him a member of the United Firm" (History of the Church, *vol. 1:340*). *This revelation was received March 15, 1833, at Kirtland, Ohio* (History of the Church, *vol. 1:333*).

1. Verily, thus saith the Lord, I give unto the united order, organized agreeable to the commandment previously given, a revelation and commandment concerning my servant Shederlaomach, (Frederick G. Williams,) that ye shall receive him into the order. What I say unto one, I say unto all.

2. And again, I say unto you my servant Shederlaomach, (Frederick G. Williams,) you shall be a lively member in this order, and inasmuch as you are faithful in keeping all former commandments, you shall be blessed for ever. Amen.

Section 93

The Prophet Joseph Smith received this revelation May 6, 1833, at Kirtland, Ohio. Worshiping properly is one of several principles revealed in this revelation (History of the Church, vol. 1:343).

1. Verily, thus saith the Lord, it shall come to pass that every soul who forsaketh their sins and cometh unto me, and calleth on my name, and obeyeth my voice, and keepeth my commandments, shall see my face and know that I am,
2. And that I am the true light that lighteth every man that cometh into the world;
3. And that I am in the Father, and the Father in me, and the Father and I are one:
4. The Father because he gave me of his fulness, and the Son because I was in the world and made flesh my tabernacle, and dwelt among the sons of men.
5. I was in the world and received of my Father, and the works of him were plainly manifest;
6. And John saw and bore record of the fulness of my glory, and the fulness of John's record is hereafter to be revealed:
7. And he bore record, saying, I saw his glory that he was in the beginning before the world was;
8. Therefore in the beginning the Word was, for he was the Word, even the messenger of salvation,
9. The light and the Redeemer of the world; the Spirit of truth, who came into the world, because the world was made by him, and in him was the life of men and the light of men.
10. The worlds were made by him; men were made by him; all things were made by him, and through him, and of him.
11. And I, John, bear record that I beheld his glory, as the glory of the Only Begotten of the Father, full of grace and truth, even the Spirit of truth, which came and dwelt in the flesh, and dwelt among us.
12. And I, John, saw that he received not of the fulness at the first, but received grace for grace:
13. And he received not of the fulness at first, but continued from grace to grace, until he received a fulness;
14. And thus he was called the Son of God, because he received not of the fulness at the first.

15. And I, John, bear record, and lo, the heavens were opened, and the Holy Ghost descended upon him in the form of a dove, and sat upon him, and there came a voice out of heaven saying, This is my beloved Son.

16. And I, John, bear record that he received a fulness of the glory of the Father;

17. And he received all power, both in heaven and on earth, and the glory of the Father was with him, for he dwelt in him.

18. And it shall come to pass, that if you are faithful you shall receive the fulness of the record of John.

19. I give unto you these sayings that you may understand and know how to worship, and know what you worship, that you may come unto the Father in my name, and in due time receive of his fulness.

20. For if you keep my commandments you shall receive of his fulness, and be glorified in me as I am in the Father; therefore, I say unto you, you shall receive grace for grace.

21. And now, verily I say unto you, I was in the beginning with the Father, and am the firstborn;

22. And all those who are begotten through me are partakers of the glory of the same, and are the church of the first-born.

23. Ye were also in the beginning with the Father; that which is Spirit, even the Spirit of truth,

24. And truth is knowledge of things as they are, and as they were, and as they are to come;

25. And whatsoever is more or less than this is the spirit of that wicked one who was a liar from the beginning.

26. The Spirit of truth is of God. I am the Spirit of truth, and John bore record of me, saying—He received a fulness of truth, yea, even of all truth;

27. And no man receiveth a fulness unless he keepeth his commandments.

28. He that keepeth his commandments receiveth truth and light, until he is glorified in truth and knoweth all things.

29. Man was also in the beginning with God. Intelligence, or the light of truth, was not created or made, neither indeed can be.

30. All truth is independent in that sphere in which God has placed it, to act for itself, as all intelligence also, otherwise there is no existence.

31. Behold, here is the agency of man, and here is the condemnation of man, because that which was from the beginning is plainly manifest unto them, and they receive not the light.

32. And every man whose spirit receiveth not the light is under condemnation.

33. For man is spirit. The elements are eternal, and spirit and element, inseparably connected, receive a fulness of joy;

34. And when separated, man cannot receive a fulness of joy.

35. The elements are the tabernacle of God; yea, man is the tabernacle of God, even temples; and whatsoever temple is defiled, God shall destroy that temple.

36. The glory of God is intelligence, or, in other words, light and truth;

37. Light and truth forsaketh that evil one.

38. Every spirit of man was innocent in the beginning, and God having redeemed man from the fall, men became again in their infant state, innocent before God.

39. And that wicked one cometh and taketh away light and truth, through disobedience, from the children of men, and because of the tradition of their fathers.

40. But I have commanded you to bring up your children in light and truth;

41. But verily I say unto you, my servant Frederick G. Williams, you have continued under this condemnation;

42. You have not taught your children light and truth, according to the commandments, and that wicked one hath power, as yet, over you, and this is the cause of your affliction.

43. And now a commandment I give unto you, if you will be delivered, you shall set in order your own house, for there are many things that are not right in your house.

44. Verily, I say unto my servant Sidney Rigdon, that in some things he hath not kept the commandments concerning his children; therefore, firstly set in order thy house.

45. Verily, I say unto my servant Joseph Smith, jun., or, in other words, I will call you friends, for you are my friends, and ye shall have an inheritance with me.

46. I called you servants for the world's sake, and ye are their servants for my sake;

47. And now, verily, I say unto Joseph Smith, jun., you have not kept the commandments, and must needs stand rebuked before the Lord.

48. Your family must needs repent and forsake some things, and give more earnest heed unto your sayings, or be removed out of their place.

49. What I say unto one I say unto all; pray always lest that wicked one have power in you, and remove you out of your place.

50. My servant Newel K. Whitney, also a bishop of my church, hath need to be chastened, and set in order his family, and see that they are more diligent and concerned at home, and pray always, or they shall be removed out of their place.

51. Now, I say unto you, my friends, let my servant Sidney Rigdon go on his journey, and make haste, and also proclaim the acceptable year of the Lord, and the gospel of salvation, as I shall give him utterance, and by your prayer of faith with one consent, I will uphold him.

52. And let my servant Joseph Smith, jun., and Frederick G. Williams, make haste also, and it shall be given them even according to the prayer of faith, and inasmuch as you keep my sayings, you shall not be confounded in this world, nor in the world to come.

53. And verily, I say unto you, that it is my will that you should hasten to translate my scriptures, and to obtain a knowledge of history, and of countries, and of kingdoms, of laws of God and man, and all this for the salvation of Zion. Amen.

ection 94

The Church did not own any buildings at this period of time (May 1833). Because of the growth of the Church it became necessary to pursue the possibility of building a meeting house where the Elders might gather to receive instruction. A committee composed of Hyrum Smith, Reynolds Cahoon, and Jared Carter was appointed by a conference to obtain subscriptions for the purpose of erecting such a building. On May 6, 1833, at Kirtland, Ohio, the Prophet Joseph Smith received this revelation, which contains instructions pertaining to Church buildings (History of the Church, vol. 1:346).

1. And again, verily I say unto you, my friends, a commandment I give unto you, that ye shall commence a work of laying out and preparing a beginning and foundation of the city of the Stake of Zion, here in the land of Kirtland, beginning at my house.
2. And behold it must be done according to the pattern which I have given unto you.
3. And let the first lot on the south, be consecrated unto me for the building of an house, for the Presidency, for the work of the Presidency, in obtaining revelations; and for the work of the ministry of the Presidency, in all things pertaining to the church and kingdom.
4. Verily I say unto you, that it shall be built fifty-five by sixty-five feet in the width thereof and in the length thereof, in the inner court;
5. And there shall be a lower court and a higher court, according to the pattern which shall be given unto you hereafter;
6. And it shall be dedicated unto the Lord from the foundation thereof, according to the order of the Priesthood, according to the pattern which shall be given unto you hereafter.
7. And it shall be wholly dedicated unto the Lord for the work of the Presidency.
8. And ye shall not suffer any unclean thing to come in unto it; and my glory shall be there, and my presence shall be there;
9. But if there shall come into it any unclean thing, my glory shall not be there; and my presence shall not come into it.
10. And again, verily I say unto you, the second lot on the south shall be dedicated unto me for the building of a house unto me, for the work of the printing of the translation of my scriptures, and all things whatsoever I shall command you;
11. And it shall be fifty-five by sixty-five feet in the width thereof and the length thereof, in the inner court; and there shall be a lower and a higher court;
12. And this house shall be wholly dedicated unto the Lord from the foundation thereof, for the work of the printing, in all things whatsoever I

shall command you, to be holy, undefiled, according to the pattern in all things, as it shall be given unto you.

13. And on the third lot shall my servant Hyrum Smith receive his inheritance,

14. And on the first and second lots on the north shall my servants Reynolds Cahoon and Jared Carter receive their inheritances.

15. That they may do the work which I have appointed unto them, to be a committee to build mine houses, according to the commandment, which I, the Lord God, have given unto you.

16. These two houses are not to be built until I give unto you a commandment concerning them.

17. And now I give unto you no more at this time. Amen.

Section 95

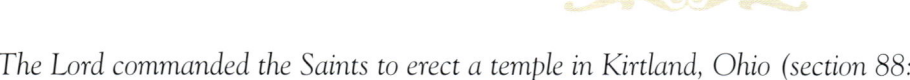

The Lord commanded the Saints to erect a temple in Kirtland, Ohio (section 88:119). This command was not adhered to with the diligence necessary to accomplish the work. On June 1, 1833, at Kirtland, Ohio, the Lord gave this revelation to the Prophet Joseph Smith in which He chastised the Saints for failure to begin to build the Kirtland Temple (History of the Church, vol. 1:349–350).

1. Verily, thus saith the Lord unto you, whom I love, and whom I love I also chasten, that their sins may be forgiven, for with the chastisement I prepare a way for their deliverance in all things out of temptation, and I have loved you.
2. Wherefore ye must needs be chastened and stand rebuked before my face
3. For ye have sinned against me a very grievous sin, in that ye have not considered the great commandment in all things, that I have given unto you concerning the building of mine house,
4. For the preparation wherewith I design to prepare mine apostles to prune my vineyard for the last time, that I may bring to pass my strange act, that I may pour out my Spirit upon all flesh.
5. But behold, verily I say unto you, that there are many who have been ordained among you, whom I have called, but few of them are chosen;
6. They who are not chosen have sinned a very grievous sin, in that they are walking in darkness at noon-day;
7. And for this cause I gave unto you a commandment that you should call your solemn assembly, that your fastings and your mourning might come up into the ears of the Lord of Sabaoth, which is by interpretation, the Creator of the first day, the beginning and the end.
8. Yea, verily I say unto you, I gave unto you a commandment that you should build an house, in the which house I design to endow those whom I have chosen with power from on high;
9. For this is the promise of the Father unto you; therefore I command you to tarry, even as mine apostles at Jerusalem;
10. Nevertheless my servants sinned a very grievous sin, and contentions arose in the school of the prophets, which was very grievous unto me, saith your Lord; therefore I sent them forth to be chastened.
11. Verily I say unto you, it is my will that you should build a house. If you keep my commandments, you shall have power to build it;

12. If you keep not my commandments, the love of the Father shall not continue with you, therefore you shall walk in darkness.

13. Now here is wisdom, and the mind of the Lord; let the house be built, not after the manner of the world, for I give not unto you that ye shall live after the manner of the world;

14. Therefore let it be built after the manner which I shall show unto three of you, whom ye shall appoint and ordain unto this power.

15. And the size thereof shall be fifty and five feet in width, and let it be sixty-five feet in length, in the inner court thereof;

16. And let the lower part of the inner court be dedicated unto me for your sacrament offering, and for your preaching, and your fasting, and your praying, and the offering up your most holy desires unto me, saith your Lord.

17. And let the higher part of the inner court be dedicated unto me, for the school of mine apostles, saith Son Ahman; or, in other words, Alphus; or, in other words, Omegus; even Jesus Christ your Lord. Amen.

THE SAINTS JOYOUSLY LABOR TO BUILD THE KIRTLAND TEMPLE

Verily I say unto you, it is my will that you should build a house. If you keep my commandments you shall have power to build it.

D&C 95:11

Section 96

The Church purchased several parcels of land in Kirtland, Ohio, upon which they might build a stake of Zion. One such purchase was the farm of Peter French. The conference could not agree on how the farm should be divided into lots for the Saints to settle upon. The Prophet Joseph Smith inquired of the Lord pertaining to this matter, and received this revelation June 4, 1833, at Kirtland, Ohio (History of the Church, vol. 1:352).

1. Behold, I say unto you, Here is wisdom, whereby ye may know how to act concerning this matter, for it is expedient in me that this Stake that I have set for the strength of Zion should be made strong;
2. Therefore let my servant Ahashdah (Newel K. Whitney) take charge of the place which is named among you, upon which I design to build mine holy house;
3. And again, let it be divided into lots according to wisdom, for the benefit of those who seek inheritances, as it shall be determined in council among you.
4. Therefore, take heed that ye see to this matter, and that portion that is necessary to benefit mine order, for the purpose of bringing forth my word to the children of men;
5. For behold, verily I say unto you, this is the most expedient in me, that my word should go forth unto the children of men, for the purpose of subduing the hearts of the children of men for your good. Even so. Amen.
6. And again, verily I say unto you, it is wisdom and expedient in me, that my servant Zombre (John Johnson) whose offering I have accepted, and whose prayers I have heard, unto whom I give a promise of eternal life inasmuch as he keepeth my commandments from henceforth,
7. For he is a descendant of Seth, (Joseph,) and a partaker of the blessings of the promise made unto his fathers.
8. Verily I say unto you, it is expedient in me that he should become a member of the order, that he may assist in bringing forth my word unto the children of men;
9. Therefore ye shall ordain him unto this blessing, and he shall seek diligently to take away incumbrances that are upon the house named among you, that he may dwell therein. Even so. Amen.

Section 97

Mob action had taken place against the Saints in Jackson County, Missouri, in an attempt to drive them from the county. To prevent bloodshed, the brethren on July 23 signed an agreement that they would leave the county. At Kirtland, Ohio, August 2, 1833, the Prophet Joseph Smith received this revelation (History of the Church, vol. 1:400).

1. Verily I say unto you my friends, I speak unto you with my voice, even the voice of my Spirit, that I may show unto you my will concerning your brethren in the land of Zion, many of whom are truly humble and are seeking diligently to learn wisdom and to find truth.
2. Verily, verily I say unto you, blessed are such, for they shall obtain, for I, the Lord, show mercy unto all the meek, and upon all whomsoever I will, that I may be justified when I shall bring them into judgment.
3. Behold, I say unto you, concerning the school in Zion, I, the Lord, am well pleased that there should be a school in Zion, and also with my servant Parley P. Pratt, for he abideth in me;
4. And inasmuch as he continueth to abide in me; he shall continue to preside over the school in the land of Zion, until I shall give unto him other commandments;
5. And I will bless him with a multiplicity of blessings, in expounding all scriptures and mysteries to the edification of the school, and of the church in Zion;
6. And to the residue of the school, I, the Lord, am willing to show mercy, nevertheless there are those that must needs be chastened, and their works shall be made known.
7. The ax is laid at the root of the trees, and every tree that bringeth not forth good fruit, shall be hewn down and cast into the fire: I, the Lord, have spoken it.
8. Verily I say unto you, all among them who know their hearts are honest, and are broken, and their spirits contrite, and are willing to observe their covenants by sacrifice; yea, every sacrifice which I, the Lord, shall command, they are accepted of me,
9. For I, the Lord, will cause them to bring forth as a very fruitful tree which is planted in a goodly land, by a pure stream, that yieldeth much precious fruit.
10. Verily, I say unto you, that it is my will that an house should be built unto me in the land

MOBS IN MISSOURI SET FIRE TO THE SAINTS' FARMS AND POSSESSIONS

of Zion, like unto the pattern which I have given you;

11. Yea, let it be built speedily, by the tithing of my people:

12. Behold, this is the tithing and the sacrifice which I, the Lord, require at their hands, that there may be an house built unto me for the salvation of Zion,

13. For a place of thanksgiving for all saints, and for a place of instruction for all those who are called to the work of the ministry in all their several callings and offices,

14. That they may be perfected in the understanding of their ministry—in theory, in principle, and in doctrine—in all things pertaining to the kingdom of God on the earth, the keys of which kingdom have been conferred upon you.

15. And inasmuch as my people build an house unto me in the name of the Lord, and do not suffer any unclean thing to come into it that it be not defiled, my glory shall rest upon it;

16. Yea, and my presence shall be there, for I will come into it, and all the pure in heart that shall come into it shall see God;

17. But if it be defiled I will not come into it, and my glory shall not be there, for I will not come into unholy temples.

18. And, now, behold, if Zion do these things she shall prosper, and spread herself and become very glorious, very great, and very terrible,

19. And the nations of the earth shall honor her, and shall say, surely Zion is the city of our God, and surely Zion cannot fall, neither be moved out of her place, for God is there, and the hand of the Lord is there,

20. And he hath sworn by the power of his might, to be her salvation and her high tower;

21. Therefore, verily, thus saith the Lord, let Zion rejoice, for this is Zion—THE PURE IN HEART; therefore, let Zion rejoice, while all the wicked shall mourn;

22. For behold, and lo, vengeance cometh speedily upon the ungodly as the whirlwind, and who shall escape it;

23. The Lord's scourge shall pass over by night and by day, and the report thereof shall vex all people; yet, it shall not be stayed until the Lord come;

24. For the indignation of the Lord is kindled against their abominations and all their wicked works;

25. Nevertheless Zion shall escape if she observe to do all things whatsoever I have commanded her,

26. But if she observe not to do whatsoever I have commanded her, I will visit her according to all her works, with sore affliction, with pestilence, with plague, with sword, with vengeance, with devouring fire;

27. Nevertheless, let it be read this once in their ears, that I, the Lord, have accepted of her offering, and if she sin no more, none of these things shall come upon her,

28. And I will bless her with blessings, and multiply a multiplicity of blessings upon her, and upon her generations forever and ever, saith the Lord your God. Amen.

Section 98

Because of mob violence against the Saints in Missouri, and a desire on the part of the Saints to retaliate for the wrongs they endured, the Lord gave this revelation to the Prophet Joseph Smith, August 6, 1833, at Kirtland, Ohio (History of the Church, vol. 1:403).

1. Verily I say unto you my friends, fear not, let your hearts be comforted; yea, rejoice evermore, and in everything give thanks,

2. Waiting patiently on the Lord, for your prayers have entered into the ears of the Lord of Sabaoth, and are recorded with this seal and testament; the Lord hath sworn and decreed that they shall be granted;

3. Therefore he giveth this promise unto you, with an immutable covenant that they shall be fulfilled and all things wherewith you have been afflicted, shall work together for your good, and to my name's glory, saith the Lord.

4. And now, verily I say unto you concerning the laws of the land, it is my will that my people should observe to do all things whatsoever I command them;

5. And that law of the land which is constitutional, supporting that principle of freedom in maintaining rights and privileges, belongs to all mankind, and is justifiable before me;

6. Therefore, I, the Lord, justify you, and your brethren of my church, in befriending that law which is the constitutional law of the land;

7. And as pertaining to law of man, whatsoever is more or less than these, cometh of evil.

8. I, the Lord God, make you free, therefore ye are free indeed; and the law also maketh you free;

9. Nevertheless, when the wicked rule the people mourn;

10. Wherefore, honest men, and wise men should be sought for diligently, and good men and wise men ye should observe to uphold; otherwise whatsoever is less than these cometh of evil.

11. And I give unto you a commandment, that ye shall forsake all evil and cleave unto all good, that ye shall live by every word which proceedeth forth out of the mouth of God;

12. For he will give unto the faithful line upon line, precept upon precept; and I will try you and prove you herewith;

13. And whoso layeth down his life in my cause, for my name's sake, shall find it again, even life eternal:

14. Therefore be not afraid of your enemies, for I have decreed in my heart, saith the Lord, that I will prove you in all things, whether you will abide in my covenant, even unto death, that you may be found worthy;

15. For if ye will not abide in my covenant, ye are not worthy of me;

16. Therefore renounce war and proclaim peace, and seek diligently to turn the hearts of their children to their fathers, and the hearts of the fathers to the children;

17. And again, the hearts of the Jews unto the prophets, and the prophets unto the Jews, lest I come and smite the whole earth with a curse, and all flesh be consumed before me.

18. Let not your hearts be troubled, for in my Father's house are many mansions, and I have prepared a place for you, and where my Father and I am, there ye shall be also.

19. Behold, I, the Lord, am not well pleased with many who are in the church at Kirtland,

20. For they do not forsake their sins, and their wicked ways, the pride of their hearts, and their covetousness, and all their detestable things, and observe the words of wisdom and eternal life which I have given unto them.

21. Verily I say unto you, that I, the Lord, will chasten them, and will do whatsoever I list, if they do not repent and observe all things whatsoever I have said unto them.

22. And again I say unto you, if ye observe to do whatsoever I command you, I, the Lord, will turn away all wrath and indignation from you, and the gates of hell shall not prevail against you.

23. Now I speak unto you concerning your families; if men will smite you, or your families, once, and ye bear it patiently and revile not against them, neither seek revenge, ye shall be rewarded;

24. But if ye bear it not patiently, it shall be accounted unto you as being meted out a just measure unto you.

25. And again, if your enemy shall smite you the second time, and you revile not against your enemy, and bear it patiently, your reward shall be an hundred fold.

26. And again, if he shall smite you the third time, and ye bear it patiently, your reward shall be doubled unto you four fold;

27. And these three testimonies shall stand against your enemy if he repent not, and shall not be blotted out.

28. And now verily I say unto you, if that enemy shall escape my vengeance, that he be not brought into judgment before me, then ye shall see to it that ye warn him in my name, that he come no more upon you, neither upon your family, even your children's children unto the third and fourth generation;

29. And then if he shall come upon you, or your children, or your children's children unto the third and fourth generation; I have delivered thine enemy into thine hands,

30. And then if thou wilt spare him, thou shalt be rewarded for thy righteousness; and also thy children and thy children's children unto the third and fourth generation;

31. Nevertheless thine enemy is in thine hands, and if thou rewardest him according to his works, thou art justified, if he has sought thy life, and thy life is endangered by him, thine enemy is in thine hands and thou art justified.

32. Behold, this is the law I gave unto my servant Nephi, and thy fathers Joseph, and Jacob, and Isaac, and Abraham, and all mine ancient prophets and apostles.

33. And again, his is the law that I gave unto mine ancients, that they should not go out unto battle against any nation, kindred, tongue, or people, save I, the Lord, commanded them.

34. And if any nation, tongue, or people, should proclaim war against them, they should first lift a standard of peace unto that people, nation, or tongue;

35. And if that people did not accept the offering of peace neither the second nor the third time, they should bring these testimonies before the Lord;

36. Then I, the Lord, would give unto them a commandment, and justify them in going out to battle against that nation, tongue, or people,

37. And I, the Lord, would fight their battles, and their children's battles, and their children's children's, until they had avenged themselves on all their enemies, to the third and fourth generation.

38. Behold, this is an ensample unto all people, saith the Lord your God, for justification before me.

39. And again, verily I say unto you, if after thine enemy has come upon thee the first time, he repent and come unto thee praying thy forgiveness, thou shalt forgive him, and shall hold it no more as a testimony against thine enemy,

40. And so on unto the second and third time; and as oft as thine enemy repenteth of the trespass wherewith he has trespassed against thee, thou shalt forgive him, until seventy times seven:

41. And if he trespass against thee and repent not the first time, nevertheless thou shalt forgive him;

42. And if he trespass against thee the second time, and repent not, nevertheless thou shalt forgive him;

43. And if he trespass against thee the third time, and repent not, thou shalt also forgive him;

44. But if he trespass against thee the fourth time, thou shalt not forgive him, but shalt bring these testimonies before the Lord, and they shall not be blotted out until he repent and reward thee four fold in all things wherewith he has trespassed against thee;

45. And if he do this, thou shalt forgive him with all thine heart, and if he do not this, I the Lord, will avenge thee of thine enemy an hundred fold;

46. And upon his children, and upon his children's children of all them that hate me, unto the third and fourth generation;

47. But if the children shall repent, or the children's children, and turn to the Lord their God, with all their hearts, and with all their might, mind, and strength, and restore four fold for all their trespasses, wherewith they have trespassed, or wherewith their fathers have trespassed, or their father's fathers, then thine indignation shall be turned away,

48. And vengeance shall no more come upon them, saith the Lord thy God, and their trespasses shall never be brought any more as a testimony before the Lord against them. Amen.

SECTION 99

This revelation was received by the Prophet Joseph Smith in August 1832, at Hiram, Ohio. John Murdock is called by the Lord to proclaim His gospel in the eastern part of the United States.

1. Behold, thus saith the Lord unto my servant John Murdock, thou art called to go into the eastern countries from house to house, from village to village, and from city to city, to proclaim mine everlasting gospel unto the inhabitants thereof, in the midst of persecution and wickedness;

2. And who receiveth you receiveth me, and you shall have power to declare my word in the demonstration of my Holy Spirit;

3. And who receiveth you as a little child, receiveth my kingdom, and blessed are they, for they shall obtain mercy;

4. And whoso rejecteth you shall be rejected of my Father and his house; and you shall cleanse your feet in the secret places by the way for a testimony against them.

5. And behold, and lo, I come quickly to judgment, to convince all of their ungodly deeds which they have committed against me, as it is written of me in the volume of the book.

6. And now, verily I say unto you, that it is not expedient that you should go until your children are provided for, and kindly sent up unto the bishop in Zion;

7. And after a few years, if thou desirest of me, thou mayest go up also unto the goodly land, to possess thine inheritance:

8. Otherwise thou shalt continue proclaiming my gospel until thou be taken. Amen.

Section 100

On October 5, 1833, the Prophet Joseph Smith, Sidney Rigdon, and Freeman Nickerson started on a mission to Canada. They arrived at Perrysburg, New York, on October 12, where the Prophet Joseph Smith received this revelation (History of the Church, vol. 1:416–419).

1. Verily, thus saith the Lord unto you, my friends Sidney, and Joseph, your families are well; they are in mine hands, and I will do with them as seemeth me good; for in me there is all power;

2. Therefore, follow me, and listen to the counsel which I shall give unto you.

3. Behold, and lo, I have much people in this place, in the regions round about, and an effectual door shall be opened in the regions round about in this eastern land.

4. Therefore, I, the Lord, have suffered you to come unto this place; for thus it was expedient in me for the salvation of souls;

5. Therefore, verily, I say unto you, lift up your voices unto this people, speak the thoughts that I shall put into your hearts, and you shall not be confounded before men;

6. For it shall be given you in the very hour, yea, in the very moment, what ye shall say.

7. But a commandment I give unto you, that ye shall declare whatsoever things ye declare in my name, in solemnity of heart, in the spirit of meekness, in all things.

8. And I give unto you this promise, that inasmuch as ye do this, the Holy Ghost shall be shed forth in bearing record unto all things whatsoever ye shall say.

9. And it is expedient in me that you, my servant Sidney, should be a spokesman unto this people; yea, verily, I will ordain you unto this calling, even to be a spokesman unto my servant Joseph;

10. And I will give unto him power to be mighty in testimony;

11. And I will give unto thee power to be mighty in expounding all scriptures, that thou mayest be a spokesman unto him, and he shall be a revelator unto thee, that thou mayest know the certainty of all things pertaining to the things of my kingdom on the earth.

12. Therefore, continue your journey and let your hearts rejoice; for behold, and lo, I am with you even unto the end.

13. And now I give unto you a word concerning Zion. Zion shall be redeemed, although she is chastened for a little season.

14. Thy brethren, my servants Orson Hyde, and John Gould, are in my hands, and inasmuch as they keep my commandments, they shall be saved.

15. Therefore let your hearts be comforted, for all things shall work together for good to them that walk uprightly, and to the sanctification of the church;

16. For I will raise up unto myself a pure people, that will serve me in righteousness;

17. And all that call on the name of the Lord, and keep his commandments, shall be saved. Even so. Amen.

Section 101

Violent mob action began against the Saints in Jackson County, Missouri, October 31, 1833. By November 7, the Saints were forced to flee the county. Most of the Saints fled to Clay County where they were treated with some kindness. On December 16, 1833, at Kirtland, Ohio, the Prophet Joseph Smith received this revelation explaining why the Saints were expelled from Jackson County, Missouri (History of the Church, vol. 1:458).

1. Verily I say unto you, concerning your brethren who have been afflicted, and persecuted, and cast out from the land of their inheritance,
2. I, the Lord, have suffered the affliction to come upon them, wherewith they have been afflicted, in consequence of their transgressions;
3. Yet I will own them, and they shall be mine in that day when I shall come to make up my jewels.
4. Therefore, they must needs be chastened and tried, even as Abraham, who was commanded to offer up his only son,
5. For all those who will not endure chastening, but deny me, cannot be sanctified.
6. Behold, I say unto you, there were jarrings, and contentions, and envyings, and strifes, and lustful and covetous desires among them; therefore by these things they polluted their inheritances.
7. They were slow to hearken unto the voice of the Lord their God, therefore the Lord their God is slow to hearken unto their prayers, to answer them in the day of their trouble.
8. In the day of their peace they esteemed lightly my counsel; but, in the day of their trouble, of necessity they feel after me.
9. Verily I say unto you, notwithstanding their sins, my bowels are filled with compassion towards them: I will not utterly cast them off; and in the day of wrath I will remember mercy.
10. I have sworn, and the decree hath gone forth by a former commandment which I have given unto you, that I would let fall the sword of mine indignation in behalf of my people; and even as I have said, it shall come to pass.
11. Mine indignation is soon to be poured out without measure upon all nations, and this will I do when the cup of their iniquity is full.
12. And in that day all who are found upon the watch tower, or in other words, all mine Israel shall be saved.
13. And they that have been scattered shall be gathered;
14. And all they who have mourned shall be comforted;

15. And all they who have given their lives for my name shall be crowned.

16. Therefore, let your hearts be comforted concerning Zion; for all flesh is in mine hands: be still and know that I am God.

17. Zion shall not be moved out of her place, notwithstanding her children are scattered.

18. They that remain, and are pure in heart, shall return, and come to their inheritances, they and their children, with songs of everlasting joy, to build up the waste places of Zion;

19. And all these things that the prophets might be fulfilled.

20. And, behold, there is none other place appointed than that which I have appointed; neither shall there be any other place appointed than that which I have appointed, for the work of the gathering of my saints,

21. Until the day cometh when there is found no more room for them; and then I have other places which I will appoint unto them, and they shall be called Stakes, for the curtains, or the strength of Zion.

22. Behold, it is my will, that all they who call on my name, and worship me according to mine everlasting gospel, should gather together, and stand in holy places,

23. And prepare for the revelation which is to come, when the vail of the covering of my temple, in my tabernacle, which hideth the earth, shall be taken off, and all flesh shall see me together.

24. And every corruptible thing, both of man, or of the beasts of the field, or of the fowls of the heavens, or of the fish of the sea, that dwell upon all the face of the earth, shall be consumed;

25. And also that of element shall melt with fervent heat; and all things shall become new, that my knowledge and glory may dwell upon all the earth.

26. And in that day the enmity of man, and the enmity of beasts, yea, the enmity of all flesh, shall cease from before my face.

27. And in that day whatsoever any man shall ask, it shall be given unto him.

28. And in that day Satan shall not have power to tempt any man.

29. And there shall be no sorrow because there is no death.

30. In that day an infant shall not die until he is old, and his life shall be as the age of a tree,

31. And when he dies he shall not sleep, (that is to say in the earth,) but shall be changed in the twinkling of an eye, and shall be caught up, and his rest shall be glorious.

32. Yea, verily I say unto you, in that day when the Lord shall come, he shall reveal all things—

33. Things which have passed, and hidden things which no man knew—things of the earth, by which it was made, and the purpose and the end thereof—

34. Things most precious—things that are above, and things that are beneath—things that are in the earth, and upon the earth, and in heaven.

35. And all they who suffer persecution for my name, and endure in faith, though they are called to lay down their lives for my sake, yet shall they partake of all this glory.

36. Wherefore, fear not even unto death; for in this world your joy is not full, but in me your joy is full.

37. Therefore, care not for the body, neither the life of the body; but care for the soul, and for the life of the soul;

38. And seek the face of the Lord always, that in patience ye may possess your souls, and ye shall have eternal life.

39. When men are called unto mine everlasting gospel, and covenant with an everlasting covenant, they are accounted as the salt of the earth, and the savor of men;

40. They are called to be the savor of men. Therefore, if that salt of the earth lose its savor, behold, it is thenceforth good for nothing, only to be cast out, and trodden under the feet of men.

41. Behold, here is wisdom concerning the children of Zion, even many, but not all; they were found transgressors, therefore they must needs be chastened:

42. He that exalteth himself shall be abased, and he that abaseth himself shall be exalted.

43. And now, I will show unto you a parable, that you may know my will concerning the redemption of Zion.

44. A certain nobleman had a spot of land, very choice; and he said unto his servants, Go ye unto my vineyard, even upon this very choice piece of land, and plant twelve olive trees,

45. And set watchmen round about them, and build a tower, that one may overlook the land round about, to be a watchman upon the tower, that mine olive trees may not be broken down, when the enemy shall come to spoil and take upon themselves the fruit of my vineyard.

46. Now, the servants of the nobleman went and did as their lord commanded them; and planted the olive trees, and built a hedge round about, and set watchmen, and began to build a tower.

47. And while they were yet laying the foundation thereof, they began to say among themselves, And what need hath my lord of this tower?

48. And consulted for a long time, saying among themselves, What need hath my lord of this tower, seeing this is a time of peace?

49. Might not this money be given to the exchangers? for there is no need of these things!

50. And while they were at variance one with another they became very slothful, and they hearkened not unto the commandments of their lord,

51. And the enemy came by night, and broke down the hedge, and the servants of the nobleman arose and were affrighted, and fled; and the enemy destroyed their works, and broke down the olive trees.

52. Now, behold, the nobleman, the lord of the vineyard, called upon his servants, and said unto them, Why! what is the cause of this great evil?

53. Ought ye not to have done even as I commanded you? and after ye had planted the vineyard, and built the hedge round about, and set watchmen upon the walls thereof, built the tower also, and set a watchman upon the tower, and watched for my vineyard, and not have fallen asleep, lest the enemy should come upon you?

54. And behold, the watchman upon the tower would have seen the enemy while he was yet afar off, and then ye could have made ready and kept the enemy from breaking down the hedge thereof, and saved my vineyard from the hands of the destroyer.

55. And the lord of the vineyard said unto one of his servants, Go and gather together the residue of my servants, and take all the strength of mine house, which are my warriors, my young men, and they that are of middle age also among all my servants, who are the strength of mine house, save those only whom I have appointed to tarry;

56. And go ye straightway unto the land of my vineyard, and redeem my vineyard, for it is mine, I have bought it with money.

57. Therefore, get ye straightway unto my land; break down the walls of mine enemies; throw down their tower, and scatter their watchmen:

58. And inasmuch as they gather together against you, avenge me of mine enemies, that by and by I may come with the residue of mine house, and possess the land.

59. And the servant said unto his lord, When shall these things be?

60. And he said unto his servant, When I will, go ye straightway, and do all things whatsoever I have commanded you;

61. And this shall be my seal and blessing upon you—a faithful and wise steward in the midst of mine house, a ruler in my kingdom.

62. And his servant went straightway, and did all things whatsoever his lord commanded him, and after many days all things were fulfilled.

63. Again, verily I say unto you, I will show unto you wisdom in me concerning all the churches, inasmuch as they are willing to be guided in a right and proper way for their salvation,

64. That the work of the gathering together of my saints may continue, that I may build them up unto my name upon holy places; for the time of harvest is come, and my word must needs be fulfilled.

65. Therefore, I must gather together my people, according to the parable of the wheat and the tares, that the wheat may be secured in the garners to possess eternal life, and be crowned with celestial glory when I shall come in the kingdom of my Father, to reward every man according as his work shall be,

66. While the tares shall be bound in bundles, and their bands made strong, that they may be burned with unquenchable fire.

67. Therefore, a commandment I give unto all the churches, that they shall continue to gather together unto the places which I have appointed.

68. Nevertheless, as I have said unto you in a former commandment, let not your gathering be in haste, nor by flight; but let all things be prepared before you:

69. And in order that all things be prepared before you, observe the commandment which I have given concerning these things,

70. Which saith, or teacheth, to purchase all the lands by money, which can be purchased for money, in the region round about the land which I have appointed to be the land of Zion, for the beginning of the gathering of my saints;

71. All the land which can be purchased in Jackson county, and the counties round about, and leave the residue in mine hand.

72. Now, verily I say unto you, let all the churches gather together all their monies; let these things be done in their time, but not in haste, and observe to have all things prepared before you.

73. And let honorable men be appointed, even wise men and send them to purchase these lands;

74. And the churches in the eastern countries, when they are built up, if they will hearken unto this counsel, they may buy lands and gather together upon them, and in this way they may establish Zion.

75. There is even now already in store a sufficient, yea, even abundance, to redeem Zion, and establish her waste places, no more to be thrown down, were the churches, who call themselves after my name, willing to hearken to my voice.

76. And again I say unto you, those who have been scattered by their enemies, it is my will that they should continue to importune for redress, and redemption, by the hands of those who are placed as rulers and are in authority over you,

77. According to the laws and constitution of the people, which I have suffered to be established, and should be maintained for the rights and protection of all flesh, according to just and holy principles,

78. That every man may act in doctrine and principle pertaining to futurity, according to the moral agency which I have given unto him, that every man may be accountable for his own sins in the day of judgment.

79. Therefore, it is not right that any man should be in bondage one to another.

80. And for this purpose have I established the constitution of this land, by the hands of wise men whom I raised up unto this very purpose, and redeemed the land by the shedding of blood.

81. Now, unto what shall I liken the children of Zion? I will liken them unto the parable of the woman and the unjust judge (for men ought always to pray and not to faint) which saith,

82. There was in a city a judge which feared not God, neither regarded man.

BRIGHAM YOUNG
AS SENIOR ASPOSTLE
DIRECTS THE ORDERLY
EVACUATION OF
THE SAINTS FROM
MISSOURI

. . . they that have been scattered shall be gathered. And all they who have mourned shall be comforted. And all they who have given their lives for my name shall be crowned. Therefore, let your hearts be comforted concerning Zion; for all flesh is mine hands; be still and know that I am God.

D&C 101:13–16

83. And there was a widow in that city, and she came unto him saying, Avenge me of mine adversary.

84. And he would not for a while, but afterward he said within himself, Though I fear not God, nor regard man, yet because this widow troubleth me I will avenge her, lest by her continual coming she weary me.

85. Thus will I liken the children of Zion.

86. Let them importune at the feet of the judge;

87. And if he heed them not, let them importune at the feet of the Governor;

88. And if the Governor heed them not, let them importune at the feet of the President;

89. And if the President heed them not, then will the Lord arise and come forth out of his hiding place, and in his fury vex the nation,

90. And in his hot displeasure, and in his fierce anger, in his time, will cut off those wicked, unfaithful, and unjust stewards, and appoint them their portion among hypocrites, and unbelievers;

91. Even in outer darkness, where there is weeping, and wailing, and gnashing of teeth.

92. Pray ye, therefore, that their ears may be opened unto your cries, that I may be merciful unto them, that these things may not come upon them.

93. What I have said unto you, must needs be, that all men may be left without excuse;

94. That wise men and rulers may hear and know that which they have never considered;

95. That I may proceed to bring to pass my act, my strange act, and perform my work, my strange work, that men may discern between the righteous and the wicked, saith your God.

96. And again, I say unto you, it is contrary to my commandment and my will that my servant Sidney Gilbert should sell my storehouse, which I have appointed unto my people, into the hands of mine enemies.

97. Let not that which I have appointed be polluted by mine enemies, by the consent of those who call themselves after my name;

98. For this is a very sore and grievous sin against me, and against my people, in consequence of those things which I have decreed and are soon to befall the nations.

99. Therefore, it is my will that my people should claim, and hold claim upon that which I have appointed unto them, though they should not be permitted to dwell thereon;

100. Nevertheless, I do not say they shall not dwell thereon; for inasmuch as they bring forth fruit and works meet for my kingdom, they shall dwell thereon;

101. They shall build, and another shall not inherit it; they shall plant vineyards, and they shall eat the fruit thereof. Even so. Amen.

Section 102

This section contains the minutes of the organization of the First High Council of the Church at Kirtland, Ohio, February 17, 1834. On February 18, the Prophet Joseph Smith revised and corrected these minutes. On February 19, the corrected minutes were presented to the council and were unanimously approved (History of the Church, vol. 2:28–31).

1. This day a general council of twenty-four High Priests assembled at the house of Joseph Smith, Jun., by revelation, and proceeded to organize the High Council of the Church of Christ, which was to consist of twelve High Priests, and one or three Presidents as the case might require.

2. The High Council was appointed by revelation for the purpose of settling important difficulties which might arise in the church, which could not be settled by the church or the bishop's council to the satisfaction of the parties.

3. Joseph Smith, jun., Sidney Rigdon and Frederick G. Williams were acknowledged Presidents by the voice of the council; and Joseph Smith, sen., John Smith, Joseph Coe, John Johnson, Martin Harris, John S. Carter, Jared Carter, Oliver Cowdery, Samuel H. Smith, Orson Hyde, Sylvester Smith, and Luke Johnson, Hgh Priests, were chosen to be a standing Council for the church, by the unanimous voice of the Council.

4. The above-named councilors were then asked whether they accepted their appointments and whether they would act in that office according to the law of heaven; to which they all answered that they accepted their appointments, and would fill their offices according to the grace of God bestowed upon them.

5. The number composing the council, who voted in the name and for the church, in appointing the above-named councilors were forty-three, as follows—Nine High Priests, seventeen elders, four priests, and thirteen members.

6. Voted: that the High Council cannot have power to act without seven of the above-named councilors, or their regularly appointed successors are present.

7. These seven shall have power to appoint other High Priests, whom they may consider worthy and capable to act in the place of absent councilors.

8. Voted: that whenever any vacancy shall occur by the death, removal from office for transgression, or

removal from the bounds of this church government, of any one of the above-named councilors, it shall be filled by the nomination of the President or Presidents, and sanctioned by the voice of a general council of High Priests, convened for that purpose, to act in the name of the church.

9. The President of the church, who is also the President of the council, is appointed by revelation, and acknowledged in his administration, by the voice of the church;

10. And it is according to the dignity of his office that he should preside over the Council of the church; and it is his privilege to be assisted by two other Presidents, appointed after the same manner that he himself was appointed;

11. And in case of the absence of one or both of those who are appointed to assist him, he has power to preside over the Council without an assistant: and in case he himself is absent, the other Presidents have power to preside in his stead, both or either of them.

12. Whenever an High Council of the church of Christ is regularly organized, according to the foregoing pattern, it shall be the duty of the twelve councilors to cast lots by numbers, and thereby ascertain, who of the twelve shall speak first, commencing with number one, and so in succession to number twelve.

13. Whenever this Council convenes to act upon any case, the twelve councilors shall consider whether it is a difficult one or not; if it is not, two only of the councilors shall speak upon it, according to the form above written.

14. But if it is thought to be difficult, four shall be appointed; and if more difficult, six; but in no case shall more than six be appointed to speak.

15. The accused, in all cases, has a right to one half of the Council, to prevent insult or injustice;

16. And the councilors appointed to speak before the Council are to present the case, after the evidence is examined, in its true light before the Council, and every man is to speak according to equity and justice.

17. Those councilors who draw even numbers, that is 2, 4, 6, 8, 10, and 12, are the individuals who are to stand up in behalf of the accused, and prevent insult or injustice.

18. In all cases the accuser and the accused shall have a privilege of speaking for themselves before the Council, after the evidences are heard, and the councilors who are appointed to speak on the case, have finished their remarks.

19. After the evidences are heard, the councilors, accuser and accused have spoken, the President shall give a decision according to the understanding which he shall have of the case, and call upon the twelve councilors to sanction the same by their vote.

20. But should the remaining councilors, who have not spoken, or any one of them, after hearing the evidences and pleadings impartially, discover an error in the decision of the President, they can manifest it, and the case shall have a re-hearing;

21. And if, after a careful re-hearing, any additional light is shown upon the case, the decision shall be altered accordingly;

22. But in case no additional light is given, the first decision shall stand, the majority of the Council having power to determine the same.

23. In case of difficulty respecting doctrine or principle, (if there is not a sufficiency written to make the case clear to the minds of the council,) the President may inquire and obtain the mind of the Lord by revelation.

24. The High Priests, when abroad, have power to Call and Organize a council after the manner of the foregoing, to settle difficulties, when the parties, or either of them shall request it.

25. And the said council of High Priests shall have power to appoint one of their own number, to preside over such council for the time being.

26. It shall be the duty of said council to transmit, immediately, a copy of their proceedings, with a full statement of the testimony accompanying their decision, to the High Council of the seat of the First Presidency of the Church.

27. Should the parties, or either of them be dissatisfied with the decision of said council, they may appeal to the High Council of the seat of the First Presidency of the church, and have a re-hearing, which case shall there be conducted, according to the former pattern written, as though no such decision had been made.

28. This council of High Priests abroad is only to be called on the most difficult cases of church matters; and no common or ordinary case is to be sufficient to call such council.

29. The traveling or located High Priests abroad, have power to say whether it is necessary to call such a council or not.

30. There is a distinction between the High Council or traveling High Priests abroad, and the traveling High Council composed of the Twelve apostles, in their decisions.

31. From the decision of the former there can be an appeal, but from the decision of the latter there cannot.

32. The latter can only be called in question by the general authorities of the church in case of transgression.

33. Resolved, that the President or Presidents of the seat of the First Presidency of the church, shall have power to determine whether any such case, as may be appealed, is justly entitled to a re-hearing, after examining the appeal and the evidences and statements accompanying it.

34. The twelve councilors then proceeded to cast lots or ballot, to ascertain who should speak first, and the following was the result, namely:—

1 Oliver Cowdery,
2 Joseph Coe,
3 Samuel H. Smith,
4 Luke Johnson,
5 John S. Carter,
6 Sylvester Smith,
7 John Johnson,
8 Orson Hyde,
9 Jared Carter,
10 Joseph Smith, Sen.,
11 John Smith,
12 Martin Harris.

After prayer, the conference adjourned.

OLIVER COWDERY,
ORSON HYDE, Clerks.

Section 103

Parley P. Pratt and Lyman Wight, delegates from the brethren in Missouri, arrived at Kirtland, Ohio, to report on the conditions of the Saints who had been driven from Jackson County, Missouri. The Prophet Joseph Smith received this revelation February 24, 1834, at Kirtland, Ohio. In this revelation the Lord commanded the Saints in Ohio to contribute money and provisions, and to organize a company of men (Zions Camp) to go to Missouri to aid the scattered Saints (History of the Church, vol. 2:36–39).

1. Verily I say unto you, my friends, behold I will give unto you a revelation and commandment, that you may know how to act in the discharge of your duties concerning the salvation and redemption of your brethren, who have been scattered on the land of Zion;

2. Being driven and smitten by the hands of mine enemies, on whom I will pour out my wrath without measure in mine own time;

3. For I have suffered them thus far, that they might fill up the measure of their iniquities, that their cup might be full;

4. And that those who call themselves after my name might be chastened for a little season with a sore and grievous chastisement, because they did not hearken altogether unto the precepts and commandments which I gave unto them.

5. But verily I say unto you, that I have decreed a decree which my people shall realize, inasmuch as they hearken from this very hour, unto the counsel which I, the Lord their God, shall give unto them.

6. Behold they shall, for I have decreed it, begin to prevail against mine enemies from this very hour,

7. And by hearkening to observe all the words which I, the Lord their God, shall speak unto them, they shall never cease to prevail until the kingdoms of the world are subdued under my feet, and the earth is given unto the saints, to possess it for ever and ever.

8. But inasmuch as they keep not my commandments, and hearken not to observe all my words, the kingdoms of the world shall prevail against them,

9. For they were set to be a light unto the world, and to be the saviors of men;

10. And inasmuch as they are not the saviors of men, they are as salt that has lost its savor, and is thenceforth good for nothing but to be cast out and trodden under foot of men.

11. But verily I say unto you, I have decreed that your brethren which have been scattered shall return to the land of their inheritances, and build up the waste places of Zion;

12. For after much tribulation, as I have said unto you in a former commandment, cometh the blessing.

13. Behold, this is the blessing which I have promised after your tribulations, and the tribulations of your brethren; your redemption, and the redemption of your brethren, even their restoration to the land of Zion, to be established no more to be thrown down;

14. Nevertheless, if they pollute their inheritances, they shall be thrown down, for I will not spare them if they pollute their inheritances.

15. Behold, I say unto you, the redemption of Zion must needs come by power;

16. Therefore, I will raise up unto my people a man, who shall lead them like as Moses led the children of Israel,

17. For ye are the children of Israel, and of the seed of Abraham, and ye must needs be led out of bondage by power, and with a stretched out arm:

18. And as your fathers were led at the first, even so shall the redemption of Zion be.

19. Therefore let not your hearts faint, for I say not unto you as I said unto your fathers, mine angel shall go up before you, but not my presence,

20. But I say unto you, mine angels shall go up before you, and also my presence, and in time ye shall possess the goodly land.

21. Verily, verily I say unto you, that my servant Baurak Ale (Joseph Smith, jr.) is the man to whom I likened the servant to whom the Lord of the vineyard spake in the parable which I have given unto you.

22. Therefore let my servant Baurak Ale (Joseph Smith, jr.) say unto the strength of my house, my young men and the middle aged, gather yourselves together unto the land of Zion, upon the land which I have bought with money that has been consecrated unto me;

23. And let all the churches send up wise men with their moneys, and purchase lands even as I have commanded them;

24. And inasmuch as mine enemies come against you to drive you from my goodly land, which I have consecrated to be the land of Zion; even from your own lands after these testimonies, which ye have brought before me, against them, ye shall curse them;

25. And whomsoever ye curse, I will curse, and ye shall avenge me of mine enemies;

26. And my presence shall be with you even in avenging me of mine enemies, unto the third and fourth generation of them that hate me.

27. Let no man be afraid to lay down his life for my sake, for whoso layeth down his life for my sake shall find it again.

28. And whoso is not willing to lay down his life for my sake, is not my disciple.

29. It is my will that my servant Sidney Rigdon shall lift up his voice in the congregations in the eastern countries, in preparing the churches to keep the commandments which I have given unto them ,concerning the restoration and redemption of Zion.

30. It is my will that my servant Parley P. Pratt and my servant Lyman Wight should not return to the land of their brethren, until they have obtained companies to go up unto the land of Zion, by tens, or by twenties, or by fifties, or by an hundred, until they have obtained to the number of five hundred of the strength of my house.

31. Behold this is my will; ask and ye shall receive, but men do not always do my will;

32. Therefore, if you cannot obtain five hundred, seek diligently, that peradventure you may obtain three hundred;

33. And if ye cannot obtain three hundred, seek diligently, that peradventure ye may obtain one hundred.

34. But verily I say unto you, a commandment I give unto you, that ye shall not go up unto the land of Zion, until you have obtained a hundred of the strength of my house, to go up with you unto the land of Zion.

35. Therefore as I said unto you, ask and ye shall receive; pray earnestly that peradventure my servant Baurak Ale (Joseph Smith, jr.) may go with you, and preside in the midst of my people, and organize my kingdom upon the consecrated land, and establish the children of Zion upon the laws and commandments which have been, and which shall be given unto you.

36. All victory and glory is brought to pass unto you through your diligence, faithfulness and prayers of faith.

37. Let my servant Parley P. Pratt journey with my servant Joseph Smith, jr.

38. Let my servant Lyman Wight journey with my servant Sidney Rigdon.

39. Let my servant Hyrum Smith journey with my servant Frederick G. Williams.

40. Let my servant Orson Hyde journey with my servant Orson Pratt, whithersoever my servant Joseph Smith, jr., shall counsel them, in obtaining the fulfilment of these commandments which I have given unto you, and leave the residue in my hands. Even so. Amen.

Section 104

Early in 1834, the Church in Kirtland, Ohio, and Zion (Jackson County, Missouri) was experiencing financial difficulties. The United Firm (United Order) had been organized to aid the Church financially. In this revelation the Lord restructures this organization for the benefit of the Church and the poor. This revelation was received by the Prophet Joseph Smith, April 23, 1834, at Kirtland, Ohio (History of the Church, vol. 2:54).

1. Verily I say unto you, my friends, I give unto you counsel, and a commandment, concerning all the properties which belong to the order which I commanded to be organized and established, to be an united order, and an everlasting order for the benefit of my church, and for the salvation of men until I come,

2. With promise immutable and unchangeable, that inasmuch as those whom I commanded were faithful they should be blessed with a multiplicity of blessings;

3. But inasmuch as they were not faithful they were nigh unto cursing.

4. Therefore, inasmuch as some of my servants have not kept the commandment, but have broken the covenant through covetousness, and with feigned words, I have cursed them with a very sore and grievous curse;

5. For I, the Lord, have decreed in my heart, that inasmuch as any man belonging to the order, shall be found a transgressor, or, in other words, shall break the covenant with which ye are bound, he shall be cursed in his life, and shall be trodden down by whom I will,

6. For I, the Lord, am not to be mocked in these things;

7. And all this that the innocent among you may not be condemned with the unjust, and that the guilty among you may not escape, because I, the Lord, have promised unto you a crown of glory at my right hand.

8. Therefore inasmuch as you are found transgressors, you cannot escape my wrath in your lives;

9. Inasmuch as ye are cut off for transgression, ye cannot escape the buffetings of Satan, until the day of redemption.

10. And I now give unto you power from this very hour, that if any man among you, of the order, is found a transgressor, and repenteth not of the evil, that ye shall deliver him over unto the buffetings of Satan, and he shall not have power to bring evil upon you.

11. It is wisdom in me: therefore, a commandment I give unto you, that ye shall organize yourselves and appoint every man his stewardship,

12. That every man may give an account unto me of the stewardship which is appointed unto him;

13. For it is expedient that I, the Lord, should make every man accountable, as stewards over earthly blessings, which I have made and prepared for my creatures.

14. I, the Lord, stretched out the heavens, and built the earth as a very handiwork, and all things therein are mine:

15. And it is my purpose to provide for my saints, for all things are mine;

16. But it must needs be done in mine own way; and behold this is the way that I, the Lord, have decreed to provide for my saints, that the poor shall be exalted, in that the rich are made low;

17. For the earth is full, and there is enough and to spare; yea, I prepared all things, and have given unto the children of men to be agents unto themselves.

18. Therefore, if any man shall take of the abundance which I have made, and impart not his portion, according to the law of my gospel, unto the poor and the needy, he shall, with the wicked, lift up his eyes in hell, being in torment.

19. And now, verily I say unto you, concerning the properties of the order.

20. Let my servant Pelagoram (Sidney Rigdon) have appointed unto him the place where he now resides and the lot of Tahhannes (the tannery) for his stewardship, for his support while he is laboring in my vineyard, even as I will when I shall command him;

21. And let all things be done according to the counsel of the order, and united consent or voice of the order, which dwell in the land of Shinehah. (Kirtland.)

22. And this stewardship and blessing, I, the Lord, confer upon my servant Pelagoram, (Sidney Rigdon,) for a blessing upon him, and his seed after him;

23. And I will multiply blessings upon him, inasmuch as he shall be humble before me.

24. And again, let my servant Mahemson (Martin Harris) have appointed unto him, for his stewardship, the lot of land which my servant Zombre (John Johnson) obtained in exchange for his former inheritance, for him and his seed after him;

25. And inasmuch as he is faithful, I will multiply blessings upon him, and his seed after him.

26. And let my servant Mahemson (Martin Harris) devote his moneys for the proclaiming of my words, according as my servant Gazelam (Joseph Smith, jr.) shall direct.

27. And again, let my servant Shederlaomach (Frederick G. Williams) have the place upon which he now dwells.

28. And let my servant Olihah (Oliver Cowdery) have the lot which is set off joining the house, which is to be for the Laneshine-house (printing office) which is lot number one, and also the lot upon which his father resides.

29. And let my servants Shederlaomach (Frederick G. Williams) and Olihah (Oliver Cowdery) have the Laneshine-house, (printing office,) and all things that pertain unto it;

30. And this shall be their stewardship which shall be appointed unto them:

31. And inasmuch as they are faithful, behold I will bless, and multiply blessings upon them,

32. And this is the beginning of the stewardship which I have appointed them, for them and their seed after them;

33. And, inasmuch as they are faithful, I will multiply blessings upon them, and their seed after them, even a multiplicity of blessings.

34. And again, let my servant Zombre (John Johnson) have the house in which he lives, and the inheritance—all, save the ground which has been reserved for the building of my houses,

which pertains to that inheritance, and those lots which have been named for my servant Oliahah. (Oliver Cowdery.)

35. And, inasmuch as he is faithful, I will multiply blessings upon him.

36. And it is my will that he should sell the lots that are laid off for the building up of the city of my saints, inasmuch as it shall be made known to him by the voice of the Spirit, and according to the counsel of the order, and by the voice of the order.

37. And this is the beginning of the stewardship which I have appointed unto him, for a blessing unto him, and his seed after him;

38. And, inasmuch as he is faithful, I will multiply a multiplicity of blessings upon him.

39. And again, let my servant Ahashdah (Newel K. Whitney) have appointed unto him the houses and lot where he now resides, and the lot and building on which the Ozondah (mercantile establishment) stands, and also the lot which is on the corner south of the Ozondah (mercantile establishment), and also the lot on which the Shule (ashery) is situated.

40. And all this I have appointed unto my servant Ahashdah, (Newel K. Whitney,) for his stewardship, for a blessing upon him and his seed after him, for the benefit of the Ozondah (mercantile establishment) of my order which I have established for my Stake in the land of Shinehah; (Kirtland;)

41. Yea, verily, this is the stewardship which I have appointed unto my servant Ahashdah, (N. K. Whitney,) even this whole Ozondah, (mercantile establishment,) him and his agent, and his seed after him;

42. And, inasmuch as he is faithful in keeping my commandments which I have given unto him, I will multiply blessings upon him, and his seed after him, even a multiplicity of blessings.

43. And again, let my servant Gazelam (Joseph Smith, jr.) have appointed unto him the lot which is laid off for the building of my house, which is forty rods long and twelve wide, and also the inheritance upon which his father resides;

44. And this is the beginning of the stewardship which I have appointed unto him, for a blessing upon him, and upon his father;

45. For, behold, I have reserved an inheritance for his father, for his support; therefore he shall be reckoned in the house of my servant Gazelam, (Joseph Smith, jr.,)

46. And I will multiply blessings upon the house of my servant Gazelam, (Joseph Smith, jr.,) inasmuch as he is faithful, even a multiplicity of blessings.

47. And now, a commandment I give unto you concerning Zion, that you shall no longer be bound as an United Order to your brethren of Zion, only on this wise.

48. After you are organized, you shall be called the United Order of the Stake of Zion, the city of Shinehah. (Kirtland.) And your brethren, after they are organized, shall be called the United Order of the City of Zion;

49. And they shall be organized in their own names, and in their own name; and they shall do their business in their own name, and in their own names;

50. And you shall do your business in your own name, and in your own names.

51. And this I have commanded to be done for your salvation, and also for their salvation, in consequence of their being driven out, and that which is to come.

52. The covenants being broken through transgression, by covetousness and feigned words;

53. Therefore, you are dissolved as a United Order with your brethren, that you are not bound only up to this hour unto them, only on this wise, as I said, by loan as shall be agreed by this order in council, as your circumstances will admit and the voice of the council direct.

54. And again, a commandment I give unto you concerning your stewardship which I have appointed unto you.

55. Behold, all these properties are mine, or else your faith is vain, and ye are found hypocrites, and the covenants which ye have made unto me are broken;

56. And if the properties are mine, then ye are stewards, otherwise ye are no stewards.

57. But, verily I say unto you, I have appointed unto you to be stewards over mine house, even stewards indeed;

58. And for this purpose I have commanded you to organize yourselves, even to Shinelah (print) my words, the fulness of my scriptures, the revelations which I have given unto you, and which I shall, hereafter, from time to time give unto you,

59. For the purpose of building up my church and kingdom on the earth, and to prepare my people for the time when I shall dwell with them, which is nigh at hand.

60. And ye shall prepare for yourselves a treasury, and consecrate it unto my name;

61. And ye shall appoint one among you to keep the treasury, and he shall be ordained unto this blessing;

62. And there shall be a seal upon the treasury, and all the sacred things shall be delivered into the treasury, and no man among you shall call it his own, or any part of it, for it shall belong to you all with one accord;

63. And I give it unto you from this very hour :and now see to it, that ye go to and make use of the stewardship which I have appointed unto you, exclusive of the sacred things, for the purpose of Shinelane (printing) these sacred things as I have said;

64. And the avails of the sacred things shall be had in the treasury, and a seal shall be upon it, and it shall not be used or taken out of the treasury by any one, neither shall the seal be loosed which shall be placed upon it only by the voice of the order, or by commandment.

65. And thus shall ye preserve the avails of the sacred things in the treasury, for sacred and holy purposes:

66. And this shall be called the sacred treasury of the Lord; and a seal shall be kept upon it that it may be holy and consecrated unto the Lord.

67. And again, there shall be another treasury prepared, and a treasurer appointed to keep the treasury, and a seal shall be placed upon it;

68. And all moneys that you receive in your stewardships, by improving upon the properties which I have appointed unto you, in houses, or in lands, or in cattle, or in all things save it be the holy and sacred writings, which I have reserved unto myself for holy and sacred purposes, shall be cast into the treasury as fast as you receive moneys, by hundreds, or by fifties, or by twenties, or by tens, or by fives;

69. Or in other words, if any man among you obtain five talents, (dollars,) let him cast them into the treasury; or if he obtain ten, or twenty, or fifty, or an hundred, let him do likewise;

70. And let not any man among you say that it is his own, for it shall not be called his, nor any part of it,

71. And there shall not any part of it be used, or taken out of the treasury, only by the voice and common consent of the order.

72. And this shall be the voice and common consent of the order; that any man among you say to the treasurer; I have need of this to help me in my stewardship;

73. If it be five talents, (dollars,) or if it be ten talents, (dollars,) or twenty, or fifty, or an hundred, the treasurer shall give unto him the sum which he requires, to help him in his stewardship,

74. Until he be found a transgressor, and it is manifest before the council of the order plainly, that he is an unfaithful and an unwise steward;

75. But so long as he is in full fellowship, and is faithful, and wise in his stewardship, this shall be his token unto the treasurer, that the treasurer shall not withhold.

76. But in case of transgression, the treasurer shall be subject unto the council and voice of the order.

77. And in case the treasurer is found an unfaithful, and an unwise steward, he shall be subject to the council and voice of the order, and shall be removed out of his place, and another shall be appointed in his stead.

78. And again, verily I say unto you, concerning your debts, behold it is my will that you shall pay all your debts;

79. And it is my will that you shall humble yourselves before me, and obtain this blessing by your diligence and humility, and the prayer of faith;

80. And inasmuch as you are diligent and humble, and exercise the prayer of faith, behold, I will soften the hearts of those to whom you are in debt, until I shall send means unto you for your deliverance.

81. Therefore write speedily unto Cainhannoch, (New York), and write according to that which shall be dictated by my Spirit, and I will soften the hearts of those to whom you are in debt, that it shall be taken away out of their minds to bring affliction upon you.

82. And inasmuch as ye are humble and faithful, and call upon my name, behold, I will give you the victory.

83. I give unto you a promise, that you shall be delivered this once out of your bondage;

84. Inasmuch as you obtain a chance to loan money by hundreds, or thousands, even until you shall loan enough to deliver yourselves from bondage, it is your privilege;

85. And pledge the properties which I have put into your hands, this once, by giving your names by common consent or otherwise, as it shall seem good unto you.

86. I give unto you this privilege, this once, and behold, if you proceed to do the things which I have laid before you, according to my commandments, all these things are mine, and ye are my stewards, and the master will not suffer his house to be broken up. Even so. Amen.

THE MEN OF ZION'S CAMP SEEK REFUGE FROM A STORM

ection 105

In February 1834, the Lord gave a revelation (section 103) to the Prophet Joseph Smith in which the Saints in Ohio were instructed to contribute money and provisions, and to organize a company of men (Zions Camp) to go to Missouri to assist the scattered Saints. Zions Camp arrived at Fishing River, Clay County, Missouri, June 22, 1834, at which time this revelation was given to the Prophet Joseph Smith (History of the Church, vol. 2:108).

1. Verily I say unto you who have assembled yourselves together that you may learn my will concerning the redemption of mine afflicted people.
2. Behold, I say unto you, were it not for the transgressions of my people, speaking concerning the church and not individuals, they might have been redeemed even now;
3. But behold, they have not learned to be obedient to the things which I required at their hands, but are full of all manner of evil, and do not impart of their substance, as becometh saints, to the poor and afflicted among them,
4. And are not united according to the union required by the law of the celestial kingdom;
5. And Zion cannot be built up unless it is by the principles of the law of the celestial kingdom, otherwise I cannot receive her unto myself.
6. And my people must needs be chastened until they learn obedience, if it must needs be, by the things which they suffer.
7. I speak not concerning those who are appointed to lead my people, who are the first elders of my church, for they are not all under this condemnation;
8. But I speak concerning my churches abroad—there are many who will say, Where is their God? Behold, he will deliver them in time of trouble, otherwise we will not go up unto Zion, and will keep our moneys.
9. Therefore, in consequence of the transgressions of my people, it is expedient in me that mine elders should wait for a little season for the redemption of Zion,
10. That they themselves may be prepared, and that my people may be taught more perfectly, and have experience, and know more perfectly concerning their duty, and the things which I require at their hands.
11. And this cannot be brought to pass until mine elders are endowed with power from on high;
12. For behold, I have prepared a great endowment and blessing to be poured out upon them, inasmuch as they are faithful and continue in humility before me;

13. Therefore it is expedient in me that mine elders should wait for a little season, for the redemption of Zion;

14. For behold, I do not require at their hands to fight the battles of Zion; for, as I said in a former commandment, even so will I fulfil. I will fight your battles.

15. Behold, the destroyer I have sent forth to destroy and lay waste mine enemies: and not many years hence they shall not be left to pollute mine heritage, and to blaspheme my name upon the lands which I have consecrated for the gathering together of my saints.

16. Behold, I have commanded my servant Baurak Ale (Joseph Smith, jr.) to say unto the strength of my house, even my warriors, my young men, and middle-aged, to gather together for the redemption of my people, and throw down the towers of mine enemies, and scatter their watchmen;

17. But the strength of mine house have not hearkened unto my words;

18. But inasmuch as there are those who have hearkened unto my words, I have prepared a blessing and an endowment for them, if they continue faithful.

19. I have heard their prayers, and will accept their offering; and it is expedient in me, that they should be brought thus far for a trial of their faith.

20. And now, verily I say unto you, a commandment I give unto you, that as many as have come up hither, that can stay in the region round about, let them stay;

21. And those that cannot stay, who have families in the east, let them tarry for a little season, inasmuch as my servant Joseph shall appoint unto them;

22. For I will counsel him concerning this matter, and all things whatsoever he shall appoint unto them shall be fulfilled.

23. And let all my people who dwell in the regions round about be very faithful, and prayerful, and humble before me, and reveal not the things which I have revealed unto them, until it is wisdom in me that they should be revealed.

24. Talk not of judgments, neither boast of faith nor of mighty works, but carefully gather together, as much in one region as can be consistently with the feelings of the people;

25. And behold, I will give unto you favor and grace in their eyes, that you may rest in peace and safety, while you are saying unto the people, Execute judgment and justice for us according to law, and redress us of our wrongs.

26. Now, behold, I say unto you, my friends, in this way you may find favor in the eyes of the people, until the army of Israel becomes very great;

27. And I will soften the hearts of the people, as I did the heart of Pharaoh, from time to time, until my servant Baurak Ale, (Joseph Smith, jr.,) and Baneemy, (mine elders,) whom I have appointed, shall have time to gather up the strength of my house,

28. And to have sent wise men, to fulfil that which I have commanded concerning the purchasing of all the lands in Jackson county that can be purchased, and in the adjoining counties round about;

29. For it is my will that these lands should be purchased, and after they are purchased that my saints should possess them according to the laws of consecration which I have given;

30. And after these lands are purchased, I will hold the armies of Israel guiltless in taking possession of their own lands, which they have previously purchased with their moneys, and of throwing down the towers of mine enemies that may be upon them, and scattering their watchmen, and avenging me of mine enemies unto the third and fourth generation of them that hate me.

31. But firstly let my army become very great, and let it be sanctified before me, that it may become fair as the sun, and clear as the moon, and that

her banners may be terrible unto all nations;

32. That the kingdoms of this world may be constrained to acknowledge, that the kingdom of Zion is in very deed the kingdom of our God and his Christ; therefore, let us become subject unto her laws.

33. Verily I say unto you, it is expedient in me that the first elders of my church should receive their endowment from on high in my house which I have commanded to be built unto my name in the land of Kirtland;

34. And let those commandments which I have given concerning Zion and her law be executed, and fulfilled, after her redemption.

35. There has been a day of calling, but the time has come for a day of choosing, and let those be chosen that are worthy;

36. And it shall be manifest unto my servant, by the voice of the Spirit, those that are chosen, and they shall be sanctified;

37. And inasmuch as they follow the counsel which they receive, they shall have power after many days to accomplish all things pertaining to Zion.

38. And again I say unto you, sue for peace, not only to the people that have smitten you, but also to all people;

39. And lift up an ensign of peace, and make a proclamation of peace unto the ends of the earth;

40. And make proposals for peace unto those who have smitten you, according to the voice of the Spirit which is in you, and all things shall work together for your good;

41. Therefore, be faithful, and behold, and lo, I am with you even unto the end. Even so. Amen.

Section 106

In Kirtland, Ohio, a school for the Elders had been organized, "wherein they might be more perfectly instructed in the great things of God." While preparing for the school, the Prophet Joseph Smith received this revelation, November 25, 1834 (History of the Church, vol. 2:169–170).

1. It is my will that my servant Warren A. Cowdery should be appointed and ordained a presiding High Priest over my church, in the land of Freedom and the regions round about;

2. And should preach my everlasting gospel, and lift up his voice and warn the people, not only in his own place, but in the adjoining countries,

3. And devote his whole time in this high and holy calling which I now give unto him, seeking diligently the kingdom of heaven and its righteousness, and all things necessary shall be added thereunto, for the laborer is worthy of his hire.

4. And again, verily I say unto you the coming of the Lord draweth nigh, and it overtaketh the world as a thief in the night:

5. Therefore, gird up your loins that you may be the children of light, and that day shall not overtake you as a thief.

6. And again, verily I say unto you, there was joy in heaven when my servant Warren bowed to my scepter, and separated himself from the crafts of men:

7. Therefore, blessed is my servant Warren, for I will have mercy on him, and notwithstanding the vanity of his heart, I will lift him up, inasmuch as he will humble himself before me;

8. And I will give him grace and assurance wherewith he may stand, and if he continue to be a faithful witness and a light unto the church, I have prepared a crown for him in the mansions of my Father. Even so. Amen.

Section 107

In Kirtland, Ohio, March 12, 1835, the Twelve Apostles met in council meeting. The Prophet Joseph Smith proposed that the Twelve take their first mission to the eastern states. Not knowing how long it would be before they would meet in council again, the Twelve asked the Prophet Joseph Smith if he would inquire of the Lord and obtain a revelation for the Twelve, "that we may look upon it when we are separated, that our hearts may be comforted." This revelation was received March 28, 1835, at Kirtland, Ohio (History of the Church, vol. 2:209–210).

1. There are, in the church, two Priesthoods, namely, the Melchisedek and Aaronic, including the Levitical priesthood.
2. Why the first is called the Melchisedek Priesthood is because Melchisedek was such a great High Priest.
3. Before his day it was called *the Holy Priesthood, after the order of the Son of God;*
4. But out of respect or reverence to the name of the Supreme Being, to avoid the too frequent repetition of his name, they, the church, in ancient days, called that Priesthood after Melchisedek, or the Melchisedek Priesthood.
5. All other authorities or offices in the church are appendages to this Priesthood;
6. But there are two divisions or grand heads—one is the Melchisedek Priesthood, and the other is the Aaronic, or Levitical priesthood.
7. The office of an elder comes under the Priesthood of Melchisedek.
8. The Melchisedek Priesthood holds the right of Presidency, and has power and authority over all the offices in the church in all ages of the world, to administer in spiritual things.
9. The Presidency of the High Priesthood, after the order of Melchisedek, have a right to officiate in all the offices in the church.
10. High Priests after the order of the Melchisedek Priesthood have a right to officiate in their own standing, under the direction of the Presidency, in administering spiritual things; and also in the office of an elder, priest, (of the Levitical order,), teacher, deacon, and member.
11. An elder has a right to officiate in his stead when the High Priest is not present.
12. The High Priest and elder are to administer in spiritual things, agreeable to the covenants and commandments of the church; and they have a right to officiate in all these offices of the church when there are no higher authorities present.
13. The second priesthood is called the priesthood of Aaron, because it was conferred upon Aaron and his seed, throughout all their generations.

14. Why it is called the lesser priesthood, is because it is an appendage to the greater or the Melchisedek Priesthood, and has power in administering outward ordinances.

15. The bishopric is the presidency of this priesthood and holds the keys or authority of the same.

16. No man has a legal right to this office, to hold the keys of this priesthood, except he be a literal descendant of Aaron.

17. But as a High Priest of the Melchisedek Priesthood has authority to officiate in all the lesser offices, he may officiate in the office of bishop when no literal descendant of Aaron can be found, provided he is called and set apart and ordained unto this power by the hands of the Presidency of the Melchisedek Priesthood.

18. The power and authority of the Higher, or Melchisedek Priesthood, is to hold the keys of all the spiritual blessings of the church—

19. To have the privilege of receiving the mysteries of the kingdom of heaven—to have the heavens opened unto them—to commune with the general assembly and church of the first born, and to enjoy the communion and presence of God the Father, and Jesus the Mediator of the new covenant.

20. The power and authority of the lesser, or Aaronic priesthood, is to hold the keys of the ministering of angels, and to administer in outward ordinances, the letter of the gospel—the baptism of repentance for the remission of sins, agreeable to the covenants and commandments.

21. Of necessity there are presidents, or presiding offices growing out of, or appointed of or from among those who are ordained to the several offices in these two priesthoods.

22. Of the Melchisedek Priesthood, three Presiding High Priests, chosen by the body, appointed and ordained to that office, and upheld by the confidence, faith, and prayer of the church, form a quorum of the Presidency of the church.

23. The Twelve traveling councilors are called to be the Twelve apostles, or special witnesses of the name of Christ in all the world; thus differing from other officers in the church in the duties of their calling.

24. And they form a quorum, equal in authority and power to the three Presidents previously mentioned.

25. The seventy are also called to preach the gospel, and to be especial witnesses unto the Gentiles and in all the world. Thus differing from other officers in the church in the duties of their calling;

26. And they form a quorum, equal in authority to that of the Twelve special witnesses or apostles just named.

27. And every decision made by either of these quorums, must be by the unanimous voice of the same; that is, every member in each quorum must be agreed to its decisions, in order to make their decisions of the same power or validity one with the other.

28. (A majority may form a quorum, when circumstances render it impossible to be otherwise.)

29. Unless this is the case, their decisions are not entitled to the same blessings which the decisions of a quorum of three Presidents were anciently, who were ordained after the order of Melchisedek, and were righteous and holy men.

30. The decisions of these quorums, or either of them, are to be made in all righteousness, in holiness, and lowliness of heart, meekness and long suffering, and in faith, and virtue, and knowledge, temperance, patience, godliness, brotherly kindness and charity;

31. Because the promise is, if these things abound in them, they shall not be unfruitful in the knowledge of the Lord.

32. And in case that any decision of these quorums is made in unrighteousness, it may be brought before a general assembly of the several

quorums, which constitute the spiritual authorities of the church, otherwise there can be no appeal from their decision.

33. The Twelve are a traveling presiding High Council, to officiate in the name of the Lord, under the direction of the Presidency of the church, agreeable to the institution of heaven; to build up the church, and regulate all the affairs of the same in all nations; first unto the Gentiles, and secondly unto the Jews.

34. The seventy are to act in the name of the Lord, under the direction of the Twelve or the traveling High Council, in building up the church and regulating all the affairs of the same in all nations—first unto the Gentiles and then to the Jews;

35. The Twelve being sent out, holding the keys, to open the door by the proclamation of the gospel of Jesus Christ—and first unto the Gentiles and then unto the Jews.

36. The standing High Councils, at the Stakes of Zion, form a quorum equal in authority, in the affairs of the church, in all their decisions, to the quorum of the Presidency, or to the traveling High Council.

37. The High Council in Zion form a quorum equal in authority, in the affairs of the church, in all their decisions, to the Councils of the Twelve at the Stakes of Zion.

38. It is the duty of the traveling High Council to call upon the seventy, when they need assistance, to fill the several calls for preaching and administering the gospel, instead of any others.

39. It is the duty of the Twelve, in all large branches of the church, to ordain evangelical ministers, as they shall be designated unto them by revelation.

40. The order of this Priesthood was confirmed to be handed down from father to son, and rightly belongs to the literal descendants of the chosen seed, to whom the promises were made.

41. This order was instituted in the days of Adam, and came down by lineage in the following manner—

42. From Adam to Seth, who was ordained by Adam at the age of 69 years, and was blessed by him three years previous to his (Adam's) death, and received the promise of God by his father, that his posterity should be the chosen of the Lord, and that they should be preserved unto the end of the earth,

43. Because he (Seth) was a perfect man, and his likeness was the express likeness of his father's, insomuch that he seemed to be like unto his father in all things, and could be distinguished from him only by his age.

44. Enos was ordained at the age of 134 years and four months, by the hand of Adam.

45. God called upon Cainan in the wilderness, in the fortieth year of his age, and he met Adam in journeying to the place Shedolamak. He was 87 years old when he received his ordination.

46. Mahalaleel was 496 years and seven days old when he was ordained by the hand of Adam, who also blessed him.

47. Jared was 200 years old when he was ordained under the hand of Adam, who also blessed him.

48. Enoch was 25 years old when he was ordained under the hand of Adam, and he was 65 and Adam blessed him.

49. And he saw the Lord, and he walked with him, and was before his face continually; and he walked with God 365 years, making him 430 years old when he was translated.

50. Methuselah was 100 years old when he was ordained under the hand of Adam.

51. Lamech was 32 years old when he was ordained under the hand of Seth.

52. Noah was 10 years old when he was ordained under the hand of Methuselah.

53. Three years previous to the death of Adam, he called Seth, Enos, Cainan, Mahalaleel, Jared,

Enoch, and Methuselah, who were all High Priests, with the residue of his posterity who were righteous, into the valley of Adam-ondi-Ahman, and there bestowed upon them his last blessing.

54. And the Lord appeared unto them, and they rose up and blessed Adam, and called him Michael, the Prince, the Archangel.

55. And the Lord administered comfort unto Adam, and said unto him; I have set thee to be at the head—a multitude of nations shall come of thee, and thou art a prince over them for ever.

56. And Adam stood up in the midst of the congregation, and notwithstanding he was bowed down with age, being full of the Holy Ghost, predicted whatsoever should befall his posterity unto the latest generation.

57. These things were all written in the book of Enoch, and are to be testified of in due time.

58. It is the duty of the Twelve, also, to ordain and set in order all the other officers of the church, agreeable to the revelation which says:

59. To the church of Christ in the land of Zion, in addition to the church laws respecting church business—

60. Verily, I say unto you, says the Lord of Hosts, there must needs be presiding elders to preside over those who are of the office of an elder;

61. And also priests to preside over those who are of the office of a priest;

62. And also teachers to preside over those who are of the office of a teacher; in like manner, and also the deacons;

63. Wherefore, from deacon to teacher, and from teacher to priest, and from priest to elder, severally as they are appointed, according to the covenants and commandments of the church.

64. Then comes the High Priesthood, which is the greatest of all;

65. Wherefore it must needs be that one be appointed of the High Priesthood to preside over the priesthood, and he shall be called President of the High Priesthood of the church;

66. Or, in other words, the Presiding High Priest over the High Priesthood of the church.

67. From the same comes the administering of ordinances and blessings upon the church, by the laying on of the hands.

68. Wherefore the office of a bishop is not equal unto it; for the office of a bishop is in administering all temporal things;

69. Nevertheless a bishop must be chosen from the High Priesthood, unless he is a literal descendant of Aaron;

70. For unless he is a literal descendant of Aaron he cannot hold the keys of that priesthood.

71. Nevertheless, a High Priest, that is, after the order of Melchisedek, may be set apart unto the ministering of temporal things, having a knowledge of them by the spirit of truth,

72. And also to be a judge in Israel, to do the business of the church, to sit in judgment upon transgressors upon testimony as it shall be laid before him according to the laws, by the assistance of his counselors, whom he has chosen, or will choose among the elders of the church.

73. This is the duty of a bishop who is not a literal descendant of Aaron, but has been ordained to the High Priesthood after the order of Melchisedek.

74. Thus shall he be a judge, even a common judge among the inhabitants of Zion, or in a Stake of Zion, or in any branch of the church where he shall be set apart unto this ministry, until the borders of Zion are enlarged, and it becomes necessary to have other bishops or judges in Zion, or elsewhere;

75. And inasmuch as there are other bishops appointed they shall act in the same office.

76. But a literal descendant of Aaron has a legal right to the presidency of this priesthood, to the keys of this ministry, to act in the office of bishop

THE LORD APPEARED UNTO ADAM AT ADAM-ONDI-AHMAN

independently, without counselors, except in a case where a president of the High Priesthood, after the order of Melchisedek, is tried, to sit as a judge in Israel.

77. And the decision of either of these councils, agreeable to the commandment which says,

78. Again, verily, I say unto you, the most important business of the church, and the most difficult cases of the church, inasmuch as there is not satisfaction upon the decision of the bishop or judges, it shall be handed over and carried up unto the Council of the church, before the Presidency of the High Priesthood;

79. And the Presidency of the Council of the High Priesthood shall have power to call other High Priests, even twelve, to assist as counselors; and thus the Presidency of the High Priesthood and its counselors shall have power to decide upon testimony according to the laws of the church.

80. And after this decision it shall be had in remembrance no more before the Lord; for this is the highest Council of the church of God, and a final decision upon controversies in spiritual matters.

81. There is not any person belonging to the church who is exempt from this Council of the church.

82. And inasmuch as a President of the High Priesthood shall transgress, he shall be had in remembrance before the common council of the church, who shall be assisted by twelve counselors of the High Priesthood;

83. And their decision upon his head shall be an end of controversy concerning him.

84. Thus, none shall be exempted from the justice and the laws of God, that all things may be done in order and in solemnity before him, according to truth and righteousness.

85. And again, verily I say unto you, the duty of a president over the office of a deacon is to preside over twelve deacons, to sit in council with them, and to teach them their duty—edifying one another, as it is given according to the covenants.

86. And also the duty of the president over the office of the teachers is to preside over twenty-four of the teachers, and to sit in council with them, teaching them the duties of their office, as given in the covenants.

87. Also the duty of the president over the priesthood of Aaron is to preside over forty-eight priests, and sit in council with them, to teach them the duties of their office, as is given in the covenants.

88. This president is to be a bishop; for this is one of the duties of this priesthood.

89. Again, the duty of the president over the office of elders is to preside over ninety-six elders, and to sit in council with them, and to teach them according to the covenants.

90. This presidency is a distinct one from that of the seventy, and is designed for those who do not travel into all the world.

91. And again, the duty of the President of the office of the High Priesthood is to preside over the whole church, and to be like unto Moses.

92. Behold, here is wisdom; yea, to be a seer, a revelator, a translator, and a prophet, having all the gifts of God which he bestows upon the head of the church.

93. And it is according to the vision, showing the order of the seventy, that they should have seven presidents to preside over them, chosen out of the number of the seventy;

94. And the seventh president of these presidents is to preside over the six;

95. And these seven presidents are to choose other seventy besides the first seventy, to whom they belong, and are to preside over them;

96. And also other seventy, until seven times seventy, if the labor in the vineyard of necessity requires it.

97. And these seventy are to be traveling ministers unto the Gentiles first, and also unto the Jews;

98. Whereas other officers of the church, who belong not unto the Twelve, neither to the Seventy, are not under the responsibility to travel among all nations, but are to travel as their circumstances shall allow, notwithstanding they may hold as high and responsible offices in the church.

99. Wherefore now let every man learn his duty, and to act in the office in which he is appointed, in all diligence.

100. He that is slothful shall not be counted worthy to stand, and he that learns not his duty and shows himself not approved, shall not be counted worthy to stand. Even so. Amen.

ECTION 108

Lyman Sherman came to the Prophet Joseph Smith and asked to have the word of the Lord through him. He said, "I have been wrought upon to make known to you my feelings and desires, and was promised that I should have a revelation which should make known my duty." This revelation was received December 26, 1835, at Kirtland, Ohio (History of the Church, vol. 2:345).

1. Verily, thus saith the Lord unto you, my servant Lyman, your sins are forgiven you, because you have obeyed my voice in coming up hither this morning to receive counsel of him whom I have appointed.

2. Therefore, let your soul be at rest concerning your spiritual standing, and resist no more my voice;

3. And arise up and be more careful henceforth, in observing your vows which you have made, and do make, and you shall be blessed with exceeding great blessings.

4. Wait patiently until the solemn assembly shall be called of my servants, then you shall be remembered with the first of mine elders, and receive right by ordination with the rest of mine elders, whom I have chosen.

5. Behold, this is the promise of the Father unto you if you continue faithful;

6. And it shall be fulfilled upon you in that day that you shall have right to preach my gospel wheresoever I shall send you, from henceforth from that time.

7. Therefore, strengthen your brethren in all your conversation, in all your prayers, and in all your exhortations, and in all your doings.

8. And behold! and lo! I am with you to bless you and deliver you for ever. Amen.

SECTION 109

The Prophet Joseph Smith informs us that, "The following prayer was given by Revelation to Joseph, the Seer, and was repeated in the Kirtland Temple at the time of its Dedication, March 27, 1836" (History of the Church, *vol. 2:420*).

1. Thanks be to thy name O Lord God of Israel, who keepest covenant and showest mercy unto thy servants who walk uprightly before thee, with all their hearts.

2. Thou who hast commanded thy servants to build a house to thy name in this place. (Kirtland.)

3. And now thou beholdest, O Lord, that thy servants have done according to thy commandment,

4. And now we ask thee, Holy Father, in the name of Jesus Christ, the Son of thy bosom, in whose name alone, salvation can be administered to the children of men, we ask thee, O Lord, to accept of this house, the workmanship of the hands of us, thy servants, which thou didst command us to build;

5. For thou knowest that we have done this work through great tribulation; and out of our poverty we have given of our substance, to build a house to thy name, that the Son of man might have a place to manifest himself to his people.

6. And as thou hast said in a revelation, given to us, calling us thy friends, saying, "Call your solemn assembly, as I have commanded you;

7. And as all have not faith, seek ye diligently, and teach one another words of wisdom; yea, seek ye out of the best books, words of wisdom, seek learning even by study, and also by faith.

8. Organize yourselves; prepare every needful thing, and establish a house, even a house of prayer, a house of fasting, a house of faith, a house of learning, a house of glory, a house of order, a house of God,

9. That your incomings may be in the name of the Lord, that your outgoings may be in the name of the Lord, that all your salutations may be in the name of the Lord, with uplifted hands unto the Most High."

10. And now, Holy Father, we ask thee to assist us, thy people, with thy grace, in calling our solemn assembly, that it may be done to thy honor and to thy divine acceptance,

KIRTLAND TEMPLE

*Thanks be to thy name,
O Lord God of Israel . . .
Thou who hast commanded
thy servants to build a house
to thy name in this place . . .
And now thou beholdest,
O Lord, that thy servants
have done according to thy
commandment.*

D&C 109:1–3

11. And in a manner that we may be found worthy, in thy sight, to secure a fulfilment of the promises which thou hast made unto us, thy people, in the revelations given unto us;

12. That thy glory may rest down upon thy people, and upon this thy house, which we now dedicate to thee, that it may be sanctified and consecrated to be holy, and that thy holy presence may be continually in this house,

13. And that all people who shall enter upon the threshold of the Lord's house, may feel thy power, and feel constrained to acknowledge that thou hast sanctified it, and that it is thy house, a place of thy holiness.

14. And do thou grant, Holy Father, that all those who shall worship in this house, may be taught words of wisdom out of the best books, and that they may seek learning even by study, and also by faith, as thou hast said;

15. And that they may grow up in thee, and receive a fulness of the Holy Ghost, and be organized according to thy laws, and be prepared to obtain every needful thing;

16. And that this house may be a house of prayer, a house of fasting, a house of faith, a house of glory and of God, even thy house;

17. That all the incomings of thy people, into this house, may be in the name of the Lord;

18. That all their outgoings from this house may be in the name of the Lord;

19. And that all their salutations may be in the name of the Lord, with holy hands, uplifted to the Most High;

20. And that no unclean thing shall be permitted to come into thy house to pollute it;

21. And when thy people transgress, any of them, they may speedily repent, and return unto thee, and find favor in thy sight, and be restored to the blessings which thou hast ordained to be poured out upon those who shall reverence thee in thy house.

22. And we ask thee, Holy Father, that thy servants may go forth from this house, armed with thy power, and that thy name may be upon them, and thy glory be round about them, and thine angels have charge over them;

23. And from this place they may bear exceedingly great and glorious tidings, in truth, unto the ends of the earth, that they may know that this is thy work, and that thou hast put forth thy hand, to fulfil that which thou hast spoken by the mouths of the prophets, concerning the last days.

24. We ask thee, Holy Father, to establish the people that shall worship, and honorably hold a name and standing in this thy house, to all generations, and for eternity;

25. That no weapon formed against them shall prosper; that he who diggeth a pit for them shall fall into the same himself;

26. That no combination of wickedness shall have power to rise up and prevail over thy people upon whom thy name shall be put in this house;

27. And if any people shall rise against this people, that thine anger be kindled against them,

28. And if they shall smite this people, thou wilt smite them, thou wilt fight for thy people as thou didst in the day of battle, that they may be delivered from the hands of all their enemies.

29. We ask thee, Holy Father, to confound, and astonish, and bring to shame and confusion, all those who have spread lying reports, abroad, over the world, against thy servant, or servants, if they will not repent, when the everlasting gospel shall be proclaimed in their ears,

30. And that all their works may be brought to naught, and be swept away by the hail, and by the judgments which thou wilt send upon them in thine anger, that there may be an end to lyings and slanders against thy people;

31. For thou knowest, O Lord, that thy servants have been innocent before thee in bearing record of thy name, for which they have suffered these things;

32. Therefore we plead before thee a full and complete deliverance from under this yoke;

33. Break it off, O Lord; break it off from the necks of thy servants, by thy power, that we may rise up in the midst of this generation and do thy work.

34. O Jehovah, have mercy upon this people, and as all men sin, forgive the transgressions of thy people, and let them be blotted out forever.

35. Let the anointing of thy ministers be sealed upon them with power from on high;

36. Let it be fulfilled upon them, as upon those on the day of Pentecost, let the gift of tongues be poured out upon thy people, even cloven tongues as of fire, and the interpretation thereof,

37. And let thy house be filled, as with a rushing mighty wind, with thy glory.

38. Put upon thy servants the testimony of the covenant, that when they go out and proclaim thy word, they may seal up the law, and prepare the hearts of thy saints for all those judgments thou art about to send, in thy wrath, upon the inhabitants of the earth, because of their transgressions, that thy people may not faint in the day of trouble.

39. And whatsoever city thy servants shall enter, and the people of that city receive their testimony, let thy peace and thy salvation be upon that city, that they may gather out of that city the righteous, that they may come forth to Zion, or to her Stakes, the places of thine appointment, with songs of everlasting joy;

40. And until this be accomplished, let not thy judgments fall upon that city.

41. And whatsoever city thy servants shall enter, and the people of that city receive not the testimony of thy servants, and thy servants warn them to save themselves from this untoward generation, let it be upon that city according to that which thou hast spoken by the mouths of thy prophets;

42. But deliver thou, O Jehovah, we beseech thee, thy servants from their hands, and cleanse them from their blood.

43. O Lord, we delight not in the destruction of our fellow men! their souls are precious before thee;

44. But thy word must be fulfilled; help thy servants to say, with thy grace assisting them, thy will be done, O Lord, and not ours.

45. We know that thou hast spoken by the mouth of thy prophets terrible things concerning the wicked, in the last days—that thou wilt pour out thy judgments, without measure;

46. Therefore, O Lord, deliver thy people from the calamity of the wicked; enable thy servants to seal up the law, and bind up the testimony, that they may be prepared against the day of burning.

47. We ask thee, Holy Father, to remember those who have been driven (by the inhabitants of Jackson County, Missouri) from the lands of their inheritance, and break off, O Lord, this yoke of affliction that has been put upon them.

48. Thou knowest, O Lord, that they have been greatly oppressed and afflicted by wicked men, and our hearts flow out with sorrow, because of their grievous burdens.

49. O Lord, how long wilt thou suffer this people to bear this affliction, and the cries of their innocent ones to ascend up in thine ears, and their blood come up in testimony before thee, and not make a display of thy testimony in their behalf?

50. Have mercy, O Lord, upon that wicked mob, who have driven thy people, that they may cease to spoil, that they may repent of their sins, if repentance is to be found;

51. But if they will not, make bare thine arm, O Lord, and redeem that which thou didst appoint a Zion unto thy people!

52. And if it cannot be otherwise, that the cause of thy people may not fail before thee, may thine

anger be kindled, and thine indignation fall upon them, that they may be wasted away, both root and branch, from under heaven;

53. But inasmuch as they will repent, thou art gracious and merciful, and wilt turn away thy wrath, when thou lookest upon the face of thine anointed.

54. Have mercy, O Lord, upon all the nations of the earth, have mercy upon the rulers of our land; may those principles which were so honorably and nobly defended, viz., the Constitution of our land, by our fathers, be established for ever;

55. Remember the kings, the princes, the nobles, and the great ones of the earth, and all people, and the churches, all the poor, the needy, and afflicted ones of the earth,

56. That their hearts may be softened, when thy servants shall go out from thy house, O Jehovah, to bear testimony of thy name, that their prejudices may give way before the truth, and thy people may obtain favor in the sight of all,

57. That all the ends of the earth may know that we thy servants have heard thy voice, and that thou hast sent us,

58. That from among all these, thy servants the sons of Jacob may gather out the righteous to build a holy city to thy name, as thou hast commanded them.

59. We ask thee to appoint upon Zion other Stakes besides this one which thou hast appointed, that the gathering of thy people may roll on in great power and majesty, that thy work may be cut short in righteousness.

60. Now these words, O Lord, we have spoken before thee, concerning the revelations and commandments which thou hast given unto us, who are identified with the Gentiles;

61. But thou knowest that thou hast a great love for the children of Jacob, who have been scattered upon the mountains, for a long time, in a cloudy and dark day;

62. We therefore ask thee to have mercy upon the children of Jacob, that Jerusalem, from this hour, may begin to be redeemed,

63. And the yoke of bondage may begin to be broken off from the house of David,

64. And the children of Judah may begin to return to the lands which thou didst give to Abraham, their father;

65. And cause that the remnants of Jacob, who have been cursed and smitten, because of their transgression, be converted from their wild and savage condition, to the fulness of the everlasting gospel,

66. That they may lay down their weapons of bloodshed, and cease their rebellions,

67. And may all the scattered remnants of Israel, who have been driven to the ends of the earth, come to a knowledge of the truth, believe in the Messiah, and be redeemed from oppression, and rejoice before thee.

68. O Lord, remember thy servant, Joseph Smith, junior, and all his afflictions and persecutions, how he has covenanted with Jehovah, and vowed to thee, O mighty God of Jacob, and the commandments which thou hast given unto him, and that he hath sincerely striven to do thy will.

69. Have mercy, O Lord, upon his wife and children, that they may be exalted in thy presence, and preserved by thy fostering hand;

70. Have mercy upon all their immediate connexions, that their prejudices may be broken up, and swept away as with a flood, that they may be converted and redeemed with Israel, and know that thou art God.

71. Remember, O Lord, the presidents, even all the presidents of thy church, that thy right hand may exalt them, with all their families, and their immediate connexions, that their names may be perpetuated, and had in everlasting remembrance, from generation to generation.

72. Remember all thy church, O Lord, with all their families, and all their immediate connexions,

with all their sick and afflicted ones, with all the poor and meek of the earth, that the kingdom which thou hast set up without hands, may become a great mountain, and fill the whole earth;

73. That thy church may come forth out of the wilderness of darkness, and shine forth fair as the moon, clear as the sun, and terrible as an army with banners,

74. And be adorned as a bride for that day when thou shalt unvail the heavens, and cause the mountains to flow down at thy presence, and the valleys to be exalted, the rough places made smooth; that thy glory may fill the earth,

75. That when the trump shall sound for the dead we shall be caught up in the cloud to meet thee, that we may ever be with the Lord,

76. That our garments may be pure, that we may be clothed upon with robes of righteousness, with palms in our hands, and crowns of glory upon our heads, and reap eternal joy for all our sufferings.

77. O Lord God Almighty, hear us in these our petitions, and answer us from heaven, thy holy habitation, where thou sittest enthroned, with glory, honor, power, majesty, might, dominion, truth, justice, judgment, mercy, and an infinity of fulness, from everlasting to everlasting.

78. O hear, O hear, O hear us, O Lord, and answer these petitions, and accept the dedication of this house unto thee, the work of our hands, which we have built unto thy name!

79. And also this church, to put upon it thy name; and help us by the power of thy Spirit, that we may mingle our voices with those bright, shining seraphs around thy throne, with acclamations of praise, singing, Hosanna to God and the Lamb;

80. And let these thine anointed ones be clothed with salvation, and thy saints shout aloud for joy. Amen, and Amen.

THE SAVIOR APPEARS TO JOSEPH SMITH AND OLIVER COWDERY IN THE KIRTLAND TEMPLE

Section 110

After the dedication of the Kirtland Temple (March 27, 1836), the Saints held sacred meetings throughout the week in the temple. The following Sabbath, April 3, 1836, the Saints met in this sacred edifice to worship the Lord. The Prophet Joseph Smith informs us, "In the afternoon, I assisted the other Presidents in distributing the Lord's Supper to the Church, receiving it from the Twelve, whose privilege it was to officiate at the sacred desk this day. After having performed this service to my brethren, I retired to the pulpit, the veils being dropped, and bowed myself, with Oliver Cowdery, in solemn and silent prayer. After rising from prayer, the following vision was opened to both of us" (History of the Church, vol. 2:434–435).

1. The vail was taken from our minds, and the eyes of our understanding were opened.

2. We saw the Lord standing upon the breast work of the pulpit, before us, and under his feet was a paved work of pure gold in color like amber.

3. His eyes were as a flame of fire, the hair of his head was white like the pure snow, his countenance shone above the brightness of the sun, and his voice was as the sound of the rushing of great waters, even the voice of Jehovah, saying—

4. I am the first and the last, I am he who liveth, I am he who was slain, I am your advocate with the Father.

5. Behold, your sins are forgiven you, you are clean before me, therefore lift up your heads and rejoice,

6. Let the hearts of your brethren rejoice, and let the hearts of all my people rejoice, who have, with their might, built this house to my name,

7. For behold, I have accepted this house, and my name shall be here, and I will manifest myself to my people in mercy in this house,

8. Yea, I will appear unto my servants, and speak unto them with mine own voice, if my people will keep my commandments, and do not pollute this holy house,

9. Yea the hearts of thousands and tens of thousands shall greatly rejoice in consequence of the blessings which shall be poured out, and the endowment with which my servants have been endowed in this house;

10. And the fame of this house shall spread to foreign lands, and this is the beginning of the blessing which shall be poured out upon the heads of my people. Even so. Amen.

11. After this vision closed, the heavens were again opened unto us, and Moses appeared before us, and committed unto us the keys of the

gathering of Israel from the four parts of the earth, and the leading of the ten tribes from the land of the north.

12. After this, Elias appeared, and committed the dispensation of the gospel of Abraham, saying, that in us, and our seed, all generations after us should be blessed.

13. After this vision had closed, another great and glorious vision burst upon us, for Elijah the prophet, who was taken to heaven without tasting death, stood before us, and said—

14. Behold, the time has fully come, which was spoken of by the mouth of Malachi, testifying that he (Elijah) should be sent before the great and dreadful day of the Lord come,

15. To turn the hearts of the fathers to the children, and the children to the fathers, lest the whole earth be smitten with a curse.

16. Therefore the keys of this dispensation are committed into your hands, and by this ye may know that the great and dreadful day of the Lord is near, even at the doors.

SECTION 111

Due to the heavy financial burden the Church was under at this time, the Prophet Joseph Smith, Sidney Rigdon, Hyrum Smith, and Oliver Cowdery traveled to Salem, Massachusetts, to secure, if possible, money that was unclaimed. Failing to secure this money, the brethren engaged in preaching the gospel in and around Salem, Massachusetts. The Prophet Joseph Smith received this revelation August 6, 1836, at Salem, Massachusetts (History of the Church, vol. 2:463–465).

1. I, the Lord your God, am not displeased with your coming this journey, notwithstanding your follies;
2. I have much treasure in this city for you, for the benefit of Zion; and many people in this city whom I will gather out in due time for the benefit of Zion, through your instrumentality!
3. Therefore it is expedient that you should form acquaintance with men in this city, as you shall be led, and as it shall be given you;
4. And it shall come to pass in due time, that I will give this city into your hands, that you shall have power over it, insomuch that they shall not discover your secret parts; and its wealth pertaining to gold and silver shall be yours.
5. Concern not yourselves about your debts, for I will give you power to pay them.
6. Concern not yourselves about Zion, for I will deal mercifully with her.
7. Tarry in this place, and in the regions round about;
8. And the place where it is my will that you should tarry, for the main, shall be signalized unto you by the peace and power of my Spirit, that shall flow unto you.
9. This place you may obtain by hire, &c. And inquire diligently concerning the more ancient inhabitants and founders of this city;
10. For there are more treasures than one for you in this city;
11. Therefore be ye as wise as serpents and yet without sin, and I will order all things for your good, as fast as ye are able to receive them. Amen.

HEBER C. KIMBALL PREACHES THE GOSPEL IN ENGLAND

SECTION 112

The spirit of apostasy, due to worldly endeavors, took root among some members of the Church in Kirtland, Ohio. This attitude affected every quorum of the priesthood. For the salvation of the Church, the Lord revealed to the Prophet Joseph Smith that Heber C. Kimball serve a mission in England (History of the Church, vol. 2:487–489). The same day that Heber C. Kimball preached the first gospel message in England, the Prophet Joseph Smith received this revelation July 23, 1837, at Kirtland, Ohio. This revelation is addressed to Thomas B. Marsh, President of the Quorum of the Twelve Apostles (History of the Church, vol. 2:499).

1. Verily, thus saith the Lord unto you my servant Thomas, I have heard thy prayers and thine alms have come up as a memorial before me, in behalf of those thy brethren who were chosen to bear testimony of my name, and to send it abroad among all nations, kindreds, tongues, and people, and ordained through the instrumentality of my servants.

2. Verily I say unto you, there have been some few things in thine heart and with thee with which I, the Lord, was not well pleased;

3. Nevertheless, inasmuch as thou hast abased thyself thou shalt be exalted; therefore all thy sins are forgiven thee.

4. Let thy heart be of good cheer before my face, and thou shalt bear record of my name, not only unto the Gentiles, but also unto the Jews; and thou shalt send forth my word unto the ends of the earth.

5. Contend thou, therefore, morning by morning, and day after day let thy warning voice go forth, and when the night cometh, let not the inhabitants of the earth slumber because of thy speech.

6. Let thy habitation be known in Zion, and remove not thy house, for I, the Lord, have a great work for thee to do, in publishing my name among the children of men;

7. Therefore, gird up thy loins for the work. Let thy feet be shod also, for thou art chosen, and thy path lieth among the mountains, and among many nations;

8. And by thy word many high ones shall be brought low, and by thy word many low ones shall be exalted.

9. Thy voice shall be a rebuke unto the transgressor, and at thy rebuke let the tongue of the slanderer cease its perverseness.

10. Be thou humble, and the Lord thy God shall lead thee by the hand, and give thee answer to thy prayers.

11. I know thy heart, and have heard thy prayers concerning thy brethren. Be not partial towards them in love above many others, but let thy love be for them as for thyself; and let thy love abound unto all men, and unto all who love my name.

12. And pray for thy brethren of the Twelve. Admonish them sharply for my name's sake, and let them be admonished for all their sins, and be ye faithful before me unto my name.

13. And after their temptations, and much tribulation, behold, I, the Lord, will feel after them, and if they harden not their hearts, and stiffen not their necks against me, they shall be converted, and I will heal them.

14. Now, I say unto you, and what I say unto you, I say unto all the Twelve, Arise and gird up your loins, take up your cross, follow me, and feed my sheep.

15. Exalt not yourselves; rebel not against my servant Joseph, for verily I say unto you, I am with him and my hand shall be over him; and the keys which I have given unto him, and also to youward, shall not be taken from him till I come.

16. Verily I say unto you, my servant Thomas, Thou art the man whom I have chosen to hold the keys of my kingdom (as pertaining to the Twelve) abroad among all nations,

17. That thou mayest be my servant to unlock the door of the kingdom in all places where my servant Joseph, and my servant Sidney, and my servant Hyrum, cannot come;

18. For on them have I laid the burden of all the churches for a little season;

19. Wherefore, whithersoever they shall send you, go ye, and I will be with you; and in whatsoever place ye shall proclaim my name, an effectual door shall be opened unto you, that they may receive my word;

20. Whosoever receiveth my word receiveth me, and whosoever receiveth me, receiveth those (the First Presidency) whom I have sent, whom I have made counselors for my name's sake unto you.

21. And again, I say unto you, That whosoever ye shall send in my name, by the voice of your brethren, the Twelve, duly recommended and authorized by you, shall have power to open the door of my kingdom unto any nation whithersoever ye shall send them,

22. Inasmuch as they shall humble themselves before me, and abide in my word, and hearken to the voice of my Spirit.

23. Verily, verily I say unto you, Darkness covereth the earth, and gross darkness the minds of the people, and all flesh has become corrupt before my face.

24. Behold, vengeance cometh speedily upon the inhabitants of the earth, a day of wrath, a day of burning, a day of desolation, of weeping, of mourning, and of lamentation, and as a whirlwind it shall come upon all the face of the earth, saith the Lord.

25. And upon my house shall it begin, and from my house shall it go forth, saith the Lord.

26. First among those among you, saith the Lord, who have professed to know my name and have not known me, and have blasphemed against me in the midst of my house, saith the Lord.

27. Therefore, see to it that ye trouble not yourselves concerning the affairs of my church in this place, saith the Lord;

28. But purify your hearts before me, and then go ye into all the world, and preach my gospel unto every creature who has not received it,

29. And he that believeth and is baptized shall be saved, and he that believeth not, and is not baptized, shall be damned.

30. For unto you, (the Twelve,) and those (the First Presidency) who are appointed with you, to be your counselors and your leaders, is the power of this priesthood given, for the last days and for

the last time, in the which is the dispensation of the fulness of times.

31. Which power you hold in connection with all those who have received a dispensation at any time from the beginning of the creation;

32. For verily I say unto you, the keys of the dispensation which ye have received, have come down from the fathers; and last of all, being sent down from heaven unto you.

33. Verily I say unto you, Behold how great is your calling. Cleanse your hearts and your garments, lest the blood of this generation be required at your hands.

34. Be faithful until I come, for I come quickly, and my reward is with me to recompense every man according as his work shall be. I am Alpha and Omega. Amen.

JOSEPH BLESSES EPHRAIM AND MANASSEH, THROUGH WHOSE LINEAGE THE SAVIOR DESCENDS

Section 113

The Prophet Joseph Smith arrived at Far West, Missouri, March 14, 1838. Some of the brethren had questions pertaining to the writings of Isaiah. This section is an answer to their inquiries, given in March 1838 (History of the Church, vol. 3:8–10).

1. Who is the Stem of Jesse spoken of in the 1st, 2nd, 3rd, 4th, and 5th verses of the 11th chapter of Isaiah?

2. Verily thus saith the Lord, it is Christ.

3. What is the rod spoken of in the first verse of the 11th chapter of Isaiah that should come of the Stem of Jesse?

4. Behold thus saith the Lord, it is a servant in the hands of Christ, who is partly a descendant of Jesse as well as of Ephraim, or of the house of Joseph, on whom there is laid much power.

5. What is the root of Jesse spoken of in the 10th verse of the 11th chapter?

6. Behold thus saith the Lord, it is a descendant of Jesse, as well as of Joseph, unto whom rightly belongs the Priesthood, and the keys of the Kingdom, for an ensign, and for the gathering of my people in the last days.

7. Questions by Elias Higbee, as follows—"What is meant by the command in Isaiah, 52d chapter, 1st verse, which saith, put on thy strength, O Zion? And what people had Isaiah reference to?"

8. He had reference to those whom God should call in the last days, who should hold the power of Priesthood to bring again Zion, and the redemption of Israel; and to put on her strength is to put on the authority of the Priesthood, which she (Zion) has a right to by lineage; also to return to that power which she had lost.

9. "What are we to understand by Zion loosing herself from the bands of her neck, 2d verse?"

10. We are to understand that the scattered remnants are exhorted to return to the Lord from whence they have fallen, which if they do, the promise of the Lord is that he will speak to them, or give them revelation. See the 6th, 7th, and 8th verses. The bands of her neck are the curses of God upon her, or the remnants of Israel in their scattered condition among the Gentiles.

Section 114

This revelation is given through the Prophet Joseph Smith to David W. Patten at Far West, Missouri, April 17, 1838. Elder Patten, a member of the Council of the Twelve Apostles, is instructed by the Lord to settle his affairs and prepare to serve a mission the following spring (History of the Church, vol. 3:23).

1. Verily thus saith the Lord, it is wisdom in my servant David W. Patten, that he settle up all his business as soon as he possibly can, and make a disposition of his merchandise, that he may perform a mission unto me next spring, in company with others, even Twelve including himself, to testify of my name, and bear glad tidings unto all the world;

2. For verily thus saith the Lord, that inasmuch as there are those among you who deny my name, others shall be planted in their stead, and receive their bishopric. Amen.

Section 115

The Lord addresses this revelation to the leaders and all the people of The Church of Jesus Christ of Latter-day Saints. The Lord makes known His will concerning the building up of Far West, Missouri, and the building of the Lord's House. This revelation was received by the Prophet Joseph Smith at Far West, Missouri, April 26, 1838 (History of the Church, vol. 3:23).

1. Verily thus saith the Lord unto you, my servant Joseph Smith, jr., and also my servant Sidney Rigdon, and also my servant Hyrum Smith, and your counselors who are and shall be appointed hereafter;

2. And also unto you my servant Edward Partridge, and his counselors;

3. And also unto my faithful servants, who are of the High Council of my church in Zion (for thus it shall be called) and unto all the elders and people of my Church of Jesus Christ of Latter-day Saints, scattered abroad in all the world;

4. For thus shall my church be called in the last days, even The Church of Jesus Christ of Latter-day Saints.

5. Verily I say unto you all, Arise and shine forth, that thy light may be a standard for the nations,

6. And that the gathering together upon the land of Zion, and upon her Stakes, may be for a defense, and for a refuge from the storm, and from wrath when it shall be poured out without mixture upon the whole earth.

7. Let the city, Far West, be a holy and consecrated land unto me, and it shall be called most holy, for the ground upon which thou standest is holy;

8. Therefore I command you to build a house unto me, for the gathering together of my saints, that they may worship me;

9. And let there be a beginning of this work, and a foundation, and a preparatory work, this following summer;

10. And let the beginning be made on the 4th day of July next; and from that time forth let my people labor diligently to build a house unto my name,

11. And in one year from this day let them recommence laying the foundation of my house:

12. Thus let them from that time forth labor diligently until it shall be finished, from the corner stone thereof unto the top thereof, until there shall not anything remain that is not finished.

13. Verily I say unto you, let not my servant Joseph, neither my servant Sidney, neither my servant Hyrum, get in debt any more for the building of an house unto my name;

A SCENE IN
FAR WEST, MISSOURI

And again, verily I say unto you, it is my will that the city of Far West should be built up speedily by the gathering of my saints.

D&C 115:17

14. But let a house be built unto my name according to the pattern which I will show unto them.

15. And if my people build it not according to the pattern which I shall show unto their Presidency, I will not accept it at their hands;

16. But if my people do build it according to the pattern which I shall show unto their Presidency, even my servant Joseph and his counselors, then I will accept it at the hands of my people.

17. And again, verily I say unto you, it is my will that the city of Far West should be built up speedily by the gathering of my saints,

18. And also that other places should be appointed for Stakes in the regions round about, as they shall be manifested unto my servant Joseph, from time to time;

19. For behold, I will be with him, and I will sanctify him before the people, for unto him have I given the keys of this kingdom and ministry. Even so. Amen.

SECTION 116

The Prophet Joseph Smith and a number of the brethren left Far West, Missouri, and traveled north to Caldwell and Daviess Counties to locate lands for the gathering of the Saints. Near Wight's Ferry at Spring Hill in Daviess County, Missouri, May 19, 1838, the Prophet Joseph Smith received this revelation in which the Lord reveals the location of Adam-ondi-Ahman (History of the Church, vol. 3:34–35).

1. ADAM-ONDI-AHMAN, because, said he, it is the place where Adam shall come to visit his people, or the Ancient of days shall sit, as spoken of by Daniel the prophet.

ECTION 117

The Lord commanded the Saints to gather and build up Far West, Missouri, speedily (section 115:17). It appears that Newel K. Whitney and William Marks were slow to respond to this command. The Lord directed this revelation to these brethren and others through the Prophet Joseph Smith July 8, 1838, at Far West, Missouri (History of the Church, vol. 3:45).

1. Verily thus saith the Lord unto my servant William Marks, and also unto my servant N. K. Whitney, let them settle up their business speedily and journey from the land of Kirtland, before I, the Lord, send again the snows upon the earth;
2. Let them awake, and arise, and come forth, and not tarry, for I, the Lord, command it;
3. Therefore if they tarry it shall not be well with them.
4. Let them repent of all their sins, and of all their covetous desires, before me, saith the Lord, for what is property unto me saith the Lord?
5. Let the properties of Kirtland be turned out for debts, saith the Lord. Let them go, saith the Lord, and whatsoever remaineth, let it remain in your hands, saith the Lord;
6. For have I not the fowls of heaven, and also the fish of the sea, and the beasts of the mountains? Have I not made the earth? Do I not hold the destinies of all the armies of the nations of the earth?
7. Therefore will I not make solitary places to bud and to blossom, and to bring forth in abundance, saith the Lord.
8. Is there not room enough on the mountains of Adam-ondi-Ahman, and upon the plains of Olaha Shinehah, or the land where Adam dwelt, that you should covet that which is but the drop, and neglect the more weighty matters?
9. Therefore come up hither unto the land of my people, even Zion.
10. Let my servant William Marks be faithful over a few things, and he shall be a ruler over many. Let him preside in the midst of my people in the city of Far West, and let him be blessed with the blessings of my people.
11. Let my servant N. K. Whitney be ashamed of the Nicholatine band and of all their secret abominations, and of all his littleness of soul before me, saith the Lord, and come up to the land of Adam-ondi-Ahman, and be a bishop unto my people, saith the Lord, not in name but in deed, saith the Lord.

12. And again, I say unto you, I remember my servant Oliver Granger, behold, verily I say unto him, that his name shall be had in sacred remembrance from generation to generation, for ever and ever, saith the Lord.

13. Therefore let him contend earnestly for the redemption of the First Presidency of my church, saith the Lord, and when he falls he shall rise again, for his sacrifice shall be more sacred unto me than his increase, saith the Lord:

14. Therefore let him come up hither speedily, unto the land of Zion, and in the due time he shall be made a merchant unto my name, saith the Lord, for the benefit of my people;

15. Therefore let no man despise my servant Oliver Granger, but let the blessings of my people be on him for ever and ever.

16. And again, verily I say unto you, let all my servants in the land of Kirtland remember the Lord their God, and mine house also, to keep and preserve it holy, and to overthrow the money changers in mine own due time, saith the Lord. Even so. Amen.

SECTION 118

Four members of the Quorum of the Twelve Apostles had succumbed to the apostate feelings that existed among some members of the Church in Kirtland, Ohio, during the years 1837 and 1838. They were released from the Quorum, and the Prophet Joseph Smith sought to know the will of the Lord concerning filling the vacancies. This revelation was received July 8, 1838, at Far West, Missouri (History of the Church, vol. 3:46).

1. Verily, thus saith the Lord, let a conference be held immediately, let the Twelve be organized, and let men be appointed to supply the place of those who are fallen.

2. Let my servant Thomas remain for a season in the land of Zion, to publish my word.

3. Let the residue continue to preach from that hour, and if they will do this in all lowliness of heart, in meekness and humility, and long-suffering, I, the Lord, give unto them a promise that I will provide for their families, and an effectual door shall be opened for them, from henceforth;

4. And next spring let them depart to go over the great waters, and there promulgate my gospel, the fulness thereof, and bear record of my name.

5. Let them take leave of my saints in the city Far West, on the 26 day of April next, on the building spot of my house, saith the Lord.

6. Let my servant John Taylor, and also my servant John E. Page, and also my servant Wilford Woodruff, and also my servant Willard Richards, be appointed to fill the places of those who have fallen, and be officially notified of their appointment.

Section 119

The Prophet Joseph Smith said: "O Lord! Show unto thy servant how much thou requirest of the properties of thy people for a tithing." This revelation was received July 8, 1838, at Far West, Missouri (History of the Church, vol. 3:44).

1. Verily, thus saith the Lord, I require all their surplus property to be put into the hands of the bishop of my church in Zion,

2. For the building of mine house, and for the laying of the foundation of Zion and for the Priesthood, and for the debts of the Presidency of my church;

3. And this shall be the beginning of the tithing of my people;

4. And after that, those who have thus been tithed, shall pay one-tenth of all their interest annually; and this shall be a standing law unto them for ever, for my holy Priesthood, saith the Lord.

5. Verily I say unto you, it shall come to pass, that all those who gather unto the land of Zion shall be tithed of their surplus properties, and shall observe this law or they shall not be found worthy to abide among you.

6. And I say unto you, if my people observe not this law, to keep it holy, and by this law sanctify the land of Zion unto me, that my statutes and my judgments may be kept thereon, that it may be most holy, behold, verily I say unto you, it shall not be a land of Zion unto you;

7. And this shall be an ensample unto all the Stakes of Zion. Even so. Amen.

# SECTION 120

This revelation was received by the Prophet Joseph Smith, July 8, 1838, at Far West, Missouri, "making known the disposition of the properties tithed and named in the preceding revelation" (section 119), (History of the Church, vol. 3:44).

1. Verily, thus saith the Lord, the time is now come, that it shall be disposed of by a Council, composed of the First Presidency of my church, and of the bishop and his council, and by my High Council; and by mine own voice unto them, saith the Lord. Even so. Amen.

ection 121

The Prophet Joseph Smith, Hyrum Smith, Lyman Wight, Caleb Baldwin, and Alexander McRae were held in Liberty Jail, Clay County, Missouri, waiting trial on false charges. The Prophet Joseph Smith addressed an epistle "To the Church of Latter-day Saints at Quincy, Illinois, and Scattered Abroad, and to Bishop Partridge in Particular." This epistle is dated Liberty Jail, Clay County, Missouri, March 25, 1839 and signed by the five brethren. Sections 121, 122, and 123 are extracts from this epistle (History of the Church, vol. 3:289–305).

1. O God! where art thou? And where is the pavilion that covereth thy hiding place?

2. How long shall thy hand be stayed, and thine eye, yea thy pure eye, behold from the eternal heavens the wrongs of thy people and of thy servants, and thine ear be penetrated with their cries?

3. Yea, O Lord, how long shall they suffer these wrongs and unlawful oppressions, before thine heart shall be softened towards them, and thy bowels be moved with compassion towards them?

4. O Lord God Almighty, maker of heaven, earth, and seas, and of all things that in them are and who controllest and subjectest the devil, and the dark and benighted dominion of Sheole! Stretch forth thy hand; let thine eye pierce; let thy pavilion be taken up; let thy hiding place no longer be covered; let thine ear be inclined; let thine heart be softened, and thy bowels moved with compassion toward us;

5. Let thine anger be kindled against our enemies; and in the fury of thine heart, with thy sword avenge us of our wrongs;

6. Remember thy suffering saints, O our God! and thy servants will rejoice in thy name forever.

7. My son, peace be unto thy soul; thine adversity and thine afflictions shall be but a small moment;

8. And then, if thou endure it well, God shall exalt thee on high; thou shalt triumph over all thy foes;

9. Thy friends do stand by thee, and they shall hail thee again, with warm hearts and friendly hands;

10. Thou art not yet as Job; thy friends do not contend against thee, neither charge thee with transgression, as they did Job;

11. And they who do charge thee with transgression, their hope shall be blasted, and their prospects shall melt away as the hoar frost melteth before the burning rays of the rising sun;

12. And also that God hath set his hand and seal, to change the times and seasons, and to blind their minds, that they may not understand his marvelous workings; that he may prove them also and take them in their own craftiness;

35. Because their hearts are set so much upon the things of this world, and aspire to the honors of men, that they do not learn this one lesson—

36. That the rights of the priesthood are inseparably connected with the powers of heaven, and that the powers of heaven cannot be controlled nor handled only upon the principles of righteousness.

37. That they may be conferred upon us, it is true; but when we undertake to cover our sins, or to gratify our pride, our vain ambition, or to exercise control, or dominion, or compulsion upon the souls of the children of men, in any degree of unrighteousness, behold, the heavens withdraw themselves; the Spirit of the Lord is grieved; and when it is withdrawn, Amen to the Priesthood, or the authority of that man.

38. Behold! ere he is aware, he is left unto himself, to kick against the pricks; to persecute the saints, and to fight against God.

39. We have learned, by sad experience, that it is the nature and disposition of almost all men, as soon as they get a little authority, as they suppose, they will immediately begin to exercise unrighteous dominion.

40. Hence many are called, but few are chosen.

41. No power or influence can or ought to be maintained by virtue of the Priesthood, only by persuasion, by long-suffering, by gentleness, and meekness, and by love unfeigned;

42. By kindness, and pure knowledge, which shall greatly enlarge the soul without hypocrisy, and without guile,

43. Reproving betimes with sharpness, when moved upon by the Holy Ghost, and then showing forth afterwards an increase of love toward him whom thou hast reproved, lest he esteem thee to be his enemy;

44. That he may know that thy faithfulness is stronger than the cords of death;

45. Let thy bowels also be full of charity towards all men, and to the household of faith, and let virtue garnish thy thoughts unceasingly, then shall thy confidence wax strong in the presence of God, and the doctrine of the Priesthood shall distil upon thy soul as the dews from heaven.

46. The Holy Ghost shall be thy constant companion, and thy sceptre an unchanging sceptre of righteousness and truth, and thy dominion shall be an everlasting dominion, and without compulsory means it shall flow unto thee for ever and ever.

Section 122

This section is an extract from an epistle written by the Prophet Joseph Smith and his companions dated Liberty Jail, Clay County, Missouri, March 25, 1839 (see historical background, section 121), (History of the Church, vol. 3:289–305).

1. The ends of the earth shall enquire after thy name, and fools shall have thee in derision, and hell shall rage against thee,
2. While the pure in heart, and the wise, and the noble, and the virtuous, shall seek counsel, and authority, and blessings constantly from under thy hand,
3. And thy people shall never be turned against thee by the testimony of traitors;
4. And although their influence shall cast thee into trouble, and into bars and walls, thou shalt be had in honor, and but for a small moment and thy voice shall be more terrible in the midst of thine enemies, than the fierce lion, because of thy righteousness; and thy God shall stand by thee for ever and ever.
5. If thou art called to pass through tribulation; if thou art in perils among false brethren; if thou art in perils among robbers; if thou art in perils by land or by sea;
6. If thou art accused with all manner of false accusations; if thine enemies fall upon thee; if they tear thee from the society of thy father and mother and brethren and sisters; and if with a drawn sword thine enemies tear thee from the bosom of thy wife, and of thine offspring, and thine elder son, although but six years of age, shall cling to thy garments, and shall say, My father, my father, why can't you stay with us? O, my father, what are the men going to do with you? and if then he shall be thrust from thee by the sword, and thou be dragged to prison, and thine enemies prowl around thee like wolves for the blood of the lamb;
7. And if thou shouldst be cast into the pit, or into the hands of murderers, and the sentence of death passed upon thee; if thou be cast into the deep; if the billowing surge conspire against thee; if fierce winds become thine enemy; if the heavens gather blackness, and all the elements combine to hedge up the way; and above all, if the very jaws of hell shall gape open the mouth wide after thee, know thou, my son, that all these things shall give thee experience, and shall be for thy good.

FEAR NOT WHAT MAN CAN DO, FOR GOD SHALL BE WITH YOU FOREVER AND EVER (D&C 122:9).

8. The Son of Man hath descended below them all; art thou greater than he?

9. Therefore, hold on thy way, and the Priesthood shall remain with thee, for their bounds are set, they cannot pass. Thy days are known, and thy years shall not be numbered less; therefore, fear not what man can do, for God shall be with you for ever and ever.

JOSEPH SMITH INSTRUCTS THE SAINTS IN WRITING WHILE HE IS IMPRISONED IN LIBERTY JAIL

Section 123

This section is an extract from an epistle written by the Prophet Joseph Smith and his companions dated Liberty Jail, Clay County, Missouri March 25, 1839 (see historical background, section 121), (History of the Church, vol. 3:289–305).

1. And again, we would suggest for your consideration the propriety of all the saints gathering up a knowledge of all the facts, and sufferings and abuses put upon them by the people of this State,
2. And also of all the property and amount of damages which they have sustained, both of character and personal injuries, as well as real property;
3. And also the names of all persons that have had a hand in their oppressions, as far as they can get hold of them and find them out;
4. And perhaps a committee can be appointed to find out these things, and to take statements, and affidavits, and also to gather up the libelous publications that are afloat,
5. And all that are in the magazines, and in the encyclopedias, and all the libelous histories that are published, and are writing, and by whom, and present the whole concatenation of diabolical rascality, and nefarious and murderous impositions that have been practised upon this people,
6. That we may not only publish to all the world, but present them to the heads of government in all their dark and hellish hue, as the last effort which is enjoined on us by our Heavenly Father, before we can fully and completely claim that promise which shall call him forth from his hiding place, and also that the whole nation may be left without excuse before he can send forth the power of his mighty arm.
7. It is an imperious duty that we owe to God, to angels, with whom we shall be brought to stand, and also to ourselves, to our wives and children, who have been made to bow down with grief, sorrow, and care, under the most damning hand of murder, tyranny, and oppression, supported, and urged on, and upheld by the influence of that spirit which hath so strongly riveted the creeds of the fathers, who have inherited lies, upon the hearts of the children, and filled the world with confusion, and has been growing stronger and stronger, and is now the very main-spring of all

corruption, and the whole earth groans under the weight of its iniquity.

8. It is an iron yoke, it is a strong band; they are the very handcuffs, and chains, and shackles, and fetters of hell.

9. Therefore, it is an imperious duty that we owe, not only to our own wives and children, but to the widows and fatherless, whose husbands and fathers have been murdered under its iron hand;

10. Which dark and blackening deeds are enough to make hell itself shudder, and to stand aghast and pale, and the hands of the very devil to tremble and palsy.

11. And also it is an imperious duty that we owe to all the rising generation, and to all the pure in heart;

12. (For there are many yet on the earth among all sects, parties, and denominations, who are blinded by the subtle craftiness of men, whereby they lie in wait to deceive, and who are only kept from the truth because they know not where to find it;)

13. Therefore, that we should waste and wear out our lives in bringing to light all the hidden things of darkness, wherein we know them; and they are truly manifest from heaven.

14. These should then be attended to with great earnestness.

15. Let no man count them as small things; for there is much which lieth in futurity, pertaining to the saints, which depends upon these things.

16. You know, brethren, that a very large ship is benefited very much by a very small helm in the time of a storm, by being kept workways with the wind and the waves.

17. Therefore, dearly beloved brethren, let us cheerfully do all things that lie in our power, and then may we stand still with the utmost assurance, to see the salvation of God, and for his arm to be revealed.

Section 124

Because of the extermination order issued by Governor Boggs of the State of Missouri, the Saints were driven from that state. The majority of the Latter-day Saints sought refuge in the state of Illinois. The Church purchased land in Commerce, which was later named Nauvoo. On January 19, 1841, at Nauvoo, Illinois, the Prophet Joseph Smith received this revelation in which the Lord gives direction and counsel for the building of a Stake of Zion in Nauvoo (History of the Church, vol. 4:274).

1. Verily, thus saith the Lord unto you, my servant Joseph Smith, I am well pleased with your offering and acknowledgments, which you have made, for unto this end have I raised you up, that I might show forth my wisdom through the weak things of the earth.

2. Your prayers are acceptable before me, and in answer to them I say unto you, that you are now called immediately to make a solemn proclamation of my gospel, and of this Stake which I have planted to be a corner stone of Zion, which shall be polished with the refinement which is after the similitude of a palace.

3. This proclamation shall be made to all the kings of the world—to the four corners thereof—to the honorable President elect, and the high minded Governors of the nation in which you live, and to all the nations of the earth scattered abroad.

4. Let it be written in the spirit of meekness and by the power of the Holy Ghost, which shall be in you at the time of the writing of the same;

5. For it shall be given you by the Holy Ghost to know my will concerning those kings and authorities, even what shall befall them in a time to come.

6. For, behold! I am about to call upon them to give heed to the light and glory of Zion, for the set time has come to favor her.

7. Call ye, therefore, upon them with loud proclamation, and with your testimony, fearing them not, for they are as grass, and all their glory as the flower thereof which soon falleth, that they may be left also without excuse,

8. And that I may visit them in the day of visitation, when I shall unvail the face of my covering, to appoint the portion of the oppressor among hypocrites, where there is gnashing of teeth, if they reject my servants and my testimony which I have revealed unto them.

9. And again, I will visit and soften their hearts, many of them for your good, that ye may find grace in their eyes, that they may come to the

light of truth, and the Gentiles to the exaltation or lifting up of Zion.

10. For the day of my visitation cometh speedily, in an hour when ye think not of, and where shall be the safety of my people, and refuge for those who shall be left of them?

11. Awake! O kings of the earth! Come ye, O come ye, with your gold and your silver, to the help of my people, to the house of the daughters of Zion.

12. And again, verily I say unto you, Let my servant Robert B. Thompson help you to write this proclamation, for I am well pleased with him, and that he should be with you;

13. Let him, therefore, hearken to your counsel, and I will bless him with a multiplicity of blessings; let him be faithful and true in all things from henceforth, and he shall be great in mine eyes;

14. But let him remember that his stewardship will I require at his hands.

15. And again, verily I say unto you, Blessed is my servant Hyrum Smith, for I, the Lord, love him because of the integrity of his heart, and because he loveth that which is right before me, saith the Lord.

16. Again let my servant John C. Bennett, help you in your labor in sending my word to the kings and people of the earth, and stand by you, even you my servant Joseph Smith, in the hour of affliction, and his reward shall not fail if he receive counsel.

17. And for his love he shall be great, for he shall be mine if he do this, saith the Lord. I have seen the work which he hath done, which I accept, if he continue, and will crown him with blessings and great glory.

18. And again, I say unto you, that it is my will that my servant Lyman Wight should continue in preaching for Zion, in the spirit of meekness, confessing me before the world, and I will bear him up as on eagles' wings, and he shall beget glory and honor to himself and unto my name.

19. That when he shall finish his work, that I may receive him unto myself, even as I did my servant David Patten, who is with me at this time, and also my servant Edward Partridge, and also my aged servant Joseph Smith, sen., who sitteth with Abraham at his right hand, and blessed and holy is he, for he is mine.

20. And again, verily I say unto you, my servant George Miller is without guile; he may be trusted because of the integrity of his heart; and for the love which he has to my testimony I, the Lord, love him;

21. I therefore say unto you, I seal upon his head the office of a bishopric, like unto my servant Edward Partridge, that he may receive the consecrations of mine house, that he may administer blessings upon the heads of the poor of my people, saith the Lord. Let no man despise my servant George, for he shall honor me.

22. Let my servant George, and my servant Lyman, and my servant John Snider, and others, build a house unto my name, such an one as my servant Joseph shall show unto them, upon the place which he shall show unto them also.

23. And it shall be for a house for boarding, a house that strangers may come from afar to lodge therein: therefore let it be a good house, worthy of all acceptation, that the weary traveler may find health and safety while he shall contemplate the word of the Lord; and the corner stone I have appointed for Zion.

24. This house shall be a healthful habitation if it be built unto my name, and if the governor which shall be appointed unto it shall not suffer any pollution to come upon it. It shall be holy, or the Lord your God will not dwell therein.

25. And again, verily I say unto you, Let all my saints come from afar;

26. And send ye swift messengers, yea, chosen messengers, and say unto them; come ye, with all your gold, and your silver, and your precious

stones, and with all your antiquities; and with all who have knowledge of antiquities, that will come, may come, and bring the box tree, and the fir tree, and the pine tree, together with all the precious trees of the earth;

27. And with iron, with copper, and with brass, and with zinc, and with all your precious things of the earth, and build a house to my name, for the Most High to dwell therein;

28. For there is not a place found on earth that he may come to and restore again that which was lost unto you, or which he hath taken away, even the fulness of the Priesthood;

29. For a baptismal font there is not upon the earth, that they, my saints, may be baptized for those who are dead;

30. For this ordinance belongeth to my house, and cannot be acceptable to me, only in the days of your poverty, wherein ye are not able to build a house unto me.

31. But I command you, all ye my saints, to build a house unto me; and I grant unto you a sufficient time to build a house unto me; and during this time your baptisms shall be acceptable unto me.

32. But behold, at the end of this appointment, your baptisms for your dead shall not be acceptable unto me; and if you do not these things at the end of the appointment, ye shall be rejected as a church, with your dead, saith the Lord your God.

33. For verily I say unto you, that after you have had sufficient time to build a house to me, wherein the ordinance of baptizing for the dead belongeth, and for which the same was instituted from before the foundation of the world, your baptisms for your dead cannot be acceptable unto me,

34. For therein are the keys of the holy priesthood ordained, that you may receive honor and glory.

35. And after this time, your baptisms for the dead, by those who are scattered abroad, are not acceptable unto me, saith the Lord;

36. For it is ordained that in Zion, and in her stakes, and in Jerusalem, those places which I have appointed for refuge, shall be the places for your baptisms for your dead.

37. And again, verily I say unto you, How shall your washings be acceptable unto me, except ye perform them in a house which you have built to my name?

38. For, for this cause I commanded Moses that he should build a tabernacle, that they should bear it with them in the wilderness, and to build a house in the land of promise, that those ordinances might be revealed which had been hid from before the world was;

39. Therefore, verily I say unto you, that your anointings, and your washings, and your baptisms for the dead, and your solemn assemblies, and your memorials for your sacrifices, by the sons of Levi, and for your oracles in your most holy places, wherein you receive conversations, and your statutes and judgments, for the beginning of the revelations and foundation of Zion, and for the glory, honor, and endowment of all her municipals, are ordained by the ordinance of my holy house which my people are always commanded to build unto my holy name.

40. And verily I say unto you, Let this house be built unto my name, that I may reveal mine ordinances therein, unto my people;

41. For I deign to reveal unto my church, things which have been kept hid from before the foundation of the world, things that pertain to the dispensation of the fulness of times;

42. And I will show unto my servant Joseph all things pertaining to this house, and the priesthood thereof, and the place whereon it shall be built;

43. And ye shall build it on the place where you have contemplated building it, for that is the spot which I have chosen for you to build it;

44. If ye labor with all your might, I will consecrate that spot that it shall be made holy;

45. And if my people will hearken unto my voice, and unto the voice of my servants whom I have appointed to lead my people, behold, verily I say unto you, they shall not be moved out of their place.

46. But if they will not hearken to my voice, nor unto the voice of these men whom I have appointed, they shall not be blest, because they pollute mine holy grounds, and mine holy ordinances, and charters, and my holy words which I give unto them.

47. And it shall come to pass, That if you build a house unto my name, and do not do the things that I say, I will not perform the oath which I make unto you, neither fulfil the promises which ye expect at my hands, saith the Lord;

48. For instead of blessings, ye, by your own works, bring cursings, wrath, indignation, and judgments upon your own heads, by your follies, and by all your abominations, which you practise before me, saith the Lord.

49. Verily, verily I say unto you, That when I give a commandment to any of the sons of men, to do a work unto my name, and those sons of men go with all their might, and with all they have, to perform that work, and cease not their diligence, and their enemies come upon them, and hinder them from performing that work, behold, it behooveth me to require that work no more at the hands of those sons of men, but to accept of their offerings.

50. And the iniquity and transgression of my holy laws and commandments, I will visit upon the heads of those who hindered my work, unto the third and fourth generation, so long as they repent not, and hate me, saith the Lord God.

51. Therefore for this cause have I accepted the offerings of those whom I commanded to build up a city and a house unto my name, in Jackson county, Missouri, and were hindered by their enemies, saith the Lord your God:

52. And I will answer judgment, wrath, and indignation, wailing, and anguish, and gnashing of teeth upon their heads, unto the third and fourth generation, so long as they repent not and hate me, saith the Lord your God.

53. And this I make an example unto you, for your consolation concerning all those who have been commanded to do a work, and have been hindered by the hands of their enemies, and by oppression, saith the Lord your God;

54. For I am the Lord your God, and will save all those of your brethren who have been pure in heart, and have been slain in the land of Missouri, saith the Lord.

55. And again, verily I say unto you, I command you again to build a house to my name, even in this place, that you may prove yourselves unto me that ye are faithful in all things whatsoever I command you, that I may bless you, and crown you with honor, immortality, and eternal life.

56. And now I say unto you, as pertaining to my boarding house which I have commanded you to build for the boarding of strangers, let it be built unto my name, and let my name be named upon it, and let my servant Joseph, and his house have place therein, from generation to generation;

57. For this anointing have I put upon his head, that his blessing shall also be put upon the head of his posterity after him,

58. And as I said unto Abraham concerning the kindreds of the earth, even so I say unto my servant Joseph: In thee and in thy seed shall the kindred of the earth be blessed.

59. Therefore, let my servant Joseph and his seed after him have place in that house, from generation to generation, for ever and ever, saith the Lord,

60. And let the name of that house be called Nauvoo house, and let it be a delightful habitation for man, and a resting place for the weary traveler, that he may contemplate the glory of Zion, and the glory of this, the corner-stone thereof;

61. That he may receive also the counsel from those whom I have set to be as plants of renown, and as watchmen upon her walls.

62. Behold, verily I say unto you, let my servant George Miller, and my servant Lyman Wight, and my servant John Snider, and my servant Peter Haws, organize themselves, and appoint one of them to be a president over their quorum for the purpose of building that house.

63. And they shall form a constitution whereby they may receive stock for the building of that house.

64. And they shall not receive less than fifty dollars for a share of stock in that house, and they shall be permitted to receive fifteen thousand dollars from any one man for stock in that house;

65. But they shall not be permitted to receive over fifteen thousand dollars stock from any one man;

66. And they shall not be permitted to receive under fifty dollars for a share of stock from any one man in that house;

67. And they shall not be permitted to receive any man, as a stockholder in this house, except the same shall pay his stock into their hands at the time he receives stock;

68. And in proportion to the amount of stock he pays into their hands, he shall receive stock in that house; but if he pays nothing into their hands, he shall not receive any stock in that house.

69. And if any pay stock into their hands, it shall be for stock in that house, for himself and for his generation after him, from generation to generation, so long as he and his heirs shall hold that stock, and do not sell or convey the stock away out of their hands by their own free will and act, if you will do my will, saith the Lord your God.

70. And again, verily I say unto you, if my servant George Miller, and my servant Lyman Wight, and my servant John Snider, and my servant Peter Haws, receive any stock into their hands, in moneys, or in properties wherein they receive the real value of moneys, they shall not appropriate any portion of that stock to any other purpose, only in that house;

71. And if they do appropriate any portion of that stock any where else, only in that house, without the consent of the stockholder, and do not repay fourfold for the stock which they appropriate any where else, only in that house, they shall be accursed, and shall be moved out of their place, saith the Lord God, for I, the Lord, am God, and cannot be mocked in any of these things.

72. Verily I say unto you, Let my servant Joseph pay stock into their hands for the building of that house, as seemeth him good; but my servant Joseph cannot pay over fifteen thousand dollars stock in that house, nor under fifty dollars; neither can any other man, saith the Lord.

73. And there are others also who wish to know my will concerning them, for they have asked it at my hands.

74. Therefore I say unto you concerning my servant Vinson Knight, if he will do my will, let him put stock into that house for himself, and for his generation after him, from generation to generation.

75. And let him lift up his voice long and loud, in the midst of the people, to plead the cause of the poor and the needy, and let him not fail, neither let his heart faint, and I will accept of his offerings, for they shall not be unto me as the offerings of Cain, for he shall be mine, saith the Lord.

76. Let his family rejoice and turn away their hearts from affliction, for I have chosen him and anointed him, and he shall be honored in the midst of his house, for I will forgive all his sins, saith the Lord. Amen.

77. Verily I say unto you, let my servant Hyrum put stock into that house as seemeth him good, for himself and his generation after him, from generation to generation.

78. Let my servant Isaac Galland put stock into that house, for I, the Lord, love him for the work

JOSEPH SMITH PREACHES TO THE SAINTS

And if my people will hearken unto my voice, and unto the voice of my servants whom I have appointed to lead my people, behold, verily I say unto you, they shall not be moved out of their place.

D&C 124:45

he hath done, and will forgive all his sins; therefore, let him be remembered for an interest in that house from generation to generation.

79. Let my servant Isaac Galland be appointed among you, and be ordained by my servant William Marks, and be blessed of him, to go with my servant Hyrum, to accomplish the work that my servant Joseph shall point out to them, and they shall be greatly blessed.

80. Let my servant William Marks pay stock into that house, as it seemeth him good, for himself and his generation, from generation to generation.

81. Let my servant Henry G. Sherwood pay stock into that house, as seemeth him good, for himself and his seed after him, from generation to generation.

82. Let my servant William Law pay stock into that house, for himself and his seed after him, from generation to generation.

83. If he will do my will let him not take his family unto the eastern lands, even unto Kirtland; nevertheless, I, the Lord, will build up Kirtland, but I, the Lord, have a scourge prepared for the inhabitants thereof.

84. And with my servant Almon Babbitt, there are many things with which I am not well pleased; behold, he aspireth to establish his counsel instead of the counsel which I have ordained, even that of the Presidency of my church, and he setteth up a golden calf for the worship of my people.

85. Let no man go from this place who has come here essaying to keep my commandments.

86. If they live here let them live unto me; and if they die let them die unto me; for they shall rest from all their labors here, and shall continue their works.

87. Therefore let my servant William put his trust in me, and cease to fear concerning his family, because of the sickness of the land. If ye love me, keep my commandments, and the sickness of the land shall redound to your glory.

88. Let my servant William go and proclaim my everlasting gospel with a loud voice, and with great joy, as he shall be moved upon by my Spirit, unto the inhabitants of Warsaw, and also unto the inhabitants of Carthage, and also unto the inhabitants of Burlington, and also unto the inhabitants of Madison, and await patiently and diligently for further instructions at my general conference, saith the Lord.

89. If he will do my will let him from henceforth hearken to the counsel of my servant Joseph, and with his interest support the cause of the poor and publish the new translation of my holy word unto the inhabitants of the earth;

90. And if he will do this, I will bless him with a multiplicity of blessings, that he shall not be forsaken, nor his seed be found begging bread.

91. And again, verily I say unto you, Let my servant William be appointed, ordained, and anointed, as a counselor unto my servant Joseph, in the room of my servant Hyrum, that my servant Hyrum may take the office of Priesthood and Patriarch, which was appointed unto him by his father, by blessing and also by right,

92. That from henceforth he shall hold the keys of the patriarchal blessings upon the heads of all my people,

93. That whoever he blesses shall be blessed, and whoever he curses shall be cursed; that whatsoever he shall bind on earth shall be bound in heaven; and whatsoever he shall loose on earth shall be loosed in heaven;

94. And from this time forth I appoint unto him that he may be a prophet, and a seer, and a revelator unto my church, as well as my servant Joseph,

95. That he may act in concert also with my servant Joseph, and that he shall receive counsel from my servant Joseph, who shall show unto him the keys whereby he may ask and receive, and be crowned with the same blessing, and

glory, and honor, and Priesthood, and gifts of the Priesthood that once were put upon him that was my servant Oliver Cowdery;

96. That my servant Hyrum may bear record of the things which I shall show unto him, that his name may be had in honorable remembrance from generation to generation, for ever and ever.

97. Let my servant William Law also receive the keys by which he may ask and receive blessings; let him be humble before me, and be without guile, and he shall receive of my Spirit, even the Comforter, which shall manifest unto him the truth of all things, and shall give him in the very hour, what he shall say.

98. And these signs shall follow him; he shall heal the sick, he shall cast out devils, and shall be delivered from those who would administer unto him deadly poison;

99. And he shall be led in paths where the poisonous serpent cannot lay hold upon his heel, and he shall mount up in the imagination of his thoughts as upon eagles' wings;

100. And what if I will that he should raise the dead, let him not withhold his voice.

101. Therefore, let my servant William cry aloud and spare not, with joy and rejoicing, and with hosannas to him that sitteth upon the throne for ever and ever, saith the Lord your God.

102. Behold, I say unto you, I have a mission in store for my servant William, and my servant Hyrum, and for them alone; and let my servant Joseph tarry at home, for he is needed: the remainder I will show unto you hereafter. Even so. Amen.

103. And again, verily I say unto you, if my servant Sidney will serve me and be counselor unto my servant Joseph, let him arise and come up and stand in the office of his calling, and humble himself before me;

104. And if he will offer unto me an acceptable offering, and acknowledgments, and remain with my people, behold, I, the Lord your God, will heal him that he shall be healed; and he shall lift up his voice again on the mountains, and be a spokesman before my face.

105. Let him come and locate his family in the neighborhood in which my servant Joseph resides,

106. And in all his journeyings let him lift up his voice as with the sound of a trump, and warn the inhabitants of the earth to flee the wrath to come;

107. Let him assist my servant Joseph; and also let my servant William Law assist my servant Joseph, in making a solemn proclamation unto the kings of the earth, even as I have before said unto you.

108. If my servant Sidney will do my will, let him not remove his family unto the eastern lands, but let him change their habitation, even as I have said.

109. Behold, it is not my will that he shall seek to find safety and refuge out of the city which I have appointed unto you, even the city of Nauvoo.

110. Verily I say unto you, even now, if he will hearken unto my voice, it shall be well with him. Even so. Amen.

111. And again, verily I say unto you, Let my servant Amos Davies pay stock into the hands of those whom I have appointed to build a house for boarding, even the Nauvoo House;

112. This let him do if he will have an interest, and let him hearken unto the counsel of my servant Joseph, and labor with his own hands that he may obtain the confidence of men;

113. And when he shall prove himself faithful in all things that shall be entrusted unto his care, yea, even a few things, he shall be made ruler over many;

114. Let him therefore abase himself that he may be exalted. Even so. Amen.

115. And again, verily I say unto you, if my servant Robert D. Foster will obey my voice, let him

build a house for my servant Joseph, according to the contract which he has made with him, as the door shall be open to him from time to time;

116. And let him repent of all his folly, and clothe himself with charity, and cease to do evil, and lay aside all his hard speeches;

117. And pay stock also into the hands of the quorum of the Nauvoo House, for himself and for his generation after him, from generation to generation.

118. And hearken unto the counsel of my servants Joseph, and Hyrum, and William Law, and unto the authorities which I have called to lay the foundation of Zion, and it shall be well with him for ever and ever. Even so. Amen.

119. And again, verily I say unto you, Let no man pay stock to the quorum of the Nauvoo House, unless he shall be a believer in the Book of Mormon, and the revelations I have given unto you, saith the Lord your God;

120. For that which is more or less than this cometh of evil, and shall be attended with cursings and not blessings, saith the Lord your God. Even so. Amen.

121. And again, verily I say unto you, Let the quorum of the Nauvoo House have a just recompense of wages for all their labors which they do in building the Nauvoo House, and let their wages be as shall be agreed among themselves, as pertaining to the price thereof;

122. And let every man who pays stock bear his proportion of their wages, if it must needs be, for their support, saith the Lord; otherwise, their labors shall be accounted unto them for stock in that house. Even so. Amen.

123. Verily I say unto you, I now give unto you the officers belonging to my Priesthood, that ye may hold the keys thereof, even the Priesthood which is after the order of Melchizedek, which is after the order of mine Only Begotten Son.

124. First, I give unto you Hyrum Smith to be a patriarch unto you, to hold the sealing blessings of my church, even the Holy Spirit of promise, whereby ye are sealed up unto the day of redemption, that ye may not fall notwithstanding the hour of temptation that may come upon you.

125. I give unto you my servant Joseph to be a presiding elder over all my church, to be a translator, a revelator, a seer and prophet.

126. I give unto him for counselors my servant Sidney Rigdon and my servant William Law, that these may constitute a quorum and First Presidency, to receive the oracles for the whole church.

127. I give unto you my servant Brigham Young, to be a president over the Twelve traveling Council,

128. Which Twelve hold the keys to open up the authority of my kingdom upon the four corners of the earth, and after that to send my word to every creature.

129. They are—Heber C. Kimball, Parley P. Pratt, Orson Pratt, Orson Hyde, William Smith, John Taylor, John E. Page, Wilford Woodruff, Willard Richards, George A. Smith;

130. David Patten I have taken unto myself; behold, his Priesthood no man taketh from him; but, verily I say unto you, another may be appointed unto the same calling.

131. And again, I say unto you, I give unto you a High Council, for the corner stone of Zion;

132. Viz., Samuel Bent, H. G. Sherwood, George W. Harris, Charles C. Rich, Thomas Grover, Newel Knight, David Dort, Dunbar Wilson; (Seymour Brunson I have taken unto myself; no man taketh his priesthood, but another may be appointed unto the same Priesthood in his stead; and verily I say unto you, let my servant Aaron Johnson be ordained unto this calling in his stead;) David Fullmer, Alpheus Cutler, William Huntington.

133. And again, I give unto you Don C. Smith, to be a president over a quorum of High Priests;

134. Which ordinance is instituted for the purpose of qualifying those who shall be appointed

standing presidents or servants over different Stakes scattered abroad,

135. And they may travel also if they choose, but rather be ordained for standing presidents, this is the office of their calling, saith the Lord your God.

136. I give unto him Amasa Lyman, and Noah Packard, for counselors, that they may preside over the quorum of High Priests of my church, saith the Lord.

137. And again, I say unto you, I give unto you John A. Hicks, Samuel Williams, and Jesse Baker, which Priesthood is to preside over the quorum of elders, which quorum is instituted for standing ministers, nevertheless they may travel, yet they are ordained to be standing ministers to my church, saith the Lord.

138. And again, I give unto you Joseph Young, Josiah Butterfield, Daniel Miles, Henry Herriman, Zera Pulsipher, Levi Hancock, James Foster, to preside over the quorum of seventies,

139. Which quorum is instituted for traveling elders to bear record of my name in all the world, wherever the traveling High Council, mine apostles, shall send them to prepare a way before my face.

140. The difference between this quorum and the quorum of elders is, that one is to travel continually, and the other is to preside over the churches from time to time; the one has the responsibility of presiding from time to time, and the other has no responsibility of presiding, saith the Lord your God.

141. And again, I say unto you I give unto you Vinson Knight, Samuel H. Smith, and Shadrach Roundy, if he will receive it, to preside over the bishopric; a knowledge of said bishopric is given unto you in the Book of Doctrine and Covenants.

142. And again, I say unto you, Samuel Rolfe and his counselors for priests, and the president of the teachers and his counselors, and also the president of the deacons and his counselors, and also the president of the stake and his counselors;

143. The above offices I have given unto you, and the keys thereof, for helps and for governments, for the work of the ministry and the perfecting of my saints;

144. And a commandment I give unto you that you should fill all these offices and approve of those names which I have mentioned, or else disapprove of them at my general conference,

145. And that ye should prepare rooms for all these offices in my house when you build it unto my name, saith the Lord your God. Even so. Amen.

THE SAINTS LABOR TOGETHER TO BUILD THE NAUVOO TEMPLE

Section 125

Some of the Saints driven from the State of Missouri settled in the Territory of Iowa. Later the Lord directed the Saints to gather in Nauvoo, Illinois, and erect a temple, "for the Most High to dwell therein" (section 124:25–27). The Saints living on the Territory side of the Mississippi River desired to know if they should move to the Illinois side to be in harmony with the Lord's counsel. This revelation was received by the Prophet Joseph Smith March 1841, at Nauvoo, Illinois (History of the Church, vol. 4:311).

1. "What is the will of the Lord, concerning the saints in the Territory of Iowa?"

2. Verily, thus saith the Lord, I say unto you, if those who call themselves by my name, and are essaying to be my saints, if they will do my will and keep my commandments concerning them; let them gather themselves together, unto the places which I shall appoint unto them by my servant Joseph, and build up cities unto my name, that they may be prepared for that which is in store for a time to come.

3. Let them build up a city unto my name upon the land opposite the city of Nauvoo, and let the name of Zarahemla be named upon it.

4. And let all those who come from the east, and the west, and the north, and the south, that have desires to dwell therein, take up their inheritance in the same, as well as in the city of Nashville, or in the city of Nauvoo, and in all the Stakes which I have appointed, saith the Lord.

BRIGHAM YOUNG AND JOSEPH SMITH CONVERSE TOGETHER IN NAUVOO AFTER BRIGHAM RETURNS FROM HIS MISSION TO ENGLAND

SECTION 126

On July 1, 1841, Brigham Young, President of the Quorum of the Twelve Apostles, arrived with several members of the Quorum at Nauvoo, Illinois, from their mission to England. At the home of Brigham Young, July 9, 1841, the Prophet Joseph Smith received this revelation (History of the Church, vol. 4:382).

1. Dear and well-beloved brother Brigham Young, verily thus saith the Lord unto you, my servant Brigham, it is no more required at your hand to leave your family as in times past, for your offering is acceptable to me;

2. I have seen your labor and toil in journeyings for my name.

3. I therefore command you to send my word abroad, and take special care of your family from this time, henceforth, and for ever. Amen.

SECTION 127

The enemies of the Prophet Joseph Smith in the states of Illinois and Missouri were pursuing him with vicious intent. For his protection and the safety of Church members, the Prophet secluded himself from public activities for a season (section 127:1). From his place of concealment the Prophet wrote two letters (sections 127–128) to the Saints at Nauvoo giving directions on baptism for the dead. This letter (section 127) was written September 1, 1842, at Nauvoo, Illinois (History of the Church, vol. 5:142).

1. Forasmuch as the Lord has revealed unto me that my enemies, both in Missouri and this State, were again in the pursuit of me; and inasmuch as they pursue me without a cause, and have not the least shadow or coloring of justice or right on their side, in the getting up of their prosecutions against me; and inasmuch as their pretensions are all founded in falsehood of the blackest dye, I have thought it expedient and wisdom in me to leave the place for a short season, for my own safety, and the safety of this people. I would say to all those with whom I have business, that I have left my affairs with agents and clerks, who will transact all business in a prompt and proper manner, and will see that all my debts are canceled in due time, by turning out property, or otherwise, as the case may require, or as the circumstances may admit of. When I learn that the storm is fully blown over, then I will return to you again.

2. And as for the perils which I am called to pass through, they seem but a small thing to me, as the envy and wrath of man have been my common lot all the days of my life; and for what cause it seems mysterious, unless I was ordained from before the foundation of the world for some good end, or bad, as you may choose to call it. Judge ye for yourselves. God knoweth all these things, whether it be good or bad. But nevertheless, deep water is what I am wont to swim in. It all has become a second nature to me, and I feel like Paul, to glory in tribulation, for to this day has the God of my fathers delivered me out of them all, and will deliver me from henceforth; for behold, and lo, I shall triumph over all my enemies, for the Lord God hath spoken it.

3. Let all the saints rejoice, therefore, and be exceedingly glad, for Israel's God is their God, and he will mete out a just recompense of reward upon the heads of all their oppressors.

4. And again, verily thus saith the Lord, Let the work of my temple, and all the works which I have appointed unto you, be continued on and not cease; and let your diligence, and your perseverance, and patience, and your works be redoubled,

and you shall in nowise lose your reward, saith the Lord of Hosts. And if they persecute you, so persecuted they the prophets and righteous men that were before you. For all this there is a reward in heaven.

5. And again, I give unto you a word in relation to the baptism for your dead.

6. Verily, thus saith the Lord unto you concerning your dead: When any of you are baptized for your dead, let there be a Recorder, and let him be eye witness of your baptisms; let him hear with his ears, that he may testify of a truth, saith the Lord;

7. That in all your recordings it may be recorded in heaven; whatsoever you bind on earth, may be bound in heaven; whatsoever you loose on earth, may be loosed in heaven;

8. For I am about to restore many things to the earth, pertaining to the Priesthood, saith the Lord of Hosts.

9. And again, let all the records be had in order, that they may be put in the archives of my Holy Temple, to be held in remembrance from generation to generation, saith the Lord of hosts.

10. I will say to all the saints, that I desired, with exceedingly great desire, to have addressed them from the stand, on the subject of baptism for the dead, on the following sabbath. But inasmuch as it is out of my power to do so, I will write the word of the Lord from time to time, on that subject, and send it to you by mail, as well as many other things.

11. I now close my letter for the present, for the want of more time; for the enemy is on the alert, and as the Savior said, the prince of this world cometh, but he hath nothing in me.

12. Behold, my prayer to God is, that you all may be saved. And I subscribe myself your servant in the Lord, Prophet and Seer of the Church of Jesus Christ of Latter-day Saints.

JOSEPH SMITH.

Section 128

While in seclusion from his enemies, the Prophet Joseph Smith wrote this letter September 6, 1842, at Nauvoo, Illinois, to the Church giving further directions on baptism for the dead (see historical background, section 127), (History of the Church, vol. 5:148).

1. As I stated to you in my letter before I left my place, that I would write to you from time to time, and give you information in relation to many subjects, I now resume the subject of the baptism for the dead, as that subject seems to occupy my mind, and press itself upon my feelings the strongest, since I have been pursued by my enemies.

2. I wrote a few words of revelation to you concerning a recorder. I have had a few additional views in relation to this matter, which I now certify. That is, it was declared in my former letter that there should be a recorder, who should be eye witness, and also to hear with his ears, that he might make a record of a truth before the Lord.

3. Now, in relation to this matter, it would be very difficult for one recorder to be present at all times, and do all the business. To obviate this difficulty, there can be a recorder appointed in each ward of the city, who is well qualified for taking accurate minutes; and let him be very particular and precise in taking the whole proceedings, certifying in his record that he saw with his eyes, and heard with his ears, giving the date, and names, &c., so forth, and the history of the whole transaction; naming also some three individuals that are present, if there be any present, who can at any time when called upon, certify to the same, that in the mouth of two or three witnesses, every word may be established.

4. Then let there be a general recorder, to whom these other records can be handed, being attended with certificates over their own signatures, certifying that the record they have made is true. Then the general church recorder can enter the record on the general church book, with the certificates and all the attending witnesses, with his own statement that he verily believes the above statement and records to be true, from his knowledge of the general character and appointment of those men by the church. And when this is done on the general church book, the record shall be just as holy, and shall answer the ordinance just the same as if he had seen with his eyes, and

heard with his ears, and made a record of the same on the general church book.

5. You may think this order of things to be very particular, but let me tell you, that it is only to answer the will of God, by conforming to the ordinance and preparation that the Lord ordained and prepared before the foundation of the world, for the salvation of the dead who should die without a knowledge of the gospel.

6. And further I want you to remember that John the Revelator was contemplating this very subject in relation to the dead, when he declared, as you will find recorded in Revelations xx. 12—"And I saw the dead, small and great, stand before God; and the books were opened; and another book was opened, which was the book of life; and the dead were judged out of those things which were written in the books, according to their works."

7. You will discover in this quotation, that the books were opened; and another book was opened, which was the book of life; but the dead were judged out of those things which were written in the books, according to their works; consequently the books spoken of must be the books which contained the record of their works; and refer to the records which are kept on the earth. And the book which was the book of life, is the record which is kept in heaven; the principle agreeing precisely with the doctrine which is commanded you in the revelation contained in the letter which I wrote to you previously to my leaving my place—that in all your recordings it may be recorded in heaven.

8. Now the nature of this ordinance consists in the power of the Priesthood, by the revelation of Jesus Christ, wherein it is granted, that whatsoever you bind on earth, shall be bound in heaven, and whatsoever you loose on earth, shall be loosed in heaven. Or, in other words, taking a different view of the translation, whatsoever you record on earth, shall be recorded in heaven; and whatsoever you do not record on earth, shall not be recorded in heaven; for out of the books shall your dead be judged, according to their own works, whether they themselves have attended to the ordinances in their own *propria persona*, or by the means of their own agents, according to the ordinance which God has prepared for their salvation from before the foundation of the world, according to the records which they have kept concerning their dead.

9. It may seem to some to be a very bold doctrine that we talk of—a power which records or binds on earth, and binds in heaven. Nevertheless in all ages of the world, whenever the Lord has given a dispensation of the Priesthood to any man by actual revelation, or any set of men, this power has always been given. Hence, whatsoever those men did in authority, in the name of the Lord, and did it truly and faithfully, and kept a proper and faithful record of the same, it became a law on earth and in heaven, and could not be annulled, according to the decrees of the great Jehovah. This is a faithful saying! Who can hear it?

10. And again, for the precedent, Matthew xvi. 18, 19, "And I say also unto thee, that thou art Peter: and upon this rock I will build my church; and the gates of hell shall not prevail against it; and I will give unto thee the keys of the kingdom of heaven, and whatsoever thou shalt bind on earth, shall be bound in heaven; and whatsoever thou shalt loose on earth, shall be loosed in heaven."

11. Now the great and grand secret of the whole matter, and the *summum bonum* of the whole subject that is lying before us, consists in obtaining the powers of the Holy Priesthood. For him to whom these keys are given, there is no difficulty in obtaining a knowledge of facts in relation to the salvation of the children of men, both as well for the dead as for the living.

12. Herein is glory and honor, and immortality and eternal life. The ordinance of baptism by

water, to be immersed therein in order to answer to the likeness of the dead, that one principle might accord with the other. To be immersed in the water and come forth out of the water is in the likeness of the resurrection of the dead in coming forth out of their graves; hence this ordinance was instituted to form a relationship with the ordinance of baptism for the dead, being in likeness of the dead.

13. Consequently the baptismal font was instituted as a simile of the grave and was commanded to be in a place underneath where the living are wont to assemble, to show forth the living and the dead and that all things may have their likeness, and that they may accord one with another; that which is earthly conforming to that which is heavenly, as Paul hath declared, 1 Corinthians xv. 46, 47, and 48.

14. "Howbeit that was not first which is spiritual, but that which is natural, and afterwards that which is spiritual. The first man is of the earth, earthy; the second man is the Lord, from heaven. As is the earthy, such are they also that are earthy; and as is the heavenly, such are they also that are heavenly." And as are the records on the earth in relation to your dead, which are truly made out, so also are the records in heaven. This, therefore, is the sealing and binding power, and, in one sense of the word, the keys of the kingdom which consist in the key of knowledge.

15. And now, my dearly beloved brethren and sisters, let me assure you that these are principles in relation to the dead, and the living, that cannot be lightly passed over, as pertaining to our salvation. For their salvation is necessary, and essential to our salvation, as Paul says concerning the fathers, "that they without us cannot be made perfect;" either can we without our dead be made perfect.

16. And now, in relation to the baptism for the dead, I will give you another quotation of Paul, 1. Corinthians xv. 29, "Else what shall they do which are baptized for the dead, if the dead rise not at all; why are they then baptized for the dead?"

17. And again, in connection with this quotation, I will give you a quotation from one of the prophets, who had his eye fixed on the restoration of the Priesthood, the glories to be revealed in the last days, and in an especial manner this most glorious of all subjects belonging to the everlasting gospel, viz., the baptism for the dead; for Malachi says, last chapter, verses 5th and 6th, "Behold, I will send you Elijah the prophet, before the coming of the great and dreadful day of the Lord; and he shall turn the heart of the fathers to the children, and the heart of the children to their fathers, lest I come and smite the earth with a curse.

18. I might have rendered a plainer translation to this, but it is sufficiently plain to suit my purpose as it stands. It is sufficient to know, in this case, that the earth will be smitten with a curse, unless there is a welding link of some kind or other, between the fathers and the children, upon some subject or other, and behold what is that subject? It is the baptism for the dead. For we without them cannot be made perfect; neither can they without us be made perfect. Neither can they nor we, be made perfect, without those who have died in the gospel also; for it is necessary in the ushering in of the dispensation of the fulness of times; which dispensation is now beginning to usher in, that a whole and complete and perfect union, and welding together of dispensations, and keys, and powers, and glories should take place, and be revealed from the days of Adam even to the present time; and not only this, but those things which never have been revealed from the foundation of the world, but have been kept hid from the wise and prudent, shall be revealed unto babes and sucklings in this the dispensation of the fulness of times.

19. Now, what do we hear in the gospel which we have received? "A voice of gladness! A voice of mercy from heaven; and a voice of truth out of the earth; glad tidings for the dead; a voice of gladness for the living and the dead; glad tidings of great joy; how beautiful upon the mountains are the feet of those that bring glad tidings of good things; and that say unto Zion; behold! thy God reigneth. As the dews of Carmel, so shall the knowledge of God descend upon them."

20. And again, what do we hear? Glad tidings from Cumorah! Moroni, an angel from heaven, declaring the fulfilment of the prophets—the book to be revealed. A voice of the Lord in the wilderness of Fayette, Seneca county, declaring the three witnesses to bear record of the book. The voice of Michael on the banks of the Susquehanna, detecting the devil when he appeared as an angel of light. The voice of Peter, James, and John in the wilderness between Harmony, Susquehanna county, and Colesville, Broome county, on the Susquehanna river, declaring themselves as possessing the keys of the kingdom, and of the dispensation of the fulness of times.

21. And again, the voice of God in the chamber of old father Whitmer, in Fayette, Seneca county, and at sundry times, and in divers places through all the travels and tribulations of this Church of Jesus Christ of Latter-day Saints. And the voice of Michael, the archangel; the voice of Gabriel, and of Raphael, and of divers angels, from Michael or Adam, down to the present time, all declaring their dispensation, their rights, their keys, their honors, their majesty and glory, and the power of their Priesthood; giving line upon line, precept upon precept; here a little, and there a little—giving us consolation by holding forth that which is to come, confirming our hope.

22. Brethren, shall we not go on in so great a cause? Go forward and not backward. Courage, brethren; and on, on to the victory! Let your hearts rejoice, and be exceedingly glad. Let the earth break forth into singing. Let the dead speak forth anthems of eternal praise to the King Immanuel, who hath ordained before the world was, that which would enable us to redeem them out of their prison; for the prisoners shall go free.

23. Let the mountains shout for joy, and all ye valleys cry aloud; and all ye seas and dry lands tell the wonders of your Eternal King. And ye rivers, and brooks, and rills flow down with gladness. Let the woods and all the trees of the field praise the Lord; and ye solid rocks weep for joy. And let the sun, moon, and the morning stars sing together, and let all the sons of God shout for joy. And let the eternal creations declare his name for ever and ever. And again I say, how glorious is the voice we hear from heaven, proclaiming in our ears, glory, and salvation, and honor, and immortality, and eternal life; kingdoms, principalities, and powers.

24. Behold the great day of the Lord is at hand, and who can abide the day of his coming, and who can stand when he appeareth; for he is like a refiner's fire, and like fuller's soap; and he shall sit as a refiner and purifier of silver, and he shall purify the sons of Levi, and purge them as gold and silver, that they may offer unto the Lord an offering in righteousness. Let us therefore, as a church and a people, and as Latter-day Saints offer unto the Lord an offering in righteousness; and let us present in his holy temple, when it is finished, a book containing the records of our dead, which shall be worthy of all acceptation.

25. Brethren, I have many things to say to you on the subject; but shall now close for the present, and continue the subject another time. I am, as ever, your humble servant and never deviating friend.

JOSEPH SMITH.

JOSEPH SMITH PREACHES TO THE SAINTS IN NAUVOO

SECTION 129

On February 9, 1843, at Nauvoo, Illinois, the Prophet Joseph Smith gave to the Saints, "Three Grand Keys by which Good or Bad Angels or Spirits may be Known" (History of the Church, vol. 5:267).

1. There are two kinds of beings in heaven—viz., angels who are resurrected personages, having bodies of flesh and bones.

2. For instance, Jesus said, "Handle me and see, for a spirit hath not flesh and bones, as ye see me have."

3. 2nd. The spirits of just men made perfect—they who are not resurrected, but inherit the same glory.

4. When a messenger comes, saying he has a message from God, offer him your hand, and request him to shake hands with you.

5. If he be an angel, he will do so, and you will feel his hand.

6. If he be the spirit of a just man made perfect, he will come in his glory; for that is the only way he can appear.

7. Ask him to shake hands with you, but he will not move, because it is contrary to the order of heaven for a just man to deceive; but he will still deliver his message.

8. If it be the Devil as an angel of light, when you ask him to shake hands, he will offer you his hand, and you will not feel anything: you may therefore detect him.

9. These are three grand keys whereby you may know whether any administration is from God.

SECTION 130

This section contains "Important Items of Instruction given by Joseph the Prophet at Ramus, Illinois, April 2nd 1843" (History of the Church, *vol. 5:323–325*).

1. When the Savior shall appear, we shall see him as he is. We shall see that he is a man like ourselves;

2. And that same sociality which exists among us here will exist among us there, only it will be coupled with eternal glory, which glory we do not now enjoy.

3. (John XIV. 23.) The appearing of the Father and the Son, in that verse, is a *personal* appearance; and the idea that the Father and the Son dwell in a man's heart, is an old sectarian notion, and is false.

4. In answer to the question, "is not the reckoning of God's time, angel's time, prophet's time, and man's time according to the planet on which they reside?"

5. I answer, yes. But there are no angels who minister to this earth but those who do belong or have belonged to it.

6. The angels do not reside on a planet like this earth.

7. But they reside in the presence of God, on a globe like a sea of glass and fire, where all things for their glory are manifest—past, present, and future, and are continually before the Lord.

8. The place where God resides is a great Urim and Thummim.

9. This earth, in its sanctified and immortal state, will be made like unto crystal and will be a Urim and Thummim to the inhabitants who dwell thereon, whereby all things pertaining to an inferior kingdom, or all kingdoms of a lower order, will be manifest to those who dwell on it; and this earth will be Christ's.

10. Then the white stone mentioned in Revelations ii. 17, will become a Urim and Thummim to each individual who receives one, whereby things pertaining to a higher order of kingdoms, even all kingdoms will be made known;

11. And a white stone is given to each of those who come into the celestial kingdom, whereon is a new name written, which no man knoweth save he that receiveth it. The new name is the key word.

12. I prophesy, in the name of the Lord God, that the commencement of the difficulties which will

cause much bloodshed previous to the coming of the Son of Man will be in South Carolina.

13. It may probably arise through the slave question. This a voice declared to me, while I was praying earnestly on the subject, December 25th, 1832.

14. I was once praying very earnestly to know the time of the coming of the Son of Man, when I heard a voice repeat the following—

15. "Joseph, my son, if thou livest until thou art eighty-five years old, thou shalt see the face of the Son of Man: therefore let this suffice, and trouble me no more on this matter."

16. I was left thus, without being able to decide whether this coming referred to the beginning of the millennium or to some previous appearing, or whether I should die and thus see his face.

17. I believe the coming of the Son of Man will not be any sooner than that time.

18. Whatever principle of intelligence we attain unto in this life, it will rise with us in the resurrection;

19. And if a person gains more knowledge and intelligence in this life through his diligence and obedience than another, he will have so much the advantage in the world to come.

20. There is a law, irrevocably decreed in heaven before the foundations of this world, upon which all blessings are predicated;

21. And when we obtain any blessing from God, it is by obedience to that law upon which it is predicated.

22. The Father has a body of flesh and bones as tangible as man's; the Son also; but the Holy Ghost has not a body of flesh and bones, but is a personage of Spirit. Were it not so, the Holy Ghost could not dwell in us.

23. A man may receive the Holy Ghost, and it may descend upon him and not tarry with him.

SECTION 131

This section contains inspired statements given by the Prophet Joseph Smith, May 16 and 17, 1843, at Ramus, Illinois (History of the Church, vol. 5:392–393).

1. In the celestial glory there are three heavens or degrees;
2. And in order to obtain the highest, a man must enter into this Order of the Priesthood; (meaning the new and everlasting covenant of marriage;)
3. And if he does not he cannot obtain it.
4. He may enter into the other, but that is the end of his kingdom: he cannot have an increase.
5. (May 17th, 1843.) The more sure word of prophecy (mentioned by Peter) means a man's knowing that he is sealed up unto eternal life, by revelation and the spirit of prophecy, through the power of the Holy Priesthood.
6. It is impossible for a man to be saved in ignorance.
7. There is no such thing as immaterial matter. All spirit is matter, but it is more fine or pure, and can only be discerned by purer eyes.
8. We cannot see it; but when our bodies are purified, we shall see that it is all matter.

Section 132

The Prophet Joseph Smith inquired of the Lord pertaining to prophets living in Old Testament times having more than one wife (section 132:1–2). This revelation is an answer to his inquiry and was written July 12, 1843, at Nauvoo, Illinois. (History of the Church, vol. 5:501).

1. Verily, thus saith the Lord unto you, my servant Joseph, that inasmuch as you have inquired of my hand, to know and understand wherein I, the Lord, justified my servants Abraham, Isaac and Jacob; as also Moses, David and Solomon, my servants, as touching the principle and doctrine of their having many wives and concubines:

2. Behold! and lo, I am the Lord thy God, and will answer thee as touching this matter:

3. Therefore, prepare thy heart to receive and obey the instructions which I am about to give unto you; for all those who have this law revealed unto them must obey the same;

4. For behold! I reveal unto you a new and an everlasting covenant; and if ye abide not that covenant, then are ye damned; for no one can reject this covenant, and be permitted to enter into my glory;

5. For all who will have a blessing at my hands, shall abide the law which was appointed for that blessing, and the conditions thereof, as were instituted from before the foundation of the world:

6. And as pertaining to the new and everlasting covenant, it was instituted for the fulness of my glory; and he that receiveth a fulness thereof, must and shall abide the law, or he shall be damned, saith the Lord God.

7. And verily I say unto you, that the conditions of this law are these—All covenants, contracts, bonds, obligations, oaths, vows, performances, connections, associations, or expectations, that are not made, and entered into, and sealed, by the Holy Spirit of promise, of him who is anointed, both as well for time and for all eternity, and that too most holy, by revelation and commandment through the medium of mine anointed, whom I have appointed on the earth to hold this power, (and I have appointed unto my servant Joseph to hold this power in the last days, and there is never but one on the earth at a time, on whom this power and the keys of this Priesthood are conferred) are of no efficacy, virtue or force, in and after the resurrection from the dead; for all contracts that are not made unto this end, have an end when men are dead.

8. Behold! mine house is a house of order, saith the Lord God, and not a house of confusion.

9. Will I accept of an offering, saith the Lord, that is not made in my name!

10. Or, will I receive at your hands that which I have not appointed!

11. And will I appoint unto you, saith the Lord, except it be by law, even as I and my Father ordained unto you, before the world was!

12. I am the Lord thy God, and I give unto you this commandment, that no man shall come unto the Father but by me, or by my word, which is my law, saith the Lord;

13. And everything that is in the world, whether it be ordained of men, by thrones or principalities, or powers, or things of name, whatsoever they may be, that are not by me, or by my word, saith the Lord, shall be thrown down, and shall not remain after men are dead, neither in nor after the resurrection, saith the Lord your God;

14. For whatsoever things remain are by me; and whatsoever things are not by me, shall be shaken and destroyed.

15. Therefore, if a man marry him a wife in the world, and he marry her not by me, nor by my word; and he covenant with her so long as he is in the world, and she with him, their covenant and marriage are not of force when they are dead, and when they are out of the world; therefore, they are not bound by any law when they are out of the world;

16. Therefore, when they are out of the world, they neither marry, nor are given in marriage; but are appointed angels in heaven, which angels are ministering servants, to minister for those who are worthy of a far more, and an exceeding, and an eternal weight of glory;

17. For these angels did not abide my law, therefore, they cannot be enlarged, but remain separately and singly, without exaltation, in their saved condition, to all eternity, and from henceforth are not Gods, but are angels of God, for ever and ever.

18. And again, verily I say unto you, if a man marry a wife, and make a covenant with her for time and for all eternity, if that covenant is not by me, or by my word, which is my law, and is not sealed by the Holy Spirit of promise, through him whom I have anointed and appointed unto this power—then it is not valid, neither of force when they are out of the world, because they are not joined by me, saith the Lord, neither by my word; when they are out of the world, it cannot be received there, because the angels and the Gods are appointed there, by whom they cannot pass; they cannot, therefore, inherit my glory, for my house is a house of order, saith the Lord God.

19. And again, verily I say unto you, if a man marry a wife by my word, which is my law, and by the new and everlasting covenant, and it is sealed unto them by the Holy Spirit of promise, by him who is anointed unto whom I have appointed this power, and the keys of this Priesthood; and it shall be said unto them, ye shall come forth in the first resurrection; and if it be after the first resurrection, in the next resurrection; and shall inherit thrones, kingdoms, principalities, and powers, dominions, all heights and depths—then shall it be written in the Lamb's Book of Life, that he shall commit no murder whereby to shed innocent blood, and if ye abide in my covenant, and commit no murder whereby to shed innocent blood, it shall be done unto them in all things whatsoever my servant hath put upon them, in time, and through all eternity, and shall be of full force when they are out of the world; and they shall pass by the angels, and the Gods, which are set there, to their exaltation and glory in all things, as hath been sealed upon their heads, which glory shall be a fulness and a continuation of the seeds for ever and ever.

20. Then shall they be Gods, because they have no end; therefore shall they be from everlasting to everlasting, because they continue; then shall they be above all, because all things are subject unto them. Then shall they be Gods, because they have all power, and the angels are subject unto them.

21. Verily, verily I say unto you, except ye abide my law, ye cannot attain to this glory;

22. For strait is the gate, and narrow the way that leadeth unto the exaltation and continuation of the lives, and few there be that find it, because ye receive me not in the world, neither do ye know me.

23. But if ye receive me in the world, then shall ye know me, and shall receive your exaltation, that where I am, ye shall be also.

24. This is eternal lives, to know the only wise and true God, and Jesus Christ, whom he hath sent. I am he. Receive ye, therefore, my law.

25. Broad is the gate, and wide the way that leadeth to the deaths, and many there are that go in thereat; because they receive me not, neither do they abide in my law.

26. Verily, verily I say unto you, if a man marry a wife according to my word, and they are sealed by the Holy Spirit of promise, according to mine appointment, and he or she shall commit any sin or transgression of the new and everlasting covenant whatever, and all manner of blasphemies, and if they commit no murder, wherein they shed innocent blood—yet they shall come forth in the first resurrection, and enter into their exaltation; but they shall be destroyed in the flesh, and shall be delivered unto the buffetings of Satan unto the day of redemption, saith the Lord God.

27. The blasphemy against the Holy Ghost, which shall not be forgiven in the world, nor out of the world, is in that ye commit murder, wherein ye shed innocent blood, and assent unto my death, after ye have received my new and everlasting covenant, saith the Lord God; and he that abideth not this law, can in no wise enter into my glory, but shall be damned, saith the Lord.

28. I am the Lord thy God, and will give unto thee the law of my Holy Priesthood, as was ordained by me, and my Father before the world was.

29. Abraham received all things, whatsoever he received, by revelation and commandment, by my word, saith the Lord, and hath entered into his exaltation, and sitteth upon his throne.

30. Abraham received promises concerning his seed, and of the fruit of his loins,—from whose loins ye are, namely, my servant Joseph—which were to continue so long as they were in the world; and as touching Abraham and his seed, out of the world they should continue; both in the world and out of the world should they continue as innumerable as the stars; or, if ye were to count the sand upon the sea shore, ye could not number them.

31. This promise is yours, also, because ye are of Abraham, and the promise was made unto Abraham; and by this law is the continuation of the works of my Father, wherein he glorified himself.

32. Go ye, therefore, and do the works of Abraham; enter ye into my law, and ye shall be saved.

33. But if ye enter not into my law ye cannot receive the promise of my Father which he made unto Abraham.

34. God commanded Abraham, and Sarah gave Hagar to Abraham to wife. And why did she do it? Because this was the law, and from Hagar sprang many people. This, therefore, was fulfilling, among other things, the promises.

35. Was Abraham, therefore, under condemnation? Verily, I say unto you, Nay; for I, the Lord, commanded it.

36. Abraham was commanded to offer his son Isaac; nevertheless, it was written, thou shalt not kill. Abraham, however, did not refuse, and it was accounted unto him for righteousness.

37. Abraham received concubines, and they bear him children, and it was accounted unto him for righteousness, because they were given unto him, and he abode in my law, as Isaac also, and Jacob did none other things than that which they were commanded; and because they did none other things than that which they were commanded, they have entered into their exaltation, according to the promises, and sit upon thrones, and are not angels, but are Gods.

38. David also received many wives and concubines, and also Solomon and Moses my servants; as also many others of my servants, from the beginning of creation until this time; and in nothing did they sin, save in those things which they received not of me.

39. David's wives and concubines were given unto him, of me, by the hand of Nathan, my servant, and others of the prophets who had the keys of this power; and in none of these things did he sin against me, save in the case of Uriah and his wife; and, therefore he hath fallen from his exaltation, and received his portion: and he shall not inherit them out of the world; for I gave them unto another, saith the Lord.

40. I am the Lord thy God, and I gave unto thee, my servant Joseph, an appointment, and restore all things; ask what ye will, and it shall be given unto you according to my word:

41. And as ye have asked concerning adultery—verily, verily I say unto you, if a man receiveth a wife in the new and everlasting covenant, and if she be with another man, and I have not appointed unto her by the holy anointing, she hath committed adultery, and shall be destroyed.

42. If she be not in the new and everlasting covenant, and she be with another man, she has committed adultery;

43. And if her husband be with another woman, and he was under a vow, he hath broken his vow, and hath committed adultery,

44. And if she hath not committed adultery, but is innocent, and hath not broken her vow, and she knoweth it, and I reveal it unto you, my servant Joseph, then shall you have power, by the power of my Holy Priesthood, to take her, and give her unto him that hath not committed adultery, but hath been faithful; for he shall be made ruler over many;

45. For I have conferred upon you the keys and power of the Priesthood, wherein I restore all things, and make known unto you all things in due time.

46. And verily, verily I say unto you, that whatsoever you seal on earth, shall be sealed in heaven; and whatsoever you bind on earth, in my name, and by my word, saith the Lord, it shall be eternally bound in the heavens; and whosesoever sins you remit on earth shall be remitted eternally in the heavens; and whosesoever sins you retain on earth, shall be retained in heaven.

47. And again, verily I say, whomsoever you bless, I will bless, and whomsoever you curse, I will curse, saith the Lord; for I, the Lord, am thy God.

48. And again, verily I say unto you, my servant Joseph, that whatsoever you give on earth, and to whomsoever you give any one on earth, by my word, and according to my law, it shall be visited with blessings, and not cursings, and with my power, saith the Lord, and shall be without condemnation on earth, and in heaven;

49. For I am the Lord thy God, and will be with thee even unto the end of the world, and through all eternity; for verily, I seal upon you your exaltation, and prepare a throne for you in the kingdom of my Father, with Abraham your father.

50. Behold, I have seen your sacrifices, and will forgive all your sins; I have seen your sacrifices in obedience to that which I have told you; go, therefore, and I make a way for your escape, as I accepted the offering of Abraham, of his son Isaac.

51. Verily, I say unto you, a commandment I give unto mine handmaid, Emma Smith, your wife, whom I have given unto you, that she stay herself, and partake not of that which I commanded you to offer unto her; for I did it, saith the Lord, to prove you all, as I did Abraham; and that I might require an offering at your hand, by covenant and sacrifice;

52. And let mine handmaid, Emma Smith, receive all those that have been given unto my servant Joseph, and who are virtuous and pure before me; and those who are not pure, and have said they were pure, shall be destroyed, saith the Lord God;

53. For I am the Lord thy God, and ye shall obey my voice; and I give unto my servant Joseph, that he shall be made ruler over many things, for he hath been faithful over a few things, and from henceforth I will strengthen him.

54. And I command mine handmaid, Emma Smith, to abide and cleave unto my servant Joseph, and to none else. But if she will not abide this commandment, she shall be destroyed, saith the Lord; for I am the Lord thy God, and will destroy her, if she abide not in my law;

55. But if she will not abide this commandment, then shall my servant Joseph do all things for her, even as he hath said; and I will bless him and multiply him and give unto him an hundred-fold in this world, of fathers and mothers, brothers and sisters, houses and lands, wives and children, and crowns of eternal lives in the eternal worlds.

56. And again, verily I say, let mine handmaid forgive my servant Joseph his trespasses; and then shall she be forgiven her trespasses, wherein she has trespassed against me; and I, the Lord thy God, will bless her, and multiply her, and make her heart to rejoice.

57. And again, I say, let not my servant Joseph put his property out of his hands, lest an enemy come and destroy him; for Satan seeketh to destroy; for I am the Lord thy God, and he is my servant; and behold, and lo, I am with him, as I was with Abraham, thy father, even unto his exaltation and glory.

58. Now, as touching the law of the Priesthood, there are many things pertaining thereunto.

59. Verily, if a man be called of my Father, as was Aaron, by mine own voice, and by the voice of him that sent me; and I have endowed him with the keys of the power of this Priesthood, if he do anything in my name, and according to my law, and by my word, he will not commit sin, and I will justify him.

60. Let no one, therefore, set on my servant Joseph; for I will justify him; for he shall do the sacrifice which I require at his hands, for his transgressions, saith the Lord your God.

61. And again, as pertaining to the law of the Priesthood: If any man espouse a virgin, and desire to espouse another, and the first give her consent; and if he espouse the second, and they are virgins, and have vowed to no other man, then is he justified; he cannot commit adultery, for they are given unto him; for he cannot commit adultery with that that belongeth unto him and to no one else;

62. And if he have ten virgins given unto him by this law, he cannot commit adultery, for they belong to him, and they are given unto him, therefore is he justified.

63. But if one or either of the ten virgins, after she is espoused, shall be with another man; she has committed adultery, and shall be destroyed; for they are given unto him to multiply and replenish the earth, according to my commandment, and to fulfil the promise which was given by my Father before the foundation of the world; and for their exaltation in the eternal worlds, that they may bear the souls of men; for herein is the work of my Father continued, that he may be glorified.

EMMA HALE SMITH, WIFE OF THE PROPHET JOSEPH SMITH

64. And again, verily, verily I say unto you, if any man have a wife, who holds the keys of this power, and he teaches unto her the law of my Priesthood, as pertaining to these things, then shall she believe, and administer unto him, or she shall be destroyed, saith the Lord your God, for I will destroy her; for I will magnify my name upon all those who receive and abide in my law.

65. Therefore, it shall be lawful in me, if she receive not this law, for him to receive all things, whatsoever I, the Lord his God, will give unto him, because she did not administer unto him according to my word; and she then becomes the transgressor; and he is exempt from the law of Sarah, who administered unto Abraham according to the law, when I commanded Abraham to take Hagar to wife.

66. And now, as pertaining to this law, verily, verily I say unto you, I will reveal more unto you, hereafter; therefore, let this suffice for the present. Behold, I am Alpha and Omega. Amen.

ection 133

The Prophet Joseph Smith informs us, "At this time there were many things which the Elders desired to know relative to preaching the Gospel to the inhabitants of the earth, and concerning the gathering; and in order to walk by the true light, and be instructed from on high, on the 3rd of November, 1831, (at Hiram, Ohio) I inquired of the Lord and received the following important revelation." This revelation is known as an appendix (History of the Church, vol. 1:229).

1. Hearken, O ye people of my church, saith the Lord your God, and hear the word of the Lord concerning you:

2. The Lord who shall suddenly come to his temple; the Lord who shall come down upon the world with a curse to judgment; yea, upon all the nations that forget God, and upon all the ungodly among you.

3. For he shall make bare his holy arm in the eyes of all the nations, and all the ends of the earth shall see the salvation of their God.

4. Wherefore, prepare ye, prepare ye, O my people; sanctify yourselves; gather ye together, O ye people of my church, upon the land of Zion, all you that have not been commanded to tarry.

5. Go ye out from Babylon. Be ye clean that bear the vessels of the Lord.

6. Call your solemn assemblies, and speak often one to another. And let every man call upon the name of the Lord;

7. Yea, verily I say unto you again, the time has come when the voice of the Lord is unto you, go ye out of Babylon; gather ye out from among the nations, from the four winds, from one end of heaven to the other.

8. Send forth the elders of my church unto the nations which are afar off; unto the islands of the sea; send forth unto foreign lands; call upon all nations; firstly, upon the Gentiles, and then upon the Jews.

9. And behold, and lo, this shall be their cry, and the voice of the Lord unto all people: Go ye forth unto the land of Zion, that the borders of my people may be enlarged, and that her Stakes may be strengthened, and that Zion may go forth unto the regions round about;

10. Yea, let the cry go forth among all people: Awake and arise and go forth to meet the Bridegroom: behold and lo, the Bridegroom cometh, go ye out to meet him. Prepare yourselves for the great day of the Lord.

11. Watch, therefore, for ye know neither the day nor the hour.

12. Let them therefore, who are among the Gentiles, flee unto Zion.

13. And let them who be of Judah flee unto Jerusalem, unto the mountains of the Lord's house.

14. Go ye out from among the nations, even from Babylon, from the midst of wickedness, which is spiritual Babylon.

15. But verily, thus saith the Lord, Let not your flight be in haste, but let all things be prepared before you; and he that goeth, let him not look back, lest sudden destruction shall come upon him.

16. Hearken and hear, O ye inhabitants of the earth. Listen ye elders of my church together, and hear the voice of the Lord, for he calleth upon all men, and he commandeth all men everywhere to repent;

17. For, behold, the Lord God hath sent forth the angel crying through the midst of heaven, saying, Prepare ye the way of the Lord, and make his paths straight for the hour of his coming is nigh,

18. When the Lamb shall stand upon Mount Zion, and with him a hundred and forty-four thousand, having his Father's name written on their foreheads:

19. Wherefore, prepare ye for the coming of the Bridegroom; go ye, go ye out to meet him,

20. For behold, he shall stand upon the mount of Olivet, and upon the mighty ocean, even the great deep, and upon the islands of the sea, and upon the land of Zion;

21. And he shall utter his voice out of Zion, and he shall speak from Jerusalem, and his voice shall be heard among all people,

22. And it shall be a voice as the voice of many waters, and as the voice of a great thunder, which shall break down the mountains, and the valleys shall not be found;

23. He shall command the great deep, and it shall be driven back into the north countries, and the islands shall become one land,

24. And the land of Jerusalem and the land of Zion shall be turned back into their own place, and the earth shall be like as it was in the days before it was divided.

25. And the Lord, even the Savior, shall stand in the midst of his people, and shall reign over all flesh.

26. And they who are in the north countries shall come in remembrance before the Lord, and their prophets shall hear his voice, and shall no longer stay themselves, and they shall smite the rocks, and the ice shall flow down at their presence.

27. And an highway shall be cast up in the midst of the great deep.

28. Their enemies shall become a prey unto them,

29. And in the barren deserts there shall come forth pools of living water; and the parched ground shall no longer be a thirsty land.

30. And they shall bring forth their rich treasures unto the children of Ephraim my servants.

31. And the boundaries of the everlasting hills shall tremble at their presence.

32. And there shall they fall down and be crowned with glory, even in Zion, by the hands of the servants of the Lord, even the children of Ephraim;

33. And they shall be filled with songs of everlasting joy.

34. Behold, this is the blessing of the everlasting God upon the tribes of Israel, and the richer blessing upon the head of Ephraim and his fellows.

35. And they also of the tribe of Judah, after their pain, shall be sanctified in holiness before the Lord to dwell in his presence, day and night, for ever and ever.

36. And now, verily saith the Lord, That these things might be known among you, O inhabitants of the earth, I have sent forth mine angel, flying through the midst of heaven, having the everlasting gospel, who hath appeared unto some, and hath committed it unto man, who shall appear unto many that dwell on the earth;

37. And this gospel shall be preached unto every nation, and kindred, tongue, and people,

38. And the servants of God shall go forth, saying, with a loud voice, Fear God and give glory to him, for the hour of his judgment is come:

39. And worship him that made heaven, and earth, and the sea, and the fountains of waters,

40. Calling upon the name of the Lord day and night, saying, O that thou wouldst rend the heavens, that thou wouldst come down, that the mountains might flow down at thy presence.

41. And it shall be answered upon their heads, for the presence of the Lord shall be as the melting fire that burneth, and as the fire which causeth the waters to boil.

42. O Lord thou shalt come down to make thy name known to thine adversaries, and all nations shall tremble at thy presence.

43. When thou doest terrible things—things they look not for;

44. Yea, when thou comest down, and the mountains flow down at thy presence, thou shalt meet him who rejoiceth and worketh righteousness, who remembereth thee in thy ways;

45. For since the beginning of the world have not men heard nor perceived by the ear, neither hath any eye seen, O God, besides thee, how great things thou hast prepared for him that waiteth for thee.

46. And it shall be said, Who is this that cometh down from God in heaven with dyed garments; yea, from the regions which are not known, clothed in his glorious apparel, traveling in the greatness of his strength?

47. And he shall say, I am he who spake in righteousness, mighty to save.

48. And the Lord shall be red in his apparel, and his garments like him that treadeth in the wine vat,

49. And so great shall be the glory of his presence, that the sun shall hide his face in shame; and the moon shall withhold its light; and the stars shall be hurled from their places;

50. And his voice shall be heard, I have trodden the wine-press alone, and have brought judgment upon all people; and none were with me;

51. And I have trampled them in my fury, and I did tread upon them in mine anger, and their blood have I sprinkled upon my garments, and stained all my raiment; for this was the day of vengeance which was in my heart.

52. And now the year of my redeemed is come, and they shall mention the loving kindness of their Lord, and all that he has bestowed upon them according to his goodness, and according to his loving kindness, for ever and ever.

53. In all their afflictions he was afflicted. And the angel of his presence saved them; and in his love, and in his pity, he redeemed them, and bear them, and carried them all the days of old;

54. Yea, and Enoch also, and they who were with him; the prophets who were before him; and Noah also, and they who were before him; and Moses also, and they who were before him;

55. And from Moses to Elijah; and from Elijah to John, who were with Christ in his resurrection, and the holy apostles, with Abraham, Isaac, and Jacob, shall be in the presence of the Lamb.

56. And the graves of the saints shall be opened; and they shall come forth and stand on the right hand of the Lamb, when he shall stand upon Mount Zion, and upon the holy city, the New Jerusalem, and they shall sing the song of the Lamb, day and night, for ever and ever.

57. And for this cause, that men might be made partakers of the glories which were to be revealed, the Lord sent forth the fulness of his gospel, his everlasting covenant, reasoning in plainness and simplicity,

58. To prepare the weak for those things which are coming on the earth, and for the Lord's errand in the day when the weak shall confound the wise, and the little one become a strong nation, and two should put their tens of thousands to flight;

59. And by the weak things of the earth the Lord shall thresh the nations by the power of his Spirit.

60. And for this cause these commandments were given; they were commanded to be kept from the world in the day that they were given, but now are to go forth unto all flesh.

61. And this according to the mind and will of the Lord, who ruleth over all flesh.

62. And unto him that repenteth and sanctifieth himself before the Lord, shall be given eternal life;

63. And upon them that hearken not to the voice of the Lord, shall be fulfilled that which was written by the Prophet Moses, that they should be cut off from among the people.

64. And also that which was written by the prophet Malachi; for, behold, the day cometh that shall burn as an oven, and all the proud, yea, and all that do wickedly, shall be stubble; and the day that cometh shall burn them up, saith the Lord of hosts, that it shall leave them neither root nor branch.

65. Wherefore, this shall be the answer of the Lord unto them—

66. In that day when I came unto mine own, no man among you received me, and you were driven out.

67. When I called again, there was none of you to answer, yet my arm was not shortened at all, that I could not redeem, neither my power to deliver.

68. Behold, at my rebuke I dry up the sea. I make the rivers a wilderness; their fish stinketh, and dieth for thirst.

69. I clothe the heavens with blackness, and make sackcloth their covering.

70. And this shall ye have of my hand, ye shall lie down in sorrow.

71. Behold and lo, there are none to deliver you, for ye obeyed not my voice when I called to you out of the heavens; ye believed not my servants, and when they were sent unto you ye received them not;

72. Wherefore they sealed up the testimony and bound up the law, and ye were delivered over unto darkness;

73. These shall go away into outer darkness where there is weeping, and wailing, and gnashing of teeth.

74. Behold the Lord your God hath spoken it. Amen.

Section 134

This section is an article written by Oliver Cowdery on "Governments and Laws in General," which was presented to the conference assembled August 17, 1835, at Kirtland, Ohio, and was unanimously accepted. Since 1835, this article has appeared in each edition of the Doctrine and Covenants (History of the Church, vol. 2:247).

1. We believe that governments were instituted of God for the benefit of man, and that he holds men accountable for their acts in relation to them, either in making laws and administering them, for the good and safety of society.

2. We believe that no government can exist in peace, except such laws are framed and held inviolate as will secure to each individual the free exercise of conscience, the right and control of property, and the protection of life.

3. We believe that all governments necessarily require civil officers and magistrates to enforce the laws of the same, and that such as will administer the law in equity and justice, should be sought for and upheld by the voice of the people (if a republic,) or the will of the sovereign.

4. We believe that religion is instituted of God, and that men are amenable to him, and to him only, for the exercise of it, unless their religious opinions prompt them to infringe upon the rights and liberties of others; but we do not believe that human law has a right to interfere in prescribing rules of worship to bind the consciences of men, nor dictate forms for public or private devotion; that the civil magistrate should restrain crime, but never control conscience; should punish guilt, but never suppress the freedom of the soul.

5. We believe that all men are bound to sustain and uphold the respective governments in which they reside, while protected in their inherent and inalienable rights by the laws of such governments; and that sedition and rebellion are unbecoming every citizen thus protected, and should be punished accordingly; and that all governments have a right to enact such laws as in their own judgment are best calculated to secure the public interest, at the same time, however, holding sacred the freedom of conscience.

6. We believe that every man should be honored in his station: rulers and magistrates as such, being placed for the protection of the innocent, and the punishment of the guilty; and that to the laws, all men owe respect and deference, as without them peace and harmony would be supplanted by

anarchy and terror; human laws being instituted for the express purpose of regulating our interests as individuals and nations, between man and man, and divine laws given of heaven, prescribing rules on spiritual concerns, for faith and worship, both to be answered by man to his Maker.

7. We believe that rulers, states, and governments, have a right, and are bound to enact laws for the protection of all citizens in the free exercise of their religious belief; but we do not believe that they have a right in justice, to deprive citizens of this privilege, or proscribe them in their opinions, so long as a regard and reverence are shown to the laws, and such religious opinions do not justify sedition nor conspiracy.

8. We believe that the commission of crime should be punished according to the nature of the offense; that murder, treason, robbery, theft, and the breach of the general peace, in all respects, should be punished according to their criminality, and their tendency to evil among men, by the laws of that government in which the offense is committed; and for the public peace and tranquility, all men should step forward and use their ability in bringing offenders against good laws to punishment.

9. We do not believe it just to mingle religious influence with civil government, whereby one religious society is fostered, and another proscribed in its spiritual privileges, and the individual rights of its members as citizens, denied.

10. We believe that all religious societies have a right to deal with their members for disorderly conduct according to the rules and regulations of such societies, provided that such dealings be for fellowship and good standing; but we do not believe that any religious society has authority to try men on the right of property or life, to take from them this world's goods, or to put them in jeopardy of either life or limb, neither to inflict any physical punishment upon them, they can only excommunicate them from their society, and withdraw from them their fellowship.

11. We believe that men should appeal to the civil law for redress of all wrongs and grievances, where personal abuse is inflicted, or the right of property or character infringed, where such laws exist as will protect the same; but we believe that all men are justified in defending themselves, their friends, and property, and the government, from the unlawful assaults and encroachments of all persons, in times of exigency, where immediate appeal cannot be made to the laws, and relief afforded.

12. We believe it just to preach the gospel to the nations of the earth, and warn the righteous to save themselves from the corruption of the world; but we do not believe it right to interfere with bond servants, neither preach the gospel to, nor baptize them, contrary to the will and wish of their masters, nor to meddle with or influence them in the least, to cause them to be dissatisfied with their situations in this life, thereby jeopardizing the lives of men; such interference we believe to be unlawful and unjust, and dangerous to the peace of every government allowing human beings to be held in servitude.

JOSEPH AND HYRUM SMITH
"IN LIFE THEY WERE NOT DIVIDED, AND IN DEATH THEY WERE NOT SEPARATED."

Section 135

This section is an article on the martyrdom of the Prophet Joseph Smith and Hyrum Smith written by John Taylor, a member of the Quorum of Twelve Apostles. It constitutes, "the official statement of the martyrdom of the Prophet and the Patriarch" (History of the Church, vol. 6:629).

1. To seal the testimony of this book and the Book of Mormon, we announce the Martyrdom of Joseph Smith the Prophet, and Hyrum Smith the Patriarch. They were shot in Carthage jail, on the 27th of June, 1844, about five o'clock p.m., by an armed mob, painted black—of from 150 to 200 persons. Hyrum was shot first and fell calmly, exclaiming, "I am a dead man?" Joseph leaped from the window, and was shot dead in the attempt, exclaiming, "O Lord my God!" They were both shot after they were dead in a brutal manner, and both received four balls.

2. John Taylor, and Willard Richards, two of the Twelve, were the only persons in the room at the time; the former was wounded in a savage manner with four balls, but has since recovered; the latter, through the providence of God, escaped, "without even a hole in his robe."

3. Joseph Smith, the Prophet and Seer of the Lord, has done more (save Jesus only) for the salvation of men in this world, than any other man that ever lived in it. In the short space of twenty years, he has brought forth the Book of Mormon, which he translated by the gift and power of God, and has been the means of publishing it on two continents; has sent the fulness of the everlasting gospel which it contained to the four quarters of the earth; has brought forth the revelations and commandments which compose this Book of Doctrine and Covenants, and many other wise documents and instructions for the benefit of the children of men; gathered many thousands of the Latter-day Saints, founded a great city; and left a fame and name that cannot be slain. He lived great, and he died great in the eyes of God and his people, and like most of the Lord's anointed in ancient times, has sealed his mission and his works with his own blood—and so has his brother Hyrum. In life they were not divided, and in death they were not separated!

4. When Joseph went to Carthage to deliver himself up to the pretended requirements of the law, two or three days previous to his assassination, he said, "I am going like a lamb to the slaughter; but

THEY DIED FOR GLORY; AND GLORY IS THEIR ETERNAL REWARD (D&C 135:6).

THE SAINTS CROSS
THE MISSOURI RIVER
UNDER ADVERSE
WEATHER CONDITIONS

*Let all the people of
the Church of Jesus Christ of
Latter-day Saints,
and those who journey with
them, be organized into
companies, with a covenant
and promise to keep all
commandments and statutes
of the Lord our God.*

D&C 136:2

JOSEPH SMITH RECEIVES REVELATION IN THE KIRTLAND TEMPLE

# SECTION 137

On January 21, 1836, at Kirtland, Ohio, the Prophet Joseph Smith and other leaders of the Church were attending to ordinance work in the Kirtland, Ohio, Temple. While engaged in this sacred Priesthood endeavor, the Heavens were opened unto them, and the Prophet beheld the Celestial Kingdom (History of the Church, vol. 2:380–381). Although the Prophet Joseph included this revelation in his manuscript History of the Church, *it was not included in the present edition of the Doctrine and Covenants until 1981.*

1. The heavens were opened upon us, and I beheld the celestial kingdom of God, and the glory thereof, whether in the body or out I cannot tell.

2. I saw the transcendent beauty of the gate through which the heirs of that kingdom will enter, which was like unto circling flames of fire;

3. Also the blazing throne of God, whereon was seated the Father and the Son.

4. I saw the beautiful streets of that kingdom, which had the appearance of being paved with gold.

5. I saw Father Adam and Abraham; and my father and my mother; my brother Alvin, that has long since slept;

6. And marveled how it was that he had obtained an inheritance in that kingdom, seeing that he had departed this life before the Lord had set his hand to gather Israel the second time, and had not been baptized for the remission of sins.

7. Thus came the voice of the Lord unto me, saying: All who have died without a knowledge of this gospel, who would have received it if they had been permitted to tarry, shall be heirs of the celestial kingdom of God;

8. Also all that shall die henceforth without a knowledge of it, who would have received it with all their hearts, shall be heirs of that kingdom.

9. For I, the Lord, will judge all men according to their works, according to the desire of their hearts.

10. And I also beheld that all children who die before they arrive at the years of accountability are saved in the celestial kingdom of heaven.

PRESIDENT JOSEPH F. SMITH, TO WHOM SECTION 138 WAS REVEALED

Section 138

President Joseph F. Smith informs us that on October 3, 1918, while he was pondering the events of the Savior's Atonement and subsequent visit to the Spirit World, the eyes of his understanding were open and this vision of the Spirit World was opened to him (section 138:1–11). This revelation (vision) was written at the conclusion of the October 1918 general conference of the Church, and was submitted to the counselors in the First Presidency, the Council of the Twelve Apostles, and the Patriarch to the Church on October 31, 1918. This revelation was included in the 1981 edition of the Doctrine and Covenants.

1. On the third of October, in the year nineteen hundred and eighteen, I sat in my room pondering over the scriptures;

2. And reflecting upon the great atoning sacrifice that was made by the Son of God, for the redemption of the world;

3. And the great and wonderful love made manifest by the Father and the Son in the coming of the Redeemer into the world;

4. That through his atonement, and by obedience to the principles of the gospel, mankind might be saved.

5. While I was thus engaged, my mind reverted to the writings of the apostle Peter, to the primitive saints scattered abroad throughout Pontus, Galatia, Cappadocia, and other parts of Asia, where the gospel had been preached after the crucifixion of the Lord.

6. I opened the Bible and read the third and fourth chapters of the first epistle of Peter, and as I read I was greatly impressed, more than I had ever been before with the following passages:

7. "For Christ also hath once suffered for sins, the just for the unjust, that he might bring us to God, being put to death in the flesh, but quickened by the Spirit:

8. "By which also he went and preached unto the spirits in prison;

9. "Which sometime were disobedient, when once the long suffering of God waited in the days of Noah, while the ark was a preparing, wherein few, that is, eight souls were saved by water." (1. Peter 3:18-20.)

10. "For, for this cause was the gospel preached also to them that are dead, that they might be judged according to men in the flesh, but live according to God in the spirit." (1. Peter 4:6.)

11. As I pondered over these things which are written, the eyes of my understanding were opened, and the Spirit of the Lord rested upon me, and I saw the hosts of the dead, both small and great.

12. And there were gathered together in one place an innumerable company of the spirits of

the just, who had been faithful in the testimony of Jesus while they lived in mortality;

13. And who had offered sacrifice in the similitude of the great sacrifice of the Son of God, and had suffered tribulation in their Redeemer's name.

14. All these had departed the mortal life, firm in the hope of a glorious resurrection, through the grace of God the Father and his Only Begotten Son, Jesus Christ.

15. I beheld that they were filled with joy and gladness, and were rejoicing together because the day of their deliverance was at hand.

16. They were assembled awaiting the advent of the Son of God into the spirit world, to declare their redemption from the bands of death.

17. Their sleeping dust was to be restored unto its perfect frame bone to his bone, and the sinews and the flesh upon them, the spirit and the body to be united never again to be divided, that they might receive a fulness of joy.

18. While this vast multitude waited and conversed, rejoicing in the hour of their deliverance from the chains of death, the Son of God appeared, declaring liberty to the captives who had been faithful;

19. And there he preached to them the everlasting gospel, the doctrine of the resurrection and the redemption of mankind from the fall, and from individual sins on conditions of repentance.

20. But unto the wicked he did not go, and among the ungodly and the unrepentant who had defiled themselves while in the flesh, his voice was not raised;

21. Neither did the rebellious who rejected the testimonies and the warnings of the ancient prophets behold his presence, nor look upon his face.

22. Where these were, darkness reigned, but among the righteous there was peace;

23. And the saints rejoiced in their redemption, and bowed the knee and acknowledged the Son of God as their Redeemer and Deliverer from death and the chains of hell.

24. Their countenances shone, and the radiance from the presence of the Lord rested upon them and they sang praises unto his holy name.

25. I marveled, for I understood that the Savior spent about three years in his ministry among the Jews and those of the house of Israel, endeavoring to teach them the everlasting gospel and call them unto repentance;

26. And yet, notwithstanding his mighty works, and miracles, and proclamation of the truth, in great power and authority, there were but few who hearkened to his voice, and rejoiced in his presence, and received salvation at his hands.

27. But his ministry among those who were dead was limited to the brief time intervening between the crucifixion and his resurrection;

28. And I wondered at the words of Peter—wherein he said that the Son of God preached unto the spirits in prison, who sometime were disobedient, when once the long-suffering of God waited in the days of Noah—and how it was possible for him to preach to those spirits and perform the necessary labor among them in so short a time.

29. And as I wondered, my eyes were opened, and my understanding quickened, and I perceived that the Lord went not in person among the wicked and the disobedient who had rejected the truth, to teach them;

30. But behold, from among the righteous, he organized his forces and appointed messengers, clothed with power and authority, and commissioned them to go forth and carry the light of the gospel to them that were in darkness, even to all the spirits of men; and thus was the gospel preached to the dead.

31. And the chosen messengers went forth to declare the acceptable day of the Lord and proclaim liberty to the captives who were bound,

even unto all who would repent of their sins and receive the gospel.

32. Thus was the gospel preached to those who had died in their sins, without a knowledge of the truth, or in transgression, having rejected the prophets.

33. These were taught faith in God, repentance from sin, vicarious baptism for the remission of sins, the gift of the Holy Ghost by the laying on of hands.

34. And all other principles of the gospel that were necessary for them to know in order to qualify themselves that they might be judged according to men in the flesh, but live according to God in the spirit.

35. And so it was made known among the dead, both small and great, the unrighteous as well and the faithful, that redemption had been wrought through the sacrifice of the Son of God upon the cross.

36. Thus was it made known that our Redeemer spent his time during his sojourn in the world of spirits, instructing and preparing the faithful spirits of the prophets who had testified of him in the flesh.

37. That they might carry the message of redemption unto all the dead, unto whom he could not go personally, because of their rebellion and transgression, that they through the ministration of his servants might also hear his words.

38. Among the great and mighty ones who were assembled in this vast congregation of the righteous were Father Adam, the Ancient of Days and father of all,

39. And our glorious Mother Eve, with many of her faithful daughters who had lived through the ages and worshiped the true and living God.

40. Abel, the first martyr, was there, and his brother Seth, one of the mighty ones, who was in the express image of his father, Adam.

41. Noah, who gave warning of the flood; Shem, the great high priest; Abraham, the father of the faithful; Isaac, Jacob, and Moses, the great lawgiver of Israel;

42. And Isaiah, who declared by prophecy that the Redeemer was anointed to bind up the broken-hearted, to proclaim liberty to the captives, and the opening of the prison to them that were bound, were also there.

43. Moreover, Ezekiel, who was shown in vision the great valley of dry bones, which were to be clothed upon with flesh, to come forth again in the resurrection of the dead, living souls;

44. Daniel, who foresaw and foretold the establishment of the kingdom of God in the latter days, never again to be destroyed nor given to other people;

45. Elias, who was with Moses on the Mount of Transfiguration;

46. And Malachi, the prophet who testified of the coming of Elijah—of whom also Moroni spake to the Prophet Joseph Smith, declaring that he should come before the ushering in of the great and dreadful day of the Lord—were also there.

47. The Prophet Elijah was to plant in the hearts of the children the promises made to their fathers.

48. Foreshadowing the great work to be done in the temples of the Lord in the dispensation of the fulness of times, for the redemption of the dead, and the sealing of the children to their parents, lest the whole earth be smitten with a curse and utterly wasted at his coming.

49. All these and many more, even the prophets who dwelt among the Nephites and testified of the coming of the Son of God, mingled in the vast assembly and waited for their deliverance,

50. For the dead had looked upon the long absence of their spirits from their bodies as a bondage.

51. These the Lord taught, and gave them power to come forth, after his resurrection from the

dead, to enter into his Father's kingdom and there to be crowned with immortality and eternal life.

52. And continue thence forth their labor as had been promised by the Lord, and be partakers of all blessings which were held in reserve for them that love him.

53. The Prophet Joseph Smith, and my father, Hyrum Smith, Brigham Young, John Taylor, Wilford Woodruff, and other choice spirits who were reserved to come forth in the fulness of times to take part in laying the foundations of the great latter-day work,

54. Including the building of the temples and the performance of ordinances therein for the redemption of the dead, were also in the spirit world.

55. I observed that they were also among the noble and great ones who were chosen in the beginning to be rulers in the Church of God.

56. Even before they were born, they, with many others, received their first lessons in the world of spirits and were prepared to come forth in the due time of the Lord to labor in his vineyard for the salvation of the souls of men.

57. I beheld that the faithful elders of this dispensation, when they depart from mortal life, continue their labors in the preaching of the gospel of repentance and redemption, through the sacrifice of the Only Begotten Son of God, among those who are in darkness and under the bondage of sin in the great world of the spirits of the dead.

58. The dead who repent will be redeemed, through obedience to the ordinances of the house of God.

59. And after they have paid the penalty of their transgressions, and are washed clean, shall receive a reward according to their works, for they are heirs of salvation.

60. Thus was the vision of the redemption of the dead revealed to me, and I bear record, and I know that this record is true, through the blessing of our Lord and Savior, Jesus Christ, even so, Amen.

Official Declaration

To Whom it may Concern:

 Press dispatches having been sent for political purposes, from Salt Lake City, which have been widely published, to the effect that the Utah Commission, in their recent report to the Secretary of the Interior, allege that plural marriages are still being solemnized and that forty or more such marriages have been contracted in Utah since last June or during the past year, also that in public discourses the leaders of the Church have taught, encouraged and urged the continuance of the practice of polygamy—

 I, therefore, as President of the Church of Jesus Christ of Latter-day Saints, do hereby, in the most solemn manner, declare that these charges are false. We are not teaching polygamy or plural marriage, nor permitting any person to enter into its practice, and I deny that either forty or any other number of plural marriages have during that period been solemnized in our Temples or in any other place in the Territory.

 One case has been reported, in which the parties allege that the marriage was performed in the Endowment House, in Salt Lake City, in the Spring of 1889, but I have not been able to learn who performed the ceremony; whatever was done in this matter was without my knowledge. In consequence of this alleged occurrence the Endowment House was, by my instructions, taken down without delay.

 Inasmuch as laws have been enacted by Congress forbidding plural marriages, which laws have been pronounced constitutional by the court of last resort, I hereby declare my intention to submit to those laws, and to use my influence with the members of the Church over which I preside to have them do likewise.

There is nothing in my teachings to the Church or in those of my associates, during the time specified, which can be reasonably construed to inculcate or encourage polygamy; and when any Elder of the Church has used language which appeared to convey any such teaching, he has been promptly reproved. And I now publicly declare that my advice to the Latter-day Saints is to refrain from contracting any marriage forbidden by the law of the land.

WILFORD WOODRUFF
President of the Church of Jesus Christ
of Latter-day Saints.

President Lorenzo Snow offered the following:

"I move that, recognizing Wilford Woodruff as the President of the Church of Jesus Christ of Latter-day Saints, and the only man on the earth at the present time who holds the keys of the sealing ordinances, we consider him fully authorized by virtue of his position to issue the Manifesto which has been read in our hearing, and which is dated September 24th, 1890, and that as a Church in General Conference assembled, we accept his declaration concerning plural marriages as authoritative and binding."

The vote to sustain the foregoing motion was unanimous.

Salt Lake City, Utah, October 6, 1890.

EXCERPTS

FROM THREE ADDRESSES BY PRESIDENT WILFORD WOODRUFF REGARDING THE MANIFESTO

The Lord will never permit me or any other man who stands as President of this Church to lead you astray. It is not in the programme. It is not in the mind of God. If I were to attempt that, the Lord would remove me out of my place, and so He will any other man who attempts to lead the children of men astray from the oracles of God and from their duty. (Sixty-first Semiannual General Conference of the Church, Monday, October 6, 1890, Salt Lake City, Utah. Reported in Deseret Evening News, October 11, 1890, p. 2.)

It matters not who lives or who dies, or who is called to lead this Church, they have got to lead it by the inspiration of Almighty God. If they do not do it that way, they cannot do it at all. . . .
I have had some revelations of late, and very important ones to me, and I will tell you what the Lord has said to me. Let me bring your minds to what is termed the manifesto . . .

The Lord has told me to ask the Latter-day Saints a question, and He also told me that if they would listen to what I said to them and answer the question put to them, by the Spirit and power of God, they would all answer alike, and they would all believe alike with regard to this matter.

The question is this: Which is the wisest course for the Latter-day Saints to pursue—to continue to attempt to practice plural marriage, with the laws of the nation against it and the opposition of sixty millions of people, and at the cost of the confiscation and loss of all the Temples, and the stopping of all the ordinances therein, both for the living and the dead, and the imprisonment of the First Presidency and Twelve and the heads of families in the Church, and the confiscation of personal property of the people (all of which of themselves would stop the practice); or, after doing and suffering what we have through our adherence to this principle to cease the practice and submit to the law, and through doing so leave the Prophets, Apostles and fathers at home, so that they can instruct the people and attend to the duties

A VIEW OF FIRST AVENUE IN SALT LAKE CITY IN THE EARLY 1900s

of the Church, and also leave the Temples in the hands of the Saints, so that they can attend to the ordinances of the Gospel, both for the living and the dead?

The Lord showed me by vision and revelation exactly what would take place if we did not stop this practice. If we had not stopped it, you would have had no use for . . . any of the men in this temple at Logan; for all ordinances would be stopped throughout the land of Zion. Confusion would reign throughout Israel, and many men would be made prisoners. This trouble would have come upon the whole Church, and we should have been compelled to stop the practice. Now, the question is, whether it should be stopped in this manner, or in the way the Lord has manifested to us, and leave our Prophets and Apostles and fathers free men, and the temples in the hands of the people, so that the dead may be redeemed. A large number has already been delivered from the prison house in the spirit world by this people, and shall the work go on or stop? This is the question I lay before the Latter-day Saints. You have to judge for yourselves. I want you to answer it for yourselves. I shall not answer it; but I say to you that is exactly the condition we as a people would have been in had we not taken the course we have.

. . . I saw exactly what would come to pass if there was not something done. I have had this spirit upon me for a long time. But I want to say this: I should have let all the temples go out of our hands; I should have gone to prison myself, and let every other man go there, had not the God of heaven commanded me to do what I did do; and when the hour came that I was commanded to do that, it was all clear to me. I went before the Lord, and I wrote what the Lord told me to write . . .

I leave this with you, for you to contemplate and consider. The Lord is at work with us. (Cache Stake Conference, Logan, Utah, Sunday, November 1, 1891. Reported in *Deseret Weekly*, November 14, 1891.)

Now I will tell you what was manifested to me and what the Son of God performed in this thing. . . . All these things would have come to pass, as God Almighty lives, had not that Manifesto been given. Therefore, the Son of God felt disposed to have that thing presented to the Church and to the world for purposes in his own mind. The Lord had decreed the establishment of Zion. He had decreed the finishing of this temple. He had decreed that the salvation of the living and the dead should be given in these valleys of the mountains. And Almighty God decreed that the Devil should not thwart it. If you can understand that, that is a key to it. (From a discourse at the sixth session of the dedication of the Salt Lake Temple, April 1893. Typescript of Dedicatory Services, Archives, Church Historical Department, Salt Lake City, Utah.)

ABOUT OFFICIAL DECLARATION 2

After much fasting, prayer, and meditation regarding this matter, a revelation was received in June of 1978 by Spencer W. Kimball in which the Lord made known his desire that all worthy male members of the Church should receive priesthood and temple blessings.

The Quorum of the Twelve Apostles and President Kimball's counselors approved it unanimously. It was later ratified unanimously by a vote of the general membership of The Church of Jesus Christ of Latter-Day Saints at the Semiannual General Conference on September 30, 1978.

THE PEARL OF GREAT PRICE

A SELECTION FROM THE REVELATIONS,
TRANSLATIONS, AND NARRATIONS OF
JOSEPH SMITH

FIRST PROPHET, SEER, AND REVELATOR TO
THE CHURCH OF JESUS CHRIST OF
LATTER-DAY SAINTS

INTRODUCTORY NOTE

The Pearl of Great Price is "a selection form revelations, translations, and narrations of Joseph Smith." It contains some visions of Moses as revealed to the Prophet, a translation of records found in Egypt, some of the writings of Joseph Smith, and the Articles of Faith. The Pearl of Great Price, therefore, also contains much matter which refers to the past. In it we obtain a clearer view of the Creation, the fall, and redemption, and a fuller account of the history of Abraham and the effect of his mission to Egypt. It was necessary that these things should be more clearly revealed in this dispensation. For this is the time when the hearts of the children are to be turned to their fathers, as well as the hearts of the fathers to their children, and this implies that the children should know something about their fathers and ancestors, and their work in the past on which they have built in all ages, and are still building. Through the Book of Abraham, in the Pearl of Great Price, a great deal of light has been shed upon the history of Egypt, to which country European civilization is so highly indebted.

THE LORD APPEARS TO HIS SERVANT MOSES

THE PEARL OF GREAT PRICE

THE BOOK OF MOSES

CHAPTER 1

VISIONS OF MOSES

As revealed to Joseph Smith the Prophet, in June, 1830.

1. The words of God, which he spake unto Moses at a time when Moses was caught up into an exceedingly high mountain,
2. And he saw God face to face, and he talked with him, and the glory of God was upon Moses; therefore Moses could endure his presence.
3. And God spake unto Moses, saying: Behold, I am the Lord God Almighty, and Endless is my name; for I am without beginning of days or end of years; and is not this endless?
4. And, behold, thou art my son; wherefore look, and I will show thee the workmanship of mine hands; but not all, for my works are without end, and also my words, for they never cease.
5. Wherefore, no man can behold all my works, except he behold all my glory; and no man can behold all my glory, and afterwards remain in the flesh on the earth.
6. And I have a work for thee, Moses, my son; and thou art in the similitude of mine Only Begotten; and mine Only Begotten is and shall be the Savior, for he is full of grace and truth; but there is no God beside me, and all things are present with me, for I know them all.
7. And now, behold, this one thing I show unto thee, Moses, my son; for thou art in the world, and now I show it unto thee.
8. And it came to pass that Moses looked, and beheld the world upon which he was created; and Moses beheld the world and the ends thereof, and all the children of men which are, and which were created; of the same he greatly marveled and wondered.
9. And the presence of God withdrew from Moses, that his glory was not upon Moses; and Moses was left unto himself. And as he was left unto himself, he fell unto the earth.

10. And it came to pass that it was for the space of many hours before Moses did again receive his natural strength like unto man; and he said unto himself: Now, for this cause I know that man is nothing, which thing I never had supposed.

11. But now mine own eyes have beheld God; but not my natural, but my spiritual eyes, for my natural eyes could not have beheld; for I should have withered and died in his presence; but his glory was upon me; and I beheld his face, for I was transfigured before him.

12. And it came to pass that when Moses had said these words, behold, Satan came tempting him, saying: Moses, son of man, worship me.

13. And it came to pass that Moses looked upon Satan and said: Who art thou? For behold, I am a son of God, in the similitude of his Only Begotten; and where is thy glory, that I should worship thee?

14. For behold, I could not look upon God, except his glory should come upon me, and I were strengthened before him. But I can look upon thee in the natural man. Is it not so, surely?

15. Blessed be the name of my God, for his Spirit hath not altogether withdrawn from me, or else where is thy glory, for it is darkness unto me? And I can judge between thee and God; for God said unto me: Worship God, for him only shalt thou serve.

16. Get thee hence, Satan; deceive me not; for God said unto me: Thou art after the similitude of mine Only Begotten.

17. And he also gave me commandments when he called unto me out of the burning bush, saying: Call upon God in the name of mine Only Begotten, and worship me.

18. And again Moses said: I will not cease to call upon God, I have other things to inquire of him: for his glory has been upon me, wherefore I can judge between him and thee. Depart hence, Satan.

19. And now, when Moses had said these words, Satan cried with a loud voice, and rent upon the earth, and commanded, saying: I am the Only Begotten, worship me.

20. And it came to pass that Moses began to fear exceedingly; and as he began to fear, he saw the bitterness of hell. Nevertheless, calling upon God, he received strength, and he commanded, saying: Depart from me, Satan, for this one God only will I worship, which is the God of glory.

21. And now Satan began to tremble, and the earth shook; and Moses received strength, and called upon God, saying: In the name of the Only Begotten, depart hence, Satan.

22. And it came to pass that Satan cried with a loud voice, with weeping, and wailing, and gnashing of teeth; and he departed hence, even from the presence of Moses, that he beheld him not.

23. And now of this thing Moses bore record; but because of wickedness it is not had among the children of men.

24. And it came to pass that when Satan had departed from the presence of Moses, that Moses lifted up his eyes unto heaven, being filled with the Holy Ghost, which beareth record of the Father and the Son;

25. And calling upon the name of God, he beheld his glory again, for it was upon him; and he heard a voice, saying: Blessed art thou, Moses, for I, the Almighty, have chosen thee, and thou shalt be made stronger than many waters; for they shall obey thy command as if thou wert God.

26. And lo, I am with thee, even unto the end of thy days; for thou shalt deliver my people from bondage, even Israel my chosen.

27. And it came to pass, as the voice was still speaking, Moses cast his eyes and beheld the earth, yea, even all of it; and there was not a particle of it which he did not behold, discerning it by the Spirit of God.

28. And he beheld also the inhabitants thereof, and there was not a soul which he beheld not;

and he discerned them by the Spirit of God; and their numbers were great, even numberless as the sand upon the sea shore.

29. And he beheld many lands; and each land was called earth, and there were inhabitants on the face thereof.

30. And it came to pass that Moses called upon God, saying: Tell me, I pray thee, why these things are so, and by what thou madest them?

31. And behold, the glory of the Lord was upon Moses, so that Moses stood in the presence of God, and talked with him face to face. And the Lord God said unto Moses: For mine own purpose have I made these things. Here is wisdom and it remaineth in me.

32. And by the word of my power, have I created them, which is mine Only Begotten Son, who is full of grace and truth.

33. And worlds without number have I created; and I also created them for mine own purpose; and by the Son I created them, which is mine Only Begotten.

34. And the first man of all men have I called Adam, which is many.

35. But only an account of this earth, and the inhabitants thereof, give I unto you. For behold, there are many worlds that have passed away by the word of my power. And there are many that now stand, and innumerable are they unto man; but all things are numbered unto me, for they are mine and I know them.

36. And it came to pass that Moses spake unto the Lord, saying: Be merciful unto thy servant, O God, and tell me concerning this earth, and the inhabitants thereof, and also the heavens, and then thy servant will be content.

37. And the Lord God spake unto Moses, saying: The heavens, they are many, and they cannot be numbered unto man; but they are numbered unto me, for they are mine.

38. And as one earth shall pass away, and the heavens thereof, even so shall another come; and there is no end to my works, neither to my words.

39. For behold, this is my work and my glory—to bring to pass the immortality and eternal life of man.

40. And now, Moses, my son, I will speak unto thee concerning this earth upon which thou standest; and thou shalt write the things which I shall speak.

41. And in a day when the children of men shall esteem my words as naught and take many of them from the book which thou shalt write, behold, I will raise up another like unto thee; and they shall be had again among the children of men—among as many as shall believe.

42. These words were spoken unto Moses in the mount, the name of which shall not be known among the children of men. And now they are spoken unto you. Show them not unto any except them that believe. Even so. Amen.

CHAPTER 2

THE WRITINGS OF MOSES
As revealed to Joseph Smith the Prophet, in December, 1830.

1. And it came to pass that the Lord spake unto Moses, saying: Behold, I reveal unto you concerning this Heaven, and this Earth; write the words which I speak. I am the Beginning and the End, the Almighty God; by mine Only Begotten I created these things; yea, in the beginning I created the heaven, and the earth upon which thou standest.

2. And the earth was without form, and void; and I caused darkness to come up upon the face of the deep; and my Spirit moved upon the face of the water; for I am God.

3. And I, God, said: Let there be light; and there was light.

4. And I, God, saw the light; and that light was good. And I, God, divided the light from the darkness.

5. And I, God, called the light Day; and the darkness, I called Night; and this I did by the word of my power, and it was done as I spake; and the evening and the morning were the first day.

6. And again, I, God, said: Let there be a firmament in the midst of the water, and it was so, even as I spake; and I said: Let it divide the waters from the waters; and it was done;

7. And I, God, made the firmament and divided the waters, yea, the great waters under the firmament from the waters which were above the firmament, and it was so even as I spake.

8. And I, God, called the firmament Heaven; and the evening and the morning were the second day.

9. And I, God, said: Let the water under the heaven be gathered together unto one place, and it was so; and I, God, said: Let there be dry land; and it was so.

10. And I, God, called the dry land Earth; and the gathering together of the waters, called I the Sea; and I, God, saw that all things which I had made were good.

11. And I, God, said: Let the earth bring forth grass, the herb yielding seed, the fruit tree yielding fruit, after his kind, and the tree yielding fruit, whose seed should be in itself upon the earth, and it was so even as I spake.

12. And the earth brought forth grass, every herb yielding seed after his kind, and the tree yielding fruit, whose seed should be in itself, after his kind, and I, God, saw that all things which I had made were good;

13. And the evening and the morning were the third day.

14. And I, God, said: Let there be lights in the firmament of the heaven, to divide the day from the night, and let them be for signs, and for seasons, and for days, and for years;

15. And let them be for lights in the firmament of the heaven to give light upon the earth; and it was so.

16. And I, God, made two great lights; the greater light to rule the day, and the lesser light to rule the night, and the greater light was the sun, and the lesser light was the moon; and the stars also were made even according to my word.

17. And I, God, set them in the firmament of the heaven to give light upon the earth,

18. And the sun to rule over the day, and the moon to rule over the night, and to divide the light from the darkness; and I, God, saw that all things which I had made were good;

19. And the evening and the morning were the fourth day.

20. And I, God, said: Let the waters bring forth abundantly the moving creature that hath life, and fowl which may fly above the earth in the open firmament of heaven.

21. And I, God, created great whales, and every living creature that moveth, which the waters brought forth abundantly, after their kind, and every winged fowl after his kind; and I, God, saw that all things which I had created were good.

22. And I, God, blessed them, saying: Be fruitful, and multiply, and fill the waters in the sea; and let fowl multiply in the earth;

23. And the evening and the morning were the fifth day.

24. And I, God, said: Let the earth bring forth the living creature after his kind, cattle, and creeping things, and beasts of the earth after their kind, and it was so;

25. And I, God, made the beasts of the earth after their kind, and cattle after their kind, and everything which creepeth upon the earth after his kind; and I, God, saw that all these things were good.

26. And I, God, said unto mine Only Begotten, which was with me from the beginning: Let us make man in our image, after our likeness; and it was so.

And I, God, said: Let them have dominion over the fishes of the sea, and over the fowl of the air, and over the cattle, and over all the earth, and over every creeping thing that creepeth upon the earth.

27. And I, God, created man in mine own image, in the image of mine Only Begotten created I him; male and female created I them.

28. And I, God, blessed them, and said unto them: Be fruitful, and multiply, and replenish the earth, and subdue it, and have dominion over the fish of the sea, and over the fowl of the air, and over every living thing that moveth upon the earth.

29. And I, God, said unto man: Behold, I have given you every herb bearing seed, which is upon the face of all the earth, and every tree in the which shall be the fruit of a tree yielding seed; to you it shall be for meat.

30. And to every beast of the earth, and to every fowl of the air, and to everything that creepeth upon the earth, wherein I grant life, there shall be given every clean herb for meat; and it was so, even as I spake.

31. And I, God, saw everything that I had made, and, behold, all things which I had made were very good; and the evening and the morning were the sixth day.

CHAPTER 3

THE WRITINGS OF MOSES
As revealed to Joseph Smith the Prophet, in December, 1830—continued

1. Thus the heaven and the earth were finished, and all the host of them.

2. And on the seventh day I, God, ended my work, and all things which I had made; and I rested on the seventh day from all my work, and all things which I had made were finished, and I, God, saw that they were good;

3. And I, God, blessed the seventh day, and sanctified it; because that in it I had rested from all my work which I, God, had created and made.

4. And now, behold, I say unto you, that these are the generations of the heaven and of the earth, when they were created, in the day that I, the Lord God, made the heaven and the earth.

5. And every plant of the field before it was in the earth, and every herb of the field before it grew. For I, the Lord God, created all things, of which I have spoken, spiritually, before they were naturally upon the face of the earth. For I, the Lord God, had not caused it to rain upon the face of the earth. And I, the Lord God, had created all the children of men; and not yet a man to till the ground; for in heaven created I them; and there was not yet flesh upon the earth, neither in the water, neither in the air;

6. But I, the Lord God, spake, and there went up a mist from the earth, and watered the whole face of the ground.

7. And I, the Lord God, formed man from the dust of the ground, and breathed into his nostrils the breath of life; and man became a living soul, the first flesh upon the earth, the first man also; nevertheless, all things were before created; but spiritually were they created and made according to my word.

8. And I, the Lord God, planted a garden eastward in Eden, and there I put the man whom I had formed.

9. And out of the ground made I, the Lord God, to grow every tree, naturally, that is pleasant to the sight of man; and man could behold it. And it became also a living soul. For it was spiritual in the day that I created it; for it remaineth in the sphere in which I, God, created it, yea, even all things which I prepared for the use of man; and man saw that it was good for food. And I, the Lord God, planted the tree of life also in the

midst of the garden, and also the tree of knowledge of good and evil.

10. And I, the Lord God, caused a river to go out of Eden to water the garden; and from thence it was parted, and became into four heads.

11. And I, the Lord God, called the name of the first Pison, and it compasseth the whole land of Havilah, where I, the Lord God, created much gold;

12. And the gold of that land was good, and there was bdellium and the onyx stone.

13. And the name of the second river was called Gihon; the same that compasseth the whole land of Ethiopia.

14. And the name of the third river was Hiddekel; that which goeth toward the east of Assyria. And the fourth river was the Euphrates.

15. And I, the Lord God, took the man, and put him into the Garden of Eden, to dress it, and to keep it.

16. And I, the Lord God, commanded the man, saying: Of every tree of the garden thou mayest freely eat,

17. But of the tree of the knowledge of good and evil, thou shalt not eat of it, nevertheless, thou mayest choose for thyself, for it is given unto thee; but, remember that I forbid it, for in the day thou eatest thereof thou shalt surely die.

18. And I, the Lord God, said unto mine Only Begotten, that it was not good that the man should be alone; wherefore, I will make an help meet for him.

19. And out of the ground I, the Lord God, formed every beast of the field, and every fowl of the air; and commanded that they should come unto Adam, to see what he would call them; and they were also living souls; for I, God, breathed into them the breath of life, and commanded that whatsoever Adam called every living creature, that should be the name thereof.

20. And Adam gave names to all cattle, and to the fowl of the air, and to every beast of the field; but as for Adam, there was not found an help meet for him.

21. And I, the Lord God, caused a deep sleep to fall upon Adam; and he slept, and I took one of his ribs and closed up the flesh in the stead thereof;

22. And the rib which I, the Lord God, had taken from man, made I a woman, and brought her unto the man.

23. And Adam said: This I know now is bone of my bones, and flesh of my flesh; she shall be called Woman, because she was taken out of man.

24. Therefore shall a man leave his father and his mother, and shall cleave unto his wife; and they shall be one flesh.

25. And they were both naked, the man and his wife, and were not ashamed.

CHAPTER 4

THE WRITINGS OF MOSES
As revealed to Joseph Smith the Prophet, in December, 1830—continued

1. And I, the Lord God, spake unto Moses, saying: That Satan, whom thou hast commanded in the name of mine Only Begotten, is the same which was from the beginning, and he came before me, saying, Behold—here am I, send me, I will be thy son, and I will redeem all mankind, that one soul shall not be lost, and surely I will do it; wherefore give me thine honor.

2. But, behold, my Beloved Son, which was my Beloved and Chosen from the beginning, said unto me—Father, thy will be done, and the glory be thine forever.

3. Wherefore, because that Satan rebelled against me, and sought to destroy the agency of man, which I, the Lord God, had given him, and also, that I should give unto him mine own power; by

the power of mine Only Begotten, I caused that he should be cast down;

4. And he became Satan, yea, even the devil, the father of all lies, to deceive and to blind men, and to lead them captive at his will, even as many as would not hearken unto my voice.

5. And now the serpent was more subtle than any beast of the field which I, the Lord God, had made.

6. And Satan put it into the heart of the serpent, (for he had drawn away many after him,) and he sought also to beguile Eve, for he knew not the mind of God, wherefore he sought to destroy the world.

7. And he said unto the woman: Yea, hath God said—Ye shall not eat of every tree of the garden? (And he spake by the mouth of the serpent.)

8. And the woman said unto the serpent: We may eat of the fruit of the trees of the garden;

9. But of the fruit of the tree which thou beholdest in the midst of the garden, God hath said—Ye shall not eat of it, neither shall ye touch it, lest ye die.

10. And the serpent said unto the woman: Ye shall not surely die;

11. For God doth know that in the day ye eat thereof, then your eyes shall be opened, and ye shall be as gods, knowing good and evil.

12. And when the woman saw that the tree was good for food, and that it became pleasant to the eyes, and a tree to be desired to make her wise, she took of the fruit thereof, and did eat, and also gave unto her husband with her, and he did eat.

13. And the eyes of them both were opened, and they knew that they had been naked. And they sewed fig leaves together and made themselves aprons.

14. And they heard the voice of the Lord God, as they were walking in the garden, in the cool of the day; and Adam and his wife went to hide themselves from the presence of the Lord God amongst the trees of the garden.

15. And I, the Lord God, called unto Adam, and said unto him: Where goest thou?

16. And he said: I heard thy voice in the garden, and I was afraid, because I beheld that I was naked, and I hid myself.

17. And I, the Lord God, said unto Adam: Who told thee thou wast naked? Hast thou eaten of the tree whereof I commanded thee that thou shouldst not eat, if so thou shouldst surely die?

18. And the man said: The woman thou gavest me, and commandest that she should remain with me, she gave me of the fruit of the tree and I did eat.

19. And I, the Lord God, said unto the woman: What is this thing which thou hast done? And the woman said: The serpent beguiled me, and I did eat.

20. And I, the Lord God, said unto the serpent: Because thou hast done this thou shalt be cursed above all cattle, and above every beast of the field; upon thy belly shalt thou go, and dust shalt thou eat all the days of thy life;

21. And I will put enmity between thee and the woman, between thy seed and her seed; and he shall bruise thy head, and thou shalt bruise his heel.

22. Unto the woman, I, the Lord God, said: I will greatly multiply thy sorrow and thy conception. In sorrow thou shalt bring forth children, and thy desire shall be to thy husband, and he shall rule over thee.

23. And unto Adam, I, the Lord God, said: Because thou hast hearkened unto the voice of thy wife, and hast eaten of the fruit of the tree of which I commanded thee, saying—Thou shalt not eat of it, cursed shall be the ground for thy sake; in sorrow shalt thou eat of it all the days of thy life.

24. Thorns also, and thistles shall it bring forth to thee, and thou shalt eat the herb of the field.

25. By the sweat of thy face shalt thou eat bread, until thou shalt return unto the ground—for thou shalt surely die—for out of it wast thou taken: for dust thou wast, and unto dust shalt thou return.

26. And Adam called his wife's name Eve, because she was the mother of all living; for thus have I, the Lord God, called the first of all women, which are many.

27. Unto Adam, and also unto his wife, did I, the Lord God, make coats of skins, and clothed them.

28. And I, the Lord God, said unto mine Only Begotten: Behold, the man is become as one of us to know good and evil; and now lest he put forth his hand and partake also of the tree of life, and eat and live forever,

29. Therefore I, the Lord God, will send him forth from the Garden of Eden, to till the ground from whence he was taken;

30. For as I, the Lord God, liveth, even so my words cannot return void, for as they go forth out of my mouth they must be fulfilled.

31. So I drove out the man, and I placed at the east of the Garden of Eden, cherubim and a flaming sword, which turned every way to keep the way of the tree of life.

32. (And these are the words which I spake unto my servant Moses, and they are true even as I will; and I have spoken them unto you, see thou show them unto no man, until I command you, except to them that believe.) Amen.

CHAPTER 5

THE WRITINGS OF MOSES
As revealed to Joseph Smith the Prophet, in December, 1830—continued

1. And it came to pass that after I, the Lord God, had driven them out, that Adam began to till the earth, and to have dominion over all the beasts of the field, and to eat his bread by the sweat of his brow, as I the Lord had commanded him. And Eve, also, his wife, did labor with him.

2. And Adam knew his wife, and she bare unto him sons and daughters, and they began to multiply and to replenish the earth.

3. And from that time forth, the sons and daughters of Adam began to divide two and two in the land, and to till the land, and to tend flocks, and they also begat sons and daughters.

4. And Adam and Eve, his wife, called upon the name of the Lord, and they heard the voice of the Lord from the way toward the Garden of Eden, speaking unto them, and they saw him not; for they were shut out from his presence.

5. And he gave unto them commandments, that they should worship the Lord their God, and should offer the firstlings of their flocks, for an offering unto the Lord. And Adam was obedient unto the commandments of the Lord.

6. And after many days an angel of the Lord appeared unto Adam, saying: Why dost thou offer sacrifices unto the Lord? And Adam said unto him: I know not, save the Lord commanded me.

7. And then the angel spake, saying: This thing is a similitude of the sacrifice of the Only Begotten of the Father, which is full of grace and truth.

8. Wherefore, thou shalt do all that thou doest in the name of the Son, and thou shalt repent and call upon God in the name of the Son forevermore.

9. And in that day the Holy Ghost fell upon Adam, which beareth record of the Father and the Son, saying: I am the Only Begotten of the Father from the beginning, henceforth and forever, that as thou hast fallen thou mayest be redeemed, and all mankind, even as many as will.

10. And in that day Adam blessed God and was filled, and began to prophesy concerning all the families of the earth, saying: Blessed be the name of God, for because of my transgression my eyes are opened, and in this life I shall have joy, and again in the flesh I shall see God.

11. And Eve, his wife, heard all these things and was glad, saying: Were it not for our transgression

we never should have had seed, and never should have known good and evil, and the joy of our redemption, and the eternal life which God giveth unto all the obedient.

12. And Adam and Eve blessed the name of God, and they made all things known unto their sons and their daughters.

13. And Satan came among them, saying: I am also a son of God; and he commanded them, saying: Believe it not; and they believed it not, and they loved Satan more than God. And men began from that time forth to be carnal, sensual, and devilish.

14. And the Lord God called upon men by the Holy Ghost everywhere and commanded them that they should repent;

15. And as many as believed in the Son, and repented of their sins, should be saved; and as many as believed not and repented not, should be damned; and the words went forth out of the mouth of God in a firm decree; wherefore they must be fulfilled.

16. And Adam and Eve, his wife ceased not to call upon God. And Adam knew Eve his wife, and she conceived and bare Cain, and said: I have gotten a man from the Lord; wherefore he may not reject his words. But behold, Cain hearkened not, saying: Who is the Lord, that I should know him?

17. And she again conceived and bare his brother Abel. And Abel hearkened unto the voice of the Lord. And Abel was a keeper of sheep, but Cain was a tiller of the ground.

18. And Cain loved Satan more than God. And Satan commanded him, saying: Make an offering unto the Lord.

19. And in process of time it came to pass that Cain brought of the fruit of the ground an offering unto the Lord.

20. And Abel he also brought of the firstlings of his flock, and of the fat thereof. And the Lord had respect unto Abel, and to his offering;

21. But unto Cain, and to his offering, he had not respect. Now Satan knew this, and it pleased him. And Cain was very wroth, and his countenance fell.

22. And the Lord said unto Cain: Why art thou wroth? Why is thy countenance fallen?

23. If thou doest well, thou shalt be accepted. And if thou doest not well, sin lieth at the door, and Satan desireth to have thee; and except thou shalt hearken unto my commandments, I will deliver thee up, and it shall be unto thee according to his desire. And thou shalt rule over him;

24. For from this time forth thou shalt be the father of his lies; thou shalt be called Perdition; for thou wast also before the world.

25. And it shall be said in time to come—That these abominations were had from Cain; for he rejected the greater counsel which was had from God; and this is a cursing which I will put upon thee, except thou repent.

26. And Cain was wroth, and listened not any more to the voice of the Lord, neither to Abel, his brother, who walked in holiness before the Lord.

27. And Adam and his wife mourned before the Lord, because of Cain and his brethren.

28. And it came to pass that Cain took one of his brothers' daughters to wife, and they loved Satan more than God.

29. And Satan said unto Cain: Swear unto me by thy throat, and if thou tell it thou shalt die; and swear thy brethren by their heads, and by the living God, that they tell it not; for if they tell it, they shall surely die; and this that thy father may not know it; and this day I will deliver thy brother Abel into thine hands.

30. And Satan sware unto Cain that he would do according to his commands. And all these things were done in secret.

31. And Cain said: Truly I am Mahan, the master of this great secret, that I may murder and get

gain. Wherefore Cain was called Master Mahan, and he gloried in his wickedness.

32. And Cain went into the field, and Cain talked with Abel, his brother. And it came to pass that while they were in the field, Cain rose up against Abel, his brother, and slew him.

33. And Cain gloried in that which he had done, saying: I am free; surely the flocks of my brother falleth into my hands.

34. And the Lord said unto Cain: Where is Abel, thy brother? And he said: I know not. Am I my brother's keeper?

35. And the Lord said: What hast thou done? The voice of thy brother's blood cries unto me from the ground.

36. And now thou shalt be cursed from the earth which hath opened her mouth to receive thy brother's blood from thy hand.

37. When thou tillest the ground it shall not henceforth yield unto thee her strength. A fugitive and a vagabond shalt thou be in the earth.

38. And Cain said unto the Lord: Satan tempted me because of my brother's flocks. And I was wroth also; for his offering thou didst accept and not mine; my punishment is greater than I can bear.

39. Behold thou hast driven me out this day from the face of the Lord, and from thy face shall I be hid; and I shall be a fugitive and a vagabond in the earth; and it shall come to pass, that he that findeth me will slay me, because of mine iniquities, for these things are not hid from the Lord.

40. And I the Lord said unto him: Whosoever slayeth thee, vengeance shall be taken on him sevenfold. And I the Lord set a mark upon Cain, lest any finding him should kill him.

41. And Cain was shut out from the presence of the Lord, and with his wife and many of his brethren dwelt in the land of Nod, on the east of Eden.

42. And Cain knew his wife, and she conceived and bare Enoch, and he also begat many sons and daughters. And he builded a city, and he called the name of the city after the name of his son, Enoch.

43. And unto Enoch was born Irad, and other sons and daughters. And Irad begat Mahujael, and other sons and daughters. And Mahujael begat Methusael, and other sons and daughters. And Methusael begat Lamech.

44. And Lamech took unto himself two wives; the name of one being Adah, and the name of the other, Zillah.

45. And Adah bare Jabal; he was the father of such as dwell in tents, and they were keepers of cattle; and his brother's name was Jubal, who was the father of all such as handle the harp and organ.

46. And Zillah, she also bare Tubal Cain, an instructor of every artificer in brass and iron. And the sister of Tubal Cain was called Naamah.

47. And Lamech said unto his wives, Adah and Zillah: Hear my voice, ye wives of Lamech, hearken unto my speech; for I have slain a man to my wounding, and a young man to my hurt.

48. If Cain shall be avenged sevenfold, truly Lamech shall be seventy and seven fold;

49. For Lamech having entered into a covenant with Satan, after the manner of Cain, wherein he became Master Mahan, master of that great secret which was administered unto Cain by Satan; and Irad, the son of Enoch, having known their secret, began to reveal it unto the sons of Adam;

50. Wherefore Lamech, being angry, slew him, not like unto Cain, his brother Abel, for the sake of getting gain, but he slew him for the oath's sake.

51. For, from the days of Cain, there was a secret combination, and their works were in the dark, and they knew every man his brother.

52. Wherefore the Lord cursed Lamech, and his house, and all them that had covenanted with Satan; for they kept not the commandments of God, and it displeased God, and he ministered not unto them, and their works were abominations, and began to spread among all the sons of men.

53. And it was among the sons of men, and among the daughters of men these things were not spoken, because that Lamech had spoken the secret unto his wives, and they rebelled against him, and declared these things abroad, and had not compassion;

54. Wherefore Lamech was despised, and cast out, and came not among the sons of men, lest he should die.

55. And thus the works of darkness began to prevail among all the sons of men.

56. And God cursed the earth with a sore curse, and was angry with the wicked, with all the sons of men whom he had made;

57. For they would not hearken unto his voice, nor believe on his Only Begotten Son, even him whom he declared should come in the meridian of time, who was prepared from before the foundation of the world.

58. And thus the Gospel began to be preached, from the beginning, being declared by holy angels sent forth from the presence of God, and by his own voice, and by the gift of the Holy Ghost.

59. And thus all things were confirmed unto Adam, by an holy ordinance, and the Gospel preached, and a decree sent forth, that it should be in the world, until the end thereof; and thus it was. Amen.

CHAPTER 6

THE WRITINGS OF MOSES
As revealed to Joseph Smith the Prophet, in December, 1830—continued

1. And Adam hearkened unto the voice of God, and called upon his sons to repent.

2. And Adam knew his wife again, and she bare a son, and he called his name Seth. And Adam glorified the name of God; for he said: God hath appointed me another seed, instead of Abel, whom Cain slew.

3. And God revealed himself unto Seth, and he rebelled not, but offered an acceptable sacrifice, like unto his brother Abel. And to him also was born a son, and he called his name Enos.

4. And then began these men to call upon the name of the Lord, and the Lord blessed them;

5. And a book of remembrance was kept, in the which was recorded, in the language of Adam, for it was given unto as many as called upon God to write by the spirit of inspiration;

6. And by them their children were taught to read and write, having a language which was pure and undefiled.

7. Now this same Priesthood, which was in the beginning, shall be in the end of the world also.

8. Now this prophecy Adam spake, as he was moved upon by the Holy Ghost, and a genealogy was kept of the children of God. And this was the book of the generations of Adam, saying: In the day that God created man, in the likeness of God made he him;

9. In the image of his own body, male and female, created he them, and blessed them, and called their name Adam, in the day when they were created and became living souls in the land upon the footstool of God.

10. And Adam lived one hundred and thirty years, and begat a son in his own likeness, after his own image, and called his name Seth.

11. And the days of Adam, after he had begotten Seth, were eight hundred years, and he begat many sons and daughters;

12. And all the days that Adam lived were nine hundred and thirty years, and he died.

13. Seth lived one hundred and five years, and begat Enos, and prophesied in all his days, and taught his son Enos in the ways of God; wherefore Enos prophesied also.

14. And Seth lived, after he begat Enos, eight hundred and seven years, and begat many sons and daughters.

15. And the children of men were numerous upon all the face of the land. And in those days Satan had great dominion among men, and raged in their hearts; and from thenceforth came wars and bloodshed; and a man's hand was against his own brother, in administering death, because of secret works, seeking for power.

16. All the days of Seth were nine hundred and twelve years, and he died.

17. And Enos lived ninety years, and begat Cainan. And Enos and the residue of the people of God came out from the land, which was called Shulon, and dwelt in a land of promise, which he called after his own son, whom he had named Cainan.

18. And Enos lived, after he begat Cainan, eight hundred and fifteen years, and begat many sons and daughters. And all the days of Enos were nine hundred and five years, and he died.

19. And Cainan lived seventy years, and begat Mahalaleel; and Cainan lived after he begat Mahalaleel eight hundred and forty years, and begat sons and daughters. And all the days of Cainan were nine hundred and ten years, and he died.

20. And Mahalaleel lived sixty-five years, and begat Jared; and Mahalaleel lived, after he begat Jared, eight hundred and thirty years, and begat sons and daughters. And all the days of Mahalaleel were eight hundred and ninety-five years, and he died.

21. And Jared lived one hundred and sixty-two years, and begat Enoch; and Jared lived, after he begat Enoch, eight hundred years, and begat sons and daughters. And Jared taught Enoch in all the ways of God.

22. And this is the genealogy of the sons of Adam, who was the son of God, with whom God, himself, conversed.

23. And they were preachers of righteousness, and spake and prophesied, and called upon all men, everywhere, to repent; and faith was taught unto the children of men.

24. And it came to pass that all the days of Jared were nine hundred and sixty-two years, and he died.

25. And Enoch lived sixty-five years, and begat Methuselah.

26. And it came to pass that Enoch journeyed in the land, among the people; and as he journeyed, the Spirit of God descended out of heaven, and abode upon him.

27. And he heard a voice from heaven, saying: Enoch, my son, prophesy unto this people, and say unto them—Repent, for thus saith the Lord: I am angry with this people, and my fierce anger is kindled against them; for their hearts have waxed hard, and their ears are dull of hearing, and their eyes cannot see afar off;

28. And for these many generations, ever since the day that I created them, have they gone astray, and have denied me, and have sought their own counsels in the dark; and in their own abominations have they devised murder, and have not kept the commandments, which I gave unto their father, Adam.

29. Wherefore, they have foresworn themselves, and, by their oaths, they have brought upon themselves death; and a hell I have prepared for them, if they repent not;

30. And this is a decree, which I have sent forth in the beginning of the world, from my own mouth, from the foundation thereof, and by the mouths of my servants, thy fathers, have I decreed it, even as it shall be sent forth in the world, unto the ends thereof.

31. And when Enoch had heard these words, he bowed himself to the earth, before the Lord, and spake before the Lord, saying: Why is it that I have found favor in thy sight, and am but a lad, and all the people hate me; for I am slow of speech; wherefore am I thy servant?

32. And the Lord said unto Enoch: Go forth and do as I have commanded thee, and no man shall pierce thee. Open thy mouth, and it shall be filled, and I will give thee utterance, for all flesh is in my hands, and I will do as seemeth me good.

33. Say unto this people: Choose ye this day, to serve the Lord God who made you.

34. Behold my Spirit is upon you, wherefore all thy words will I justify; and the mountains shall flee before you, and the rivers shall turn from their course; and thou shalt abide in me, and I in you; therefore walk with me.

35. And the Lord spake unto Enoch, and said unto him: Anoint thine eyes with clay, and wash them, and thou shalt see. And he did so.

36. And he beheld the spirits that God had created; and he beheld also things which were not visible to the natural eye; and from thenceforth came the saying abroad in the land: A seer hath the Lord raised up unto his people.

37. And it came to pass that Enoch went forth in the land, among the people, standing upon the hills and the high places, and cried with a loud voice, testifying against their works; and all men were offended because of him.

38. And they came forth to hear him, upon the high places, saying unto the tent keepers: Tarry ye here and keep the tents, while we go yonder to behold the seer, for he prophesieth, and there is a strange thing in the land; a wild man hath come among us.

39. And it came to pass when they heard him, no man laid hands on him; for fear came on all them that heard him; for he walked with God.

40. And there came a man unto him, whose name was Mahijah, and said unto him: Tell us plainly who thou art, and from whence thou comest?

41. And he said unto them: I came out from the land of Cainan, the land of my fathers, a land of righteousness unto this day. And my father taught me in all the ways of God.

42. And it came to pass, as I journeyed from the land of Cainan, by the sea east, I beheld a vision; and lo, the heavens I saw, and the Lord spake with me, and gave me commandment; wherefore, for this cause, to keep the commandment, I speak forth these words.

43. And Enoch continued his speech, saying: The Lord which spake with me, the same is the God of heaven, and he is my God, and your God, and ye are my brethren, and why counsel ye yourselves, and deny the God of heaven?

44. The heavens he made; the earth is his footstool; and the foundation thereof is his. Behold, he laid it, an host of men hath he brought in upon the face thereof.

45. And death hath come upon our fathers; nevertheless we know them, and cannot deny, and even the first of all we know, even Adam.

46. For a book of remembrance we have written among us, according to the pattern given by the finger of God; and it is given in our own language.

47. And as Enoch spake forth the words of God, the people trembled, and could not stand in his presence.

48. And he said unto them: Because that Adam fell, we are; and by his fall came death; and we are made partakers of misery and woe.

49. Behold Satan hath come among the children of men, and tempteth them to worship him; and men have become carnal, sensual, and devilish, and are shut out from the presence of God.

50. But God hath made known unto our fathers that all men must repent.

51. And he called upon our father Adam by his own voice, saying: I am God; I made the world, and men before they were in the flesh.

52. And he also said unto him: If thou wilt turn unto me, and hearken unto my voice, and believe, and repent of all thy transgressions, and be baptized, even in water, in the name of mine

Only Begotten Son, who is full of grace and truth, which is Jesus Christ, the only name which shall be given under heaven, whereby salvation shall come unto the children of men, ye shall receive the gift of the Holy Ghost, asking all things in his name, and whatsoever ye shall ask, it shall be given you.

53. And our father Adam spake unto the Lord, and said: Why is it that men must repent and be baptized in water? And the Lord said unto Adam: Behold I have forgiven thee thy transgression in the Garden of Eden.

54. Hence came the saying abroad among the people, That the Son of God hath atoned for original guilt, wherein the sins of the parents cannot be answered upon the heads of the children, for they are whole from the foundation of the world.

55. And the Lord spake unto Adam, saying: Inasmuch as thy children are conceived in sin, even so when they begin to grow up, sin conceiveth in their hearts, and they taste the bitter, that they may know to prize the good.

56. And it is given unto them to know good from evil; wherefore they are agents unto themselves, and I have given unto you another law and commandment.

57. Wherefore teach it unto your children, that all men, everywhere, must repent, or they can in nowise inherit the kingdom of God, for no unclean thing can dwell there, or dwell in his presence; for, in the language of Adam, Man of Holiness is his name, and the name of his Only Begotten is the Son of Man, even Jesus Christ, a righteous Judge, who shall come in the meridian of time.

58. Therefore I give unto you a commandment, to teach these things freely unto your children, saying:

59. That by reason of transgression cometh the fall, which fall bringeth death, and inasmuch as ye were born into the world by water, and blood, and the spirit, which I have made, and so became of dust a living soul, even so ye must be born again into the kingdom of heaven, of water, and of the Spirit, and be cleansed by blood, even the blood of mine Only Begotten; that ye might be sanctified from all sin, and enjoy the words of eternal life in this world, and eternal life in the world to come, even immortal glory;

60. For by the water ye keep the commandment; by the Spirit ye are justified, and by the blood ye are sanctified;

61. Therefore it is given to abide in you; the record of heaven; the Comforter; the peaceable things of immortal glory; the truth of all things; that which quickeneth all things, which maketh alive all things; that which knoweth all things, and hath all power, according to wisdom, mercy, truth, justice, and judgment.

62. And now, behold, I say unto you: This is the plan of salvation unto all men, through the blood of mine Only Begotten, who shall come in the meridian of time.

63. And behold, all things have their likeness, and all things are created and made to bear record of me, both things which are temporal, and things which are spiritual; things which are in the heavens above, and things which are on the earth, and things which are in the earth, and things which are under the earth, both above and beneath: all things bear record of me.

64. And it came to pass, when the Lord had spoken with Adam, our father, that Adam cried unto the Lord, and he was caught away by the Spirit of the Lord, and was carried down into the water, and was laid under the water, and was brought forth out of the water.

65. And thus he was baptized, and the Spirit of God descended upon him, and thus he was born of the Spirit, and became quickened in the inner man.

66. And he heard a voice out of heaven, saying: Thou art baptized with fire, and with the Holy Ghost. This is the record of the Father, and the Son, from henceforth and for ever;

67. And thou art after the order of him who was without beginning of days or end of years, from all eternity to all eternity.

68. Behold, thou art one in me, a son of God; and thus may all become my sons. Amen.

CHAPTER 7

THE WRITINGS OF MOSES
As revealed to Joseph Smith the Prophet, in December, 1830—continued

1. And it came to pass that Enoch continued his speech, saying: Behold, our father Adam taught these things, and many have believed and become the sons of God, and many have believed not, and have perished in their sins, and are looking forth with fear, in torment, for the fiery indignation of the wrath of God to be poured out upon them.

2. And from that time forth Enoch began to prophesy, saying unto the people, that: As I was journeying, and stood upon the place Mahujah, and cried unto the Lord, there came a voice out of heaven, saying—Turn ye, and get ye upon the mount Simeon.

3. And it came to pass that I turned and went up on the mount; and as I stood upon the mount, I beheld the heavens open, and I was clothed upon with glory;

4. And I saw the Lord; and he stood before my face, and he talked with me, even as a man talketh one with another, face to face; and he said unto me: Look, and I will show unto thee the world for the space of many generations.

5. And it came to pass that I beheld in the valley of Shum, and lo, a great people which dwelt in tents, which were the people of Shum.

6. And again the Lord said unto me: Look; and I looked towards the north, and I beheld the people of Canaan, which dwelt in tents.

7. And the Lord said unto me: Prophesy; and I prophesied, saying: Behold the people of Canaan, which are numerous, shall go forth in battle array against the people of Shum, and shall slay them that they shall utterly be destroyed; and the people of Canaan shall divide themselves in the land, and the land shall be barren and unfruitful, and none other people shall dwell there but the people of Canaan;

8. For behold, the Lord shall curse the land with much heat, and the barrenness thereof shall go forth forever; and there was a blackness came upon all the children of Canaan, that they were despised among all people.

9. And it came to pass that the Lord said unto me: Look; and I looked, and I beheld the land of Sharon, and the land of Enoch, and the land of Omner, and the land of Heni, and the land of Shem, and the land of Haner, and the land of Hanannihah, and all the inhabitants thereof;

10. And the Lord said unto me: Go to this people, and say unto them—Repent, lest I come out and smite them with a curse, and they die.

11. And he gave unto me a commandment that I should baptize in the name of the Father, and of the Son, which is full of grace and truth, and of the Holy Ghost, which beareth record of the Father and the Son.

12. And it came to pass that Enoch continued to call upon all the people, save it were the people of Canaan, to repent;

13. And so great was the faith of Enoch, that he led the people of God, and their enemies came to battle against them; and he spake the word of the Lord, and the earth trembled, and the mountains fled, even according to his command; and the rivers of water were turned out of their course; and the roar of the lions was heard out of the wilderness; and all nations feared greatly, so powerful was the word of Enoch, and so great was the power of the language which God had given him.

14. There also came up a land out of the depth of the sea, and so great was the fear of the enemies of the people of God, that they fled and stood afar off and went upon the land which came up out of the depth of the sea.

15. And the giants of the land, also, stood afar off; and there went forth a curse upon all people that fought against God;

16. And from that time forth there were wars and bloodshed among them; but the Lord came and dwelt with his people, and they dwelt in righteousness.

17. The fear of the Lord was upon all nations, so great was the glory of the Lord, which was upon his people. And the Lord blessed the land, and they were blessed upon the mountains, and upon the high places, and did flourish.

18. And the Lord called his people ZION, because they were of one heart and one mind, and dwelt in righteousness; and there was no poor among them.

19. And Enoch continued his preaching in righteousness unto the people of God. And it came to pass in his days, that he built a city that was called the City of Holiness, even ZION.

20. And it came to pass that Enoch talked with the Lord; and he said unto the Lord: Surely Zion shall dwell in safety forever. But the Lord said unto Enoch: Zion have I blessed, but the residue of the people have I cursed.

21. And it came to pass that the Lord showed unto Enoch all the inhabitants of the earth; and he beheld, and lo, Zion, in process of time, was taken up into heaven. And the Lord said unto Enoch: Behold mine abode forever.

22. And Enoch also beheld the residue of the people which were the sons of Adam; and they were a mixture of all the seed of Adam save it were the seed of Cain, for the seed of Cain were black, and had not place among them.

23. And after that Zion was taken up into heaven, Enoch beheld, and lo, all the nations of the earth were before him;

24. And there came generation upon generation; and Enoch was high and lifted up, even in the bosom of the Father, and of the Son of Man; and behold, the power of Satan was upon all the face of the earth.

25. And he saw angels descending out of heaven; and he heard a loud voice saying: Wo, wo be unto the inhabitants of the earth.

26. And he beheld Satan; and he had a great chain in his hand, and it veiled the whole face of the earth with darkness; and he looked up and laughed, and his angels rejoiced.

27. And Enoch beheld angels descending out of heaven, bearing testimony of the Father and Son; and the Holy Ghost fell on many, and they were caught up by the powers of heaven into Zion.

28. And it came to pass that the God of heaven looked upon the residue of the people, and he wept; and Enoch bore record of it, saying: How is it that the heavens weep, and shed forth their tears as the rain upon the mountains?

29. And Enoch said unto the Lord: How is it that thou canst weep, seeing thou art holy, and from all eternity to all eternity?

30. And were it possible that man could number the particles of the earth, yea, millions of earths like this, it would not be a beginning to the number of thy creations; and thy curtains are stretched out still; and yet thou art there, and thy bosom is there; and also thou art just; thou art merciful and kind forever;

31. And thou hast taken Zion to thine own bosom, from all thy creations, from all eternity to all eternity; and naught but peace, justice, and truth is the habitation of thy throne; and mercy shall go before thy face and have no end; how is it thou canst weep?

32. The Lord said unto Enoch: Behold these thy brethren; they are the workmanship of mine own

hands, and I gave unto them their knowledge, in the day I created them; and in the Garden of Eden, gave I unto man his agency;

33. And unto thy brethren have I said, and also given commandment, that they should love one another, and that they should choose me, their Father; but behold, they are without affection, and they hate their own blood;

34. And the fire of mine indignation is kindled against them; and in my hot displeasure will I send in the floods upon them, for my fierce anger is kindled against them.

35. Behold, I am God; Man of Holiness is my name; Man of Counsel is my name; and Endless and Eternal is my name, also.

36. Wherefore, I can stretch forth mine hands and hold all the creations which I have made; and mine eye can pierce them also, and among all the workmanship of mine hands there has not been so great wickedness as among thy brethren.

37. But behold, their sins shall be upon the heads of their fathers; Satan shall be their father, and misery shall be their doom; and the whole heavens shall weep over them, even all the workmanship of mine hands; wherefore should not the heavens weep, seeing these shall suffer?

38. But behold, these which thine eyes are upon shall perish in the floods; and behold, I will shut them up; a prison have I prepared for them.

39. And That which I have chosen hath pled before my face. Wherefore, he suffereth for their sins; inasmuch as they will repent in the day that my Chosen shall return unto me, and until that day they shall be in torment;

40. Wherefore, for this shall the heavens weep, yea, and all the workmanship of mine hands.

41. And it came to pass that the Lord spake unto Enoch, and told Enoch all the doings of the children of men; wherefore Enoch knew, and looked upon their wickedness, and their misery, and wept and stretched forth his arms, and his heart swelled wide as eternity; and his bowels yearned; and all eternity shook.

42. And Enoch also saw Noah, and his family; that the posterity of all the sons of Noah should be saved with a temporal salvation;

43. Wherefore Enoch saw that Noah built an ark; and that the Lord smiled upon it, and held it in his own hand; but upon the residue of the wicked the floods came and swallowed them up.

44. And as Enoch saw this, he had bitterness of soul, and wept over his brethren, and said unto the heavens: I will refuse to be comforted; but the Lord said unto Enoch: Lift up your heart, and be glad; and look.

45. And it came to pass that Enoch looked; and from Noah, he beheld all the families of the earth; and he cried unto the Lord, saying: When shall the day of the Lord come? When shall the blood of the Righteous be shed, that all they that mourn may be sanctified and have eternal life?

46. And the Lord said: It shall be in the meridian of time, in the days of wickedness and vengeance.

47. And behold, Enoch saw the day of the coming of the Son of Man, even in the flesh; and his soul rejoiced, saying: The Righteous is lifted up, and the Lamb is slain from the foundation of the world; and through faith I am in the bosom of the Father, and behold, Zion is with me.

48. And it came to pass that Enoch looked upon the earth; and he heard a voice from the bowels thereof, saying: Wo, wo is me, the mother of men; I am pained, I am weary, because of the wickedness of my children. When shall I rest, and be cleansed from the filthiness which is gone forth out of me? When will my Creator sanctify me, that I may rest, and righteousness for a season abide upon my face?

49. And when Enoch heard the earth mourn, he wept, and cried unto the Lord, saying: O Lord,

wilt thou not have compassion upon the earth? Wilt thou not bless the children of Noah?

50. And it came to pass that Enoch continued his cry unto the Lord, saying: I ask thee, O Lord, in the name of thine Only Begotten, even Jesus Christ, that thou wilt have mercy upon Noah and his seed, that the earth might never more be covered by the floods.

51. And the Lord could not withhold; and he covenanted with Enoch, and sware unto him with an oath, that he would stay the floods; that he would call upon the children of Noah;

52. And he sent forth an unalterable decree, that a remnant of his seed should always be found among all nations, while the earth should stand;

53. And the Lord said: Blessed is he through whose seed Messiah shall come; for he saith—I am Messiah, the King of Zion, the Rock of Heaven, which is broad as eternity; whoso cometh in at the gate and climbeth up by me shall never fall; wherefore, blessed are they of whom I have spoken, for they shall come forth with songs of everlasting joy.

54. And it came to pass that Enoch cried unto the Lord, saying: When the Son of Man cometh in the flesh, shall the earth rest? I pray thee, show me these things.

55. And the Lord said unto Enoch: Look, and he looked and beheld the Son of Man lifted up on the cross, after the manner of men;

56. And he heard a loud voice; and the heavens were veiled; and all the creations of God mourned; and the earth groaned; and the rocks were rent; and the saints arose, and were crowned at the right hand of the Son of Man, with crowns of glory;

57. And as many of the spirits as were in prison came forth, and stood on the right hand of God; and the remainder were reserved in chains of darkness until the judgment of the great day.

58. And again Enoch wept and cried unto the Lord, saying: When shall the earth rest?

59. And Enoch beheld the Son of Man ascend up unto the Father; and he called unto the Lord, saying: Wilt thou not come again upon the earth? Forasmuch as thou art God, and I know thee, and thou hast sworn unto me, and commanded me that I should ask in the name of thine Only Begotten; thou hast made me, and given unto me a right to thy throne, and not of myself, but through thine own grace; wherefore, I ask thee if thou wilt not come again on the earth.

60. And the Lord said unto Enoch: As I live, even so will I come in the last days, in the days of wickedness and vengeance, to fulfil the oath which I have made unto you concerning the children of Noah;

61. And the day shall come that the earth shall rest, but before that day the heavens shall be darkened, and a veil of darkness shall cover the earth; and the heavens shall shake, and also the earth; and great tribulations shall be among the children of men, but my people will I preserve;

62. And righteousness will I send down out of heaven; and truth will I send forth out of the earth, to bear testimony of mine Only Begotten; his resurrection from the dead; yea, and also the resurrection of all men; and righteousness and truth will I cause to sweep the earth as with a flood, to gather out mine elect from the four quarters of the earth, unto a place which I shall prepare, an Holy City, that my people may gird up their loins, and be looking forth for the time of my coming; for there shall be my tabernacle, and it shall be called Zion, a New Jerusalem.

63. And the Lord said unto Enoch: Then shalt thou and all thy city meet them there, and we will receive them into our bosom, and they shall see us; and we will fall upon their necks, and they shall fall upon our necks, and we will kiss each other;

64. And there shall be mine abode, and it shall be Zion, which shall come forth out of all the creations which I have made; and for the space of a thousand years the earth shall rest.

65. And it came to pass that Enoch saw the day of the coming of the Son of Man, in the last days, to dwell on the earth in righteousness for the space of a thousand years;

66. But before that day he saw great tribulations among the wicked; and he also saw the sea, that it was troubled, and men's hearts failing them, looking forth with fear for the judgments of the Almighty God, which should come upon the wicked.

67. And the Lord showed Enoch all things, even unto the end of the world; and he saw the day of the righteous, the hour of their redemption; and received a fulness of joy;

68. And all the days of Zion, in the days of Enoch, were three hundred and sixty-five years.

69. And Enoch and all his people walked with God, and he dwelt in the midst of Zion; and it came to pass that Zion was not, for God received it up into his own bosom; and from thence went forth the saying, Zion is Fled.

CHAPTER 8

THE WRITINGS OF MOSES
As revealed to Joseph Smith the Prophet, in December, 1830—continued

1. And all the days of Enoch were four hundred and thirty years.

2. And it came to pass that Methuselah, the son of Enoch, was not taken, that the covenants of the Lord might be fulfilled, which he made to Enoch; for he truly covenanted with Enoch that Noah should be of the fruit of his loins.

3. And it came to pass that Methuselah prophesied that from his loins should spring all the kingdoms of the earth (through Noah), and he took glory unto himself.

4. And there came forth a great famine into the land, and the Lord cursed the earth with a sore curse, and many of the inhabitants thereof died.

5. And it came to pass that Methuselah lived one hundred and eighty-seven years, and begat Lamech;

6. And Methuselah lived, after he begat Lamech, seven hundred and eighty-two years, and begat sons and daughters;

7. And all the days of Methuselah were nine hundred and sixty-nine years, and he died.

8. And Lamech lived one hundred and eighty-two years, and begat a son,

9. And he called his name Noah, saying: This son shall comfort us concerning our work and toil of our hands, because of the ground which the Lord hath cursed.

10. And Lamech lived, after he begat Noah, five hundred and ninety-five years, and begat sons and daughters;

11. And all the days of Lamech were seven hundred and seventy-seven years, and he died.

12. And Noah was four hundred and fifty years old, and begat Japheth; and forty-two years afterward he begat Shem of her who was the mother of Japheth, and when he was five hundred years old he begat Ham.

13. And Noah and his sons hearkened unto the Lord, and gave heed, and they were called the sons of God.

14. And when these men began to multiply on the face of the earth, and daughters were born unto them, the sons of men saw that those daughters were fair, and they took them wives, even as they chose.

15. And the Lord said unto Noah: The daughters of thy sons have sold themselves; for behold mine anger is kindled against the sons of men, for they will not hearken to my voice.

16. And it came to pass that Noah prophesied, and taught the things of God, even as it was in the beginning.

17. And the Lord said unto Noah: My Spirit shall not always strive with man, for he shall know that all flesh shall die; yet his days shall be an hundred and twenty years; and if men do not repent, I will send in the floods upon them.

18. And in those days there were giants on the earth, and they sought Noah to take away his life; but the Lord was with Noah, and the power of the Lord was upon him.

19. And the Lord ordained Noah after his own order, and commanded him that he should go forth and declare his Gospel unto the children of men, even as it was given unto Enoch.

20. And it came to pass that Noah called upon the children of men that they should repent; but they hearkened not unto his words;

21. And also, after that they had heard him, they came up before him, saying: Behold, we are the sons of God; have we not taken unto ourselves the daughters of men? And are we not eating and drinking, and marrying and giving in marriage? And our wives bear unto us children, and the same are mighty men, which are like unto men of old, men of great renown. And they hearkened not unto the words of Noah.

22. And God saw that the wickedness of men had become great in the earth; and every man was lifted up in the imagination of the thoughts of his heart, being only evil continually.

23. And it came to pass that Noah continued his preaching unto the people, saying: Hearken, and give heed unto my words;

24. Believe and repent of your sins and be baptized in the name of Jesus Christ, the Son of God, even as our fathers, and ye shall receive the Holy Ghost, that ye may have all things made manifest; and if ye do not this, the floods will come in upon you; nevertheless they hearkened not.

25. And it repented Noah, and his heart was pained that the Lord had made man on the earth, and it grieved him at the heart.

26. And the Lord said: I will destroy man whom I have created, from the face of the earth, both man and beast, and the creeping things, and the fowls of the air; for it repenteth Noah that I have created them, and that I have made them; and he hath called upon me; for they have sought his life.

27. And thus Noah found grace in the eyes of the Lord; for Noah was a just man, and perfect in his generation; and he walked with God, as did also his three sons, Shem, Ham, and Japheth.

28. The earth was corrupt before God, and it was filled with violence.

29. And God looked upon the earth, and, behold, it was corrupt, for all flesh had corrupted its way upon the earth.

30. And God said unto Noah: The end of all flesh is come before me, for the earth is filled with violence, and behold I will destroy all flesh from off the earth.

# THE BOOK OF ABRAHAM

Translated from the Papyrus, by Joseph Smith.

A Translation of some ancient Records, that have fallen into our hands from the catacombs of Egypt; The writings of Abraham while he was in Egypt, called the Book of Abraham, written by his own hand, upon papyrus.

CHAPTER 1

1. In the land of the Chaldeans, at the residence of my father, I, Abraham, saw that it was needful for me to obtain another place of residence;

2. And, finding there was greater happiness and peace and rest for me, I sought for the blessings of the fathers, and the right whereunto I should be ordained to administer the same; having been myself a follower of righteousness, desiring also to be one who possessed great knowledge, and to be a greater follower of righteousness, and to possess a greater knowledge, and to be a father of many nations, a prince of peace, and desiring to receive instructions, and to keep the commandments of God, I became a rightful heir, a High Priest, holding the right belonging to the fathers.

3. It was conferred upon me from the fathers; it came down from the fathers, from the beginning of time, yea, even from the beginning, or before the foundations of the earth, down to the present time, even the right of the first-born, or the first man, who is Adam, our first father, through the fathers, unto me.

4. I sought for mine appointment unto the Priesthood according to the appointment of God unto the fathers concerning the seed.

5. My fathers having turned from their righteousness, and from the holy commandments which the Lord their God had given unto them, unto the worshiping of the gods of the heathen, utterly refused to hearken to my voice;

6. For their hearts were set to do evil, and were wholly turned to the god of Elkenah, and the god of Libnah, and the god of Mahmackrah, and the god of Korash, and the god of Pharaoh, king of Egypt;

7. Therefore they turned their hearts to the sacrifice of the heathen in offering up their children unto their dumb idols, and hearkened not unto my voice, but endeavored to take away my life by the hand of the priest of Elkenah. The priest of Elkenah was also the priest of Pharaoh.

8. Now, at this time it was the custom of the priest of Pharaoh, the king of Egypt, to offer up upon the altar which was built in the land of Chaldea, for the offering unto these strange gods, men, women, and children.

9. And it came to pass that the priest made an offering unto the god of Pharaoh, and also unto the god of Shagreel, even after the manner of the Egyptians. Now the god of Shagreel was the sun.

10. Even the thank-offering of a child did the priest of Pharaoh offer upon the altar which stood by the hill called Potiphar's Hill, at the head of the plain of Olishem.

11. Now, this priest had offered upon this altar three virgins at one time, who were the daughters of Onitah, one of the royal descent directly from the loins of Ham. These virgins were offered up because of their virtue; they would not bow down to worship gods of wood or of stone, therefore they were killed upon this altar, and it was done after the manner of the Egyptians.

12. And it came to pass that the priests laid violence upon me, that they might slay me also, as they did those virgins upon this altar; and that you may have a knowledge of this altar, I will refer you to the representation at the commencement of this record.

13. It was made after the form of a bedstead, such as was had among the Chaldeans, and it stood before the gods of Elkenah, Libnah, Mahmackrah, Korash, and also a god like unto that of Pharaoh, king of Egypt.

14. That you may have an understanding of these gods, I have given you the fashion of them in the figures at the beginning, which manner of the figures is called by the Chaldeans Rahleenos, which signifies hieroglyphics.

15. And as they lifted up their hands upon me, that they might offer me up and take away my life, behold, I lifted up my voice unto the Lord my God, and the Lord hearkened and heard, and he filled me with the vision of the Almighty, and the angel of his presence stood by me, and immediately unloosed my bands;

16. And his voice was unto me: Abraham, Abraham, behold, my name is Jehovah, and I have heard thee, and have come down to deliver thee, and to take thee away from thy father's house, and from all thy kins-folk, into a strange land which thou knowest not of;

17. And this because they have turned their hearts away from me, to worship the god of Elkenah, and the god of Libnah, and the god of Mahmackrah, and the god of Korash, and the god of Pharaoh, king of Egypt; therefore I have come down to visit them, and to destroy him who hath lifted up his hand against thee, Abraham, my son, to take away thy life.

18. Behold, I will lead thee by my hand, and I will take thee, to put upon thee my name, even the Priesthood of thy father, and my power shall be over thee.

19. As it was with Noah so shall it be with thee; but through thy ministry my name shall be known in the earth forever, for I am thy God.

20. Behold, Potiphar's Hill was in the land of Ur, of Chaldea. And the Lord broke down the altar of Elkenah, and of the gods of the land, and utterly destroyed them, and smote the priest that he died; and there was great mourning in Chaldea, and also in the court of Pharaoh; which Pharaoh signifies king by royal blood.

21. Now this king of Egypt was a descendant from the loins of Ham, and was a partaker of the blood of the Canaanites by birth.

22. From this descent sprang all the Egyptians, and thus the blood of the Canaanites was preserved in the land.

23. The land of Egypt being first discovered by a woman, who was the daughter of Ham, and the daughter of Egypt, which in the Chaldean signifies Egypt, which signifies that which is forbidden.

AN EGYPTIAN PRIEST ATTEMPTING TO SLAY ABRAHAM ON A SACRIFICIAL ALTAR

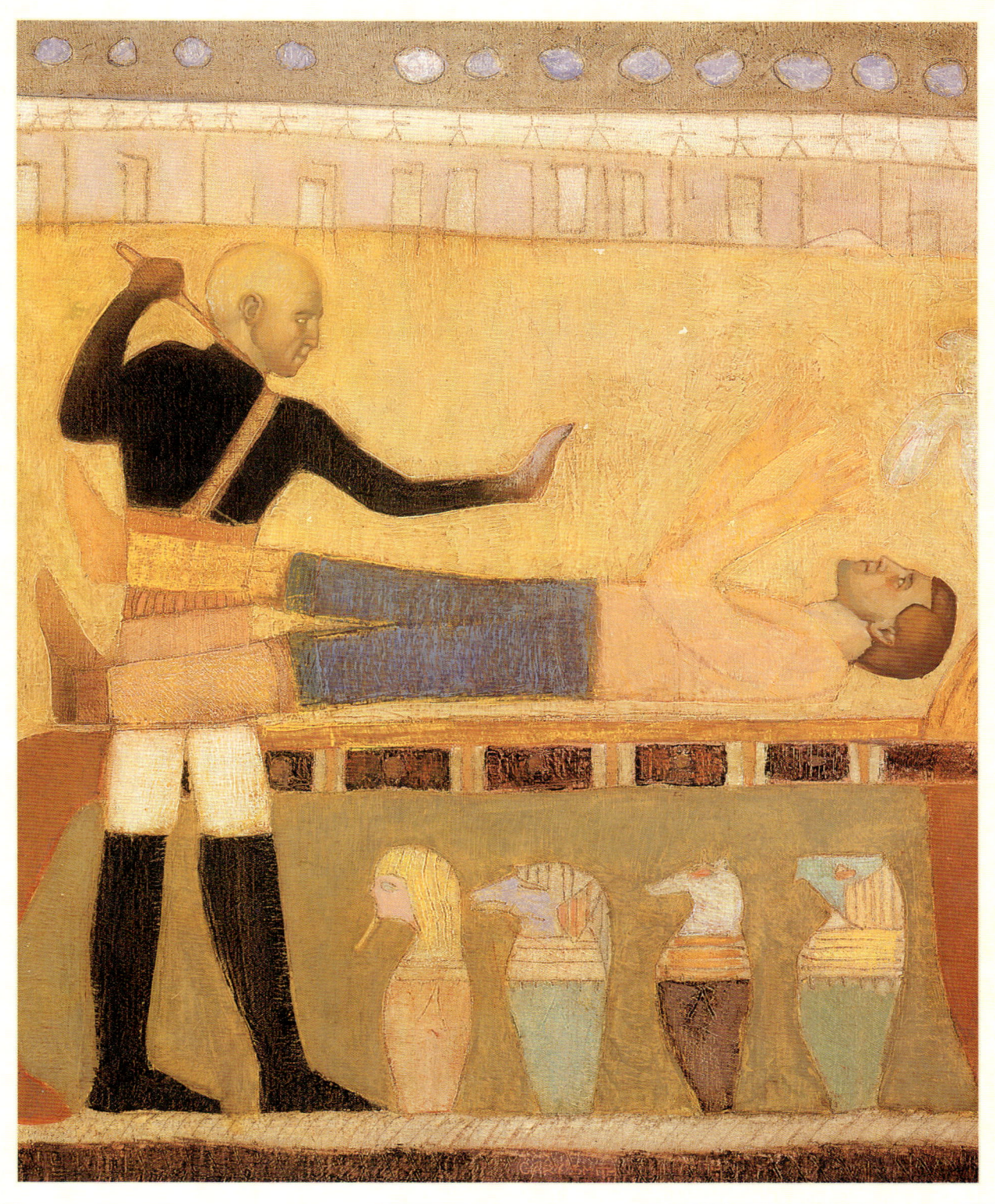

24. When this woman discovered the land it was under water, who afterward settled her sons in it; and thus, from Ham, sprang that race which preserved the curse in the land.

25. Now the first government of Egypt was established by Pharaoh, the eldest son of Egyptus, the daughter of Ham, and it was after the manner of the government of Ham, which was patriarchal.

26. Pharaoh, being a righteous man, established his kingdom and judged his people wisely and justly all his days, seeking earnestly to imitate that order established by the fathers in the first generations, in the days of the first patriarchal reign, even in the reign of Adam, and also of Noah, his father, who blessed him with the blessings of the earth, and with the blessings of wisdom, but cursed him as pertaining to the Priesthood.

27. Now, Pharaoh being of that lineage by which he could not have the right of Priesthood, notwithstanding the Pharaohs would fain claim it from Noah, through Ham, therefore my father was led away by their idolatry;

28. But I shall endeavor, hereafter, to delineate the chronology running back from myself to the beginning of the creation, for the records have come into my hands, which I hold unto this present time.

29. Now, after the priest of Elkenah was smitten that he died, there came a fulfilment of those things which were said unto me concerning the land of Chaldea, that there should be a famine in the land.

30. Accordingly a famine prevailed throughout all the land of Chaldea, and my father was sorely tormented because of the famine, and he repented of the evil which he had determined against me, to take away my life.

31. But the records of the fathers, even the patriarchs, concerning the right of Priesthood, the Lord my God preserved in mine own hands; therefore a knowledge of the beginning of the creation, and also of the planets, and of the stars, as they were made known unto the fathers, have I kept even unto this day, and I shall endeavor to write some of these things upon this record, for the benefit of my posterity that shall come after me.

CHAPTER 2

1. Now the Lord God caused the famine to wax sore in the land of Ur, insomuch that Haran, my brother, died; but Terah, my father, yet lived in the land of Ur, of the Chaldees.

2. And it came to pass that I, Abraham, took Sarai to wife, and Nehor, my brother, took Milcah to wife, who were the daughters of Haran.

3. Now the Lord had said unto me: Abraham, get thee out of thy country, and from thy kindred, and from thy father's house, unto a land that I will show thee.

4. Therefore I left the land of Ur, of the Chaldees, to go into the land of Canaan; and I took Lot, my brother's son, and his wife, and Sarai my wife; and also my father followed after me, unto the land which we denominated Haran.

5. And the famine abated; and my father tarried in Haran and dwelt there, as there were many flocks in Haran; and my father turned again unto his idolatry, therefore he continued in Haran.

6. But I, Abraham, and Lot, my brother's son, prayed unto the Lord, and the Lord appeared unto me, and said unto me: Arise, and take Lot with thee; for I have purposed to take thee away out of Haran, and to make of thee a minister to bear my name in a strange land which I will give unto thy seed after thee for an everlasting possession, when they hearken to my voice.

7. For I am the Lord thy God; I dwell in heaven; the earth is my footstool; I stretch my hand over the sea, and it obeys my voice; I cause the wind

and the fire to be my chariot; I say to the mountains—Depart hence—and behold, they are taken away by a whirlwind, in an instant, suddenly.

8. My name is Jehovah, and I know the end from the beginning; therefore my hand shall be over thee.

9. And I will make of thee a great nation, and I will bless thee above measure, and make thy name great among all nations, and thou shalt be a blessing unto thy seed after thee, that in their hands they shall bear this ministry and Priesthood unto all nations;

10. And I will bless them through thy name; for as many as receive this Gospel shall be called after thy name, and shall be accounted thy seed, and shall rise up and bless thee, as their father;

11. And I will bless them that bless thee, and curse them that curse thee; and in thee (that is, in thy Priesthood) and in thy seed (that is, thy Priesthood,) for I give unto thee a promise that this right shall continue in thee, and in thy seed after thee (that is to say, the literal seed, or the seed of the body) shall all the families of the earth be blessed, even with the blessings of the Gospel, which are the blessings of salvation, even of life eternal.

12. Now, after the Lord had withdrawn from speaking to me, and withdrawn his face from me, I said in my heart: Thy servant has sought thee earnestly; now I have found thee;

13. Thou didst send thine angel to deliver me from the gods of Elkenah, and I will do well to hearken unto thy voice, therefore let thy servant rise up and depart in peace.

14. So I, Abraham, departed as the Lord had said unto me, and Lot with me; and I, Abraham, was sixty and two years old when I departed out of Haran.

15. And I took Sarai, whom I took to wife when I was in Ur, in Chaldea, and Lot, my brother's son, and all our substance that we had gathered, and the souls that we had won in Haran, and came forth in the way to the land of Canaan, and dwelt in tents as we came on our way;

16. Therefore, eternity was our covering and our rock and our salvation, as we journeyed from Haran by the way of Jershon, to come to the land of Canaan.

17. Now I, Abraham, built an altar in the land of Jershon, and made an offering unto the Lord, and prayed that the famine might be turned away from my father's house, that they might not perish.

18. And then we passed from Jershon through the land unto the place of Sechem; it was situated in the plains of Moreh, and we had already come into the borders of the land of the Canaanites, and I offered sacrifice there in the plains of Moreh, and called on the Lord devoutly, because we had already come into the land of this idolatrous nation.

19. And the Lord appeared unto me in answer to my prayers, and said unto me: Unto thy seed will I give this land.

20. And I, Abraham, arose from the place of the altar which I had built unto the Lord, and removed from thence unto a mountain on the east of Bethel, and pitched my tent there, Bethel on the west, and Hai on the east; and there I built another altar unto the Lord, and called again upon the name of the Lord.

21. And I, Abraham, journeyed, going on still towards the south; and there was a continuation of a famine in the land; and I, Abraham, concluded to go down into Egypt, to sojourn there, for the famine became very grievous.

22. And it came to pass when I was come near to enter into Egypt, the Lord said unto me: Behold, Sarai, thy wife, is a very fair woman to look upon;

23. Therefore it shall come to pass, when the Egyptians shall see her, they will say—She is his

wife; and they will kill you, but they will save her alive; therefore see that ye do on this wise:

24. Let her say unto the Egyptians, she is thy sister, and thy soul shall live.

25. And it came to pass that I, Abraham, told Sarai, my wife, all that the Lord had said unto me—Therefore say unto them, I pray thee, thou art my sister, that it may be well with me for thy sake, and my soul shall live because of thee.

CHAPTER 3

1. And I, Abraham, had the Urim and Thummim, which the Lord my God had given unto me, in Ur of the Chaldees;

2. And I saw the stars, that they were very great, and that one of them was nearest unto the throne of God; and there were many great ones which were near unto it;

3. And the Lord said unto me: These are the governing ones; and the name of the great one is Kolob, because it is near unto me, for I am the Lord thy God: I have set this one to govern all those which belong to the same order as that upon which thou standest.

4. And the Lord said unto me, by the Urim and Thummim, that Kolob was after the manner of the Lord, according to its times and seasons in the revolutions thereof; that one revolution was a day unto the Lord, after his manner of reckoning, it being one thousand years according to the time appointed unto that whereon thou standest. This is the reckoning of the Lord's time, according to the reckoning of Kolob.

5. And the Lord said unto me: The planet which is the lesser light, lesser than that which is to rule the day, even the night, is above or greater than that upon which thou standest in point of reckoning, for it moveth in order more slow; this is in order because it standeth above the earth upon which thou standest, therefore the reckoning of its time is not so many as to its number of days, and of months, and of years.

6. And the Lord said unto me: Now, Abraham, these two facts exist, behold thine eyes see it; it is given unto thee to know the times of reckoning, and the set time, yea, the set time of the earth upon which thou standest, and the set time of the greater light which is set to rule the day, and the set time of the lesser light which is set to rule the night.

7. Now the set time of the lesser light is a longer time as to its reckoning than the reckoning of the time of the earth upon which thou standest.

8. And where these two facts exist, there shall be another fact above them, that is, there shall be another planet whose reckoning of time shall be longer still;

9. And thus there shall be the reckoning of the time of one planet above another, until thou come nigh unto Kolob, which Kolob is after the reckoning of the Lord's time; which Kolob is set nigh unto the throne of God, to govern all those planets which belong to the same order as that upon which thou standest.

10. And it is given unto thee to know the set time of all the stars that are set to give light, until thou come near unto the throne of God.

11. Thus I, Abraham, talked with the Lord, face to face, as one man talketh with another; and he told me of the works which his hands had made;

12. And he said unto me: My son, my son, (and his hand was stretched out,) behold I will show you all these. And he put his hand upon mine eyes, and I saw those things which his hands had made, which were many; and they multiplied before mine eyes, and I could not see the end thereof.

13. And he said unto me: This is Shinehah, which is the sun. And he said unto me: Kokob, which is star. And he said unto me: Olea, which

is the moon. And he said unto me: Kokaubeam, which signifies stars, or all the great lights, which were in the firmament of heaven.

14. And it was in the night time when the Lord spake these words unto me: I will multiply thee, and thy seed after thee, like unto these; and if thou canst count the number of sands, so shall be the number of thy seeds.

15. And the Lord said unto me: Abraham, I show these things unto thee before ye go into Egypt, that ye may declare all these words.

16. If two things exist, and there be one above the other, there shall be greater things above them; therefore Kolob is the greatest of all the Kokaubeam that thou hast seen, because it is nearest unto me.

17. Now, if there be two things, one above the other, and the moon be above the earth, then it may be that a planet or a star may exist above it; and there is nothing that the Lord thy God shall take in his heart to do but what he will do it.

18. Howbeit that he made the greater star; as, also, if there be two spirits, and one shall be more intelligent than the other, yet these two spirits, notwithstanding one is more intelligent than the other, have no beginning; they existed before, they shall have no end, they shall exist after, for they are gnolaum, or eternal.

19. And the Lord said unto me: These two facts do exist, that there are two spirits, one being more intelligent than the other; there shall be another more intelligent than they; I am the Lord thy God, I am more intelligent than they all.

20. The Lord thy God sent his angel to deliver thee from the hands of the priest of Elkenah.

21. I dwell in the midst of them all; I now, therefore, have come down unto thee to deliver unto thee the works which my hands have made, wherein my wisdom excelleth them all, for I rule in the heavens above, and in the earth beneath, in all wisdom and prudence, over all the intelligences thine eyes have seen from the beginning; I came down in the beginning in the midst of all the intelligences thou hast seen.

22. Now the Lord had shown unto me, Abraham, the intelligences that were organized before the world was; and among all these there were many of the noble and great ones;

23. And God saw these souls that they were good, and he stood in the midst of them, and he said: These I will make my rulers; for he stood among those that were spirits, and he saw that they were good; and he said unto me: Abraham, thou art one of them; thou wast chosen before thou wast born.

24. And there stood one among them that was like unto God, and he said unto those who were with him: We will go down, for there is space there, and we will take of these materials, and we will make an earth whereon these may dwell;

25. And we will prove them herewith, to see if they will do all things whatsoever the Lord their God shall command them;

26. And they who keep their first estate shall be added upon; and they who keep not their first estate shall not have glory in the same kingdom with those who keep their first estate; and they who keep their second estate shall have glory added upon their heads for ever and ever.

27. And the Lord said: Whom shall I send? And one answered like unto the Son of Man: Here am I, send me. And another answered and said: Here am I, send me. And the Lord said: I will send the first.

28. And the second was angry, and kept not his first estate; and, at that day, many followed after him.

CHAPTER 4

1. And then the Lord said: Let us go down. And they went down at the beginning, and they, that is the Gods, organized and formed the heavens and the earth.

2. And the earth, after it was formed, was empty and desolate, because they had not formed anything but the earth; and darkness reigned upon the face of the deep, and the Spirit of the Gods was brooding upon the face of the waters.

3. And they (the Gods) said: Let there be light; and there was light.

4. And they (the Gods) comprehended the light, for it was bright; and they divided the light, or caused it to be divided, from the darkness.

5. And the Gods called the light Day, and the darkness they called Night. And it came to pass that from the evening until morning they called night; and from the morning until the evening they called day; and this was the first, or the beginning, of that which they called day and night.

6. And the Gods also said: Let there be an expanse in the midst of the waters, and it shall divide the waters from the waters.

7. And the Gods ordered the expanse, so that it divided the waters which were under the expanse from the waters which were above the expanse; and it was so, even as they ordered.

8. And the Gods called the expanse, Heaven. And it came to pass that it was from evening until morning that they called night; and it came to pass that it was from morning until evening that they called day; and this was the second time that they called night and day.

9. And the Gods ordered, saying: Let the waters under the heaven be gathered together unto one place, and let the earth come up dry; and it was so as they ordered;

10. And the Gods pronounced the dry land, earth; and the gathering together of the waters, pronounced they, great waters; and the Gods saw that they were obeyed.

11. And the Gods said: Let us prepare the earth to bring forth grass; the herb yielding seed; the fruit tree yielding fruit, after his kind, whose seed in itself yieldeth its own likeness upon the earth; and it was so, even as they ordered.

12. And the Gods organized the earth to bring forth grass from its own seed, and the herb to bring forth herb from its own seed, yielding seed after his kind; and the earth to bring forth the tree from its own seed, yielding fruit, whose seed could only bring forth the same in itself, after his kind; and the Gods saw that they were obeyed.

13. And it came to pass that they numbered the days; from the evening until the morning they called night; and it came to pass, from the morning until the evening they called day; and it was the third time.

14. And the Gods organized the lights in the expanse of the heaven, and caused them to divide the day from the night; and organized them to be for signs and for seasons, and for days and for years;

15. And organized them to be for lights in the expanse of the heaven to give light upon the earth; and it was so.

16. And the Gods organized the two great lights, the greater light to rule the day, and the lesser light to rule the night; with the lesser light they set the stars also;

17. And the Gods set them in the expanse of the heavens, to give light upon the earth, and to rule over the day and over the night, and to cause to divide the light from the darkness.

18. And the Gods watched those things which they had ordered until they obeyed.

19. And it came to pass that it was from evening until morning that it was night; and it came to pass that it was from morning until evening that it was day; and it was the fourth time.

20. And the Gods said: Let us prepare the waters to bring forth abundantly the moving creatures that have life; and the fowl, that they may fly above the earth in the open expanse of heaven.

21. And the Gods prepared the waters that they might bring forth great whales, and every living creature that moveth, which the waters were to bring forth abundantly after their kind; and every winged fowl after their kind. And the Gods saw that they would be obeyed, and that their plan was good.

22. And the Gods said: We will bless them, and cause them to be fruitful and multiply, and fill the waters in the seas or great waters; and cause the fowl to multiply in the earth.

23. And it came to pass that it was from evening until morning that they called night; and it came to pass that it was from morning until evening that they called day; and it was the fifth time.

24. And the Gods prepared the earth to bring forth the living creature after his kind, cattle and creeping things, and beasts of the earth after their kind; and it was so, as they had said.

25. And the Gods organized the earth to bring forth the beasts after their kind, and cattle after their kind, and every thing that creepeth upon the earth after its kind; and the Gods saw they would obey.

26. And the Gods took counsel among themselves and said: Let us go down and form man in our image, after our likeness; and we will give them dominion over the fish of the sea, and over the fowl of the air, and over the cattle, and over all the earth, and over every creeping thing that creepeth upon the earth.

27. So the Gods went down to organize man in their own image, in the image of the Gods to form they him, male and female to form they them.

28. And the Gods said: We will bless them. And the Gods said: We will cause them to be fruitful and multiply, and replenish the earth, and subdue it, and to have dominion over the fish of the sea, and over the fowl of the air, and over every living thing that moveth upon the earth.

29. And the Gods said: Behold, we will give them every herb bearing seed that shall come upon the face of all the earth, and every tree which shall have fruit upon it; yea the fruit of the tree yielding seed to them we will give it; it shall be for their meat.

30. And to every beast of the earth, and to every fowl of the air, and to every thing that creepeth upon the earth, behold, we will give them life, and also we will give to them every green herb for meat, and all these things shall be thus organized.

31. And the Gods said: We will do everything that we have said, and organize them; and behold, they shall be very obedient. And it came to pass that it was from evening until morning they called night; and it came to pass that it was from morning until evening that they called day; and they numbered the sixth time.

CHAPTER 5

1. And thus we will finish the heavens and the earth, and all the hosts of them.

2. And the Gods said among themselves: On the seventh time we will end our work, which we have counseled; and we will rest on the seventh time from all our work which we have counseled.

3. And the Gods concluded upon the seventh time, because that on the seventh time they would rest from all their works which they (the Gods) counseled among themselves to form; and sanctified it. And thus were their decisions at the time that they counseled among themselves to form the heavens and the earth.

4. And the Gods came down and formed these the generations of the heavens and of the earth,

when they were formed in the day that the Gods formed the earth and the heavens,

5. According to all that which they had said concerning every plant of the field before it was in the earth, and every herb of the field before it grew; for the Gods had not caused it to rain upon the earth when they counseled to do them, and had not formed a man to till the ground.

6. But there went up a mist from the earth, and watered the whole face of the ground.

7. And the Gods formed man from the dust of the ground, and took his spirit, (that is, the man's spirit,) and put it into him; and breathed into his nostrils the breath of life, and man became a living soul.

8. And the Gods planted a garden, eastward in Eden, and there they put the man, whose spirit they had put into the body which they had formed.

9. And out of the ground made the Gods to grow every tree that is pleasant to the sight and good for food; the tree of life, also, in the midst of the garden, and the tree of knowledge of good and evil.

10. There was a river running out of Eden, to water the garden, and from thence it was parted and became into four heads.

11. And the Gods took the man and put him in the Garden of Eden, to dress it and to keep it.

12. And the Gods commanded the man, saying: Of every tree of the garden thou mayest freely eat,

13. But of the tree of knowledge of good and evil, thou shalt not eat of it; for in the time that thou eatest thereof, thou shalt surely die. Now I, Abraham, saw that it was after the Lord's time, which was after the time of Kolob; for as yet the Gods had not appointed unto Adam his reckoning.

14. And the Gods said: Let us make an help-meet for the man, for it is not good that the man should be alone, therefore we will form an help-meet for him.

15. And the Gods caused a deep sleep to fall upon Adam; and he slept, and they took one of his ribs, and closed up the flesh in the stead thereof;

16. And of the rib which the Gods had taken from man, formed they a woman, and brought her unto the man.

17. And Adam said: This was bone of my bones, and flesh of my flesh; now she shall be called Woman, because she was taken out of man;

18. Therefore shall a man leave his father and his mother, and shall cleave unto his wife, and they shall be one flesh.

19. And they were both naked, the man and his wife, and were not ashamed.

20. And out of the ground the Gods formed every beast of the field, and every fowl of the air, and brought them unto Adam to see what he would call them; and whatsoever Adam called every living creature, that should be the name thereof.

21. And Adam gave names to all cattle, to the fowl of the air, to every beast of the field; and for Adam, there was found an help-meet for him.

THE PROPHET JOSEPH SMITH—"BLESSED TO OPEN THE LAST DISPENSATION"

Writings of Joseph Smith

An Extract from a Translation of the Bible

Being the twenty-fourth chapter of Matthew, commencing with the last verse of the twenty-third chapter, King James' Translation.

1. For I say unto you, that ye shall not see me henceforth and know that I am he of whom it is written by the prophets, until ye shall say: Blessed is he who cometh in the name of the Lord, in the clouds of heaven, and all the holy angels with him. Then understood his disciples that he should come again on the earth, after that he was glorified and crowned on the right hand of God.

2. And Jesus went out, and departed from the temple; and his disciples came to him, for to hear him, saying: Master, show us concerning the buildings of the temple, as thou hast said—They shall be thrown down, and left unto you desolate.

3. And Jesus said unto them: See ye not all these things, and do ye not understand them? Verily I say unto you, there shall not be left here, upon this temple, one stone upon another that shall not be thrown down.

4. And Jesus left them, and went upon the Mount of Olives. And as he sat upon the Mount of Olives, the disciples came unto him privately, saying: Tell us when shall these things be which thou hast said concerning the destruction of the temple, and the Jews; and what is the sign of thy coming, and of the end of the world, or the destruction of the wicked, which is the end of the world?

5. And Jesus answered, and said unto them: Take heed that no man deceive you;

6. For many shall come in my name, saying—I am Christ—and shall deceive many;

7. Then shall they deliver you up to be afflicted, and shall kill you, and ye shall be hated of all nations, for my name's sake;

8. And then shall many be offended, and shall betray one another;

9. And many false prophets shall arise, and shall deceive many;

10. And because iniquity shall abound, the love of many shall wax cold;

11. But he that remaineth steadfast and is not overcome, the same shall be saved.

12. When you, therefore, shall see the abomination of desolation, spoken of by Daniel the prophet, concerning the destruction of Jerusalem, then you shall stand in the holy place; whoso readeth let him understand.
13. Then let them who are in Judea flee into the mountains;
14. Let him who is on the housetop flee, and not return to take anything out of his house;
15. Neither let him who is in the field return back to take his clothes;
16. And woe unto them that are with child, and unto them that give suck in those days;
17. Therefore, pray ye the Lord that your flight be not in the winter, neither on the Sabbath day;
18. For then, in those days, shall be great tribulations on the Jews, and upon the inhabitants of Jerusalem, such as was not before sent upon Israel, of God, since the beginning of their kingdom until this time; no, nor ever shall be sent again upon Israel.
19. All things which have befallen them, are only the beginning of the sorrows which shall come upon them.
20. And except those days should be shortened, there should none of their flesh be saved; but for the elect's sake, according to the covenant, those days shall be shortened.
21. Behold, these things I have spoken unto you concerning the Jews; and again, after the tribulation of those days which shall come upon Jerusalem, if any man shall say unto you, Lo, here is Christ, or there, believe him not;
22. For in those days there shall also arise false Christs, and false prophets, and shall show great signs and wonders, insomuch, that, if possible, they shall deceive the very elect, who are the elect according to the covenant.
23. Behold, I speak these things unto you for the elect's sake; and you also shall hear of wars, and rumors of wars; see that ye be not troubled, for all I have told you must come to pass; but the end is not yet.
24. Behold, I have told you before;
25. Wherefore, if they shall say unto you: Behold, he is in the desert; go not forth; Behold, he is in the secret chambers; believe it not;
26. For as the light of the morning cometh out of the east, and shineth even unto the west, and covereth the whole earth, so shall also the coming of the Son of Man be.
27. And now I show unto you a parable. Behold, wheresoever the carcass is, there will the eagles be gathered together; so likewise shall mine elect be gathered from the four quarters of the earth.
28. And they shall hear of wars, and rumors of wars.
29. Behold I speak for mine elect's sake; for nation shall rise against nation, and kingdom against kingdom; there shall be famines, and pestilences, and earthquakes, in divers places.
30. And again, because iniquity shall abound, the love of many shall wax cold; but he that shall not be overcome, the same shall be saved.
31. And again, this Gospel of the Kingdom shall be preached in all the world, for a witness unto all nations, and then shall the end come, or the destruction of the wicked;
32. And again shall the abomination of desolation, spoken of by Daniel the prophet, be fulfilled.
33. And immediately after the tribulation of those days, the sun shall be darkened, and the moon shall not give her light, and the stars shall fall from heaven, and the powers of heaven shall be shaken.
34. Verily, I say unto you, this generation, in which these things shall be shown forth, shall not pass away until all I have told you shall be fulfilled.
35. Although, the days will come, that heaven and earth shall pass away; yet my words shall not pass away, but all shall be fulfilled.
36. And, as I said before, after the tribulation of those days, and the powers of the heavens shall

be shaken; then shall appear the sign of the Son of Man in heaven, and then shall all the tribes of the earth mourn; and they shall see the Son of Man coming in the clouds of heaven, with power and great glory;

37. And whoso treasureth up my word, shall not be deceived, for the Son of Man shall come, and he shall send his angels before him with the great sound of a trumpet, and they shall gather together the remainder of his elect from the four winds, from one end of heaven to the other.

38. Now learn a parable of the fig tree:—when its branches are yet tender, and it begins to put forth leaves, you know that summer is nigh at hand;

39. So likewise, mine elect, when they shall see all these things, they shall know that he is near, even at the doors;

40. But of that day, and hour, no one knoweth; no, not the angels of God in heaven, but my Father only.

41. But as it was in the days of Noah, so it shall be also at the coming of the Son of Man;

42. For it shall be with them, as it was in the days which were before the flood; for until the day that Noah entered into the ark they were eating and drinking, marrying and giving in marriage;

43. And knew not until the flood came, and took them all away; so shall also the coming of the Son of Man be.

44. Then shall be fulfilled that which is written, that in the last days, two shall be in the field, the one shall be taken, and the other left;

45. Two shall be grinding at the mill, the one shall be taken, and the other left;

46. And what I say unto one, I say unto all men; watch, therefore, for you know not at what hour your Lord doth come.

47. But know this, if the good man of the house had known in what watch the thief would come, he would have watched, and would not have suffered his house to have been broken up, but would have been ready.

48. Therefore be ye also ready, for in such an hour as ye think not, the Son of Man cometh.

49. Who, then, is a faithful and wise servant, whom his lord hath made ruler over his household, to give them meat in due season?

50. Blessed is that servant whom his lord, when he cometh, shall find so doing; and verily I say unto you, he shall make him ruler over all his goods.

51. But if that evil servant shall say in his heart: My lord delayeth his coming,

52. And shall begin to smite his fellow-servants, and to eat and drink with the drunken,

53. The lord of that servant shall come in a day when he looketh not for him, and in an hour that he is not aware of,

54. And shall cut him asunder, and shall appoint him his portion with the hypocrites; there shall be weeping and gnashing of teeth.

55. And thus cometh the end of the wicked, according to the prophecy of Moses, saying: They shall be cut off from among the people; but the end of the earth is not yet, but bye and bye.

JOSEPH SMITH STUDYING THE BIBLE

Joseph Smith

Extracts from the History of Joseph Smith

1. Owing to the many reports which have been put in circulation by evil-disposed and designing persons, in relation to the rise and progress of the Church of Jesus Christ of Latter-day Saints, all of which have been designed by the authors thereof to militate against its character as a Church and its progress in the world—I have been induced to write this history, to disabuse the public mind, and put all inquirers after truth in possession of the facts, as they have transpired, in relation both to myself and the Church, so far as I have such facts in my possession.

2. In this history I shall present the various events in relation to this Church, in truth and righteousness, as they have transpired, or as they at present exist, being now the eighth year since the organization of the said Church.

3. I was born in the year of our Lord one thousand eight hundred and five, on the twenty-third day of December, in the town of Sharon, Windsor county, state of Vermont. My father, Joseph Smith, Senior, left the state of Vermont, and moved to Palmyra, Ontario (now Wayne) county, in the state of New York, when I was in my tenth year, or thereabouts. In about four years after my father's arrival in Palmyra, he moved with his family into Manchester in the same county of Ontario.

4. His family consisted of eleven souls, namely—my father, Joseph Smith; my mother, Lucy Smith (whose name, previous to her marriage, was Mack, daughter of Solomon Mack); my brothers, Alvin, (who died November 19th, 1823, in the 26th year of his age,) Hyrum, myself, Samuel Harrison, William, Don Carlos; and my sisters Sophronia, Catherine, and Lucy.

5. Some time in the second year after our removal to Manchester, there was in the place where we lived an unusual excitement on the subject of religion. It commenced with the Methodists, but soon became general among all the sects in that region of country. Indeed, the whole district of country seemed affected by it, and great multitudes united themselves to the

different religious parties, which created no small stir and division amongst the people, some crying, "Lo, here!" and others, "Lo, there!" Some were contending for the Methodist faith, some for the Presbyterian, and some for the Baptist.

6. For notwithstanding the great love which the converts to these different faiths expressed at the time of their conversion, and the great zeal manifested by the respective clergy, who were active in getting up and promoting this extraordinary scene of religious feeling, in order to have everybody converted, as they were pleased to call it, let them join what sect they pleased—yet when the converts began to file off, some to one party and some to another, it was seen that the seemingly good feelings of both the priests and the converts were more pretended than real; for a scene of great confusion and bad feeling ensued—priest contending against priest, and convert against convert; so that all their good feelings one for another, if they ever had any, were entirely lost in a strife of words and a contest about opinions.

7. I was at this time in my fifteenth year. My father's family was proselyted to the Presbyterian faith, and four of them joined that church, namely—my mother Lucy; my brothers Hyrum and Samuel Harrison; and my sister Sophronia.

8. During this time of great excitement, my mind was called up to serious reflection and great uneasiness; but though my feelings were deep and often poignant, still I kept myself aloof from all these parties, though I attended their several meetings as often as occasion would permit. In process of time my mind became somewhat partial to the Methodist sect, and I felt some desire to be united with them; but so great were the confusion and strife among the different denominations, that it was impossible for a person young as I was, and so unacquainted with men and things, to come to any certain conclusion who was right and who was wrong.

9. My mind at times was greatly excited, the cry and tumult were so great and incessant. The Presbyterians were most decided against the Baptists and Methodists, and used all the powers of both reason and sophistry to prove their errors, or, at least, to make the people think they were in error. On the other hand, the Baptists and Methodists in their turn were equally zealous in endeavoring to establish their own tenets and disprove all others.

10. In the midst of this war of words and tumult of opinions, I often said to myself, What is to be done? Who of all these parties are right; or, are they all wrong together? If any one of them be right, which is it, and how shall I know it?

11. While I was laboring under the extreme difficulties caused by the contests of these parties of religionists, I was one day reading the Epistle of James, first chapter and fifth verse, which reads: *If any of you lack wisdom, let him ask of God, that giveth to all men liberally, and upbraideth not; and it shall be given him.*

12. Never did any passage of scripture come with more power to the heart of man than this did at this time to mine. It seemed to enter with great force into every feeling of my heart. I reflected on it again and again, knowing that if any person needed wisdom from God, I did; for how to act I did not know, and unless I could get more wisdom than I then had, I would never know; for the teachers of religion of the different sects understood the same passages of scripture so differently as to destroy all confidence in settling the question by an appeal to the Bible.

13. At length I came to the conclusion that I must either remain in darkness and confusion, or else I must do as James directs, that is, ask of God. I at length came to the determination to "ask of God," concluding that if he gave wisdom to them that lacked wisdom, and would give liberally, and not upbraid, I might venture.

14. So, in accordance with this, my determination to ask of God, I retired to the woods to make the attempt. It was on the morning of a beautiful, clear day, early in the spring of eighteen hundred and twenty. It was the first time in my life that I had made such an attempt, for amidst all my anxieties I had never as yet made the attempt to pray vocally.

15. After I had retired to the place where I had previously designed to go, having looked around me, and finding myself alone, I kneeled down and began to offer up the desires of my heart to God. I had scarcely done so, when immediately I was seized upon by some power which entirely overcame me, and had such an astonishing influence over me as to bind my tongue so that I could not speak. Thick darkness gathered around me, and it seemed to me for a time as if I were doomed to sudden destruction.

16. But, exerting all my powers to call upon God to deliver me out of the power of this enemy which had seized upon me, and at the very moment when I was ready to sink into despair and abandon myself to destruction—not to an imaginary ruin, but to the power of some actual being from the unseen world, who had such marvelous power as I had never before felt in any being—just at this moment of great alarm, I saw a pillar of light exactly over my head, above the brightness of the sun, which descended gradually until it fell upon me.

17. It no sooner appeared than I found myself delivered from the enemy which held me bound. When the light rested upon me I saw two personages, whose brightness and glory defy all description, standing above me in the air. One of them spake unto me, calling me by name and said, pointing to the other—*This is my beloved Son, hear Him!*

18. My object in going to inquire of the Lord was to know which of all the sects was right, that I might know which to join. No sooner, therefore, did I get possession of myself, so as to be able to speak, than I asked the personages who stood above me in the light, which of all the sects was right—and which I should join.

19. I was answered that I must join none of them, for they were all wrong; and the personage who addressed me said that all their creeds were an abomination in his sight; that those professors were all corrupt; that "they draw near to me with their lips, but their hearts are far from me; they teach for doctrines the commandments of men, having a form of godliness, but they deny the power thereof."

20. He again forbade me to join with any of them; and many other things did he say unto me, which I cannot write at this time. When I came to myself again, I found myself lying on my back, looking up into heaven.

21. Some few days after I had this vision, I happened to be in company with one of the Methodist preachers, who was very active in the before mentioned religious excitement; and, conversing with him on the subject of religion, I took occasion to give him an account of the vision which I had had. I was greatly surprised at his behavior; he treated my communication not only lightly, but with great contempt, saying it was all of the devil, that there were no such things as visions or revelations in these days; that all such things had ceased with the apostles, and that there would never be any more of them.

22. I soon found, however, that my telling the story had excited a great deal of prejudice against me among professors of religion, and was the cause of great persecution, which continued to increase; and though I was an obscure boy, only between fourteen and fifteen years of age, and my circumstances in life such as to make a boy of no consequence in the world, yet men of high standing would take notice sufficient to excite the

public mind against me, and create a bitter persecution; and this was common among all the sects—all united to persecute me.

23. It caused me serious reflection then, and often has since, how very strange it was that an obscure boy, of a little over fourteen years of age, and one, too, who was doomed to the necessity of obtaining a scanty maintenance by his daily labor, should be thought a character of sufficient importance to attract the attention of the great ones of the most popular sects of the day, and in a manner to create in them a spirit of the most bitter persecution and reviling. But strange or not, so it was, and it was often the cause of great sorrow to myself.

24. However, it was nevertheless a fact that I had beheld a vision. I have thought since, that I felt much like Paul, when he made his defence before King Agrippa, and related the account of the vision he had when he saw a light, and heard a voice; but still there were but few who believed him; some said he was dishonest, others said he was mad; and he was ridiculed and reviled. But all this did not destroy the reality of his vision. He had seen a vision, he knew he had, and all the persecution under heaven could not make it otherwise; and though they should persecute him unto death, yet he knew, and would know to his latest breath, that he had both seen a light and heard a voice speaking unto him, and all the world could not make him think or believe otherwise.

25. So it was with me. I had actually seen a light, and in the midst of that light I saw two personages, and they did in reality speak to me; and though I was hated and persecuted for saying that I had seen a vision, yet it was true; and while they were persecuting me, reviling me, and speaking all manner of evil against me falsely for so saying, I was led to say in my heart: Why persecute me for telling the truth? I have actually seen a vision, and who am I that I can withstand God, or why does the world think to make me deny what I have actually seen? For I had seen a vision; I knew it, and I knew that God knew it, and I could not deny it, neither dared I do it, at least I knew that by so doing I would offend God, and come under condemnation.

26. I had now got my mind satisfied so far as the sectarian world was concerned; that it was not my duty to join with any of them, but to continue as I was until further directed. I had found the testimony of James to be true, that a man who lacked wisdom might ask of God, and obtain, and not be upbraided.

27. I continued to pursue my common vocations in life until the twenty-first of September, one thousand eight hundred and twenty-three, all the time suffering severe persecution at the hands of all classes of men, both religious and irreligious, because I continued to affirm that I had seen a vision.

28. During the space of time which intervened between the time I had the vision and the year eighteen hundred and twenty-three—having been forbidden to join any of the religious sects of the day, and being of very tender years, and persecuted by those who ought to have been my friends and to have treated me kindly, and if they supposed me to be deluded to have endeavored in a proper and affectionate manner to have reclaimed me,—I was left to all kinds of temptations; and, mingling with all kinds of society, I frequently fell into many foolish errors, and displayed the weakness of youth, and the foibles of human nature; which, I am sorry to say, led me into divers temptations, offensive in the sight of God.

29. In consequence of these things, I often felt condemned for my weakness and imperfections; when, on the evening of the above-mentioned twenty-first of September, after I had retired to

my bed for the night, I betook myself to prayer and supplication to Almighty God for forgiveness of all my sins and follies, and also for a manifestation to me, that I might know of my state and standing before him; for I had full confidence in obtaining a divine manifestation, as I previously had one.

30. While I was thus in the act of calling upon God, I discovered a light appearing in my room, which continued to increase until the room was lighter than at noonday, when immediately a personage appeared at my bedside, standing in the air, for his feet did not touch the floor.

31. He had on a loose robe of most exquisite whiteness. It was a whiteness beyond anything earthly I had ever seen; nor do I believe that any earthly thing could be made to appear so exceedingly white and brilliant. His hands were naked, and his arms also, a little above the wrist; so, also, were his feet naked, as were his legs, a little above the ankles. His head and neck were also bare. I could discover that he had no other clothing on but this robe, as it was open, so that I could see into his bosom.

32. Not only was his robe exceedingly white, but his whole person was glorious beyond description, and his countenance truly like lightning. The room was exceedingly light, but not so very bright as immediately around his person. When I first looked upon him, I was afraid; but the fear soon left me.

33. He called me by name, and said unto me that he was a messenger sent from the presence of God to me, and that his name was Moroni; that God had a work for me to do; and that my name should be had for good and evil among all nations, kindreds, and tongues, or that it should be both good and evil spoken of among all people.

34. He said there was a book deposited, written upon gold plates, giving an account of the former inhabitants of this continent, and the source from whence they sprang. He also said that the fulness of the everlasting Gospel was contained in it, as delivered by the Savior to the ancient inhabitants;

35. Also, that there were two stones in silver bows—and these stones, fastened to a breastplate, constituted what is called the Urim and Thummim—deposited with the plates, and the possession and use of these stones were what constituted "seers" in ancient or former times; and that God had prepared them for the purpose of translating the book.

36. After telling me these things, he commenced quoting the prophecies of the Old Testament. He first quoted part of the third chapter of Malachi, and he quoted also the fourth or last chapter of the same prophecy, though with a little variation from the way it reads in our Bibles. Instead of quoting the first verse as it reads in our books, he quoted it thus:

37. *For behold, the day cometh that shall burn as an oven, and all the proud, yea, and all that do wickedly shall burn as stubble; for they that come shall burn them, saith the Lord of Hosts, that it shall leave them neither root nor branch.*

38. And again, he quoted the fifth verse thus: *Behold, I will reveal unto you the Priesthood, by the hand of Elijah the prophet, before the coming of the great and dreadful day of the Lord.*

39. He also quoted the next verse differently: *And he shall plant in the hearts of the children the promises made to the fathers, and the hearts of the children shall turn to their fathers. If it were not so, the whole earth would be utterly wasted at his coming.*

40. In addition to these, he quoted the eleventh chapter of Isaiah, saying that it was about to be fulfilled. He quoted also the third chapter of Acts, twenty-second and twenty-third verses, precisely as they stand in our New Testament. He

THE SACRED GROVE

So, in accordance with this my determination to ask of God, I retired to the woods to make the attempt. It was on the morning of a beautiful clear day, early in the spring of eighteen hundred and twenty.

JS–H 1:24

said that that Prophet was Christ; but the day had not yet come when they who would not hear his voice should be cut off from among the people, but soon would come.

41. He also quoted the second chapter of Joel, from the twenty-eighth verse to the last. He also said that this was not yet fulfilled, but was soon to be. And he further stated that the fulness of the Gentiles was soon to come in. He quoted many other passages of scripture, and offered many explanations which cannot be mentioned here.

42. Again, he told me, that when I got those plates of which he had spoken—for the time that they should be obtained was not yet fulfilled—I should not show them to any person; neither the breastplate with the Urim and Thummim; only to those to whom I should be commanded to show them; if I did I should be destroyed. While he was conversing with me about the plates, the vision was opened to my mind that I could see the place where the plates were deposited, and that so clearly and distinctly that I knew the place again when I visited it.

43. After this communication, I saw the light in the room begin to gather immediately around the person of him who had been speaking to me, and it continued to do so, until the room was again left dark, except just around him, when instantly I saw, as it were, a conduit open right up into heaven, and he ascended till he entirely disappeared, and the room was left as it had been before this heavenly light had made its appearance.

44. I lay musing on the singularity of the scene, and marveling greatly at what had been told to me by this extraordinary messenger; when, in the midst of my meditation, I suddenly discovered that my room was again beginning to get lighted, and in an instant, as it were, the same heavenly messenger was again by my bedside.

45. He commenced, and again related the very same things which he had done at his first visit, without the least variation; which having done, he informed me of great judgments which were coming upon the earth, with great desolations by famine, sword, and pestilence; and that these grievous judgments would come on the earth in this generation. Having related these things, he again ascended as he had done before.

46. By this time, so deep were the impressions made on my mind, that sleep had fled from my eyes, and I lay overwhelmed in astonishment at what I had both seen and heard. But what was my surprise when again I beheld the same messenger at my bedside, and heard him rehearse or repeat over again to me the same things as before; and added a caution to me, telling me that Satan would try to tempt me, (in consequence of the indigent circumstances of my father's family,) to get the plates for the purpose of getting rich. This he forbade me, saying that I must have no other object in view in getting the plates but to glorify God, and must not be influenced by any other motive than that of building his kingdom; otherwise I could not get them.

47. After this third visit, he again ascended into heaven as before, and I was again left to ponder on the strangeness of what I had just experienced; when almost immediately after the heavenly messenger had ascended from me for the third time, the cock crowed, and I found that day was approaching, so that our interviews must have occupied the whole of that night.

48. I shortly after arose from my bed, and, as usual, went to the necessary labors of the day; but, in attempting to work as at other times, I found my strength so exhausted as to render me entirely unable. My father, who was laboring along with me, discovered something to be wrong with me, and told me to go home. I started with the intention of going to the house; but, in attempting to cross the fence out of the field

where we were, my strength entirely failed me, and I fell helpless on the ground, and for a time was quite unconscious of anything.

49. The first thing that I can recollect was a voice speaking unto me, calling me by name. I looked up, and beheld the same messenger standing over my head, surrounded by light as before. He then again related unto me all that he had related to me the previous night, and commanded me to go to my father and tell him of the vision and commandments which I had received.

50. I obeyed; I returned to my father in the field, and rehearsed the whole matter to him. He replied to me that it was of God, and told me to go and do as commanded by the messenger. I left the field, and went to the place where the messenger had told me the plates were deposited; and owing to the distinctness of the vision which I had had concerning it, I knew the place the instant that I arrived there.

51. Convenient to the village of Manchester, Ontario county, New York, stands a hill of considerable size, and the most elevated of any in the neighborhood. On the west side of this hill, not far from the top, under a stone of considerable size, lay the plates, deposited in a stone box. This stone was thick and rounding in the middle on the upper side, and thinner towards the edges, so that the middle part of it was visible above the ground, but the edge all around was covered with earth.

52. Having removed the earth, I obtained a lever, which I got fixed under the edge of the stone, and with a little exertion raised it up. I looked in, and there indeed did I behold the plates, the Urim and Thummim, and the breastplate, as stated by the messenger. The box in which they lay was formed by laying stones together in some kind of cement. In the bottom of the box were laid two stones crossways of the box, and on these stones lay the plates and the other things with them.

53. I made an attempt to take them out, but was forbidden by the messenger, and was again informed that the time for bringing them forth had not yet arrived, neither would it, until four years from that time; but he told me that I should come to that place precisely in one year from that time, and that he would there meet with me, and that I should continue to do so until the time should come for obtaining the plates.

54. Accordingly, as I had been commanded, I went at the end of each year, and at each time I found the same messenger there, and received instruction and intelligence from him at each of our interviews, respecting what the Lord was going to do, and how and in what manner his kingdom was to be conducted in the last days.

55. As my father's worldly circumstances were very limited, we were under the necessity of laboring with our hands, hiring out by day's work and otherwise, as we could get opportunity. Sometimes we were at home, and sometimes abroad, and by continuous labor, were enabled to get a comfortable maintenance.

56. In the year 1823 my father's family met with a great affliction by the death of my eldest brother, Alvin. In the month of October, 1825, I hired with an old gentleman by the name of Josiah Stoal, who lived in Chenango county, state of New York. He had heard something of a silver mine having been opened by the Spaniards in Harmony, Susquehanna county, state of Pennsylvania; and had, previous to my hiring to him, been digging, in order, if possible, to discover the mine. After I went to live with him, he took me, with the rest of his hands, to dig for the silver mine, at which I continued to work for nearly a month, without success in our undertaking, and finally I prevailed with the old gentleman to cease digging after it. Hence arose the very prevalent story of my having been a money-digger.

57. During the time that I was thus employed, I was put to board with a Mr. Isaac Hale, of that place; it was there I first saw my wife (his daughter), Emma Hale. On the 18th of January, 1827, we were married, while I was yet employed in the service of Mr. Stoal.

58. Owing to my continuing to assert that I had seen a vision, persecution still followed me, and my wife's father's family were very much opposed to our being married. I was, therefore, under the necessity of taking her elsewhere; so we went and were married at the house of Squire Tarbill, in South Bainbridge, Chenango county, New York. Immediately after my marriage, I left Mr. Stoal's, and went to my father's, and farmed with him that season.

59. At length the time arrived for obtaining the plates, the Urim and Thummim, and the breastplate. On the twenty-second day of September, one thousand eight hundred and twenty-seven, having gone as usual at the end of another year to the place where they were deposited, the same heavenly messenger delivered them up to me with this charge: that I should be responsible for them; that if I should let them go carelessly, or through any neglect of mine, I should be cut off; but that if I would use all my endeavors to preserve them, until he, the messenger, should call for them, they should be protected.

60. I soon found out the reason why I had received such strict charges to keep them safe, and why it was that the messenger had said that when I had done what was required at my hand, he would call for them. For no sooner was it known that I had them, than the most strenuous exertions were used to get them from me. Every stratagem that could be invented was resorted to for that purpose. The persecution became more bitter and severe than before, and multitudes were on the alert continually to get them from me if possible. But by the wisdom of God, they remained safe in my hands, until I had accomplished by them what was required at my hand. When, according to arrangements, the messenger called for them, I delivered them up to him; and he has them in his charge until this day, being the second day of May, one thousand eight hundred and thirty-eight.

61. The excitement, however, still continued, and rumor with her thousand tongues was all the time employed in circulating falsehoods about my father's family, and about myself. If I were to relate a thousandth part of them, it would fill up volumes. The persecution, however, became so intolerable that I was under the necessity of leaving Manchester, and going with my wife to Susquehanna county, in the State of Pennsylvania. While preparing to start,—being very poor, and the persecution so heavy upon us that there was no probability that we would ever be otherwise,—in the midst of our afflictions we found a friend in a gentleman by the name of Martin Harris, who came to us and gave me fifty dollars to assist us on our journey. Mr. Harris was a resident of Palmyra township, Wayne county, in the state of New York, and a farmer of respectability.

62. By this timely aid was I enabled to reach the place of my destination in Pennsylvania; and immediately after my arrival there I commenced copying the characters off the plates. I copied a considerable number of them, and by means of the Urim and Thummim I translated some of them, which I did between the time I arrived at the house of my wife's father, in the month of December, and the February following.

63. Sometime in this month of February, the aforementioned Mr. Martin Harris came to our place, got the characters which I had drawn off the plates, and started with them to the city of New York. For what took place relative to him and the characters, I refer to his own account of

the circumstances, as he related them to me after his return, which was as follows:

64. I went to the city of New York, and presented the characters which had been translated, with the translation thereof, to Professor Charles Anthon, a gentleman celebrated for his literary attainments. Professor Anthon stated that the translation was correct, more so than any he had before seen translated from the Egyptian. I then showed him those which were not yet translated, and he said that they were Egyptian, Chaldaic, Assyriac, and Arabic; and he said they were true characters. He gave me a certificate, certifying to the people of Palmyra that they were true characters, and that the translation of such of them as had been translated was also correct. I took the certificate and put it into my pocket, and was just leaving the house, when Mr. Anthon called me back, and asked me how the young man found out that there were gold plates in the place where he found them. I answered that an angel of God had revealed it unto him.

65. He then said to me, "Let me see that certificate." I accordingly took it out of my pocket and gave it to him, when he took it and tore it to pieces, saying that there was no such thing now as ministering of angels, and that if I would bring the plates to him he would translate them. I informed him that part of the plates were sealed, and that I was forbidden to bring them. He replied, "I cannot read a sealed book." I left him and went to Dr. Mitchell, who sanctioned what Professor Anthon had said respecting both the characters and the translation.

66. On the 5th day of April, 1829, Oliver Cowdery came to my house, until which time I had never seen him. He stated to me that having been teaching school in the neighborhood where my father resided, and my father being one of those who sent to the school, he went to board for a season at his house, and while there the family related to him the circumstances of my having received the plates, and accordingly he had come to make inquiries of me.

67. Two days after the arrival of Mr. Cowdery (being the 7th of April) I commenced to translate the Book of Mormon, and he began to write for me.

68. We still continued the work of translation, when, in the ensuing month (May, 1829), we on a certain day went into the woods to pray and inquire of the Lord respecting baptism for the remission of sins, that we found mentioned in the translation of the plates. While we were thus employed, praying and calling upon the Lord, a messenger from heaven descended in a cloud of light, and having laid his hands upon us, he ordained us, saying:

69. *Upon you my fellow servants, in the name of Messiah, I confer the Priesthood of Aaron, which holds the keys of the ministering of angels, and of the gospel of repentance, and of baptism by immersion for the remission of sins; and this shall never be taken again from the earth, until the sons of Levi do offer again an offering unto the Lord in righteousness.*

70. He said this Aaronic Priesthood had not the power of laying on hands for the gift of the Holy Ghost, but that this should be conferred on us hereafter; and he commanded us to go and be baptized, and gave us directions that I should baptize Oliver Cowdery, and that afterwards he should baptize me.

71. Accordingly we went and were baptized. I baptized him first, and afterwards he baptized me—after which I laid my hands upon his head and ordained him to the Aaronic Priesthood, and afterwards he laid his hands on me and ordained me to the same Priesthood—for so we were commanded.*

72. The messenger who visited us on this occasion and conferred this Priesthood upon us, said that his name was John, the same that is called

John the Baptist in the New Testament, and that he acted under the direction of Peter, James, and John, who held the keys of the Priesthood of Melchesidek, which Priesthood, he said, would in due time be conferred on us, and that I should be called the first Elder of the Church, and he (Oliver Cowdery) the second. It was on the fifteenth day of May, 1829, that we were ordained under the hand of this messenger, and baptized.

73. Immediately on our coming up out of the water after we had been baptized, we experienced great and glorious blessings from our Heavenly Father. No sooner had I baptized Oliver Cowdery, than the Holy Ghost fell upon him, and he stood up and prophesied many things which should shortly come to pass. And again, so soon as I had been baptized by him, I also had the spirit of prophecy, when, standing up, I prophesied concerning the rise of this church, and many other things connected with the Church, and this generation of the children of men. We were filled with the Holy Ghost, and rejoiced in the God of our salvation.

74. Our minds being now enlightened, we began to have the scriptures laid open to our understandings, and the true meaning and intention of their more mysterious passages revealed unto us in a manner which we never could attain to previously, nor ever before had thought of. In the meantime we were forced to keep secret the circumstances of having received the Priesthood and our having been baptized, owing to a spirit of persecution which had already manifested itself in the neighborhood.

75. We had been threatened with being mobbed, from time to time, and this, too, by professors of religion. And their intentions of mobbing us were only counteracted by the influence of my wife's father's family (under Divine providence), who had become very friendly to me, and who were opposed to mobs, and were willing that I should be allowed to continue the work of translation without interruption; and therefore offered and promised us protection from all unlawful proceedings, as far as in them lay.

CHAPTER FOOTNOTE

* Oliver Cowdery describes these events thus: "These were days never to be forgotten—to sit under the sound of a voice dictated by the inspiration of heaven, awakened the utmost gratitude of this bosom! Day after day I continued, uninterrupted, to write from his mouth, as he translated with the Urim and Thummim, or, as the Nephites would have said, 'Interpreters,' the history or record called 'The Book of Mormon.'

"To notice, in even few words, the interesting account given by Mormon and his faithful son Moroni, of a people once beloved and favored of heaven, would supersede my present design; I shall therefore defer this to a future period, and, as I said in the introduction, pass more directly to some few incidents immediately connected with the rise of this Church, which may be entertaining to some thousands who have stepped forward amid the frowns of bigots and the calumny of hypocrites, and embraced the Gospel of Christ.

"No men, in their sober senses, could translate and write the directions given to the Nephites from the mouth of the Savior, of the precise manner in which men should build up His Church, and especially when corruption had spread an uncertainty over all forms and systems practiced among men, without desiring a privilege of showing the willingness of the heart by being buried in the liquid grave, to answer a 'good conscience by the resurrection of Jesus Christ.'

"After writing the account given of the Savior's ministry to the remnant of the seed of Jacob, upon this continent, it was easy to be seen, as the prophet said would be, that darkness covered the earth and gross darkness the minds of the people. On reflecting further it was easy to be seen that amid the great strife and noise concerning religion, none had authority from God to administer the ordinances of the Gospel. For the question might be asked, have men authority to administer in the name of Christ, who deny revelations, when His testimony is no less than the spirit of prophecy, and His religion based, built, and sustained by immediate revelations, in all ages of the world when He has had a people on earth? If these facts were buried, and carefully concealed by men whose craft would have been in danger if once permitted to shine in the faces of men, they were no longer to us; and we only waited for the commandment to be given 'Arise and be baptized.'

"This was not long desired before it was realized. The Lord, who is rich in mercy, and ever willing to answer the consistent prayer of the humble, after we had called upon Him in a fervent manner, aside from the abodes of men, condescended to manifest to us His will. On a sudden, as from the midst of eternity, the voice of the Redeemer spake peace to us. While the vail was parted and the angel of God came down clothed with glory, and delivered the anxiously looked for message, and the keys of the Gospel of repentance. What joy! what wonder! what amazement! While the world was racked and distracted—while millions were groping as the blind for the wall, and while all men were resting upon uncertainty, as a general mass, our eyes beheld, our ears heard, as in the 'blaze of day;' yes, more—above the glitter of the May sunbeam, which then shed its brilliancy over the face of nature! Then his voice, though mild, pierced to the center, and his words, 'I am thy fellow-servant,' dispelled every fear. We listened, we gazed, we admired! 'Twas the voice of an angel, from glory, 'twas a message from the Most High! And as we heard we rejoiced, while His love enkindled upon our souls, and we were wrapped in the vision of the Almighty! Where was room for doubt? Nowhere; uncertainty had fled, doubt had sunk no more to rise, while fiction and deception had fled forever!

"But, dear brother, think, further think for a moment, what joy filled our hearts, and with what surprise we must have bowed, (for who would not have bowed the knee for such a blessing?) when we received under his hand the Holy Priesthood as he said, 'Upon you my fellow-servants, in the name of Messiah, I confer this Priesthood and this authority, which shall remain upon earth, that the sons of Levi may yet offer an offering unto the Lord in righteousness!'

"I shall not attempt to paint to you the feelings of this heart, nor the majestic beauty and glory which surrounded us on this occasion; but you will believe me when I say, that earth, nor men, with the eloquence of time, cannot begin to clothe language in as interesting and sublime a manner as this holy personage. No; nor has this earth power to give the joy, to bestow the peace, or comprehend the wisdom which was contained in each sentence as they were delivered by the power of the Holy Spirit! Man may deceive his fellow-men, deception may follow deception, and the children of the wicked one may have power to seduce the foolish and untaught, till naught but fiction feeds the many, and the fruit of falsehood carries in its current the giddy to the grave; but one touch with the finger of his love, yes, one ray of glory from the upper world, or one word from the mouth of the Savior, from the bosom of eternity, strikes it all into insignificance, and blots it forever from the mind. The assurance that we were in the presence of an angel, the certainty that we heard the voice of Jesus, and the truth unsullied as it flowed from a pure personage, dictated by the will of God, is to me past description, and I shall ever look upon this expression of the Savior's goodness with wonder and thanksgiving while I am permitted to tarry; and in those mansions where perfection dwells and sin never comes, I hope to adore in that day which shall never cease."—*Times and Seasons*.

The Articles of Faith
Of the Church of Jesus Christ of Latter-day Saints

1. We believe in God, the Eternal Father, and in His Son, Jesus Christ, and in the Holy Ghost.
2. We believe that men will be punished for their own sins, and not for Adam's transgression.
3. We believe that through the atonement of Christ, all mankind may be saved, by obedience to the laws and ordinances of the Gospel.
4. We believe that the first principles and ordinances of the Gospel are:— (1) Faith in the Lord Jesus Christ; (2) Repentance; (3) Baptism by immersion for the remission of sins; (4) Laying on of Hands for the Gift of the Holy Ghost.
5. We believe that a man must be called of God, by prophecy, and by the laying on of hands, by those who are in authority, to preach the Gospel and administer in the ordinances thereof.
6. We believe in the same organization that existed in the Primitive Church, viz., apostles, prophets, pastors, teachers, evangelists, etc.
7. We believe in the gift of tongues, prophecy, revelation, visions, healing, interpretation of tongues, etc.
8. We believe the Bible to be the word of God, as far as it is translated correctly; we also believe the Book of Mormon to be the word of God.
9. We believe all that God has revealed, all that He does now reveal, and we believe that He will yet reveal many great and important things pertaining to the Kingdom of God.
10. We believe in the literal gathering of Israel and in the restoration of the Ten Tribes; that Zion will be built upon this [the American] continent; that Christ will reign personally upon the earth; and, that the earth will be renewed and receive its paradisiacal glory.
11. We claim the privilege of worshiping Almighty God according to the dictates of our own conscience, and allow all men the same privilege, let them worship how, where, or what they may.
12. We believe in being subject to kings, presidents, rulers, and magistrates, in obeying, honoring, and sustaining the law.
13. We believe in being honest, true, chaste, benevolent, virtuous, and in doing good to *all men*; indeed, we may say that we follow the admonition of Paul, We believe all things, we hope all things, we have endured many things, and hope to be able to endure all things. If there is anything virtuous, lovely, or of good report or praiseworthy, we seek after these things.

—Joseph Smith.

People in the Doctrine and Covenants

Ashley, Major Noble
Born: 3 March 1798
Section: 75

Babbitt, Almon Whiting
Born: 1 October 1812
Died: 7 September 1856
Section: 124

Baker, Jesse
Born: 23 January 1778
Died: 1 November 1846
Section: 124

Baldwin, Wheeler
Born: 7 March 1793
Died: 11 May 1887
Section: 52

Basset, Herman A.
Born: 1814
Died: 1876
Section: 52

Bennett, John Cook
Born: 4 August 1804
Died: 5 August 1867
Section: 124

Benson, Ezra T.
Born: 22 February 1811
Died: 3 September 1869
Section: 136

Bent, Samuel
Born: 19 July 1778
Died: 16 August 1846
Section: 124

Billings, Titus
Born: 24 or 25 March 1793
Died: 6 February 1866
Section: 63

Boggs, Lilburn W.
Born: 14 December 1792
Died: 19 March 1861
Section: 124

Booth, Ezra
Born: 1792
Sections: 52, 64, 71

Boynton, John Farnham
Born: 20 September 1811
Died: 20 October 1890
Section: Testimony of the Twelve Apostles

BRUNSON, SEYMOUR
Born: 18 September 1799
Died: 10 August 1840
Sections: 75, 124

BURNETT, STEPHEN
Born: 1814
Sections: 75, 80

BURROUGHS, PHILIP
Born: 1795
Section: 30

BUTTERFIELD, JOSIAH
Born: 13 March 1795
Died: 3 March 1871
Section: 124

CAHOON, REYNOLDS
Born: 30 April 1790
Died: 29 April 1861
Sections: 52, 61, 75, 94

CARTER, GIDEON HAYDEN (HADEN)
Born: 1798
Died: 25 October 1838
Section: 75

CARTER, JARED
Born: 14 June 1801
Died: July 1855
Sections: 52, 79, 94, 102

CARTER, JOHN SIMS
Born: 1796
Died: 26 June 1834
Section: 102

CARTER, SIMEON
Born: 7 June 1794
Died: 3 February 1869
Sections: 52, 75

CARTER, WILLIAM
Section: 52

COE, JOSEPH
Born: 12 November 1784
Died: 17 October 1854
Sections: 55, 102

COLTRIN, ZEBEDEE
Born: 7 September 1804
Died: 2 July 1887
Section: 52

COPLEY, LEMAN
Born: 1781
Died: December 1862
Sections: 49, 54

CORRILL, JOHN
Born: 17 September 1794
Sections: 50, 52

COVILL, JAMES
Sections: 39, 40

COWDERY, OLIVER
Born: 3 October 1806
Died: 3 March 1850
Sections: 6–9, 13, 17–18, 20, 21, 10, 12, 23–24, 26, 28, 30, 32, 55, 57, 58, 61, 63, 67, 68, 70, 82, 102, 104, 110, 111, 124

COWDERY, WARREN A.
Born: 5 or 17 October 1788
Died: 23 February 1851
Section: 106

CUTLER, ALPHEUS
Born: 29 February 1784
Died: 10 August 1864
Section: 124

DAVIES, AMOS
Born: 20 September 1813
Died: 22 March 1872
Section: 124

DODDS, ASA
Born: 1793
Section: 75

DORT, DAVID D.
Born: 6 January 1793
Died: 10 March 1841
Section: 124

EAMES, RUGGLES
Section: 75

FOSTER, JAMES
Born: 1 April 1775
Died: 21 December 1841
Section: 124

FOSTER, ROBERT D.
Born: 14 March 1811
Section: 124

FULLER, EDSON
Born: 1809
Section: 52

FULLMER, DAVID
Born: 7 July 1803
Died: 21 October 1879
Section: 124

GALLAND, ISAAC
Born: 15 May 1791
Died: 27 September 1858
Section: 124

GAUSE, JESSE
Born: 1784 or 1785
Section: 81

GILBERT, ALGERNON SIDNEY
Born: 28 December 1789
Died: 29 June 1834
Sections: 53, 57, 61, 64, 82, 90

GOULD, JOHN
Born: 11 May 1808
Died: 9 May 1851
Section: 100

Granger, Oliver
Born: 7 February 1794
Died: 25 August 1841
Section: 117

Griffin, Selah J.
Born: 17 March 1799
Sections: 52, 56

Grover, Thomas
Born: 22 July 1807
Died: 20 February 1886
Section: 124

Hancock, Levi Ward
Born: 7 April 1803
Died: 10 June 1882
Sections: 52, 124

Hancock, Solomon
Born: 5 or 14 August 1793
Died: 2 December 1847
Section: 52

Harris, Emer
Born: 29 May 1781
Died: 28 November 1869
Section: 75

Harris, George Washington
Born: 1 April 1780
Died: 1857
Section: 124

Harris, Martin
Born: 18 May 1783
Died: 10 July 1875
Sections: 3, 5, 10, 17, 19, 52, 58, 70, 82, 102, 104

Haws, Peter
Born: 17 February 1795
Died: 1862
Section: 124

Herriman, Henry
Born: 9 June 1804
Died: 17 May 1891
Section: 124

Hicks, John A.
Born: 1810
Section: 124

Higbee, Elias
Born: 23 October 1795
Died: 8 June 1843
Section: 113

Humphrey, Solomon
Born: 23 September 1775
Died: September 1834
Section: 52

Huntington Sr., William Sr
Born: 28 March 1784
Died: 19 August 1846
Section: 124

HYDE, ORSON
Born: 8 January 1805
Died: 28 November 1878
Sections: Testimony of the Twelve Apostles, 68, 75, 100, 102, 103, 124

JAQUES, VIENNA
Born: 10 June 1787
Died: 7 February 1884
Section: 90

JAMES, GEORGE FITCH
Born: 1797
Died: November 1864
Section: 52

JOHNSON, AARON
Born: 22 June 1806
Died: 10 May 1877
Section: 124

JOHNSON, JOHN
Born: 11 April 1778
Died: 30 July 1843
Sections: 102, 104

JOHNSON, LUKE S.
Born: 3 November 1807
Died: 9 December 1861
Sections: 68, 75, 102

JOHNSON, LYMAN EUGENE
Born: 24 October 1811
Died: 20 December 1856
Sections: Testimony of the Twelve Apostles, 68, 75

KIMBALL, HEBER CHASE
Born: 13 June 1801
Died: 22 June 1868
Sections: Testimony of the Twelve Apostles, 124

KIMBALL, SPENCER WOOLLEY
Born: 28 March 1895
Died: 5 November 1985
About Official Declaration—2

KNIGHT SR., JOSEPH
Born: 3 November 1772
Died: 2 February 1847
Section: 12, 23

KNIGHT, NEWEL
Born: 13 September 1800
Died: 11 January 1847
Sections: 52, 54, 56, 72, 124

KNIGHT, VINSON
Born: 14 March 1804
Died: 31 July 1842
Sections: 124, 141

LAW, WILLIAM
Born: 8 September 1809
Died: 12 January 1892
Section: 124

LEE, ANN
Born: 29 February 1736
Died: 8 September 1784
Section: 49

LYMAN, AMASA MASON
Born: 30 March 1813
Died: 4 February 1877
Sections: 124, 136

MARKS, WILLIAM
Born: 15 November 1792
Died: 22 May 1872
Sections: 117, 124

MARSH, THOMAS BALDWIN
Born: 1 November 1799
Died: January 1866
Sections: Testimony of the Twelve Apostles, 31, 52, 56, 75, 112, 118

McLELLIN, WILLIAM E.
Born: 18 January 1806
Died: 24 April 1883
Sections: Testimony of the Twelve Apostles, 66, 68, 75, 90

MILES, DANIEL SANBORN
Born: 23 July 1772
Died: 12 October 1845
Section: 124

MILLER, GEORGE
Born: 27 November 1794
Died: 1856
Section: 124

MORLEY, ISAAC
Born: 11 March 1786
Died: 24 June 1865
Section: 52, 64

MURDOCK, JOHN
Born: 15 July 1792
Died: 23 December 1871
Section: 52, 99

PACKARD, NOAH
Born: 7 May 1796
Died: 7 or 17 February 1859
Section: 124

PAGE, HIRAM
Born: 1800
Died: 12 August 1852
Section: 28

PAGE, JOHN EDWARD
Born: 25 February 1799
Died: 14 October 1867
Section: 118, 124

PARTRIDGE, EDWARD
Born: 27 August 1793
Died: 27 May 1840
Sections: 36, 41, 42, 50, 51, 52, 57, 58, 60, 64, 82, 115, 124

PATTEN, DAVID W.
Born: 14 November 1799
Died: 25 October 1838
Sections: Testimony of the Twelve Apostles, 14, 124, 130

PETERSON, ZIBA
Died: 1849
Sections: 32, 58

PHELPS, WILLIAM WINES
 Born: 17 February 1792
 Died: 6 March 1872
 Sections: 55, 57, 58, 61, 67, 70, 85

PRATT, ORSON
 Born: 19 September 1811
 Died: 3 October 1881
 Sections: Testimony of the Twelve Apostles, 34, 52, 75, 124, 136

PRATT, PARLEY P.
 Born: 12 April 1807
 Died: 13 May 1857
 Sections: Testimony of the Twelve Apostles, 32, 49, 50, 52, 97, 103, 124

PULSIPHER, ZERA
 Born: 24 June 1789
 Died: 1 January 1872
 Section: 124

RICH, CHARLES C.
 Born: 21 August 1809
 Died: 17 November 1883
 Section: 124

RICHARDS, WILLIARD
 Born: 24 June 1804
 Died: 11 March 1854
 Sections: 118, 124, 135

RIGDON, SIDNEY
 Born: 19 February 1793
 Died: 14 July 1876
 Sections: 35, 36, 37, 40, 41, 44, 49, 52, 58, 61, 63, 70, 71, 73, 76, 90, 93, 100, 103, 111, 115, 124

RIGGS, BURR
Born: 17 April 1811
Died: 8 June 1860
Section: 75

ROLFE, SAMUEL JONES
Born: 26 August 1794 or 1796
Died: July 1867
Section: 124

ROUNDY, SHADRACH
Born: 1 January 1789
Died: 4 July 1872
Section: 124

RYDER, SYMONDS
Born: 20 November 1792
Died: 1 August 1970
Section: 52

SCOTT, JACOB
Section: 52

SHERMAN, LYMAN ROYAL
Born: 22 May 1804
Died: 27 January 1839
Section: 108

SHERWOOD, HENRY GARLIE
Born: 20 April 1785
Died: 24 November 1862 or 1867
Sections: 24, 132

SMITH, ALVIN
Born: 11 February 1798 or 1799
Died: 19 November 1823
Section: 137

SMITH, DON CARLOS
Born: 25 March 1816
Died: 7 August 1841
Section: 124

SMITH, EDEN
Born: 1806
Died: 7 December 1851
Sections: 75, 80

SMITH, EMMA
Born: 10 July 1804
Died: 30 April 1879
Sections: 25, 132

SMITH, GEORGE A.
Born: 26 June 1817
Died: 1 September 1875
Sections: 124, 136

SMITH, HYRUM
Born: 9 February 1800
Died: 27 June 1844
Sections: 11, 23, 52, 75, 94, 111, 115, 124, 135, 138

SMITH, JOHN
Born: 16 July 1781
Died: 23 May 1854
Section: 102

SMITH JR., JOSEPH
Born: 23 December 1805
Died: 27 June 1844

SMITH SR., JOSEPH
Born: 12 July 1771
Died: 14 September 1840
Sections: 4, 23, 90, 102, 124

SMITH, JOSEPH F.
Born: 13 November 1838
Died: 19 November 1918
Section: 138

SMITH, SAMUEL HARRISON
Born: 13 March 1808
Died: 30 July 1844
Sections: 23, 52, 61, 66, 75, 102, 124

SMITH, SYLVESTER
Born: 1805
Sections: 75, 102

SMITH, WILLIAM
Born: 13 March 1811
Died: 13 November 1893
Section: 124

SNIDER, JOHN
Born: 11 February 1800
Died: 18 December 1875
Section: 124

SNOW, ERASTUS
Born: 9 November 1818
Died: 28 May 1888
Section: 136

STANTON, DANIEL
Born: 28 May 1795
Died: 26 October 1872
Section: 75

SWEET, NORTHROP
Born: 1802
Section: 33

TAYLOR, JOHN
Born: 1 November 1808
Died: 25 July 1887
Sections: 118, 124, 135, 138

THAYRE, EZRA
Born: 14 October 1791
Sections: 33, 52, 54, 56, 75

THOMPSON, ROBERT BLASHEL
Born: 1 October 1811
Died: 27 August 1841
Section: 124

WAKEFIELD, JOSEPH H.
Born: About 1792
Sections: 50, 52

WELTON, MICAH BALDWIN
Born: 13 August 1792
Died: 9 August 1861
Sections: 75

WHITLOCK, HARVEY G.
Born: 1809
Section: 52

WHITMER, DAVID
Born: 7 January 1805
Died: 25 January 1888
Sections: 14, 17–18, 30, 52

WHITMER, JOHN
Born: 27 August 1802
Died: 11 July 1878
Sections: 15, 26, 30, 47, 69, 70

WHITMER JR., PETER
Born: 27 September 1809
Died: 22 September 1836
Sections: 16, 30

WHITMER SR., PETER
Born: 14 April 1773
Died: 12 August 1854
Sections: 14, 21, 34, 128

WHITNEY, NEWEL K.
Born: 5 February 1795
Died: 23 September 1850
Sections: 63, 64, 72, 84, 93, 96, 104, 117

WIGHT, LYMAN
Born: 9 May 1796
Died: 31 March 1858
Sections: 52, 103, 124

WILLIAMS, FREDERICK G.
Born: 28 October 1787
Died: 10 or 25 October 1842
Sections: 64, 81, 90, 92, 93, 102, 104

WILLIAMS, SAMUEL
Born: 22 March 1789
Died: 10 November 1855
Section: 124

WILSON, CALVES
Section: 75

WILSON, LEWIS DUNBAR
Born: 2 June 1805
Died: 11 March 1856
Sections 124

WOODRUFF, WILFORD
Born: 1 March 1807
Died: 2 September 1898
Sections: 118, 124, 136, 138, Official Declaration—1

YOUNG, BRIGHAM
Born: 1 June 1801
Died: 29 August 1877
Sections: Testimony of the Twelve Apostles, 124, 126, 136, 138

YOUNG, JOSEPH
Born: 7 April 1797
Died: 16 July 1881
Section: 124

A Concordance to the Doctrine and Covenants

By ELDER JOHN A. WIDTSOE.

Salt Lake City, Utah. Published by the Deseret Sunday School Union. 1906.

PREFACE.

This concordance was constructed during my spare hours in the years 1896–1898. It was revised and slightly extended in 1904; again revised, and cut down in size in 1905.

The necessity for such a work was first impressed upon me by an exhaustive study of the Book of Doctrine and Covenants carried on for several years by an Elder's Quorum of which I was a member. Since then, the Sunday Schools and the Young Ladies' Mutual Improvement Associations have published outlines for the study of the Book; and there seems to be a general interest among the people in the marvelous Book of Latter-day Revelations. There is therefore a greater need than ever before for a suitable concordance to the Book. This concordance has been constructed in the hope that it may aid in making God's latter-day word more accessible, better known and more thoroughly appreciated among the members of the Church.

Concordance making is not a work for vacation times. Yet the wearisome routine, which can not be avoided in such labors, has been more than compensated for, by the glorious visions of revealed truth that have sprung from every page of the Book. Thus, whatever reward is due for the work represented by this concordance I have already received.

I render herewith my thanks to my mother Anna C. Widtsoe and to my brother Osborne Widtsoe, for much valuable help in the preparation of this concordance.

The Book of Doctrine and Covenants is a mighty evidence of the divine inspiration of the Prophet Joseph Smith. The study of this holy Book has greatly strengthened my love for the Gospel. My mother first taught me the Gospel; by her guiding care it has become the abiding joy of my life. In grateful acknowledgement of her teachings, I dedicate the labors and love represented by this concordance to my Mother. Logan, Utah, Jan. 31st, 1905.

WHAT THE CONCORDANCE IS.

In the construction of this concordance the attempt has been made, (1) to group every complete idea with every other similar idea found in the Book of Doctrine and Covenants, (2) to classify the references under such keywords that quotations from the Book can be located if some leading word is remembered, (3) to enable the student to find easily all that the Book has to say on any subject, and (4) to compress the work into a volume of a size suitable for the workers at home, and the missionaries abroad. This concordance is not, therefore, a catalogue of all the **words** of the Book: it is rather a catalogue of the **ideas** that the Book contains.

The governing principles of brevity and conciseness have led to some omissions (1) a few expressions that occur very frequently, as forms of introduction or ending, have been referred to a few times only, (2) occasional statements of evident meaning only to the people to whom they were given, have not been indexed, (3) the keywords have been confined very largely to nouns and verbs; other parts of speech have been used only in cases where they appeared to possess distinctive value in identifying quotations, (4) only the leading nouns and verbs have been used as keywords, (5) statements that would probably seldom if ever be referred to have not been indexed.

In some cases, also, ideas have been classified under keywords not found in the Book, but of common occurrence today.

Cross references have been added to aid those who are not accustomed to the use of indexes.

HOW TO USE THE CONCORDANCE.

A concordance does not take the place of the Book to which it is an index. No quotation should be taken as it stands in the concordance. Every reference should be verified and read with the context. The references are given by section and verse. The given verse usually refers to the exact place where the word or sentence occurs. In many cases, however, the idea in question continues through several verses, and the verse indicated refers in a general way to the place where it may be found. The verses just preceding and succeeding any verse to which the concordance refers, should always be read to make sure that all and the full meaning has been gained. Moreover, it very seldom happens that the reference in the concordance contains the complete idea as found in the Book.

To find a quotation which is remembered more or less distinctly, try to recall some distinctive word in the quotation. Look over all the references under that word. If the quotation is not found, try another word. If the quotation cannot be found by this method consider the general subject with which it deals, and examine the reference under this subject. By this method the quotation will finally be found, unless, indeed, it is one of the few excluded from the concordance.

Suppose for an illustration that it is desired to find the statement that "the rebellious are not of the blood of Ephraim." This statement deals primarily with the rebellious, and under the heading "Rebellious," the statement is ascribed to section 64:36. The important fact concerning the rebellious is that they are not of Ephraim, and under that heading, "Ephraim," the reference is also found. The word "blood" in this quotation is only incidental in the meaning of the expression, and, therefore, section 64:36 will not be found classified under the heading "Blood." Take as another illustration the command, "Let every man esteem his brother as himself." The essential idea there is that our brother should be esteemed, and under "Brother," it is found that the passage occurs in Section 32:24. Under "Esteem," also, the reference occurs. "Man" in this quotation is general in sense, and the reference is not found under that heading.

To find what the Book has to say concerning a given subject look up that subject, and its references. Then, look up all the cross references in the same manner. Thus, all the main references to the subject and related subjects, will be found. The constant use of cross references is important in studying a book like the Doctrine and Covenants, which frequently refers to the same subject under various names.

For instance, to learn thoroughly what the Book has to say about sin it is necessary to examine the references under "Sin," and also those under Abomination, Break, Evil, Fall, Guilty, Offender, Sinner, Son of Perdition, Rebellious, Temptation, Transgression, Trespass, and perhaps others that will occur to the student.

AARON See also Gift of Aaron, Priesthood Aaronic,
- 8   6–9   Gift of Aaron
- 27   8   Ordained even as Aaron
- 28   3   Obedient like unto Aaron
- 68   16   Literal descendants of Aaron have legal right
-       19   High Priest may be bishop if no son of Aaron
-       20   Literal descendant of Aaron must be called
-       21   Literal descendant may claim anointing, if
-       21   Priesthood of Aaron descends from father to
- 84   18   Lord confirmed priesthood on Aaron and seed
-       27   Lesser priesthood with Israel, through Aaron
-       30   Lesser priesthood confirmed upon Aaron and
-       31   Sons of Aaron to offer sacrifice in House of
-       32   Sons of Moses and Aaron filled with glory,
-       34   Who receive priesthood sons of Aaron
- 88   8   Hold gift of Aaron in your hands
- 107   13   Priesthood conferred on Aaron and sons for-
-       16   Legal right belongs to descendant of Aaron
-       69   Bishop chosen from High Priesthood unless
-       76   Literal descendant of Aaron may act without
-       76   Literal descendant of Aaron right to pre-
- 132   59   Aaron called by the Father

AARONIC See also Aaron
- 13   hd   John the Baptist conferred Aaronic Priest-
- 107   1   Melchizedek and Aaronic including Levitical

ABEL
- 84   16   Abel received priesthood from Adam

ABOMINATION
- 3   18   Destroyed because of abominations
- 10   21   Hearts full of abominations
- 29   21   Abominations shall not reign
- 50   4   Seen abominations in church
- 84   117   Set forth desolation of abomination
- 88   85   Desolation of abomination awaits wicked
-       94   Fate of church, mother of abomination
- 97   24   Lord's indignation against abominations

ABOVE
- 132   20   Above because all things subject

ABRAHAM See also Jew Israel
- 27   10   With Abraham your father
- 84   13   Esaias blessed by Abraham
-       14   Abraham received priesthood from Melchis-
-       34   Who receive priesthood seed of Abraham
- 98   32   Law given to Abraham
- 101   4   Chastened as Abraham
-       4   Abraham to offer up only son
- 103   17   Ye are of Israel and Abraham
- 109   64   Land given to Abraham
- 110   12   Elias commits dispensation of gospel of
- 124   19   Joseph Smith Sen. with Abraham at right
-       58   As I said to Abraham
- 132   29   Abraham received all by revelation and com-
-       29   Abraham hath entered his exaltation
-       30   Abraham and his seed to continue
-       31   Promise yours who are of Abraham
-       32   Do the works of Abraham
-       34   Sarah gave Abraham Hagar to wife
-       35   Abraham not under condemnation for Hagar
-       36   Abraham commanded to offer up Isaac
-       37   Abraham received concubines for righteous-
-       49   Throne with Abraham your father
-       65   Sarah administered to Abraham with Hagar
- 133   55   Abraham in presence of Lamb
- 136   21   Lord, God of our fathers, Abraham, Isaac and
-       37   From Adam to Abraham
-       37   From Abraham to Moses

ABUNDANCE
- 49   19   That man might have abundance
- 70   13   Abundance through manifestation of Spirit
- 117   7   Make solitary places bring abundance
- 104   18   Who imparts not to poor of abundance, in

ABUSE
- 123   1   Gather facts of abuse of the people

ACCOMPLISH
- 45   72   Not know works until accomplished
- 105   37   Who follow counsel shall accomplish all

ACCORD
- 128   12   That one principle might accord with another

ACCOUNT
- 10   38   Account engraven
-       39   More particular account of plates of Nephi
- 50   34   Who receiveth of God let him account
- 72   3   Steward render account in time and eternity

ACCOUNTABLE
- 101   78   Every man accountable for his own sins
- 134   1   Men accountable in relation to Governments
- 104   13   Every man accountable as steward over

ACCOUNTABILITY
- 18   42   Children to be baptized at years of accounta-
- 20   71   Members must have years of accountability

ACCUSED
- 102   15   Accused has right to one half of the Council
-       18   Accuser and accused allowed to speak

ACKNOWLEDGE
- 5   28   Except acknowledge wrong will not grant
- 81   3   God acknowledges Joseph Smith
- 102   9   President of Church acknowledged by church

ACQUAINTANCE
- 111   3   Expedient to form acquaintance with men

ACT
- 1   3   Secret act of rebellious revealed
- 68   8   Act in authority given
- 95   4   Bring to pass my strange act
- 88   108   Reveal secret acts in first thousand years
-       109   Reveal secret acts in second thousand years
- 101   78   Act in doctrine and principle pertaining to
-       95   Bring to pass my strange act

ADAM
- 27   11   Michael or Adam, etc.
- 29   34   Adam, father, created by God

ADAM continued

29	35	Adam received no temporal commandments
	35	Adam an agent unto himself
	36	Adam tempted of devil
	40	Adam became subject to devil
	40	Devil tempted Adam
	40	Adam transgressed commandment
20	42	The Gospel promised Adam and his seed
84	16	Abel received priesthood from Adam
	16	Adam was the first man
107	42	Seth ordained by Adam
	42	Adam ordained Enos
	43	Seth the express likeness of Adam
	46	Adam ordained Mahalaleel
	45	Cainan met Adam on way to Shedolamak
	47	Adam ordained Jared
	48	Adam ordained Enoch
	50	Adam ordained Methuselah
	55	Lord administered comfort to Adam
	55	Adam to be a prince of nations
	56	Adam prophesies of his posterity
	41	Order instituted in days of Adam
	53	Last blessing of Adam upon his posterity at
	54	Lord appeared to Adam and his posterity at
	54	Adam's posterity blessed him
	54	Adam Michael, Prince, Archangel
	56	Adam predicted what should befall his pos-
116	1	Adam-ondi-Ahman, where Adam visit his
117	8	Olaha Shinehah where Adam dwelt
128	18	Mysteries from days of Adam revealed now
	21	Michael or Adam
136	37	From Adam to Abraham

ADAM-ONDI-AHMAN

78	15	Who hath established Adam-ondi-Ahman
107	53	Last blessing of Adam upon his posterity at
	54	Lord appeared to Adam and his posterity at
116	1	The place located same: where Adam shall
117	8	Room on mountains of Adam-ondi-Ahman
	11	Come to Adam-ondi-Ahman and be bishop

ADD

11	22	Study all, and all things shall be added
	23	All things shall be added
106	3	Seek, all necessary added

ADDITION

5	11	Addition to your testimony

ADMINISTRATION

20	73	Administration of baptism
46	15	Given to some to know differences of ad-

ADMONISH

6	19	Admonish him in his faults

ADULTERER

42	24	Adulterer to be cast out
	25	Adulterer if repentant, forgiven
	26	Adulterer, second time, not forgiven
	76	How received back
	80–81	Adulterer dealt with according to law of
63	15	Warning to adulterers
76	103	Adulterers receive telestial glory

ADULTERY

42	24	Shalt not commit adultery
	75	Adulterers to be cast out
	80	Adultery tried before two elders of church
59	6	Shalt not commit adultery
63	16	Who commit adultery in their hearts shall
132	41	Adultery defined
	43–44	Husband looses his wife by adultery
	44	Who shall receive adulterer's wife
	62	If ten virgins cannot commit adultery

ADVERSITY

121	7	Adversity and affliction of small moment

ADVERSARY see also Devil, Satan

3	8	Supported you against darts of adversary
50	7	Hypocrites give adversary power
82	5	Adversary spreads his dominion
133	42	Make name known to adversaries

ADVOCATE see also Christ, Jesus, Son

29	5, 45:3, 62:1, 110:4, I am your advocate	

AFFLICTED

52	40	Disciple remembers poor, needy, sick and
105	3	Impart to afflicted

AFFLICTION

24	1	Lifted out of affliction
	8	Joseph Smith to have many afflictions
30	6	Be afflicted in his afflictions
31	9	Be patient in afflictions
97	26	Sore afflictions if disobedient
98	3	Affliction work to your good and God's glory
101	2	Affliction through transgression
121	7	Adversity and afflictions of small moment
133	53	Afflicted in their afflictions

AGENCY

29	36	Third part of heaven turned because of agency
	40	Agency through temptation
93	31	Here is agency of man
101	78	That all may act according to moral agency

AGENT

29	35	Adam an agent unto himself
51	8	Agent to care for money left to people
	12	Money lending through agent
58	28	Power to be agents to themselves
	49	Agents for lands in Zion
64	29	Agents on Lord's errand
84	113	Bishop to employ agent
90	22	Bishop's agent, a man of God and strong
104	17	Men agents unto themselves
128	8	Whether ordinances attended by oneself or

AGREE

27	18	Be agreed in all things

41	2	Assemble and agree on my word	28		John ordained by angel at eight days old

AGREEMENT
    42   3   Shall receive if agreed

AHMAN see also Jesus
    78   20   Redeemer, even Son Ahman
    95   17   Son Ahman, Jesus Christ

ALAM
    82   11

ALBANY
    84   114   Warn Albany of desolation and abolishment

ALM
    88   2   Alms of prayers come up
    112   1   Alms come as memorial to God

AMBITION
    121   37   Grieves Spirit to have vain ambition

AMEN
    88   135   Salutation answered by Amen
    121   37   Amen to Priesthood of man

ANCIENT
    8   1   Shall receive knowledge of ancient records
    98   33   Law to ancients concerning battles
    111   9   Inquire about ancient inhabitants

ANCIENT OF DAYS see also Adam
    27   11   Adam, ancient of days
    116   1   Where Ancient of Days shall sit

ANGEL
    2   hd   Words spoken by angel
    7   6   I will make him a ministering angel
    13   hd   John the Baptist an angel
          1   Keys of ministering of angels
    20   6   Holy angel, countenance as lightning
          10   Gospel confirmed by ministering of angels
    27   16   Sent angels to commit gospel
          35   Revelations by ministering of angels
    29   28   Devils and angels
          42   Angels sent to declare gospel
    38   12   Angels awaiting great command
    43   25   God calls by ministering of angels
    45   45   Angel shall sound trump
    49   7   Angels know not Christ's coming
          23   Events when angel sound trumpet
    62   3   Angels see testimony and rejoice
    63   54   Angels to pluck out wicked for the fire
    67   13   Cannot now abide ministering of angels
    76   21   Saw holy angels worshiping at the throne
          25   Angel in authority rebelled against the Only
          25   Angel thrust down from God and Son
          33   Suffer with devil and his angels in eternity
          67   Come to an innumerable company of angels
          88   Telestial receive by ministering angels
    77   8   Four angels of John explained
          9   Ascending angel of John explained
          12   Seven angels explained
    84   26   Lesser priesthood holds the key of minister-
          28   John ordained by angel at eight days old
          42   Given angels charge concerning you
          88   Angels shall bear you up
    86   5   Angels crying to the Lord to reap
          5   Angels waiting to be sent forth
    88   2   Angels rejoice over you
          92   Angels fly through the midst of heaven cry-
        92–112   Mission of the seven angels
    89   21   Promise that destroying angel pass them by
    90   34   Repent, angels rejoice
          20   My angel and presence shall go before you
    107   20   Aaronic priesthood holds keys of ministering
    123   7   Be brought to stand with angels
    128   20   Michael detecting devil as angel of light
          21   Voice of divers angels from Michael to Adam
          21   Angels declaring their dispensation and priest
    129   hd   Keys to know angels or spirits
          1   Angels are resurrected, with bodies of flesh
          4   How to distinguish between good and bad
          5   Can feel the hand of an angel
          8   To know devil, as an angel of light
    130   4   Angel's time according to residence
          5   Angels ministering to earth belong to it
          6   Angels do not reside on planet like earth
          7   Angels reside in the presence of God
    132   16   Who marry without the covenant are made
          17   These angels did not abide law
          18   Appointed angels to pass
          19   Shall pass by angels and Gods
          20   Gods because of power and subjection of
          37   Isaac and Jacob gods, not angels
    133   17   Angel crying through midst of heaven
          36   Mission of angel flying in midst of heaven
          53   Angel of his presence saved them
    136   37   Mine angels, ministering servants

ANGER
    1   13   The anger of the Lord is kindled
    5   8   Mine anger kindled against them
    10   24   Satan stirreth hearts to anger
    19   15   Smite you by my anger
    56   1   Anger against rebellious
    60   2   Angry with those that hide their talent
    61   31   Anger kindled against wickedness
    63   2   Lord's anger against wicked
          27   That world may not be stirred to anger
          28   Satan makes anger against you
    82   6   Anger of God kindled against inhabitants
    101   90   In hot displeasure and fierce anger
    121   5   Let anger kindle against enemies
    133   51   Tread on them in anger

ANGRY
    61   20   Lord was angry yesterday, today
    63   11   With whom angry, God not pleased
    88   87   Stars angry and cast down as figs

ANIMAL
- 29 24 Animals to be new
- 89 15 Animals for man in hunger or famine

ANIMAL continued
- 89 17 Barley for useful animals and mild drinks

ANOINT
- 68 20 Literal descendant of Aaron must be called, anointed and ordained by First President
-     21 They may claim their anointing
-     26 May claim their anointing
- 109 35 Let anointing be sealed
-     80 Anointed ones clothed with salvation
- 121 16 Cursed who lift heel against anointed
- 124 39 Anointings to be done in Temple
-     57 This anointing upon his head
-     76 Chosen and anointed him
-     91 Appointed ordained and anointed a counselor
- 132 7 Mine anointed holds sealing power

ANSWER
- 113 hd Answers to questions in Scripture
- 133 67 None to answer yet arm not shortened

ANTHEM
- 128 22 Let dead speak anthem of praise

APOCRYPHA
- 91   1 Mostly true
-      3 Not needful to translate Apocrypha
-      4 Whoso reads let him understand

APOLLOS
- 76 99 Telestial, those of Paul, Apollos, and Cephas

APOSTASY
- 58 32–33 Cause of apostasy

APOSTATES
- 20 83 Names blotted out of book
- 41   1 Heaviest of all curses upon apostates
- 76 34–38 Fate of apostates
-     42 Fate of apostates
-     48 Fate of apostates
- 85   2 Record of apostates to be kept
-     11 Apostates to have no inheritance
- 86   3 Babylon, the apostate, the whore

APOSTLE
- 1   14 Who will not heed apostles be cut off
- 18   9 Speak, as Paul, mine apostle
-     32 Duties of Apostles
- 19   8 To know as mine apostles
- 20   2 Joseph Smith ordained as an apostle of Jesus
-      3 Oliver Cowdery called of God an apostle
-     38 An Apostle is an elder; his calling to baptize
-     38 Duties of apostles
- 21   1 Joseph Smith be called apostle
- 27 12 Apostles and especial witnesses
- 29 10 Spoken by apostles fulfilled
-     12 First apostles on day of judgment
- 35   6 Apostles of old conferred Holy Ghost
- 49 11 Peter mine apostle
- 52   9 Say only what apostles written
-     36 Declare only prophets and apostles
- 63 21 Pattern shown apostles upon mount
-     52 Why apostles preached resurrection of dead
- 64 39 Who are not apostles shall be known
- 74   2 Circumcision in days of Apostles
-      5 Commandment not of Lord but of Apostle
- 84 63 Apostles, even God's High Priests
-    108 How ancient Apostles built up church
- 95   4 Prepare apostles to prune vineyard
-      9 Command even as apostles at Jerusalem
-     17 House for school of apostles
- 98 32 Law given to ancient apostles
- 107 23 Quorum of apostles special witnesses of name
-     24 Quorum of Apostles same authority as Presi-
-     26 Quorum of Seventy of equal authority with
-     33 Twelve a traveling presiding High Council
-     33 Apostles to officiate under direction of Presi-
-     33 Duties of Apostles
-     34 The Seventy to act under direction of apostles
-     35 Twelve to open door by proclamation of gos-
-     36 Stake, standing high councils of equal author-
-     38 Traveling High Council to call upon seventy
-     39 Twelve to ordain evangelical ministers as re-
- 112 12 Admonish the Apostles
-     12 Pray for the twelve
-     15 Instructions for humility, etc.
-     16 President of apostles hold keys of kingdom
-     17 Apostle quorum to act for presidency
-     19 Apostles go where Presidency send
-     21 Send missionaries by voice of Twelve
-     21 President to send missionaries by voice of
-     30 First Presidency counselors and leaders of
-     30 Power of priesthood given to Apostles and
- 136 37 Jesus and his apostles

APOSTLES, TWELVE, see also Twelve
- 18 hd Calling of twelve apostles made known
- 102 30 High Council of High Priests and High Council of Twelve Apostles not the same
-     31 No appeal from High Council of Twelve
-     32 Their decisions called in question by general authorities only
- 107 58 Twelve to ordain all other officers in church
- 112 hd Word to Thomas B. Marsh concerning Twelve
- 118 1 Let Twelve be organized
-      4 Apostles called to cross great waters
- 124 127 Brigham Young to be President of Twelve
-     128 Twelve hold keys to open authority of king-
-     129 Members of quorum of Twelve enumerated
-     139 Seventies under direction of Apostles
-     139 Apostles traveling High Council
- 136 3 Twelve Apostles in charge of journeying to

APPAREL
- 133 46 Who comes in glorious apparel
-     48 Lord shall be red in apparel

APPEAL
11	18	Appeal to my Spirit
	102	From what church court appeals may be
	33	First Presidency to determine if appeal en-
107	32	Manner of appeal from decision

APPENDIX
133	hd	Revelation called appendix

APPENDAGE
107	14	Called lesser priesthood because an appendage
84	29	Office of an elder appendage to the High
	5	All other authorities appendages to priesthood
84	30	Offices of teacher and deacon appendages to

APPOINT
51	3	Appoint portion to each man
118	1	Appoint men to supply places of fallen
124	91	Appointed, ordained and anointed a counselor
132	10	Will receive what not appointed
	11	Appoint only by law previously ordained

APPOINTMENT
84	107	Lesser priesthood to go before to make ap-
118	6	Officially notified of appointment

ARCHANGEL
29	26, 88:112, 107:54, 128:21, Michael the archangel	

ARCHIVE
127	9	Records placed in archives of Holy Temple

ARISE
88	124	Arise early that your bodies may be invigorated
133	10	Arise to meet bridegroom

ARK
85	8	Who steady ark of God shall fall

ARM
1	19	Man not trust in arm of flesh
3	8	He would have extended his arm
90	10	Arm of Lord in power to convincing
133	67	None to answer yet arm not shortened

ARMY
5	14	Church terrible as army with banners
60	4	God rules among armies
88	111	Satan loosed to gather armies
	112	Michael to gather armies, hosts of heaven
	113	Devil and armies to battle with Michael and
105	26	Until army of Israel becomes great
	30	After purchase, armies guiltless in taking
	31	How Israel's army should be

ASHAMED
90	17	Be not ashamed

ASHLEY, MAJOR N.
75	17	Mission for Major N. Ashley

ASK
4	7	Ask and ye shall receive
8	1	Receive knowledge of whatsoever you shall
	9	What you ask by faith will grant
	10	Ask not for what you ought not
	11	Ask to know mysteries of God, etc.
9	7	Took no thought save to ask me
	8	Ask if it be right
10	21	Will not ask because deeds are evil
14	8	Ask in faith believing
	8	Ask the Father in my name
42	56	Ask and Scriptures given
46	28	Ask in Spirit, receive in Spirit
50	29	Ask, if pure, and given you

ASSEMBLY
76	67	General assembly and church of Enoch and
88	70	Call a solemn assembly
95	7	Solemn assembly that fastings and mournings
107	32	General assembly spiritual authorities
108	4	Wait patiently until solemn assembly
124	39	Solemn assemblies to be held in Temple
133	6	Call solemn assemblies

ATONEMENT see also Jesus
19	16–19	Purpose of atonement
29	1	Arm of mercy atoned for sins
45	4	For the glory of God
74	7	Children are holy and sanctified through atone-
76	39–41	Christ's atonement
	69	Perfect atonement through shedding of

ATHIRST
84	80	Missionaries not go hungry or athirst

AUTHORITY see also Priesthood, General Author-
1	6	This is mine authority and authority of my
28	3	Declare commandments with authority
42	11	Only ordained has authority
63	62	Condemnation to use Lord's name without
68	8	Act in authority given
76	25	Angel in authority rebelled against Only Be-
84	21	Power of godliness not manifest without auth-
	101	God's vengeance if the authorities do not heed
	76	Importune rulers and authority for redress and
107	5	All authorities in church appendages to Mel-
	32	General assembly spiritual authorities
109	55	Remember civil authorities
113	8	To put on strength is authority of priesthood
121	37	If Spirit of Lord grieved Priesthood and auth-
	39	Men with little authority exercise unrighteous
122	2	Those who seek counsel, authority, and bless-
124	6	Authorities called to heed Zion
	118	Authorities called to lay foundation
	128	Twelve hold keys to open authority of king-
128	9	When done in authority becomes law

AUTHORIZE
112	21	Duly authorized shall have power

AVENGE see also Punish, Chasten
87	7	Blood of saints to be avenged on enemies
98	37	Until avenged on enemies
	45	Will avenge thee of enemy if
103	25	Avenge me of mine enemies
	26	My presence in avenging enemies
121	5	Avenge wrong with sword

AXE
    97   7   Axe laid at the root of trees
BABBITT, ALMON
    124   84   Not pleased with Almon Babbitt
BABE
    128   18   Hidden things revealed to babes in this dis-
BABYLON see also World, Wicked
    1   16   Babylon shall fall
    35   11   Desolations upon Babylon to be shown
    64   24   Spare none that remains in Babylon
    86   3   Babylon, the apostate, the whore
    133   5   Come out from Babylon
            7   Go out of Babylon
           14   Wickedness is spiritual Babylon
BACK
    133   15   Look not back lest destruction
BACKBITE
    20   54   Teacher to see that there is no backbiting
BACKWARD
    128   22   Go forward not backward
BAKER, JESSE
    124 137   of presidency of elders
BALDWIN, WHEELER
    52   31   Wheeler Baldwin called
BALLOT
    102   34   Ballot of first High Council for order of speech
BANEEMY
    105   27   Mine elders
BAPTISM
    13   1   Keys of baptism by immersion
    18   42   Time of baptism of children
           42   Baptism for men, women and children
    19   31   Remission of sins by baptism and by fire
    20   37   Who shall be baptized
           68   Duty of members after baptism
           69   Walk of members after baptism
           72   Manner of administering
           74   Manner of baptism
    22   2   Hundred baptisms avail not
    33   11   Repent and be baptized
           11   Baptism for the remission of sins
           11   Baptism by water and the Holy Ghost
    35   5   Baptism by water unto repentance
    39   6   Baptism by water in the gospel
           6   Baptism by fire in the gospel
           20   Baptism with water
    68   25   Parents to teach children baptism
           25   Baptism and Holy Ghost at eight years
           27   Children baptized when eight years
    84   27   Baptism part of preparatory gospel
    107   20   Baptism function of Aaronic priesthood
    128   12   Baptism in likeness of resurrection of dead
           12   Why ordinance instituted
           13   Where the baptismal font should be placed
           13   Baptismal font a simile of grave

BAPTISM FOR DEAD see also, Baptism, Baptize,
    124   29   Baptismal font for baptism of dead
           30   Baptism for dead must take place in a temple
           31   What baptism acceptable before temple built
           32   Unless attended to church rejected
           35   By these scattered not acceptable
           36   Places of refuge to be for baptism of dead
           39   Baptism for dead to be done in temple
    127   6   A recorder to be witness of baptism for dead
    128   1   The subject continued
           2   Recorder of baptism for dead
           2   Eye-witness to baptism for dead
           3   Recorder for baptism for dead in every ward
           3   Three witnesses required for baptism for dead
           4   Records of baptism for dead placed with gen-
           5   Order of record of baptisms for dead particular
           5   Baptism for dead ordained before foundations
           18   Earth cursed without baptism for dead
BAPTISM RE-
    22   hd   Section 22 concerning Re-baptism
BAPTISMAL
    124   29   Baptismal font for baptism of dead
BAPTIZE
    18   7   As thou hast been baptized he hath fulfilled
           22   Baptized in name of Jesus Christ shall
           22   As repent and baptized, be saved
           29   Twelve to baptize in my name
           29   Baptize as is written
           41   Repent and be baptized
    20   25   Who believe and baptized saved
           46   Priests may baptize
           58   Teachers and deacons cannot baptize
    20   73   Baptized in name of Father, Son and Holy
    22   hd   Must be baptized to enter church
    49   13   Be baptized in name of Jesus Christ
    52   10   Baptizing by water
    68   8   Baptize in name of Father, Son, and Holy
           9   Believeth and is baptized shall be saved
    76   51   Baptized after manner of His burial
    84   28   John baptized while in childhood
           64   Baptized by water for remission of sins
           64   Baptized shall receive Holy Ghost
    112   29   Who believes and baptized be saved
           29   Believe not, not baptized, damned
    124   33   Instituted before foundation of world
BARLEY
    89   17   Barley for useful animals and mild drinks
BARNS
    121   20   Their barns shall perish
BARREN
    133   29   Pools of living water in barren deserts
BASKET
    121   20   Their baskets not full
BASSETT, HEMAN
    52   37   Take away from Heman Basset

BATTLE
45	70	No battle against Zion
88	113	Devil and armies to battle with Michael and
	114	Battle of the great God
	115	Michael fight the battles of saints
98	33	Law to ancients concerning battle
	36	Lord commands and justifies battle
	37	When does the Lord fight his people's battles
	38	Ensample for justification of battle
105	14	God will fight battles of Zion

BEAR
1	8	Who bearing tidings to world shall have power
50	40	Cannot bear all things now
64	20	Tempted above what he is able to bear
78	18	Cannot bear all things now
84	88	Angels shall bear you up
132	63	Work continued by bearing souls
	63	Exaltation to bear souls of men
133	53	Bear and carried all days of old
136	37	Cannot yet bear my glory

BEAST
29	24	Beasts to be new
49	19	Beasts for use of man
77	2	Four beasts of John explained
89	14	Grain staff of life for man and beast
	17	Rye for fowls, swine and beasts of field
101	26	Enmity of man and beast shall cease

BED
88	124	Retire to thy bed early

BEGINNING
3	15	Counsel trampled on from beginning
5	14	This the beginning of church
8	12	I spake from beginning
22	1	This new and everlasting covenant from be-
29	33	Works of God have no beginning
61	14	Lord in beginning blessed water
	17	In beginning cursed land
63	8	Sign-seekers from beginning
76	13	Son was in bosom of Father from beginning
	13	Things ordained from beginning
93	21	First-born, in the beginning with Father
	23	Ye were in beginning with Father
	25	Spirit of wicked, liar from the beginning
	29	Man was in beginning with God
	38	Spirit of man innocent in beginning
110	10	Shall be beginning of blessings

BELIEF
34	4	Blessed because of belief

BELIEVE
3	20	Lamanites might believe gospel
5	7	If would not believe words, would not you
8	1	Shall receive what ask for believing
11	10	Believing in power of Jesus Christ
	14	Shall know, in faith believing
14	8	Ask in faith believing
20	29	All men must repent and believe
	25	Who believes and baptized saved
	26	All who believe be saved
46	14	Given to some to believe
49	12	Believe on name of Lord Jesus
58	64	Signs follow these who believe
66	2	Blessed who believe on Christ's name
68	9	Believeth and is baptized shall be saved
	10	Who believeth blest with signs
84	64	Every soul who believeth shall
112	29	Who believes and is baptized

BELIEVER
74	5	Marriage of believer and unbeliever
84	65	Signs to follow believers
	71	Poison not hurt believers

BELLY
56	17	Bellies not satisfied
89	7	Strong drinks not for belly, for washing bodies
	9	Hot drinks not for body or belly

BENEATH
63	59	I from above, but power beneath
84	100	Lord brought Zion from beneath

BENEFIT
70	8	Benefits shall be consecrated
	15	Commandment for benefit of saints
91	6	Who receives not by spirit not benefited
104	hd	Concerning order for benefit of poor

BENJAMIN, KING
10	41	Translate to reign of King Benjamin

BENNETT, J.C.
124	16	J.C. Bennett to help Joseph

BENSON, EZRA T.
136	12	Ezra T. Benson and Erastus Snow organize

BENT, SAMUEL
124	132	Samuel Bent member of High Council

BIBLE see also, Holy Word, Holy Scripture.
42	12	Fulness of Gospel in Bible and Book of Mor-

BILLINGS, TITUS
63	39	Words to Titus Billings

BIND see also Seal, Temple.
43	9	Bind yourselves to act in holiness
45	55	Satan shall be bound
82	10	Lord bound when you do what I say
88	84	To bind up the law
127	7	Bind on earth bound in heaven
128	8	Power of priesthood to bind on earth and in
	9	Priesthood of all ages had power to bind on
	14	This is sealing or binding power
132	46	Bind on earth, bound in heaven
133	72	Bind up law for disobedient

BISHOP
20	66	Traveling bishops may ordain without vote
	67	Bishop to be ordained by whose direction
41	9	Edward Partridge to be Bishop to the church
	9	Duties of bishop to the church

BISHOP–BLESS

BISHOP continued

42	31	Bishop to have counselors
	31	Bishop to receive donations for the poor
	34	As appointed by bishop and council
42	71	Bishop and counselors and families to be supported by the church
	71	Elders or High Priests to assist him
	82	Bishop to be present at trials
48	6	Act in appointment of presidency
51	5	Portion consecrated to the bishop for poor
	12	Money lending through bishop
	13	Bishop to keep the excess of meat and money
	13	Let bishop appoint storehouse
51	14	Bishop to reserve enough for his wants
53	4	Sidney Gilbert to be agent appointed by bishop
57	15	Bishop to make preparation for gathering
58	35	Lay monies before bishop
64	40	Bishop is a judge
	40	Bishops and counselors condemned if not faithful
68	14	Other bishops to minister as the first
	15	Bishops to be worthy high priests
	15	Bishops appointed by First Presidency
	16	First born of sons of Aaron have legal right
	19	High priest may be bishop if no son of Aaron
	19	Bishop set apart and ordained by First Presi-
	22	Bishop can only be tried before First Presi-
	23	If bishop guilty shall be condemned
	24	If bishop repents shall be forgiven
70	11	Bishop not exempt from law
72	2	Bishop to be appointed in this part
	5	Elders render account to bishop
	6	Record of stewardship handed to bishop
	7	Duty of bishop known by commandment and
	8	Newel K. Whitney to be bishop
	10	Bishop to keep storehouse
	10	Bishop to receive funds of church
	11	Bishop to take account of elders
	14	Labors of faithful answer debt to bishop
	15	Every man must lay all before bishop
	16	Every elder give account to bishop
	17	From bishop renders man acceptable
	19	Elder, who accounts to bishop be recommended
	20	Stewards of literary concern have claim on
	25	Certificates presented to bishop
	25	Certificate from three elders or bishop
84	29	Bishop a necessary appendage to High Priest-
	104	Send monies to bishop
	112	Bishop to search after the poor
	112	Bishop to travel
	113	Bishop to employ an agent
85	1	Record of those who receive from bishop
90	22	Bishop's agent, a man of God and strong faith
	22	Bishop's agent to have riches in store
	35	Not well pleased with bishop
99	6	Children sent to bishop of Zion
107	16	Legal right belongs to descendant of Aaron
	17	High Priest may act as bishop
	17	Bishop to be ordained by Presidency of High
	68	Bishop administer temporal things
	68	Office of Bishop not equal to High Priesthood
	69	Bishop chosen from High Priesthood unless
	71	Duties of Bishop who is High Priest
	72	Counselors he has chosen
	72	Bishop to be a judge: manner of his judging
	73	Duty of bishop who is not descendant

Bishops to be common judges in Zion

107	76	Literal descendants of Aaron may act
	78	Cases undecided in Bishop's court brought to
	88	Bishop to be president of priests
117	11	Be bishop in deed not name
119	1	Surplus property put into hands of bishop
120	1	Bishop to aid in disposition of tithing
124	20	A bishop characterized

BISHOPRIC see also Bishop

82	12	Covenant to manage affairs of bishopric
107	15	Bishopric presidency of Aaronic Priesthood
114	2	Others receive their bishopric
124	141	Presidents over bishopric
	21	George Miller receives bishopric

BITTER

29	39	Taste bitter to know sweet

BLASPHEME

112	26	Punishment for blasphemed
132	27	Blasphemy against Holy Ghost explained

BLESS

1	28	If humble, blessed from on high
6	9	Shall be blessed if
	10	Blessed because of thy gift
	14	Blessed for what thou hast done
	30	Blessed to dwell with God in glory
	30	Blessed are ye if they do unto you as unto me
	31	Blessed are they, if they reject not
11	9	Assist, and you shall be blessed
14	11	If faithful shall be blessed
15	5	Blessed are you for speaking my words
16	5	Blessed are you for speaking my words
19	37	Hosanna blessed be name of Lord
21	9	Bless those who labor
24	3	Bless temporally and spiritually
34	4	Blessed because of belief
	5	Blessed because called to ministry
38	14	Blessed through mercy of God
41	1	Delight to bless my people
50	5	Blessed are faithful
	36	Blessed are you now hearing
59	1	Blessed are they how have come according to
	3	Blessed who stand on land of Zion
	12–17	Blessing upon those who observe Sabbath
61	14	Lord in beginning blessed waters
	17	In last days blessed land

63	30	Blessed if Zion obtained by purchase	138		Receive only who are clean from blood
	49	Blessed are dead that die in the Lord	101	80	I redeemed land by shedding of blood
	50	Who lives when Christ comes is blessed, but	112	33	Lest blood of generation required of your hand
66	2	Blessed for receiving everlasting covenant	130	12	Bloodshed before Christ's coming to begin in
84	60	Blessed if you receive	132	19	Shedding of innocent blood cancels sealings
86	11	Blessed if continue in goodness		27	Shedding of innocent blood is blasphemy
97	1	Blessed who seek wisdom and truth	133	51	Sprinkled garments with blood
132	47	Whom you bless I will bless	135	7	Innocent blood—Carthage, shall come forth
136	11	With pure hearts, in faith, be blessed	136	36	Innocent blood cries from ground against

BLESSING

BLOSSOM

10	50	Left blessing upon this land in prayers	117	7	Make solitary places bud and blossom

BOARDING HOUSE

18	45	My blessings above all things	124	22	Boarding house to be built
19	38	Pray and great shall be your blessing		56	Let my name be upon house

BOAST

20	70	Blessing of children	3	4	If he boasts in strength must fall
58	4	After tribulations blessings		13	Boasted in own wisdom
	32	God revokes blessing	50	33	Boast not against false spirit
61	37	Humble and blessings yours	84	73	Commandment not to boast of gift
67	3	Blessing lost through fears in heart	105	24	Boast not of faith, etc.

BODY see also, Spirit, Soul

75	19	Blessing upon house that receives you	19	18	God suffered in body
78	17	Are little children and understand not bless-	27	2	My body laid down for you
	18	Blessings of Kingdom yours	45	17	Absence of spirits from body a bondage
103	12	After much tribulation comes blessing	59	19	Nature to strengthen body
104	13	Earthly blessings prepared for my creatures	76	70	Whose bodies are celestial
	46	Blessings as faithful		78	Bodies terrestial
105	12	Endowment and blessing for faithful and hum-	84	33	Sanctified by Spirit to renewing bodies
107	67	Administering of ordinances and blessings		109	Body how stand without feet
122	2	Those who seek counsel, authority and bless-		110	Body hath need of every member
124	97	Keys by which to receive blessings	88	15	Spirit and body the soul
	124	Patriarch holds sealing blessings of church		27	Righteous die, rise spiritual body
130	20	All blessings predicated on law		28	Celestial spirit receives natural body
	21	Blessing obtained by obedience to its law		67	Body filled with light comprehends all
132	5	All who have a blessing shall abide the law		67	Bodies filled with light if eyes single to glory

BLIND

19	40	Canst thou run as a blind guide	89	7	Strong drinks not for belly, for washing bodies
35	9	Blind made to see		9	Hot drinks not for body or belly
58	11	Blind come to marriage of Lamb	101	37	Care not for body but soul
78	10	Through Satan become blind and	129	1	Angels are resurrected with bodies of flesh and
84	69	In my name open eyes of blind	130	22	Father has body of flesh and bones
123	12	Blinded by craftiness		22	Son has body of flesh and bones

BLOOD

			131	8	When bodies pure see spirit matter

BOND see also Bondage

27	2	My blood shed for remission of sin			
29	17	My blood shall not cleanse them	78	11	Organize by bond that cannot be broken
45	41	Shall behold blood	82	11	Bound by bond that cannot break by trans-
49	21	Don't shed blood without need	134	12	Not preach gospel to bond servants without

BONDAGE see also Bond

58	53	Lest no inheritance save by blood			
63	28	Satan plans shedding of blood	19	35	Release thyself from bondage
	29	Zion obtained by purchase not blood	45	17	Absence of spirits from body a bondage
	31	Forbidden to shed blood	84	50	Bondage of sin
	31	Punishment for shedding blood	101	79	Not right for a man to be in bondage
76	69	Perfect atonement through shedding of Christ's	103	17	Must be led from bondage by power
87	6	Earth mourn by bloodshed	104	83	Shall be delivered from bondage

BONE

	7	Cry and blood of saints cease to come up	29	19	Flesh fall from bones
88	75	Clean from blood of			
	87	Moon bathed in blood			
	94	Who shed blood of saints			

BONE continued
85	6	Still small voice makes bones to quake
89	18	Marrow to their bones
129	1	Angels are resurrected, with bodies of flesh
130	22	Father has body of flesh and bones
	22	Son has body of flesh and bones

BOOK   see also, School, Learn, Teach
20	82	List of names of church to be kept in a book
55	4	Write books for schools in church
77	6	Book of seven seals explained
	14	Little book eaten by John
88	2	Recorded in book of names of
	118	Seek wisdom from best books
90	15	Become acquainted with all good books
99	5	Written in volume of book
109	14	Wisdom out of best books
128	6	Books from which dead are judged explained
	7	Books by which dead judged are records kept
	8	Dead judged out of books
	24	Books of records of dead

BOOK OF COMMANDMENTS
1	6	Inhabitants of earth given book of command-
	6	Preface to book of commandments
67	6	If any can make the like of one commandment
	8	Its truth proved

BOOK OF DOCTRINE AND COVENANTS
67	4	How to test the truth of Doctrine and Cov-
	9	No unrighteousness in Doctrine and Covenants
135	1	Martyrdom of Joseph and Hyrum the seal of

BOOK OF ENOCH
107	57	Things written in book of Enoch

BOOK OF LAW
85	5	Names not found in the Book of Law
	7	Inheritances whose names in the Book of Law
	11	Fate of High Priesthood whose names not in

BOOK OF LIFE
128	7	Book of life is record kept in heaven
132	19	Written in the Lamb's Book of Life

BOOK OF MORMON   see also Plates of Nephi, Plate,
1	29	Power to translate Book of Mormon
3	hd	Section 2 concerning lost mss of first part
6	17	Witness that work is true
10	hd	Section 10 concerning alteration of mss of
17	hd	Revelation given to three witnesses
18	4	In it all things concerning
19	26	Book of Mormon contains truth and the word
	27	Book of Mormon word to Gentile
20	8–9	Book of Mormon contains fulness of Gospel
	10	Book of Mormon given by inspiration, etc.
	13	Book of Mormon testimony to world
24	1	Joseph Smith called and chosen to write Book
27	5	Contains fulness of everlasting Gospel
	5	Moroni sent to reveal it
33	16	Given for instruction
42	12	Fulness of Gospel in Bible and Book of Mor-
84	57	New covenant, even Book of Mormon
124	119	Not allowed to pay stock unless believer in
128	20	The book to be revealed
	20	Where three witnesses declared
135	1	Martyrdom of Joseph and Hyrum the seal of
	3	Book of Mormon translated by power of God

BOOK OF REMEMBRANCE
85	9	Not in book of remembrance no inheritance

BOOTH, EZRA
52	23	Isaac Morley and Ezra Booth called
64	15	Angry with Ezra Booth

BORN
5	16	Born of water and of the Spirit
76	32	Better for sons of perdition not to have been

BORROW
136	25	Return what is borrowed

BOSOM
9	8	Bosom shall burn if right
76	25	Who was in bosom of Father
88	13	God in bosom of eternity
109	4	Jesus Christ, son of thy bosom

BOSTON
84	114	Warn Boston of desolation and abolishment

BOUND
88	38	Every law has bounds and conditions
121	30	If bounds set to heaven, etc.
122	9	Bounds of enemies set
133	72	Bound up the law

BOW
5	24	If he bow in mighty prayer I will grant
88	104	Every knee shall bow
106	6	Joy in heaven when Warren bowed

BOWEL
84	101	Truth established in bowels of earth
85	7	His bowels a fountain of truth
101	9	Bowels filled with compassion
121	3	Let bowels be moved with compassion
	45	Bowels be full of charity to household of faith

BRANCH
10	60	Branch of house of Jacob
72	23	Ensample to all branches of church
107	39	Evangelical ministers in large branches

BREAD   see also   Sacrament, Wine
20	40	Administer bread and wine
	75	Bread of Sacrament
	77	Blessing on bread

BREAK   see also Sin
1	15	Have broken everlasting covenant
	19	Weak to break down mighty
3	13	Broken sacred promises
5	27	If he deny he will break covenant
54	4	A broken covenant void
56	18	Have broken hearts and contrite spirits
88	35	What breaketh law not sanctified by law
97	8	Blessings on broken honest hearts and contrite

104	86	Master not suffer house broken up	64	23	Who is tithed shall not burn
				24	Burning cometh after today

BREASTPLATE
  17   1   Shall have view of breastplate
  27 16 Breastplate of righteousness

BREASTWORK
 110 2   Saw Lord on breastwork of pulpit

BRIDEGROOM see also, Jesus
  33 17 Be ready for Bridegroom
  65   3 Make ready for Bridegroom
  88 92 Bridegroom comes, meet him
 133 10 Go and meet Bridegroom
       19 Prepare for coming of Bridegroom

BRIMSTONE
  63 17 Lake of fire and brimstone
  76 36 Who shall go to the lake of fire and brimstone

BRING
   6   6 Seek to bring forth cause of Zion
        9 Assist to bring forth my work
      11 Bring many to knowledge of truth
  10 61 Will bring to light marvelous works
  11   6 Seek to bring forth cause of Zion
  12   6 Seek to bring forth cause of Zion
  14 10 Must bring forth Gospel

BROOK
 128 23 Brooks flow with gladness

BROOME COUNTY
 128 20 Peter, James and John at Broome Co.

BROTHER
  38 24 Esteem your brother
  61 32 More labor needed among brethren than
 136 20 Covet not thy brothers

BRUNSON, SEYMOUR
  75 33 Mission for Seymour Brunson
 124 132 No man takes his priesthood

BUD
 117 7 Make solitary places bud and blossom

BUILD
  10 52 Bring gospel to build up
      54 Not to destroy but to build up church
      56 Who build up churches to themselves King-
  52 33 Build not on another's foundation
  63   4 Lord builds what he pleases
  94 15 Committee to build the Lord's houses
  95   3 Grievous sin in not building Lord's house
      11 Keep commandments, power to build
  97 15 Build temple in name of Lord
 101 101 Build and another shall not inherit
 104 59 Print words to build up church
 124 62 Committee to build temple
 136 19 No power to build up himself without counsel

BURLINGTON
 124 88 Wm. Marks to preach in Burlington

BURN
   9   8 Bosom shall burn if right
  29   9 I will burn them up

BURNETT, STEPHEN
  75 35 Mission for Stephen Burnett
  80   1 Words to Stephen Burnett

BURROUGH, PHILIP
  30 10 Labor at Philip Burrough's

BRUISES
  89   8 Tobacco for bruises

BURY
  60 13 Bury not thy talent
  76 51 Buried in water in his name

BUSINESS see also Government
  20 62 Conferences to do church business
  64 29 On the Lord's business
  70   5 Their business in church of God
 104 49 Do business in our own names
 107 72 Bishop to do business of church
      78 Most important business of church shall

BUTTERFIELD, J.
 124 138 J. Butterfield a president of Seventies

CAESAR
  63 26 Lord renders to Caesar Caesar's

CAHOON, REYNOLDS
  52 30, 61:35, 75:32, 94:14, Reynolds Cahoon

CAIN
 124 75 His offering not like Cain

CAINAN
 107 45 God called Cainan in wilderness
      45 Cainan met Adam, on way to Shedolamak
      53 Cainan a High Priest

CALEB
  84   8 Caleb received priesthood from Elihu

CALL see also Calling Chasten, Missionaries
   3 10 Repent, thou art still called
   4   3 Called if desire to serve
   6   4 Called who will thrust in sickle and reap
   9 14 Work wherewith I have called you
  11 15 Not suppose you are called until called
  12   4 Whoso will, is called of God
       9 Give heed, then you are called
  18   8 Marvel not that I have called him
       9 Called with calling of Paul mine Apostle
      14 Called to cry repentance
      24 In what name called at last day
      26 Others called to declare my gospel
  20   2 Joseph Smith, Jr., called of God
       3 Oliver Cowdery called of God an Apostle
      11 God does call men to his work
  43 20 Call nations to repent
  65   5 Call upon Lord to extend his kingdom
  88 85 Not called, for garments not yet clean
      85 Continue in vineyard till Lord calls
      62 Call when I am near
      71 Let these warned call and ponder

CALL continued
- 95　5　Many ordained and called; few chosen
- 101　39　Saints accounted as salt and savor of earth
- 　　40　Called to be savor of men
- 121　34　Many called, few chosen
- 124　7　Call with testimony
- 132　59　A man called is justified in his acts
- 136　32　Wisdom by humbling and calling

CALLING see also Call
- 18　32　According to callings and gifts
- 20　27　Who believe in calling of God shall be saved
- 23　2　Make known thy calling
- 　　3　Thy calling to exhortion
- 24　9　Attend to thy calling
- 84　33　Who magnify calling are sanctified
- 　　109　Every man labor in own calling
- 105　35　Day of calling now choosing

CAMP OF THE LORD
- 61　29　Way for saints of camp of the Lord to journey

CAMP OF ISRAEL
- 136　1　Will concerning camp of Israel

CANAL
- 61　23　Save it be upon canal

CAPTAIN
- 136　3　Companies with captains of hundreds, fifties,

CARE
- 39　9　Rejected God because of cares of the world
- 63　64　Speak of sacred things with care
- 101　37　Care not for body but soul

CARMEL
- 128　19　As dews of Carmel so knowledge of God des-

CARNAL
- 3　4　If follow carnal desires he must fall
- 67　10　Not see God with carnal but spiritual mind

CARNAL COMMANDMENT
- 84　27　Carnal commandments part of preparatory

CARTHAGE
- 124　88　Wm. Marks to preach in Carthage

CARTER, GIDEON
- 75　34　Mission for Gideon Carter

CARTER, JARED
- 52　38　Jared Carter ordained a priest
- 79　1　Command for Jared Carter
- 94　14　Jared Carter to receive inheritance on second
- 102　3　Jared Carter member of first High Council

CARTER, JOHN S.
- 102　3　John S. Carter member of first High Council

CARTER, SIMEON
- 52　27　Simeon Carter called
- 75　30　Mission for Simeon Carter

CARTER, WILLIAM
- 52　31　William Carter called

CASE
- 102　13　Number of speakers for different cases
- 107　78　Most difficult cases shall

CAST
- 46　3　Cast none out of public meetings

CATTLE
- 89　8　Tobacco for sick cattle

CAUGHT UP
- 88　96　Saints shall be quickened and caught up
- 101　31　Shall be caught up

CAUSE
- 6　6　Seek to establish cause of Zion
- 10　26　Causeth to catch in own snare
- 24　10　Cannot say enough in my cause
- 58　27　Men anxiously engaged in good cause
- 　　6　Sent you for this cause

CELESTIAL see also Terrestrial, Telestial Glory,
- 76　70　Who shall receive celestial glory
- 　　70　Celestial glory, like glory of sun, like glory
- 　　71　Terrestrial and celestial glories compared
- 　　87　Terrestrial receive through celestial
- 　　92　Glory of celestial excels all things
- 　　92　God reigns in celestial world
- 　　94　Who dwell in his presence are church of first
- 　　94　Celestial received of fulness of grace
- 　　95　Celestial equal in power, might, dominion
- 　　96　Glory of celestial one, as sun
- 78　7　For place in celestial world must prepare and
- 　　14　Ensample, that church shall stand above all
- 88　2　Names in book of sanctified of celestial world
- 　　4　Eternal life, glory of celestial world
- 　　5　Celestial glory defined
- 　　20　Bodies of celestial kingdom to possess earth
- 　　20　Why celestial bodies created
- 　　24　Celestial law brings celestial glory
- 　　25　Earth abides celestial law
- 　　28　Celestial spirit receive natural body
- 105　4　Law of union of celestial kingdom
- 　　5　Zion built only by law of celestial kingdom
- 130　10　White stone become Urim and Thummim for
- 　　11　White stone and new name for all of celestial
- 131　1　In celestial glory are three heavens
- 　　2　The only way to obtain the highest degree

CELESTIAL MARRIAGE see also Marriage
- 132　7　Conditions of the law
- 　　19–20　The blessings that follow
- 　　38　Practiced from beginning of creations
- 　　39　Prophets with keys of celestial marriage

CEPHAS
- 76　99　Telestial, those of Paul, Apollos and Cephas

CERTIFICATE see also Recommend
- 20　64　Certificate taken by lower priesthood
- 　　84　Member removing to take certificate
- 72　17　Certificate or "Recommend" from bishop ren-
- 　　17　Certificate answers for inheritance
- 　　18　Man not accepted without certificate
- 　　25　Members must bring recommend or certificate
- 　　25　Certificate presented to bishop

	25	Certificate from three elders or bishop
	26	Without certificate unwise steward

CHAMBER

128	21	Voice of God in chamber of Father Whitmer

CHANGE

43	32	Shall be changed in a twinkling of eye
63	51	Changed in twinkling of an eye

CHARIOT

62	7	Saints may ride in chariots

CHARITY

4	5	Charity qualifies him for the work
	6	Remember charity
6	19	Have charity, etc.
12	8	Not assist, unless having charity
18	19	Not charity, can do nothing
88	125	Bond of charity, bond of perfectness and peace
	125	Clothe yourselves in charity
121	45	Bowels be full of charity to household of
124	116	Clothe himself with charity

CHASTEN see also Punish, Avenge, Affliction

1	27	As sinned they might be chastened
42	90	Offend many chastened before many
	92	Offend in secret, chastened in secret
61	8	Chastened of all sins
64	8	My disciples were chastened for not forgiving
75	7	Commandment to chasten for murmuring
87	6	Indignation and chastening of God
90	36	Lord chasten Zion
95	1	Whom I love I chasten
	2	Must be chastened and stand rebuked
	10	Chastened because of contention
98	21	Chasten if they do not repent
100	13	Zion chastened
101	4	Chastened as Abraham
	5	Who will not endure chastening not sanctified
	41	Transgressors need be chastened
103	4	Chastened for not hearkening
105	6	Chastened to learn obedience

CHASTISEMENT

95	1	Chastisement deliverance from temptation
136	31	Who bears not chastisement not worthy

CHEER

61	36	Be of good cheer, little children
78	18	Good cheer, I will lead you

CHEERFULLY

123	17	Let us do cheerfully what lies

CHILDREN see also Parents, Father, Family, seed

2	2	Hearts of children turn to fathers
	2	Shall plant promises in hearts of children
5	6	Deliver words unto children of men
18	42	Children to be baptized at years of account-
20	70	Children to be blessed
	70	Duty of members having children
27	9	Turning hearts of children to fathers
29	46	Children redeemed from beginning through
	47	Satan cannot tempt children until accountable
45	58	Children grow up without sin to salvation
50	40	Ye are little children
55	4	Special books that children receive pleasing
61	36	Be of good cheer, little children
63	51	Children shall grow up until old but
68	25	Parents responsible if children not taught
	25	Sin of untaught children upon parents
	26	Law of Zion concerning parents and children
	27	Children baptized when eight years
	28	Parents to teach children to pray
	31	Lord not pleased that children grow in wicked-
74	1	Children of one unbelieving parent made holy
	3	Unbelieving husband wanted children circum-
	4	Children unholy in not believing gospel of
	6	False tradition that children are unholy
	7	Children are holy and sanctified through atone-
78	17	Are little children and understand not bless-
83	4	Children have claim upon parents until of age
	5	Children, of age, can claim inheritance from
93	40	Children to be brought up in light and truth
	42	Affliction from not bringing up children prop-
98	16	Turn hearts of children and fathers to each
	45–46	Children punished for father's sins
	47	Forgive if children repent of father's tres-
99	3	Receive as child, they receive kingdom, and
101	81	Children of Zion likened to parable of woman
106	5	Be like children of light
110	15	Elijah commits keys of turning hearts of
128	18	Baptism for dead welding link between father
132	37	Children born of Abraham by concubines

CHILDREN OF KINGDOM

41	6	Give not things of children of kingdom to dogs

CHILDREN OF MEN see also Man

4	1	Work to come forth to children of men
6	1	Great and marvelous work to children of men
18	6	Children of men are stirred to repentance
38	11	Among children of men in presence of hosts

CHOOSE

1	4	My disciples chosen in these last days
3	9	Joseph chosen to do work of Lord
19	9	You that are chosen
19	10	Repent, thou art still chosen
29	4	Ye are chosen from the world
37	4	Let every man choose
55	1	Thou art called and chosen
95	5	Many ordained and called; few chosen
	6	They not chosen who sin grievously
	8	House to endow who are chosen
105	35	Chosen who are worthy
	36	Manifest by Spirit who are chosen
112	7	Chosen, path among mountains
121	34	Many called, few are chosen
	35	Not chosen for aspirations to world and honor
124	76	Chosen and anointed him

CHRIST see also Jesus, Jesus Christ, Son
18	21	Take upon you name of Christ
20	22	Christ suffered temptations but gave no heed
	23	Christ was crucified, died, and rose again
	24	Christ ascended into heaven
	24	Christ reigns according to will of Father
38	21	In time, no king or rulers, but Christ
43	21	Christ a man
76	28	God and his Christ
	59	They are Christ's and Christ is God's
	62	Dwell in presence of God and Christ forever
	73	Christ preached Gospel to spirits in prison
	85	Last resurrection when Christ has finished his
	100	Of Christ, but receive not gospel
	106	Christ subdued enemies at fullness of times
	107	Christ deliver kingdom to Father
	107	Christ trodden wine-press alone
	108	Christ crowned with glory, on throne of power
	112	Telestial cannot get where God and Christ
86	9	Been hid from world with Christ
88	7	This is light of Christ
105	32	Kingdom of Zion that of God and Christ
113	1	Stem of Jesse is Christ
130	9	This earth will be Christ's
133	55	Who were with Christ in resurrection

CHRIST'S COMING
5	19	Earth consumed by coming
29	14	Signs of Christ's coming
45	26	Christ delayeth his coming
	39	Sign of coming of the Son of Man
	44	Christ's coming
45	56	Parable of virgins fulfilled at Christ's coming
49	6	Coming of Christ nigh at hand
	7	No man or angel knoweth Christ's coming
	22	Christ comes not as woman
	22	Christ comes not as a man traveling
	23	Sure signs of Christ's coming
	24	What must precede Christ's coming
51	20	Christ's coming in an hour ye think not
61	38	Christ comes when you think not
	38	Look for Christ's coming
	39	Pray to abide Christ's coming
63	50	Who lives when Christ comes is blessed, but
64	23	Called today to Christ's coming
68	11	To you given to know signs of Christ's coming
77	12	The preparation for his coming
	13	Things to be accomplished before Christ's
88	98	Who shall be with him in his first coming
	99	Who are Christ's at his coming
97	23	Scourge not stayed until Christ's coming
101	35	The faithful who die shall partake of the
106	4	Lord's coming nigh and overtaketh
128	24	Who can abide Christ's coming
130	12	Bloodshed before Christ's coming to begin in
	15	Joseph's answer to the time of Christ's com-
	15	Trouble me no more concerning Christ's com-
	17	Joseph's opinion of the time of Christ's com-
133	17	Hour of coming nigh
	18	Events of Christ's coming
	19	Prepare for coming of bridegroom
	49	The Glory of Christ's coming described

CHURCH see also Gospel, Assembly, Faithful,
1	hd	Covenants and Commandments of Lord to
	1	Hearken people of my church
	30	Bring church out of obscurity
	30	Only true and living church
5	14	How the church appears
	14	This is the beginning of church
10	53	Will establish my church among them
	54	Not to destroy but to build up church
	55	Who belongs to church not fear
	56	Who build up churches unto themselves,
	67	Whosoever repenteth is my church
	68	Is not my church
	69	Who is of church will I
11	16	My word, rock, church and gospel
18	hd	Building of church of Christ according to full-
	4	Foundation of my church and gospel
	5	Build church on foundation of gospel and
	20	Contend against no church, save
20	1	Date and manner of establishment of Church
	2	Joseph Smith first elder of church
	3	Oliver Cowdery to be elder of church
	33	Let church take heed
	53	Teacher to watch over the church
	71	Cannot be received into church until account-
	81	Duty of churches to be represented at con-
	82	Names of members to be kept in a book
21	2	Joseph Smith inspired to found church
	3	Date of foundation
	4	Church to heed words and commandments of
	5	Word of Joseph Smith as from mouth of God
22	hd	Church established in the year
	hd	Must be baptized to enter church
	3	Church built as of old
	3	Last covenant and church
	3	Church built because of dead works
24	3	Church shall support thee
	18	Church shall give what thou needest
25		Emma Smith ordained to exhort the church
26	2	Church to be governed by common consent
28	2	Revelations and commandments for the church to be received only by Joseph
29	21	Church; the great whore
33	5	Church called out of wilderness
	13	Church built upon this rock
41	3	How to govern the church
42	8	Build up my church in every region
43	8	Instruct, that may know how to direct church
45	64	Build up churches

50	37	Strengthen churches by exhortation
51	10	Another church not to be given money from
55	4	Write books for schools in church
57	11	Printer unto church, etc.
58	23	Laws of Church
	48	Let them build up churches
60	9	This for good of churches
63	63	Church repent of sins
64	37	Church like a judge over nations
69	3	History of important things concerning church
70	5	Business in church of God
	10	None exempt from law who belong to church
73	hd	Church established in last days
75	24	Duty of church to support families of mis-
	26	Support of church for families of missionaries
76	67	General assembly and church of Enoch and of
77	5	Seven churches
78	4	City of Enoch for everlasting order unto
	14	Ensample, that church shall stand above all
	21	Ye are church of first born
82	hd	Order given to Enoch and church
	18	Common property of whole church
84	2	Church established for restoration of people
	34	Who receive priesthood are church
	55	Church under condemnation for vanity and
	76	Church must preach Gospel
	108	How ancient apostles built up church
86	3	Tares drive church into wilderness
88	94	Fate of church, mother of abominations
	94	Great church is tares of earth
90	4	Oracles through you to church
	13	Joseph Smith to preside over church and
	15	Set in order churches
100	15	All things work for good of church
101	63	Wisdom concerning salvation of all churches
102	hd	Minutes of organization of High Council of
	9	President of church acknowledged by church
104	59	Print words to build up churches
106	8	Reward of light to church
107	72	Bishop to do business of church
	80	Highest council in church
	82	Before common council of church
112	24	Vengeance to begin with church
115	4	Name of church to be Church of Jesus Christ
124	32	Church rejected unless work for dead
	126	First Presidency to receive oracles for church
127	12	Subscribe, servant, prophet, seer of Church of
128	21	Trials and tribulations of this church
136	2	Let church be organized into companies

CHURCH ARTICLE
33	14	Keep them
42	13	Church articles to be observed

CHURCH COVENANT
33	14	Keep them
42	67	Church covenants to be received

CHURCH OF FIRST BORN see also Church
76	54	They are church of First Born
	67	General assembly and church of Enoch and of
	94	Who dwell in his presence are church of First
77	11	144 thousand to bring souls to church of First

CHURCH GOVERNMENT
20	hd	Section 20 on Church Government
41	3	Remarks on
42	59	Laws for church government where found

CHURCH MONEY
60	10	Church money to be given to returning elders

CHURCH, PROPERTY OF
38	36	Men to govern property of church
51	5–9	Property of church, how to deal with
	10	Church property not given to another church
	11	Church property may be lent to another church
101	98	Sore and grievous sin to sell to enemies God's

CINCINNATI
60	6	Brethren to go to Cincinnati
61	30	Lift voice against people of Cincinnati

CIRCUMCISE
74	3	Circumcised and subject to law of Moses
	3	Unbelieving husband wanted children circum-

CITY see also City of Heritage
63	31	Scourged from city to city
84	93	Wash feet against city
	94	Wo to city that rejects you
	117	Go to great and notable cities
94	1	Lay foundation of city of stake of Zion
96	hd	City or stake of Kirtland
104	36	Lots laid off for building of city
111	4	Will give this city into your hands
125	2	Build cities unto my name
133	56	Mount Zion and holy city Jerusalem

CITY OF HERITAGE see also Zion, New Jerusalem,
58	13	Zion, city of heritage of God

CIVIL see also Government
109	55	Remember civil authorities
134	9	Religious influence and civil government sep-
	11	Men should apply to civil law for

CLEAN see also Pure, Cleanse
38	10	Pleased only with the clean
	10	Not all are clean
	42	Be ye clean that bear
88	75	That I may testify you are clean
	85	Not called, for garments not yet clean
	86	Let your hands be clean
	138	Receive only those who are clean from blood
90	36	Chasten Zion until clean
133	5	Be clean that bear the vessels of the Lord

CLEANLINESS
42	41	All things in cleanliness before me

CLEAVE
88	40	Intelligence cleaveth to intelligence
	40	Light cleaveth unto light

CLERK
- 85 1 Lord's clerk to keep General Church Record

CLOTHE
- 84 81 No thought for what shall clothe
-     89 Who receives will clothe you
-     90 Who clothes you, lose no reward
-     101 Earth clothed with glory of God
- 88 125 Clothe yourselves in charity
- 133 69 Clothe heavens with blackness

CLOUD
- 34 7   Shall come in cloud with
- 45 44 Christ seen in clouds of heaven
-     45 Meet Christ in a cloud
- 76 63 Come with him in clouds of heaven
- 78 21 Will take you up in cloud
- 84 5   Cloud of God's glory upon the Temple

COAT
- 24 18 Missionary shall not take two coats, etc.
- 84 78 Neither purse, scrip nor two coats
-     105 Take new, cast old to poor

COLD
- 89 13 Flesh used in winter, cold, or famine

COE, JOSEPH
- 55 6   Joseph Coe called
- 102 3   Joseph Coe member of first High Council

COLESVILLE
- 24 3, 26:1, 37:2, Go to church in Colesville
- 128 20 Peter, James and John at Colesville

COLTRIN, ZEBEDEE
- 52 29 Zebedee Coltrin called

COMFORT
- 101 14 Who mourned shall be comforted

COMFORTER see also Holy Spirit, Holy Ghost,
- 21 9   Comforter manifests that Jesus was crucified
- 24 5   Write what is given by Comforter
- 28 4   If led by Comforter speak
- 31 11 Comforter shall give you what to do
- 42 16 Speak and prophesy by Comforter
-     17 Comforter beareth record of Father and Son
-     17 Comforter knoweth all things
- 50 14 Comforter sent to teach truth
-     17 Spirit of truth
- 52 9   Say only what taught by Comforter
- 75 10 Comforter to teach all expedient things
-     10 Call on name of Lord for Comforter
-     27 Comforter to tell missionaries where to go
- 79 2   Comforter to teach truth
- 88 3   Comforter, Holy Spirit of Promise
-     3   Comforter abide in your hearts
-     3   Comforter promised disciples in John's
-     4   Comforter promise of eternal life
- 90 11 Comforter for revelation of Jesus
-     14 Receive revelations as manifest by Comforter
- 124 97 Receive of Spirit even Comforter

COMING see also Christ's Coming
- 2   3   Earth would be wasted at its coming

COMMAND see also Commandment, Law
- 1   5   I Lord have commanded; none shall stay
- 5   21 Command you, Joseph, to repent
-     26 I, Lord, command Martin Harris to say
-     29 If case I command you Joseph to say
-     34 Will provide means to accomplish command
-     34 Stop until I command thee
- 9   13 Do this thing I have commanded you shall
- 18 9   Command all men to repent
- 28 6   Shall not command head
- 29 6   United according to command
- 56 4   I command and revoke as good
-     3   Who obeys not command, cut off
- 58 26 God, not command in all things
-     29 Who waits to be commanded is damned
-     32 Result of disobeying the Lord's command
- 98 22 Obey command and wrath and indignation
- 101 60 Do all things I command
-     67 Command to gather
- 105 28 Send wise men to fulfill commandments
- 132 37 Isaac and Jacob did only what was command-
- 133 16 All men commanded to repent
-     23 Shall command the deep

COMMANDMENT see also Command, Law, Obedi-
- 1   hd Commandment of Lord to church
-     6   Preface to book of commandments
-     17–20 Relation of commandments to servants
-     18 Gave commandments to others
-     24 The purpose of these commandment
-     24 Commandments given after manner of their
-     30 Commandments were given to found church
-     32 Who does commandments shall be forgiven
-     37 Search these commandments
-     37 Commandments are true and faithful
- 3   5   How strict were your commandments
-     6   Transgressed commandments of God
-     10 Repent of what is contrary to commandments
- 5   22 Be firm in keeping commandments
-     28 Must covenant to keep commandments
-     33 Commandments given that thy days may be
-     35 If faithful in keeping commandments shall
- 6   9   Bring forth work according to commandments
-     20 Be faithful and diligent in keeping command-
- 10 34 I give you commandments
-     56 Who keep not commandments shall
- 11 9   Bring forth work according to commandments
-     20 Your work to keep my commandments
- 14 7   If you will keep commandments shall have
- 15 5   Words given according to commandment
- 17 8   If ye do commandments shall
- 18 43 After that you must keep my commandments
-     46 If keep not commandments you cannot

19	32	Last commandment concerning this matter
28	2	Commandments for the church to be received
	5	Not write by way of commandment
29	35	Commandments of God spiritual, not carnal,
30	8	Keep commandments shall have eternal life
38	35	Commandment regarding care for the poor
42		Commandments to the church
	4	First commandment
	29	If thou lovest me keep all my commandments
43	2	Commandment for a law
46		Revelation vs. Commandment
	7	Seduced by commandments of men
56	6	Commandment revoked for stiff-neckedness
58	2	Blessed, keep my commandments
	29	Who keepeth commandment with slothfulness
	29	Who receiveth commandment with doubtful
	30	Not guiltless who obeys not commandments
59	1	Blessed, who have come according to com-
	4	Who shall receive many commandments
61	13	Commandment given for your good
	18	Commandment to one, commandment to all
63	13	Many turned away from commandments
	23	Who keeps commandments will give mysteries
67	4	A testimony of truth of commandments
	6	If any make the like of one commandment
68	hd	Items in addition to commandments
70	3	Stewards over revelations and commandments
	15	Commandment for benefit of saints
71	4	Prepare for commandments to come
	11	My commandments true and faithful
74	5	Commandment not of Lord but of apostle
75	4	Proclaim truth according to revelations and
	7	Commandment to chasten for murmurings
76	52	Cleansed from sin by keeping commandments
78	13	Ensample for accomplishing commandments
84	61	Forgive sins with this commandment
	86	A commandment to all faithful called to the
90	32	Write this commandment
93	20	Keep commandments and receive fullness
	27	Fullness only by keeping commandments
	28	Truth and light of commandments kept
95	11	Keep commandments, power to build
103	8	Keep not commandments world shall prevail
	31–34	Obey a commandment as far as possible
124	87	If love me, keep commandments
132	29	Abraham received all by revelation and com-
133	60	These commandments were kept from world,
	60	Why the latter day commandments were given
	60	Then commandments to go to all flesh
136	2	With covenant and promise to keep command-
	42	Be diligent in keeping my commandments

COMMITTEE
94	15	Committee to build the Lord's houses
123	4	Committee to aid in gathering history of

COMMON COUNCIL
107	82	Before common council of church

COMPANY
103	30	Companies of various sizes to go to Zion
136	2	Let church be organized into companies
	3	Companies with captains of hundreds, fifties,

COMPASSION see also Mercy, Merciful
64	2	I will have compassion
88	40	Mercy hath compassion on mercy
121	3	Let bowels be moved with compassion

COMPEL
58	26	Who is compelled, not a wise servant

COMPREHEND
6	21	Light shineth, darkness comprehendeth not
88	6	Jesus comprehended all things
	48	Came to his own was not comprehended
	49	Day when shall comprehend God
	67	Body filled with light comprehends all

COMPULSION
121	37	If exercise compulsion upon souls

CONCUBINE see also Marriage
132	37	Abraham received concubines for righteous-
	38	David received many wives and concubines
	38	Solomon received many wives and concubines

CONDEMN see also Punishment, Condemnation
5	27	If he break covenant he is condemned
6	35	I do not condemn you
9	12	Neither of you have I condemned
64	9	Who does not forgive stands condemned
	40	Bishop and counselors condemned if not faith-
75	21	You shall judge and condemn who
104	7	That innocent not condemned
136	39	Joseph Smith died that wicked be condemned

CONDEMNATION see also Condemn, Punishment
5	18	Condemnation if harden hearts
10	23	Shall turn to condemnation
20	15	Who harden their hearts in unbelief shall turn
42	81	Condemnation by the mouth of two witnesses
63	11	Signs shown in wrath unto condemnation
	62	Condemnation to use Lord's name without
	64	Condemnation without prayer
	66	Overcome through patience else greater con-
67	8	Under condemnation if accept not God's word
76	48	Ordained to their condemnation
82	3	Who sins against greater light receives great-
84	55	Vanity and unbelief brought church under con-
	56	This condemnation rests on children of Zion
	57	Condemned until repent
88	65	Ask anything not expedient shall turn to
	100	Time for resurrection of spirits under con-
93	31	Here is condemnation of man
	32	Who receives not light is under condemnation
132	48	What you give is without condemnation
136	33	Spirit to condemnation of ungodly

CONDITION
- 18   12   Bring men unto him on conditions of repent-
- 46   15   God suits mercies according to conditions
- 88   38   Every law has bounds and conditions
-         39   Who abide not conditions of law are not jus-

CONFER
- 13   1   In the name of Messiah I confer
- 67   14   Conferred by hands of Joseph Smith Jr.

CONFERENCE see also Meeting, Assembly
- 20   61   Frequency of conferences
-         61   Elders of church to meet in conference
-         62   Conferences to do church business
-         64   Conference may issue license
-         67   General conference to direct some ordinations
-         81   Churches to send teachers to the conferences
-         81   Conferences held by elders of church
-         82   List of names sent to conference
- 28   10   Preside over conference by voice of it
- 44   2   Elders called together for conference
- 58   58   Conference meeting to be called
-         58   As ruled by conference
- 68   hd   Will of Lord to conference concerning
- 72   7   Duty of bishop known by commandments and
- 73   hd   What elders shall do to conference
-         2   Missions known by voice of conference
- 75   hd   Revelation given in conference
- 124   144   Approve or disapprove of names for offices
-         88   Await instructions from general conference

CONFESS see also Acknowledge, Sin, Repent
- 19   20   Confess your sins
- 42   88   Offender confess, reconciled
- 58   43   If repented, will confess
- 59   12   Confess sins to brethren and Lord
-         21   Offend unless confess His hand
- 61   2   Mercy, who confess sins
- 64   7   Sins forgiven if confessed
- 76   110   Every tongue confess

CONFIDENCE
- 107   22   Presidency upheld by confidence
- 121   45   Then confidence in presence of God wax strong
- 124   112   Labor, may obtain confidence

CONFIRM see also Holy Ghost, Ordain, Baptism,
- 20   10   Gospel confirmed by ministering of angels
-         68   What shall precede confirmation
- 27   12   Confirmed to be apostles
- 33   15   Confirm those with faith
- 52   10   Confirming by water's edge
- 84   42   Priesthood I now confirm
-         48   Father teaches of renewed and confirmed cov-

CONFIRMATION MEETING
- 46   6   Do not cast non-members out of confirmation

CONFOUND
- 49   27   Shall not be confounded
- 71   7   Confound your enemies
- 84   116   Trust and not be confounded
- 93   52   Not confounded if
- 100   5   Speak and shall not be confounded
- 133   58   When weak confound the wise

CONFUSION
- 63   24   Confusion brings pestilence
- 123   7   Which has filled world with confusion
- 132   8   My house of order not confusion

CONGREGATION see also Meeting
- 52   10   Preach in every congregation
- 88   129   President to be seen and heard by congrega-

CONSCIENCE
- 134   2   Free exercise of conscience in peaceable gov-
-         4   Conscience not controlled by human law

CONSECRATE PROPERTY see also United Order
- 42   30   Consecrate of properties for poor
- 51   5   Consecrated property cannot be claimed by a

CONSECRATE see also United Order
- 51   16   I consecrate this land
- 52   2   Land I will consecrate in Missouri
- 58   57   Sidney Rigdon to dedicate land of Zion
- 70   8   Benefits shall be consecrated
- 84   31   House of Lord built in this generation on con-
- 103   35   Kingdom on consecrated land
- 105   15   Lands consecrated for gathering

CONSECRATION see also United Order
- 42   32   Property received by consecration
-         39   Consecrated property of sinner
- 51   Consecration of property
- 83   6   Storehouse kept by consecration of church
- 105   29   Saints possess lands according to laws of

CONSENT, COMMON see also Consent, Majority,
- 26   2   All things done by common consent
- 28   13   All things done by common consent

CONSENT
- 93   51   Prayer of faith with one consent
- 101   97   Let not enemies pollute by your consent
- 104   21   Things done by united consent

CONSOLATION
- 124   53   Example for consolation for oppression
- 128   21   Giving consolation by confirming hope

CONSTITUTION see also Law, United States
- 101   77   I have suffered to establish constitution
-         77   Laws and constitution are of holy and just
-         80   I established constitution of this land
-         80   Constitution by men raised up for the purpose
- 109   54   Let constitution be established forever

CONSTITUTIONAL LAW
- 98   5   Constitutional law to be befriended
-         5   Constitutional law for all mankind
-         6   Justified in befriending constitutional law

CONSUME see also Christ's Coming
- 5   19   Earth consumed by coming
- 63   34   Consume wicked with fire
- 101   24   Every corruptible thing consumed

CONTEND
- 18   20   Contend against no church, save
- 90   36   Lord will contend with strong of Zion
- 136   23   Cease to contend

CONTENTION see also Contend
- 10   63   Satan doth stir hearts to contention
- 74   3   Contention concerning circumcision
- 95   10   Chastened because of contention
-       10   Contentions in school of prophets
- 101   6   Contentions pollute inheritances

CONTINUE
- 88   40   Justice continueth her course
- 132   30   Abraham and his seed to continue
-       63   Work continued by bearing souls

CONTINUATION
- 132   19   Glory is fullness and continuation of seed
-       22   Narrow way to continuation of lives

CONTRITE see also Humble
- 21   9   Remission of sins unto contrite heart
- 52   15   Prayer with contrite heart accepted
-       16   Speech with contrite heart accepted
- 54   3   Be humble and contrite
- 55   3   Receive Holy Spirit if contrite
-       18   Have broken hearts and contrite spirits
- 59   8   Offer the Lord spirit contrite
- 97   8   Blessings on broken honest hearts and con-
- 136   33   Spirit sent to enlighten humble and contrite

CONTROVERSY
- 107   80   Final decision in spiritual controversies

CONVERSATION
- 20   69   Manifest by conversation
- 108   7   Strengthen brethren in conversation
- 124   39   Conversations in temples

COPLEY, LEMON
- 49   hd   Section 49 given to Lemon Copley and

CORINTHIANS
- 74   hd   Explanation of Corinthians 7:14
- 128   13   Cor. xv. 46–48 explained
-       16   I. Corinthians xv. 29 explained

CORN
- 89   17   Corn for the ox

CORNER STONE
- 124   2   Stake, as corner stone of Zion
-       60   Contemplated glory of corner stone
-       131   A high council for corner stone of Zion

CORRIL, JOHN
- 50   38   Mentioned
- 52   7   John Corril to travel

CORRUPTION
- 38   12   Corruption causeth silence to reign
- 123   7   Is the main-spring of corruption

COUNCIL
- 78   9   Brethren to sit in council with saints of Zion
- 90   16   Presidency to preside in council
- 107   78   Cases undecided in Bishop's Court brought to
-       80   Highest council in church of Christ
-       81   No member exempt from council
- 121   32   Was ordained in Council of Eternal God before

COUNCIL OF CHURCH See also Church Government
- 107   82   Before the common council of church

COUNCIL, HIGH
- 20   67   High Council to direct some ordinations
- 42   34   As appointed by High Council of Church
- 102   hd   Minutes of organization of High Council of
-       1–34   Power and procedure of High Council
- 107   34   Twelve a traveling presiding High Council
-       36   Stake standing High Councils of equal auth-
-       36   Twelve traveling High Council
-       37   High Council in Zion of equal authority with
- 115   3   Name to be High Council of Church in Zion
- 120   1   High Council to aid in disposition of tithing
- 124   131   A High Council for corner stone of Zion
-       132   Members enumerated
-       139   Apostles traveling High Council

COUNCILS OF TWELVE
- 107   37   High Council in Zion, of equal authority with
- 124   127   Brigham Young the president

COUNSEL
- 1   19   Man should not counsel fellow man
- 3   4   Sets at nought counsels of God must fall
-       7   Men set at nought counsels of God
-       13   Set at nought God's counsels
-       15   Suffered counsel to be trampled upon
- 19   33   Misery if thou slight counsels
- 22   4   Seek not to counsel your God
- 24   1   I have counseled thee
- 56   14   Not pardoned for seeking counsel in own way
- 58   25   As counsel between themselves and me
- 63   55   Received not counsel and grieved spirit
- 64   20   Counsel wrongfully to your hurt
- 78   2   Listen to counsel that salvation may be unto
-       16   Under counsel of Holy One
- 100   2   Listen to counsel
- 101   8   Esteemed counsel lightly in peace
- 103   5   A decree to people if they hearken to counsel
- 105   22   I will counsel Joseph
-       37   Who follow counsel shall accomplish all things
- 108   1   Blessed for receiving counsel
- 122   2   Those who seek counsel, authority and blessing
- 124   16   Reward not fail if receive counsel
-       61   Counsel from the plants of renown
-       84   Counsel ordained in presidency of church
-       84   Do not establish own counsel
-       89   My will to hearken to counsel
- 136   19   No power to build up himself without counsel
-       19   Folly made manifest without counsel

COUNSELOR
- 42   31   Counselors to bishop to be
-       71   Bishop and counselors and families to be sup-
- 58   18   Judge by assistance of counselors

COUNSELOR continued
- 64 40 Bishop and counselors condemned if not faith-
- 90 6   Counselors equal with Joseph Smith Jr.
- 107 72 Bishop chooses counselors
-     76 Descendant of Aaron cannot try president of High Priesthood without counselors
-     76 Literal descendant of Aaron may act without
-     79 Presidency of high priesthood call twelve
- 112 30 First Presidency counselors and leaders of
- 124 91 Appointed, ordained and anointed a counselor
-     126 Counselors and president form quorum of First
-     136 Counselors to president of High Priests
-     142 Counselors to presidents

COUNTRY
- 88 79 Learn of countries
- 93 53 Obtain knowledge of countries
- 133 23 Great deep driven back to north countries
-     26 Coming of those in north countries

COURSE
- 3   2   God's course one eternal round
- 35 1   Whose course is one eternal round
- 88 40 Justice continueth her course
-     43 Courses of heavens and earth fixed

COURT
- 64 12 How to deal with offender who does not repent
- 95 16 Inner court of temple
- 102   From what church court appeals may be taken
-     2   Cases from Bishop's Court to High Council
- 107 78 Cases undecided in Bishop's Court brought to

COVENANT see also Promise, Oath
- 1   hd Covenants of Lord to church
-     15 Have broken everlasting covenant
-     22 That everlasting covenant might be estab-
- 5   3   Entered into covenant with me
-     27 If he deny he will break covenant
-     27 If he break covenant he is condemned
-     28 Except he covenant will not grant
- 22 1   Old covenants done away with
-     1   This new covenant from beginning
- 25 13 Cleave to covenants
- 28 12 Nothing appointed contrary to church cov-
- 38 20 A covenant of the Lord with the church
- 39 11 Covenant to recover people
- 40 3   Covenant breaker to be dealt with as seemeth
- 42 13 Covenants to be observed
- 52 2   Heirs according to the covenant
- 54 4   A broken covenant void
-     6   Who keeps covenants receives mercy
- 66 2   Blessed for receiving everlasting covenant
- 68 hd Items in addition to covenants
- 76 69 Jesus, mediator of new covenant
- 82 11 Bound by covenant that cannot break by
-     12 Covenant to manage affairs of poor
-     15 Bind yourselves by this covenant
- 84 39 Oath and covenant of priesthood
-     40 Receive priesthood receive oath and covenant
-     41 Who breaks covenant of priesthood no forgive-
-     48 Father teaches of renewed and confirmed
-     48 Covenant for the sake of the world
-     99 Election of grace by faith and covenant of
- 88 131 Prayers in token of covenant
- 90 24 Remember covenant
- 97 8   Accepted if covenants observed by sacrifice
- 98 3   Immutable covenant that prayers be fulfilled
-     15 Not abide covenant, not worthy
- 107 19 Jesus Mediator of new covenant
- 109 1   Lord who keepest covenant
- 132 hd Eternity of marriage covenant
-     4   Reject this covenant and be damned
-     6   New and everlasting covenant instituted for
-     7   Only contracts sealed for time and eternity
-     51 I require offering by covenant and sacrifice
- 133 57 Gospel, everlasting covenant reasoning in plain-
- 136 2   With covenant and promise to keep command-
-     4   Covenant to walk in ordinances of Lord

COVET
- 19 26 Shalt not covet own property
- 117 8   Covet a drop, neglect weighty matters
- 136 20 Covet not thy brothers

COVETOUS
- 88 123 Cease to be covetous

COVETOUSNESS
- 104 4   Cursed because of covetousness

COVILL, JAMES
- 39 hd Section 39 given to James Covill
- 40 1   Covenant and fall of James Covill

COWDERY, OLIVER
- 6   22 If you desire further witness remember night
-     28 Unto you and Joseph the keys of this gift
-     9   Oliver Cowdery to continue translating
- Sections 7, 17, 18, 23, 24, 26, 28 given to Oliver Cowdery
- 8   1   Shall receive knowledge of old records
- 13 hd John the Baptist laid hands on
- 18 1   Oliver Cowdery have desired to know
-     9   I speak unto Oliver Cowdery
-     37 Oliver Cowdery and David Whitmer to search
- 20 30 Oliver Cowdery called of God
- 21 10 Joseph Smith to be ordained by Oliver
-     11 Oliver Cowdery an elder
-     12 Oliver Cowdery the first preacher
- 23 1   Oliver Cowdery under no condemnation
- 27 8   Oliver Cowdery ordained by John
- 28 1   Oliver Cowdery to be heard in his teachings
-     5   Oliver Cowdery not to write church by way of
- 30 5   Peter Whitmer to journey with Oliver Cowdery
-     6   Given power to build churches among Laman-
-     7   None above Oliver Cowdery save Joseph
- 32 1   Parley P. Pratt to go with Oliver Cowdery

37	3	Oliver Cowdery mentioned
47	3	Oliver Cowdery appointed to another office
55	4	W. W. Phelps to assist Oliver Cowdery in
57	13	Oliver Cowdery to assist W. W. Phelps
58	58	Oliver Cowdery to return
60	6	Oliver Cowdery to go to Cincinnati
61	23	Oliver Cowdery not to travel upon waters
	30	Commandment to
63	46	Words concerning
68	32	Oliver Cowdery to carry sayings to Zion
69	1	Oliver Cowdery not trusted with command-
70	1	Oliver Cowdery mentioned
102	3	Oliver Cowdery member of first High Council
	34	Clerk to first High Council
104	28	His inheritance appointed
	29	Oliver Cowdery to have printing office
110	hd	Visions to Joseph Smith and Oliver Cowdery
124	95	Who was my servant Oliver Cowdery
	104	Oliver Cowdery again a spokesman

COWDERY, WARREN A.
106 1 W. A. Cowdery to be a presiding High Priest

CRAFTINESS
76 75 Fate of honorable men, blinded by craftiness

CREATE
14	9	Who created heavens and earth
20	18	Created man, male and female
29	31	Things created spiritually and temporally
76	24	Worlds were created through him
88	20	Why the earth was created
93	29	Intelligence not created

CREATION see also Create, Creator, Foundation
29	31	Creation by power of spirit
	32	Two spiritual and two temporal creations
49	17	Man's creation before world was
	17	Purpose of creation of earth
59	18	All creation for use of man
77	3	Destined order of creation
88	25	Earth fills measure of creation
128	23	Let eternal creations declare his name
132	28	Practiced from beginning of creations

CREATOR see also Create, Creation
88 41 God the creator of all
95 7 Lord of Sabath, Creator of First Day, etc.

CREATURE
77 2 Spirit of every creature in likeness of its form
78 14 Church independent above other creatures

CRIME
134 8 Manner in which crime should be punished

CROWN see also Salvation
20	14	Shall receive crown of eternal life
25	15	Shall receive crown of righteousness
29	12	Crowns upon their heads
58	4	Crowned with glory
59	2	Faithful receive crown
66	12	Shall have crown of eternal life
75	28	Provide for family and not lose his crown
76	79	Receive not crown of kingdom
	108	Christ crowned with glory on throne of power
78	15	Crown prepared for you
79	3	If faithful, crowned with sheaves
81	6	If faithful, have crown of immortality
88	107	Angels crowned with glory of might
101	15	Given lives for my name crowned
104	7	Crown of glory at my right hand
106	8	Prepared crown in mansions
133	32	Crowned in Zion by children of Ephraim

CRUCIFY see also Jesus
20	23	Christ was crucified, died, and rose again
45	52	Jesus, Son of God, that was crucified
53	2	Crucified for sins of world
54	1	Alpha and Omega crucified
76	35	Crucified him to themselves

CRY
6	22	Night when you cried in your heart
87	7	Cry and blood of saints cease to come up
101	92	Pray that their ears open to cries
133	9	The cry of the missionaries
	17	Angel crying through midst of heaven
136	36	Innocent blood cries from ground against

CRYSTAL
130 9 This earth made like a crystal

CUMBER
66 10 Seek not to be cumbered

CUMORAH
128 20 Glad tidings from Cumorah

CUNNING
10 12 Devil sought to lay cunning plan
  23 Satan laid a cunning plan
  43 My wisdom greater than cunning

CURSE see also Damn, Cursing, Apostate
27	9	That earth may not be smitten with curse
38	18	A land upon which there is no curse
41	1	Curse those who hear not
45	32	Wicked shall curse God and die
61	14	Last days cursed waters
	17	In beginning cursed land
103	24	Curse enemies if driven from Zion
	25	Whom ye curse I curse
113	10	Bands of neck curses of God
121	16	Cursed who lift heel against anointed
	16	Cursed who cry sinned when not sinned
128	18	Earth cursed without baptism for dead
132	47	Whom you curse I will curse
133	2	Come upon world with curse to judgment

CURSING
24 4 Cursing, if they receive thee not
  15 Cursing for those who receive you not
104 3 Not faithful nigh unto cursing

CURTAIN see also Stakes
    88   95   Curtain of heaven unfolded and Lord's face
   101   21   Called Stakes, for the curtains, or the strength

CUT OFF see also Wicked, Apostate
     1   14   The day cometh when wicked cut off
    50   8   Hypocrites cut off
    51   2   Cut off if not organized
    52   6   Cut off if not faithful
    56   3   Who obeys not command, cut off
    63   63   Cut off if not repentant
    85   11   Cut off to have no inheritance
   104   9   Cut off by transgressions cannot escape buf-

CUTLER, ALPHEUS
   124 132   Alpheus Cutler member of High Council

DAMN see also Curse
    42   60   Disobeyer shall be damned
    58   29   Who receiveth commandment with doubtful
         29   Who keepeth commandment with slothfulness
         29   Who waits to be commanded is damned
    68   9   Who believeth not shall be damned
    84   74   Unbelievers to be damned
   112   29   Believe not, not baptized, damned
   132   4   Reject this covenant and be damned

DAMNATION see also Damn
    19   7   Written eternal damnation
   121   23   Generation of vipers not escape damnation

DANCE
   136   28   If merry praise with dancing, etc.

DARKNESS see also Light
     1   30   Bring church out of darkness
     6   21   Light shineth, darkness comprehendeth not
    10   21   Love darkness better than light
    14   9   I cannot be hid in darkness
    24   1   Delivered from darkness
    50   23   Not edify is darkness
         25   Chase darkness from you
    57   10   Gospel to those who sit in darkness
    77   8   Power to cast down to darkness
    84   49   World groaneth under darkness
    95   6   Sin to walk in darkness it noon-day
   101   91   In darkness with weeping, etc.
   112   23   Darkness covers the earth
   123   13   Bring hidden things of darkness
   133   72   Disobedient delivered unto darkness

DAUGHTER
    25   1   They are sons and daughters of my kingdom
    76   24   Inhabitants of earth begotten sons and daugh-
   124   11   Bring gold and silver to house of daughters

DAVIES, AMOS
   124 111   Amos Davies to pay stock to Nauvoo house

DAVID
   109   63   Yoke broken from house of David
   132   38   David received many wives and concubines
         39   David lost exaltation for Uriah and his wife
         39   David lost his wives

DAY
     1   9   Day when wrath of God shall be poured
         14   Day when wicked cut off
     2   1   Before great and dreadful day of Lord
     4   2   Blameless before God at last day
     5   33   That days may be prolonged I give you com-
     6   3   Reap while day lasts
    19   3   At last great day of judgment
    51   17   Day not given
    87   8   Day of Lord cometh quickly
   101   62   Fulfilled after many days
   106   5   Day may not overtake you as thief
   121   31   Their appointed days
   133   11   Watch, for neither day nor hour known
         40   Call upon Lord day and night
         56   Sing song of Lamb day and night

DAY OF CHRIST'S COMING
    29   12   Day of coming in a pillar of fire
    63   53

DAY OF JUDGMENT See also End of World
    10   23   Shame and condemnation at day of judgment
    29   12   Twelve at day of judgment
    41   12   Keeping of words to be answered upon day of
    60   15   Testimony in day of judgment
    70   4   Account of stewardship in day of judgment
    75   22   More tolerable for heathen in day of judgment
   101   78   Accountable for own sins on day of judgment

DEACON see also Aaronic Priesthood
    20   39   Apostle may ordain deacons
         48   Priest may ordain deacons
         57   Teachers to be assisted by the deacons
         58   Deacons may not baptize
         59   Deacons may warn, teach, etc.
         60   How ordained
         64   Deacon may take certificate
         84   Deacons may sign recommend
    84   30   Deacon necessary appendage to lesser priest-
        111   Deacons standing ministers to church
    88 127   High priests down to deacons
   107   10   High Priest may officiate instead of Deacon
         62   Presiding deacons presiding
         63   Deacon to teacher
         85   Duties of president over twelve deacons
   124 142   To be a president of deacons and counselors

DEAD see also Temple, Baptism for Dead, Death,
    18   12   He hath risen from the dead
    29   13   Dead shall come forth
         26   Dead shall awake at the trump of Michael
    42   45   Weep for the dead
    63   49   Blessed are dead that die in the Lord
         49   Dead shall arise
    76   16   Speaking of resurrection of dead
    88   14   Redemption through resurrection from dead
         16   Resurrection from dead the redemption of soul
         97   Dead caught up to pillar of heaven

DEAF–DELIVER

	101	The rest of the dead live not till end of thou-
110		Dispensation of work for dead committed
124	100	If will to raise dead, withhold not voice
128	5	Salvation of dead without gospel ordained be-
	6	Books from which dead are judged explained
	7	Books by which dead are judged are records
	8	Dead judged out of books
	11	Who has keys of Holy Priesthood receives
	12	Baptism, in likeness of resurrection of dead
	14	As records of dead on earth so in heaven
	15	Salvation of dead essential to that of living
	18	Dead not perfect without living
	19	A voice of gladness for living and dead in
	22	Let dead speak anthem of praise
	22	King Immanuel ordained redemption of pris-
	24	Present worthy record of dead in temple

DEAF
35	9	Deaf made to hear
58	11	Deaf come to marriage of Lamb
84	69	In my name unstop ears of deaf

DEATH see also Dead, Die, Immortality
7	2	Give me power over death
18	11	Redeemer suffered death in the flesh
29	41	First death is last death
	41	Last death is spiritual
	41	Adam's spiritual death
	42	Not come to Adam and his seed until
	43	Through natural death to immortality
42	44	Die in me, live in me
	46	Righteous shall not taste death
	47	Death of unrighteous bitter
	48	Sick, not appointed unto death, shall be healed
45	2	Hearken lest death overtake you
57	10	Who sit in region and shadow of death
58	2	Blessed in life or death who
63	3	Those die whom the Lord will
	17	Who shall meet second death
	51	Death during the Millennium
64	7	Who have not sinned unto death
76	37	Only ones on whom second death shall have
	59	Death is theirs
	74	Concerning those who receive not gospel in
88	116	They shall no more see death
98	14	Will prove you unto death
101	29	No sorrow because no death
	36	Fear not even unto death
110	13	Elijah tasted not death
121	44	Faithfulness stronger than cords of death
124	130	A man's priesthood remains after death
128	12	In likeness of death and resurrection
132	13	Whatever without my word ceases at death
	15	Marriage without word, only to death
	18	Marriage for time and eternity without
	19	Marriage for time and eternity within
	25	Wide the way to death

	27	Whereby assent to my death
135	3	In life not divided, in death not separated

DEBT
19	35	Pay the debt thou hast contracted
64	27	Forbidden to get in debt to enemies
72	13	Labors of faithful answer debt to bishop
104	78	Pay all your debts
	85	Privilege, once, to pledge properties for debt
111	5	Concern not about debts; I will pay
115	13	Not in debt for building of Lord's house
117	5	Let properties of Kirtland turn out for debt
119	2	Surplus property for debts of First Presidency
136	25	If debt can't be paid, tell neighbor

DECEIVE
10	25	Satan saith: deceive to destroy
	28	Wo to him who lieth to deceive
46	8	Beware, lest ye are deceived
52	14	Pattern that be not deceived
	14	Satan deceiveth nations
129	7	Contrary to order of heaven for just man to

DECEIVER
50	6	Deceivers brought to judgment

DECISION see also Church Government
102	19–32	Decisions of high council
107	27	Decision of quorum must be unanimous if
	30	How the decisions of quorums of priesthood
	32	Manner of appeal from decision
	78	Cases undecided in Bishop's Court brought to
	80	Final decision in spiritual controversies

DEDICATE
58	57	Sidney Rigdon to dedicate land of Zion
94	6	House for Presidency dedicated from founda
109	hd	Prayer at dedication of Kirtland Temple
	12	House we now dedicate

DEED
10	21	Love darkness because deeds are evil
19	3	Judging every man to his deeds
51	5	Transgressor can claim only portion deeded
56	13	Inheritance according to deeds

DEEP
133	20	Shall stand on great deep
	23	Great deep driven dark to north countries
	27	Highway cast up in deep

DEFENSE
115	6	Gathering for a defense and refuge

DEFILE see also Pollute
93	35	Will destroy defiled temple
97	17	If temple defiled God leaves it

DELIVER
3	11	Thou shalt be delivered up except
8	4	Gift shall deliver thee
95	1	Chastisement deliverance from temptation
133	67	Power to redeem or deliver not shortened
	71	None to deliver disobedient

DENOMINATION
123	12	Many pure in heart among denominations

DENY
5	27	If he deny he will break covenant
11	25	Deny not the spirit of revelation
39	16	Lord cannot deny his word
76	35	Punishment for denying the Holy Spirit
101	5	Who deny me not sanctified
114	2	Others planted instead of who deny

DESCEND
88	6	Jesus descended below all things

DESCENDANT
107	40	Priesthood belongs rightly to descendants of

DESERT
133	29	Pools of living water in barren deserts

DESIRE
3	4	If follow carnal desires he must fall
4	3	Desire to serve God are called
6	3	Who desire to reap let him
	8	If you desire you shall be means of
	20	Spoken because of thy desires
	27	Good desires; to lay up treasures in heaven
7	3	Because desirest shall tarry
	5	Good desire to speedily come to my kingdom
	8	Ye shall have according to desires
10	46	Prophets desired Gospel should come forth
11	3	Desireth to reap, thrust in
	8	As you desire, it shall be done
	10	Gift if thou wilt desire
	14	By this shall know what you desire
	17	According to your desires it shall be done
	21	If you desire shall have my Spirit and my
12	7	Who have desires to establish work
18	1	Given because of desire
	38	By their desires you shall know them
67	1	Whose desires come up before me
88	121	Cease from all lustful desires
95	16	House for holy desires

DESOLATION
63	37	Desolation come upon the wicked
84	114	Warn cities of desolation and abolishment
88	85	Desolation of abomination awaits wicked
112	24	Day of desolation to come

DESPISE
35	13	Despised to thresh nations

DESTROY
3	18	Destroy, because of iniquity and abomination
	18	Lord has suffered to destroy brethren
	33	Many lie in wait to destroy thee
10	6	They have sought to destroy you
	12	Devil sought to destroy this work
	19	Therefore we will destroy him
	25	Catch a man in a lie to destroy him
	27	Seeking to destroy souls
	43	I will not suffer they destroy
	52	Do not bring gospel to destroy
	54	Not to destroy but to build up church
17	4	That Joseph Smith may not be destroyed
63	4	Lord destroys whom he pleases
64	17	Satan seeketh to destroy soul
93	35	Will destroy defiled temple
132	57	Satan seeketh to destroy
	63	Committed adultery and shall be destroyed
	64	Wife must obey law of Priesthood or be de-

DESTROYER
61	19	Destroyer rideth upon waters
105	15	Destroyer sent to waste enemies

DESTRUCTION
19	33	If slight counsels
38	13	Mystery to cause destruction
61	5	Decreed destruction upon waters
	31	People ripe for destruction
109	43	We delight not in destruction
133	15	Look not back lest destruction

DETROIT
52	8	By way of Detroit

DEVIL see also Adversary, Satan, Lucifer, Hell,
1	35	Devil shall have power
10	12	Devil sought to lay cunning plan
29	28	Fire everlasting for devil and his angels
	29	Devil cannot return from where he is
	36	Devil before Adam
	36	Rebellion of the devil
	37	Devil and his angels, manner of becoming
	39	Temptation of devil necessary
	40	Devil tempted Adam
35	9	Devils cast out by faith
76	28	Satan, Serpent, Devil, who rebelled
	33	Suffer with devil and his angels in eternity
	36	With the devil and his angels
	44	Devil reigns where worm dieth not
	85	Not redeemed from devil until last resurrec-
84	67	In my name cast out devils
88	110	Satan, serpent, devil, bound for thousand
	113	Devil and armies to battle with Michael and
	114	Devil hath no more power over saints
121	4	God controlleth devil
123	10	Enough to make hands of devil tremble
124	98	Sign to cast out devils
128	20	Michael detecting devil as angel of light
129	8	To know devil, as an angel of light
	8	Cannot feel devil's hand

DEVIL, CHURCH OF
18	20	Save church of devil

DEVIL, KINGDOM OF
10	56	Who build up Kingdom of Devil

DEVILISH
20	20	By transgression man became devilish

DEW
128	19	As dews of Carmel, so knowledge of God des-

DIE
20	23	Christ was crucified, died, and rose again
59	2	Who die, shall rest from labors
63	49	Blessed are dead that die in the Lord
	50	Who lives when Christ comes is blessed, but
76	72	Who died without law
88	26	Earth sanctified, die and quickened
	27	Righteous die, rise spiritual body
101	30	Then infant not die until old
	31	When dies shall not sleep but changed
	35	The faithful who die shall partake of the glory
124	86	If die, die unto me

DIFFICULTY
42	88	Private settlement of difficulties
102	2	High Council to settle difficulties
	24	High Priests when abroad may call council to

DILIGENCE
21	7	Diligence I know
70	15	Reward of diligence, etc.
103	36	Victory and glory through diligence, etc.
104	79	Blessing by diligence
107	99	Act in office with diligence
127	4	Redouble your diligence
130	19	Knowledge and intelligence gained by dil-

DILIGENT
18	8	If diligent shall be blessed unto eternal life
59	4	Diligent blessed with revelations
75	29	Let every man be diligent
136	42	Be diligent in keeping my commandments

DIRECTOR
3	15	Counsel of director trampled upon
17	1	Miraculous directors give to Lehi

DISCERN
33	1	Discerner of thoughts and intents
46	23	Some given discerning of Spirit
101	95	Man may discern between righteous and wick-

DISCIPLE
1	4	Warning by mouths of disciples of last days
	5	Disciples shall go forth, not be stayed
10	46	Disciples desired Gospel should come forth
	59	I said unto disciples
18	27	Who shall desire my name
	27	Twelve shall be my disciples
41	5	Disciple receiveth and doeth law
45	16	Show it to you as to my disciples while in the
	32	Disciples stand in holy places
52	40	Disciple remembers poor, needy, sick and
58	52	Disciples to purchase Zion
63	38	Disciples in Kirtland arrange their affairs
64	8	My disciples were chastened for not forgiving
	19	What disciples must know, that they perish
84	91	By this know my disciples
103	28	Who will not lay down life, not disciple

DISOBEDIENCE see also Disobedient
30	3	David Whitmer left to himself because of
42	60	Disobeyer shall be damned
93	39	Light and truth lost through disobedience
97	26	Results of disobedience
103	8	If disobedient world shall prevail
121	17	Cry transgression because children of dis-

DISOBEDIENT see also Disobedience
133	63	Their punishment
	71	None to deliver disobedient
	72	Disobedient delivered unto darkness

DISPENSATION
27	13	Keys committed to Peter, etc.
110	16	Dispensation of work for dead committed
	12	Elias commits dispensation of gospel of Abra-
112	30	Last days, dispensation of fullness of times
	31	Power of priesthood held in connection with
	32	Keys of this dispensation come down from
121	31	All knowledge revealed in dispensation of ful-
128	18	Welding together of dispensations now
	18	Dispensation of fulness of times ushering in
	20	Peter, James and John claim keys to dispen-
	21	Angels declaring their dispensation and priest-

DISSENSION
10	48	Become Lamanites by dissensions

DIVIDE
12	2	Word to dividing asunder of joints and marrow
133	24	Earth be, as before divided

DO see also Church Government, Principle
1	32	Who does commandments shall be forgiven
101	60	Do all things I command
136	17	Go and do as told

DOCTRINE
10	62	Only doctrine which is in me
	63	Contention from Satan concerning doctrine
	67	This is my doctrine
11	16	Know of a surety my doctrine
46	7	Seduced by doctrines of devils
88	77	Teach each other doctrine of kingdom
	78	instructed in principle, theory, doctrine and
97	14	Perfected in doctrine
101	78	Act in doctrine and principle pertaining to
102	23	In difficulty of doctrine or principle president
121	45	Doctrine of priesthood distil on soul

DODDS, ASA
75	15	Mission for Asa Dodds

DOMINION
1	35	Devil shall have power over his own dominion
76	95	Celestial equal in power, might, dominion
	111	Dominion according to word
	114	Surpass understanding in dominion
121	29	Dominions revealed to the valiant
	46	Dominion flow to thee without

DONATIONS see also Poor, Offerings
42	31	Donations for the poor to be made to the
	32	Remarks on donations
	37	One cast out can not receive back his donation

DORT, DAVID
    124 132 David Dort member of High Council
DOUBT
    6 36 Doubt not
    60 7 Declare word without doubting
DOVE
    93 15 Holy Ghost in the form of dove
DREADFUL
    2 1 Before great and dreadful day of Lord
DRINK
    19 18 God, not drink bitter cup
    27 2 Mattereth not what ye shall eat or drink for
        3 Not purchase strong drink of enemies
        5 I will drink of the fruit of the vine
    84 81 No thought for what shall drink
    89 5 To drink strong drinks not good
        7 Strong drinks not for belly, for washing body
        9 Hot drinks not for body or belly
        17 Barley and other grains for mild drinks
DROP
    117 8 Covet a drop, neglect weighty matters
DRUNKENNESS
    136 24 Cease drunkenness
DRY LAND
    128 23 Dry lands tell wonders of eternal king
DUMB
    35 9 Dumb made to speak
DUST
    24 15, 60:15, 75:20, Dust of feet as a testimony
    63 51 Shall not sleep in dust
    77 12 Man formed from dust of earth
DUTY
    23 3 Thy duty to the church
    101 100 Who learns not duty not worthy
    105 10 Must know duty before redemption
    107 99 Let every man learn his duty
    123 hd Duty in relation to persecution
        9 An imperious duty we owe to all
EAGLE
    124 99 Mount in imagination as on eagle's wings
EAMES, RUGGLES
    75 35 Mission for Ruggles Eames
EAR
    1 2 No ear that shall not hear
    43 22 Shall make ears tingle
    76 10 Know what ear has not heard
    78 2 Speak in your ears words of wisdom
    84 69 In my name unstop ears of deaf
    97 27 Whisper once in ears
    101 92 Pray that their ears open to cries
    133 45 Ear not heard great things prepared for him
EARNESTNESS
    123 14 Attend with earnestness
EARTH see World, Ground
    1 35 Peace shall be taken from earth
        38 Earth, yet not word, pass away
    2 3 Earth would be wasted at its coming
    7 6 Heirs of salvation who dwell on earth
    10 27 Goeth up and down, to and fro in earth
    13 1 Priesthood of Aaron never again taken from
    14 9 Who created heavens and earth
    20 17 God framer of heaven and earth
    27 9 Mission of Elijah that the earth may not be
    29 9 Wickedness not upon the earth
        9 Earth is ripe
        13 Earth shall quake
        23 Earth and heaven shall be consumed
        23 New earth
        26 Before earth pass away shall
    38 17 Earth is my footstool
    43 18 Earth shall tremble
        32 Shall pass away as by fire
    45 48 Earth shall tremble
        58 Earth given for an inheritance
    49 16 That earth answers end of creation
        19 Cometh of earth for food
    50 27 Things of earth subject to ordained
    56 11 Though earth pass away words shall not
    59 2 Who live shall inherit earth
        3 Earth bring forth in strength
        21 Earth shall be transfigured.
    77 1 Sea of glass is sanctified earth
        6 Seven thousand years the temporal existence
        12 Man formed from dust of earth
        12 Earth will be sanctified in seventh thousand
    84 101 Heavens smiled upon earth
        101 Earth travailed and brought forth strength
        101 Earth clothed with glory of God
    88 10 Jesus Christ the light and power of earth
        18 Why the earth must be sanctified
        19 Destiny of earth
        20 Who shall possess the earth
        20 Why the earth was created
        25 Earth fills measure of creation
        26 Earth sanctified, die, and quickened
        43 Heavens and earth comprehend earth and
        43 Courses of heaven and earth fixed
        45 Earth rolls upon her wings
        87 Earth shall tremble and reel as drunken
    93 17 Son received all power on earth and heaven
    101 23 Vail which hideth earth
        25 That knowledge and glory dwell upon earth
        33 Shall reveal how and why earth was made
    103 7 Earth given saints for ever
    104 14 Lord built earth as handy work
        17 Enough and spare for all on earth
    117 6 Have I not made earth
    121 4 Maker of heaven, earth and seas
    123 7 Earth groans under weight of iniquity
    128 5 Baptism for dead ordained before foundation

EARTHLY

	7	Record of earth, recorded in heaven
	18	Earth cursed without baptism for dead
	19	Truth out of earth in Gospel
	22	Let earth break into singing
130	5	Angels ministering to earth belong to it
	6	Angels do not reside on planet like earth
	9	Sanctified earth a Urim and Thummim for
	9	This earth will be Christ's like a crystal
133	24	Earth be, as before divided
	39	Worship him who made earth, etc.

EARTHLY

78	6	Not equal in earthly, not equal heavenly

EARTHQUAKE

43	25	God calls by earthquakes
87	6	God's wrath shown by earthquakes
88	89	After your testimony that of earthquakes

EAST

77	9	Angel ascending from east

EAT

27	2	Mattereth not what ye shall eat or drink for
64	34	Willing and obedient shall eat the good of the
84	81	No thought for what shall eat

EDEN, GARDEN OF

29	41	Adam cast out

EFFORT

123	6	Publish as last effort

EGYPT

136	22	I led Israel out of Egypt

ELDER see also Melchisedek Priesthood

20	2	Joseph Smith the first elder
	3	Oliver Cowdery second elder
	5	First elder entangled in vanities
	16	Elders of church bear witness
	39	Apostle may ordain elders
	45	Duties of
	52	Priest to assist the elders
	60	How ordained
	61	Elders of church to meet in conference
	63	Elders to receive licenses by vote
	64	Certificates of ordination presented to an elder
	66	Elder may ordain without vote of church
	70	Children to be brought unto the elders
	76	Elder to administer sacrament
	81	Conferences held by elders of church
	82	One of the elders to keep a book of names
	84	Elder may sign recommend
21	1	Joseph Smith be called elder
29	hd	Section 29 given in presence of six elders
41	2	Commandment to elders of church
42	1	Revelation to elders of church
	12	Elders to preach principles of Gospel
	31	Lay before two elders or High Priests
	44	Elders to heal the sick
	71	Elder to assist bishop
43	16	Elders of church to be taught from on high
44	1	Elders called together for conference
46	2	Elders of church to conduct meetings as guid-
52	1	Elders called by voice of Spirit
53	3	Take ordinance even if elder
67	1	Elders whose prayers I have heard
68	hd	Will of Lord to conference concerning certain
	7	Word of Lord unto all faithful elders
72	5	Elders render account to bishop
	16	Every elder give account to bishop
	19	Elder, who accounts to bishop be recommended
	25	Certificates from three elders or bishop
73	hd	What elders shall do to conference
	5	Pattern to elders until further knowledge
77	5	Four and twenty elders mentioned by John
84	1	Revelation to Joseph Smith and six elders
	29	Elder a necessary appendage to High Priest
	111	Elders to travel
88	72	I will send elders to them
102	5	Seventeen elders voted on first High Council
105	11	No redemption until elders endowed with pow-
	33	First elders receive endowment in my house
107	7	Elder under Melchisedek priesthood
	10	High Priest may officiate instead of elder
	11	Elder officiate when High Priest absent
	12	An elder to officiate when no higher authority
	60	Presiding elders necessary
	63	Priest to elder
	89	Duties of presidents over 96 elders
	90	Presidency of elders distinct from that of
124	125	Joseph Smith a presiding elder
	137	Quorum of elders ordained standing ministers
	137	Elders may travel
	139	Severity a quorum for traveling elders
	140	Elders have responsibility of presiding
	140	Difference between seventies and elders
133	8	Send elders unto all nations
136	41	Elders and people received my kingdom

ELECT see also Redeem

25	3	Emma Smith an elect lady
	34	Who receive priesthood are elect of God
84	99	Redeemed by election of grace

ELEMENT

93	33	Elements are eternal
	33	Spirit and element together only receive ful-
	35	Elements are tabernacle of God
101	25	That of element melt with heat

ELIAS

27	6	Bring to pass the restoration of all things
	7	Elias visited Zacharias
76	100	Of Elias but receive not Gospel
	9	Elias to restore all things
	14	John Is Elias, the restorer
110	12	Elias commits dispensation of Gospel of Abra-

ELIHU

84	9	Elihu received priesthood from Jeremy

ELIJAH
- 2　1　Reveal priesthood by hand of Elijah
- 27　9　Mission of Elijah that the earth may not be
- 35　4　Prepare way before Elijah
- 　　110　Dispensation of work for dead committed
- 　　13　Elijah tasted not death
- 　　15　Elijah commits keys of turning hearts of
- 133　55　From Elijah to John
- 　　55　From Moses to Elijah

ENCYCLOPEDIA
- 123　5　Keep history of report of church in ency-

END see also Day of Judgment, Christ's Coming
- 6　13　Saved if hold out to end
- 10　3　At end of the world
- 　　6　Endless torment, not, no end
- 29　23　The end shall come
- 　　33　Works of God have no end
- 88　66　Truth hath no end
- 　　106　It is finished: the end
- 132　20　Gods because they have no end

END OF EARTH see also Day of Judgment
- 38　5　Judgment cometh at end of earth
- 43　21　The end mentioned
- 　　31　End of earth discussed
- 88　101　Spirits that live not till end of earth
- 121　32　Reserved until end of world

ENDLESS
- 19　4　I, God am endless
- 　　6　Endless torment, not, no end
- 　　12　Endless punishment is God's punishment

ENDOW see also Endowment, Temple
- 38　32　There endowed with power
- 43　16　Sanctify yourselves and be endowed
- 95　　House to endow with power from high
- 　　8　House to endow who are chosen
- 105　11　No redemption until elders endowed with
- 132　59　A man endowed with keys of priesthood justi-

ENDOWMENT see also Endow, Temple
- 105　12　Endowment and blessing for faithful and
- 　　18　Blessing and endowment for obedient
- 　　33　First elders receive endowment in my house in
- 110　9　Rejoice in consequence of endowment

ENDURE see also Faithful
- 10　69　Who endureth will I establish
- 14　7　If you endure shall have eternal life
- 18　22　Endure to the end and shall be saved
- 20　29　Must endure in faith
- 50　5　Blessed who endure
- 53　7　He saved only who endures to the end
- 63　20　Who endureth shall overcome
- 　　47　Who is faithful and endures shall overcome
- 101　35　Who suffer persecution but endure shall par-
- 121　8　If endure, God will exalt

ENEMY
- 8　4　Gift shall deliver thee from enemies
- 24　1　Delivered from thine enemies
- 27　3　Not purchase strong drink of enemies
- 38　12　The enemy is combined
- 　　28　Enemy in secret chambers seeketh your life
- 42　43　Enemy not nourish a sick
- 　　80　An enemy not to testify
- 44　5　That your enemies may have no power
- 52　42　Missouri now land of enemies
- 54　3　To escape enemies repent
- 63　31　Enemies if shed blood
- 64　27　Forbidden to get in debt to enemies
- 65　6　That enemies may be subdued
- 71　7　Confound your enemies
- 　　7　Meet enemies in public and private
- 76　61　All enemies subdued by God
- 　　106　Christ subdued enemies at fulness of times
- 87　7　Blood of saints to be avenged on enemies
- 98　　Law of treatment of enemies
- 　　14　Be not afraid of enemies
- 　　23　If men smite once, seek not revenge, be re-
- 　　25　If men smite, twice, no revenge, reward hun-
- 　　27　Testimonies against enemy if he repent not
- 　　28　Warn enemy if he smite more than thrice
- 　　29　Enemy delivered if warned
- 　　30　If enemy spared, rewarded for righteousness
- 　　31　Just to reward enemy according to works
- 　　39　If enemy repent, and prays forgiveness, for-
- 　　40　Forgive enemy seventy times seven if he re-
- 　　44　Bring forth trespass as testimony
- 　　45　Forgive enemy if
- 　　45　Will avenge thee of enemy if
- 101　51　Enemy came by night
- 　　53　Don't fall asleep lest enemy
- 　　54　Watchman to see enemy while afar off
- 　　57　Avenge me of my enemies
- 　　96　Sidney Gilbert not to sell storehouse to enemies
- 　　97　Let not enemies pollute by your consent
- 　　98　Sore and grievous sin to sell to enemies God's
- 103　2　Will pour wrath upon enemy
- 　　6　Saints begin to prevail against enemies from
- 　　24　Curse enemies if driven from Zion
- 　　25　Avenge me of mine enemies
- 105　15　Destroyer sent to waste enemies
- 　　15　God's enemies to be destroyed
- 　　30　Vengence on enemies to third and fourth gen-
- 121　5　Let anger kindle against enemies
- 　　43　Reprove, lest esteem thee enemy
- 122　9　Bounds of enemies set
- 124　50　Punishment of those who hinder work
- 　　50　Answer judgment, etc. on enemies
- 　　53　Example when hindered by enemies
- 127　1　Enemies pursue with a cause
- 　　2　Shall triumph over enemies
- 133　28　Enemies become a prey
- 136　17　Enemies not stop work

ENGRAVING–ETERNITY

	30	Fear not enemies
	40	Delivered from enemies in witness of my name
	42	Keep commandments lest enemy triumph

ENGRAVING
8	1	Knowledge of engravings of records
10	41	Translate engravings of plates of Nephi

ENJOY
88	32	Enjoy what willing to receive

ENLIGHTEN
6	15	Enlightened by Spirit of Truth
11	13	My Spirit shall enlighten your mind
84	46	Spirit enlightens every man

ENOCH
76	57	Order of Melchisedek after Enoch, after Only
	67	General assembly and church of Enoch and
	100	Of Enoch, but receive not Gospel
78	hd	Enoch, Joseph Smith, Jr.
	4	City of Enoch for everlasting order unto
	9	Gazelam or Enoch (Joseph Smith, Jr.)
82	hd	Order given to Enoch in his day
84	15	Enoch received priesthood
96	hd	Enoch Joseph Smith. Jr.
107	48	Enoch ordained at 25
	49	Enoch before face of God continually
	49	Enoch translated at 430
	53	Enoch a High Priest
133	54	Enoch and prophets before him

ENOCH, CITY OF
45	12	City of Enoch, etc.

ENOS
107	44	Enos ordained by Adam
	53	Enos a High Priest

ENSAMPLE
68	2	The Ensample to all missionaries
72	23	Ensample to all branches of church
78	13	Ensample for accomplishing commandments
	14	Ensample, that church shall stand above all
98	38	Ensample for justification of battle

ENSIGN
64	42	Zion an ensign unto people
105	39	Lift up ensign of peace

ENVY
127	2	Envy and wrath my common lot

ENVYING
101	6	Envyings pollute inheritances

EPHRAIM
27	5	Moroni has keys of stick of Ephraim
64	36	Rebellious not of Ephraim and are plucked out
113	4	Descendant of Jesse and Ephraim or Joseph
133	30	Bring treasure to children of Ephraim
	32	Crowned in Zion by children of Ephraim
	32	Children of Ephraim, servants of
	34	Richer blessing upon Ephraim

EQUAL
70	14	Shall be equal in temporal things
	14	Manifestations of Spirit not abundant if
76	95	Celestial equal in power, might, dominion
78	6	Not equal in earthly, not equal heavenly
82	17	You are to be equal
88	107	Saints equal with him
	122	Every man have equal privilege

EQUALITY
51	9	Equality of church members

EQUITY
102	16	Speak according to equity

ESAIAS
76	100	Of Esaias, but receive not gospel
84	12	Esaias received priesthood from God
	13	Esaias blessed by Abraham

ESTABLISH
1	22	Everlasting covenant established
6	31	Words which shall be established by testimony
	28	Word established by two or three witnesses
22	hd	Church established in year
128	3	Every word established in mouth of two or

ESTEEM
38	24	Esteem your brother

ESPECIAL WITNESS
27	12	Apostles and especial witnesses

ETERNAL see also Eternity
3	2	God's course one eternal round
19	hd	Commandment by Him who is Eternal
	7	Written eternal damnation
	11	Eternal punishment is God's punishment
20	17	God is eternal
	28	Father, Son and Holy Ghost eternal
29	44	Eternal damnation to those who repent not
93	33	Elements are eternal
98	13	Lay down life and find life eternal
121	32	Eternal God of all other Gods
	32	Enter eternal presence
	32	Was ordained in Council of Eternal God before
128	23	Seas and lands tell wonders of Eternal King
132	24	Eternal life to know God and Jesus Christ

ETERNITY
38	1	Wide expanse of eternity before the world was
	12	Eternity is pained
	20	Shall possess inheritance in eternity
	39	Shall have riches of eternity
39	22	Gathered to me in eternity
43	34	Let solemnities of eternity be upon you
68	31	Saints should seek earnestly riches of eternity
72	3	Steward render account in time and eternity
76	4	The same from eternity to eternity
	8	Shall know wonders of eternity
78	18	Riches of eternity yours
88	13	God in bosom, of eternity
132	hd	Eternity of marriage covenant and
	7	Sealed for time and eternity by Holy Spirit of
	18	Marriage for time and eternity without coven-

ETERNITY continued
        19   Marriage for time and eternity within coven-
ETHER
  135 4   Paragraph from Ether read by
EUROPE
  118 4   The mission to Europe called
EVANGELICAL MINISTER see also Patriarch
  107 39   Twelve to ordain evangelical ministers as re-
EVERLASTING COVENANT see also United Order
  1   15   Have broken everlasting covenant
       22   That everlasting covenant might be estab-
  6   3   Treasure everlasting salvation
  45 9   Everlasting covenant now sent same as from
  78 11   Organize by bond that cannot be broken
       12   Who breaks everlasting covenant shall lose,
EVIDENCE
  102 16   Case presented according to evidence
EVIL   see also Sin
  10 21   Love darkness because deeds are evil
  20 54   Teachers to see there is no evil speaking
  27 15   That ye :nay withstand evil day
  64 16   Sought evil and Lord withheld Spirit
       17   Repent of evil and be forgiven
  76 17   Who have done evil, in resurrection of unjust
  93 37   Light and truth forsake evil one
  98 11   Forsake evil cleave unto good
  124 116 Cease to do evil
       120 What is more or less of evil
  136 21   Evil to take name of Lord in vain
       23   Cease to speak evil
EVIL DAY
  5   24   He exalts himself before me
  49 10   Exalted, laid low
  63 55   Exalteth himself in heart
  104 16   Poor shall be exalted
  112 3   Exalted as abased
       8   Many low exalted
  121 8   If endure, God will exalt
  124 114 Abase he may be exalted
  132 17   Who marry without covenant are saved but not
EXALTATION see also Exalt, Salvation
  124 9   Gentiles come to exaltation of Zion
  132 22   Way to exaltation is narrow
       29   Abraham hath entered his exaltation
       37   Isaac and Jacob have entered their exaltation
       37   Obedience necessary for exaltation
       49   Seal your exaltation upon you
       63   Exaltation to bear souls of men
EXAMPLE
  51 18   Example for organizing other churches
  88 136 Example for salvation in house of Lord, School
  124 53   Example for consolation for oppression
EXCESS
  59 20   Avoid excess
  70 7   Excess given into my storehouse
  88 69   Cast away excess of laughter
EXECUTE
  88 40   Who governeth and executeth all things
EXEMPT
  10 28   Not exempt from justice of God
EXERCISE
  6   11   Thou shalt exercise thy gift
EXHORTATION
  50 37   Strengthen churches by exhortation
  108 7   Strengthen brethren in exhortations
EXPEDIENT see also Wisdom
  9   3   Not expedient that you translate now
  18 18   Holy Ghost manifesteth what is expedient
  88 65   Ask anything not expedient shall turn to con-
       78   Instructed in all expedient to understand
  96 5   Most expedient that word go forth
  100 4   Expedient for salvation of souls
  105 13   Expedient that elders wait
  127 1   Expedient to leave for safety
EXPELLED
  20 83   Names of the expelled to be blotted out
EXPERIENCE
  105 10   Redemption delayed to give people experience.
  122 7   All trials give experience and be for your good
EXTORTION
  59 20   Not used by extortion
EYE
  29 19   Eyes fall from sockets
  43 32   Shall be changed in a twinkling of eye
  58 3   Cannot behold God's design with natural eyes
  59 18   Nature to please eye
  67 2   Mine eyes are upon you
  76 10   Know what eye has not seen
       19   Lord touched eyes of understanding
  84 69   In my name open eyes of blind
       98   All see eye to eye
  88 11   Light through him, who enlighteneth eyes
  110 1   Eyes of our understanding opened
       3   Eyes as flame of fire
  121 24   Eye see and know all works
  128 2   Eye witness to baptism for dead
  133 45   No eye seen great things for him who waits
EZEKIEL
  29 21 Words of Ezekiel to come to pass
EZRA
  85 12   Ezra 2:61–62 referred to
FACE
  17 1   Brother of Jared face to face
  88 68   He will unvail his face
       95   Curtain of heaven unfolded and Lord's face
  101 38   Seek face of God always
  124 8   When unvail face of covering
  133 49   Sun shall hide face in shame
FAIL
  124 75   Not fail nor his heart faint

FAINT				76	53	Who overcome by faith
	89	20	Walk and be not faint	84	99	Election of grace by faith and covenant of
	103	19	Let not hearts faint	85	2	Record of faith of members to be kept
	124	75	Not fail nor his heart faint	88	118	As all have not faith, seek and teach
FAITH			see also Believe, Faithful, Know, Knowledge,		118	Seek learning by study and faith
	1	21	Faith might increase in earth		119	Establish a house of faith
	3	20	Glorified through faith	90	22	Bishop's agent, a man of God and strong faith
	4	5	Faith qualifies him for the work	93	51	By prayer of faith uphold him
		6	Remember faith	104	55	Properties mine or faith vain
	5	24	If in faith, I will grant	105	19	Brought for trial of faith
		28	Except exercise faith will not grant		24	Boast not of faith, etc.
	6	12	Make known gift only of thy faith	107	22	Presidency upheld by faith
		19	Have faith, etc.	136	42	Keep commandments lest faith fail
	8	1	Receive if ask in faith	FAITHFUL see also Believer, Faithfulness, Endure		
		10	Without faith, nothing, ask in faith	1	37	Commandments true and faithful
		11	According to your faith shall it be done	3	8	You should have been faithful
	10	47	Granted according to faith	5	35	If faithful thou shalt be lifted up
		48	Their faith that gospel came to Lamanites	6	13	If faithful shall be saved
		49	Faith that gospel came to other nations	27	18	If faithful be caught up
	11	10	Gift, if thou desire in faith	34	11	If faithful I am with you
		14	Shall know, in faith believing	44	2	If faithful pour out Spirit
		17	According to your faith it shall be done	51	19	Faithful steward shall inherit eternal life
	12	8	Not assist, unless having faith	52	4	If faithful shall know what to do
	14	8	Ask in faith believing		13	Faithful shall be made ruler
	17	2	By your faith shall obtain a view		34	Faithful kept and blessed with fruit
		3	After faith shall testify		43	Faithful crowned with joy
		5	Seen them because he had faith		44	Faithful lifted up at last day
		7	You have received same power faith and gift	58	2	Blessed is the faithful in tribulation
	18	18	Ask Father in my name in faith and	59	4	Faithful blessed with revelations, etc.
		19	Not faith, can do nothing	60	3	Talent taken away if not faithful
	19	31	Declare faith on the Savior	61	6	Faithful shall not perish by waters
	20	25	Who receive in faith	62	6	The faithful to see Missouri
	27	17	Taking the shield of faith	62	9	With the faithful always
	29	6	Ask in faith shall receive	63	47	Who is faithful and endures shall overcome
		43	Eternal life through faith	66	8	Who is faithful shall be strong
	33	12	Faith or not be saved	70	17	Faithful over many things
		15	Confirmed who has faith	71	11	My commandments true and faithful
	35	9	What can be done by faith	72	4	Faithful inherit mansions of Father
	37	2	Preach in Colesville for they have much faith		13	Labors of faithful answer debt to bishop
	41	3	By prayer of faith receive my law	75	5	If faithful laden with many sheaves, etc.
	42	23	Lust after a woman, deny the faith		13	With the faithful to the end
		48	All may be healed by faith		16	Faithful shall overcome all things
		52	Who have small faith may become my sons	76	6	Wonderful blessings promised the faithful
		52	Bear infirmities of weak in faith		7	Faithful shall know all mysteries of kingdom
	52	20	According to men's faith it shall be done	78	22	Who is faithful shall inherit
	53	3	Preach faith, etc.	79	3	If faithful, crowned with sheaves
	61	9	Overcome through faith	81	6	If faithful have crown of immortality
		18	Faith fail and caught in snares	83	3	Women, not faithful, no fellowship, but retain
	63	9	Faith comes not by signs	84	33	The faithful are sanctified
		11	Without faith no man pleases God		86	A commandment to all faithful called to the
		11	Signs come by faith	90	31	In peace as she is faithful
		12	Seek not signs and wonders for faith	93	18	If faithful fulness of John's record
		16	Who commit adultery in their hearts shall	97	9	Faithful compared to fruitful tree
		20	Who endureth in faith shall overcome	98	12	Give faithful precept upon precept
	68	25	Parents to teach children faith	101	35	The faithful who die shall partake of the

FAITHFUL continued
- 61 Faithful steward a ruler in kingdom
- 61 Seal of the faithful
- 104 2 Faithful with multiplicity of blessings
- 3 Not faithful nigh unto cursing
- 82 Victory, if humble and faithful
- 105 12 Endowment and blessing for faithful and
- 106 8 Reward of faithful witness
- 117 10 Be faithful over few, ruler over many
- 124 55 Prove faithful in all things
- 13 If faithful and true great in mine eyes
- 113 Faithful in few shall be ruler over many
- 132 53 Faithful over few, ruler over many
- 136 37 Shall behold glory if faithful

FAITHFULNESS see also Faithful
- 63 37 Take faithfulness upon his loins
- 103 36 Victory and glory through faithfulness
- 121 44 Faithfulness stronger than cords of death

FALL see also Sin
- 20 32 Possibility that man may fall from grace
- 50 44 Buildeth upon this rock, never fall
- 76 27 Lucifer is fallen!
- 88 89 Men fall, not able to stand
- 93 38 The effect of redemption from the fall
- 117 13 He falls shall rise again
- 118 1 Appoint men to supply places of fallen

FALSE
- 121 11 Punishment of those who charge transgression
- 18 Punishment for those who swear falsely

FALSEHOOD
- 127 1 Pretensions founded in falsehood

FAMILY see also Husband, Children, Parents
- 19 34 Impart all save support of family
- 20 47 Priests to exhort to attend to family duties
- 23 3 Duty because of family
- 51 3 Portion according to families
- 75 24 Duty of church to support families of mission-
- 28 Provide for family and not lose their crown
- 90 25 Let your families be small
- 93 48 Family needs repent or removed
- 98 23 Speak concerning families
- 100 1 Your families well
- 118 3 Families provided for
- 124 87 Cease to fear for sickness of family
- 136 11 Blessed in your families

FAMINE
- 43 25 God calls by famines
- 87 6 God's wrath shown by famines
- 89 13 Flesh used in winter, cold or famine
- 15 Animals for man in hunger or famine

FAR WEST
- 115 7 Far West, holy, consecrated land
- 17 Far West to be built by gathering of saints
- 117 10 William Marks to preside in Far West
- 118 5 Leave Far West on April 26th

FASTING
- 59 14 How to fast and pray
- 16 Blessings of fasting and prayer
- 14 Fasting is joy
- 88 76 Continue in prayer and fasting
- 119 Establish a house of fasting
- 97 7 Solemn assembly that fastings and mournings
- 16 House for fasting

FATHER see also God, Lord, Parents, Children
- 2 2 Hearts of children turn to fathers
- 3 17 Knowledge of Savior through fathers
- 18 Dwindle because of iniquity of fathers
- 20 Lamanites might come to knowledge of fath-
- 18 18 Ask father in my name in faith and
- 23 Jesus Christ name-given of Father
- 40 Warship the Father in my name
- 19 2 Accomplished and finished will of Father
- 24 I came by will of Father
- 20 28 Father, Son, and Holy Ghost one God
- 27 Holy Ghost beareth record of Father and Son
- 27 9 Turning hearts of fathers to children
- 11 Adam, father of all
- 14 Those whom my Father hath given me
- 29 5 I am your advocate with the Father
- 34 Adam, father, created of God
- 48 Given children that things required of fathers
- 31 13 Redeemer by will of Father
- 35 2 Father one with Jesus Christ
- 50 43 Father and Jesus one
- 63 34 Come down from presence of Father
- 66 12 Father full of grace and truth
- 68 8 Baptize in name of Father, Son, and Holy
- 12 Seal to eternal life whom the Father record
- 76 13 Son was in bosom of Father from the begin-
- 13 Things ordained by Father through Son
- 20 Son on right hand of Father
- 23 Only Begotten of Father
- 25 Only Begotten loved by Father
- 43 Jesus glorifies Father
- 77 Presence of Son, not fulness of Father
- 107 Christ deliver kingdom of Father
- 81 6 Mansions in house of Father
- 84 37 Who receives Lord receives Father
- 38 Who receives Father receives kingdom
- 40 Receive priesthood receive oath and covenant of the Father
- 47 Cometh to God even Father
- 63 Ye, whom Father hath given me
- 83 Father knoweth your need
- 99 Election of grace by faith and covenant of
- 93 3 In Father, Father in me, I and Father one
- 4 Why Father and Son one
- 5 In the world and received of Father
- 16 When the Son received fulness of Father
- 17 Father dwelt in him

	20	Son glorified in Father
	21	First born, in beginning with Father
	23	Ye were in beginning with Father
98	16	Turn hearts of children and fathers to each
	18	Many mansions in Father's house
	47	Forgive is children repent of father's tres-
99	4	My Father and his house
103	18	As fathers were led so redemption of Zion
	19	Said to fathers, my angel, not presence, before
104	45	Father reckoned in house of Joseph Smith Jr.
107	40	Priesthood handed from father to son
110	4	I am advocate with Father
	15	Elijah commits keys of turning hearts of
112	32	Keys of this dispensation come down from
123	6	Call Heavenly Father from hiding place
	7	Fathers inherited lies
128	18	Baptism for dead welding link between fath-
130	3	False that Father and Son dwell in man's
	22	Father has body of flesh and bones
132	12	Cannot come to Father unless by me
	59	Aaron called by the Father
136	21	Lord, God of fathers, Abraham, Isaac, Jacob

FATHERLESS

136	8	That cries of fatherless come not against

FAULT

6	19	Admonish him in his faults
20	80	How to deal with members who are in fault
88	124	Cease to find fault

FAVOR

105	25	How to find favor with people

FAYETTE

18	hd	Section 18 given in Fayette
24	3	Go to church in Fayette
128	20	Voice of Lord at Fayette, Seneca County

FEAR

1	7	Fear and tremble for decrees shall be fulfilled
3	7	Should not fear man more than God
6	33	Fear not to do good
9	11	You feared and time is passed
10	55	Whosoever belongeth to my church need not
	55	Who do not fear me shall
30	11	Not fearing what man can do
38	30	Not fear if prepared
45	39	Who feareth me shall look for
	74	Fear shall seize upon nations
60	2	Hide not talent for fear
63	6	Let rebellious fear and tremble
	16	Who commit adultery in their hearts shall fear
	17	Fearful shall die second death
	33	Fear shall come upon every man
67	10	Leave fears and see God
	3	Blessing lost through fears in hearts
76	5	Lord is merciful to those who fear
88	91	Fear shall come upon them
101	36	Fear not unto death
122	9	Fear not what man can do
124	87	Cease to fear for sickness of family
133	38	Fear God, give him glory
136	17	Fear not enemies

FEED

84	89	Who receives will feed you
	90	Who feeds you, lose no reward

FEEL

9	8	Shall feel if it is right
101	8	In trouble feel after me

FEIGN

104	4	Cursed for feigned words

FELLOW BEING

81	4	Greatest good to fellow beings

FELLOW MAN

1	10	Measure to fellow man

FELLOWSHIP see also Member

83	2	Women shall have fellowship in church
88	133	President's salutation of fellowship
104	75	In full fellowship a token

FEMALE

20	18	Created man, male and female

FIELD

6	3	Field is white to harvest
88	51	Parable of workers in the field
136	11	Blessed in your Fields

FIERCENESS

76	107	Wine press of God's fierceness of wrath
88	106	Fierceness of wrath of God

FIG TREE

45	37	Parable of the fig-tree

FILTHY

88	35	They remain filthy still
	102	Remain filthy to Last Day

FIND

88	63	Seek and ye shall find
	83	Who seeks early shall find and not forsaken

FIRE

7	6	I will make him as flaming fire
19	31	Remission of sins by baptism and by fire
29	12	Coming in a pillar of fire
	28	Fire everlasting for devil and his angels
33	11	Baptism by fire
43	32	Earth shall pass away as by fire
	33	Wicked go away into fire
45	41	Shall behold fire
63	34	Consume wicked with fire
	17	Lake of fire and brimstone
	54	Angels to pluck out wicked for the fire
76	36	Who shall go to lake of fire and brimstone
	44	Where fire is not quenched
	105	Who suffer vengeance of eternal fire
97	7	Tree of bad fruit cast into fire
	26	Devouring fire if disobedient
110	3	Eyes as flame of fire

FIRE continued
    130   7   Globe like sea of glass and fire
    133 41 Presence of Lord as melting fire

FIRM
    5   22 Be firm in keeping commandments

FIRMAMENT
    76   81 Moon in firmament
          109 Firmament of heaven

FIRST
    29   30 First shall be last; last shall be first
    110 4   I am first and last

FIRST BORN see Jesus
    68   16 First born among Aaron right to bishopric
          17 First born holds right of presidency
    93   21 First born in beginning with Father

FIRST FRUIT
    88   98 First fruits of Christ

FISH
    29   24 Fishes to be new
    133 68 Fish stinks and dies of thirst

FLEE
    133 12 Who among Gentiles flee to Zion

FLATTER
    10   25 Satan flattereth
          26 Flattereth them and draggeth souls
    10   29 Flattereth to do iniquity
    121 20 Despised by whom flattered

FLESH see also Man, Meat
    1   19 Man not trust in arm of flesh
    18   11 Redeemer suffered death in the flesh
    20   26 Christ came in meridian of time in the flesh
    29   19 Flesh fall from their bones
    38   11 All flesh corrupt
    45   13 See City of Enoch in the flesh
    49   21 Don't waste flesh without need
    61   6   All flesh in mine hand
          15 No flesh will be safe upon waters
    67   11 No man see God in flesh unless quickened by
    76   73 Judged according to men in the flesh
          74 Concerning those who receive not gospel in
    84   21 Power of Godliness not manifest in the flesh
    86   9   Lawful heirs to priesthood according to the
    88   99 Might receive gospel and be judged as in the
    89   12 Flesh used by man sparingly
          13 Flesh used in winter, cold or famine
    93   4   I made flesh my tabernacle
    129 1   Angels are resurrected with bodies of flesh and
    130 22 Son has body of flesh and bones
          22 Father has body of flesh and bones
    132 26 Shall be destroyed in the flesh

FLIGHT
    58   56 Gathering not in flight
    63   37 Declare God's word by word and flight
    101 68 Gather not in haste or flight, but prepared
    133 15 Let not flight in haste
          58 Two put ten thousand to flight

FLOCK
    6   34 Fear not little flock
    88   72 I will care for your flocks
    136 11 Blessed in your flocks

FLY
    29   18 Flies to come upon earth

FOE
    121 8   Triumph over foes

FOLD
    10   59 Other sheep not of this fold

FOLLY
    45   49 Laughed, shall see folly
    136 19 Folly made manifest without counsel

FONT
    124 29 Baptismal font for baptism of dead
    128 13 Where the baptismal font should be placed
          13 Baptismal font a simile of grave

FOOD
    49   19 Beasts, fowls, etc. food for man
    59   13 Food may be prepared on Sunday
          19 Nature for food
    70   16 Commandment for food
    89   16 Grain good for food of man

FOOL
    122 1   Fools have thee in derision

FOOT
    6   37 Prints of nails in hands and feet
    24   15 Cleansing of feet as a testimony
    27   16 Feet shod with gospel of peace
    45   48 Lord set foot on this mount
    60   15 Wash feet as testimony against
    75   20 Shake off dust of feet as testimony
    84   92 Wash feet against him who receives you not
          109 Head to feet, have no need
    88   74 Cleanse your hands and feet
    99   4   Cleanse feet as testimony
    112 7   Let feet be shod
    128 19 How beautiful on mountains are feet of

FOOTSTOOL
    38   17 Earth is my footstool

FOREHEAD
    77   9   Sealed servants of God in foreheads
    133 18 Names written on foreheads

FORGIVE see also Forgiveness, Repentance
    1   32 Who repents shall be forgiven
          32 Who does commandments shall be forgiven
    64   7   How the Lord forgives sins
          8   My disciples were chastened for not forgiving
          9   Who does not forgive stands condemned
          10 You must forgive all men
    82   1   I forgive who forgive
    84   61 Forgive sins with this commandment

95　1　Chasten that sins be forgiven
98　39　If enemy repent and prays forgiveness, forgive
　　40　Forgive enemy seventy times seventy if he re-
　　41　Forgive first trespass
　　42　Forgive second trespass
　　43　Forgive third trespass
　　45　Forgive enemy if
　　47　Forgive if children repent of father's trespass
132　27　Blasphemy against Holy Ghost never forgiven

FORGIVENESS see also Forgive
42　79　Murderer hath no forgiveness
76　34　No forgiveness for sons of perdition
84　41　Who breaks covenant of priesthood no for-

FORNICATOR
42　76, 77 How received back

FOSTER, JAMES
124　138　James Foster a president of Seventies

FOSTER, ROBT. D.
124　115　Robert D. Foster to build house

FOUNDATION see also Creation
18　4　Foundation of my church, my gospel
　　5　Build church on foundation of gospel and
21　2　Foundation of church laid by inspiration
45　1　Hearken to him who made foundation of earth
52　33　Build not on another's foundation
58　7　Honored of laying foundation
64　33　Laying foundation of great work
94　6　House for Presidency dedicated from founda-
124　33　Temples instituted before foundation of world
　　41　Reveal things hid from foundation of world
　　118　Authorities called to lay foundation
127　2　Unless ordained from foundation of world for
128　5　Baptism for dead ordained before foundations
130　20　Law decreed before foundation of earth
132　5　Law before foundation of world
136　38　Joseph Smith laid foundation of work

FOWL
29　24　Fowls to be new
49　19　Fowls for use of man
77　2　Happiness of man creeping things and fowls
89　15　Grains for fowls of air
　　17　Rye for fowls, swine and beasts of field

FRAUD
57　8　Sell goods without fraud

FREE
10　51　It might be free to all
38　22　You shall be free people
98　8　God and the law make you free
136　27　Free gift to steward

FREE　WILL
58　27　Men must do much of their own free will

FREEDOM
98　5　Principle of freedom for all mankind
106　1　Land of freedom

FRIEND
82　22　Make friends with mammon of unrighteous-
84　63　Ye are my friends
　　77　Friends from henceforth
93　45　Call your friends for
121　9　Friends hail with warm hearts and friendly

FRUIT
84　58　Fruit meet for Father's kingdom
89　11　Every herb and fruit may be used
　　16　All fruit good for man
97　7　Tree of bad fruit hewn and cast
　　9　Faithful compared to fruitful tree
101　101　Plant vineyard shall eat the fruit

FRUSTRATE
3　1　Works of God cannot be frustrated
　　3　Remember work of God not frustrated

FULFIL
1　7　What I decreed shall be fulfilled
　　18　Might be fulfilled which was written by proph-
　　37　Prophecies and promises fulfilled
　　38　Word shall be fulfilled
3　19　Promises of Lord might be fulfilled
5　4　No gift until purpose is fulfilled
18　7　As thou hast been baptized he hath fulfilled
58　31　Does the Lord promise and not fulfil
85　10　As Lord speaks, will fulfil
101　62　Fulfilled after many days
　　64　Word must be fulfilled
105　28　Send wise men to fulfil commands
128　20　Moroni declaring fulfillment of prophets

FULLER, EDSON
52　28　Edson Fuller called

FULLMER, DAVID
124　132　David Fullmer member of High Council

FULNESS see also Fulness of Gospel
42　15　Until fulness of scriptures come
59　16　Fulness of earth from fasting and prayer
76　20　Received of fulness of Son
　　56　They who have received of his fulness
　　76　Receive glory, but not fulness
　　77　Presence of Son not fulness of Father
　　86　Telestial receive not fulness
　　94　Celestial glory receive fulness of grace
84　24　Rest is fulness of glory
88　29　Who are quickened by portion receive fulness
93　4　Father gave Jesus fulness
　　14　Son received not fulness at first
　　33　Spirit and element together only receive
　　16　When the Son received fulness of Father
　　20　Keep commandments and receive fulness
　　27　Fulness only by keeping commandments
121　27　Knowledge reserved for fulness of
124　28　A temple needed to restore fulness of priest-
132　6　Who receives fulness must obey law

FULNESS continued
- 6   New and everlasting covenant instituted for
- 19   Glory is fulness and continuation of seed

FULNESS OF GOSPEL see also Fulness, Church,
- 1   23   Fulness of gospel might be proclaimed
- 14   10   Bring forth fulness of gospel
- 20   9   Book of Mormon contains fulness of gospel
- 35   12   Fulness of gospel given to this generation
-        17   Fulness of gospel by Joseph
- 39   11   Fulness of gospel to recover my people
-        11   Fulness of gospel sent out in last days
- 42   12   Fulness of Gospel in Bible and Book of Mor-
- 45   28   Times of Gentiles to bring fulness of gospel
-        29   Fulness of gospel not received by them
- 66   2   Everlasting covenant is fulness of gospel
- 76   14   Record is fulness of gospel of Jesus Christ
- 90   11   Every man shall bear fulness of gospel in own
- 133   57   Why the fulness of gospel sent out

FULLNESS OF TIMES see also Gospel
- 27   13   Gospel for the fulness of times
- 76   106   Who are cast to hell until fulness of times
-        106   Christ subdued enemies at fulness of times
- 112   30   Last days dispensation of fulness of times
- 121   31   All knowledge revealed in dispensation of ful-
- 124   41   Things that pertain to fulness of times
- 128   18   Hidden things revealed to babes in this dispen-
-        18   Dispensation of fulness of times ushering in
- 128   20   Peter, James and John claim keys to dispen-

FUTURE
- 76   8   Will show them the future
- 88   79   Learn of the Future
- 130   7   The future known in presence of God

FUTURITY
- 101   78   Act in doctrine and principle pertaining to
- 123   15   Much of futurity depends on small things

GABRIEL
- 128   21   Voice of Gabriel and Raphael

GAD
- 84   11   Gad received priesthood from Esaias

GALLAND, ISAAC
- 124   78   Isaac Galland put stock in Temple
-        79   Isaac Galland to be ordained by William

GARMENT
- 20   6   Garments of angel pure and white
- 42   40   Let thy garments be plain
-        40   Let garments be the work of own hands
- 82   14   Zion put on beautiful garments
- 133   46   Who comes in dyed garments
-        48   Garments like treader of wine vat
-        51   Sprinkled garments with blood

GATE
- 22   2   Not enter straight gate by law of Moses
-        4   Enter at gate
- 43   7   In at gate be ordained

GATE OF HELL
- 17   8   10:69, 18:5, 21:6, 98:22 Shall not prevail

GATHER see also Gathering
- 6   32   Two or three gathered in my name, there am I
- 29   8   Elect gathering in one place
- 42   9   Gathered to New Jerusalem
-        36   My people gather in me
- 45   43   Remnant gathered
-        64   Gather from east to west
- 77   14   Ordinance to gather Israel
- 84   100   Lord gathered all things in one
- 101   13   Scattered shall be gathered
-        22   My will to gather in holy place
-        65   Gather people according to parable of wheat
- 105   24   Gather as much as possible in one place
- 110   11   Moses commits keys of gathering Israel
- 115   17   Far West to be built by gathering of saints
- 119   5   Who gather shall be tithed of surplus prop-
- 133   4   Gather who are not commanded to tarry
-        7   Gather from the nations

GATHERING see also Gather
- 31   8   Prepare against gathering
- 57   1   Missouri consecrated for gathering
-        15   Concerning gathering to Missouri
- 58   56   Manner of gathering
- 62   6   Gathering that promise fulfilled
- 63   36   Why saints should assemble in Zion
- 64   24   Spare none that remain in Babylon
- 77   15   Prophets to Jews before gathering
- 84   2   Gathering of saints to stand upon Mount Zion
-        4   New Jerusalem built by gathering of saints
- 101   20   None other place for gathering until
-        64   That work of gathering may continue
-        68   Gather not in haste or flight, but prepared
-        70   Lands for beginning of gathering
-        74   Zion established by gathering
- 105   15   Lands consecrated for gathering
- 115   6   Gathering for a defence and refuge
- 133   9   The purpose of gathering

GENERAL AUTHORITIES see also Authority,
- 102   32   Their decisions called in question by general

GENERAL CHURCH RECORDER
- 128   4   Records of baptism for dead placed with Gen-

GENERATION
- 5   9   Made known to future generations
-        10   Generation shall have word through you
- 10   53   If generation harden not their hearts
- 11   9   Say only repentance to this generation
- 45   31   Men standing in that generation shall
- 76   8   Show the things of many generations
- 84   31   House of Lord built in this generation on
- 98   37   Avenged on third and fourth generation
- 112   33   Lest blood of generation required of your hand

GENTILE
- 14   10   Bring gospel from Gentiles
- 18   26   Gospel unto Jew and Gentile

19	27	Book of Mormon word to Gentile
20	9	The fulness of gospel to Gentiles
35	7	A great work among Gentiles
42	39	Riches of Gentiles for poor of Israel
45	9	Gentiles seek the everlasting covenant
57	4	Unto line between Jew and Gentile
86	11	A light unto Gentiles
87	5	Remnants to vex Gentiles
88	84	Go forth among Gentiles
90	9	Word to Gentiles and then to Jews
107	25	Especial witnesses unto Gentiles
133	12	Who among Gentiles flee to Zion
124	9	Gentiles come to exaltation of Zion

GIFT see also Spirit, Interpretation

3	11	Shalt have no more gift except
5	4	First gift bestowed upon you
	31	Except, thou shalt have gift no more
6	10	Thou hast a gift
	10	Blessed because of thy gift
6	11	Thou shalt exercise thy gift.
	12	Make known gift only of thy faith
	13	No gift greater than salvation
	25	Grant you a gift to translate as Joseph
	28	Gift which shall bring to light this ministry
8	4	Gift shall deliver thee
	5	Remember your gift
	6	Not all your gift
	8	Gift of Aaron, gift of God
10	7	Sought to destroy your gift
	18	Will say he has no gift
11	10	Gift, if thou desire in faith
14	7	Eternal life is God's greatest gift
17	7	You have received same power faith and gift
18	32	According to callings and gifts
20	27	Who believe in gifts of God shall be saved
46	8	Seek the best gifts
	9	Gifts given for what purpose
	10	Remember what gifts are given to church
	11	Gift given to every man by Spirit of God
	12	Not all gifts to every man
	13	The gifts enumerated
	26	All gifts come from God
	27	All gifts to be discerned by the bishops and
	29	Some have all gifts
84	73	Speak not of gifts before world
	73	Gifts given for profit and salvation
	103	Missionary without families send gift to
88	33	What profits a gift not received
	33	Rejoiceth not in giver of gifts
107	92	President of church all God's gifts

GILBERT, SIDNEY

53	hd	Section 53 given to Sidney Gilbert
	1	Sidney Gilbert's prayer heard
	5	Sidney Gilbert to travel with
57	6	Sidney Gilbert to stand in his office
	8	Sidney Gilbert to establish a store
61	7	Mission of Sidney Gilbert
64	18	Commission to Sidney Gilbert
	26	Words to
90	35	Mentioned
101	96	Sidney Gilbert not to sell storehouse to enemies

GIVE

43	16	Give as I have spoken
82	3	Much given, much required
84	85	Given you in very hour the portion for each
132	48	What you give is without condemnation
	62	Justified because given to him

GLADNESS see also Joy

19	39	Lifting thy heart for gladness
128	19	A voice of gladness for living and dead in

GLASS

130	7	Globe like sea of glass and fire

GLORIFY

3	20	Glorified through faith in his name
64	13	That God may be glorified
76	43	Jesus glorifies Father
93	20	Son glorified in Father
	28	Man glorified in truth

GLORIOUS

78	19	Who is thankful shall be glorious
97	18	Zion shall become glorious
101	31	His rest shall be glorious
128	23	How glorious is voice from heaven
133	46	Who comes in glorious apparel

GLORY see also Kingdoms, Celestial, Terrestrial,

4	5	Keep eye single to glory of God
6	30	You shall dwell with me in glory
7	3	Tarry, till I come in glory
19	7	Work for my name's glory
	19	Glory to the Father
24	11	In me he shall have glory
29	12	In glory as I am
43	10	Glory shall be added to
	25	God calls by glory
45	16	Signs when Christ comes in glory
	44	Christ clothed with glory
	59	Lord's glory upon them
	67	Glory of Lord in New Jerusalem
49	6	Son of Man taken seat on the right hand of his
58	4	Crowned with glory
	4	Glory to follow tribulation
63	12	Signs for God's glory, etc.
	66	Exceeding and eternal weight of glory
64	3	For my glory and your salvation sins are for-
65	5	Clothed in brightness and glory
	6	God be glorified on earth as in heaven
66	2	Partakers of glories revealed in last days
75	5	Faithful crowned with glory
76	6	Glory of faithful eternal
	19	Glory of Lord shone about

GLORY continued
	20	Behold the glory of Son
	61	Let no man glory in man, but in God
	76	Receive glory but not fulness
	81, 119	Various degrees of glory compared
78	4	Cause, to glory of Father
	8	All things be done to my glory
81	4	Will promote glory of God
84	5	Cloud of God's glory upon the temple
	24	Rest is fulness of glory
	82	Kingdoms of world in their glory not like a
	101	Earth clothed with glory of God
88	22	Who cannot abide the law cannot abide the
	24	Who cannot abide any glory
	28	Your glory which quickens bodies
	32	Fate of those who receive neither of the three
88	67	Bodies filled with light if eyes single to glory
	107	Saints filled with glory and receive inherit-
	107	Angels crowned with glory of might
	110	This is the glory of God and the sanctified
	119	Establish a house of glory
93	6	John saw and bore record of my glory
	22	Begotten of Son partakers of glory
	36	Glory of God is intelligence or light and truth
94	8	Glory and presence of God in house of the
	9	If any unclean, my glory and presence depart
97	15	My glory rest upon temple
98	3	Affliction work to your good and God's glory
101	35	Who lay down life shall receive glory
103	36	Victory and glory through diligence, etc.
109	37	Glory, as a rushing mighty wind
124	7	Glory as falling flower
	18	Beget glory and honor by preaching
	87	Sickness of land redound to glory
127	2	I glory in tribulation
128	12	Herein is glory
	18	Welding together of glory now
	21	Angels declaring their glory
129	3	Spirits of just men perfect, not resurrected, but same glory
130	2	Do not now enjoy eternal life
132	4	Reject this covenant and be damned
	6	New and everlasting covenant is instituted for fulness of glory
	19	Glory is fulness and continuation of seed
	21	Except abide law, not attain glory
133	38	Fear God, give him glory
	49	The glory of Christ's coming described
	57	Gospel that men partake glory
135	6	They lived, died for and will inherit glory
136	31	Trials to prepare for glory of Zion
	37	Shall behold glory if faithful

GOD see also Lord, Jesus, Jesus Christ, Son
1	9	Day when wrath of God shall be poured
	16	Men walketh after image of his own God
	20	Every man might speak name of God
	24	These commandments of God
	29	Power to translate through mercy of God
3	1	Works of God cannot be frustrated
	2	God walks not in crooked paths
	2	God's course one eternal round
	3	Remember work of God not frustrated
	4	A just God
	7	Should not fear man more than God
	8	God will have extended arm
	10	Remember God is merciful
4	2	Blameless before God
	3	If desires to serve God called
	5	Eye single to glory of God qualify
5	3	God commanded you
	5	Shown me by the power of God
6	2	The nature of God's word
	7	Mysteries of God shall be unfolded
	13	Greatest gift of God
	16	None else save God knowest thy thoughts
	23	What greater witness than from God
	32	God in the midst of you
8	1	Lord Your God and Redeemer
	8	Gift of Aaron, Gift of God
	12	I spake from beginning
11	2	I am God
	4	The same is called of God
14	9	Jesus Christ, son of living God
18	10	Worth of souls great in sight of God
	33	Jesus Christ your Lord and God
19	10	I am endless
	16	I God suffered these that
	18	Caused God to tremble
20	6	God ministered by an holy angel
	12	Same God today, yesterday and forever
	17	By these things we know that there is God
	19	God only being to worship
	28	Father, Son, and Holy Ghost one God
21	5	Word of Joseph Smith as from mouth of God
22	4	Seek not to counsel God
25	15	Cannot come where God is unless
27	1	Jesus Christ your Lord, God and Redeemer
29	11	God dwell on earth a thousand years
	12	God in glory
	33	God's work have no end to God
30	17	God is eternal
41	1	God delighteth to bless his people
45	1	God the creator of all things
	15	God will reason with men
50	12	God reasons like a man that we may under-
	15	Not justified to receive false spirits of God
	17	God speaks only by spirit of truth
56	4	God commanded and revokes as seemeth good
59	21	How man offends God
62	1	God your advocate

GOD'S CALL–GOSPEL

63	6	All flesh knows I am God
	11	With whom angry, God not pleased
	11	Without faith, no man pleases God
64	11	Let God judge between me and thee
	13	That God may be glorified
	19	Why God speaks
65	6	God be glorified on earth as in Heaven
67	10	Privilege to see God
	11	No man see God in flesh unless quickened by
	12	Natural man cannot abide presence of God
76	1	No savior besides God
	2	His doings none can find out
	3	His purposes fail not
	4	The same from eternity to eternity
	22	Testimony that God lives
	24	Inhabitants of earth begotten sons and daugh-
	24	Worlds were created through him
	58	They are Gods, sons of God
	59	They are Christ's and Christ is God's
	62	Dwell in presence of God
	70	Celestial glory, like glory of sun or God
	92	God reigns upon his throne
	92	God reigns in celestial world
	112	Telestial cannot get where Christ and God
	118	Through Spirit bear his presence in flesh
78	15	God Holy one of Zion
84	12	Esaias received priesthood from God
	22	Without it not see God and live
	23	That Israel might see God
	47	Cometh to God even Father
	47	Who hearkens to Spirit comes to God
	101	God stands in midst of people
	119	God will reign with people
87	6	Indignation and chastening of God
88	12	Light from God to fill space
	13	God in midst of things
	13	Light is life, law, power of God
	13	God in bosom of eternity
	41	The attributes of God
	44	These are one year with God
	47	Who has seen the least seen God
	49	Day when you shall comprehend God
	114	Battle of the great God
93	1	Shall see face of God
	29	Man was in the beginning with God
	35	Man tabernacle of God
	36	Glory of God is intelligence
97	16	Pure in heart shall see God in temple
98	8	God and the law make you free
105	32	Kingdom of Zion that of God and Christ
110	8	I will appear if
121	4	God controlleth devil
	28	One God or many, shall be manifest
	45	Then confidence in presence of God wax strong
122	9	God shall be with you
128	19	Unto Zion, thy God reigneth
	19	As dews of Carmel, so knowledge of God des-
	21	Voice of God in chamber of father Whitmer
	24	God like refiner's fire or fuller's soap
129	9	Three grand keys for administration
130	4	God's time according to residence
	7	Angels reside in the presence of God
	7	Past, present and future known in presence of
	8	God's residence a great Urim and Thummim
132	17	Who marry without covenant become not Gods
	18	Appointed Gods They cannot pass
	19	Shall pass by angels and Gods
	20	Gods because they have no end
	20	Gods because of power and subjection of
	24	Eternal life to know God and Jesus Christ
	37	Isaac and Jacob gods not angels
133	41	The glory of God's presence described
	74	Lord God hath spoken it
134	39	How God's laws may be revoked or held in
136	21	Evil to take name of Lord in vain

GOD'S CALL
43	25	God calls upon men in many ways. Some
99	6–8	Length of God's call

GODLINESS see also God
19	10	Behold mystery of godliness
84	20	Godliness manifest in ordinances
	21	Power of godliness not manifest in the flesh

GOLD
110	2	Work pure gold like amber
124	11	Bring gold and silver to house of daughters of

GOOD
6	13	If will do good shall be saved
	33	Fear not to do good
	33	Sow good reap good
10	20	Iniquity against the good
11	8	Be means of doing good
33	4	None, save few, doeth good
58	28	Who do good cannot lose reward
76	17	Who have done good in resurrection of just
81	4	Greatest good to fellow beings
82	6	None doeth good
	16	Wisdom for your good
90	24	All things work for your good
98	3	Affliction work to your good and God's glory
	10	Uphold wise and good men
	11	Forsake evil cleave unto good
100	15	All things work for good of church
105	40	All things work for good
122	7	All trials give experience and be for your good
124	9	Will soften their hearts for your good
127	2	Unless ordained from foundation of world for

GOSPEL
6	26	Records kept back contain much gospel
10	45	Greater views on gospel
	45	Remainder contains those parts of gospel

GOSPEL continued

	48	Their faith that gospel came to Lamanites
	49	Gospel made known to other nations
	52	Bring gospel to build up
	62	Gospel ministered to them
11	24	Build upon my rock, my gospel
14	10	Fulness of gospel unto house of Israel
18	hd	Building of church according to fulness of
	17	My gospel rock and salvation
	26	Gospel unto Jew and Gentile
	28	Twelve called to preach gospel
	32	Declare gospel according to Holy Ghost
20	8–9	Book of Mormon contains fulness of Gospel
	10	Gospel given by inspiration
	10	Gospel confirmed by ministering of angels
24	12	Declare my gospel at all times and in all places
25	1	Who receive gospel are sons and daughters of
27	5	Book of Mormon contains fulness of everlast-
	13	Keys committed to Peter, etc.
	16	Feet shod with gospel of peace
28	16	Declare gospel with rejoicing
29	42	The gospel promised Adam and his seed
33	12	This is my gospel
39	6	What is the gospel
	18	If receive gospel stay judgment
50	14	Gospel to be preached by Spirit
57	10	Gospel preached to those in darkness
58	64	Gospel preached to every creature
60	14	Manner of preaching gospel
65	2	Gospel roll to ends of earth
74	2	Circumcision among Jews who believe not
	4	Believe not gospel because unholy
76	50	Testimony of Gospel of Christ
	73	Christ preached gospel to spirits in prison
	74	Concerning those who receive not gospel in
	82	Fate of those who refuse gospel
	100	Who receive not gospel, but who say they are
77	8	Who have power to commit gospel to all na-
	11	Gospel administered by 144 thousand
84	19	Melchisedek priesthood administers gospel
	75	Preach gospel to all who have not received it
	76	Who must preach the gospel
88	78	Instructed in principle, theory, doctrine and
	99	Might receive gospel and be judged as in the
	103	Fifth angel to commit gospel
	123	What gospel required
90	11	Every man shall hear fulness of gospel in own
93	51	Gospel as I give utterance
107	35	Twelve to open door by proclamation of gospel
110	12	Elias commits dispensation of gospel of Abra-
112	28	Preach gospel to every creature not received
118	4	Gospel to be taken across great waters
124	2	Make solemn proclamation of gospel
	3	Proclaim gospel to all authorities
128	5	Salvation of dead without gospel ordained be-
	18	Not perfect unless died in gospel
	19	A voice of gladness for living and dead in
133	57	Gospel that men partake glory
134	12	Not preach gospel to bond servants without

GOULD, JOHN

100	14	John Gould mentioned

GOVERN

31	9	Govern in meekness
88	34	What is governed by law preserved by law
	40	Who governeth and executeth all things

GOVERNMENT see also Common Consent

124	143	Officers of priesthood for government
134	hd	Of governments and laws in general
	1	God's and man's relation to government
	2	Conditions of peace in government
	3	Government requires officers and magistrates
	5	Governments to be upheld
	9	Religious influence and civil government sepa-

GRACE see also Mercy, Kindness, Love

17	8	My grace is sufficient
20	4	This according to grace of our Lord and Savior
	30	Justification through grace of Jesus Christ is
	31	Sanctification through grace of Jesus Christ is
	32	Possibility that man may fall from grace
50	40	Ye must grow in grace, etc.
66	12	Father full of grace and truth
76	94	Celestial received of fulness of grace
84	99	Redeemed by election of grace
	99	Election of grace by faith and covenant of
88	78	Teach and grace shall attend you
93	11	Son full of grace and truth
	13	Son received grace for grace
	20	Shall receive grace for grace
102	4	Fill an office according to grace bestowed
105	26	Give you grace in their eyes
106	8	Will give grace and assurance to stand

GRAIN

89	14	Grain staff of life for man and beast
	16	Grain good for food of man

GRANGER, OLIVER

117	hd	Concerning Oliver Granger and
	12	His name to be held in remembrance
	13	Oliver Granger contend for redemption of
	14	Oliver Granger to be merchant

GRAPE

89	6	Pure wine of
124	7	Grape of vine

GRAVE

29	26	Graves shall be opened
88	97	Who have slept in graves come forth
128	13	Baptismal font a simile of grave
133	56	Graves of saints shall be opened

GREAT

64	33	Out of small things proceedeth the great
124	13	If faithful and true great in mine eyes

GREAT BRITAIN
87 3 Great Britain called upon for aid
GREAT DAY
43 17 Great day of Lord at hand
58 11 Supper prepared for great day
133 10 Prepare for great day of Lord
GREATEST
50 26 Who is ordained is greatest
GREEDINESS
56 17 Poor not to be greedy
68 31 Lord not pleased for eyes full of greediness
GRIFFIN, SELAH J.
52 32 Selah J. Griffin called
56 5 Commandment revoked
GROUND see also Earth
89 16 Fruit below ground for man
    16 Fruit above ground for man
133 29 Parched ground not thirsty land
136 36 Innocent blood cries from ground against
GROVER, THOMAS
124 132 Thomas Grover member of High Council
GROW
50 40 Ye must grow in grace, etc.
GUILE
121 42 Enlarge souls without guile
124 97 Be humble and without guile
GUILTY see also Sin
68 23 Guilty by unimpeachable testimony
104 7 This that guilty may not escape
HAGAR
132 34 Sarah gave Abraham Hagar to wife
    35 Abraham not under condemnation for Hagar
    65 Sarah administered to Abraham with Hagar
HAILSTORM
29 16 Hailstorm sent to destroy crops
43 25 God calls by hailstorms
HAIR
110 3 Hair white as snow
HANCOCK, LEVI
52 29 Levi Hancock called
124 138 Levi Hancock as president of Seventies
HANCOCK, SOLOMON
52 27 Solomon Hancock called
HAND
3 2 God turns not to right hand or left
6 37 Prints of nails in hands and feet
8 8 Hold gift of Aaron in your hands
19 5 Wailing to those on my left hand
42 18 Church lift hands against
60 7 Lift holy hands upon them
63 37 Man take righteousness in his hands
65 2 Stone cut out without hands
81 5 Lift up hands that hang down
88 74 Cleanse your hands and feet
86 Let your hands be clean
120 Salutations with uplifted hands
88 132 Salute with uplifted hands
129 4 Offer messenger from God, hand
    8 Cannot feel Devil's hand
131 9 Hail with friendly hands
HAPPINESS
72 2 Heaven paradise of God happiness of man
77 2 Happiness of man creeping things and fowls
HARD
2 54 Teacher to see there is no hardness
19 15 Sufferings hard to bear you know not
124 116 Lay aside hard speeches
HARM
42 7 Do not harm thy neighbor
10 25 Deceive etc., no harm
HARMONY
128 20 Peter, James and John at Harmony, etc.
HARRIS, EMER
75 30 Mission for Emer Harris
HARRIS, MARTIN
3 hd Section 3 concerning mss. taken from Martin
5 1 As Martin Harris desires witness
    4 Martin Harris exalts himself
    26 Martin Harris shall say no more
    32 If Martin Harris humbleth not himself will
17 hd Section 17 given to Martin Harris and
19 hd Section 19 given to Martin Harris
52 24 Martin Harris called
58 35 Martin Harris to be example to church
    38 Words concerning Martin Harris
70 1 Martin Harris mentioned
102 3 Martin Harris member of first High Council
104 24 Mahemson
    24 Inheritance of Martin Harris appointed
    26 Martin Harris to use his monies for church
HARRIS, G. W.
124 132 G. W. Harris member of High Council
HARVEST
4 4 Field is white to harvest
45 2 Summer past, harvest ended souls not saved
101 64 Time of harvest come
HASTE
58 56 Gathering not in haste
60 8 Preach not in haste
61 7 Be in haste upon mission
    21 Let them take journey in haste
101 68 Gather not in haste or flight but prepared
    72 Be not in haste
133 15 Let not flight in haste
HASTEN
52 43 Will hasten city
88 73 Will hasten my work in its time
HAWS, PETER
124 62 Committee to build temple

17 Great for his love

HEAD
- 28 6 Shall not command head
- 50 30 As head, spirits subject to you

HEAD OF CHURCH see also First Presidency
- 28 6 Head of church not to be commanded
-     7 Head of church holds keys of mysteries and
- 46 29 All gifts, to be head

HEAL see also Health
- 24 13 Healing the sick at request of the sick
- 42 44 Manner of healing the sick
-     48 Who has faith shall be healed
- 46 19 Some given to have faith to be healed
-     20 Given to have faith to heal
- 84 68 In my name heal the sick
- 124 98 Sign to heal sick

HEALTH see also Word of Wisdom, Heal, Sick
- 89 18 Health in their navel
-     21 The great health promised those who keep the

HEAR
- 1 2 No ear that shall not hear
-    11 All that will hear may hear
-    14 Who will not hear be cut off
- 42 50 Who have faith shall hear
- 67 1 Elders whose prayers I have heard
- 88 104 Every ear shall hear
- 133 21 Voice heard among all people

HEARKEN see also Obey, Heed
- 5 5 Wo if not hearken
- 45 2 Hearken lest ye die
- 84 46 Light to him who hearkens to Spirit
-     47 Who hearkens to Spirit comes to God
- 103 4 Chastened for not hearkening
-     5 A decree to people if they hearken to counsel
- 124 46 Pollute if not hearken
- 133 63 Who hearken not be cut off

HEART
- 1 2 No heart that shall not be penetrated
- 5 18 Condemnation if harden hearts
-    24 In sincerity of heart
- 8 2 Will tell in heart by Holy Ghost
- 10 10 Satan put it into hearts to alter words
-    24 Satan stirreth hearts to anger against
- 11 10 Desire with an honest heart
- 19 28 Pray vocally as in heart
-    39 Lifting thy heart for gladness
- 42 69 Lift up your hearts
- 45 26 Men's hearts shall fail
-    55 Satan to have no place in hearts
- 56 18 Blessed are poor who are pure in heart
-    18 Whose hearts broken and spirits contrite
- 58 29 Who receiveth commandment with doubtful
- 59 18 Nature to gladden heart
- 61 2 Confess sins with humble heart
- 63 55 Exalteth himself in heart
- 64 22 Lord requires hearts of men
-    34 Lord requireth heart and willing mind
- 67 1 Whose hearts I know
-    3 Blessing lost through fears in hearts
- 84 88 Spirit shall be in your hearts
- 88 3 Comforter abide in your hearts
-    62 Ponder sayings in your hearts
-    91 Men's hearts shall fail
- 110 15 Elijah commits keys of turning hearts of chil-
- 124 9 Will soften their hearts for your good
-    54 Save all pure in heart
- 130 3 False that Father and Son dwell in man's

HEATHEN
- 45 54 Heathen nations shall be redeemed
- 75 22 More tolerable for heathen than unbeliever

HEAVEN see also Glory, High Kingdom, Celestial,
- 1 8 Power to seal on earth and heaven
-   13 The sword of the Lord is bathed in heaven
-   17 Spake unto Joseph Smith Jr. from heaven
- 14 9 Who created heavens and earth
- 20 17 God framer of heaven and earth
- 21 6 Cause heavens to shake
- 29 23 New heaven
- 35 24 Heaven shake for your good
- 45 1 Who made heaven and
- 49 6 Son of man reigneth in heavens
-    23 Look for heaven to be shaken
- 50 27 Things of heaven subject to ordained
- 56 11 Though heavens pass away words shall not
- 62 3 Testimony recorded in heaven
- 63 34 Lord will come down in heaven
- 67 2 Heavens and earth in my hands
- 76 25 The rebellion in heaven
-    26 Heavens wept over Lucifer
-    68 Whose names written in heaven
-    68 God and Christ judge in heaven
-   109 Firmament of heaven
- 77 2 Heaven paradise of God happiness of man
-    8 Power to shut up heavens
- 84 101 Heavens smiled upon earth
-   118 Starry heavens tremble
- 88 43 Courses of heavens and earth fixed
-    43 Heavens and earth comprehend earth and
-    79 Learn of heaven
-    92 Angels fly through midst of heaven, crying
-    93 Great sign shall appear in heaven
-    95 Silence in heaven for half an hour
-    97 Dead caught up to pillar of heaven
-   103 Angel flying through midst of heaven
-   112 Michael to gather armies, hosts of heaven
- 106 6 Joy in heaven when Warren bowed
- 112 32 Keys of this dispensation come down from
- 121 36 Power of heaven acts only on principles of
- 127 7 Your record recorded in heaven
- 128 7 Book of life is record kept in heaven
-    9 If faithful record, law on earth and in heaven

	14	As records of dead on earth, so in heaven
	19	A voice of mercy from heaven
	23	How glorious is voice from heaven
129	1	Two kinds of beings in heaven
	7	Contrary to order of heaven for just man to
131	1	In celestial glory are three heavens
132	46	Seal on earth sealed in heaven
	46	Sins remitted on earth remitted in heaven
133	17	Angel crying through midst of heaven
	36	Mission of angel flying in midst of heaven
	69	Clothe heavens with blackness
	71	Obey my voice out of heavens

HEAVENLY
78	6	Not equal in earthly, nor equal heavenly

HEED
1	14	Who heed not prophets cut off
12	9	Give heed, then you are called
50	35	Kingdom, by giving heed

HEIR see also Glory, Member
7	6	Minister to heirs of salvation on earth
52	2	Heirs according to the covenant
70	8	Heirs according to laws of kingdom
76	88	Telestial, heirs of salvation
86	9	Lawful heirs to priesthood according to the

HELL see also Devil, Satan, Gates of Hell, Torment
6	34	Let earth and hell combine against you
10	26	Draggeth their souls to hell
17	8	Gates of hell shall not prevail
29	38	Hell prepared from beginning for devil
63	4	Lord able to cast soul to hell
76	84	Fate of those thrust to hell
	106	Who are cast to hell until fulness of times
88	113	Devil to gather armies, hosts of hell
104	18	In hell, in torment, who imparts not to poor
121	23	Generation of vipers not escape damnation of
122	1	Hell shall rage against thee
123	8	Hand-cuffs, etc. of hell
	10	Enough to make hell shudder

HELM
123	16	Large ship benefited by small helm

HERB see also Word of Wisdom
42	43	Sick, to be nourished with herbs, etc.
89	10	All wholesome herbs for man
	11	Use herb and fruit with prudence and thanks

HEREDITARY
68	20–21	Ordination necessary where priesthood

HERRIMAN, H.
124	138	H. Herriman a president of seventies

HICKS, JOHN A.
124	137	Of presidency of elders

HIDDEN
6	27	Scriptures hidden because of iniquity
7	hd	Section 7 from hidden parchment
86	9	Been hid from world with Christ
101	33	Hidden things revealed
124	38	Ordinance hid from foundation
	41	Reveal things hid from foundation of world

HIGBEE, ELIAS
113	7	Question by Elias Higbee

HIGH see also Heaven
58	47	Call upon high to repent
112	8	High brought low by word

HIGH PRIEST see also Priesthood, Melchisedek
20	66	High Priests may ordain without vote of
	67	High Priest to be ordained by whose direction
42	31	Lay before elder or high priest
	71	High Priest to assist bishop
68	15	Bishops to be worthy high priests
	19	High Priest may be bishop if no son of Aaron
	19	High Priest of Melchisedek Priesthood may of
72	1	Who are high priests of church
77	11	High Priests ordained to order of God the 144
84	63	Ye are Apostles, even God's High Priests
	111	High Priests to travel
88	127	High priests down to deacons
102	1	High Council to consist of twelve High Priests
	5	Nine High Priests voted on first High Council
	7	Majority has power to appoint High Priests
	8	Nominations for High Council sanctioned by
	24	High Priests when abroad may call council to
	28	When have High Priests abroad the right to
	30	High Council of High Priests and High Council of Twelve Apostles not the same
	30	May appeal from High Council of High Priests
106	1	Warren A. Cowdery to be presiding High
107	2	Melchisedek a great High Priest
	10	May officiate in office and for elder, priest, etc.
	12	A High Priest to officiate when no higher
	17	High Priest may act as Bishop
	22	Presidency of church to be three High Priests
	53	Seth to Methuselah High Priests
	66	Presiding High Priest of High Priesthood of
	71	High Priest may minister temporal things
124	133	Don C. Smith to be president of High Priest
	134	Purpose of High Priest quorum
	135	High Priests standing presidents
	135	May travel if they choose
	136	Counselors to president of High Priests

HILL
35	24,	39:13, 49:25, Zion rejoice upon hills
133	31	Boundaries of everlasting hills tremble

HINDER
124	50	Punishment of those who hinder works
	53	Example for all hindered works

HIRE
31	5,	84:79, 106:3, Laborer worthy of his hire
70	12	To administer spiritual things worthy of hire

HISTORIAN [CHURCH]
47	4	Church Historian given by Comforter to write
69	3	John Whitmer to be church historian

HISTORIAN [CHURCH]
85	1	Lord's clerk to keep General Church Record

HISTORY see also Record, Church Historian
47	1	Regular history kept
69	3	History of important things concerning church
	5	Missionaries to send accounts of their labors
85	1	Lord's clerk to keep a history
	3	Names of those who pay no tithing not to be
93	53	Obtain knowledge of history
123	1	History of persecutions, lost property, libels
	5	Keep history of all libelous histories
	6	Publish history of persecutions as last effort
	15	Importance of keeping a history of persecu-

HOLINESS
20	69	Walking in holiness before the Lord
38	24	Practice holiness
43	9	Covenant to act in holiness
46	33	Practice holiness continually
82	14	Zion must increase in holiness and beauty
133	35	Sanctified in holiness

HOLY see also Sacred
33	16	Holy Scriptures given for instruction
35	23	Prove words of prophecy by holy prophets
45	12	Day sought by holy men
	13	Holy men strangers and pilgrims on earth
	32	Disciples stand in holy places
	44	Christ with holy angels
59	9	See Sunday
60	7	I can make you holy
63	49	Inheritance in Holy City
76	66	Heavenly place the holiest
78	16	Michael has keys of salvation under Holy One
84	59	Children of kingdom shall not Pollute Holy
87	8	Stand in holy places
96	2	Upon which design to build Holy House
115	7	Far West called most holy
101	22	I will to gather in holy places
	64	Call on name in holy places
	77	Laws and constitution are of holy and just
104	65	Avails of sacred things for holy purposes
	68	Profits on holy, sacred writings used for same
121	26	Knowledge not revealed

HOLY GHOST see also Holy Spirit, Comforter
8	2	Holy Ghost shall dwell in your heart
	2	Tell by the Holy Ghost in your mind
14	8	Holy Ghost giveth utterance
18	18	Holy Ghost manifesteth all things
	32	Twelve to act according to power of Holy
	32	Gospel according to Holy Ghost
19	31	By fire, even the Holy Ghost
20	26	Prophets spake as inspired by Holy Ghost
	27	Holy Ghost beareth record of Father and Son
	28	Father, Son and Holy Ghost one God
	35	Revelations by Holy Ghost
	43	Apostles may confer Holy Ghost
	45	Conduct meetings as led by Holy Ghost
	60	Ordained by power of Holy Ghost
21	2	Inspired by Holy Ghost
33	11	Baptism by Holy Ghost
	15	Laying on of hands for Holy Ghost
35	6	Holy Ghost to be received
	19	Holy Ghost knoweth all things
39	6	Holy Ghost showeth and teacheth all things
68	3	Speak as moved by Holy Ghost
	4	What said when moved by Holy Ghost is mind
	8	Baptize in name of Father, Son and Holy
	25	Baptism and Holy Ghost at eight years
	27	Children receive Holy Ghost at eight years
76	114	Understood by power of Holy Ghost
84	27	John filled with Holy Ghost from mother's
	64	Baptized shall receive Holy Ghost
93	15	Holy Ghost in form of dove
	15	Holy Ghost comes to the Son
100	8	Holy Ghost in bearing record
121	46	Then Holy Ghost constant companion
124	5	Know my will by Holy Ghost
130	22	Holy Ghost has not body of flesh and bones
	22	How the Holy Ghost may dwell in us
	23	Holy Ghost may descend but not tarry
132	27	Blasphemy against Holy Ghost never forgiven

HOLY GHOST, GIFT OF see also Confirm
39	23	Gift of Holy Ghost to follow baptism with
49	14	Gift of Holy Ghost received
53	3	Preach gift of Holy Ghost

HOLY SPIRIT see also Holy Ghost, Comforter
44	2	Holy Spirit poured on assemblage of elders
45	57	Who have Holy Spirit for guide will
46	2	Notwithstanding conduct meeting by Holy
55	3	Receive Holy Spirit if contrite
76	35	Punishment for denying the Holy Spirit
	52	Holy Spirit received by laying on of hands
	53	Holy Spirit of promise shed upon the just and
	83	Who deny not Holy Spirit
	116	Things known only by Holy Spirit
88	3	Comforter, Holy Spirit of Promise
99	2	Word in demonstration of Holy Spirit
121	26	Gives knowledge by Holy Spirit
124	124	Sealing blessings even Holy Spirit of Promise
132	7	Sealed for time and eternity by Holy Spirit
132	26	Sealed by Holy Spirit of Promise

HONEST see also Pay
98	10	Seek for honest men
51	9	Every man deal honestly

HONOR
43	25	God calls by honor
75	5	Faithful crowned with honor
76	5	Delight to honor those who serve in righteous-
84	102	Honor to God
97	19	Nations shall honor Zion
121	35	Not chosen because aspirations to world and

HOPE
124	18	Beget glory and honor by preaching
128	12	Herein is honor
	21	Angels declaring their honors
	23	Glorious voice declaring honor

HOPE
4	5	Hope qualifies him for the work
6	19	Have hope, etc.
12	8	Not assist, unless having hope
18	19	Not hope, can do nothing
128	21	Giving consolation by confirming hope

HORSE
89	17	Oats for the horse

HOST OF HEAVEN
29	11	With hosts of heaven
	36	Devil turned one third of Host of Heaven
38	1	Seraphic hosts of heaven before world was

HOUR
1	35	Hour not yet but nigh
33	3	It is the eleventh hour
84	85	Given you in very hour the portion for each
88	58	Every man in his hour, time and season
	61	Every kingdom in hour, time and season
133	11	Watch for neither day or hour known

HOUSE see also Temple, House of Lord
19	36	Leave thy house and home
70	16	Commandment for houses
75	19	Blessing upon house that receives you
81	6	Mansions in house of Father
84	94	Wo to house that rejects you
88	119	Houses to be established
	127	House for presidency of school of prophets
93	43	Set in order your own house
124	11	Bring gold and silver to house of daughters
	22	Boarding house to be built
	27	Build house for Most High to dwell
132	8	My house of order not confusion
136	11	Blessed in your houses

HOUSE OF GOD see also Temple, House of Lord
85	7	Mighty one sent to set house of God in order
88	134	Unworthy not to pollute God's house
	128–136	Order of meetings in house of God
105	33	Receive endowment in God's house

HOUSE OF THE LORD see also Temple
58	9	Supper of house of Lord
84	31	House of Lord in this generation built on con-
	31	Sons of Moses and Aaron to offer in House of
88	136	Example for salutation in house of Lord,
	137	As Spirit give utterance in House of Lord
	137	House of Lord, School of Prophets, Sanctuary,
94	15	Committee to build the Lord's houses
95	3	Grievous sin in not building Lord's house
	8	House to endow who are chosen
	11	Commandment to build a house
97	10	Will, that house be built in Zion
	11	House to be built by tithing
	12	House, built for salvation of Zion
104	43	Size of lot for Lord's house
112	25	Vengeance to begin with Lord's house
115	8	Build an house in Far West unto me
	13	Not in debt for building of Lord's house
	14	Lord's house built after pattern given to
	15	Not accepted if not built after pattern
	16	Lord's house accepted if built after pattern
117	16	Keep Lord's house holy
119	2	Lord's house built by surplus property
121	19	Perjurer severed from ordinances of mine
133	13	Unto mountains of Lord's house

HUMBLE see also Contrite
1	28	Humble, they be strong
5	24	Does not humble himself sufficiently
	24	If he humble himself in mighty prayer I will
	28	Except humble himself, will not grant
	32	If Martin Harris humbleth not himself will
11	12	Spirit which leadeth to walk humbly
12	8	Not assist unless humble
29	2	Save all who humble themselves
54	3	Be humble and contrite
61	37	Humble and blessing yours
67	10	Be humble and see God
104	23	Multiply blessings if humble
	82	Victory if humble and faithful
105	12	Endowment and blessing for humble and
106	7	Will lift up, spite of vanity of heart, if humble
112	10	If humble prayers answered
124	97	Be humble and without guile
136	32	Wisdom by humbling and calling
	33	Spirit sent to enlighten humble and contrite

HUMPHREY, SOLOMON
52	35	Solomon Humphrey called

HUNGER
89	15	Animals for man in hunger or famine

HUNTINGTON, WM.
124	132	Wm. Huntington a High Councilor

HUSBAND see also Family, Children, Parents, Wife,
25	5	Office of Emma Smith to Joseph Smith
25	14	Let thy soul delight in thy husband
74	1	Unbelieving husband sanctified by wife
83	2	Women have claim on husbands for mainten-
132	43	Husband loses his wife by adultery

HYDE, ORSON
68	hd	Section 68 given to Orson Hyde and
	1	Orson Hyde called by his ordinance to preach
	7	Words unto
75	13	Mission for Orson Hyde
100	14	Orson Hyde mentioned
102	3	Orson Hyde member of first High Council
	34	Clerk to first High Council
103	40	Orson Hyde journey with Orson Pratt
124	129	Orson Hyde an Apostle

HYPOCRISY
121	42	Pure knowledge to enlarge soul without

HYPOCRITE
50	6	Hypocrites brought to judgment
	7	Hypocrites give adversary power
	8	Hypocrites shall be detected and cut off
64	39	Hypocrites proved by church
101	90	Fate of hypocrites
104	55	Else found hypocrites
124	8	Portion of oppressor among hypocrites

ICE
133	26	Ice flow down at their presence

IDLE see also Idler, Labor
42	42	Be not idle, he shall
60	13	Don't idle away any time
75	3	Be not idle, but labor
88	69	Cast away idle thoughts
	124	Cease to be idle

IDLER see also Idle
42	42	Idler not to eat the bread nor
68	30	Idler had in remembrance by the Lord
	31	Lord not pleased with idlers
75	29	Idler to have no place in church

IDOL
1	16	Substance of a god that of an idol
	16	Idol waxeth old and shall perish

IDOLATRY
52	39	Labor that no idolatry practiced

IDUMEA
1	36	Idumea or world

IGNORANCE see also Intelligence
131	6	Impossible to be saved in ignorance
136	32	Let ignorant learn wisdom by

IMMATERIAL
131	7	No immaterial matter

IMAGINATION
124	99	Mount in imagination as on eagle's wings

IMMERSION see also Baptism
13	1	Keys of baptism by immersion
20	74	Baptism by immersion

IMMANUEL, KING
128	12	In likeness of death and resurrection
	22	King Immanuel ordained redemption of pris-

IMMORTALITY see also Death
29	43	Through natural death to immortality
75	5	Faithful crowned with immortality
81	6	If faithful have crown of immortality
128	12	Herein is immortality
	23	Glorious voice declaring immortality

IMPART
11	13	I will impart of my Spirit
88	123	Learn to impart as gospel requires

IMPORTUNE
101	76	Importune rulers and authority for redress
	86	Importune all authorities

IMPURE see also Unclean
121	33	How long rolling waters impure
132	52	Impure, said to be pure, destroyed

INHERITANCE
38	20	A land for your eternal inheritance
45	58	Earth given for inheritance
	65	Riches to purchase inheritance
	66	Inheritance called New Jerusalem
48	4	Purchase lands for inheritance
51	4	Inheritance held until transgress
52	5	Land of inheritance shall be made known
	42	Missouri land of inheritance
55	5	Planted in land of inheritance
56	13	Inheritance according to deeds
57	5	Purchase land for eternal inheritance
58	36	Every man to receive inheritance
	44	Inheritance not yet for all
	53	Lest no inheritance save by blood
63	20	Endureth shall receive inheritance
	48	Sends treasure to Zion receive inheritance
	49	Inheritance in holy city
64	30	Saints shall obtain inheritance
70	16	Commandment for inheritance
72	17	Certificate answered for inheritance
83	2	Woman remain on inheritance if faithful
	5	Children of age claim inheritance
85	1	Record of those who receive inheritance
	2	Record of apostates with inheritances
	7	Arrange inheritances by lot
	9	Not in book of remembrance no inheritance
	11	Apostates to have no inheritance
88	107	Saints receive glory and inheritance
101	6	Inheritances polluted by sin
	18	Pure in heart come to inheritance
103	14	Not spare if pollute inheritances

INIQUITY see also Wicked
1	3	Iniquities of rebellious spoken on housetops
3	18	Dwindled because of iniquity of fathers
6	27	Scriptures hidden because of iniquity
10	20	Stirreth up to iniquity
	29	Flattereth to do iniquity
18	6	World is ripening in iniquity
20	54	Teacher see that there is no iniquity
45	50	Watch for iniquity, hewn down
103	3	Suffer to fill measure of iniquity
123	7	Earth groans under weight of iniquity

INNOCENT see also Pure
93	38	Man becomes again innocent
	38	Spirit of man innocent in beginning
132	19	Shedding innocent blood cancels sealings
	27	Shedding innocent blood blasphemy against
136	36	Innocent blood cries from ground

INQUIRE see also Learn
6	11	If inquire shall know mysteries
	14	Blessed, inquired and received

		15	Inquire and I did enlighten
30	3		Left to inquire for yourself

INSPIRATION
20	10	Gospel given by inspiration

INSPIRE
20	7		Commandments that inspired him
	11		God does inspire men
	26		Prophets spake as inspired by Holy Ghost
21	2		Inspired of Holy Ghost

INSTRUCT see also Learn
1	26	As sought wisdom be instructed
43	8	Instructed how to act upon my law
88	78	Instructed in principle, theory, doctrine

INTEGRITY
124	15	Love Hyrum Smith for integrity

INTELLIGENCE see also Ignorance, Knowledge.
88	40	Intelligence cleaveth to intelligence
93	29	Intelligence not created
	29	Intelligence spirit of truth
	30	Truth and intelligence independent
	36	Glory of God is intelligence or light
130	18	Gained will rise in resurrection
	19	Intelligence here advantage in next world
	19	Gained by diligence and obedience

INTERPRETATION see also Gifts, Tongues
46	25	Given the interpretation of tongues,

INSTRUCTION see also Knowledge
55	4	Special books that children receive
97	13	House of instruction

IOWA
125	1	Will concerning saints in Iowa

ISAAC see also Jew, Israel
27	10	With Isaac your father
98	32	Law given to Isaac
132	36	Abraham commanded to offer up
	37	Isaac abode in the law
133	5	Isaac in presence of Lamb
136	21	God of fathers Abraham, Isaac and Jacob

ISAIAH
76	100	Of Isaiah, but receive not the gospel
113		Verses in Isaiah explained

ISHMAELITE
3	18	Testimony of Jesus to Ishmaelites

ISLAND see also Sea
1	1	Ye upon islands of sea listen
133	8	Send elders to islands of sea
	20	Shall stand on islands of sea
	23	Islands become one land

ISRAEL see also Jew, Saints, Abraham, Isaac
8	3	Moses brought Israel to Red Sea
14	10	Bring gospel to house of Israel
18	6	Gentiles and Israel stirred to repentance
35	25	Israel saved by keys given
38	33	Israel shall be saved
39	11	My people, of Israel
42	39	Riches of gentiles for poor of Israel
61	25	Pitch tents like Israel
84	23	Moses taught priesthood to Israel
	23	That Israel might see God
	24	Israel lost priesthood by sin
	26	Lesser priesthood continued with Israel
	27	Lesser priesthood through Aaron until John
	28	John to prepare Israel for Christ
	99	Lord redeemed people Israel
86	11	Through priesthood savior to Israel
101	12	All mine Israel saved
103	17	Ye are of Israel and Abraham
110	11	Moses commits keys of gathering Israel
113	10	Scattered condition curses of God
	10	Scattered remnants exhorted to return
133	34	The blessing upon tribes of Israel
136	22	I led Israel out of Egypt
	22	Stretched in last days to save Israel

JACKSON COUNTY see also New Jerusalem
57	hd	In Zion in Jackson county
58	hd	In Zion in Jackson county
101	71	Buy land in Jackson county
105	28	My will to purchase land in Jackson

JACOB see also Israel, Jews
27	10	With Jacob your father
49	24	Jacob shall flourish in wilderness
52	2	People, remnant of Jacob
98	32	Law given to Jacob
109	58	Sons of Jacob may build holy city
	61	Hast great love for children of Jacob
132	37	Jacob abode in the law
133	55	Jacob in presence of Lamb
136	21	God of fathers Abraham, Isaac, Jacob

JACOBITE
3	17	How knowledge of Savior come to Jacobites

JAMES see also Church, Apostles
7	7	Minister to him and James
27	12	Keys committed to Peter, James and John
128	20	Peter, James and John claim keys

JAMES, GEORGE
52	38	George James ordained a priest

JAQUES, VIENNA
90	28	Mentioned

JARED
107	47	Jared ordained by Adam at 200
	53	Jared a high priest

JARED, BROTHER OF
17	1	Talked with Lord face to face

JEALOUSY
67	10	Leave jealousy and see God

JEHOVAH see also Jesus
109	34	Appeal to Jehovah in dedicatory prayer
	68	Joseph Smith covenanted with Jehovah
110	3	Voice and appearance described
128	9	According to decrees of great Jehovah

JEREMY
- 84 10 Jeremy received priesthood from God

JERUSALEM
- 33 8 Nephi journeyed from Jerusalem
- 77 15 Two prophets to build Jerusalem after Jews
- 109 62 Let Jerusalem be redeemed
- 124 36 Baptism for dead in Jerusalem
- 133 13 Of Judah flee to Jerusalem
-   21 Shall speak from Jerusalem
-   24 Jerusalem and Zion in own place
-   56 Mount Zion and holy city of Jerusalem

JESSE
- 113 1 Stem of Jesse is Christ
-   4 Rod of Jesse, servant of much power
-   4 Descendant partly of Jesse and Ephraim or
-   6 Root of Jesse Explained

JESUS CHRIST
- 3 20 Rely on merits of Jesus Christ
- 15 1 Words of Jesus Christ
- 18 23 Saved only by name of Jesus Christ
-   41 Must be baptized in name of
-   22 Baptized in name of
-   23 Jesus Christ name given of the Father
- 19 24 Came by will of Father
- 20 1 1830 years since coming of Jesus in flesh
-   75–78 Sacrament in remembrance of Lord Jesus
-   30 Justification through grace of Jesus is true
-   31 Sanctification through grace of Jesus is true
-   70 Lay hands upon them in the name of
- 21 9 Crucified for the sins of the world
- 31 13 Redeemer by will of Father
- 34 2 Jesus, light that shineth in darkness
- 35 2 Crucified for the sins of world
-   2 One with the Father
- 38 2 Knoweth all things
-   21 To be king
- 39 3 Came in the meridian of time
- 45 3 Christ's pleadings for man
-   7 Christ's names
-   18 Words of to disciples at Jerusalem
- 46 13 To some given to know Jesus
- 50 43 Father and Jesus one
-   44 Jesus the Good Shepherd and Stone of Israel
- 51 21 Jesus Christ cometh quickly
- 59 5 Serve God in name of Jesus
- 62 1 Jesus Christ knows weakness of men
- 68 6 Son of living God, was, is and shall be
- 74 7 Children sanctified through atonement of
- 76 14 The Son
-   14 Saw and conversed with Jesus Christ
-   41 Crucified for the world, to sanctify, etc.
-   43 Glorifies the Father
-   69 Perfect atonement through
- 85 45 Light is Spirit of Jesus Christ
- 88 6 Omnipresence of Jesus Christ
-   6 The light of truth
-   7 Light and power of sun, moon and stars
-   10 The light and power of the earth
- 107 19 Mediator of the new covenant
- 109 4 Jesus Christ Son of Thy bosom
- 132 24 Eternal life to know God and Jesus Christ
- 135 3 Joseph Smith did more, save Jesus, for
- 136 37 From Moses to Jesus
-   37 From Jesus to Joseph Smith

JETHRO
- 84 6 Father-in-law to Moses
-   6 Moses received holy priesthood from Jethro
-   7 Jethro received priesthood from Caleb

JEW see also Israel, Abraham, Isaac, Jacob
- 3 16 Knowledge of Savior through testimony of
- 18 26 Gospel unto Jew and Gentile
- 19 27 Lamanites a remnant of the Jews
- 20 9 Fulness of the Gospel to Jews
- 45 25 Jews to be gathered
-   52 Jews will know that Christ is Lord
-   53 Jews shall weep and lament
- 57 4 Unto line between Jew and Gentile
- 74 2 Circumcision among Jews who believe not
- 77 15 Two prophets to Jews in last days
- 90 9 Word to Gentiles then to Jews
- 98 33 Turn hearts of Jews and prophets to each
- 107 33 First to Gentiles then to Jews

JOB
- 121 10 Friends charged Job with transgression

JOHN see also Church, Apostle
- 7 hd Translated from parchment written by John
- 7 2 John desired to have power over death
-   6 Promise to John
- 27 12 With Peter, James and John
-   13 Keys of kingdom committed to Peter, James
- 61 14 Cursed waters by mouth of John
- 76 15 John 5:29 translated
- 77 hd Key to St. John's revelation
- 88 3 Testimony of John
- 93 6 John saw and bore record of my glory
-   6 Fulness of John's record to be revealed
-   11 John's record of the Son's glory
-   18 If faithful, fulness of John's record
- 128 20 Peter, James and John claim keys, etc
- 130 3 John 14:23 explained

JOHN THE BAPTIST
- 13 hd Words spoken by John the Baptist
-   hd John the Baptist an angel
-   hd John the Baptist laid hands on Joseph and
- 27 7 John the son of Zacharias
-   7 John to be filled with the spirit of Elias
-   7 John's birth foretold
-   8 John sent to ordain Joseph and Oliver
- 35 4 John called to prepare the way
- 76 100 Of John, but receive not the Gospel

77	14	John is Elias, the restorer	109	80	May saints shout for joy
	14	John to gather Israel	133	33	Filled with songs of everlasting joy
84	27	Lesser priesthood through Aaron until John	JUDAH see also Israel		
	27	Filled with Holy Ghost from mother's womb	109	64	May children of Judah return
	28	John baptized while in childhood	133	13	Of Judah flee to Jerusalem
	28	Ordained by an angel at eight days		35	After pain, be sanctified
	28	John's mission	JUDGE see also Judgment, God		
133	55	From Elijah to John	10	37	Cannot always judge righteous
JOHNSON, AARON			11	12	Spirit which leadeth to judge right
124	132	Aaron Johnson member of the high council	19	3	Judging every man according to his works
JOHNSON, JOHN			20	13	World shall be judged by great witnesses
96	6	Zombre to become member of order		13	Come to knowledge of this world shall be
102	3	Member of first high council	58	17	Whoso standeth in mission is a judge
104	24	Zombre		18	Judge by assistance of counselors
	34	inheritance appointed		18	Judge of testimony
JOHNSON, LUKE				20	Let God rule judge
68	hd	Given to Luke Johnson	64	37	Church like a judge over nations
	7	Words unto		38	Inhabitants of Zion shall judge in Zion
75	9	To go with W. E. M'Lellin	76	68	God and Christ judge in heaven
102	3	Member of First High Council	77	12	All things judged in 7th thousand years
JOHNSON, LYMAN			88	99	Might receive gospel and be judged as in
68	hd	Given to Lyman Johnson	101	81	Parable of woman and unjust judge
	7	Words unto		86	Importune at feet of judge
75	14	Mission for Lyman Johnson	107	72	Bishop a judge, manner of his judging
JOINT			JUDGMENT see also Judge, Justice		
6	2	To dividing of joints and marrow	1	36	Lord shall come in judgment
JOSEPH see also Smith, Joseph			3	13	Dependent upon own judgment
3	9	Chosen to do work of God	19	5	I revoke not judgments
5	9	Things entrusted unto you, Joseph	29	30	My judgments not given to men
	21	Command you, Joseph, to repent	39	18	Judgment stayed if receive gospel
6	18	Stand by Joseph faithfully	61	2	Known according to their judgments
9	12	Given Joseph sufficient strength	62	8	Act according to judgment
JOSEPH (the son of Jacob)			82	4	Justice and judgment penalty of God's law
90	10	Heathen nations, house of Joseph		23	Judgment is mine, I will repay
96	7	John Johnson a descendant of Joseph	84	87	Teach world of judgment to come
98	32	Law given to Joseph	88	35	What breaketh law not sanctified by
113	4	Descendant of Jesse and Ephraim or Joseph		40	Judgment goes before face of him
132	30	Ye are from Joseph		84	Prepare saints for judgment
JOSEPHITE				92	Prepare for judgment is come
3	17	How knowledge of Savior come to Josephites	99	5	I come quickly to judgment
JOURNEY			105	24	Talk not of judgment
52	33	Journey not in another's track	107	72	Judgment upon transgressors upon testimony
61	34	A way for journeying of saints	121	24	Swift judgment in season
JOY see also Gladness, Praise			124	39	Judgment in temples
6	31	Joy in fruit of your labors	136	42	Keep commandments lest judgment
18	16	Your joy, bring many souls unto me	JUST see also Justice, Law		
42	61	Ask and know what brings joy	38	26	God is just
45	71	Songs of everlasting joy	51	19	Just steward shall inherit eternal life
51	19	Faithful steward enter the joy of his Lord	58	18	Judge by testimony of just
59	14	Fasting is joy	76	17	Done good, in resurrection of just
66	11	Push many to Zion with songs of joy		50	Testimony concerning resurrection of just
93	33	Spirit and element receive fulness of joy		53	Holy Spirit of promise upon just and true
101	18	Return to Zion with songs of joy		69	Just men made perfect through Jesus
	36	In this world joy not full	98	31	Just to reward enemy according to works
106	6	Joy in heaven when Warren bowed	101	77	Laws and constitution holy and just

JUST continued
- 129 3   Spirits of just men made perfect
-       6   Spirit of just man comes only in glory
-       7   Contrary to heaven for just man to deceive

JUSTICE see also Injustice, Judgment, Just
- 38   26   Parable of justice
- 82   4   Justice and judgment penalty of God's law
- 84 102   God full of justice
- 88   35   What breaketh law not sanctified by
-       40   Justice claims her own
- 102 16   Speak according to justice
- 107 81   Manner of justice in the church
-       84   None exempt from justice and laws of God

JUSTIFICATION
- 20   30   Justification through grace is true
- 98   38   Ensample for Justification

JUSTIFY
- 88   39   Abide not conditions, not justified
- 132 59   Man endowed with keys of priesthood
-       62   Justified because given to him

KEY see also Power, Authority, Church, Priesthood
- 6   28   Keys of the gift of translation
- 7   7   To you three give keys of this ministry
- 13   1   Keys of ministering of angels, etc.
- 27   5   Keys of record of stick of Ephraim
-        6   Keys of restoration of things
-        9   Keys of turning hearts of fathers
- 28   7   Given Joseph Smith keys of mysteries
- 35   18   Joseph and successor hold keys of mysteries
- 35   25   Israel led by keys given
- 42   69   Kingdom or keys of church
- 64   5   Keys of mysteries not taken from Joseph
- 84   26   Lesser priesthood holds keys of ministering
- 110 11   Moses commits keys of gathering
- 112 32   Keys of this dispensation from fathers and
- 124 34   Keys of priesthood in temples
-       92   Keys of patriarchal blessings
-       97   Keys by which to receive blessings
-      128   twelve hold keys to open authority of
-      143   Key of officers of priesthood
- 128 11   Has keys of holy priesthood receives facts
-       18   Welding together of keys now
-       20   Peter, James and John claim keys of
-       21   Angels declaring their keys
- 129   9   Three grand keys of administration
-       hd   Keys to know angels or spirits
- 132 39   Prophets with keys of celestial marriage
-       59   Endowed with keys of priesthood justified

KEY OF KINGDOM
- 27   13   Keys of kingdom committed to Peter, James
- 65   2   Committed to man
- 81   2   Belong to first presidency
- 90   3   Belong to Joseph Smith in and out of the
-        6   Equal with Joseph Smith in keys of kingdom
- 97   14   Keys of kingdom conferred upon you
- 112 16   Thomas B. Marsh to hold keys of kingdom
- 128 14   Keys of kingdom are keys of knowledge
-       20   Peter, James and John claim keys of

KILL see also Blood, Murder
- 42   19   Thou shalt not kill
-       79   Murderers, how dealt with
- 59   6   Thou shalt not kill

KIMBALL, HEBER C.
- 124 129   Heber C. Kimball an apostle

KINDNESS see also Grace, Love
- 4   6   Remember brotherly kindness
- 121 42   Power of priesthood by kindness
- 133 52   Bestowed according to loving kindness
-       52   Mention loving kindness of Lord

KING see also God
- 1   23   Gospel proclaimed before kings
- 76   56   They are priests and kings
- 38   21   In time, no king or ruler but Christ
- 124   3   Proclamation of gospel to all kings
-        6   Kings called to heed Zion
-       11   Awake, O kings
-       16   Help to send word to kings
-      107   Make a solemn proclamation to kings

KINGDOM see also Heaven, Glory, Church
- 7   4   Good desire to come to my kingdom
- 29   5   Good will of Father to give you kingdom
- 35   27   Kingdom is yours until
- 42   69   Kingdom or keys of church
- 43   10   Kingdom shall be taken away
-       10   Glory added to kingdom if
- 45   1   Kingdom given to man
- 50   35   Kingdom given to father
- 52   9   Kingdom is yours
- 63   23   Keep commandments, receive mysteries of
- 64   4   Merciful for given you kingdom
-        5   Of kingdom not taken from Joseph Smith
- 76   79   Receive not crown of kingdom
-      107   Christ deliver kingdom to Father
-      114   Mysteries of kingdom great and marvelous
- 78   18   Blessings of kingdom yours
- 84   34   Who receives priesthood are kingdom
-       38   Receives Father receives kingdom
-       59   Children of kingdom shall not pollute Holy
-       74   No unbelievers in Father's kingdom
- 88   24   A kingdom not of glory
-       36   All kingdoms have a law
-       37   No space without a kingdom
-       47   Sun, moon and stars kingdoms
-       61   Every kingdom in hour, time and season
-       70   First labor in last kingdom
-       74   First laborers in last kingdom
- 93   53   Keys of kingdom conferred on you
- 99   3   Receives you as child, receives kingdom
- 103   7   Not cease to prevail until kingdoms are
- 105 32   Kingdoms of world acknowledge kingdom

128	14	Keys of kingdom are keys of knowledge
130	10	White stone, Urim and Thummim for all
	10	Pertaining to higher order of kingdom
131	4	If other marriage, no kingdom to increase
136	31	Bears not chastisement not worthy of
	41	Elders and people receive my kingdom

KIRTLAND

63	38	Disciples in Kirtland arrange their affairs
64	21	Lord will retain stronghold in Kirtland
82	13	Shinehah (Kirtland) consecrated for stake
94	2	Pattern for city in land of Kirtland
104	21	Shinehah
	40	My stake in Kirtland
	48	United order of Kirtland separated from
105	33	First elders receive endowment in my house
109	2	Commanded to build house in Kirtland
117	5	Let properties of Kirtland turn out for debt
	16	Saints in Kirtland to keep temple holy
124	83	I will build up Kirtland

KIRTLAND TEMPLE

109	hd	Prayer at dedication of Kirtland temple
110	hd	Visions in Kirtland temple
	2	Lord seen in Kirtland temple
	7	I have accepted this house
	8	Lord will appear in Kirtland temple if
	10	Fame extend to foreign lands

KNEE

76	110	All shall bow the knee
88	104	Every knee shall bow

KNIGHT, JOSEPH

12	hd	Given to Joseph Knight
23	hd	Given to Joseph Knight
	6	Words to Joseph Knight

KNIGHT, NEWEL

52	32	Newel Knight called
54	hd	Given to Newel Knight
	2	Newel Knight stand fast in office
56	6	Command to Newel Knight revoked
124	132	Newel Knight member of high council

KNIGHT, VINSON

124	74	Words to
	141	Vinson Knight to preside over bishopric

KNOCK

4	7,	6:5, 11:5, 12:5, 14:5, 66:9, 75:27, 88:63
		Knock and it shall be opened

KNOW see also Faith, Knowledge

6	11	If inquire shalt know of mysteries
	12	Make not gift known
	16	None save God knows thoughts and intents
	24	Witness things no man knoweth
11	14	Know whatsoever you desire
	16	Know of a surety my doctrine
15	3, 16:3	No man knoweth save thee and me
18	8	Purpose is known in me
19	8	To know as mine apostles

	23	Must not know lest they perish
20	17	By these things we know that there is God
76	117	Privilege of seeing and knowing for them
	94	Know as known
84	52	Who receives not knows not
93	28	Man shall know all things
121	24	Eye see and know all works
132	45	Make known all things in due time

KNOWLEDGE see also Know, Faith, Intelligence

1	28	Humble receive knowledge
3	20	Lamanites come to the knowledge
4	6	Remember knowledge
8	1	Receive knowledge of whatever you ask
	11	Receive knowledge from ancient records
20	13	Come to knowledge of this world shall be
29	49	Repentance required of those having
39	6	Holy Ghost showeth and teacheth all things
42	61	Ask and receive knowledge
46	18	Word of knowledge given to some
	18	All taught knowledge and to be wise
50	40	Ye must grow in knowledge
67	5	Sought knowledge beyond language of
69	7	Travel to obtain knowledge
84	19	Melchizedek priesthood holds key of
88	79	All knowledge to be sought
89	19	Hidden treasures of knowledge if keep word
93	24	Truth knowledge of things
	53	Obtain knowledge of history, laws, etc.
101	25	Knowledge and glory shall dwell upon earth
107	31	If these things abound not unfruitful in
	71	Knowledge by Spirit of truth
121	26	Gives knowledge by Holy Spirit
	31	All knowledge revealed in fulness of times
	33	Will pour knowledge on Latter-Day Saints
	42	Pure knowledge to enlarge soul without
128	14	Keys of kingdom are keys of knowledge
	19	As dews of Carmel so knowledge of God
130	19	More knowledge here advantage in next
	19	Knowledge gained by diligence and

LABAN, SWORD OF

17	1	Shall have view of the sword of Laban

LABOR see also Idle, Laborer, Work

10	4	Do not labor beyond strength and means
21	9	Bless those who labor
43	28	Labor in my vineyard
53	6	Ordinances come according to labor
56	17	Poor to labor
64	25	Labor while called today
68	30	Saints remember their labors in faithfulness
71	4	Labor in my vineyard
75	3	Be not idle but labor
	28	Family provider to labor in church
84	109	Every man labor in his own calling
124	86	Rest from labors, continue works
	121	Just recompense of wages for labor

LABORER continued
- 122 Labors may be accounted as stock

LABORER see also Labor
- 31 5 Laborer worthy of his hire
- 42 42 Idle shall not eat or wear with laborer

LAKE
- 63 17 Lake of fire and brimstone
- 76 36 Who shall go to lake of fire and brimstone

LAMANITE
- 3 18 Testimony of Jesus come to Lamanites
- 20 Lamanites may believe gospel
- 10 48 Become Lamanites by dissension
- 19 27 Lamanites a remnant of the Jews
- 28 8 Preach to Lamanites
- 30 6 Power to build church among Lamanites
- 49 24 Lamanites shall blossom as a rose
- 54 8 Missouri, unto borders of Lamanites
- 109 65 Remnants from wild and savage conditions

LAME
- 35 9 Lame made to walk
- 42 51 The lame shall leap
- 58 11 Lame come to marriage of Lamb

LAMECH
- 107 51 Lamech ordained at 52

LAMENTATION
- 112 24 Day of lamentations come

LAND see also America, United States
- 10 50 Blessing upon this land
- 51 This land free to all
- 19 34 Impart a part of thy lands
- 38 18 A land upon which there is no curse
- 42 35 Lands of church, how bought
- 45 63 Wars in your own lands
- 48 2 Impart of your lands to brethren
- 3 If no lands buy
- 4 Purchase land for inheritance
- 58 19 My law kept on this land
- 61 17 In last days land blessed
- 17 In beginning land cursed
- 63 27 Purchase lands
- 70 16 Commandment for lands
- 101 70 Purchase lands by money
- 73 Honorable and wise men to buy lands
- 103 20 Shall possess land in time
- 24 Land of Zion goodly land
- 105 15 Lands consecrated for gathering
- 29 Possess lands according to laws of
- 30 After purchase armies guiltless in taking
- 35 Organize kingdom on consecrated land
- 124 87 Sickness of land redound to glory
- 133 23 Islands become one land
- 29 Parched ground not thirsty land

LANESHINE HOUSE
- 104 28 Printing house

LANGUAGE
- 1 24 Commandments given after manner of their
- 52 15 Meek and edifying language of God
- 67 5 Sought knowledge beyond language of
- 90 11 Every man hear gospel in own tongue
- 15 Learn languages

LAST DAYS see also End, Christ's Coming, Times of
- 1 4 My disciples chosen in last days
- 5 35 If faithful, lifted up at last day
- 9 14 Lifted up at last day
- 17 8 Ye shall be lifted up at last day
- 18 24 In that name called at last day
- 20 1 Rise of church in last days
- 27 6 Fulfillment of things spoken of the last days
- 39 11 Fulness of gospel sent out in last days
- 46 26 Events of last days
- 43 1–35 Last days discussed
- 52 44 Faithful lifted up at last day
- 63 34 Words concerning
- 73 hd Church established in last days
- 77 15 Two prophets of Jews in last days
- 84 117 Desolation of abomination of last days
- 87 5 Wars of last days
- 88 90 Natural forces in last days
- 91 Happenings of last days
- 102 Who are to remain to last day
- 102 Remain filthy to last day
- 112 30 Last days, dispensation of fulness of times
- 136 22 Arm stretched in last days to save Israel

LAST JUDGMENT
- 38 5 Wicked kept until last judgment

LATTER-DAY SAINTS
- 121 33 Will pour knowledge upon Latter-day Saints

LAUGHTER
- 59 15 Much laughter is sin
- 88 69 Cast away excess of laughter
- 121 Cease from all laughter

LAW see also Command, Commandment
- 20 20 By transgression of holy laws man fell
- 24 17 Who shall go to law shall be cursed
- 29 34 No temporal law given of God
- 38 22 Have only my laws
- 41 3 By prayer of faith receive my law
- 4 See that my law is kept
- 5 Disciple receiveth and doeth law
- 42 59 Take for law what thou findest in
- 66 Observe laws
- 81 Dealt with according to law of God
- 43 2 Commandment for a law
- 8 Learn how to act upon my law
- 45 54 Know no law have part in first resurrection
- 51 2 People must be organized according to law
- 56 4 How God justifies changes in law
- 58 19 My law kept on this land
- 23 Laws of church
- 36 Do with monies as law directs

64	13	Justified in eyes of law
68	85	The law concerning children
70	10	None exempt from law who belong to church
76	72	Who died without law
82	15	United order according to law of God
85	11	Fate of high priesthood not in book of law
88	13	Light is life, law, power of God
	21	Who are not sanctified through law of
	22	Cannot abide law cannot abide glory
	34	What is governed by law preserved by law
	35	Seeks to become law to itself
	36	All kingdoms have a law
	38	Every law has bounds and conditions
	39	Abide not conditions of law not justified
	42	Law by which things move in times and
93	53	Obtain knowledge of laws
98		Law for treatment of enemies
	5	Law for rights and privileges justifiable
	5	Constitutional law to be befriended
	7	Law of man, more or less than these, of evil
	8	God and the law make you free
101	77	Laws and constitution holy and just
105	4	Law of union of celestial kingdom
	5	Zion built only by law of celestial kingdom
	32	Let us be subject to the laws
107	72	Judgment according to laws
	84	None exempt from justice and laws of God
109	46	Seal up law, bind up testimony
119	4	Tithing a law forever
124	49	God's laws may be revoked or held in
128	9	If faithful record, law on earth and in
132	3	Who have laws revealed must obey
	6	Who receives fulness must obey the law
	11	Appoint only by law previously ordained
	12	My word, my law
130	20	All blessings predicated on law
	21	Blessing obtained by obedience to its law
132	21	Except abide law, not obtain glory
	32	Enter law and be saved
	59	No sin to act according to law
133	72	Bind up law for disobedient
134	hd	Of governments and laws in general
	4	Relation of human law and religion
	5	Government has right to enact such laws
	6	Purposes of human and divine laws
	6	Human and divine laws answerable to
	6	Men owe respect to laws
	11	Men should apply to civil law for

LAWS OF THE LAND

42	79	Murderer to be dealt with according to laws
44	4	Organize according to laws of man
51	6	Things done according to laws of land
58	21	Laws of land, laws of God
	21	No man break laws of land
98	4	Statement concerning

LAW, WILLIAM

124	82	William Law to pay stock to temple
	91	William Law counselor in place of Hyrum
	97	William Law to receive keys
	126	To be counselor to Joseph

LAW-GIVER see also God

38		22, 45:59 I am the law-giver

LAYING ON OF HANDS see also Confirm

13	hd	John the Baptist laid hands on Joseph and
20	58	Teachers and deacons cannot lay on hands
	68	Laying on of hands to those baptized
	68	What should precede confirmation
24	9	Continue laying on of hands
33	15	Laying on of hands for Holy Ghost
53	3	Holy Spirit by laying on of hands
107	67	Administering by laying on of hands

LEADER

54	7	Appoint whom you will for leader
112	30	First Presidency counselors and leaders of

LEARN see also Inquire, Instruct, Knowledge

19		23, 58:1 Learn of me
88	79	All knowledge to be sought
	80	Learn all, prepared when sent
	123	Learn to impart as gospel requires
90	15	Study to learn
136	32	Let ignorant learn wisdom

LEARNED

58	10	Learned invited to supper of Lord

LEARNING see also Learn

88	118	Seek learning by study and faith
	119	Establish a house of learning

LEHI

17	1	Given Lehi in wilderness on borders
	1	Miraculous directors given to Lehi

LEMUELITE

3	18	Testimony of Jesus come to Lemuelites

LETTER

20	84	Member removing to take a letter or

LEVI, SONS OF

13	1	Until sons of Levi offer again
124	39	Sacrifices by sons of Levi in temples
128	24	Shall purify sons of Levi

LEVITICAL

107	1	Melchizedek and Aaronic including Levitical

LIAR see also Lie

42	21, 86	Liar to be cast out
63	17	liars shall die second death
64	39	Liars proved by church
76	103	Liars receiving telestial glory
93	25	Spirit of wicked, liar from beginning

LIBERTY

88	86	Abide in liberty, made free

LICENSE see also Certificate

20	63	Elders to receive licenses by vote
	64	Priesthood entitled to license

LICENSE continued
    57   9   Sidney Gilbert to obtain a license
LIE see also Liar, Truth, Perjurer
    10   25   Satan telleth no sin to lie
         25   Catch a man in a lie to destroy
         28   Woe to him who lieth to deceive
    42   21   Thou shalt not lie
    62   6   Lord promised and cannot lie
    76   103 Who loves and makes a lie, telestial glory
    123 7   Fathers inherited lies
LIFE see also Live
    10   70   Life and light of the world
    19   25   Shalt not seek thy neighbor's life
    50   27   Life subject to the ordained
    76   59   Life is theirs
    77   8   Power to seal unto life
    78   16   God without end of life
    85   2   Record of life of members to be kept
    86   10   Life and priesthood remain through you
    88   13   Light is life, law, power of God
    89   14   Grain staff of life for man and beast
    98   13   Lay down life and find life eternal
    101 15   Given lives for my name be crowned
         30   An infant's life like the age of a tree
         35   Though life laid down shall partake
    103 27   Who lays down life shall find it again
         28   Will not lay down life not a disciple
    128 7   Book of life is a record kept in heaven
    132 22   Narrow way to continuation of lives
    135 13   In life not divided in death not separated
LIFE ETERNAL see also Salvation
    5   22   I grant you eternal life
    6   7   Who hath eternal life is rich
    10   50   In this land might have eternal life
    14   7   Eternal life is God's greatest gift
    20   14   Receive work shall receive eternal life
    29   43   Eternal life through faith
    42   61   Ask and know what brings eternal life
    45   8   Eternal life to those who believe on my
    51   19   Faithful steward shall inherit eternal life
    59   23   Eternal life in life to come
    66   12   Shall have crown of eternal life
    68   12   Seal to eternal life whom the Father
    88   4   Comforter promise of eternal life
    101 38   Possess soul in patience for eternal life
    128 12   Herein is eternal life
         23   Glorious voice declaring eternal life
    133 62   Who repents shall have eternal life
LIGHT see also Darkness, Truth
    6   21   Light which shineth in darkness
    10   58   Light which shineth in darkness
         70   Life and light of the world
    11   11   I am light that shineth in darkness
    14   9   Light which cannot be hid
    45   28   Light break forth among those in darkness

    50   24   Who continueth in God receiveth more light
         24   Light groweth brighter and
         27   Light subject to the ordained
    82   3   Sins against greater light, greater
    84   45   Truth is light and spirit of Jesus Christ
         46   Spirit gives light to every man
    85   7   Clothed with light for a covering
    86   11   I light unto Gentiles
    88   6   Jesus Christ the light of truth
         11   Same light quickeneth understanding
         12   Light from God to fill all space
         13   Light is life, law, power of God
         40   Light cleaveth unto light
         44   Planets give light in times and seasons
         49   Light shineth, darkness comprehendeth it
         67   Body filled with light comprehends all
         87   Sun shall hide face and give no light
    93   29   Intelligence or light of truth
         32   Who receives not light is under
         36   Glory of God is intelligence or light and
    103 9   Saints to be lights and saviors
    106 8   Reward of light to church
    115 5   Light of church a standard to nations
    128 20   Michael detecting devil as angel of light
    133 49   Moon shall withhold its light
LIGHT-MINDEDNESS
    88   121 Cease from all light mindedness
LIGHTNING
    43   2   Lightning to speak to nations
         25   God calls by lightning
    87   6   God's wrath shown by lightning
    88   90   After your testimony that of lightning
LIKENESS
    128 13   All things should have their likeness
LINE
    57   4   Unto line between Jew and Gentile
    98   12   Give to faithful line upon line
    128 21   Giving line upon line
LINEAGE
    68   21   Lineage ascertained by revelation
    86   8   Priesthood continued through lineage
    107 41   Priesthood came down by lineage from
    113 8   Zion has right to priesthood by lineage
LISTENER
    50   22   Preacher and receiver understand each
LITERARY
    72   20   Stewards of literary concerns have claim on
LITTLE
    128 21   Here a little, there a little
LIVE see also Life
    42   45   Live in love
    54   9   Seek living like other men
    59   2   Who live shall inherit the earth
    63   3   Those live whom the Lord wills
         50   Who lives when Christ comes is blessed

84	20	Without it, not see God and live		70	18	Lord is merciful
	43	Shall live by word from mouth of God		82	1	I forgive who forgive
95	13	Not live after manner of world			10	Lord bound by what I say
98	11	Live by every word from mouth of God		84	3	Appointed by finger of the Lord
120	15	Salvation of dead essential to that of living			35	Receive priesthood receive the Lord
124	86	If live, live unto me			36	Receives servants receives the Lord

LOOK

6	36	Look unto me in every thought			37	Receives Lord receives Father
133	15	Look not back lest destruction			98	All filled with knowledge of Lord

LOOSE

11	21	Your tongue be loosed		85	10	As the Lord speaks will fulfil
128	8	Loose on earth and in heaven		87	7	Ears of Lord of Sabath

LORD

1	11	Voice of Lord unto ends of earth		88	2	Come unto ears of Lord
	13	Anger of the Lord is kindled			59	Lord visits all in their season
	14	Arm of the Lord shall be revealed			95	Lord's face unveiled
	16	Seek not the Lord to establish righteousness		90	10	Arm of Lord in power to convincing
	17	Lord called upon Joseph Smith			36	Lord will contend with strong of Zion
	17	Lord spake from heaven		107	49	Enoch saw Lord
	34	Willing to make things known to all flesh			45	Appeared to Adam at Adam-Ondi-Ahman
	36	Lord shall reign		110	2	The Lord seen in Kirtland temple
	38	What Lord has spoken is spoken		110	3	His voice and appearance described
	39	Lord is God			4	Who he is
3	9	Joseph chosen to do work of the Lord		128	20	Voice of Lord at Fayette
	18	Lord suffered to destroy		133	41	Presence of Lord as melting fire
10	70	Your Lord			48	Lord shall be red in apparel
17	1	Brother of Jared talked with Lord face to		136	21	God of fathers Abraham, Isaac and Jacob

LORD OF HOSTS

18	33	Jesus Christ your Lord and God		64	24	I am Lord of Hosts

LOSE

39	16	Lord cannot deny His word		3	14	Reason thou hast lost privileges
43	23	Lord shall speak to the nations		9	14	Hair of head shall not be lost
45	48	Lord set foot on this mount		10	2	Lost writings and gift
	49	Lord shall again utter his voice		50	42	None shall be lost
59	7	Thank the Lord in all things		67	3	Blessing lost through fears in hearts
	8	Sacrifice to be offered the Lord		136	26	Return what is lost

LOT

61	2	I, Lord, forgive sins		85	7	Arrange inheritances by lot
	13	Lord will reason as in days of old		102	12	Determine order by lot
	20	Lord angry yesterday, today anger turned		104	36	Lots laid off for building of city

LOVE see also Grace, Mercy, Kindness

63		What the Lord is able to do		4	5	Love qualifies him for work
	5	Lord demands obedience		12	8	Not assist unless full of love
	26	Lord renders to Caesar Caesar's		20	19	Man should love God
	32	Lord angry with wicked		42	22	Love thy wife
	34	Lord will come down in heaven			29	If thou love me serve me
	53	Speaking after manner of the Lord			45	Live in love
64	10	Lord forgive whom he will		45	27	Love of men shall wax cold
	16	Sought evil and Lord withheld his Spirit		59	5	How to love God
	24	Speaking after manner of the Lord			6	Love thy neighbor as thyself
	28	Lord can take when he pleases and pay		76	116	Gifts to those who love God
	30	Lord's words are sure		95	1	Whom I love I chasten
	34	Lord requireth heart and willing mind		112	11	Be not partial in love
65	4	Pray unto the Lord		121	41	Power of priesthood by love
	5	Call upon the Lord to extend his kingdom		124	17	Great for his love
66	13	Lord, God, Redeemer, Jesus Christ			20	Love him for love of testimony
68	hd	Will of Lord to conference concerning			78	I love him for his work
	5	Promise of the Lord to missionaries			87	If you love me, keep my commandments
	31	Lord not pleased with idlers				

LOVE continued
- 133 53 Redeemed them in his love

LOW
- 58 47 Call upon low to repent
- 104 16 The rich shall be made low
- 112 8 Many low exalted
- 8 High brought low by word

LUCIFER see also Devil, Satan
- 76 25 Lucifer's rebellion
- 26 Heavens wept over Lucifer
- 26 Perdition, Lucifer, a son of the morning

LUST see also Adulterer
- 42 23 Lust after woman deny the faith
- 23 If lust after woman, shall be cast out
- 46 8 Sign to consume upon lusts
- 63 16 Cease from all lustful desires

LYMAN, AMASA
- 124 136 A counselor in high priests quorum
- 136 14 And George A. Smith organize a company

MAGAZINE
- 123 5 Keep history of reports of church in

MAGISTRATE see also Government
- 134 3 Government requires officers and magistrates
- 6 Purpose of magistrates

MAGNIFY
- 24 2 Magnify thine office
- 66 11 How to magnify thine office

MAHALALEEL
- 82 11 Mahalaleel
- 107 46 Time of ordination
- 53 Mahalaleel a high priest

MAJORITY see also Consent
- 107 28 Majority may form a quorum

MALACHI
- 110 14 Time spoken of by Malachi has come
- 128 17 Malachi 4:5, 6 explained
- 133 64 Fulfilled as written by Malachi

MALE
- 20 18 Created man male and female

MAN see also Children of Men, Flesh
- 1 16 Man walketh in his own way
- 19 Man should not counsel fellowman
- 20 Every man might speak name of God
- 33 Spirit shall not always strive with man
- 35 Men shall know the day cometh
- 3 4 Man may have many revelations and
- 7 Should not fear man more than God
- 7 Men set at naught counsels of God
- 11 Thou shalt come as other men
- 18 42 Men to repent and be baptized
- 20 20 How man became fallen man
- 42 Man may fall from grace and
- 29 24 Men to be new
- 43 21 Christ a man
- 49 16 Man and wife shall be one flesh
- 17 Man created before the world was
- 22 Son of man comes not as a man traveling
- 58 27 Men must do much of own free will
- 18 All things for the use of man
- 21 How man offends God
- 65 2 Keys of kingdom committed to men
- 67 12 Natural man cannot abide presence of God
- 76 61 Let no man glory in man, but in God
- 77 2 Happiness of man, beast, creeping things
- 12 Man formed from dust of the earth
- 82 18 That man may improve his talents
- 84 16 Adam was first man
- 88 58 Every man in his hour, time and season
- 89 14 Grain staff of life for man and beast
- 16 Grain good for food of man
- 17 Wheat for man
- 90 11 Every man hear gospel in own tongue
- 93 28 Man shall know all things
- 29 Man was in the beginning with God
- 31 Here is agency of man
- 33 Man is a spirit
- 36 Man is temple or tabernacle of God
- 38 Spirit of man innocent in beginning
- 38 Man become again innocent
- 101 26 Enmity of man and beast cease
- 81 Men should pray and not faint
- 104 13 Every man accountable as steward over
- 122 9 Fear not what man can do
- 130 4 Man's time according to residence

MANCHESTER
- 24 3 Go to church in Manchester

MANNER
- 1 24 Commandments given after manner of their
- 63 53 Speaking after manner of the Lord

MARKS, WILLIAM
- 117 hd William Marks to leave Kirtland
- 10 To preside in Far West
- 124 79 Isaac Galland to be ordained by William
- 80 William Marks to pay stock into temple

MARRIAGE see also Celestial Marriage, Concubine
- 49 15 Marriage ordained of God
- 15 Whoso forbids to marry is not
- 16 The object of marriage
- 74 5 Marriage of believer and unbeliever
- 131 2 Celestial order of marriage
- 132 hd Concerning plurality of wives
- hd Eternity of marriage covenant
- 15 Marriage without word only to death
- 16 Neither marry nor given in marriage
- 16 Marry without covenant become ministering
- 3 Who have law revealed must obey
- 5 Law before foundation of world
- 6 Reject this covenant and be damned
- 17 Marry without covenant saved but not
- 17 Marry without covenant not God's

18		Marriage without covenant not valid after
19		Marriage in covenant valid after death
19		Blessings to those married in covenant
26		Punishment of sin for those married in

MARSH, THOMAS B.

31	1	Comfort to Thomas B. Marsh
52	22	T. B. Marsh and Ezra Thayre called
56	5	Commandment to revoked
75	31	Mission for
112	1	Words to Thomas B. Marsh
	16	To hold keys of kingdom

MARTYRDOM

135	hd	Martyrdom of Joseph and Hyrum
	1	Seal testimony of this work

MARVELOUS

4	1	Marvelous work to come forth
6	11	Great and marvelous mysteries
11	1	A great and marvelous work

MATTER

131	7	No immaterial matter
	7	All spirit is matter.
	8	When bodies pure see spirit matter

MATTHEW

128	10	Matt. 16:18 explained

MEANS

5	34	I will provide means
10	4	Do not labor more than you have means

MEASURE

1	9	Wrath of God poured without measure
	10	God shall measure according to measure e
88	25	Earth fills measure of creation
101	11	Indignation without measure upon nations
103	3	Suffer them to fill up measure of iniquity

MEAT see also Flesh

18	22	They cannot bear meat now
49	18	Forbidding to eat meat is not of God
	21	Waste of meats forbidden
51	13	Excess of meat, in storehouse

MEDIATOR see also Jesus

76	69, 107:19	Jesus mediator of new covenant

MEEK

35	15	Meek shall hear gospel
52	16	Meek and edifying language of God
88	17	Poor and meek inherit earth
97	2	Show mercy to the meek and

MEEKNESS

19	23	Walk in meekness of Spirit
25	14	Continue in spirit of meekness
31	9	Govern in meekness
63	57	Who desire in meekness shall
84	106	He may be edified in meekness
100	7	Declare in meekness
121	41	Power of priesthood by meekness
124	4	Write in meekness

MEETING

24	44	Apostles to take lead of all meetings
	45	Elders to conduct meetings as led
	49	Priests may lead in meetings
	55	Teachers to see that meetings are attended
	56	Teachers may lead meeting
42	89	Complaint filed in meeting
43	8	In meeting edify and instruct
46	2	Conduct meetings as led by Spirit
	3	Cast none out of public meetings
88	100	Conducting meetings

MELCHISEDEK see also Priesthood

76	57	Order of Melchisedek after Only Begotten
107	1	Melchisedek and Aaronic, including
	2	Melchisedek a great high priest
107	14	Aaronic priesthood an appendage to
124	123	Priesthood after Melchisedek after Only

MEMBER

20	68	Duty of members after baptism
	71	When members may be received
	82	Names of members kept in a book
	84	Member removing to take certificate
42	70	Members to have stewardships
	78	Keep all commandments and covenants
46	4	Not to be cast out of sacrament meeting
50	41	Given to Christ of the Father
	42	None shall be lost
	43	Members one with Christ
84	110	Body hath need of every member
85	2	Record of their life faith and works
72	24	Members must bring recommends
102	5	Thirteen members voted on first high
107	10	High priest may officiate instead of
134	10	Right of religious societies to deal with

MEMORIAL

112	1	Alms come as a memorial to God
124	39	Memorials for sacrifices in temples

MEN

5	21	Yield to persuasions of men no more
18	11	Redeemer suffered pain for all men
63	51	Old men shall die but

MERCIFUL see also Mercy

3	10, 38:14, 50:16, 61:2, 64:4, 70:18, God is
101	92	Pray that I may be merciful to them

MERCY

1	29	Power to translate through mercy of God
29	1	Arm of mercy atoned for sin
38	14	Blessed through mercy of God
43	25	God calls by mercy
46	15	God suits mercies to men
56	6	Who keeps covenant receives mercy
84	102	God full of mercy
88	35	Breaketh law not sanctified by mercy
	40	Mercy hath compassion on mercy

MERCY continued
- 97　2　Mercy that I may be justified
- 　　2　Show mercy to meek and
- 98　30　If enemy spared, reward for righteousness
- 99　3　Receive as a child, receive kingdom and
- 101　9　In day of wrath will have mercy
- 109　1　Lord who showeth mercy
- 　　54　Have mercy, O Lord
- 128　19　A voice of mercy from heaven

MERIDIAN OF TIME
- 20　26, 39:3　Came in meridian of time

MERRY
- 136　28　If merry, praise with singing, etc.

MESSIAH
- 13　1　In the name of Messiah I confer
- 19　27　That Jews may not look for Messiah

MESSENGER
- 45　9　Everlasting covenant a messenger
- 93　8　Son the word and messenger of salvation
- 129　4　When messenger from God comes offer

METHUSELAH
- 107　50　Methuselah ordained at 100
- 　　52　Methuselah ordained Noah
- 　　53　Methuselah a high priest

MICHAEL see also Adam
- 27　11　Michael or Adam
- 29　26　Michael to sound trump before the end
- 　　26　Michael mine archangel
- 78　16　Michael your prince
- 　　16　Michael has keys of salvation
- 88　112　Seventh angel, archangel
- 　　112　To gather armies of heaven
- 　　113　Devil and armies battle with Michael and
- 　　115　Michael to fight the battles of the Saints
- 107　54　Adam, Michael, prince, archangel
- 128　20　Voice of Michael on banks of Susquehanna
- 　　20　Michael detecting devil as angel of light
- 　　21　Michael or Adam
- 　　21　Voice of Michael the archangel

MIDDLE-AGED
- 105　16　Young and middle-aged God's warriors

MIDST
- 1　36　Lord shall reign in their midst
- 88　13　God in midst of things
- 133　36　Angel flying in the midst of heaven

MIGHT
- 4　2　Serve God with all your might
- 4, 6:3, 11:3　Thrust in sickle with might
- 76　90　Celestial equal in power, might, dominion
- 　　114　Surpass understanding in might
- 84　102　Might to God
- 88　107　Angels crowned with glory of might
- 97　20　God sworn by power of might

MIGHTY
- 1　19　Weak to break down mighty

MILES, DANIEL
- 124　138　A president of seventies

MILK
- 19　22　Milk they must receive

MILLENNIUM
- 29　11　God dwell on earth a thousand years.
- 　　22　When millennium ended
- 43　30　Millennium shall come
- 　　30　Millennium discussed
- 45　57　Millennium, etc
- 　　60　Knowledge about millennium
- 63　51　Death during millennium
- 77　1　Things concerning millennium
- 　　12　In beginning of millennium
- 101　23–34　Conditions in millennium
- 130　2　Same sociality there as here except

MILLER, GEORGE
- 124　20　George Miller without guile
- 　　21　Receives bishopric
- 　　62　Committee to build temple

MIND
- 6　15　I did enlighten thy mind
- 　　24　Speak peace to your mind
- 8　2　Will tell in mind by Holy Ghost
- 9　8　Study it out in your mind
- 10　2　Mind became darkened
- 11　13　My spirit shall enlighten your mind
- 　　20　Keep commandments with all your mind
- 64　34　Lord requireth heart and willing mind
- 67　14　Let not your minds turn back
- 68　4　Said when moved by spirit mind of God
- 84　54　Minds darkened because of unbelief
- 　　61　Remain steadfast in your minds
- 　　80　Shall not be weary in mind
- 　　85　Treasure words of life in your minds
- 88　68　Sanctify that minds become single unto God
- 95　13　Wisdom and mind of the Lord
- 112　23　Darkness covers minds of people
- 121　12　To blind their minds
- 133　61　According to mind and will of God

MINISTER
- 7　6　Minister to heirs to salvation
- 　　7　Minister to him and James
- 10　62　Gospel ministered to them
- 13　1　Keys of ministering of angels
- 20　6　God ministered by an holy angel
- 84　111　Deacons and teachers standing ministers
- 107　97　Seventy to be traveling ministers
- 124　137　Elders ordained standing ministers

MINISTRY see also Church, Priesthood
- 6　28　Gift which shall bring to light this ministry
- 7　7　To you three give keys and power of ministry
- 27　12　Bear keys of your ministry
- 84　86　A commandment to all faithful called to
- 88　84　Labor diligently in ministry

90	8	Perfected for ministry by school		2	Ensample to all missionaries
97	13	House, for instruction of ministry		5	The promise of the Lord to missionaries
	14	Be perfected in understanding of ministry		6	The record to be borne by missionaries
MIRACLES				8	Act in authority given
24	13	Miracles that may be sought	69	5	Missionaries to send accounts of their labors
	13	Require not miracles	71	1	What to expound
	14	Miracles to be performed only by request		7	Meet enemies in public and private
45	8	Miracles by those who receive Christ		9–10	Promise to missionaries
46	21	Some given working of miracles	75	3	Be not idle but labor
MISERY see also Sorrow, Pain				18	Go from house to house, etc.
19	33	Misery if thou slight counsels		19	How to treat those who receive you
76	48	Misery of eternal punishment not		20	How to treat those receive you not
MISSION see also Missionary				21	Filled with joy and gladness
58	16	Mission given shall not be given again	75	24	Duty of church to support families of
58	17	Whoso standeth in mission is a judge		25	Missionaries to go if they can receive support
73	2	Missions known by voice of conference		26	Missionaries to go anywhere
77	14	Mission and ordinance to gather		27	Comforter to tell missionaries where to go
MISSIONARY see also Call, Preach, Servant				28	Missionaries who provide for families shall
4	5	Qualifications of a missionary	79	1	Go in power of ordination
24	18	Missionaries to receive help from church	80	3	Preach and go not amiss
	18	Missionaries to go without supplies		3	Missionaries called by Jesus Christ
	19	Pattern for missionaries to follow	84	92	Wash feet against him who receives you not
28	15	Directions to be given missionaries		76	Who must preach the gospel
33	8–12	What missionaries should do		78	Neither purse, scrip nor two coats
36	5	Every man shall preach the gospel		79	Sent to prove the world
	6	What they shall preach		80	Promises of health of body and mind to
39	15	Missionaries to go into all nations		80	Missionaries not go hungry or athirst
	17	Call faithful laborers		86	A commandment to all faithful called to
	20	Prepare for time of my coming		86	Not to take purse or scrip
42	6	Missionaries to speak like angels of God		87	Sent out to reprove the world
	6	How they shall go and what do		88	How disciples treat them
	11	Missionaries not to go unless ordained		88	Promises made to
	63	Missionaries to be sent everywhere		94	Wo to place that rejects you
43	15	Missionaries to teach, not to be taught		94	Search diligently and spare not
	16	Missionaries to be taught from on high		103	Missionaries with families send gifts to
49	11	Speak like unto Peter		103	Missionary without families send gifts to
50	17	How to preach the gospel		105	Take new, cast old to poor
	38	No man to hinder missionary		106	The strong to take the weak
52	10	Missionaries to go two by two		107	Lesser priesthood to go before to make
	33	Journey not in each other's tracks	88	80	Learn all, be prepared when sent
	36	Declare only prophets and apostles		81	Sent out to testify and warn
60	8	How to preach two by two		84	Their work
	10	Money to be given returning missionaries		85	Continue in vineyard till Lord calls
	11	Missionaries to return church money if able	90	11	Every man shall hear fulness of gospel
	13	Missionaries not to idle away time	93	51	Gospel as I give utterance
	14	Instructions to missionaries		51	Prayer of faith uphold him
61	22	Missionaries to travel upon water or land	97	13	House for instruction of missionaries
	35	Missionaries to journey together, two by two		14	What they should be perfected in
62	5	Missionaries to bear record	99	4	Cleanse feet as testimony
	5	Missionaries to go two by two	100	6	Shall be given you what to say
63	57	Who desire to warn sinners, let them be	107	35	Twelve to open door by proclamation of
66	7	Missionary instructions to W E. M'Lellin	111	3	How to begin work in a city
	9	Return not until Lord shall send you	112	21	Sent by voice of Twelve
68	1	Calling of Orson Hyde		21	Presidency to send missionaries by voice of
	1	Proclaim gospel by spirit of living God		21	Duly recommended and authorized

MISSIONARY continued
- 118 3   Lord will provide for families if
- 124 3   Proclaim gospel to all authorities
-      8   Fate if servants and testimony rejected
-     18   Beget glory and honor by preaching
- 133 8   Send elders unto all nations
-      9   The cry of the missionaries
-     37   Gospel be preached to every nation
-     38   They shall go and say

MISSOURI see also New Jerusalem
- 52   2   Land I will consecrate in Missouri
-      3   Joseph Smith and Sidney Rigdon to go to
-     42   Missouri land of inheritance
- 54   8   Missouri unto borders of Lamanites
- 57   1   Missouri consecrated for gathering of saints
-      2   Missouri place for city of Zion
-      2   Missouri the land of promise
- 62   6   Rejoice in Missouri
- 84   3   New Jerusalem to be built in Missouri
- 124 54   Save those slain in Missouri

MISSOURI RIVER
- 61   5   Many destructions upon Missouri river
- 121 33   Puny arm to stop Missouri

M'LELLIN, WILLIAM E.
- 66   1   Words to
- 68   7   Words to
- 75   6   Commission revoked
- 90 36   Mentioned

MOCK
- 63 58, 104:6, 124:71 Lord not mocked

MOCKER
- 45 50   Calamity shall overcome mocker

MONEY
- 48   4   Save money
- 51   8   Agent to care for money left to people
-     13   Excess of money in storehouse
- 58 35   Lay moneys before bishop
-     36   Do with moneys as law directs
- 84 89   Who receives will give money
-     90   Who gives money, lose no reward
-    104   Money consecrated to revelations and
- 101 70   Purchase lands around Zion for money
- 104 26   Martin Harris to use his moneys for church
-     84   Your privilege to loan money

MOON see also Sun, Stars, Planets
- 5   14   Church clear as the moon
- 29 14, 34:9, 45:42   Moon turned to blood
- 76 71   Terrestrial from celestial as moon from sun
-     81   Terrestrial to telestial as moon to stars
-     97   Glory of moon is one
- 88   8   Jesus light and power of moon
-     45   Moon gives light by night
-     47   Moon a kingdom
-     87   Moon bathed in blood
- 105 31   Army clear as the moon
- 121 30   If bounds set to moon
- 128 23   Let sun, moon and stars sing together
- 133 49   Moon shall withhold its light

MORLEY, ISAAC
- 52 23   Isaac Morley and Ezra Booth called
- 64 15   Angry with Isaac Morley
-     20   Words concerning

MORONI
- 27   5   Has keys of record of stick of Ephraim
-      5   Sent to reveal Book of Mormon
- 128 20   Moroni declaring fulfilment of prophets

MOSES
- 8   3   Moses brought Israel through Red Sea
- 22   2   Cannot enter by law of Moses
- 28   2   Joseph Smith receive revelations as Moses
- 74   3   Circumcised and subject to law of Moses
- 76 100 Of Moses, but receive not the gospel
- 84   6   Father-in-law of Moses
-      6   Moses received priesthood through Jethro
-     23   Moses taught priesthood to Israel
-     25   Moses and priesthood taken away
-     31   Sons of Moses to offer sacrifice
-     32   Sons of Moses and Aaron filled with glory
-     34   Who receive priesthood sons of Moses
- 103 16   Raise a man to lead like Moses
- 107 91   President of church like Moses
- 110 11   Moses commits keys of gathering Israel
- 124 38   Moses' tabernacle for temple ordinances
- 132 38   Moses received many wives and concubines
- 133 54   Moses and they before him
-     55   From Moses to Elijah
-     63   Fulfilled as written by Moses
- 136 37   From Moses to Jesus
-     37   From Abraham to Moses

MOUNTAIN
- 49 23   Mountain to be made low
-     25   Zion flourish upon hills and mountains
- 112 7   Chosen path among mountains
- 117 8   Room on mountains of Adam-Ondi-Ahman
- 124 104 Lift his voice again on mountains
- 128 19   How beautiful upon the mountains
-     23   Let mountains shout for joy
- 133 13   Unto mountains of Lord's house
-     22   Voice shall break mountains
-     40   Mountains flow down at his presence

MOURN
- 87   6   How the inhabitants shall mourn in last days
- 97 21   Zion rejoice when wicked mourn
- 98   9   Wicked rule, people mourn
- 101 14   Who mourned shall be comforted

MOURNING
- 95   7   Assemblies that fasting and mournings come
- 112 24   Day of mourning to come

MOUTH
- 19 15   Smite you by rod of my mouth

33	8	Open your mouths they shall be filled
60	2	Elders will not open mouths
84	44	Shall live by word from mouth of God
85	7	Mouth utters eternal words

MURDER see also Kill, Blood

121	23	Wo to those who murder my people
132	19	Shedding of innocent blood cancels sealing
	26	Sin but not murder shall come forth
	27	Shedding innocent blood, blasphemy against

MURDERER

42	18	No forgiveness, but shall die
	79	Murderer hath no forgiveness
	79	To be dealt with according to law of land

MURDOCK, JOHN

52	8	John Murdock to travel
99	1	Mission for John Murdock

MURMURING

75	7	Commandment to chasten for murmurings

MUSIC

136	28	If merry, praise with music

MYSTERY see also Hide

6	11	Exercise gift to find mysteries
10	64	Unfold this great mystery
19	8	Will explain this mystery
	10	Behold mystery of godliness
28	7	Given Joseph Smith key of mysteries
	7	Keys of mysteries held by head of church
35	13	Mystery of secret chambers
	11	If inquire shall know mysteries
42	65	You shall know mysteries
	61	Ask and you shall know mysteries
84	19	Greater priesthood holdeth keys of
97	5	Blessed in expounding mysteries
107	19	Mysteries to be received

MYSTERY OF GOD

6	7	Mysteries of God shall be unfolded
8	11	Ask to know mysteries of God
11	7	Mysteries of God unfolded to you
77	6	Mysteries of God is book of seven seals
84	19	Holds keys of mysteries of God

MYSTERY OF KINGDOM

43	13	Obtained by supporting Joseph Smith
63	23	Keep commandments receive mystery of
64	5	Keys of mystery of kingdom not taken from
76	7	Will reveal hidden mysteries of kingdom
	7	Faithful shall know all
	114	Mysteries of kingdom, great and marvelous

NAME see also Member

18	23	Jesus Christ name given by Father
	24	Men must take name given of Father
	25	If they know not name cannot have place
20	82	Record of names of church to be kept
	83	General church record of names
	83	Names of those expelled to be blotted out
24	5	Call upon God in my name
63	61	Beware to take God's name in their lips
	62	Condemnation to use name of God in vain
76	68	Whose names written in heaven
82	4	Ye call upon my name for revelation
84	66	Wonderful works in God's name
85	3	Names who pay no tithing not to be kept
	7	Inheritance whose names in book of law
115	4	Name of the church
117	11	Be bishop in deed and not in name only
123	3	Keep history of names of oppressors
124	56	Let names be upon house
	144	Approve names for officers at conference
130	11	The new name is the key word
	11	New name known only to recipient
	11	New name for all celestial kingdom
133	18	Names written on foreheads
	42	Make name known to adversaries
136	21	Evil to take name of Lord in vain

NAME OF CHRIST

46	31	All things done in name of Christ
49	13	Be baptized in name of Jesus Christ
50	29	Ask in name of Jesus and

NATION see also World

10	49	Other nations possess this land
	49	Faith that gospel came to other nations
34	8	Shall tremble at coming of Lord
42	58	Scriptures to be taught to nations, etc
53	20	Call nations to repent
45	47	Arm of Lord shall fall upon nations
	49	Nations shall mourn
	75	Nations afraid of terror of God
49	10	Nations to bow to law
56	1	Visitation and wrath upon nations
58	9	Nations invited to supper
64	37	Church like a judge over nations
	42	Come from every nation to Zion
	43	Nations shall tremble because of Zion
84	96	Laid my hand upon nations to scourge
87	2	War will be poured upon all nations
	6	Hath made full end of nations
88	79	Learn of wars of nations
	105	She is fallen who made the nations drink
90	10	Heathen nations house of Joseph
97	19	Nations shall honor Zion
101	11	indignation without measure upon nations
	89	Heeds not, God's fury vex the nation
107	55	Adam to be a prince of nations
112	21	Right to open door to nations
133	2	Come on all nations that forget
	42	All nations tremble at thy presence
	58	When little become strong nation

NAUVOO

124	109	City of Nauvoo appointed
125	3	Build Zarahemla opposite Nauvoo
126	4	Take inheritance in Nauvoo

NAUVOO HOUSE
- 124　60　Call the place Nauvoo house
- 　　　60　Nauvoo house for Joseph Smith

NEED
- 51　3　Portion according to needs
- 61　12　Take what is not needful as agree
- 82　17　Every man claim according to his needs
- 84　83　Father knoweth thy need

NEEDY see also Poor
- 44　6　Visit the needy
- 52　40　Disciple remembers poor and needy
- 124　75　Plead for poor and needy

NEIGHBOR
- 19　25　Not covet thy neighbor's wife or life
- 42　27　Not speak evil or harm thy neighbor
- 45　68　Not take sword against neighbor must flee
- 59　6　Love thy neighbor as thyself
- 82　19　Seek the interest of thy neighbor
- 88　81　Who warned, warn his neighbor
- 136　25　Duties to neighbor

NEPHI
- 10　42　Publish it as the record of Nephi
- 　　　44　Have abridgment of account of Nephi
- 　　　45　Translate first part of engravings of Nephi
- 33　8　Nephi journeyed from Jerusalem
- 98　32　Law given to Nephi

NEPHI, PLATES OF see also Book of Mormon
- 10　38　Account engraven on plates of Nephi
- 　　　39　More particular account on Plates of Nephi
- 　　　41　Translate engravings of plates of Nephi
- 　　　45　Plates of Nephi give greater views

NEPHITE
- 1　29　Received record of Nephites
- 3　17　How knowledge of Savior came to Nephites
- 　　18　Lord suffered brethren to destroy
- 38　39　Do not become as Nephites

NEW
- 63　49　Old things become new
- 101　25　All things become new

NEW JERUSALEM
- 42　9　New Jerusalem to be established
- 　　35　Church to build New Jerusalem
- 　　62　Ask and site of New Jerusalem revealed
- 　　67　Covenants to establish you in New Jerusalem
- 28　9　To be on borders of the Lamanites
- 29　9　Location of New Jerusalem to be given later
- 45　66　New Jerusalem described
- 　　67　To be called Zion
- 48　5　Site of, how and when to be revealed
- 52　43　Will hasten the city in time
- 57　3　New Jerusalem located
- 84　2　Mount Zion the city of New Jerusalem
- 　　3　Where New Jerusalem shall be built
- 　　3　Dedicated by Joseph Smith and others
- 　　4　To be built by gathering of Saints
- 　　31　Temple to be built in this generation
- 124　51　Why New Jerusalem not built

NEW YORK
- 84　114　Warn New York of desolation and
- 104　81　Cainhannock

NICHOLATINE
- 117　11　N. K. Whitney ashamed of Nicholatine band

NOAH
- 84　14　Priesthood through lineage of Noah
- 　　15　Noah received priesthood
- 107　52　Noah ordained at ten years
- 133　54　Noah and they before him

NOBLE
- 58　10　Noble invited to supper of the Lord
- 122　2　Noble will seek counsel

NON-MEMBER see also Member
- 46　5　Not to be cast out of sacrament meetings
- 　　6　Not to be cast out of confirmation meetings

NORTH
- 110　11　Lead ten tribes from the north
- 133　23　Great deep driven back to north countries
- 　　26　Coming of those in north countries

NORTHERN STATES
- 87　3　Southern states divided against northern

OATS
- 89　17　Oats for the horse

OATH see also Swear, Covenant, Promise
- 84　39　Oath and covenant of priesthood
- 　　40　Receive priesthood, receive oath and

OBEDIENCE see also Obey, Obedient, Will
- 6　9　Blessed if obedient
- 21　6　Church must receive what apostle says
- 63　5　Lord demands obedience
- 82　10　No promise without obedience
- 89　18　Reward of obedience
- 97　25–28　Zion if obedient, escape scourges, etc.
- 101　43　Parable of necessity of obedience
- 105　5　Chastened to learn obedience
- 124　49　Obedience justifies results
- 130　19　Knowledge and intelligence gained by
- 　　21　Blessings obtained by obedience
- 132　37　Obedience necessary for exaltation
- 　　50　Joseph's obedience rewarded

OBEDIENT see also Obey, Obedience
- 28　3　Be obedient to commandments
- 58　2　Blessed are obedient and faithful
- 　　6　Sent to be obedient.
- 64　34　Willing and obedient eat good of land
- 105　18　Blessing and endowment for obedient
- 132　65　Wife, if not obedient the transgressor

OBEY see also Hearken, Heed
- 52　15　Prayer heard if obey
- 56　3　Who obeys not command, cut off
- 58　30　Guiltless who obeys commandment
- 59　3　Blessed who obeyed the gospel

		Offend unless obedient
21		
78	7	Must prepare and obey
103	31–34	Obey as far as possible
132	3	Have law revealed must obey
132	6	Receive fulness must obey the law
	53	Obey my voice
133	71	Obey my voice out of heavens

OFFENSE
- 54 5 Wo by whom offense cometh

OFFEND
- 42 90 Offend many, chastened before many
-     92 Offend in secret, chastened in secret
- 59 21 How man offends God
- 64 13 Do not offend your Law-giver

OFFENDER
- 42 88 Manner of prosecuting an offender
-     88 Offender confess, reconciled
-     90 Offender chastened according to offense
- 64 12 How to deal with unrepentant offender

OFFERING
- 95 16 House dedicated for sacrament offering
- 97 27 Offering of Zion accepted
- 105 19 Heard prayer accepted offering
- 124 49 Accept incomplete offering
- 132 9   Will I receive offering not in my name?
-     51 I require offering by covenant and sacrifice

OFFICE
- 24 3   Magnify thine office
- 66 11 How to magnify thine office
- 78 12 Breaks covenant, lose office
- 81 5   Stand in office appointed
- 84 109 Every man stand in his own office
- 102 4   Fill office according to grace
- 107 5   Offices in church appendages to priesthood
-     99 Act in office with diligence
- 124 143 Why offices of priesthood given
-     144 Fill offices of priesthood
-     145 Prepare rooms for offices of priesthood in

OFFICER
- 70 12 Church officer worthy of hire
- 88 127 School of prophets for all officers
- 107 58 Twelve to ordain all other officers
- 124 123 Officers of priesthood enumerated
- 134 3   Governments require officers and magistrates

OHIO
- 37 1   Assemble in Ohio
- 38 32 Will give law in Ohio
- 39 15 If people assemble in Ohio
- 48 2   Commandment regarding lands in Ohio

OLD
- 29 24 All old things pass away
- 63 49 Old things become new
- 133 53 Bear and carried all days of old

OLIVER
- 6   20 Thou art Oliver
- 23 1   I speak to you, Oliver

OMNIPRESENCE
- 88 6   Omnipresence of Jesus Christ

ONE
- 38 27 Not one, not mine
- 51 9   That ye may be one
- 61 8   One, that perish not in wickedness
-     8   Chastened that you might be one
-     18 Commandment to one, to all
- 93 49 Say to one, to all

ONLY BEGOTTEN
- 76 23 Only Begotten of the Father
-     25 Only Begotten loved by Father
-     25 Angel rebelled against Only Begotten
-     35 Punishment for denying Only Begotten
-     57 Order of Melchisedek after Enoch, after

ONE HUNDRED AND FORTY-FOUR THOUSAND
- 77 11 High Priests ordained to order of

OPEN
- 4 7, 6:5, 11:5, 12:5, 66:9, 75:27, 88:63 Knock and it shall be opened

OPPRESSOR
- 123 3   Keep history of names of oppressors
- 124 8   Portion of oppressors among hypocrites
- 127 3   A just recompense upon oppressors

ORACLE
- 90 4   Oracles through you to church
-     5   Who receive oracles, beware
- 124 39 Oracles in temple
-     136 First presidency to receive oracles

ORDAIN
- 5   17 Wait, for not yet ordained
- 7   7   I shall ordain three servants
- 18 29 Twelve ordained to baptize
-     32 Twelve ordained to ordain
- 11 60 Ordain by power of Holy Ghost
- 20 64 Those ordained may take certificate
- 25 7   Emma Smith ordained to expound scriptures
- 27 12 Ordained and confirmed to be apostles
- 50 17 Who ordained preachers by spirit
-     14 Ordained to preach the gospel
-     26 Who is ordained is greatest
-     35 Power to overcome all not ordained
- 63 45 Let him be ordained to this power
- 67 10 Ordained privileged to see God
- 76 13 Things ordained from the beginning
-     48 Ordained to their condemnation
- 77 11 Ordain to holy order of Gods
- 78 2   Ordained you from on high
- 95 5   Many ordained and called, few chosen
- 96 89 Ordained to be member of United Order
- 121 32 Ordained in council of God before world
- 124 91 Appointed, ordained, and anointed
- 127 2   Unless ordained from foundation of world

ORDER
- 28   13, 58:55   All things must be done in order
- 77   3   Destined order of creation
- 78   hd   Order of Lord to Enoch

ORDER continued
- 4   City of Enoch for everlasting order
- 85   7   Mighty one to set house of God in order
- 88   2   Order of business
- 119   Establish a house of order
- 127   Order of presidency
- 127   Order of school of prophets
- 89   2   Order and will of God in temporal salvation
- 90   15   Set in order churches
- 18, 93:43   Set your houses in order
- 96   4   Order of stakes of Zion
- 102   12   Determine order by lot
- 130   10   Higher order of kingdom
- 132   8   House of order not confusion

ORDER OF ENOCH
- 42   32, 42:53–55.
- 82   20   Order of Enoch everlasting if sin not
- 21   Punishment if obey not order of Enoch

ORDER OF GOD
- 77   11   Ordained to order of God, 144,000
- 84   18   Priesthood after holiest order of God

ORDINANCE
- 21   11   Ordination an ordinance
- 77   4   Mission and ordinance to gather
- 84   20   Godliness manifest in ordinances
- 88   139   Ordinance of washing of feet
- 107   14   Priesthood to administer outward ordinances
- 20   Aaronic priesthood for outward ordinances
- 124   38   Moses' tabernacle for temple ordinances
- 38   Temple ordinances hid from the world
- 39   Temple ordinances enumerated
- 40   Reveal mine ordinances in temple
- 136   4   Covenant to walk in ordinances of Lord

ORDINATION
- 20   60   Manner of ordaining priesthood
- 65   Ordination preceded by vote
- 66   Where there is no branch of the church
- 67   Officers of high priesthood to be ordained
- 21   11   Ordination an ordinance
- 43   7   Ordination necessary for president of church
- 68   20–21   Ordination necessary where
- 107   45   Ordination of Cainan

ORGANIZE
- 44   4   Organize according to laws of man
- 51   1–18   Directions how to organize
- 88   74   Assemble, organize, sanctify, and prepare
- 119   Organize yourselves
- 136   1   Organized into companies with promises

ORPHAN
- 83   6   Orphans to be provided for

OVERCOME
- 50   35   Power to overcome all not ordained
- 52   18   Who is overcome not of me
- 61   9   Overcome through faith
- 63   20   Who endureth shall overcome
- 66   Overcome through patience
- 75   16   Faithful shall overcome all things

OX
- 89   17   Corn for the ox

PACKARD, NOAH
- 124   136   A counselor in high priests' quorum

PAGE HIRAM
- 28   11   Written by Hiram Page from stones, false

PAGE, JOHN E.
- 118   6   Called to the apostleship
- 124   129   An apostle

PAIN
- 18   11   Redeemer suffered pain of all men
- 19   18   God to tremble for pain

PARABLE
- 38   26   Parable of the just man
- 45   56   Parable of ten virgins fulfilled
- 86   1   Parable of wheat and tares explained
- 88   51   Parable of workers in the field
- 101   43   Parable of redemption of Zion
- 44   Parable of watchman and slothful servant
- 81   Parable of woman and unjust judge
- 103   21   Joseph the man of parable of vineyard

PARADISE
- 77   2   Heaven, paradise of God, happiness of man
- 5   In the paradise of God

PARENT
- 68   25   Sin of untaught children upon parents
- 26   Law of Zion concerning parents and children
- 28   Parents to teach children to pray
- 83   4   Children have claim upon parents until
- 5   Children claim inheritance from church if

PARTRIDGE, EDWARD
- 36   hd   Given to Edward Partridge
- 41   9   To be bishop of the church
- 11   Like Nathaniel
- 42   10   To stand in his office
- 50   39   Edward Partridge not justified
- 51   1   Spoken to
- 18   Example to
- 52   24   Edward Partridge called
- 41   To take recommend
- 57   7   To stand in his office
- 58   14   Why selected
- 24   Land for Edward Partridge and counselors
- 62   To direct conference
- 60   10   To impart money
- 64   17   Edward Partridge hath sinned
- 115   2   Unto you, Edward Partridge
- 124   19   Edward Partridge with me now

PAST
- 88 79 Learn of the past
- 130 7 The past known in the presence of God

PATIENCE
- 4 6 Remember patience
- 67 13 Continue n patience until perfected
- 63 66 Overcome through patience
- 101 38 Possess soul in patience for eternal life
- 127 4 Redouble your patience

PATIENT
- 6 19 Be patient, have patience
- 11 19 Be patient until you accomplish it
- 31 9, 54:10, 64:9, Be patient until you accomplish
- 98 2 Wait patiently on the Lord

PATRIARCH
- 107 39 Twelve to ordain evangelical ministers as
- 124 92 A patriarch by blessing and right
- 93 The powers of the patriarch
- 124 Sealing blessings, even Holy Spirit of promise
- 124 Patriarchal blessings in temptation

PATTEN, DAVID W.
- 114 1 Mission for David W. Patten
- 124 19 David Patten with me now
- 130 Priesthood not taken from David

PAUL
- 18 9 Called with the calling of Paul
- 9 Speak as Paul
- 76 99 Telestial, those of Paul, Apollos and Cephas
- 128 14 I. Cor. 15:46–48 explained
- 16 I. Cor. 15:29 explained

PAY
- 19 35 Pay the debt thou hast contracted
- 42 54 Pay for all thou gettest
- 64 28 Lord take when he pleases and pay
- 104 78 Pay all your debts

PEACE
- 1 35 Peace shall be taken from the earth
- 19 23 You shall have peace in me
- 27 16 Gospel of peace
- 39 6 Comforter teacheth peace
- 45 66 New Jerusalem a land of peace
- 84 102 God full of peace
- 88 125 Charity, perfectness and peace
- 90 31 In peace as she is faithful
- 98 16 Renounce war, proclaim peace
- 34 Lift standard of peace thrice to those
- 35 If peace not accepted bring testimony to
- 105 38 Sue for peace
- 39 Lift up ensign of peace to ends of earth
- 40 Proposal of peace, who have smitten
- 134 2 Conditions of in government

PENALTY
- 82 4 Justice and judgment penalties of God's law

PEOPLE
- 1 4 Voice of warning unto all people
- 3 16 Knowledge of Savior come to all people
- 7 3 Thou shalt prophesy to people
- 10 52 Bring gospel to my people
- 42 58 Scriptures to be taught to nations, etc.
- 43 14 Reserve a pure people
- 84 99 Lord redeemed people
- 101 God stands in midst of people
- 90 15 Learn people
- 100 16 Will raise up a pure people
- 107 42 Chosen people to be descendants of Seth
- 122 3 People never turned by testimony of traitors
- 133 37 Gospel to be preached to every people
- 136 31 People must be tried because

PERDITION
- 76 26 Perdition, Lucifer, a son of the morning

PERFECT
- 76 69 Just men made perfect through Jesus
- 88 34 Governed by law perfected by law
- 90 8 Perfected for ministry by school
- 107 43 Seth was a perfect man
- 128 15 Not perfect without our dead
- 129 3 Spirits of just men, perfect, not resurrected

PERJURER
- 121 19 Perjurer severed from ordinances of
- 21 Perjurer no right to the priesthood

PERSECUTE
- 88 94 Fate of church which persecutes Saints
- 121 38 Left to persecute saints
- 127 4 Persecuted prophets before you

PERSECUTION
- 101 35 Suffer persecution but endure shall partake
- 123 4 Committee to aid in gathering history of
- 6 Publish history of persecutions as last effort
- 7 Duty to publish facts of persecution
- 15 Importance of keeping history of persecution

PESTILENCE
- 43 25 God calls by pestilences
- 63 24 Confusion brings pestilence
- 97 26 Pestilence if disobedient

PETER
- 7 4 Lord said to Peter
- 5 Peter, this was good desire
- 8 Shall have desire, for ye joy in
- 27 12 With Peter, James and John
- 13 Keys of kingdom committed to
- 49 11 Speak like Peter, Mine apostle
- 128 10 Priesthood held by Peter
- 20 Peter, James and John claim keys
- 131 5 Sure word of prophecy mentioned by Peter

PETERSON, ZIBA
- 32 hd Given to Ziba Peterson
- 3 Revelation to
- 58 60 Words concerning

PHELPS, W.W.
- 55 1 Revelation to

PHELPS, W.W. continued
	4	To assist Oliver Cowdery in printing
57	11	Printer to the church
58	40	Words concerning
61	7	Mission for
70	1	W. W. Phelps mentioned

PLAGUE
84	97	Plagues on earth until work is completed
87	6	God's wrath shown by plagues
97	26	Plagues if disobedient

PLAN
| 10 | 12–23 | Devil sought to lay clever plan |

PLANET
88	43	Heavens and earth comprehend earth and
	44	Planets give light in times and seasons
	37	Planets are kingdoms
130	4	Time reckoned according to planets

PLATES
3	19	For this purpose are plates preserved
	19	Plates which contain these records
5	1	Joseph Smith testified of plates
	2	Joseph to stand as witness to the plates
	2	No power over plates, except
	4	Have gift to translate plates
	11	I will show plates to three servants
17	1	Shall have view of plates

PLURALITY
| 132 | hd | Concerning plurality of wives |

POISON
84	71	Poison shall not hurt believers
	72	Poison of serpent not hurt believers
124	98	Sign to be delivered from poison

POOR
35	15	Poor shall hear gospel
38	35	Commandment regarding the poor
42	30	Poor shall be fed, duties to poor
	33	Poor to receive from excess of rich
	34	Poor to receive of church property
	38	What ye do to poor, ye do to me
44	6	Visit the poor
52	40	Disciple remembers poor, needy, etc.
56	16	Wo to rich who give not to poor
	17	Poor not to be greedy, to labor
	18	Blessed are poor who are pure in heart
	19	Poor shall rejoice
	20	Generations of poor inherit the earth
58	11	Poor come to marriage of the Lamb
	8	Feast for the poor
88	17	Poor and meek inherit the earth
58	47	Call upon poor to repent
72	12	Support of the poor
78	3	Organization for the poor
82	12	Covenant to manage affairs of the poor
83	6	Poor to be provided for
84	105	Take new, cast old to poor
	112	Bishop to search after poor
104	hd	Concerning order for benefit of poor
	16	Poor shall be exalted
	18	Who imparts not to poor, shall be in hell
105	3	Impart to poor
124	75	Plead for poor and needy

PORTION
51	3	Appoint portion to each man
	4	Writing to secure a portion
78	21	Appoint every man his portion

POWER
1	8	Power to seal on earth and in heaven
	29	Translate through mercy and power of God
	30	Power to found church
	35	Devil shall have power
	36	Lord shall have power over saints
3	4	Man may have power to do works
5	14	Grant power to receive testimony
10	17	God give power again
11	10	Power which speaketh unto thee
	30	Power to become sons of God
15	2	Speak with power
19	3	Power to the destroying of Satan and his
45	44	Christ clothed with power
50	27	Power subject to the ordained
	35	Power to overcome all not ordained
58	11	Day of power cometh after
61	1	Who has all power
71	6	Who receives, given power
76	31	Punishment of those who deny my power
	108	Christ crowned with glory, on throne of
79	1	Go in power of ordination
88	13	Light is life, law, power of God
93	17	Son received all power on earth and in
97	20	God sworn by power of might
100	1	All power in me
103	15	Redemption of Zion to come by power
103	17	Must be led from bondage by power
121	29	Powers revealed to the valiant
	36	Powers of heaven act only in righteousness
128	18	Welding together of power now
	23	Glorious voice declaring powers
132	20	Gods because of power and

PRAISE
52	17	Faults of praise and wisdom
58	39	Repent, for he seeks praise
84		Song of praise to God
128	22	Let dead speak anthem of praise
136	28	If merry, praise with singing

PRATT, ORSON
34	1	Words to Orson Pratt
52	26	Called
75	14	Mission for
103	40	Orson Hyde journey with Orson Pratt
124	129	Orson Pratt an apostle

PRATT–PREPARE

136	13	O. Pratt W. Woodruff organize a company

PRATT, PARLEY P.

32	hd	Given to Parley P. Pratt
	1	Revelation to
49	hd	Given to Parley P. Pratt
	3	To preach to the Shakers
50	37	Mentioned
52	26	Called
97	3	To preside over school in Zion Blessed in expounding scriptures and
103	30	Commission to
	37	To journey with Joseph Smith
124	129	Parley P. Pratt an apostle

PRAY

10	5	Pray always that ye may conquer Satan
19	28	Pray vocally and before the world
	38	Pray always and will pour out Spirit
20	33	Pray lest ye fall into temptation
	47	Exort to pray vocally and in private
23	6	Pray vocally, and in all places
31	12	Pray lest ye enter into temptation
32	4	Pray that may unfold to understanding
61	39	Pray always, not enter into temptation
65	4	Pray unto the Lord
68	28	Parents to teach children to pray
75	11	Praying that they faint not
88	126	Pray that ye faint not
95	16	House for praying
101	81	Men should pray and not faint
	92	Pray that their ears open to cries
104	80	Pray, I will soften hearts of debtors

PRAYER

5	24	If mighty prayer I will grant
10	46	Prophets and disciples desired in their
	50	Their faith in their prayers was
	47	According to faith in prayers
25	12	Song of righteous is a prayer
29	2	Save all who engage in mighty prayer
38	30	Things told because of prayers
41	3	By prayer of faith receive my law
	2	Shall receive as ye ask
46	7	Act with prayer
52	15	Prayer heard if obey and contrite in heart
63	64	Spirit received by prayer
	65	Taught by prayer through Spirit
68	33	Observes not prayers, tried before judge
	33	Prayer in the season thereof
84	61	In solemnity and spirit of prayer
88	2	Alms of prayers come up
	119	Establish a house of prayer
	131	Prayer in token of covenant
93	49	Pray lest wicked one have power
	51	By prayer of faith uphold him
98	2	Prayers recorded with this seal and
	3	Immutable covenant that prayers be fulfill
101	7	Prayers answered slowly if we are slow
105	19	Heard prayer, accepted offering
107	22	Presidency upheld by prayer
108	7	Strengthen brethren in prayer
109	hd	Prayer at dedication of Kirtland temple
112	10	If humble, prayers answered
121	hd	A prayer and prophecies
127	12	Prayer that you be saved
136	28	If merry, praise with prayer

PRAYER OF FAITH

28	13	All things done by prayer of faith
42	14	Spirit given by prayer of faith
52	9	Taught by prayer of faith
103	36	Victory and glory through prayers of faith
104	79	Blessing by prayer of faith

PREACH

11	15	Not to preach until called
18	28	Twelve called to preach
19	21	Preach naught but repentance
	30	Preach with humility
	31	How and what to preach
	37	Preach truth with a loud voice
36	5	Every man shall preach the gospel
38	41	Preaching in mildness and meekness
	41	Let preaching be warning voice
42	7	Missionaries to preach the gospel
	11	None to preach gospel unless ordained
52	9	Preach by the way
	10	Preach in every congregation
58	47	Preach by the way
60	7	How to preach the word
	8	Preach not in haste
	14	Manner of preaching
68	2	Ensample for all preaching
	8	Preach gospel to every creature
84	77	Traveling to preach gospel in my power
	85	How to preach gospel
95	16	House for preaching
107	25	Seventy to preach gospel
112	28	Preach gospel to every creature
	28	Purify hearts and preach
124	18	Beget glory and honor by preaching
133	37	Gospel to be preached to every nation, etc.

PRECEPT

98	12	Give faithful precept upon precept
128	21	Giving precept upon precept

PREFACE

1	6	Preface to book of commandments

PREPARE

1	12	Prepare ye for that which is to come
45	61	New Testament translated to prepare for
78	7	For place in celestial world must prepare
88	74	Assemble, organize, sanctify and prepare
88	80	Learn all, be prepared when sent.
	84	Prepare saints for judgment

PREPARE continued

	92	Prepare, for judgment has come
101	23	Prepare for revelation to come
	68	Gather not in haste, etc., but prepare
	72	Prepare things before you
104	59	Prepare for when I shall dwell
105	10	Must be prepared for redemption
106	8	Prepared crown in mansions
133	10	Prepare for great day of the Lord
	15	Let things be prepared

PREPARATION

| 78 | 13 | The preparation for salvation |

PREPARATORY GOSPEL

| 84 | 26 | Lesser priesthood holds keys of preparatory |

PRESENCE

67	12	Natural man cannot abide presence of God
76	62	Dwell in presence of God and Christ forever
	77	Presence of Son not fulness of Father
	94	In his presence are church of First Born
	118	Through Spirit bear His presence in the flesh
94	8	Glory and presence of God in house
	9	If unclean, my glory and presence depart
103	19	My angel, not presence, before you
	20	My angel and presence shall go before you
	26	My presence in avenging enemies
121	32	Enter eternal presence
130	7	Angels reside in presence of God
133		Glory of God's presence described
	40	Mountains flow at presence
	41	Presence of Lord as fire of boiling water
	41	Presence of Lord as melting fire
	42	All nations tremble at thy presence
	44	Mountains flow down at thy presence
	53	Angel of his presence saved them

PRESIDE

124	137	Priesthood to preside
	140	Responsibility of presiding

PRESIDENCY

48	6	Bishop act in appointment of presidency
68	15	Bishops appointed by presidency
	20	Descendant of Aaron chosen and ordained
	22	Bishop can only be tried before presidency
81	2	Keys belong always to presidency of high
88	127	House for presidency of school of prophets
	127	Order of presidency
90	12	Continue in ministry and presidency
	2–32	Items concerning presidency of church
	15	How presidency shall spend their lives
94	3	House consecrated for work of presidency
	4	Dimensions of house for presidency
	6	House for presidency dedicated from
	8	Glory and presence of God in house of
102	10	President assisted by two appointed like
	11	Assistants to president preside alone when
	26	First presidency to receive copy of action
	33	Determine if appeal entitled to re-hearing
107	8	Melchisedek priesthood holds right of
	9	Right to officiate in all offices of the church
	17	Bishop to be ordained by presidency of
	22	Presidency to be three high priests
	22	How chosen, appointed, upheld, etc.
	24	Quorum of apostles of same authority
	33	Apostles officiate under direction of
	36	Standing high councils equal in authority
	78	Undecided cases brought to presidency
	79	Presidency call twelve counselors in cases
112	17	Apostles quorum act for presidency
	19	Apostles go where presidency send
	20	Who receives first presidency receives me
	21	Presidency to send missionaries by voice of
	30	Presidency counselors and leaders to the
115	14	Lord's house after pattern given presidency
	18	Appoint stakes as manifest
116	13	Presidency not to go in debt for temple
117	13	Contend for redemption of first presidency
119	2	Surplus property for debts of first presidency
120	1	Tithing to be disposed of by presidency and
124	84	Counsel ordained in presidency of church
	126	Presidency to receive oracles of the church

PRESIDENT

88	128	President or teacher to stand in house
	129	President to be seen and heard by
	129	First in house of God; not to use loud speech
	130	The president to be an example
	132	Duties of president
88	133	President's salutation of fellowship
	140	President to administer the washing of feet
101	88	Importune at feet of president
	89	If president heed not, God's fury vex nations
102	1	One of three presidents for high council
107	21	Presidents of offices of priesthood necessary
	61	Presidents of priesthood necessary
	65	President of high priesthood of church
	85	Duties of presidents of quorums
124	3	Proclamation of gospel to all presidents
	62	Appoint one president
	134	Ordinance for qualifying presidents of
	136	Counselors to president of high priests
	138	President of quorum of seventies
	141	Presidents over bishopric
	142	Presidents of teachers and deacons
136	3	President and counselors over companies

PRESIDENT OF THE CHURCH

28	6	Head of church not to be commanded
	7	President holds keys until someone else
35	18	If not abide in God will
	19	Watch over him
43	2	Commandment for a law through president
	3	Only president to receive revelations for
	4	If power taken away has right to appoint

		7	President must be ordained
102	8		Vacancy in high council filled by president
	9		Appointed by revelation, acknowledged by
	10		Assisted by two appointed like himself
	10		According to dignity that he preside
	11		May preside over council without assistance
	23		May obtain mind of Lord by revelation
107	65		His title
	92		Seer, revelator, translator, prophet, with all
124	95		Patriarch to receive counsel from president
	125		Prophet, seer, revelator, translator

PRESIDENT OF HIGH PRIESTHOOD

20	67		To be ordained, by whose direction
107	76		Descendant of Aaron cannot try president
	82		How president is tried
	91		President like Moses

PRESIDING PATRIARCH

124	91		His office hereditary
	92		Holds keys of patriarchal blessings
	95		Presiding patriarch receive counsel from
	124		Hyrum Smith appointed patriarch of church

PRIDE

23			1, 25:14, 38:39 Beware of pride
39	9		Rejected God because of pride
56	8		Repent of pride and selfishness
90	17		Be admonished in pride
121	37		Grieves Spirit to gratify pride

PRIEST

18	32		Twelve ordained to ordain priests
20	39		Apostles may ordain priests
	46		Duties of priests
	48		Priests may ordain priests
	52		Priest is to assist the elder
	60		How ordained
	64		Priest may take certificate
	76		Priest to administer the sacrament
	82		Send by priest to conference
	84		Priest may sign recommend
38	40		Priests to go with might
42	12		Priests to preach principles of gospel
	70		Priests to have stewardships
52	38		Two priests to be ordained
76	56		They are priests and kings
84	111		Lesser priests to travel
76	57		Who are priests of the Most High
102	5		Four priests voted on first high council
107	10		High Priest may officiate instead of priest
	61		Presiding priests necessary
	63		Priest to elder
	87		Duties of president of priests
107	88		Bishop to be president of priests.
124	142		Presidency of priests

PRIESTHOOD

2	1		I will reveal priesthood
67	10		Privilege of priesthood to see God
68	21		Priesthood descending from father to son
	20–21		Ordination necessary where priesthood
78	1		Ordained to high priesthood of my church
84	6		et seq., Succession of priesthood from Adam
	17		In church of God always; priesthood eternal
	18		Priesthood after holiest order of God
84	24		Israel lost priesthood by sin
	25		Moses and priesthood taken away
	33		Who obtains and magnifies two priesthood
	34		Priesthood seed of Abraham, elect of God
	35		Receive priesthood, receive God
	39		Oath and covenant of priesthood
	40		Receive oath and covenant of Father
	41		Breaks covenant of priesthood, no
	111		What part of priesthood to travel
86	8		Priesthood continued through lineage
	9		Lawful heirs to priesthood
	10		Life and priesthood remain to restoration
	11		Through priesthood savior to Israel
94	6		Dedicated according to order of priesthood
107	hd		Section on priesthood
	1		Melchisedek and Aaronic, including Levitical
	6		Divisions are Melchisedek, Aaronic, and
	12		How priesthood is to administer in spiritual
	40		Order of priesthood handed from father to
	41		How priesthood came down by lineage from
	63		Grades of priesthood, deacon, teacher, etc.
	65		One appointed to preside over priesthood
	98		Priesthood required to travel
112	30		Power of priesthood given to presidency
	31		Priesthood held in former dispensations
113	6		Keys belong to rod of Jesse
	8		To put on strength is authority of
	8		Zion has right to priesthood by lineage
119	2		Surplus property for priesthood
121	21		Perjurer no right to priesthood
	36		Rights of priesthood connected with heaven
	37		If Spirit grieved, priesthood withdrawn
	36–41		How powers must be exercised
	45		Doctrine of priesthood distil on soul
122	9		Hold on way and priesthood will remain
124	28		Temple needed for fulness of priesthood
	34		Keys of priesthood in temples
	42		Show priesthood of temple
	123		Priesthood after Melchisedek after Only
	123		Officers of priesthood enumerated
	130		A man's priesthood remains after death
	137		Priesthood to preside
	143		Why offices of priesthood given
	144		Approve names of officers of priesthood at
124	145		Prepare rooms for officers of priesthood in
127	8		About to restore many things of priesthood
128	8		Power to bind and loose on earth and in
	9		In all ages power to bind on earth and in
	10		Priesthood possessed by Peter

PRIESTHOOD continued
- 17   Malachi foresaw restoration of priesthood
- 21   Angels declaring their priesthood, etc.
- 132   7   Power and keys to one man only
-      45   Restore all things by priesthood
-      59   Endowed with keys of priesthood, justified
-      64   Wife must obey law of priesthood

PRIESTHOOD OF AARON
- 13   1   Priesthood of Aaron, (see Aaron)

PRIESTHOOD, AARONIC
- 13   1   Never taken from the earth
-      1   What its powers are
- 68   17   First born of Aaron has right of
-      18   Only literal descendant has legal right to
-      20   Literal descendant must be tailed
- 84   18   Origin and continuation
- 107   13   Second priesthood, why so called
-      14   To administer outward ordinances
-      14   Lesser because appendage to Melchisedek
-      15   Bishopric presidency of Aaronic priesthood
-      20   Powers and authority given
-      70   Keys held by descendants of
-      76   Literal descendant of Aaron right of

PRIESTHOOD, FIRST
- 27   8   John Sent to confer first priesthood

PRIESTHOOD, HIGH
- 84   29   Elder a necessary appendage to
-      29   Bishop a necessary appendage to
- 85   11   Fate of high priesthood whose names not in
- 107   64   High priesthood greatest of all
-      65   One appointed to preside over priesthood
-      69   Bishop chosen from high priesthood unless
-      78   Undecided cases brought to presidency
-      76   Descendant of Aaron cannot try president of
-      79   Presidency of call twelve counselors in cases
-      91   President of high priesthood president of

PRIESTHOOD, HOLY
- 84   6   Moses received holy priesthood from Jethro
- 107   3   Melchisedek priesthood formerly called holy
- 128   11   Priesthood receives facts of salvation
- 132   28   Law of holy priesthood ordained before

PRIESTHOOD, LESSER
- 84   26   Holds keys of ministering of angels and
-      26   Lesser priesthood continued with Israel
-      27   With Israel through Aaron until John
-      30   Teacher and deacon necessary appendages to
-      107   To go before to make appointments, etc.
- 85   11   No inheritance, lesser priesthood
- 107   14   Aaronic priesthood

PRIESTHOOD, MELCHISEDEK
- 84   18   Aaronic priesthood abideth with Melchisedek
-      19   Administers gospel
-      19   Holds keys of mysteries and knowledge of
-      21   Power of Godliness not manifest without
-      22   Without it, cannot see God and live
- 107   2   Melchisedek priesthood, why so called
-      3   Formerly called holy priesthood
-      4   Why name changed
-      5   All authorities in church appendages in
-      7   Rights and privileges of Melchisedek
-      8   Holds right of presidency
-      8   To administer spiritual things
-      18   Its power and authority given

PRINCIPLE
- 42   12   Principles of gospel in Bible and Book of
- 88   78   Instructed in principle, theory, doctrine and
- 89   3   Word of wisdom a principle with promise
- 101   78   Act in doctrine and principle pertaining to
- 102   23   Ask for revelation in difficulty of doctrine
- 128   12   That one principle might accord with

PRINTING
- 55   4   Assist Oliver Cowdery in printing
- 58   37   Lands for house of printing
- 94   10   House for printing to be dedicated
-      11   Dimensions for house for printing
- 104   58   Print fulness of scriptures and revelation
-      59   Print words to build up church

PRINTER
- 19   35   Pay debt to printer
- 57   11   W. W. Phelps printer to the church

PRISON
- 76   73   Christ preached to spirits in prison
- 88   99   Redemption of those in prison

PRIVILEGE
- 88   122   Every man have equal privilege
- 98   5   Law for rights and privileges justifiable

PROCLAMATION
- 105   39   Proclamation for peace to ends of earth
- 124   2   Make solemn proclamation of the gospel
-      3   Proclamation to all kings and authorities
-      7   Call with loud proclamation
-      107   Make solemn proclamation to kings

PROFIT
- 104   68   What to do with profits
-      68   Profits on sacred writings used for same

PROMISE
- 58   31   Does the Lord promise and not fulfil
- 82   10   No promise without obedience
- 88   3   Comforter, Holy Spirit of promise
-      75   Fast and great promise
-      75   I may fulfil promise
- 89   3   Word of wisdom, a principle with promise
- 132   7   Sealed by Holy Spirit of promise

PROPERTY
- 42   33   Property not needed used for the poor
- 19   26   Shalt not covet own property
-      34   Impart a portion of thy property
- 42   30   Give of your properties to the poor
-      32   Every man steward over his own property
-      34   Property of church to be kept in storehouse

	34	Property to be administered by whom
	35	To be used for what purpose
51		Consecration of property
66	6	Think not of thy property
82	17	Have equal claims on property
	18	Common property of whole church
85	1	Record of those who consecrate properties
101	99	Saints to claim their own though
104	1	Counsel concerning property of united order
	55	Properties mine or faith vain
	56	Stewards if properties mine
	85	Privilege, once, to pledge properties for debt
117	4	What is property before the Lord
	5	Property of Kirtland turn out for debt
119	1	Surplus property in hands of bishop
	2	How to use surplus property
	5	Who gather shall be tithed of surplus
120	hd	Disposition of property tithing
123	2	Keep history of property lost

PROPHECY
11	25	Deny not the spirit of prophecy
35	23	Prove words of prophecy by holy prophets
131	5	The more sure word of prophecy defined

PROPHESY
7	3	Thou shalt prophesy to
34	10	Prophesy by power of Spirit
42	16	Prophesy as seemeth me good
	16	Speak and prophesy by Comforter
45	15	God will prophesy to men
46	22	Some given to prophesy

PROPHET
1	14	Who heed not prophets cut off
10	46	Prophets desired gospel should come
20	26	Believe in prophets shall be saved
	26	Spake as inspired by Holy Ghost
21	1	Joseph Smith be called prophet
52	9	Say only what prophets written
	36	Declare only prophets and apostles
58	8	Earth know mouths of prophets shall not
77	15	Two prophets to build Jerusalem after
84	hd	Joseph Smith called a prophet
95	10	Contentions in school of prophets
98	17	Turn hearts of Jews and prophets to each
107	92	President of church a prophet
124	94	Hyrum Smith a prophet, seer and revelator
127	4	Persecuted prophets before you
130	4	Prophet's time according to residence
133	54	Enoch and prophets before him
136	36	Calamity for killing prophets

PROSECUTION
42	88	Manner of prosecution in the church

PROUD
42	40	Shalt not be proud in thy heart
64	24	Proud burn as stubble
84	112	Bishop humbling rich and proud

PROVE
84	79	Sent to prove the world
98	14	Will prove you unto death
124	55	Prove faithful in all things
132	51	Command to prove Emma Smith

PROVIDE
75	28	Provide for family, not lose crown
99	6	Go not until children provided for
104	15	The way the Lord would provide for saints

PULSIPHER, ZERA
124	138	A president of seventies

PUNISHMENT
19	10	Eternal punishment is God's punishment
76	44	Everlasting, endless is eternal punishment
	45	Eternal punishment not known by any man

PURCHASE
57	5	Purchase land for everlasting inheritance
63	29	Zion obtained by purchase, not blood
	30	Blessed if Zion obtained by purchase
101	70	Purchase lands around Zion for money
103	23	Purchase lands
105	28	My will to purchase lands in Jackson county
	30	After purchase, guiltless in taking lands

PURE
35	21	Elect purified even as I am pure
58	8	Not purified shall not abide
41	12	Words pure, therefore beware
56	18	Blessed are poor who are pure in heart
97	16	Pure in heart shall see God in temple
	21	Zion is the pure in heart
100	16	Will raise up a pure people
101	18	Pure in heart return to Zion
122	2	Pure in heart will seek counsel
124	54	Save all pure in heart
131	8	When bodies pure see spirit matter
132	52	Impure, said to be pure, destroyed
136	11	With pure hearts in faith be blessed
	37	Marvel not, ye are not pure

PURGE
43	11	Purge out iniquity

PURIFY
50	28	All things yours if purified from sin
76	116	Gifts to those who purify themselves
88	74	Purify your hearts
112	28	Purify hearts and preach

PURSE
24	18, 84:78, 86	Shall not take purse nor scrip

QUICKEN
88	26	Earth sanctified, die and quickened
	28	Your glory which quickens bodies
	32	Who remain shall be quickened
	49	Comprehend, being quickened
	96	Saints shall be quickened and caught up

QUORUM
102	7	Majority has power to fill vacancies

QUORUM continued
- 107 24 Quorum of presidency of church
-      27 Decision of Quorum must be unanimous
-      28 Majority may form a quorum
-      30 Decisions of quorums of priesthood
-      32 General assembly of quorums spiritual
-      36 Quorum equal in authority
- 124 26 Quorum for building house
-      126 Quorum of first presidency

RAPHAEL
- 128 21 Voice of Gabriel and Raphael

REAP
- 6   3   Desireth to reap, thrust in
-      33 What ye sow ye shall reap
- 11   3   Reap while day lasts
- 86   5   Angels crying to the Lord to reap

REASON
- 45   10 I will reason as with men in days of old
-      15 God will reason with men
- 50   12 God will reason as man to man
- 61   13 Lord will reason as in days of old
- 133 57 Reasoning in plainness

REBEL
- 76   25 Angel in authority rebelled
-      28 Satan, serpent, Devil who rebelled

REBELLION
- 56   6   Rebellions of people in Thompson
- 76   25 The rebellion in heaven
- 87   1   War to begin at rebellion of South Carolina
- 134 5   Rebellion unbecoming citizens

REBELLIOUS
- 1   3   Shall be pierced with sorrow
-      8   Rebellious may be sealed up
- 56   1   Rebellious know mine arm and indignation
-      4   Changes answered upon rebellious
- 63   2   Lord angry at rebellious
-      6   Let rebellious fear and tremble
-      35 Rebellious shall not inherit Zion
- 64   36 Rebellious not of Ephraim and are plucked

RECEIVE
- 11   5   Ask of me, you shall receive
-      30 Receive me I will give power
- 50   34 Who receiveth of God, let him account
-      43 Receive me, receive the Father
- 62   7   Receive with thankful heart
- 71   6   Who receives given power
- 84   60 Blessed if you receive

RECOMMEND
- 20   84 Who may give recommend
-      84 Member removing to take certificate
- 52   41 Joseph Smith and others to take recommend
- 72   1–26 Regarding recommends
- 112 21 Duly recommended shall have power

RECOMPENSE
- 1   10 Lord shall come to recompense
- 56   19 Recompense come with the Lord
- 124 121 Have a just recompense of wages
- 127 3   A just recompense upon oppressors

RECONCILIATION
- 42   88 Offender confess, reconciled
- 46   4   Not partake of sacrament until

RECORD
- 1   39 Spirit beareth true record
- 6   26 Records kept back contain much gospel
- 8   1   Engravings of old records
-      11 Ancient records hid up
- 9   2   Other records have I
- 20   27 Holy Ghost beareth record of Father and
-      82 Record of names of churches to be kept
-      83 General church record of names
- 21   1   Record shall be kept
- 47   3   Church record to be kept
- 58   7   Record of land for Zion of God
- 72   6   Record handed to bishop
- 76   14 record is fulness of gospel of Jesus Christ
- 85   1   Lord's clerk to keep general church record
-      2   Record of life, faith and works
-      2   Record of apostates
-      3   Names of non-tithe payers not to be on
- 93   6   Fulness of John's record to be revealed
- 100 8   Holy Ghost is bearing record
- 127 7   Your record recorded in heaven
-      9   Have records in order
-      9   Records placed in archives of temple
- 128 4   The value of transcribed record
-      7   Dead judged by records kept on earth
-      7   Book of life is record kept in heaven
-      8   Not recorded on earth not recorded in
-      9   If record faithful, law on earth and in
-      9   Faithful record cannot be annulled
-      14 As records of dead on earth so in heaven
-      24 Present worthy record of dead in temple

RECORDER
- 127 6   Recorder to be witness of baptism for the
- 128 2   Recorder of baptisms for the dead
-      3   In every ward if necessary
-      3   Instructions to recorder for baptisms for
-      22 Recorder at baptisms for the dead

RED SEA
- 8   3   Moses brought Israel through
- 17   1   Given Lehi on borders of Red Sea

REDEEM
- 29   46 Children redeemed from beginning
- 43   29 Church shall be redeemed
- 76   38 All redeemed save sons of perdition
-      85 Not redeemed until last resurrection
- 77   12 All redeemed in seventh thousand years
- 84   99 Israel redeemed by election of grace
- 93   38 Effect of redemption from fall
- 100 13 Zion shall all be redeemed though

101	75	Zion redeemed if churches willing
105	2	Church redeemed if no transgression
133	52	Year of my redeemed is come
	53	Redeemed them in his love and pity
	67	Power to redeem not shortened
136	18	Zion to be redeemed in time

REDEEMER

10	70	Your Redeemer
18	11	Redeemer suffered that all might come unto
	12	Purpose of Redeemer's suffering
19	1	I am Redeemer of the world

REDEMPTION

29	42	Redemption through faith in Christ
35	26	Redemption is nigh
45	17	How day of redemption shall come
	46	Redemption shall be perfected
	54	Redemption of heathen nations
49	5	Only Begotten sent for redemption of world
78	12	Delivered to Satan to day of redemption
88	14	Redemption through resurrection from dead
	16	Resurrection from dead, redemption of soul
	17	Redemption of soul through him
	99	Redemption of those in prison
101	43	Parable of redemption of Zion
	76	Importune rulers for redress and redemption
103	13	After tribulation come redemption and
	15	Redemption of Zion to come by power
	18	And as fathers were led, so redemption of
104	9	Cannot escape until day of redemption
105	3	Redemption delayed by disobedience
	9	Because of transgression must wait for
	10	Redemption delayed to give people
	10	Must be prepared for redemption
	11	No redemption until elders endowed with
	34	Let Zion's law be executed after redemption
117	13	Contend for redemption of first presidency
124	124	Sealed to day of redemption by patriarch
128	22	Ordained redemption of prisoner dead
	22	Plan of redemption before the world
132	26	Delivered to Satan to day of redemption

REFUGE

45	66	New Jerusalem a city of refuge
115	6	Gathering for a defense and refuge
124	36	Places appointed for refuge

RE-HEARING

102	20	Error in decision entitles to re-hearing
	33	First presidency determine if entitled to

REJECT

6	29	If they reject, blessed are ye
	31	Blessed are they if reject not
84	92	Return not to him who rejects
	95	Wo unto them that reject me
	115	If reject, judgment is nigh
99	4	Who rejects, rejected of Father
124	8	Fate if servants and testimony rejected

132	4	Reject this covenant and be damned

RELIGION

134	4	God instituted religion
	4	Relation of human law and religion
	7	Relation of state and religion

RELIGIOUS

134	9	Religious influence and civil government
	10	Right of religious societies to deal with

RELY

3	20	Rely on merits of Jesus Christ
17	1	You must rely on my word
18	3	Rely on things that are written

REMAIN

84	98	All who remain know me
88	32	Who remain shall be quickened
	35	They remain filthy still

REMISSION OF SINS

13	1	Baptism for remission of sins
19	31	Remission of sins by baptism and by fire
21	8	Days are come unto remission of sins
	9	Jesus crucified for remission of sins
27	2	Blood shed for remission of sins
49	13	Baptize for remission of sins
53	3	Preach remission of sins
84	27	Remission of sins part of preparatory gospel

REMNANT

87	5	Remnants to vex Gentiles
113	10	Remnants exhorted to return

REMOVE

20	84	Member removing to take certificate

REMUNERATION

42	72	Bishop and counselors to receive just

REPENT

1	27	Chastened that they might repent
	32	Who repents shall be forgiven
	33	Who repents shall not lose light
3	10	Repent, thou art still called
5	19	Scourges if they repent not
10	67	Whosoever repents is my church
18	9	Command all men to repent
	13	Great is his joy that repenteth
	22	As repent and baptized be saved
	41	Repent and be baptized
18	42	All must repent
19	4	Every man must repent or suffer
20	29	All men must repent and believe
	72	Baptism to those who repent
33	11	Repent and be baptized
42	28	Sins and repents not, cast out
43	20	Call nations to repent
49	13	Repent and be baptized
	8	All men shall repent
50	39	Repent and be forgiven
54	3	Repent, to escape enemies
56	8	Repent of pride and selfishness

REPENT continued
- 58   42   Who repents is forgiven
-       48   Call upon all to repent
- 63   63   Cut off if not repentant
- 64   12   How to deal with unrepentant
-       17   Repent of evil and be forgiven
- 84   57   Condemned until repent
- 90   34   Repent, angels rejoice
- 98   21   Chasten if they do not repent
-       27   Testimonies against enemy if repent not
-       39   If enemy repents forgive him
-       40   Forgive seventy times seven if repent
-       44   What one must do to repent
-       47   Forgive if children repent of
- 104   10   Transgressor repents not, delivered to Satan
- 133   16   All men commanded to repent
-       62   Who repents shall have eternal life

REPENTANCE
- 3   20   Through repentance be saved
- 6   9   Say nothing but repentance
- 11   9   Say nothing but repentance
- 13   1   Keys of gospel of repentance
- 14   8   That you may declare repentance
- 15   6, 16:6 Most worth to declare repentance
- 18   6   Children of men are stirred to repentance
-       12   Bring men unto him on condition of
-       15   Labor all your days in crying repentance
- 19   21   Preach nought but repentance
- 20   71   Members must be capable of repentance
- 29   42   Send angels to declare repentance
-       44   Damnation to those who repent not
-       49   Repentance required of those having
- 35   5   Baptism by water unto repentance
- 39   6   Repentance in Gospel
- 53   3   Preach repentance
- 58   43   How repentance may be known
- 68   25   Parents to teach children repentance
- 84   27   Repentance part of preparatory gospel
- 98   1–48 Vengeance turned away from repentant
-       48   Trespasses removed by repentance

REPROOF
- 121   43   How reproofs should be given

REPROVE
- 84   87   Sent out to reprove the world
-       117   Reprove in righteousness
- 121   43   Reprove with sharpness when moved upon
-       43   Increase of love to reprove

REQUIRE
- 82   3   Much given, much required

RESERVE
- 5   9   Things reserved for a wise purpose
- 121   32   Reserved until end of world

RESPECT
- 134   6   Respect all men in stations

RESPECTOR
- 1   35, 8:16 God no respecter of persons

REST
- 19   9   You may enter into my rest
- 54   10   Seek early, find rest for souls
- 59   2   Who die, shall rest from their labors
-       9   Sunday a day of rest and worship
- 84   24   Rest is fulness of glory
- 121   32   Enter immortal rest

RESTORATION
- 27   6   Elias bring to pass restoration of all things
- 45   17   How restoration of Israel shall come
- 77   15   Two prophets to Jews at time of restoration
- 84   2   Church established for restoration of people
- 86   10   Priesthood remain to restoration
- 103   13   After tribulation, restoration of Zion

RESTORE
- 77   14   John, Elias, to restore all things
- 132   45   Restore all things by priesthood

RESURRECT
- 129   1   Angels are resurrected with bodies
-       3   Spirits of just men, perfect, not resurrected

RESURRECTION
- 29   13, 43:18, 45:45 First resurrection
- 42   29   Weep for those not in first resurrection
- 45   54   Know no law, part in first resurrection
- 63   18   Who shall have no part in first resurrection
-       52   Why apostles preached resurrection of the
- 76   16   Speaking of resurrection of dead
-       17   Done good or evil in resurrection of
-       39   All brought forth by resurrection of dead
-       39   Resurrection through Lamb
-       50   Testimony concerning resurrection of just
-       64   Who have part in first resurrection
-       65   Who come forth in resurrection of just
-       85   Last resurrection when work finished
-       85   Not redeemed until last resurrection
- 88   14   Redemption through resurrection
-       16   Resurrection the redemption of the soul
-       97   First resurrection
-       99   The second resurrection
-       100   The third resurrection
-       100   Resurrection of spirits under condemnation
-       98   First resurrection by voice of trump
- 128   12   Baptism likeness of resurrection
- 130   18   Intelligence gained will rise in resurrection
- 132   7   Only sealed contracts valid after resurrection
-       19   Marry within covenant, first resurrection
- 133   55   Came with Christ in resurrection

RETIRE
- 88   124   Retire to thy bed early

REVEAL
- 1   3   Secret acts of rebellion revealed
- 76   7   Will reveal for ages to come
-       7   Reveal hidden mysteries of kingdom
- 88   108   Reveal secret acts in first 1,000 years

101	32	Lord comes will reveal all things		19	Shall reward every man
105	23	Reveal not things until wisdom	58		Reward of disobedience lurketh beneath
121	29	All things revealed to the valiant		2	Reward greater in kingdom of heaven
	31	All knowledge revealed in dispensation of		26	Who is compelled receive no reward
124	40	Reveal my ordinances in temple		28	Men do good lose no reward
	41	Reveal things hidden from foundation of	63	48	Reward in world to come
128	18	Things never before, revealed now	70	15	Reward of diligence, etc.

REVELATION

3	4	Man may have many revelations	76	79	Reward of those not valiant
11	25	Deny not spirit of revelation	84	90	Reward not lost for feeding missionaries
20	35	By Holy Ghost, voice of God and angels	98	23–26	Seek not revenge, be rewarded
	35	Revelation that shall come hereafter	112	34	My reward according to works
28	2	Revelations for church received only by	124	16	Reward not fail if receive counsel

RICH

	7	Keys of sealed revelations held by head of	6	7	Who hath eternal life is rich
28	8	Not all revelations for church	38	16	I have made thee rich
32	4	Heed no revelation unless written		39	Seek correct riches and ye shall be rich
42	61	Ask and receive revelations	56	16	Lamentation of rich at last day
43	4	For church received only by the president		16	Wo unto rich who give not to poor
46	2	Revelation vs. commandment	58	10	Rich invited to supper of the Lord
59	4	Faithful blessed with revelations		47	Call upon rich to repent
68	21	Lineage ascertained by revelation	84	112	Bishop humbling rich and proud
70	3	Stewards over revelations and	104	16	The rich be made low

RICH, C. C.

124 132 Member of high council

RICHARDS, WILLARD

71	4	Prepare for revelations to come	118	6	Called to apostleship
72	21	Revelations be published	124	129	Willard Richards an apostle
75	hd	Revelation given in confidence	135	2	Present at Joseph's death

RICHES

	4	Proclaim truth according to revelation	6	7	Seek not riches, but wisdom
77	hd	Key to St. John's revelation	38	39	Riches of earth mine in give
87	hd	Revelation and prophecy on war	42	32	What to do with riches
90	14	Receive revelations as manifest		39	Riches of Gentiles for poor of Israel
94	3	House consecrated for receiving revelations	43	25	God called by riches of eternal life
101	23	Prepare for revelations to come	45	65	Gather riches to purchase
102	9	President of church appointed by revelation	56	16	Riches will canker your souls
	23	In difficulty of doctrine ask for revelation	67	2	Riches of eternity mine to give
104	58	Print fulness of scriptures and revelations	68	31	Seek earnestly riches of eternity
124	39	Revelation for foundation of Zion	78	18	Riches of eternity yours
	119	Not pay stock unless believe in revelations		19	Riches given him who is thankful
128	6	Revelations 20:12 explained	90	22	Bishops agent to have riches in store

RIDER, SIMONDS

52 37 Give to Simonds Rider

RIGDON, SIDNEY

	9	When power given by actual revelation	Sections 35, 37, 40, 44, 49, 73, 76, 100 To Sidney		
130	10	Revelations 2:17 explained	35	5	Words to
132	7	Revelation through medium of anointed		4	Called like John
	29	Abraham received all by revelation	36	2	Edward Partridge to be blessed by Sidney

REVELATOR

			41	8	To live as seemeth him good
100	11	Revelator to know with certainty	49	1	Words to Sidney Rigdon
107	92	President of church a revelator		3	To preach to the Shakers
124	94	Hyrum Smith a prophet, seer and revelator	52	41	Sidney Rigdon to take recommend
	125	President a prophet, seer and revelator		3	To go to Missouri

REVENGE

98	23–26	How to take revenge		24	Sidney Rigdon called

REVOKE

56 4 I command and revoke as good

58 50 To write

REWARD

6	33	Sow good, reap good for reward
14	11	If faithful great shall be reward
31	12	Reward lost by temptation
56	12	Reward according to what they do

RIGDON, SIDNEY continued

58		To return
57		To dedicate land of Zion
60	6	To go to Cincinnati
61	23	Not to travel upon waters
	30	Commandment to
63	55	Not pleased with
	65	Joseph and Sidney to seek a home
70	1	Mentioned
71	1	I say unto Sidney Rigdon
73	3	To translate
	5	Take journey with Sidney Rigdon
90	6	Equal with Joseph Smith in keys of kingdom
	21	Words concerning
93	44	Commanded to set his house in order
	51	To take his journey
100	1	Your family well
	9	To be spokesman for Joseph Smith
102	3	First high council presidency
103	29	Commission to Sidney Rigdon
	38	Lyman Wight journey with Sidney Rigdon
104	20	Inheritance appointed
115	1	Unto you Sidney Rigdon
124	103	Conditions of re-establishment
	126	To be counselor to Joseph

RIGGS, BURR
75 17 Mission for Burr Riggs

RIGHT
3 2 God turns not to right or left
9 8 Bosom burn if right
128 21 Angels declaring their rights

RIGHTEOUS
10 37 Cannot always judge the righteous
11 12 Spirit which leadeth to judge righteously
25 12 Song of the righteous is a prayer
29 12 Judge only the righteous
42 46 Righteous shall not taste death
45 71 Righteous gathered to Zion
63 54 Separation of righteous and wicked
67 9 What is righteous cometh from above
84 53 May know righteous from wicked
88 26 Righteous inherit the earth
27 Righteous die, rise spiritual body
100 16 Will raise up a righteous people
101 95 Men may discern between righteous and

RIGHTEOUSNESS
1 16 Seek not the Lord to establish righteousness
20 14 Who work righteousness shall
27 16 Breastplate of righteousness
29 12 Clothed in robes of righteousness
43 32 Live in righteousness changed in twinkling
45 12 Day of righteousness sought for
48 4 Obtain all ye can in righteousness
52 11 Work cut short in righteousness
58 27 Men bring to pass righteousness
59 8 Sacrifice in righteousness to the Lord
23 Reward of works of righteousness
63 37 Man take righteousness in his hands
75 5 Delight to honor those who serve in
84 97 Work cut short in righteousness
117 Reprove in righteousness
98 30 If enemy, spared, reward for righteousness
107 84 Things (lone in righteousness
109 59 Thy work cut short in righteousness
121 36 Powers of heaven act only in righteousness
46 Sceptre of righteousness and truth
128 24 As church offer in righteousness
132 36 Accounted to Abraham for righteousness
133 44 When meet him who works righteousness

ROBBER
42 84 Robber to be dealt with

ROCK
6 34 If built upon my rock, cannot
11 16 My word, rock, church and gospel
24 Build upon my rock, my gospel
18 4 Foundation of my church, my rock

ROLFE, SAMUEL
124 142 Presidency of high priests

ROUNDY, SHADRACH
124 141 To preside over bishopric

RULER
1 23 Gospel proclaimed before rulers
38 21 No king or ruler save Christ
52 13 Faithful shall be made ruler
58 20 Let no man think he is ruler
101 61 Faithful steward a ruler in kingdom
76 Importune rulers for redress
134 6 Purpose of rulers

RUN
10 4 Do not run faster than you have strength
89 20 Run and not be weary

RYE
89 17 Rye for fowls, swine and beasts of field

SABBATH DAY
68 29 Saints to keep sabbath day holy

SACRAMENT
20 40 Apostle may administer sacrament
46 Priests may administer sacrament
58 Teachers and deacons cannot administer
68 Sacrament to members just baptized
75 To be taken often in remembrance of Lord
76 Elder or priest administer sacrament
77 Manner of administering the sacrament
79 Manner of administering the wine
79 Meaning of the sacrament
27 2 Purpose of the sacrament
2 Matters not what ye eat and drink for
46 4 Not partake of sacrament until reconciliation
59 9 Sacrament on Sunday
12 Sacrament to Lord on Sunday

62	4	Offer sacrament to Most High
88	140	To precede washing of feet
89	5	Wine may be used in sacrament
95	6	House dedicated for sacrament offerings
46	5	Members not to be cast out of sacrament
	5	Nor.-members not to be cast out of

SACRED
6	12	Trifle not with sacred things
9	9	Cannot write sacred things except of me
25	11	Emma Smith make selection of sacred
63	64	What cometh from above is sacred
	64	Speak of sacred things with care
104	64	Preserve avails of sacred things in treasury
	65	Avails of sacred things for holy purpose
	68	Profits on sacred writings used for same

SACRIFICE
59	8	Sacrifice to be offered the Lord
97	12	Sacrifice required by the Lord
117	13	sacrifice more sacred than increase
124	39	Memorials for sacrifices in temple
132	51	I require offering by covenant and sacrifice

SAINT
43	29	Saints to reign with God
45	45	Saints who have slept shall come
58	54	Workman to labor for saints
61	17	Land blessed for saints
63	34	Saints shall hardly escape God's wrath
	36	Why saints should assemble in Zion
64	30	Saints shall obtain inheritance
	31	Saints seek earnestly riches of eternity
76	29	Satan makes war with saints
84	2	Saints to stand upon Mount Zion
	4	New Jerusalem to be built by gathering of
88	107	Saints filled with glory and receive
	114	Devil have no more power over saints
	115	Michael fight the battle of the saints
101	39	Saints accounted as salt of the earth
103	7	Earth given to the saints forever
	9	Saints to be lights and saviors
	10	If not saviors, like salt without savor
104	15	The way the Lord provides for saints
105	29	Saints possess lands according to
123	hd	Duty of saints in relation to persecutors

SALT
101	39	Saints accounted as salt of the earth
	40	If salt lose its savor it is
103	10	Saints not saviors, like salt without savor

SALUTATION
88	120–136	Manner of salutation in Lord's house

SALVATION
6	3	Everlasting salvation in kingdom
	13	No gift greater than salvation
11	3	Treasure up everlasting salvation
29	43	Conditions of salvation
43	25	God would save with everlasting salvation
45	58	Children grow without sin to salvation
49	5	Conditions of salvation
64	3	Forgiven sins for salvation of souls
76	88	Telestial, heir to salvation
77	12	Salvation completed in seventh thousand
78	2	Listen to counsel that salvation may be
	13	The preparation for salvation
	16	Michael has keys of salvation
82	9	Direction for salvation
84	73	Gifts given for profit and salvation
89	2	Will of God in temporal salvation
93	53	Obtain knowledge for salvation of Zion
	20	God sworn to be salvation and tower of Zion
109	4	Salvation only in name of Jesus Christ
128	5	Salvation of dead without gospel ordained
	11	Priesthood receives facts of salvation
	15	Salvation of dead essential to living
135	3	Did more, save Jesus, for salvation than

SANCTIFICATION
20	31	Through grace of Jesus Christ

SANCTIFIED
88	2	Names in book of sanctified
135	6	Names as gems for the sanctified

SANCTIFY
43	9	Sanctified by what received
76	21	Angels sanctified before throne of God
77	12	Earth sanctified on seventh day
84	33	Sanctified by Spirit to renewing bodies
88	26	Earth sanctified, die and quickened
	34	Governed by law sanctified by law
	68	Sanctify that minds become single to God
	74	Assemble, organize, sanctify and prepare
101	5	Not endure chastening not sanctified
105	36	Chosen be sanctified

SANCTUARY
88	137	House of Lord, school of Prophets, sanctuary

SARAH
132	34	Sarah gave Abraham Hager to wife
	65	Sarah administered to Abraham

SATAN
10	5	Pray always to conquer Satan
	23	Satan laid a cunning plan
	24	Satan stirreth hearts to anger
	25	Satan saith no sin to lie
	27	Goeth up and down, to and fro in the earth
	32	Satan will harden the hearts
	33	Satan thinketh to overcome testimony
	63	Doth stir hearts to contention
29	36	Rebellion of Satan
	47	Satan cannot tempt children
35	24	Satan shall tremble
43	31	Shall be bound, loosed, and reign short time
52	14	Satan will sift Lyman Wight as chaff
	14	Satan deceiveth nations
63	28	Makes anger against you

SATAN continued

	28	Plans shedding of blood
64	17	Satan seeketh to destroy soul
76	28	Satan, serpent, devil, who rebelled
	29	Makes war with saints
	30	Sufferings of those whom Satan overcomes
78	10	Through Satan become blind and
	12	Who breaks covenant delivered to Satan
84	100	Satan is bound
86	3	Reigns in the heart of Babylon
88	110	Bound for thousand years
	111	Satan loosed to gather armies
101	28	Then no power to tempt
104	9	Cannot escape buffetings of Satan
	10	Not repent, delivered to Satan
132	21	Delivered to Satan to day of redemption
	57	Seeketh to destroy

SAVE

3	20	Through repentance be saved
18	22	Repent and baptized be saved
	23	Saved only by name of Jesus Christ
20	26	Who shall be saved of mankind
	29	Must worship or cannot be saved
33	12	Not saved without faith
38	33	Israel shall be saved
42	60	Doer shall be saved
53	7	Save only those who endure to the end
76	42	Through Jesus all might be saved
	43	All God's works saved except sons of
	44	Saves all except
100	17	All who call be saved
124	54	Save all pure in heart
131	6	Impossible to be saved in ignorance
132	17	Without covenant, saved but not exalted

SAVIOR

1	20	God, Lord, Savior of the world
3	16	How knowledge of Savior comes
76	1	No Savior beside Lord God
86	11	Through priesthood savior to Israel
103	9	Saints to be lights and saviors
130	1	Savior a man like ourselves

SAVOR

101	39	Saints salt and savor of the earth
103	10	If not saviors, like salt without savor

SAY

3	2	God varies not from what is said
6	6	As you have asked, I say
10	16	Say in your hearts
24	10	Cannot say enough in my name
82	10	Lord bound by what I say
84	57	Say and do what is written
	85	Take no thought of what ye shall say
100	6	Shall be given you what to say
124	97	Give in very hour what to say

SCHOOL

55	4	Write books for schools in church
90	8	Perfected for ministry
95	17	House for school of apostles
97	3	Parley P. Pratt to preside over

SCHOOL OF PROPHETS

88	127	House for presidency of school of prophets
	136	Example for salutation in school of prophets
	137	House of Lord, school of prophets, etc.
90	7	School of prophets to be organized
95	10	Contentions in school of prophets

SCORNER

45	50	Scorner to be consumed

SCOTT, JACOB

52	28	Jacob Scott called

SCRIPTURE

6	27	Scriptures hidden because of iniquity
8	1	Old records of my scripture
10	63	Wrest scriptures and do not understand
20	11	Holy scriptures are true
24	5	Expound the scriptures
25	7	Emma Smith ordained to expound the
26	1	Devote time to study of scriptures
35	20	Scriptures given to Joseph as in God's bosom
42	56	Given and preserved in safety
	57	Not to be taught until received in full
	58	To be taught to all nations, kindreds, etc.
	59	Take for law what thou findest in scriptures
68	4	Said when moved by Holy Ghost is scripture
104	58	Print fulness of scriptures and revelations
113	hd	Answers to questions on scripture

SCROLL

88	95	As a scroll unfolded

SEA

77	1	Sea of glass is sanctified earth
88	90	After your testimony that of waves of sea
121	4	Maker of heaven, earth and seas
	30	If bounds set to the sea
128	23	Seas tell wonders of eternal King
130	7	Globe like sea of glass and fire
133	8	Send elders to islands of the sea
	68	Sea dries at my rebuke

SEAL

1	8	Power to seal on earth and in heaven
68	12	Seal to eternal life whom Father record
76	53	Sealed by Holy Ghost
77	6	Book of seven seals explained
	8	Power to seal unto life
	9	Sealed servants of God in foreheads
	10	Sixth seal for accomplishment of these
	11	Sealing of 144,000 of Israel explained
	12	Sealed unto end of all things
88	84	To seal up testimony
98	2	Prayers recorded with this seal
101	61	Seal of the faithful
104	62	Shall be a seal upon treasury

SECRET–SEVENTY

	64	Seal on treasury broken only
109	35	Let anointing be sealed
124	124	Sealed to day of redemption
129	14	This is sealing or binding power
	7	Only sealed contracts valid for time and
	7	Mine anointed holds sealing power
	19	Shedding innocent blood cancels sealings
	46	Sealed on earth sealed in heaven
	49	Seal your exaltation upon you
133	72	Sealed up testimony for disobedient
135	1	Martyrdom sealed testimony of this work
124	124	Patriarch holds sealing blessings of church

SECRET

38	28	Enemy in secret chambers seeketh your
42	64	Safety from secret combinations
	92	Offend in secret, chastened in secret
60	15	Shake dust of feet in secret
88	108	Reveal secret works in first thousand years
	109	Reveal secret works in second thousand
99	4	Cleanse feet in secret places
117	11	Be ashamed of secret abominations

SEDITION

134	5	Sedition unbecoming citizens

SEE

1	2	No eye that shall not see
14	8	Witness of things you shall see and hear
17	5	By my power has seen them
38	7	Ye cannot see me
42	49	Who has faith shall see
76	94	They see as they are seen
	109	Privilege of seeing for themselves
	117	Seeing and knowing for themselves
97	16	Pure in heart shall see God
121	24	Eye see and know all works

SEED

84	34	Become seed of Abraham
110	12	In our seed shall all be blessed
124	58	Kindred blessed in thy seed
	90	Nor his seed begging bread
132	30	Abraham and his seed to continue
	19	Glory is fulness and continuation of seed

SEEK

11	21	First seek to obtain my word
	21	Seek not to declare my words
46	8	Seek the best gifts
54	10	Who seeks early find rest for soul
88	63	Seek and ye shall find
	83	Seeks early, find and not be forsaken
	118	As all have not faith, seek and teach
106	3	Seek, all necessary added
136	20	Seek and keep pledge

SEER

4	hd	Joseph Smith called seer
21	1	Joseph Smith be called a seer
107	92	President of church a seer

124	94	Hyrum Smith a prophet, seer, etc
	125	President of church a prophet, seer, etc
127	12	Servant, prophet, seer of Church of Jesus

SELFISHNESS

56	8	Repent of pride and selfishness

SELL

57	8	Sell goods without fraud
101	98	Sore and grievous sin to sell to enemies

SENECA COUNTY

128	21	Voice of Lord at Fayette, Seneca county

SERPENT

76	28	Satan, serpent, devil, who rebelled
84	72	Poison of serpent not hurt believers
89	110	Satan, serpent, devil bound 1,000 years
111	11	Wise as serpents without sin
124	99	Where serpents not touch his heel

SERVANTS

1	hd	Covenants and commandments to his
	6	This authority of my servants
5	11	Testimony of three servants
10	5	Servant of Satan
43	25	God call by mouths of servants
58	26	Who is compelled not a wise servant
50	26	Who is ordained is greatest though a
76	112	Telestial, servants of the Most High
77	9	Sealed servants of God in foreheads
101		Parable of the slothful servant
124		Fate if reject servants and testimony
134	12	Not preach gospel to bond servants without
136	37	Mine angels, ministering servants

SERVE

4	3	Desire to serve God are called
42	29	If you love me, serve me
59	5	How to serve God

SETH

96	7	Seth for Joseph
107	41	Promise to Seth concerning posterity
	43	Seth the express likeness of Adam
	43	Seth was a perfect man
	51	Seth ordained Lamech
	53	Seth a high priest

SEVENTY

107	25	Seventy to preach gospel
	25	Especial witnesses unto Gentiles
	26	Quorum of seventy equal to apostles
	34	Duties of the seventy
	38	Traveling high council call upon seventy
	90	Presidency of elders distinct from that of
	93	Seven presidents from among seventy
	95	Presidents to choose more seventy
	97	Traveling ministers unto Gentiles and Jews
124	138	President of quorum of seventies
	139	A quorum for traveling elders
	139	Under direction of apostles
	140	Travel continually; different from elders

SHAKERS
- 49 1   Preach gospel to Shakers
-     2   Shakers not wholly right

SHERMAN, LYMAN
- 108 hd Concerning Lyman Sherman
-     1   Words to Lyman Sherman

SHERWOOD, HENRY G.
- 124 81 To pay stock to temple
-     132 Member of high council

SHIP
- 123 16 Large ship benefited by small helm

SHOW
- 5   7   Would not believe if shown
-     25 Shown me by power of God
- 10 43 Show my wisdom is greater
- 19 21 Show not until it is wisdom

SICK
- 35 9   Sick healed by faith
- 42 43 How to deal with the sick
-     48 All sick healed by faith
- 52 40 Remembers poor, needy, sick, etc.
- 66 9   Lay hands upon sick to recover
- 84 68 In my name heal the sick
- 89 8   Tobacco for sick cattle
- 124 98 Sign to heal the sick

SICKLE
- 4   4; 6:3, 4; 11:3, 4, 27; 12:3, 4; 14:3; 31:5
         Thrust in sickle

SIGN
- 29 14 Signs of Christ's coming
- 35 8   I will show signs
- 39 23 Shall look for signs of coming
- 45 16 Signs of coming discussed
- 45 39 Signs shown those who fear God
- 46 8   Sign to consume upon lusts
- 58 64 Signs follow those who believe
- 63 7   Sought signs not unto salvation
-     8   Sign-seekers from the beginning
-     9   Signs follow those who believe
-     9   Faith comes not by signs
-     10 How signs come
-     11 Signs shown in wrath unto condemnation
-     11 Signs come unto mighty works
-     12 Seek not signs and wonders for faith
- 68 10 Who believes blest with signs
-     11 To you given to know signs of
- 84 65 Signs to follow believers
- 88 93 Great signs shall appear in heaven
- 124 98 These signs shall follow him

SIMPLICITY
- 133 57 Reasoning in plainness and simplicity

SIN
- 1   31 Lord make no allowance for sin
- 10 25 Satan telleth, no sin to lie
- 13 1   Baptism for remission of sins
- 18 44 Work unto convincing of sin
- 19 20 Confess your sins
- 20 37 Spirit of Christ unto remission of sins
- 21 37 Crucified for sins of world
- 29 1   Arm of mercy atoned for sins
-     3   Sin no more lest perils come
-     3   Sin forgiven thee
-     47 Children cannot sin
- 31 5   Sins are forgiven
- 33 11 Baptisms for the remission of sins
- 45 58 Children grow without sin
- 49 8   All men under sin except
-     20 Why the world lies in sin
- 56 14 Sins come unto me and not pardoned
- 58 42 Who repenteth is forgiven of sins
-     43 How repentance for sins may be known
- 59 12 Confess sins to brethren and the Lord
-     15 Much laughter is sin
- 61 2   Mercy to those who confess their sins
- 63 63 Church repent of sins
- 64 3   Sins forgiven for my glory and salvation
-     7   How the Lord forgives sins
-     9   Greater sin not to forgive
- 68 25 Sin of untaught children upon parents
- 76 52 Cleansed from sin by keeping commandments
- 82 2   All have sinned
-     2   Refrain from sin lest sore judgment
-     3   Sins against greater light greater
-     7   To soul that sins, former sins return
-     20 Order of Enoch everlasting if you sin not
- 84 49 Whole world lies in sin
-     50 Under sin, they come not to me
-     51 Who comes not to me, under sin
-     61 Forgive sins with this commandment
- 88 35 Who willeth to abide in sin cannot
-     82 Without excuse, sin upon heads
- 93 1   Who forsakes sins sees God
- 95 1   Chasten that sins be forgiven
-     6   Those not chosen have sinned
-     6   Sin to walk in darkness at noon day
- 101 9   Compassion notwithstanding sin
- 111 11 Wise as serpents, without sin
- 121 16 Cursed who cry sin when no sin
-     17 Cry transgression because servants of sin
-     37 Grieves Spirit to cover sins
- 132 26 Punishment for common sin
-     26 Marriage within covenant not annulled by
-     26 Sin not to murder shall come forth
-     38 Cannot sin in what is received from God
-     46 Sins retained on earth retained in heaven
-     46 Sins remitted on earth remitted in heaven

SING
- 128 22 Let earth break into singing
- 136 28 If merry, break into singing, etc.

SINLESS
50	28	Sinless man possesses all things

SINNERS
41	5	Sinners to be thrown out
42		How delt with in the church
	37	Fate of a sinner in the church
	87	Sinner to be dealt with
43	18	Sinners stay and sleep
63	57	Desire to warn sinners, let them be ordained
76	30	Vision of sufferings of sinners

SLANDERER
112	9	Let Slanderer cease perverseness

SLAVE
87	4	Slaves against masters for war

SLEEP
43	18	Sleeping nation awakened
88	124	Cease to sleep longer than is necessary

SMALL
64	33	Out of small things proceedeth the great
123	15	Much of futurity depends on small things

SMELL
59	19	Nature for a smell

SMITE
98	23	If man smite once, seek not revenge
	25	Smite twice, no revenge, reward hundred
	26	Smite thrice, no revenge, reward double
105	40	Proposal of peace who have smitten

SMITH, DON C.
124	133	President of high priest quorum

SMITH, EDEN
75	36	Mission for Eden Smith
82	2	Words concerning

SMITH, EMMA
25	1	The Lord to Emma Smith
	5	Office of Emma Smith to Joseph
	7	Emma Smith ordained to expound the
132	51	Command to prove Emma Smith
	52	Emma Smith to receive those given to
	56	To forgive Joseph his trespasses

SMITH, GEORGE A.
124	129	An apostle
136	14	Amasa Lyman and George A. to organize

SMITH, HYRUM
23	hd	Given to Hyrum Smith
	3	Hyrum Smith under no condemnation
	23	Duty of church to family of Hyrum Smith
52	8	To travel
75	32	Mission for Hyrum Smith
94	13	To receive his inheritance on third lot
103	39	To travel with Frederick G. Williams
115	1	Unto you Hyrum Smith
124	15	Love Hyrum for his integrity
	77	Put stock in temple
	91	William Law counselor in place of Hyrum
	92	A patriarch by blessing and right
	94	Appointed a prophet, seer and revelator
	95	To receive counsel from Joseph Smith
	124	To be a patriarch
135	1	Martyrdom of Joseph and Hyrum the seal
	6	Lived died and will inherit glory
	6	Hyrum Smith 44 years old at death

SMITH, JOHN
102	3	Member of first high council

SMITH, JOSEPH, SENIOR
23	hd	Given to Joseph Smith Sen. and
102	23	Member of first high council
124	19	With Abraham at right hand

SMITH, JOSEPH, JR
1	17	Lord called upon Joseph Smith
	29	Power to translate Book of Mormon
	29	Received Nephite record
5	1	Borne record of plates
	2	To stand as witness of plates
	9	Generation have word through Joseph
	23	Joseph speak to Joseph
18	7	Baptized at hands of Joseph Smith
	8	Called Joseph to my own purpose
19	13	Commandments received at hands of Joseph
20	2	Ordained an apostle of Jesus Christ
	2	Called of God
	5	Entangled in vanities
	6	Ministered to by holy angels
21	1	Names to be applied to Joseph Smith
	2	Inspired to found church
	5	Word of Joseph Smith as from mouth of
	4	Church to heed words of Joseph Smith
21	8	Promise of the Lord to Joseph Smith
	9	Words given Joseph through comforter
	10	To be ordained by Oliver Cowdery
23	5	Words to Joseph Smith
24	1	Joseph Smith chosen to write Book of
	7	To devote all services to Zion
	8	To have many afflictions
	9	Not have strength in temporal labors
25	5	Office of Emma to Joseph Smith
27	8	Ordained by John
28	2	To receive revelations like Moses
	2	Alone to receive revelations for the church
	10	To preside over conference by voice
30	7	To be above Oliver
35	17	Gospel sent by Joseph Smith
	18	Or successor to hold keys of mysteries of
41	7	Joseph Smith should have house built
43	12	Uphold Joseph Smith
	13	Provide Joseph with food and
52	3	To go to Missouri
	6	Cut off if not faithful
	24	Called
	41	And others to take recommend
53	5	Take journey with Joseph Smith

SMITH, JOSEPH, JR continued
55	2	Ordained by Joseph Smith
	5	Journey with Joseph Smith
56	12	If Joseph Smith must pay the money
58	18	Joseph Smith to return
60	6	To go to Cincinnati
61	23	Not to travel upon the waters
	30	Commandment to
63	41	To discern by the Spirit
	65	And Sidney Rigdon to seek a home
64	5	Keys of mysteries not taken from
	7	Joseph Smith has sinned
67	5	Sought knowledge beyond the knowledge of
	5	Language and imperfections known
	14	Conferred by hand of Joseph Smith
70	1	Commands to Joseph Smith for the Saints
71	1	Frederick G. Williams counselor to Joseph
	2	Joseph Smith holds keys of kingdom
	3	Acknowledged and blessed of God
73	3	Joseph Smith to translate
76	11	In the Spirit
84	3	New Jerusalem dedicated by Joseph Smith
90	1	Revelation concerning his presidency of
	3	Possess keys of kingdom in this and coming
	6	Equal with Joseph in keys of the kingdom
	13	To preside over church and school
	20	Words concerning
93	47	Rebuked
	53	Command to gain knowledge
	45	I say unto my servant Joseph Smith
100	9	Sidney Rigdon to be spokesman for
100	11	Joseph Smith to be a revelator
102	1	High council organized at house of
	2	President of high council
103	21	Man of the parable of the vineyard
	35	Pray that Joseph Smith may preside
	37	Parley P. Pratt to journey with Joseph
	40	Go as Joseph Smith shall counsel
	43	Inheritance appointed
	45	Father reckoned in house of Joseph Smith
105	21	As Joseph shall appoint
109	68	Covenanted with Jehovah
110	hd	Vision to Joseph and Oliver in Kirtland
112	15	Given keys until Christ's coming
115	19	Holds keys of kingdom and ministry
122	1	How Joseph's name shall be known
	4–7	Trials to which Joseph may be subjected
	9	Promised to Joseph Smith
124	1	Why Joseph Smith was raised up
	42	Show Joseph all pertaining to the temple
	56	His blessing be upon his posterity
	58	Kindred blessed in thy seed
	59	Joseph and seed have place in house
	125	Presiding elder of the church
127	2	Envy and wrath my common lot
	12	Subscribe servant, prophet, seer, etc.
128	1	Baptism for the dead occupies Joseph's mind
130	15	Joseph's answer as to time of Christ's
132	7	Joseph Smith to hold sealing power
	48	What you give is without condemnation
	50	Joseph's obedience rewarded
	52	Emma Smith to receive those given to
	53	Faithful over few, ruler over many
	54	Emma to cleave unto Joseph or be destroyed
	55	Blessings promised to Joseph Smith
	56	Emma to forgive Joseph his trespasses
135	1	Martyrdom the seal of testimony of this
	3	Summary of Joseph's life
	3	Did more, Save Jesus, for salvation than
	4	Words before final imprisonment
	6	Lived, died for and will inherit glory
	6	Joseph Smith 38 years old at death
	7	Innocence of any crime
136	37	From Jesus to Joseph Smith
	37	Called by angels and God's voice
	38	Laid foundation of work
	39	Why Joseph's death was needful
	38	Joseph Smith was faithful

SMITH, SAMUEL H.
23	4	Samuel H. Smith called
61	35	And Reynolds Cahoon to travel together
66	8	Words concerning
75	13	Mission for Samuel H. Smith
102	3	Member of first high council
124	141	To preside over the bishopric

SMITH, SYLVESTER
75	34	Mission for
102	3	Member of first high council

SMITH, WILLIAM
124	129	William Smith an apostle

SNARE
61	18	Faith fail and caught in snares
63	15	Judgment upon adulterers as a snare
90	17	Being a snare upon souls

SNIDER, JOHN
124	22	John Snider to assist building
	62	Committee to build temple

SNOW, ERASTUS
136	12	And Erastus Snow organize a company

SOBER
6	19, 43:35, 61:38, 73:6	Be sober
18	21	Speak truth in soberness

SOCIETY
134	1	Government for safety of society
	10	Right of religious societies to deal with

SOLEMN
88	70	Call a solemn assembly
124	39	Solemn assemblies to be held in temples
133	6	Call solemn assemblies

SOLEMNITY
43	34	Let solemnities of eternity be upon you
84	61	In solemnity and spirit of prayer
100	7	Declare in solemnity of heart
107	84	Things done in solemnity

SOLOMON
132	38	Solomon received many wives and concubines

SON
9	1	I say unto you my son
20	28	Father, Son and Holy Ghost one God
42	52	Have small faith become my sons
68	8	Baptize in name of Father, Son and Holy
76	13	Son in bosom of Father from the beginning
	20	Son on right hand of Father
	20	Received of fulness of Son
	24	Inhabitants of earth sons and daughters of
	26	Lucifer, a son of the morning
	77	Presence of Son not fulness of Father
84	34	Became sons of Moses and Aaron
93	4	Why the Father and Son are one
	7	Son was in the beginning
	8	Son the Word, and Messenger of salvation
	9	The Son the Spirit of Truth
	11	Son full of grace and truth
	13	Son received grace for grace
	14	Why he is called the Son
	14	Son received not of fulness at first
	15	Holy Ghost comes to the Son
	16	When the Son received the fullness of the
93	17	Received all power on earth and in heaven
	17	The Father dwelt in the Son
	20	The Son glorified the Father
	22	Begotten of Son, partakers of glory
95	17	Son Ahman, Jesus Christ
107	40	Priesthood handed down from father to son
130	3	False that Son dwells in man's heart
	22	Son has a body of flesh and bones

SON OF GOD
6	21,	10:57, 11:28, 11:30, 14:9 The Son of God
11	30	Power to become sons of God
45	9	Receive Christ, sons of God
76	58	They are gods, sons of God
107	3	Priesthood after order of Son of God
128	23	Let sons of God shout for joy

SON OF MAN
49	6	Reigneth in the heavens
	6	On right hand of his glory
58	65	Son of man cometh
65	5	Come down to meet kingdom of God on
122	8	Descended below all trials

SONS OF PERDITION
76	32	They are sons of perdition
	33	Fate of sons of perdition
	34	No forgiveness for sons of perdition
	38	Sons of perdition not redeemed
	43	All God's works saved except sons of
	44	Torment of sons of perdition
	46	Punishment of sons of perdition

SONG
25	12	Song of the righteous is a prayer
	12	My soul delights in song of the heart
45	71	Songs of everlasting joy
66	11	Push many to Zion with songs of everlasting
84	98	Sing the new song
101	18	Return to Zion with songs of joy
133	38	Filled with songs of everlasting joy
	56	Sing song of the Lamb
84	99–101	The new song

SORCERER
63	17	Shall die second death
76	103	Receive telestial glory

SORROW
1	3	Rebellious be pierced with sorrow
101	29	No sorrow because of death

SORROWFUL
136	29	If sorrowful call upon Lord with

SOUL
4	4	Bringeth salvation to his soul
6	3	Treasure up salvation for his soul
8	4	Slay and bring souls to destruction
10	22	Lead souls to destruction
	27	Seeking to destroy souls
	13	Fill your soul with joy
15	6	That you may bring souls unto
18	10	Worth of souls is great to God
	15	Bring save one soul unto me
	13	Great joy in soul who repents
	16	Great joy if you bring many souls unto me
25	12	My soul delights in the song of the heart
	14	Let thy soul delight in thy husband
41	12	Words to be answered upon souls
45	2	Harvest ended, souls not saved
	46	Souls shall live
56	16	Riches will canker your souls
59	19	Nature to enliven soul
63	4	Lord able to cast soul to hell
88	15	Spirit and body the soul
	16	Resurrection the redemption of the soul
101	37	Care not for body but soul
117	11	Be ashamed of littleness of soul
121	37	Undue control over souls grieves spirit
	42	Enlarge soul without hypocrisy
	45	Doctrine of priesthood distil upon soul
132	63	Work continued by bearing souls
	63	Exaltation to bear souls of men
134	4	Freedom of soul not controlled by human

SOUTH CAROLINA
87	1	Begin at rebellion in South Carolina
130	12	Bloodshed before Christ's coming begin in

SOUTHERN STATES
    87   3   Southern States divided against Northern

SOW
    6   33   What ye sow, ye shall reap

SPACE
    88   12   Light from God to fill space
           37   No space without kingdom

SPEAK
    6   20   Spoken because of thy desires
    8   12   I spake from the beginning
    16   2   Speak with sharpness and power
    18   21   Speak truth in soberness
    19   37   Speak freely to all
    24   6   Given thee what to speak
    24   6   Gift of speaking
    42   27   Shalt not speak evil against neighbor
    52   16   Speech with contrite heart accepted
    60   53   Speaking after the manner of the Lord
    64   19   Why God speaks
           24   Speaking after manner of the Lord
    68   3   Speak as moved by Holy Ghost
    84   70   Dumb shall speak
    88   122   One speak at a time
    97   1   Speak by voice of Spirit
    133 6   Speak often to one another

SPEECH
    88   121   Cease from light speeches
           129   President not to use loud speech
    112 5   Let not earth slumber because of speech
    124 115   Lay aside hard speeches

SPHERE
    77   3   Destined order and sphere

SPIRIT
    1   33   Spirit will not always strive with man
           39   Spirit beareth record
    5   16   Visit with manifestations of Spirit
           16   Born of water and Spirit
    6   14   Received instructions by Spirit
    8   1   Scripture spoken by manifestation of Spirit
    11   12   This is my Spirit
           12   Spirit which leadeth to do good
           12   Put your trust in that Spirit
           13   My Spirit shall enlighten your mind
           18   Appeal to my Spirit
           21   If you desire you shall have my Spirit
    18   2   Manifested by my Spirit they are true
           35   Given by my Spirit
           47   Spoken by power of my Spirit
    19   18   God suffered in spirit
           20   Punishment when I withdraw my Spirit
           23   Walk in meekness of my Spirit
           38   Pray and I will pour out my Spirit
    27   18   Take sword of my Spirit
    29   31   Creation by power of Spirit
    33   16   Power of Spirit quickeneth all things

    42   14   Spirit given by prayer
    45   17   Absence of spirits from body a bondage
    46   7   Do what Spirit testifies
           23   Some given discerning of spirits
           28   Ask in spirit, receive in spirit
           31   Things of Spirit done in name of Christ
    50   10   Come, saith the Lord by the Spirit
           14   The Comforter
           15   Not justified in spirits not understand
           27   Spirit subject to the ordained
           30   As head, spirits subject to you
    52   19   Pattern to know spirits in all cases
    56   17   Have broken hearts and contrite spirits
           18   Whose hearts broken and spirits contrite
    57   13   Copy, correct, and prove by Spirit
    58   38   Directions given by the Spirit
    59   24   Spirit beareth record
    61   27   Given by Spirit to know his ways
           28   Do as Spirit commandeth
    62   8   Act according to directions of Spirit
    63   16   Adulterers in their hearts shall lose Spirit
           32   Lord withholds Spirit from inhabitants of
           41   Joseph Smith to discern by the Spirit
           55   Received not counsel and grieved Spirit
           64   Speak with constraint of Spirit
           64   Spirit received by prayer
    64   16   Sought evil and Lord withheld Spirit
    68   hd   Mind and will of the Lord made known by
    70   13   Abundance through manifestations of Spirit
           14   Manifestations of Spirit not abundant if
    75   1   Speak by voice of Spirit
    76   10   Enlighten them by Spirit
           12   What was done by power of Spirit
           18   Given us of the Spirit
           80   We being in the Spirit
           80   To write while in the Spirit
           73   Spirits of men kept in prison
           118   Through Spirit bear his presence in the flesh
    84   33   Sanctified by Spirit to renewing of bodies
           45   Light is Spirit of Jesus Christ
           46   Spirit gives light to every man
           47   Who hearkens to the Spirit comes to God
           88   Spirit shall be in your hearts
    88   15   Spirit and body the soul
           28   Celestial spirit receive natural body
           66   My voice is spirit and truth
           101   Spirits that live not until end of earth
           137   As Spirit gives utterance in house of the
    91   4   Spirit manifests the truth
           6   Receives not of Spirit not benefited
    93   25   Spirit of wicked, liar from the beginning
           26   Spirit of truth of God
           33   Spirit and element receive fulness of joy
           33   Man is spirit
    95   4   Pour Spirit upon all flesh

97	1	Speak by voice of Spirit	133	14	Wickedness is spiritual Babylon
	8	Blessings on contrite spirits	SPOKESMAN		
105	36	Manifest by Spirit who are chosen	88	122	Let not all be spokesmen
124	97	Receive of Spirit, even Comforter		122	Listen to sayings of spokesman
129	hd	Keys to know angels or spirits	100	9	Sidney Rigdon to be spokesman
	3	Spirits of just men made perfect	124	104	Oliver Cowdery again a spokesman
	4	How to distinguish between good and bad	STAKE		
	6	Spirit of just man comes only in glory	68	26	Organized stakes of Zion
	7	Spirit will not shake hands	82	13	Kirtland consecrated for stake of Zion
130	22	Holy Ghost is a personage of spirit		14	Stakes of Zion strengthened
131	7	All spirit is matter	94	1	Lay foundation of stakes of Zion
	8	When bodies pure see spirit matter	96	1	Stake for strength of Zion
136	33	Spirit to condemnation of ungodly		3	To be divided in lots
	33	Spirit to enlighten humble and contrite	101	21	Stakes of Zion organized when no more room

SPIRIT OF BEAST
77	2	Spirit of beast in likeness of its body		21	Called stakes, for the curtains

SPIRIT OF ELIAS
27	7	John filled with the spirit of Elias	104	40	My stake in Kirtland
			107	37	Councils of twelve at stakes of Zion
			109	39	Stakes the place of appointment

SPIRIT, EVIL
46	7	Seduced by evil spirits		59	Appoint unto Zion other stakes
			115	6	Zion and her stakes

SPIRIT, FALSE
50	2	Many false spirits		18	Appoint stakes as manifest
	31	How to treat false spirits	119	7	Tithing a law for all stakes
	31	How to know false spirit	124	2	Stake polished as marble

SPIRIT OF GOD
				2	Stake the corner stone of Zion
46	11	Gifts given to every man by Spirit of God		36	Baptism for dead in stakes
67	11	Not see God unless quickened by the Spirit		134	Qualifying presidents of stakes
				142	To be a president for stake and counselors

SPIRIT OF LORD
121	37	How Spirit of Lord is grieved	125	4	Reside in all stakes appointed
	37	Spirit grieved priesthood withdrawn	133	9	Gather that stakes be strengthened
	38	Spirit of Lord grieved, man left to himself	136	10	Help remove stakes of Zion

SPIRIT OF MAN

STANDARD
77	2	Spirit of man in likeness of his person	45	9	Covenant to be a standard
93	38	Spirit of man innocent in beginning	98	35	Should lift standard of peace thrice
			115	5	Light of church a standard for nations

SPIRIT OF REVELATION

STANTON
8	3	This is the spirit of revelation	75	33	Mission for Daniel Stanton

SPIRIT OF TRUTH

STAR
6	15	Enlightened by spirit of truth	29	14	Stars fall from heaven
50	19	Truth received by spirit of truth only	34	9	Stars refuse to shine and fall
	19	Preached by spirit of truth	45	42	Stars fall from heaven
	22	Understand by spirit of truth	76	81	Glory as the moon is to the stars
93	9	Son the spirit of truth		98	Telestial differs as stars
	11	Son even spirit of truth		98	Glory of stars one
107	71	Knowledge by spirit of truth		109	Numerous as stars in firmament

SPIRITUAL
			88	9	Jesus light and power of stars
14	11	Blessed spiritually		45	Stars give light and roll upon wings
24	7	In spiritual labors thou shalt have strength		47	Stars are kingdoms
29	32	Spiritual nature of things		87	Stars angry and cast down as figs
	34	All things spiritual to God	121	30	If bounds set to stars
	44	Redemption from spiritual fall	129	23	Let sun, moon and stars sing together
67	10	See God with spiritual mind	133	49	Stars to be hurled from their places
70	12	Administer spiritual things, worthy of hire	STATE		
72	14	Who labor in spiritual things shall	134	7	Relation of state and religion
77	2	Spiritual in likeness of temporal	STEADFAST		
107	80	Decision in spiritual difficulties	82	24	If fall not from steadfastness

STEADFAST continued
- 84   61   Remain steadfast in minds

STEAL
- 42   20   Thou shalt not steal
- 59   6   Shalt not steal

STEWARD
- 42   32   Property received by consecration
- 51   19   Faithful steward inherit eternal life
-       11   Steward of temporal things not exempt from
- 72   3   Steward render account in time and eternity
-       20   Stewards of literary concern have claim upon
- 101   61   Faithful steward a ruler in kingdom
- 104   13   Every man accountable as steward over

STEWARDSHIP
- 42   53   Stand in place of stewardship
- 69   5   Send account of stewardship
- 70   4   Account of stewardship in day of judgment
-       9   What God requires of every stewardship
- 82   11   Stewardships of church united by a covenant
- 104   56   The nature of stewardships

STIFF-NECKEDNESS
- 56   6   Commandment revoked for stiff-neckedness

ST. JOHN
- 88   141   Pattern in St. John, chapter 13

ST. LOUIS
- 60   5   Go to St. Louis
-       8   Take their journey from St. Louis

STONE
- 28   11   Things written from stone, false
- 124   2   Stake as corner stone of Zion
- 130   10   White stone become Urim and Thummim
-       11   White stone and new name for all

STOREHOUSE
- 42   34   Property of church to be kept in storehouse
-       55   Storehouse to receive what is not needed
- 51   13   Let Bishop appoint a storehouse
- 58   24   Appointed to keep storehouse
-       37   Lands for storehouse
- 70   7   Excess given into my storehouse
-       11   Agent of storehouse not exempt from law
- 72   10   Bishop to keep storehouse
- 78   3   Organization for storehouse
- 82   18   Gains cast into Lord's storehouse
- 83   6   Storehouse kept by consecration of church
- 90   23   Discharge debt that storehouse be not in
- 101   96   Sidney Gilbert not to sell storehouse to

STRANGER
- 45   13   Holy men strangers on earth

STREAM
- 97   9   As fruitful tree by pure stream

STRENGTH
- 3   4   If he boasts in strength must fall
- 10   4   Do not labor more than you have strength
- 24   12   I will give thee strength
- 59   3   Earth bring forth in strength
- 84   101   Earth prevailed and brought forth strength
- 101   21   Called stakes, curtains, or strength of Zion
- 105   16   Strength of house my warriors
- 113   16   To put on strength is authority of priesthood

STRIFE
- 60   14   Preach not with strife
- 101   6   Strifes pollute inheritances

STRIVE
- 1   33   Spirit shall not always strive with men

STRONG
- 1   19   Weak to break down strong
-       28   Humble, they be strong
- 50   16   Weak shall be made strong
- 52   17   Who tremble under power be made strong
- 66   8   Who is faithful shall be strong
- 84   106   The strong to take the weak
- 90   36   Lord will contend with strong in Zion
- 133   58   When little become strong nation

STUDY
- 9   8   You must study it out in your mind
- 11   12   Study my word past and to come
-       22   Study until you have obtained all
- 26   1   Devote time to the study of scriptures
- 88   118   Seek learning by study and faith

STUPOR
- 9   9   Not right have stupor of thought

SUBJECT
- 50   27   All things subject to ordained
-       30   As heed, spirits subject to you
- 58   22   Subject to powers that be
- 105   32   Let us be subject to laws

SUFFER
- 18   11   Redeemer suffered that all men might come
- 19   4   Every man must repent or suffer
-       15   Your sufferings be sore and exquisite
-       16   I, God suffered that
-       18   Suffering caused God to
- 76   30   Sufferings of those whom Satan overcomes
-       49   Vision of sufferings of the ungodly
- 123   1   Gather facts of suffering of the people

SUMMER
- 4   52   Summer past, harvest ended, souls not saved

SUN
- 5   14   Church fair as the sun
- 29   14   Sun shall be darkened
- 76   70   Celestial glory like glory of the sun
-       71   Terrestrial from celestial as moon from sun
- 88   7   Jesus Christ light and power of sun
-       47   The sun a kingdom
-       87   Sun shall hide face, give no light
- 128   23   Let sun, moon and stars sing together
- 133   49   Sun shall hide face in shame

SUNDAY
- 59   9   House of prayer and sacraments on Sunday
-       9   Sunday a day of rest and worship

	13	Work that may be done on Sunday

SUPPLICATION

136	29	If sorrowful, call upon Lord with

SUPPORT

19	34	Impart all save support of family
24	3	Church shall support thee
42	55	Give to church what is not needed for

SUSQUEHANNA

128	20	Peter, James and John at Susquehanna Co.
	20	Michael on banks of Susquehanna

SWEAR

63	33	Lord sworn in his wrath
88	110	Swear in name of him upon the throne
97	20	God sworn by power of might
121	18	Punishment of those who swear falsely

SWEET

29	39	Taste bitter to know sweet

SWINE

89	17	Rye for fowls, swine and beasts of the field

SWORD

1	13	Sword of the Lord bathed in heaven
	13	Shall fall upon the inhabitants of the earth
6	2,	11:2, 12:2, 14:2 Word sharper than two-
27	18	Take sword of my spirit
45	33	Men will take sword against one another
87	6	Earth mourn with sword
97	26	Sword if disobedient
101	10	Let fall sword of my indignation
121	5	Avenge wrongs with sword

SWORN

97	20	Sworn by power of might

TABERNACLE

88	137	Tabernacle of Holy Spirit
93	4	I made flesh my tabernacle
	35	Elements are tabernacle of God
	35	Man is temple or tabernacle of God
101	23	Temple in my tabernacle
124	38	Moses' tabernacle for temple ordinances

TALENT

60	2	Hide not your talents
	3	Talent taken away if not used
	13	Bury not thy talent
82	18	That man may improve his talents
	18	Man may gain other talents
104	69	Talents, dollars

TAYLOR, JOHN

118	6	John Taylor called to apostleship
124	129	John Taylor an apostle
135	2	Present at Joseph Smith's death

TEACH

38	23	Teach one another
42	13	Teach as Spirit directs
	14	Teach not unless you receive Spirit
43	15	To teach not to be taught
52	9	Taught by comforter
63	65	Taught by prayer through spirit
75	10	Comforter to teach all acceptable things
88	77	Teach each other doctrine of kingdom
	78	Teach and grace shall attend you
	118	Teach wisdom
	118	As all have not faith, seek and teach

TEACHER

18	32	Twelve ordained to ordain teachers
20	39	Apostle may ordain teachers
	48	Priest may ordain teachers
	53	Duties of teachers
	56	Teachers may lead in meetings
	57	To be assisted by deacons
	58	Teachers may not baptize or
	60	How ordained
	64	May take a certificate
	81	To be sent to conferences
	84	May sign recommend
38	40	Teacher to go with might
42	12	Teachers to preach principles of the gospel
	70	Teachers to have stewardships
84	30	Necessary appendage to lesser priesthood
84	111	Standing ministers to the church
88	122	Appoint a teacher among you
	128	Teacher to stand in house prepared
107	10	High priest may officiate instead of teacher
	62	Presiding teachers presiding
	63	Teacher to priest
	86	Duties of presidents over 24 teachers
124	142	To be president of teachers and counselors

TELESTIAL

76	81	Terrestrial to telestial as moon to stars
	86	Telestial receive not fulness in eternity
	88	Telestial receive by ministering of angels
	88	Telestial heirs to salvation
	89	Glory of telestial surpasses all understanding
	90	No man knows telestial unless revealed to
	91	Glory of terrestrial exceeds telestial
	98	Glory of telestial differs as stars
	99	Telestial those of Paul, Apollos and Cephas
	100	Receive not gospel but say they are of
	103	Includes liars, sorcerers, adulterers, etc.
	109	Telestial as numerous as stars or sands
	111	Judged according to their works
	112	Telestial cannot get where Christ and God
	112	Telestial servants of the Most High
88	21	Who shall inherit telestial kingdom
	24	Telestial law brings telestial glory
	31	Who are quickened by portion receive

TEMPERANCE

4	6	Remember temperance

TEMPERATE

6	19	Be temperate
12	8	Not assist unless being temperate

TEMPEST
43	25	God calls by tempests
88	90	After your testimony that of tempests

TEMPLE
36	8	I will suddenly come to my temple
42	36	Day when I come to temple
57	3	Place for temple in Independence designated
58	57	Sidney Rigdon to dedicate land for temple
84	3	New Jerusalem built beginning at temple lot
	4	Temple reared in this generation
	5	Cloud of God's glory upon temple
93	35	Will destroy defiled temple
	35	Man is temple or tabernacle of God
95	8	House to endow with power from on high
	13	Manner of building Lord's house
	14	Temple to be built after manner shown
	15	Dimensions of temple
97	15	How built and treated
	15	The Lord will be in it if
	16	Pure in heart shall see God in temple
	17	If temple defiled God leaves it
101	23	Vail of temple taken off, what shall happen
105	33	First elders receive endowment in
109	5	A place for Son of Man to manifest himself
124	25	Saints to come and build a temple
	26	Some things people may bring for temple
	27	Build house for Most High to dwell in
	28	Temple needed to restore fulness of
	30	Baptism for dead must take place in temple
	33	Temples instituted before foundation of
	34	Keys of priesthood in temples
	37	Washings acceptable only in temple
	38	Moses' tabernacle for temple ordinances
	39	Things received in temples
	39	People always commanded to build temples
	40	Reveal ordinances in temples
	42	Show priesthood of temple
	42	Show Joseph all pertaining to temple
	47	Temples alone insufficient
	51	Attempt to build temple accepted
	51	Why temple in Jackson county not built
	56	Command to build temple in Nauvoo
	62	Committee to build temple
	64	Receive stock for building temple
	67	Stock company for building temple
	70	Use not stock for any other purpose
	74	Stock in temple for donor and his seed
	145	Rooms for offices of priesthood in temple
127	4	Let work of temple go on
	9	Records placed in archives of holy temple
128	24	Present worthy record of dead in temple
	15	Temple ordinances cannot be lightly passed
133	2	Lord come suddenly to his temple

TEMPORAL
29	34	No things temporal to God
	35	Adam received no temporal commandments
70	11	Steward of temporal things not exempt
	14	Shall be equal in temporal things
77	2	Spiritual in likeness of temporal
89	2	Will of God in temporal salvation
107	68	Bishop to administer temporal things
	71	High priest may administer temporal things

TEMPTATION
9	13	Yield to no temptation
20	22	Christ suffered temptations but gave no heed
	33	Take heed lest they fall into temptation
29	39	Necessity of temptation
	40	Yield to temptation become subject to the
	47	Satan cannot tempt little children
31	12	Pray lest enter into temptation
	12	Reward lost through temptation
61	39	Pray always, enter not into temptation
95	1	Chastisement deliverance from temptation
112	13	Lord feel after them after temptation
124	124	Partriarchal blessing in temptation

TEMPT
10	15	Satan to tempt Lord thy God
	29	To get thee to tempt the Lord
62	1	Jesus succors the tempted
64	20	Tempted above what he is able to bear
101	28	Then Satan no power to tempt

TEN TRIBES
110	11	Lead ten tribes from the north
133	26	They in north countries shall come

TENET
19	31	Of tenets shall not talk

TERRESTRIAL GLORY
76	71	Terrestrial and telestial compared
	72	Who shall receive
	76	Receive glory but not fulness
	78	Bodies terrestrial
	79	Receive not crown of kingdom
	81	Terrestrial to telestial as moon to stars
	86	Holy Spirit through terrestrial
	87	Terrestrial receive through celestial
	91	Glory of terrestrial excels telestial
	97	Glory of terrestrial one, as moon
88	21	Who shall inherit terrestrial kingdom
	23	Terrestrial law brings terrestrial glory
	30	Quickened by portion receive fulness

TESTIFY
5	1	Joseph Smith testified of plates
17	3	Shall testify by power of God
	5	Testify that you have seen them
18	34	Testify that words are of me
	36	To testify that you heard voice
46	7	Do what Spirit testifies
88	75	That I may testify you are clean
	81	Sent out to testify and warn
121	23	Wo to those who testify against my people

TESTIMONY

3	16, 17	Knowledge of Savior through testimony
	18	Testimony of Jesus come to Lamanites, etc.
5	11	Testimony of three to the plates
	14	Power to receive testimony in this generation
	15	Testimony of three witnesses will stand forth
	18	Testimony go to the condemnation of
6	31	Words established through testimony
10	33	Satan thinketh to overpower testimony
24	15	Leave cursing as testimony against
42	80	Testimony established by two or more
	80	Testimony not established by enemy
46	15	How testimonies may be established
58	6	Hearts prepared to bear testimony
	13	Testimony might go from Zion
	18	Judge by testimony of just
	47	Bear testimony to all
60	15	Wash feet as testimony
62	3	Blessed for testimony borne
	3	Testimony recorded in heaven
67	23	Guilty by unimpeachable testimony
75	20	Shake off dust of feet as testimony
76	22	Testimony that God lives
	50	Testimony of gospel of Christ
	79	Reward of those not valiant in testimony
	82	Fate of those who refuse testimony
84	61	Bear testimony to all the world
	92	Cleanse feet with water as a testimony
88	3	In testimony of John
	84	To seal up testimony
	88	After your testimony come wrath and
	89	After your testimony that of natural forces
	90	After your testimony that of thunderings
98	27	Testimonies against enemies if he repent not
	35	If peace not accepted bring testimony
	44	Bring forth trespass as testimony
99	4	Cleanse feet as testimony
100	10	Power to be mighty in testimony
102	26	Testimony of decision to be kept
107	72	Judgment upon transgressors upon testimony
	79	Judgment upon testimony
109	46	Seal up law and bind up testimony
122	3	People never turned by testimony of traitors
124	7	Call with testimony
	8	Fate if servants and testimony rejected
	20	Love him for love of testimony
133	72	Sealed up testimony for disobedient
135	1	Martyrdom the seal of testimony of this

THANK

46	32	Give thanks for all blessings
59	7	Thank the Lord in all things
98	1	In every thing give thanks

THANKFUL

62	7	Receive with thankful heart
78	19	Who is thankful shall be glorious

THANKSGIVING

46	7	Act with thanksgiving
89	11	Use herbs and fruit with prudence and
97	13	House for thanksgiving
136	28	Praise with prayer of thanksgiving

THAYRE, EZRA

33	hd	To Ezra Thayre and
52	22	T. B. Marsh and Ezra
56	5	Commandment revoked
	8	Ezra Thayre to repent
75	31	Mission for Ezra Thayre

THEORY

88	78	Instructed in principle, theory, etc.
97	14	Perfected in theory

THIEF

42	20	Thief to be cast out
	85	Thief to be dealt with

THIRST

133	29	Parched ground not thirsty land
	68	Fish stinks for thirst

THOMPSON

56	6	Rebellions of people in Thompson

THOMPSON, R. B.

124	12	To help write the proclamation

THOUGHT

6	16	None save God knows thoughts and intents
	36	Look unto me in every thought
9	7	Took no thought save to ask me
	9	Not right, stupor of thought
88	69	Cast away idle thoughts
	109	Thoughts and intents of hearts revealed
100	5	Speak thoughts put into hearts
121	45	Let virtue garnish thoughts

THOUSAND YEARS

29	22	Thousand years ended
88	101	Live not until end of thousand years
	108	Reveal secret acts in first thousand years
	109	Reveal secret acts in second thousand years
	110	Satan bound a thousand years

THREE

6	28	Two or three witnesses
	32	Two or three in my name there I am

THRONE

76	21	Holy angels worship at throne of God
	92	God reigns upon his throne
	93	All bow in reverance before the throne
	108	Christ crowned with glory on throne of
	110	Bow and confess to him on throne
88	13	God sitteth upon throne
	40	Who sitteth upon his throne
	45	Lamb who sitteth upon throne
	110	Swear in name of him upon throne
109	79	Seraphs around thy throne
121	29	Thrones revealed to the valiant

THUNDER
- 87　6　God's wrath shown by thunder
- 43　25　God calls by thunderings
- 88　90　After your testimony that of thunderings

TIDING
- 19　29　Declare glad tidings
- 128　19　How beautiful upon the mountains are the

TIME
- 39　21　No man knoweth the time
- 60　13　Do not idle away time
- 64　32　Things must come to pass in their time
- 84　100　Time is no longer
- 88　42　Law by which things move in times and
- 　　110　When time shall be no longer
- 101　72　Do things in their time
- 121　25　Time appointed for every man
- 130　4　Time reckoned according to the planets
- 132　7　Only contracts sealed for time and eternity
- 　　18　Marriage for time and eternity without
- 　　45　Make known all things in due time
- 45　25　Jews not gathered until times of Gentiles
- 　　31　Events when times of Gentiles are fulfilled

TITHING
- 64　23　Day of tithing of my people
- 　　23　Who is tithed shall not burn
- 85　3　Names of non-tithe payers not to be kept
- 　　4　Genealogy of non-tithe payers not to be
- 97　11　House to be built by tithing
- 　　12　This is tithing I require
- 119　hd　Answer to questions on tithing
- 　　3　The beginning of tithing
- 　　4　Tithing a law forever
- 　　5　If law of tithing not observed, not Zion
- 120　1　Disposition of property tithings

TOBACCO
- 89　8　The value and use of tobacco

TOKEN
- 104　75　In full fellowship a token

TONGUE
- 46　24　Given to speak with tongues
- 　　25　Given to interpret tongues
- 75　110　Every tongue confess
- 90　11　Every man hear gospel in own tongue
- 　　15　Learn tongues

TORMENT
- 19　6　Endless torment, not without end
- 76　44　Torment of sons of perdition
- 104　18　In hell, in torment

TRACK
- 52　33　Journey not in another's tracks

TRAITOR
- 122　3　People never turned by testimony of

TRANSFIGURE
- 63　21　Earth transfigured according to pattern

TRANSFIGURATION
- 63　20　Inheritance on day of transfiguration

TRANSGRESSION
- 3　9　Because of transgression will fall
- 20　20　By transgression man became sensual and
- 　　80　How to deal with member in transgression
- 82　11　Bond that cannot be broken by transgression
- 101　2　Affliction through transgression
- 104　9　Cut off by transgressions cannot escape
- 105　9　For transgression Zion must wait for
- 121　17　Cry transgression because servants of sin

TRANSGRESSOR
- 42　10　Appoint another in transgressor's place
- 51　4　Voice of church passes on transgressor
- 82　4　Transgressors if ye keep not my sayings
- 104　8　Transgressors cannot escape wrath
- 　　10　Transgressors delivered to Satan if they do
- 105　2　Church redeemed if no transgressors
- 107　72　Judgment upon transgressor upon testimony
- 132　65　Wife transgressor if not obedient

TRANSLATE
- 1　29　Power to translate through mercy of God
- 3　12　Power and sight to translate
- 10　1　Translate by Urim and Thummim
- 37　1　Translate no more

TRANSLATION
- 6　28　Give keys of gift of translation
- 124　89　Publish new translation of holy words

TRANSLATOR
- 21　1, 107:92, 124:125 President be called

TRAVEL
- 69　7　Travel to obtain knowledge
- 84　111　What part of priesthood to travel
- 107　97　Seventy to be traveling ministers
- 　　98　Those of priesthood required to travel

TREASUURE
- 19　38　Obtain more than treasures of earth
- 89　19　Hidden treasures of knowledge if keep

TREASURER
- 104　　Duties of treasurer

TREASURY
- 104　60–68　Purpose of the treasury

TREE
- 101　30　An infant's life like the age of a tree
- 128　23　Let trees praise God

TREMBLE
- 52　17　Who trembles under power made strong
- 133　31　Boundaries of hills tremble

TRESPASS
- 64　9　Forgive his brother trespass
- 82　1　I forgive who forgive trespasses
- 98　41–43　Forgive first, second and third trespass
- 　　44　Bring fourth trespass as testimony
- 　　47　Forgive children if repent of father's
- 　　48　Trespasses removed from repentant

	46	4	Trespasser not to take sacrament until		

TRIAL

42	83	How trials are to be conducted
	88	Trials of offenders to be secret
68	22	Bishop tried only before first presidency
	33	Observe not prayers, be tried before judge
105	19	Brought for trial of faith
122	4–6	Kinds of trials enumerated
	7	Trials give experience and are for good
	8	Son of man descended below all trials

TRIAL, BISHOP'S

42	89	When conducted

TRIBULATION

54	10	Be patient in tribulation
58	2	Blessed are faithful in tribulation
	4	After tribulation blessings
78	14	Tribulation shall descend upon you
103	12	After such tribulation comes blessing
	13	After tribulation come redemption and
112	13	Lord feel after them after tribulation
127	2	I glory in tribulation

TRIFLE

6	12, 8:10	Trifle not with sacred things
32	5	Trifle not

TROUBLE

3	8	With you in time of trouble
101	8	In trouble feel after me

TRUMP

43	18	Trump of God will sound
	25	God calls by sound of trump
88	99	Angels sound their trumps

TRUMPET

77	12	Sounding of trumpets explained
	12	Trumpets, the beginning of the seventh

TRUST

1	19	Man not trust in arm of flesh
11	12	Put your trust in that Spirit
84	116	Trust and not be confounded

TRUTH

1	39	Truth abideth forever
6	22	Cried that you may know the truth
18	21	Speak truth in soberness
19	37	Preach truth with loud voice
27	16	Your loins girt with truth
45	57	Who have received truth will
50	14	Comforter sent to teach truth
	40	You must grow in knowledge of truth
58	47	Bear testimony of truth
66	12	Father full of grace and truth
67	4	A testimony of truth of commandments
75	4	Proclaim truth according to revelations
76	5	Honor those who serve in truth
	31	Punishment of those who deny truth
78	10	Satan turns hearts from truth
79	2	Comforter to teach truth
84	45	Word of Lord is truth
	45	Truth is light
	101	Truth established in bowels of earth
	102	God full of truth
85	7	His bowels a fountation of truth
88	6	Jesus the light of truth
	7	Which truth shineth
	40	Truth embraceth truth
	66	Truth hath no end
	66	My voice is spirit and truth
91	4	Spirit manifesteth truth
93	9	Son the spirit of truth
	11	Son full of grace and truth
	24	Truth defined
	26	I am the spirit of truth
93	28	Truth and light if commandments kept
	28	Man glorified in truth
	30	Truth and intelligence independent
	30	Intelligence the spirit of truth
	36	Is intelligence or light and truth
	37	Light and truth forsake evil one
	39	Light and truth lost through disobedience
97	1	Blessed who seek truth
107	84	Things done in truth
121	46	Sceptre of righteousness and truth
123	12	Kept from truth through ignorance
124	97	Comforter manifest
127	6	Make a record of truth
128	19	Truth out of earth in gospel

TRY

98	12	Faithful tried and proven herewith
136	31	People must be tried because

TWELVE

18	27	What the twelve shall do
	27	Twelve shall be my disciples
	28	What the twelve are to do
	29	Twelve to baptize
	31	I speak to the twelve
	32	Twelve ordained to ordain
	37	Oliver Cowdery and David Whitmer to
107	36	Twelve a traveling high council
118	hd	Answer to question concerning the twelve

TWO

6	32	Two or three in my name there I am also
133	58	Two put ten thousand to flight

UNBELIEF

20	15	Harden hearts in unbelief
58	15	If he repent not of unbelief
84	54	Minds darkened because of unbelief
	55	Unbelief brought church under
	76	Upbraided for hearts of unbelief

UNBELIEVER

60	15	Shake off dust against unbeliever
74	5	Marriage of believer and unbeliever
75	20–22	The fate of the unbeliever

UNBELIEVER continued
- 22 More tolerable for heathen than unbeliever
- 84 74 Unbelievers to be damned
- 85 9 Unbelievers, wailing and gnashing of teeth
- 9 His portion among unbelievers
- 88 82 Without excuse, sin upon own heads
- 101 90 Fate of unbelievers

UNBELIEVING
- 1 8 Unbelieving may be sealed up
- 63 6 Unbelieving hold their lips
- 17 Unbelieving shall die second death

UNCLEAN
- 88 124 Cease to be unclean
- 90 18 Keep uncleanness from you
- 94 9 Any unclean, glory and presence depart
- 97 15 Suffer no unclean thing in house

UNDERSTAND
- 50 11 Reason to understand
- 22 Preacher and receiver understand by Spirit
- 71 5 Who reads, understand and receive
- 116 Understand only by power of Holy Ghost
- 88 87 Instructed in all expedient to understand
- 91 4 Who so reads let him understand

UNDERSTANDING
- 29 50 God deals with those of no understanding
- 32 4 Pray that may unfold understanding
- 76 9 Understanding of prudent come to nought
- 19 Lord touched eyes of understanding
- 114 Works of God surpass understanding
- 88 11 Same light quickeneth understanding
- 97 14 Be perfected in understanding of ministry

UNFAITHFUL
- 101 90 Will cut off unfaithful stewards
- 104 3 Not faithful nigh unto cursing

UNGODLY
- 76 49 Visions of sufferings of ungodly
- 97 22 Vengeance on ungodly like whirlwind
- 136 33 Spirit of condemnation of ungodly

UNHOLY
- 97 17 God comes not into unholy temples

UNION
- 105 4 Law of union of celestial kingdom

UNITED ORDER
- 44 6 Until done according to united order
- 72 11–18 United order regulations
- 78 3, 4 An everlasting order
- 11 Organize by bond
- 15 United order a preparation
- 82 11 Commandment to enter united order
- 15 According to the laws of the Lord
- 18 For benefit of church
- 83 1–3 Rules for women and children
- 85 3 Consecration that he may tithe
- 90 24 Blessing if united order remembered
- 96 9 Ordain to be a member of united order
- 92 1 Frederick G. Williams to be a member
- 104 1 Counsel concerning property of united order
- 1 For the salvation of men
- 5 Penalty for breaking covenant
- 11 Commandment to organize
- 18 Who obeys not shall
- 21 Things to be done according to counsel of
- 48 Order of Kirtland separated from that of
- 49 Do business in own names
- 53 Dissolved as united order from brethren
- 68 What to do with profits
- 105 4 Redemption delayed because order failed
- 34 Zion's law be executed after redemption
- 34 Law of order in abeyance

UNITED STATES
- 101 80 I established constitution of this land
- 80 I redeemed land by shedding of blood

UNJUST
- 75 17 Done evil, resurrection of unjust
- 101 90 Will cut off unjust stewards

UNLEARNED
- 35 13 Unlearned to thrash nations

UNRIGHTEOUS
- 42 47 Death of unrighteous bitter
- 121 39 Little authority exercise unrighteous

UNRIGHTEOUSNESS
- 66 10 Forsake unrighteousness
- 67 9 No unrighteousness in Doctrine and
- 82 22 Friends with mammon of unrighteousness
- 107 32 Decision made in unrighteousness

UNWORTHY
- 88 134 Unworthy not to pollute God's house

UPLIFTED
- 88 120 Salutations with uplifted hands

URIAH
- 132 39 David lost exaltation for Uriah and his wife

URIM AND THUMMIM
- 10 1 Translate by
- 17 1 Given to brother of Jared
- 130 8 God's residence a great Urim and Thummim
- 9 Sanctified earth a Urim and Thummim for
- 10 White stone become Urim and Thummim

UTTER
- 76 115 Things not lawful for man to utter

UTTERANCE
- 14 8 Holy Ghost give utterance
- 93 51 Gospel as I give utterance

VAIL
- 38 8 Vail of darkness shall be rent
- 67 10 Vail rent and see God
- 101 23 Vail of temple taken off what will happen
- 23 Vail which hideth the earth
- 110 1 Vail taken from our minds

VALIANT
- 76 79 Reward of those not valiant

VALID–WAR

VALID
- 121 29 All things revealed to the valiant
- 132 7 Only sealed contracts valid after death
-      19 Marriage in the covenant valid after death

VALIDITY
- 128 9 Proper record essential to validity

VANITY
- 20 5 First elder entangled in vanities
- 84 55 Vanity brought church under condemnation
- 106 7 Will lift up, in spite of vanity, if humble

VENGEANCE
- 76 105 Who suffer vengeance of eternal fire
- 97 22 Vengeance of ungodly like whirlwind
-      26 Vengeance if disobedient
- 98   Vengeance turned away from repentant
-      46 Lord's vengeance against enemies
- 101   God's vengeance if heed not saints
- 105 30 Vengeance to third and fourth generation
- 112 25 Vengeance to begin with the Lord's house

VESSEL
- 28 42 Be clean who bear vessels of the Lord
- 76 33 Sons of perdition vessels of wrath
- 133 5 Be clean that bear vessels of the Lord

VICTORY
- 103 36 Victory and glory through diligence
- 104 82 Victory if humble and faithful

VILLAGE
- 84 93 Wash feet against village
-      94 Wo to village that rejects you

VINE
- 27 5 I will drink the fruit of the vine
- 89 16 Fruit of vine for man

VINEYARD
- 21 9 Mess laborers of my vineyard
- 24 19 Called to prune vineyard with
- 33 3 Last time to call laborers to vineyard
-      4 Vineyard has become corrupt
- 43 28, 71:4 Labor in my vineyard
- 95 4 Prepare apostles to prune vineyard
- 101 101 Plant vineyard shall eat fruit

VIRGIN
- 45 56 Parable of ten virgins fulfilled
- 63 54 Will be foolish virgins among the wise
- 132 61 May espouse another virgin
-      62 If he have ten virgins cannot commit

VIRTUE
- 4 6 Remember virtue
- 38 24, 46:33 Practice virtue
- 88 40 Virtue loveth virtue
- 121 45 Let virtue garnish thoughts
- 122 2 Virtuous will seek counsel

VOICE
- 1 2 Voice of the Lord unto all men
-    11 Voice of Lord unto ends of the earth
- 20 35 Revelations by voice of God
- 38 34 Appointed by voice of the church
- 43 18 The Lord shall utter his voice
-      23 God calls by his own voice
- 45 49 Lord shall utter his voice
- 50 45 Shall bear my voice
- 51 4 Voice of church passes on transgressor
- 52 1 Elders called by voice of Spirit
- 63 37 Lift up a warning voice
- 65 1 The voice of one who is mighty
- 68 4 Said when moved by Holy Ghost is voice of
- 71 10 Voice against you be confounded
- 85 6 Still small voice makes bones to quake
- 88 66 My voice is spirit and truth
-     90 Voice of thunder, lightning, tempest, etc.
- 97 1 Speak by voice of the Spirit
- 128 21 Voice of God heard at sundry times
-      23 How glorious is voice from heaven
- 133 21 Voice heard among all people

VOTE
- 20 63 Elders to receive licenses by vote
-      65 Ordination preceded by vote
- 102 19 Decision sanctioned by vote

VOW
- 108 3 Be careful in observing vows

WAGE
- 29 45 Wages from whom they list to obey
- 124 121 Have a just recompense of wages for labor
-       121 Wages paid as agreed

WAIT
- 5 17 Wait, for not yet ordained
- 98 2 Wait patiently on the Lord
- 133 45 Great things prepared for him who waits

WAKEFIELD, JOSEPH
- 50 37 In whom I am well pleased
- 52 35 Called

WALL
- 121 15 None left to stand by wall

WANT
- 51 3 Portion according to wants
-    14 Bishop to reserve enough for his wands
- 70 7 Excess given into my storehouse
- 82 17 Every man have claim according to wants

WAR
- 38 29 Hear of wars but know not hearts
- 45 26 Rumors of wars in last days
-      63 Prophecy on war in United States
-      63 Wars are at your doors
-      69 No war in Zion
- 63 33 Lord has decreed wars upon earth
- 87 hd Revelation and prophecy on war
-      1 War to begin with rebellion of South Carolina
-      2 War be poured out on all nations
-      4 Slaves against masters for war
-      5 Wars of last days
- 88 79 Learn of wars of nations

WAR —WHEAT

WAR continued
- 98   16   Renounce wars, proclaim peace
-       34   Standard of peace to those who proclaim war

WARD
- 128   3   In every ward and city

WARN
- 98   28   Warn enemy if he smite more than thrice
-       29   Enemy delivered if warned
- 63   57   Who desire to warn sinners
-       58   A day of warning not of many words
- 88   71   Let those warned call and ponder
-       81   Sent out to testify and warn
-       81   Who warned, warn his neighbor

WARSAW
- 124   88   William Marks preach in Warsaw

WARRIORS
- 101   55   Young and middle-aged men for warriors
- 105   16   Warriors to gather for redemption

WASHING
- 89   7   Strong drinks for washing of bodies
- 60   15   Wash Feet as testimony against
- 88   139   Members received by washing of feet
-       140   Details of washing of feet
- 124   37   Washings acceptable only in temple
-       39   Washings to be done in temple

WASTE
- 101   18   To build up waste places of Zion

WATCH
- 50   46   Watch that ye may be ready
- 61   38   Be watchful of Christ's coming
- 82   5   I say watch
- 84   11   Deacons and teachers watch over church
- 133   11   Watch, neither day nor hour known

WATCHMAN
- 101   45   Parable of watchman upon tower
-       54   Watchman to see enemy while afar off
- 105   16   Scatter watchmen of enemies
- 124   61   Set as watchmen on walls

WATER
- 5   16   Born of water and Spirit
- 10   66   May partake of waters of life freely
- 20   74   Baptism by immersion in water
- 33   11   Baptism by water
- 52   10   Baptizing by water
- 61   3   Moving swiftly upon water whilst
-       4   Many dangers upon waters
-       5   Decreed destruction upon waters
-       6   Faithful shall not perish by waters
-       14   Lord in beginning blessed waters
-       14   Last days cursed waters
-       15   No flesh be safe upon waters
-       16   None go upon waters save upright
-       16   None to go to Zion upon waters
-       18   Forewarn brethren about waters
-       19   Destroyer rideth upon waters
-       22   Missionaries travel upon water or land
-       23   Joseph and others not to travel upon waters
-       27   Power to command waters
-       28   Follow Spirit upon waters
- 76   51   Buried in water in his name
- 84   64   Baptized by water for remission of sins
-       92   Cleanse feet with water as testimony
-       94   Who sitteth upon many waters
- 110   3   Voice like rushing waters
- 118   4   Apostles called to cross great waters
- 121   33   How long rolling waters impure
- 127   2   Wont to swim in deep water
- 133   22   Voice of many waters
- 132   29   Pools of living water in barren wastes.
-       39   Worship him who made fountains of water
-       41   Presence of Lord as fire of boiling water

WAVE
- 88   90   After your testimony that of waves of sea

WAYSIDE
- 24   15   Cleansing of feet by wayside

WEAK
- 1   19   Weak things shall come forth
-    19   Weak break down mighty
-    23   Gospel proclaimed by weak
- 35   13   Weak things to thrash nations
- 42   52   Bear with infirmities of weak
- 50   16   Weak shall be made strong
- 81   5   Succor the weak
- 84   106   The strong to take the weak
- 89   3   Word of wisdom adapted to the weakest
- 124   1   Show wisdom through weak things
- 133   58   When weak confound the wise
-       58   Gospel to prepare the weak
-       59   Thresh nations with weak things

WEAKNESS
- 1   24   Commandments given servants in weakness
- 62   1   Jesus knows weakness of men

WEARY
- 64   33   Be not weary in well doing
- 89   20   Run and not be weary

WEEP
- 42   45   Weep for the dead
- 76   26   Heavens wept over Lucifer
- 112   24   Day of weeping to come

WEIGHTY
- 117   8   Covet a drop, neglect weighty matters

WELL-DOING
- 64   33   Be not weary in well-doing

WEST
- 42   64   Teach converts to fly to the west
- 45   64   Gather to the west
- 136   1   In their journeyings to the west

WHEAT
- 86   hd   Explaining parable of wheat and tares
- 89   17   Wheat for man

WHIRLWIND
- 63   6, 97:22, 112:24 Wrath comes like a

WHISPER
- 85   6   Still small voice whispereth through all

WHITE
- 20   6   White above all other whiteness
- 130   10   White stone become Urim and Thummim

WHITELOCK, HARVEY
- 52   25   Called

WHITMER, DAVID
- 14   hd   Given to David Whitmer
- 17   hd   To David Whitmer and
- 18   hd   Given to David Whitmer and
-     37   And David Whitmer to search out twelve
- 30   hd   Given to David Whitmer and
-     1   Reproved
- 52   25   Called

WHITMER, FATHER
- 128   21   Voice of God in chamber of Father Whitmer

WHITMER, JOHN
- 15   1   Hearken, my servant John
- Sections 15, 26, 30, 47 given to John Whitmer
- 30   9   To preach the gospel
- 47   1   To be church historian
- 69   2   To go with Oliver Cowdery
-     3   To be church historian
- 70   1   Mentioned

WHITMER, PETER
- Sections 16, 30 given to Peter Whitmer
- 16   1   Hearken, my servant Peter
- 30   5   Peter Whitmer to go with Oliver
- 32   2   Parley P. Pratt to go with Peter Whitmer

WHITNEY, NEWEL K.
- 63   42   Command to
- 64   26   Words to
- 72   8   To be bishop
- 84   113   Newel K. Whitney directed
- 93   50   Set his house in order
- 104   39   Inheritance appointed
- 117   1   To leave Kirtland
-     11   Be bishop in deed not in name only
-     11   Ashamed of Nicholatine band

WHORE
- 29   21   Wicked church, the great whore
- 86   3   Babylon, the apostate, the whore

WHOREMONGER
- 63   17   Shall die second death
- 76   103   Receive telestial glory

WELTON, MICAH B.
- 75   36   Mission for

WICKED
- 1   9   Wrath of God poured upon wicked
-     14   The day cometh when wicked cut off
- 3   12   Give not sacred things to wicked
- 10   1   Because writings delivered to wicked man
-     17   Wicked test God
-     37   Not tell wicked from righteous
- 29   9   Wicked shall be as stubble
-     17   Vengeance upon wicked
-     29   Wicked sent to everlasting fire
-     41   Wicked die last death
- 34   9   Great destruction for wicked
- 38   5   Wicked kept to last judgment
-     42   Go out from among wicked
- 43   33   Wicked go away into fire
-     33   No man knoweth end of wicked
- 45   32   Wicked shall curse God and die
-     67   Wicked will not come to Zion
-     68   Wicked shall be afraid of Zion
- 61   32   More labor needed among brethren than
- 63   2   Lord angry at wicked
-     6   Let wicked take heed
-     32   Lord angry at wicked
-     33   Wicked shall slay wicked
-     34   Consume wicked with fire
-     37   Desolation comes upon wicked
-     54   Angels pluck out wicked from fire
-     54   Separation of righteous from wicked
- 64   21   Wicked not overthrown for five years
-     24   Proud and wicked burn as stubble
- 84   53   May know righteous from wicked
- 88   85   Desolation of abomination awaits wicked
-     85   Punishment in this and coming world
- 93   25   Spirit of wicked liar from beginning
-     39   Wicked one taketh away light and truth
- 97   21   Zion rejoice when wicked mourn
- 98   9   Wicked rule people mourn
- 101   90   Will cut off wicked stewards
-     95   May discern between righteous and wicked
- 133   63   How the Lord will answer the wicked
-     64   Wicked burn as stubble
-     70   Fate of wicked: lay down in sorrow
- 136   39   Joseph died that wicked be condemned

WICKEDNESS
- 6   26   Records kept back because of wickedness
- 10   9   Delivered sacred things unto wicked
-     21   Hearts full of wickedness
- 61   8   One, that not perish in wickedness
-     31   Anger kindled against wickedness
- 68   31   Lord not pleased if children grow up in
- 84   96   Scourge them for wickedness
- 133   14   Wickedness is spiritual Babylon

WIDOW
- 83   6   Widows to be provided for
- 136   8   That cries of widow come not against

WIFE
- 19   25   Shalt not covet thy neighbor's wife
- 25   2   Duty of Emma Smith as a wife
-     14   Let soul delight in husband
- 42   22   Love thy wife

		WIFE continued
49	16	Lawful that man have one wife
	16	Man and wife to be one flesh
74	1	Unbelieving husband sanctified by wife
	1	Unbelieving wife sanctified by husband
83	2	Have claim on husbands for maintenance
132	hd	concerning plurality of wives
	38	How justified in having many wives of old
	39	David's wives given by Nathan
	43	Husband loses wife through adultery
	44	Who shall receive adulterer's wife
	61	Law of taking many wives
	63	Wives to multiply and replenish the earth
	63	That they may bear souls of men
	64	Wife must obey law of priesthood or
	65	Wife a transgressor if not obedient

WIGHT, LYMAN

52	7	To travel
	12	Satan will sift Lyman Wight as chaff
103	30	Commission to Lyman Wight
	38	To journey with Sidney Rigdon
124	18	To continue preaching
	62	Committee to build temple

WILDERNESS

5	14	Church out of the wilderness
49	24	Jacob shall flourish in the wilderness
86	3	Tares drive church into wilderness
88	66	In wilderness because you cannot see
128	20	A voice in wilderness of Fayette
	20	Wilderness between Harmony and Colesville
133	68	Make rivers a wilderness

WILL

3	4	If follows own will
19	2	Accomplished and finished will of Father
20	24	Christ reigns according to will of Father
21	1	Called through will of God
58	20	According to counsel of own will
63	20	Who doeth will shall overcome
68	hd	Mind and will made known by Spirit
	4	Moved by Holy Ghost is mind and will of
76	10	Power make known secrets of will
77	6	Will of God as book of seven seals
89	2	Order and will of God in temporal affairs
124	5	Know my will by Holy Ghost
	89	My will to hearken to counsel
133	61	According to mind and will of God

WILLIAMS, FREDERICK G.

64	21	Words concerning
81	1	A high priest and counselor to Joseph
90	6	Equal with Joseph Smith in keys of kingdom
	19	Provide place for Frederick G. Williams.
92	1	To be member of order
93	40–43	Commanded to gain knowledge
93	52–53	Concerning his children
102	3	Presidents of first high council
104	27	Inheritance appointed
	29	To have printing office

WILLIAMS, SAMUEL

124	127	Of presidency of elders

WILLING

1	34	Willing to make things known to all flesh
64	34	Willing and obedient eat good of land
101	75	Zion redeemed if church willing

WILSON, CALVES

75	15	Mission for

WILSON, DUNBAR

124	132	Member of high council

WINE

20	75	Wine of sacrament
	79	Blessing on wine
27	3	Not purchase wine of enemies
	4	Partake only of new wine
58	8	Feast of wine on lees
88	94	Wine of wrath of fornication
89	5	Wine may be used in sacrament
	5	To drink wine not good
	6	Pure wine of grape vine
133	48	Garments like treader of wine vat

WINE-PRESS

76	107	Christ trodden wine-press alone
88	106	Trodden wine-press alone and overcome
133	50	Have trodden wine-press alone

WING

10	65	As hen gathereth chickens under her wings
88	45	Earth roll upon her wings
124	99	Mount in imagination as on eagle's wings

WINTER

89	13	Flesh eaten in winter, cold or famine

WISDOM

1	26	As sought wisdom be instructed
6	7	Seek not for riches but wisdom
9	3	Be patient, it is wisdom in me
	6	Wisdom to have dealt with you thus
10	34	Here is wisdom
	43	My wisdom greater than cunning
11	7	Seek wisdom
	26	Time which is my wisdom
19	21	Show not until it is wisdom
28	5	Oliver to write by wisdom
37	4	Here is wisdom
38	30	Treasure wisdom
42	11	Wisdom of the God of Enoch
52	17	Fruits of praise and wisdom
76	2	Great is his wisdom
	9	Their wisdom shall be great
	9	Wisdom of wise perish before them
78	2	Speak in your ears words of wisdom
82	16	Wisdom for your good
	22	This is wisdom
88	40	Wisdom receiveth wisdom

	118	Teach wisdom	49	22	Son of Man comes not as a woman
	118	Seek wisdom from best books	63	16	Looks on woman to lust shall deny faith
89	19	Wisdom to him who keeps word of wisdom	83	3	Women, not faithful, no fellowship
95	13	Wisdom of mind of Lord		2	Women shall have fellowship in the church
97	1	Blessed who seek wisdom		2	Have claim on husbands for maintenance
101	63	Wisdom concerning salvation of all churches	101	81	Parable of woman and unjust judge
105	23	Reveal not things until wisdom	**WONDER**		
124	1	Show wisdom through weak things	35	8	I will show wonders
136	31	Let ignorant learn wisdom	45	40	Wonders shown those who fear Lord

WISE

45	57	Wise shall abide the day	63	12	Seek not signs and wonders
46	18	All taught knowledge and be wise	76	8	Shall know wonders of eternity
51	19	Wise steward inherit eternal life	128	23	Seas and lands tell wonders of eternal king

WOODRUFF, WILFORD

118	6	Called to apostleship
124	129	An apostle
136	13	And Wilford Woodruff organize a company

58	10	Wise invited to supper of Lord
63	54	Foolish virgins among wise
67	6	Most wise make commandment like unto
78	22	Who is wise shall inherit
98	10	Uphold wise and good men
101	73	Honorable and wise men to buy lands
	94	ʻWise men know what they have not
105	28	Send wise men to fulfil commandments
111	11	Wise as serpents, without sin
122	2	Wise will seek counsel
127	1	Wise to leave for safety
133	58	When weak confound the wise

WORD

1	38	Shall not pass away
5	10	Generation have word through you
	11	My words given through you
	20	My word shall be verified
6	2	The nature of God's words
	17	Witness that words are true
	20	Treasure up words in heart
	28	Word established by two or three
	31	Words which shall be established by
11	2	Sharper than two-edged sword
	16	My word, rock, church and gospel
	21	Seek not to declare my word, first obtain
	22	Study my word
12	2	Give heed to my word
16	5	Blessed for speaking my words
17	1	You must rely on my word
24	16	I will smite according to your words
29	30	Words fulfilled as spoken
	30	Word of power is power of Spirit
39	16	Cannot deny my word
41	2	Assemble and agree on my word
50	19	Word of truth received by spirit of truth
56	11	Though earth pass away words shall not
63	37	Declare both by word and flight
	58	Day of warning, not of many words
68	4	When moved by Holy Ghost is word of Lord
84	43	Live by word from mouth of God
	45	Word of Lord is truth
	60	My words, my voice
	85	Treasure words of life in your minds
85	7	Mouth utters eternal words
93	8	Son the Word, Messenger of salvation.
98	11	Live by every word from mouth of God
99	2	Word in demonstration of Holy Spirit
112	8	High brought low by word
124	128	Send my word to every creature
128	3	Word established by two or three
130	11	The new name is the key word

WITNESS

5	1	As Martin Harts has desired to witness
	11	Testimony of three witnesses
	15	Testimony of three I will send forth
	23	Concerning man that desires witness
	32	Fall in transgressions unless receive witness
6	17	Witness that work is true
	22	If desire further witness recall when you
	23	What greater witness than from God
	24	You have received a witness
	28	In mouth of two or three witnesses word
14	8	Stand as a witness
20	13	World judged by great witnesses
	16	Elders of church bear witness
42	80	Two witnesses to establish testimony
77	15	Two witnesses of John explained
106	8	Reward of faithful witness
107	23	Apostles especial witnesses of name of
	25	Seventy especial witnesses unto Gentiles
127	6	Recorder witness for baptism for dead
	6	Witness to see with eyes
128	3	Word established by two or three witnesses
	3	Three witnesses of baptism for dead
	20	Three witnesses to book declared at
136	40	Delivered from enemies in witness of my

WOE

19	5	Woes shall go forth

WOMAN

18	42	Women to repent and be baptized
42	23	Lust after woman, be cast out

WORD continued

132	12	My word, my law
	13	Without my word ceases at death
	59	No sin to act according to my word
136	24	Let words edify

WORD OF WISDOM

46	17	Word of wisdom given to some men
88	124	Sleep and rest
89	1	Nature, meaning, substance
	3	A principle with promise
	4	Why given
	18	Promises to those who keep word of wisdom
98	20	For observe not the word of wisdom

WORK

1	10	Man recompensed according to work
3	3	Remember work of God not frustrated
	9	Chosen to do work of God
4	1	Marvelous work to come forth
	5	Faith, etc., qualify him for work
	17	Witness that work is true
	35	Perform work with soberness
8	8	Gift of Aaron, work of God
10	61	Will bring to light marvelous works
11	20	Your work to keep my commandments
12	8	No one can assist in work except
18	38	By their works you shall know them
	44	By your hands I will work a marvelous work
19	3	Judging every man by his works
20	13	Come to knowledge of this work shall be
20	69	Works agreeable to holy scriptures
29	33	Works of God have no end
45	72	Not know works until accomplished
52	11	Work cut short in righteousness
59	20	Their works shall follow them
63	11	Signs come unto mighty works
76	85	Last resurrection when work finished
	111	Judged according to their works
77	6	Work of God as book of seven seals
84	66	Wonderful works in God's name
85	2	Record of works of members to be kept
88	73	Will hasten my work in its time
97	6	Need that work be done
	26	Zion visited according to works
98	31	Reward enemy according to his works
104	14	Lord built earth as handy work
105	24	Boast not of mighty works
112	34	My reward according to work
124	50	Punishment of those who hinder work
	78	I love him for his work
	86	Rest from labors, continue works
132	63	Work continued by bearing souls

WORKER

35	14	Blessings for workers of the church

WORKMANSHIP

29	25	God's workmanship not to be lost

WORLD

1	16	Image of a God in likeness of world
	23	Gospel proclaimed to all the world
10	37	Until I make all things known to the world
10	70	Life and light of the world
11	28	The light of the world
18	6	World ripening in iniquity
19	3	At end of the world
20	13	World be judged by great witnesses
25	10	Lay aside things of this world
35	18	Things sealed from foundation of world
38	1	Seraphic hosts of heaven before world was
42	65	World shall not know mysteries
43		End of the world
45	9	Everlasting covenant light to world
49	17	Man, his creation before world was
53	2	Forsake the world
	2	Crucified for sins of the world
63	27	Advantage to have claim on world
76	13	Before the world was
	24	Worlds were created through him
	41	What Jesus did for the world
77	12	World made in six days
84	48	Covenant for salve of the world
	49	Whole world lies in sin
	75	Revelation in force upon all the world
	79	Sent to prove the world
86	9	Been hid from the world with Christ
93	7	Son before world was
	9	World made by him
101	36	In this world joy not full
106	4	World overtaken as a thief in the night
121	32	Ordained before the world was
	35	Not chosen for aspirations of world and
123	7	Which has filled world with confusion
124	41	Reveal things hidden from foundation of
127	11	Prince of this world cometh
128	22	Plan of redemption laid before world
130	19	More intelligence here advantage in next
132	30	Abraham and seed continue in and out of
	49	Will be to thee to end of world

WORTH

15	6	Most worth to declare repentance
18	10	Worth of souls is great to God

WORTHY

67	14	Who worthy shall see and hear
98	15	Not abide covenant not worthy
105	35	Chosen who are worthy
107	100	Who learns not duty not worthy
	100	Slothful not counted worthy
136	31	Bears not chastisement not worthy

WORSHIP

18	40	Worship the Father in my name
20	29	All men must worship the father
42	34	Houses of worship, how built

93	19	Know what you worship
	19	That ye know how to worship
124	84	Wrong to set up golden calf to worship
133	39	Worship him who made heaven, etc.

WOUND

6	37	Behold wounds which pierced side
45	51	Wounds in body of Christ

WRATH

1	9	Day when wrath of God poured out
19	15	Smite you by my wrath
43	26	Cup of wrath is full
56	1	In day of visitation and wrath
59	21	Wrath of God kindled only against
60	7	Declare word without wrath
63	11	Signs shown in wrath unto condemnation
	33	Lord sworn in his wrath
	34	Saints hardly escape God's wrath
76	33	Sons of perdition vessels of wrath
	104	Who suffer wrath of God on earth
	107	Wine-press of God's fierceness of wrath
87	6	God's wrath shown by famine
88	85	Souls may escape wrath
	88	After your testimony come wrath and
	94	Wine of wrath of her fornication
	106	Wine-press of fierceness of God's wrath
98	22	Obey command and wrath turned away
101	8	In day of wrath will have mercy
112	24	Day of wrath to come
127	2	Envy and wrath my common lot

WRITE

1	18	Be fulfilled which was written by prophets.
9	4	Your work to write for Joseph
	9	Cannot write sacred things save of me
18	3	Rely on things that are written
	29	Baptize as is written
	30	Perform according to written words
24	6	Given thee what to write
	14	Do according to that which is written
28	5	Not write by way of commandment
32	2	Heed only what is written
46	2	Notwithstanding what is written conduct
63	56	Sidney Rigdon's writing not accepted
76	80	To write while in spirit
84	57	Say and do what is written
90	32	Write this commandment

WRITING

10	1	Because you delivered up writings
51	4	Writing to secure portion

WRONG

5	28	Except acknowledge wrong, will not
9	9	If wrong you shall forget
121	5	Avenge wrongs with sword

YEAR

77	7	7,000 years temporal existence of earth
88	44	These are one year with the Lord
93	51	Proclaim acceptable year of Lord
133	52	Year of my redeemed is come

YESTERDAY

61	20	Angry yesterday, today anger turned away

YIELD

5	21	Yield to persuasions no more
9	13	Yield to no temptation

YOUNG

101	55	Young and middle-aged men for warriors
105	16	Young and middle-aged God's warriors

YOUNG, BRIGHAM

124	127	To be president of twelve apostles
126	hd	In house of Brigham Young
	1	Mission stated
	1	Not required to leave
136	hd	Given through head

YOUNG, JOSEPH

124	138	A president of seventies

ZACHARIAS

27	7	Zacharias visited by Elias

ZARAHEMLA

125	3	Build Zarahemla opposite Nauvoo

ZION

12	6	Seek to establish cause of Zion
35	24	Shall rejoice and flourish
38	4	Take Zion of Enoch unto my bosom
39	13	To rejoice upon hills and flourish
45	67	New Jerusalem called Zion
	68	Flee to Zion for safety
	69	Every nation gathered to Zion
	70	Not battle against Zion
	70	Inhabitants of Zion terrible
49	25	Zion flourish upon hills and mountains
51	8	Established to buy land for city of Zion
58	13	Testimony might go from Zion
	13	City of heritages of God
	49	Agents for lands in Zion
	50	Sidney Rigdon to write of Zion
	52	Purchase whole country for Zion
	57	Subscription for monies for Zion
	57	Sidney Rigdon dedicate land of Zion
59	3	Blessed who stand on land of Zion
60	14	Return from Zion
61	16	None to go to Zion on waters
	24	Saints assemble unto Zion
62	4	Assemble upon Zion
63	24	Saints assemble unto Zion
	25	Zion in God's hand
	29	Zion obtained by purchase
	36	Why saints should assemble unto Zion
	40	Let monies be sent to Zion
	48	Sends treasure to Zion receive inheritance
64	22	Go with open heart to Zion
	21	After five years may go
	30	Saints shall obtain inheritance

ZION continued

	35	Rebellious shall not inherit Zion
64	38	Inhabitants of Zion shall judge in Zion
	41	Zion shall flourish
	41	Glory of Lord upon Zion
	42	Zion an ensign unto all nations
	43	Nations shall tremble because of Zion
66	11	Push many to Zion with songs
68	26	Organized stakes of Zion
	26	Law of Zion concerning parents
	32	What should not be in Zion
78	15	God, Holy One of Zion
82	14	Zion put on beautiful garments
	14	Zion increase in beauty and holiness
84	58	Scourges and judgment upon Zion
	99	Lord brought again Zion
	100	Brought Zion from above and beneath
	104	Money for establishing Zion
85	hd	Concerning Zion
90	32	Preside over Zion also
	36	Lord will contend with strong of Zion
	36	Lord chasten Zion
	37	Zion not be removed from her place
93	53	Obtain knowledge for salvation of Zion
94	1	Lay foundation for city of stake of Zion
96		Order of stake of Zion
97	3	To preside over school in Zion
	10	Will that house be built in Zion
	12	Will that house be built in Zion
	18	Zion shall prosper
	19	Zion honored by nations, cannot fall
	20	God salvation and tower of Zion
	21	Zibn is the pure in heart
	21	Zion rejoice when wicked mourn
	25	Zion if obedient to escape scourges
100	13	Zion shall be redeemed though
	16	Let hearts be comforted concerning Zion
101	17	Zion shall not be moved out
	18	To build up waste place of Zion
	18	Pure in heart shall return to Zion
	20	None other place for gathering
	21	Stakes the strength of Zion
	42	Parable of redemption of Zion
	70	Purchase lands around Zion for money
	74	Zion established by gathering
	75	Zion redeemed if churches willing
	81	Children of Zion likened to parable of
103	1	Revelation concerning those scattered in
	4	Why Zion was scattered
	13	After tribulation, redemption and restoration
	15	Redemption of Zion to come by power
	18	As fathers were led to redemption of Zion
	24	Land of Zion my goodly land
	30	Companies to go to Zion
	34	Go not to Zion with less than one hundred
104	48	Kirtland separated from order of Zion
105	5	Zion built only by law of celestial kingdom
	9	For transgression Zion must wait for
	14	God will fight battles of Zion
	15	Enemies not left to pollute Zion
	32	Kingdom of Zion that of Christ and God
	32	Kingdoms acknowledge kingdom of Zion
	34	Zion's law executed after redemption
107	74	Bishops common judges in Zion
109	51	Redeem what thou didst appoint a Zion
	59	Appoint unto Zion other stakes
111	6	Concern not about Zion
113	8	Zion has right of priesthood by lineage
115	6	Zion and her stakes
117	9	Land of my people even Zion
118	2	T. B. Marsh remain in Zion to publish
119	2	Foundation of Zion by surplus property
	5	Law of tithing not observed, not Zion
124	2	Stake as corner stone of Zion
	6	Set time come to favor Zion
	6	Authorities called to heed Zion
	9	Gentiles come to exaltation of Zion
	11	Bring gold and silver to house of Zion
	36	Baptism for dead in Zion
	39	Revelation for foundation of Zion
128	19	Unto Zion, thy God reigneth
133	9	Gather that Zion go to regions about
	12	Who among Gentiles flee to Zion
	21	Utter his voice out of Zion
	24	And Zion back in own place
136	10	Help remove to stake of Zion
	18	Zion to be redeemed in time
	31	Trials to prepare for glory of Zion

ZION, CITY OF

57	2	Missouri place for city of Zion
	3	Independence center place of city of Zion
	8	To buy land for city of Zion

ZION, MOUNT

76	66	Who shall come to Mount Zion
	66	Mount Zion holiest place of all
84	2	Gathering of Saints upon Mount Zion
	32	Filled with glory upon Mount Zion
133	18	Lamb stand upon Mount Zion
	56	Mount Zion and holy city, Jerusalem
	56	Stand with Lamb upon Mount Zion

ZORAMITE

3	17	How knowledge of Savior come to Zoramites.

Artwork

Cover and Page xix	*Sacred Grove* © Frank Magelby.
Page xxv	*Revelation Given to Joseph Smith at the Organization of the Church* by Judith Mehr © Intellectual Reserve, Inc.
Page xxviii	*Go With Me to Cumorah* © 2004 Liz Lemon Swindle. Used with permission from Foundation Arts. For print information go to www.foundationarts.com or call 1-800-366-2781.
Page xxxii	*My Servant Joseph* © 2004 Liz Lemon Swindle. Used with permission from Foundation Arts. For print information go to www.foundationarts.com or call 1-800-366-2781.
Page 4	*The Angel Moroni Appearing to Joseph Smith* by Tom Lovell © Intellectual Reserve, Inc.
Pages 6	*The Martin Harris Farm* © Al Rounds. For print information call 801-278-6789 or visit us at www.alrounds.com.
Page 16	*Joseph Smith Translating the Book of Mormon* by Del Parson © Intellectual Reserve, Inc.
Pages 26	*Hyrum Smith* © Ken Corbett.
Pages 32–33	*Susquehanna River* © Frank Magelby.
Page 36	*An Angel Shows the Gold Plates to Joseph Smith, Oliver Cowdery, and David Whitmer* © William L. Maughan.
Page 38	*Joseph Smith and Oliver Cowdery in Solemn Prayer* by Del Parson © Intellectual Reserve, Inc.
Page 44	*Printing of the First Book of Mormon* by Gary E. Smith © Intellectual Reserve, Inc. Courtesy of The Museum of Church History and Art.
Page 52	*The Organization of the Church April 6, 1830* © Robert T. Barrett.
Page 54	*A Father's Baptism* © 2004 Liz Lemon Swindle. Used with permission from Foundation Arts. For print information go to www.foundationarts.com or call 1-800-366-2781.
Page 60	*Emma's Hymns* © 2004 Liz Lemon Swindle. Used with permission from Foundation Arts. For print information go to www.foundationarts.com or call 1-800-366-2781.
Page 66–67	*The Peter Whitmer, Sr. Home* © Al Rounds. For print information call 801-278-6789 or visit us at www.alrounds.com.
Page 78–79	*Go Ye Into the Wilderness* by Robert T. Barrett © Intellectual Reserve, Inc.

Page 92	*Preparing the Way* © Joseph Brickey.	Page 228	*Fires of Rage* © 2004 Glen S. Hopkinson.
Page 104–105	*Kirtland Village* © Al Rounds. For print information call 801-278-6789 or visit us at www.alrounds.com.	Page 240–41	*Forging Onward, Ever Onward* © 2004 Glen S. Hopkinson.
Page 120	*The Seventies Sent Forth* by Del Parson © Intellectual Reserve, Inc.	Page 254	*Zion's Camp* © Judith Mehr.
		Page 263	*Christ With Adam at Adam-Ondi-Ahman* © Clark Kelley Price.
Page 130	*Independence, Missouri, 1831* © Al Rounds. For print information call 801-278-6789 or visit us at www.alrounds.com.	Page 268–69	*The Kirtland Temple* © Al Rounds. For print information call 801-278-6789 or visit us at www.alrounds.com.
Page 148	*Joseph Smith and Martin Harris Translating the Bible* © 2004 Liz Lemon Swindle. Used with permission from Foundation Arts. For print information go to www.foundationarts.com or call 1-800-366-2781.	Page 274	*Christ Appearing to Joseph Smith and Oliver Cowdery in the Kirtland Temple* © Robert T. Barrett.
		Page 278	*Heber C. Kimball Begins the Work in Preston, England* by Richard Murray © Intellectual Reserve, Inc. Courtesy of The Museum of Church History and Art.
Page 162	*Rescue of the Book of Commandments* by Clark Kelley Price © Intellectual Reserve, Inc.	Page 282	*Jacob Blessing Ephraim and Manasseh* © D. Keith Larson.
Page 166	*Joseph Preaching* © Michael Malm.		
Page 172	*John Johnson Home* © Al Rounds. For print information call 801-278-6789 or visit us at www.alrounds.com.	Page 286–87	*Far West, Missouri* © Al Rounds. For print information call 801-278-6789 or visit us at www.alrounds.com.
Page 190	*Joseph Smith and Orson Pratt* © Robert T. Barrett.	Page 296	*Liberty Jail in Winter* © Al Rounds. For print information call 801-278-6789 or visit us at www.alrounds.com.
Page 210	*Instruction From the Prophet* © Paul Mann.	Page 300	*Of One Heart: Joseph in Liberty Jail* © 2004 Liz Lemon Swindle. Used with permission from Foundation Arts. For print information go to www.foundationarts.com or call 1-800-366-2781.
Page 224	*Building of the Kirtland Temple* by Walter Rane © Intellectual Reserve, Inc. Courtesy of The Museum of Church History and Art.		

Page 302	*Joseph Smith in Liberty Jail* © Greg Olsen. By arrangement with Visions of Faith, Venice, FL. 34285. For information on art prints by Greg Olsen, contact Visions of Faith, 1-800-853-1352.
Page 310–11	*Joseph Preaching* by Theodore Gorka, © Intellectual Reserve, Inc.
Page 316	*Temple to Our God* © 2004 Glen S. Hopkinson.
Page 318	*Prophetic Welcome* © Glen Edwards.
Page 326	*Joseph Smith Preaching in Nauvoo* © Paul Mann.
Page 336	*Emma Hale Smith* image provided by Community of Christ Archives, Independence, Missouri. Used with permission
Page 344	*Joseph and Hyrum Smith Standing Near River* (Nauvoo in background) by Theodore Gorka © Intellectual Reserve, Inc.
Page 346–47	*The Martyred* © Gary E. Smith.
Page 350–51	*One More River* © 2004 Glen S. Hopkinson.
Page 354	*Joseph Smith Instructs the Apostles in the Kirtland Temple* by John Falter © Intellectual Reserve, Inc.
Page 356	*Joseph F. Smith* by Albert Salzbrenner (1865–1939) © Intellectual Reserve, Inc. Courtesy of The Museum of Church History and Art.
Page 364–65	*First Avenue* © Al Rounds. For print information call 801-278-6789 or visit us at www.alrounds.com.
Page 372	*Moses Seeing Jehovah* © Joseph Brickey.
Page 395	*Facsimile* © Gary E. Smith.
Page 404	*Brother Joseph* © David Lindsley.
Page 408	*Joseph Smith Seeks Wisdom from the Bible* by Dale Kilbourn © Intellectual Reserve, Inc. Courtesy of The Museum of Church History and Art.
Page 414–15	*Sacred Grove* © Frank Magelby.
Page 425–34	*Photographs, daguerreotypes, paintings, and etchings of various people from the Doctrine and Covenants* courtesy of Church Archives, The Church of Jesus Christ of Latter-day Saints.
Page 432	*Joseph Smith Jr.* image provided by Community of Christ Archives, Independence, Missouri. Used with permission